Public Affairs for Journalists

Public Affairs for Journalists

James Morrison

OXFORD
UNIVERSITY PRESS

OXFORD

UNIVERSITY PRESS

Great Clarendon Street, Oxford OX2 6DP

Oxford University Press is a department of the University of Oxford.
It furthers the University's objective of excellence in research, scholarship,
and education by publishing worldwide in

Oxford New York

Auckland Cape Town Dar es Salaam Hong Kong Karachi
Kuala Lumpur Madrid Melbourne Mexico City Nairobi
New Delhi Shanghai Taipei Toronto

With offices in

Argentina Austria Brazil Chile Czech Republic France Greece
Guatemala Hungary Italy Japan Poland Portugal Singapore
South Korea Switzerland Thailand Turkey Ukraine Vietnam

Oxford is a registered trade mark of Oxford University Press
in the UK and in certain other countries

Published in the United States
by Oxford University Press Inc., New York

© James Morrison and the NCTJ 2009

British Library Cataloguing in Publication Data
Data available

Library of Congress Cataloging in Publication Data
Data available

Typeset by Laserwords Private Ltd, Chennai, India
Printed in Great Britain
on acid-free paper by
Ashford Colour Press, Gosport, Hampshire

ISBN 978–0–19–955261–0

10 9 8 7 6 5 4 3 2 1

For my beloved Annalise, Scarlet, and Rosella

Preface

What are 'public affairs'?

An awful lot is expected of trainee journalists. From the day on which they first step into a regional newsroom, they will need to: know their way around the law (or, at least, to give a passable impression of understanding it); have the initiative to generate off-diary stories; display the confidence and tenacity to interview people and to persevere in the face of obfuscation; and above all, be able to take an accurate shorthand note.

But equally prominent on many editors' shopping lists of minimum requirements is the expectation that their new recruits be equipped with a rudimentary knowledge of how the world around them ticks—and that's where this book comes in. Closely based on the public affairs modules that have been a mainstay of the National Council for the Training of Journalists (NCTJ) pre-entry journalism courses for more than thirty years, it is intended to help students navigate the often bewildering network of local, regional, national, and, increasingly, global institutions that, to a greater or lesser degree, govern British people's lives.

So what exactly is (or, perhaps more correctly, are) 'public affairs'? MSN Encarta defines the term as *'issues that affect people generally, or issues arising from the relationship of the public to an organization such as a government body or a financial institution'*. This seems as good a way as any to describe the general thrust and content of this book. What you will find within these pages is a comprehensive (and, one hopes, coherent) explanation of the nature, roles, and powers of the organizations that govern the lives of citizens—and, by extension, the work of journalists—in twenty-first-century Britain. The book has been divided into two halves: the first focusing on the constitutional framework and governing institutions of the UK as a whole; the second examining the emergence, evolution, and current resurgence of various forms of local autonomy.

To ensure that the book is as accessible as possible and makes immediate sense to casual readers (not only those who will come to depend on it as their core NCTJ public affairs text), the decision has been taken to start with central government, rather than local. Some NCTJ purists (if such there are) might question this move, given that many centres have traditionally taught local government first, to prepare students for their mid-course work experience on regional papers, but I make no apologies. On sitting down to write, the logic of adopting a chronological approach—starting with the origins of parliamentary democracy—seemed inescapable. Local authorities, in the strict sense of the term, only began to emerge in the nineteenth century, so it would arguably be counter-intuitive to plunge straight into a detailed explanation of the role and structure of local government before first exploring the wider constitutional developments that made them possible.

The public affairs veterans among you will doubtless also notice one or two other quirks. For reasons that made sense to me as I began writing the book (and still do now), I have spread information on the subject of devolution through not one, but several chapters. The concept of devolution and how it came about is introduced in Chapter 1, which focuses on the evolution of the British constitution and parliamentary democracy. The parliamentary and legislative arrangements in Scotland, Wales, and Northern Ireland in the wake of devolution, however, are explained in Chapter 2, which is all about the business of the legislature in its various forms. Meanwhile, Chapter 3, which concerns the executive arm of the constitution, examines the new forms of government introduced in the three countries. In later chapters, I have tried to include the most important policy and institutional differences between the four British nations—but without becoming so obsessive about every minor variation that I bewilder the reader. Devolution is an exception, however: most core syllabus topics are handled in discrete chapters and I hope that the reader will forgive this one indulgence, which simply felt logical when I came to sit down and map the book out.

Of course, *Public Affairs for Journalists* is not the first textbook to tackle this subject; neither is it the first to receive NCTJ endorsement. Until 2002, LGcommunications published two invaluable volumes on a biannual basis to accompany its 'Public Affairs Part I' and 'Public Affairs Part II' syllabuses: *Essential Local Government* and *Essential Central Government*, both by Ron Fenney. For the past six years, these have been out of print, leaving students of these subjects—now renamed simply 'Public Affairs: Local Government' and 'Public Affairs: Central Government'—devoid of a set text (and many professional reporters short of a handy crib sheet). In the meantime, the world of government and its attendant institutions has marched steadily on—relentlessly reconfiguring, realigning, and rebranding, as journalists junior and senior have struggled to keep up.

Further, while the LGcommunication books were indispensable at the time, in light of the absence of any competing titles that so closely matched the concerns and content of the NCTJ public affairs programmes of study, they had their weaknesses. I do not presume to have avoided all of these in this first edition of *Public Affairs for Journalists*. Having taken close counsel from a number of experienced public affairs lecturers and journalists—not to mention my fellow members of the NCTJ's esteemed public affairs board—I am, however, confident that I have managed to improve on some of these areas.

One oft-cited gripe about the previous books was their lack of explicit emphasis on the 'key terms' that journalism students are expected to be able to define in their final NCTJ exams. I have sought to avoid this charge by incorporating an alphabetical glossary of these terms (fully comprehensive at the time of going to print). Another common complaint was that, by the time the books hit the shelves (or, at the very least, soon afterwards), they were already 'out of date'. To some extent, this is unavoidable, given the inherent difficulties of providing a definitive handbook for a subject so prone to changing political priorities and unexpected events. With *Public Affairs for Journalists* (as with the latest editions of McNae's *Essential Law for Journalists*), however, Oxford University Press is doing its best to counter these fears, by providing an associated Online Resource Centre and accompanying monthly e-newsletter to update students and lecturers on significant developments in local and central government between editions.

All that said, the format of the previous books had its undeniable strengths and this new book retains—and, where possible, builds on—these. An effort has been made, where possible, to include tables and charts to illustrate better some of the more technical aspects of certain topics. The book, as a whole, concludes with the glossary, and a full index and bibliography. Within the chapters themselves, whenever a new NCTJ key term is introduced, it is highlighted in the main body of the text in bold italic type, so as not to confuse it with other concepts that (however significant) are not specified as such by the NCTJ. Each chapter will also seek to provoke discussion over and above mere 'learning by rote' of its content by ending with a series of pointers towards in-depth reflection and debate.

I would like to close with a pre-emptive apology. As anyone who teaches public affairs will know, it is all but impossible for a book of this nature to be comprehensive for long, given the constantly shifting sands on which it is built. Many were the days while writing this during which I would tune in to Radio 4's *Today* programme to be greeted by yet another government announcement about the launch of a new policy, or the renaming, restructuring, or abolition of a long-standing public institution. Then there are the sudden political crises that can make the 'Westminster village' such a colourful and surprising place—but such an infuriating one, too, for those of us trying to make sense of it. In the final weeks of the editing process, as the main text of the book was about to be packed off to production (never to be tweaked again), what should occur but a wholesale collapse of the banking sector—not only in Britain, but also in the USA, mainland Europe, and beyond. As governments scrambled to avert a new global depression comparable to that of the 1930s, high street banks went bankrupt, merged, and were nationalized; in Britain, local authorities and other public bodies watched impotently while more than £1bn of taxpayers' money vanished into oblivion as the high-interest Icelandic institutions in which the money was invested capsized under the weight of their collective folly. And the UK was far from a bit player in all of this turmoil: at the centre of the storm, navigating the tortuous route to a safe haven for major economies the world over, was a resurgent Gordon Brown.

Other stop-press amendments were needed, too: the surprise return to government of Mr Brown's erstwhile arch-rival, Peter Mandelson, and Schools Secretary Ed Balls' sudden announcement of the scrapping of National Curriculum tests for 14-year-olds were among the causes of anxious-browed, late-night email 'updates' from me to my ever-patient copy-editor, Vanessa Plaister.

Who knows, by the time you pick up this book, four long months after it has gone to the printers, there might be a new prime minister, a new government, or even a new world order.

For now, however, this is it: public affairs in Britain as of October 2008.

JM

Acknowledgements

I would like to thank my unflappable research assistant, Bridget Kenning-ham, and my colleagues on the NCTJ's public affairs board, chaired by the inestimable Mandy Ball, for their support and encouragement as I wrote this book. Thanks, too, are due to the various other lecturers, journalists, and Local Government Association (LGA) experts who reviewed the chapters as I wrote them, for their invariably salient advice. Special mention must go to Ron Fenney and to David Kett—the nearest that Britain has, surely, to a public affairs guru—for the huge amount of legwork that they both did before me to make sense of the tangle of legislation and 'officialese' that bedevils local and central government today.

I would also like to thank the LGA, the Institute of Fiscal Studies (IFS), the United Nations Department of Public Information, the Directorate-General for Budget of the European Commission, the Department for Communities and Local Government (DCLG), and the Economic and Social Research Council (ESRC) for their prompt responses to requests for data, and their willingness for us to reproduce tables and charts (which we have credited where this is the case).

Thanks to the various other government departments, executive agencies, and quangos who have helped with enquiries in one way or other: HM Treasury; the Department for Work and Pensions (DWP); the Foreign and Commonwealth Office's Europe Delivery Group; the School Improvement Division of the Department for Children, Schools and Families; the Commission for Social Care Inspection; and the Department of Health.

My thanks also to Joanne Butcher, chief executive of the NCTJ, and Oxford University Press for having the foresight to commission this new textbook, after far too long without one.

This book has greatly benefited from being reviewed by a large number of reviewers:

- the Local Government Finance Team (Local Government Association);
- Caroline Abrahams (Local Government Association);

- Amanda Ball (Centre for Broadcasting and Journalism, Nottingham Trent University);

- Sandra Brown (Local Government Association);

- Cathy Duncan (assistant editor of the *South Wales Evening Post*);

- Paul Durrant (assistant editor at the Eastern Daily Press);

- Ken Eaton (Public Affairs Board, National Council for the Training of Journalists);

- Paul Francis (political editor at the Kent Messenger Group);

- Sue Green (City of Wolverhampton College);

- Janet Jones (School of Humanities, Glyndwr University);

- Gareth Knight (Local Government Association);

- Anne McDonald (Local Government Association);

- Glyn Mottershead (Centre for Journalism Studies, Cardiff School of Journalism, Media and Cultural Studies, Cardiff University);

- John Ransford (Local Government Association);

- Paul Rowinski (Strathclyde School of Journalism and Communication, University of Strathclyde);

- Milne Rowntree (School of Media, Film and Journalism, University of Ulster);

- Richard Rudin (Journalism Department, Liverpool John Moores University);

- Edward Welsh (Local Government Association);

- Martin Wheatley (Local Government Association).

The reviewers have had a very important input into the development of this book and I am grateful for their time. Any views expressed in the book are mine alone and do not necessarily reflect the views of reviewers or the NCTJ.

Finally, I would like to thank my fellow hacks in the *North Devon Journal* class of 95–97, all of whom have gone on to far greater things, in particular James Cornish, Mark Devane, Kent Upshon, Tahira Yaqoob, and Matt Radley.

Brief contents

Detailed contents

Introduction

▌ Confessions of a local council reporter

I'll never forget the name 'Mervyn Lane'. From the moment that I arrived as a naive raw recruit on the *North Devon Journal* in Barnstaple—bristling with high ideas, most of which were hugely unrealistic and some a little 'conspiracy theorist'—Mervyn and I were destined to clash. I'd been taken on as a junior reporter without a car (or, for that matter, driving licence) and was only hired on condition that I pass my test within six months of starting. Logically enough, I was immediately posted to Bideford—the area's 'second town', some ten miles west of the paper's Barnstaple headquarters—but still expected to soldier into head office each day, and cover a sprawling patch of rustic terrain into the bargain.

To top it all, I was required to generate a district edition single-handedly each week, filling three pages of news and finding at least one front-page lead without fail. Bideford being Bideford, there were few obvious sources of scoops: the edgiest events tended to be an annual Easter fair, known dubiously (but all too descriptively) as 'Cow Pat Fun Day', and the occasional drugs raid on a pint-sized sink estate at East-the-Water, the town's ungrammatically named answer to Moss Side.

Unsurprisingly, it wasn't long before I was turning to the local authority for inspiration (or, more accurately, out of desperation). Little did I know how fruitful this would be. Those wintry evenings spent pinching myself awake through meetings of Torridge District Council's planning committee invariably threw up a last-minute gem that, with a bit of creative editing (and barring news of an international sheep-rustling scam), would generate enough ire to merit a splash.

From the humdrum ('Supermarket Threat to Town Centre') to the absurd ('Ships in Our Back Garden'), Torridge seldom failed to deliver the goods. Inevitably, it was only a matter of time before I crossed swords with the venerable Mr Lane—at that time, leader of the district council's ruling Liberal Democrat group, chairman of its powerful policy and resources committee, and both a Bideford town councillor and Devon county councillor to boot.

The first of our many run-ins was sparked by a front-page story I wrote about a decision to award free parking permits to all Torridge councillors and ninety-two senior officers (dubbed 'essential users' by the council) for use in council car parks in central Bideford whenever they were on local authority business. As controversies go, this may sound small beer—there was nothing illegal or improper about the policy—but boy did it upset the locals. To understand the scale of the furore among residents and businesses, a little context is needed. Parking and the wider subject of transport were perhaps the most toxic issues facing Bidefordians. For various reasons, driving was pretty much the only way most people had of gaining access to the town for shopping or tourism, thanks to a train line that was (literally) a museum piece (take a bow, Dr Beeching), and an antediluvian bus service. The notoriously perilous North Devon Link Road and a winding, hazardous 'coastal route' were all that connected it to civilization (or Barnstaple, at any rate)—providing lifelines for those living in outlying villages. Yet, in central Bideford—in the words of one councillor, 'a medieval town with a twentieth century traffic problem'—any street wide enough to admit vehicles seemed to have been daubed with double-yellow lines, putting the limited car park spaces available at a premium. Hence the reaction.

My parking story was one of many to irritate Mr Lane during my eighteen month tenure as Bideford district reporter. But he wasn't the only local dignitary to be included in a splash on the *Journal* during this time. . .

Let's not forget George Moss, the Bideford mayor who arrived in full regalia to turn on the town's Christmas lights one November only to find out that a timer switch had done so automatically several hours earlier, at the moment at which dusk had descended. He didn't fare any better a year later, when the precautions that council engineers took to avoid a similar fiasco proved so watertight that the lights couldn't be switched on at all.

Of course, council stories don't need to emanate from committee meetings—or, for that matter, councillors. Take the case of Les Garland, a community activist from Northam—a strip of suburban housing, pock-marked with scrappy golf courses, which runs along the Torridge Estuary to the east of Bideford. Armed with little more than a tape measure, he led a one-man campaign to rid the whole of Devon of the peril of 'hazard-ously placed' A-boards. (To the uninitiated, A-boards are the signs one finds outside newsagents bearing misspelt headlines from papers such as the *Journal*.)

Insisting they posed a hazard to pedestrians, by blocking pavements and tripping people up, Les set about scouring the small print of Devon County Council's highways regulations—not to mention various Acts of Parliament—in search of a clause that would back his assertion that they contravened health and safety legislation. I clearly remember a conversation with an apoplectic county councillor, who stormed into the *Journal*'s Bideford office to inform me that the county could be faced with rewriting its entire high-ways policy, at a cost of tens of thousands of pounds, if Les were to force the issue.

Perhaps inevitably, Les had the last laugh. When I last visited North Devon, in 2003, I picked up a copy of that hallowed Bideford edition of the *Journal*. Turning to the district pages, I was greeted by a familiar visage, grinning at me over a caption about a good citizenship award he'd received for serving the local community. As I wandered down Bideford high street later that day, I couldn't help noticing several shops still had A-boards placed peril-ously distant from their doorways. But the memory of Les's beaming face reminded me that, in one way or other, his dogged devotion to civic duty had paid off.

My purpose in highlighting these anecdotal examples is to illustrate a simple point: that knowledge of public affairs (and, for the rookie journal-ist, local government especially) *matters*. Whether it be protests by angry parents over changes to school catchment areas, demands from worried residents for speed restrictions to prevent accidents on dangerous roads, or controversies about New Age traveller camps, waste disposal sites, or parasitical out-of-town superstores, local newspapers are chock-full of council-related stories on a daily and weekly basis. And to identify, research, and write up these stories in a way that is comprehensible and meaningful to their readers, journalists first need to grasp the basics of how government works and the parameters within which it operates. This book aims to make that process easier.

1

The British constitution and monarchy

▶ What is a 'constitution'?

For any state to achieve a sense of order and identity, it requires a shared set of values to be recognized and accepted by its subjects. Such values tend to be instilled by a system of fundamental laws and principles, and upheld by parliaments, courts, and other institutions established to maintain and reinforce them.

This notion of shared membership, of collective rights and responsibilities—as common to commercial companies and supranational organizations such as the European Union (EU) as to organs of any individual government—is known as a 'constitution'.

Constitutions come in all shapes, sizes, and formats. They can be formal or informal, long or short, absolute or merely advisory. Most significant, though, is the difference between the two broad types of constitution adopted by individual states: *written* and *unwritten*. Of course, for any set of ideas related to one's citizenship of a state to be communicated and sustained effectively, some kind of written record will need to exist. Yet there is an important distinction between constitutions described as 'written' and ones that are not. All constitutions of any worth comprise elements that have been written in a literal sense—for example, laws or decrees laid down in documentary form. But this does not make them 'written constitutions' per se. Written constitutions are, rather, *codified* frameworks: single manuscripts summarizing the rights, values, and responsibilities attached to membership of the states to which they relate.

For historical reasons, some states have adopted written constitutions while others have not. Although this is not universally the case, written constitutions have tended to emerge in countries where there has been a sudden change in the entire system of government caused by a political upheaval such as a war, invasion, or revolution. This was certainly the case for two of the nations with whom the term is perhaps most closely associated: France and the USA.

France's constitution derives from the *Declaration of the Rights of Man and of the Citizen*, adopted on 26 August 1789 by the National Constituent Assembly convened in the aftermath of the French Revolution, and later amended to enshrine the three abiding principles of 'liberty, equality, and fraternity'. The USA adopted its equivalent a decade after declaring independence from Britain, on 17 September 1787, at a landmark constitutional convention in Philadelphia, Pennsylvania, addressed by the Enlightenment philosopher Benjamin Franklin.

The origins and sources of the British constitution

Britain—or more accurately the 'United Kingdom of Great Britain and Northern Ireland'—is a different case entirely. The story of the UK's constitutional evolution is of, first, the gradual unification of disparate kingdoms under one national sovereign (monarch), then, in due course, the struggle for supremacy between the sovereign and the Christian Church, and ultimately between the sovereign and Parliament.

As these various power struggles have been played out, at several points in its history the UK has come close to adopting a formal framework specifying the rights and responsibilities of its citizenry, but, up to now, has stopped short of producing a definitive statement. Despite the fact that documents of one kind or another form a huge part of the constitutional framework governing the lives of its citizens, there exists no single statement of principles. Therefore, in defiance of campaigns by all manner of individuals and pressure groups—from the Chartists of 1848, to the coalition of liberal thinkers who put their names to Charter 88 a century and a half later—to all intents and purposes, Britain still has an unwritten constitution.

As such, the British constitution has clear advantages: it is *flexible* enough to be amended, added to, or subtracted from according to the will of the elected

Parliament of the day, without any of the tortuous procedures required in the USA and elsewhere whenever the slightest break with tradition is sought in the interests of political progress. Conversely, it has the disadvantage of provoking as much wrangling among lawyers, politicians, and historians as it can ever claim to circumvent, by leaving substantial layers of ambiguity around sometimes crucial issues relating to its subjects' liberties. The recent controversy about Gordon Brown's decision to sign the EU's 2007 Lisbon Treaty—seen by some as a 'European constitution' in all but name—is only one example of how easily the UK can adopt potentially significant changes to its constitutional fabric without any of the debate rendered necessary by the *rigid* rule systems of other countries. Meanwhile, the perceived assault on individuals' civil liberties represented by the raft of 'Big Brother' anti-terror legislation since the attacks on the Twin Towers on 11 September 2001, not to mention the proposed introduction of identity cards and a national DNA database, is viewed by human rights campaigners as an example of the dangers of failing to enshrine core principles in a solid constitutional statement.

So what are the primary sources of the UK's constitution? The constituent components are probably best split into the following five broad categories:

- *statute*—that is, individual laws, known as 'Acts of Parliament';
- *common law*—sometimes known as 'judge-made', or 'case' law;
- *conventions*—that is, customs, traditions, and long-standing practices;
- *treatises*—historical works of legal and/or constitutional authority;
- *treaties*—that is, EU and other international agreements.

Statute

Magna Carta (the Great Charter), signed by King John in 1215, is often cited as the foundation stone of Britain's constitution, invoking as it does the principle of *rule of law*. This embodied the inalienable right of any citizen accused of a criminal offence to a free and fair trial before their peers and, crucially, enshrined the principle that no one—not even the reigning sovereign—is 'above the law'. Of course, the idea that not even the sovereign is immune to prosecution is (like many constitutional concepts in the UK) largely a notional one. In practice, because most criminal prosecutions are instigated in the name of the Crown, if the king or queen were to be accused of a crime and brought before a court of law, this would provoke a constitutional crisis.

Perhaps more significant even than Magna Carta was the 1689 Bill of Rights, passed in the wake of the extraordinarily turbulent period stemming from the execution forty years earlier of the Anglican King Charles I, and the 11-year 'interregnum' that followed under his vanquisher, the Puritan 'Lord Protector' Oliver Cromwell. Although titular head of the Church of England, Charles was felt by many to be too sympathetic to Roman Catholicism, having married the Catholic princess Henrietta Maria of France. There was also deep unease about his invocation of the loose constitutional principle (popular among medieval monarchs) known as the 'Divine Right of Kings'—a notion that the authority of the sovereign derived from his or her relationship to God and was thus immutable. In the event, the Parliamentarians secured victory over Charles's Royalist supporters in the ensuing English Civil War (1642–51), ending centuries of rule under this premise.

The Bill of Rights itself arose out of the alliance between the Protestant-dominated Parliament and William of Orange, the Dutch king whom it helped to depose Charles's younger son, James II, during the 'Glorious Revolution' of 1688. Having worked in an uneasy stalemate with James's elder brother, Charles II, after his return from exile in France following Cromwell's death in 1660, Parliament used the ascension of his uncompromising sibling (a devout Catholic) as a pretext to cement its newly asserted authority as the supreme seat of power in Britain.

To this end, it identified James's Protestant daughter, Mary, as the rightful heir to the throne, prompting her father's flight to France. Together with her husband, William, Mary effectively deposed James as monarch. In exchange for Parliament's loyalty to the couple, they permitted the passage of the Bill, which formalized for the first time the transfer of constitutional supremacy from Crown to elected Parliament. Its central tenet was to ratify the principle that the sovereign could only in future rule *through* Parliament—rather than tell it what to do, as in the past. In other words, monarchs would henceforth have to seek the official consent of members of Parliament (MPs)—and, more particularly, government ministers—before passing legislation (Acts), declaring war, or invoking any of the other sovereign powers that they had traditionally wielded. In this way, the Bill effectively ended centuries of 'royal sovereignty' and ushered in the concept (even today a fundamental cornerstone of Britain's democracy) of *parliamentary sovereignty*.

This core constitutional principle is the one that, above all others, most symbolizes the oft-cited flexibility of an unwritten constitution. The term 'sovereignty'—also known as *political sovereignty*—refers to the notion of an individual or institution exercising supreme control over an area, people, or themselves. The concept of parliamentary sovereignty flows from this: as well as asserting the hegemony of the *institution* of Parliament over British subjects, it confers on *each individual UK Parliament*—that is, the body of MPs elected at a given general election—the authority to make its own laws and potentially to repeal any of those passed by previous Parliaments. To this extent, it prevents any one Parliament being 'bound by the actions of a predecessor'.

Many constitutional experts argue that this idea is incompatible with that of a conventional written constitution because, if we had such a document, one Parliament could theoretically use its sovereignty simply to repeal the Act that introduced it. Advocates of a codified document say that this is a bogus argument, arguing that many countries with written constitutions manage to maintain them alongside their own versions of parliamentary sovereignty without encountering such conflicts. One way of embedding written constitutions into the political fabric of a state is to compose them out of webs of interlocking legislation, rather than a single Act—making them harder to repeal. Another might be to set up an independent superior court with the power to adjudicate in constitutional disputes. A new US-style 'Supreme Court' along these lines was due to come into effect in Britain in 2009 (see pp. 20–21).

In addition to formalizing the notion of parliamentary sovereignty, the Bill of Rights granted a number of specific entitlements to all 'Englishmen'—with the exception, in certain cases, of Roman Catholics. Its main tenets are listed in Table 1.1.

The Bill also specified conditions governing the future succession of the monarchy, in light of the coronation of William and Mary over the dethroned James II:

- the flight of James from England was defined as an 'abdication';
- William and Mary were officially declared the successors of James;
- after them, the throne should pass to Mary's heirs, then her sister, Princess Anne of Denmark, and her heirs, then to heirs of William by later marriage.

Finally, the Bill also introduced a further constitutional principle that is fundamental to the working of the British Parliament. Often incorrectly described as a 'convention' (rather than as a product of statute, which it is), this is the notion of *parliamentary privilege*. In brief, parliamentary privilege enables any elected MP sitting in the House of Commons or peer in the House of Lords to make accusations about individuals or companies in open debate in the chambers without fear of prosecution for defamation.

Table 1.1 Main entitlements listed in the Bill of Rights 1689

Freedoms for all 'Englishmen'	Sanctions for Roman Catholics
Freedom from royal interference with the law—sovereigns were forbidden from establishing their own courts, or acting as judge themselves	A ban on Catholics succeeding to the English throne—reflecting the supposed fact that *'it hath been found by experience that it is inconsistent with the safety and welfare of this protestant kingdom to be governed by a papist prince'*
Freedom from being taxed without the agreement of Parliament	An obligation on newly crowned sovereigns to swear oaths of allegiance to the Church of England
Freedom to petition the monarch	
Freedom *for Protestants only* to possess 'arms for defence'	Bar on carrying weapons
Freedom from drafting into a peacetime army without Parliament's consent	
Freedom to elect MPs without interference from the sovereign	
Freedom from cruel and unusual punishments, and from excessive bail	
Freedom from fines and forfeitures without trial	

In recent years, there have been several high-profile examples of the use of parliamentary privilege by members to 'name and shame' private individuals in ways that would be considered defamatory (and might invite legal action) if they were to be repeated outside Parliament. In 2000, Peter Hain (then Foreign Office Minister for Africa) invoked parliamentary privilege to identify brothers Maurice and David Zollman as the owners of an Antwerp diamond trading business that he said was breaking **United Nations (UN)** sanctions by helping to bankroll the civil war in Angola. A year later, Peter Robinson (then deputy leader of the Democratic Unionist Party) used it to 'out' Brian Keenan and Brian Gillen as members of the Provisional Irish Republican Army (IRA) ruling army council.

A flipside of the legal protection afforded by parliamentary privilege is the fact that certain words and phrases are construed as 'unparliamentary language' and therefore unacceptable if directed at fellow members in either the Commons or Lords chambers. Most notorious is the word 'liar', which is seen to conflict constitutionally with the freedom given to members under parliamentary privilege to speak their minds. In November 1993, the Reverend Ian Paisley (then leader of the Democratic Unionists) was suspended from the Commons for five days for accusing then Prime Minister John Major of lying after it emerged that, despite previously insisting that the idea of negotiating with Northern Irish Republicans (whom he dubbed 'terrorists') would 'turn his stomach', he'd actually been holding secret talks for more than a year with Sinn Féin, the main Republican party.

Just as parliamentary privilege gives protection from being sued through the courts to MPs or peers who make defamatory statements in Parliament, it also protects the media and public from action arising out of repeating those claims. By way of further complicating explanations of this privilege, however, according to a literal interpretation of the Bill of Rights, it also protects the press from proceedings arising from *a report alleging wrongdoing in Parliament by an MP*. This contentious legal argument was used to enable *The Guardian* to defend a libel action brought in 1996 by former Conservative minister Neil Hamilton over its allegations two years earlier that he had accepted cash from Mohamed Al Fayed for asking parliamentary questions designed to further the Harrods owner's business interests. To muddy the constitutional waters further, as a sitting MP, Mr Hamilton had to obtain formal permission to sue the newspaper in the first place. In the event, a new clause was inserted into the 1996 Defamation Act (s. 13) enabling him to waive his right to parliamentary privilege by suing *The Guardian* as a private citizen. In any event, his action failed.

In November 2008, a major political row erupted about a more obscure aspect of parliamentary privilege, when it emerged that the Conservatives' immigration spokesman, Damian Green, had been arrested and questioned by police for nine hours over allegations that he unlawfully solicited leaks about government policy from a sympathetic civil servant in the Home Office. Both Opposition and government MPs united in criticising the police action. Many saw it as an abuse of the long-established constitutional right of members to conduct free and open conversations with officials in the Palace of Westminster—and a throwback to Charles I's challenge to the freedoms of Parliament in the seventeenth century. At time of writing, MPs had turned their fire on the Commons Speaker, Michael Martin, who was accused of having given his permission to officers to search Mr Green's office in the House, potentially jeopardizing the confidentiality of sensitive information relating to his constituents.

Of the UK's other key constitutional statutes, the most historically significant are the 1701 Act of Settlement and the 1706–07 Acts of Union. The former built on the newly introduced rules relating to monarchical succession in the Bill of Rights, by setting out the conditions for future sovereigns outlined in Table 1.2.

The Acts of Union, meanwhile, were twin laws passed firstly England, then in Scotland, in 1706 and 1707 respectively, formalizing the Treaty of

Table 1.2 The rules governing monarchical succession in the Act of Settlement 1701

Rule	Details
Protestants only	The Crown should pass to the Protestant descendants of the Electress Sophie of Hanover (a first cousin once removed of Queen Anne, who had inherited the throne after the death of Mary and her husband, William)
No marriages to Catholics	The monarch 'shall join in communion with the Church of England' and not marry a Roman Catholic
England for the English	If a person not native to England comes to the throne, England will not wage war for 'any dominions or territories which do not belong to the Crown of England without the consent of Parliament'
Loyalty from the Crown	No monarch may leave the 'British Isles' without the consent of Parliament (repealed by George I in 1716)
Openness before Parliament	All government matters within the jurisdiction of the Privy Council (see p. 47) should be transacted there and all such resolutions must be signed, so that Parliament is aware of who has taken such decisions
Constitutional privileges for English only	No foreigner, even if naturalized (unless born of English parents), shall be allowed to be a privy councillor or member of either House of Parliament, or hold 'any office or place of trust, either civil or military, or to have any grant of lands, tenements or hereditaments from the Crown, to himself or to any other or others in trust for him' (repealed by later citizenship laws)
Ban on election for Crown servants	No person working for the monarch or receiving a Crown pension may be a MP, to avoid 'unwelcome' royal interference in the work of Parliament
Judiciary answerable to Parliament	Judges' commissions are valid *quamdiu se bene gesserint* (during good behaviour) and can be removed only by both Houses of Parliament
Parliament has ultimate sanction	No Royal Pardon (see p. 25) can save a person from impeachment by the Commons

Table 1.3 Key statutes absorbed into the UK constitution in the twentieth century

Statute	Effect
Race Relations Acts 1965, 1968, and 1976	Outlawed discrimination on racial grounds
Government of Scotland and Government of Wales Acts 1998	Paved the way for national referenda to establish devolved power in Scotland and Wales
Human Rights Act (HRA) 1998	Incorporated into British law the *Convention on the Protection of Human Rights and Fundamental Freedoms* (commonly known as the European Convention on Human Rights), signed by the **Council of Europe** in 1950 (see p. 330–1)
House of Lords Act 1999	Removed all but 92 hereditary peers then remaining and created a 'transitional' Lords to remain until further, decisive reform was agreed by both Houses (see p. 66–70)

Union—the agreement that unified the countries as one United Kingdom under one sovereign and Parliament. Key Acts absorbed into UK law in more recent times include those listed in Table 1.3.

The penultimate Act listed in Table 1.3—the Human Rights Act (HRA) 1998—justifies some discussion here, given the growing contention by many lawyers, human rights campaigners, and constitutional experts that it conflicts with the British constitution as it previously stood. Although it received **Royal Assent** in November 1998, the Act only came into force in October 2000. Among its stipulations was that every future Bill put before Parliament must now include a preface confirming that the relevant **secretary of state** is happy that it conforms with the convention. The principal rights safeguarded by the convention are as outlined in Table 1.4.

In addition, the UK has accepted the First and Sixth (now Thirteenth) Protocols to the *European Convention on Human Rights* (ECHR), of which there are 14 altogether. The First Protocol includes additional rights for property (Art. 1), education (Art. 2), and free and fair elections (Art. 3).

Table 1.4 The Articles of the European Convention on Human Rights (ECHR)

Article	Right enshrined
1	Obligation to respect human rights
2	Life
3	Protection from torture and inhuman, or degrading, treatment
4	Protection from slavery and forced, or compulsory, labour
5	Right to liberty and security of person
6	Right to a fair trial
7	Protection from retrospective criminalization of acts or omissions
8	Protection of private and family life
9	Freedom of thought, conscience, and religion
10	Freedom of expression
11	Freedom of association and assembly
12	Right to marry and found a family
13	Freedom from discrimination
14	Prohibition of discrimination
15	Derogations
16	Exemption for political activities of aliens
17	Prohibition of abuse of rights
18	Limitations on permitted restrictions of rights

The Sixth Protocol, meanwhile, formally abolishes the death penalty in peacetime, while the Thirteenth Protocol does so in all circumstances.

The Act has, in theory, strengthened the ability of ordinary people to challenge the actions of governments, public bodies, and private companies in the UK and EU courts, by taking legal action through the *European Court of Human Rights (ECtHR)* in Strasbourg, if necessary. There are, however, some notable restrictions to its pre-eminence, and it is as yet a moot point as to how far it takes absolute precedence over national laws and conventions. There is a general consensus, for example, that the existing constitutional principle of parliamentary privilege remains unaffected by the Act. In addition, British judges—although required by it to take account of judgments in Strasbourg when making rulings in British courts—are not permitted simply to override extant parliamentary legislation that appears to contravene the terms of the Convention.

In addition, the following formal qualifications exist in relation to the implementation and enforcement of the Act:

- claims must be brought against the offending state or public body *'within one year of the action about which the complaint is being made'*;
- some rights can theoretically be breached, if not *'in accordance with the laws of the country'* that is a signatory;
- breaches are tolerated *'in the interests of national security, public safety, or the country's economic wellbeing; for the prevention of crime and disorder, the protection of health or morals, or to protect the freedom and rights of others . . .'*.

In the UK, the HRA has arguably been repeatedly breached by successive home secretaries, from David Blunkett to Jacqui Smith. The Anti-terrorism, Crime and Security Act 2001, passed in the wake of the 11 September attacks on New York, allowed the detention and deportation, without trial, of people suspected of terrorist links, and Tony Blair repeatedly threatened to amend the Act to prevent judges blocking further proposed crackdowns—particularly on the activities of extremist Islamist preachers—following the 2005 London bombings.

In Scotland, meanwhile, the Act came into force in 1998—two years ahead of England. By November 1999, the High Court had already declared unlawful the appointment of 129 temporary sheriffs (judges in the Scottish criminal courts) because they had been hired by the Lord Advocate, the member of the *Scottish Executive* responsible for prosecutions—a clear conflict with one of the constitution's fundamental guiding principles, the *separation of powers* (see p. 19–21).

One potential outcome of the adoption of the Act in the longer term could be the abolition of the Act of Settlement, which might be argued to infringe human rights by preventing non-Protestants from acceding to the throne of the UK and maintaining a system whereby the succession passes through the male line (see below). For some time, *The Guardian* has argued that the very *existence* of a monarchy is incompatible with the HRA and that it should therefore be repealed. Because it is still technically illegal, under the Treason Felony Act 1848, to advocate the monarchy's abolition, *The Guardian* recently tried to obtain a High Court declaration that the 1848 Act was incompatible with Art. 10 of the HRA. Its attempt failed, due to a loophole, because the court ruled that the Attorney General's refusal to grant immunity to its editor was not an 'act of the state'—that is, that it fell outside the HRA's remit.

The most recent twist in the newspaper's long-standing campaign for the abolition of the Act came in September 2008, when it reported that Labour MP Chris Bryant—charged by Gordon Brown during his first year as prime minister with reviewing the constitution—had recommended ending the bar on Catholics succeeding to the throne and abolishing the principle of 'eldest male primogeniture'. This is the rule stating that, following the death of a monarch, the crown should pass to his or her eldest son, over the head of any older daughter. Mr Brown's constitutional adviser, Wilf Stevenson, was said to favour legislating to end both of these traditions early in a fourth Labour term.

Besides the showpiece constitutional Acts listed in Table 1.3, a number of others have contained key clauses with serious implications for the workings of the British constitution. Among these are the myriad Parliament Acts passed in the first half of the twentieth century (discussed in more detail in Chapter 2). Perhaps the single most significant constitutional reform introduced by any of these Acts was the stipulation, in the Parliament Act 1911, that a general election must be held *a maximum of five years after the previous Parliament was convened* (in other words, a little over five years after the previous polling day). Until then, parliaments could theoretically last up to seven years, under the terms of the Septennial Act 1715. Despite this change, unlike in the USA and other countries, British parliaments still do *not* have fixed terms.

Common law

For several centuries prior to the emergence of parliamentary democracy, many laws passed in England were decided, on a case-by-case basis, by judges. When this system began to emerge in the eleventh and twelfth centuries, judicial decisions were often taken in an ad hoc way, at a very local level, leading to significant disparities from one area of the kingdom to another—in terms of the perception of what was and was not a criminal offence, and the type and severity of punishment meted out when laws were broken.

In 1166, however, the first Plantagenet king, Henry II, began the process of institutionalizing a unified national framework of common law derived from what he saw as the more reasoned judgments made in local hearings over previous decades. This new framework—which came to apply throughout England and Wales, although not Scotland—elevated some local laws to a national level, sought to eliminate arbitrary or eccentric rulings, and established a great enduring constitutional right of citizens charged with criminal offences: a jury system, which would enshrine defendants' entitlement to be tried by '12 good men and true' from among their fellow citizens. To ensure that these new practices were implemented consistently and fairly throughout the land, Henry appointed judges at his own central court and sent them around the country to adjudicate on local disputes.

Many statutes passed—and constitutional conventions that have evolved—in subsequent centuries have their roots in common law. Even now, common law is arguably sometimes 'created': judges often have to make rulings based on their interpretations of ambiguously worded Acts, or of apparent conflicts between domestic and international laws. Such 'test cases' are, in their way, common law hearings.

Conventions

Other than from formal statutes and court judgments, perhaps the single most characteristic feature of Britain's unwritten constitution is its incorporation of all manner of idiosyncratic, invariably quaint, and occasionally absurd traditions and customs. These obscure and well-worn practices have become accepted as part of Britain's constitutional framework through little more than endless repetition.

Many of the principal conventions operating in Parliament and government today are discussed in detail elsewhere in this book. These include the doctrines of *collective responsibility* and *individual ministerial responsibility*, and the tradition that the sovereign accepts the will of Parliament by rubber-stamping new legislation with the Royal Assent. Other, more amusing, conventions include the fact that the Speaker of the House of Lords (until recently the **Lord Chancellor**) sits on a woolsack and wears a wig. The annual State Opening of Parliament by the reigning monarch is heralded by a procession led by a ceremonical officer known as 'The Gentleman Usher of the Black Rod', who raps three times on the door of the Lords with (naturally) a black staff to gain permission for MPs—or 'strangers'—to enter. This ritual is derived from a confrontation between Parliament and the sovereign in 1642, when King Charles I tried to arrest five MPs, in what the Commons regarded as a breach of parliamentary privilege. Within Parliament today, a former of light 'class warfare' between the chambers remains: MPs only refer to the Lords as 'another place'.

Treatises

Just as judges often have to disentangle apparently contradictory elements of Britain's unwritten constitution when making rulings in court, so too historians, philosophers, and constitutional theorists have long struggled to make sense of it.

Of the myriad books and theses written about the UK constitution over the centuries, a handful have become so revered that they are now seen effectively to qualify as 'part of' that constitution themselves. Some are now considered so indispensable that they are often used as 'handbooks' (albeit unwieldy ones) by everyone from the **Speaker** of the House of Commons to High Court barristers and judges. Many of today's new laws and court judgments are framed in reference to the wisdom imparted in such volumes, the most celebrated of which are listed in Table 1.5.

Treaties

Over recent decades, Britain has signed many international treaties and pacts. Of these, only a handful are arguably in any way 'constitutional'—that is, legally binding. Most—such as the 1945 Charter of the United Nations and the North Atlantic Treaty, which established the **North Atlantic Treaty Organization (NATO)** military alliance in 1949—are effectively little more than membership agreements and, as such, could theoretically be 'opted out of' at any time.

Some, however—such as the ECHR, belatedly ratified by Labour in 1998—have effectively been incorporated into the UK constitution and would therefore require legislation to 'remove' the obligations that they impose on the state. There has also been considerable debate about the growing powers

Table 1.5 Seminal British constitutional treatises

Treatise	Author	Significance
A Practical Treatise on the Law, Privileges, Proceedings and Usage of Parliament (Parliamentary Practice)	Erskine May (1844)	Sir Thomas Erskine May (1815–86), first Baron Farnborough and a distinguished parliamentary officer, became Chief Librarian of the House of Commons Library and Clerk to the House of Commons. His most famous work remains the seminal examination of the role, rights, and responsibilities of Parliament.
The English Constitution	Walter Bagehot (1867)	A maths graduate from University College, London, Bagehot (1826–77) was called to the Bar, but rejected it for a career in banking and shipping. He went on to edit The Economist (the last column of which still bears his name in tribute), before writing his most esteemed work: a rumination on the relationship between Parliament and monarchy—and the contrast between the UK and US constitutions.
An Introduction to the Study of the Law of the Constitution	A. V. Dicey (1885)	Albert Venn Dicey (1835–1922) was an accomplished scholar, appointed to the Vinerian Chair of English Law at the University of Oxford in 1882, later becoming professor of law at the London School of Economics. Of all of the great constitutional treasises, Dicey's is considered the most authoritative and far-reaching. Its central thesis was that—as long ago as 1885—the 'freedom' of British subjects was under attack by an increasingly aggressive rule of law. He saw the impartiality of the courts (which he believed to be essential to preserving this freedom) as even then being under attack from governments intent on limiting fundamental civil liberties. He might well disapprove of many recent developments, given controversies over the Labour government's moves to limit defendants' rights to request trial by jury, and to imprison, tag, and/or detain 'terror suspects' without trial.

of the EU, which Britain joined (amid some controversy) in 1973, when it was still known as the European Economic Community (EEC). Recent treaties—in particular, the 2007 Lisbon Treaty—have solidified the relationship between member states and the EU's governing institutions, leading so-called 'Euro-sceptics' to claim that the UK has signed up to an 'EU constitution' by the back door and that it is now effectively part of a 'European super-state' governed from Brussels, rather than an independent, sovereign nation, as before. This is discussed further in Chapter 9.

The separation of powers in the UK

Perhaps the most fundamental guiding principle underlying the British constitution is that of the 'separation of powers'. Based on the theories of French political thinker Baron de Montesquieu (1689–1755), the *Trias Politica* is a notional model that splits the state into three branches:

- the 'executive' (the government);
- the 'legislature' (Parliament);
- the 'judiciary' (the courts).

The idea is that, to avoid arbitrary or dictatorial government, a constitutional framework is needed that does not confer too many powers on a single individual (or small group of individuals). In theory, if the executive is wholly 'separated' from the legislature and, in turn, the judiciary, each can act as a 'check and balance' on the other.

Montesquieu formulated his theory based on the workings of the UK system, although Britain's democracy arguably adheres far less strictly to this model than many that have emerged since. In practice, numerous overlaps have emerged down the centuries between the roles, powers, and even membership of the key institutions that are meant to be preserving the separation of powers, including that:

- constitutionally, the reigning monarch (as 'head of state') is titular head of all three branches of the constitution;
- until 2007, when the post was reformed (see p. 78), the Lord Chancellor was actually a member of all three institutions, as Speaker of the House of Lords (legislature), 'manager' of the legal profession (judiciary), and a minister in the *Cabinet* (executive);
- the prime minister and most other ministers are members of the government (executive) and the Parliament (legislature);
- prior to the expected establishment of an independent Supreme Court in October 2009, the Law Lords were still the UK's highest court of appeal (judiciary), as well as being members of the Lords (legislature).

Such constitutional overlaps are not confined to Britain. Many other parliamentary democracies—particularly those directly modelled on that of the UK, as in many Commonwealth countries—display a similar fusion of powers in practice, rather than the 'separation' to which they aspire. Constitutional historians are increasingly drawing a distinction in this regard between countries that practice 'presidential government' and those characterized by 'parliamentary government'. In the former (which include the USA, France, South Africa, and Australia), separation is felt to be both more practised and practicable than in countries such as Britain, where the most senior politician (the prime minister) is today drawn from among the ranks of ordinary MPs and, as such, is elected to a *constituency* in the same way as his or her peers.

In the UK, executive decisions are taken primarily by prime ministers and their ministers, before being presented for approval to Parliament (where most of them are also present, this time as voting MPs and peers like every other). In the USA and other presidential states, in contrast, the most senior elected politicians are known as presidents—who, in the absence of reigning monarchs, are also heads of state. Crucially, unlike in Britain and other parliamentary states, presidents are usually elected on different timetables to their national parliaments. The separation of powers in the USA is far more pronounced than it is in Britain because Congress (made up of the Senate and the House of Representatives—the US equivalent of Britain's Parliament) is elected in large part on a different date, and in a different manner, to the president. More crucially, the president (unlike the British prime minister) is not a member of either House; so while he or she may present policies to Congress for its approval, he or she does not preside over the ensuing debate and vote(s) within the two chambers in the way that prime ministers do in the Commons.

Another feature of the separation of powers enjoyed by presidential states is the fact that, historically, they tend to have developed a more provably independent judicial system than in many parliamentary states. To this end, the USA has a Supreme Court that is, in theory, entirely separate from the political process. Notwithstanding controversies over the president's ability to nominate judges to replace those who retire (President Bush was castigated in 2005 for choosing Harriet Miers, his former adviser and a long-time conservative ally, who later withdrew her own candidacy), this system is felt to be better than one in which judges straddle the notional divide between legislature and judiciary by serving in both a legal and legislative capacity. To this end, in 2007, Jack Straw, as inaugural Secretary of State for Justice (and de facto Lord Chancellor) announced that the Law Lords would be effectively removed from Parliament in 2009, to sit in the new US-style independent court, the creation of which was approved in the Constitutional Reform Act 2005.

Further reforms were promised by Gordon Brown during his first weeks in Downing Street, as part of a 'new constitutional settlement' for the British people. Among those mooted was a law to formalize the tradition (notably bypassed by his predecessor over Iraq) that Parliament should always have the final say on whether Britain goes to war.

The monarchy

The British sovereign is the head of what is known as a 'constitutional monarchy'. This means that, while he or she remains the UK's head of state, with the notional prerogative to govern and take major constitutional decisions, in practice she does not do so. Unlike in presidential countries, Britain's head of state is a figurehead with little real power. Instead, day-to-day decisions regarding domestic and foreign policy are left to Parliament and, more specifically, the government, led by the 'First Lord of the Treasury', or prime minister.

The authority invested in successive prime ministers to choose their own ministers, devise and draft legislation, and decide whether to take the state to war, among other things, is derived from another of those key constitutional principles: the **Royal Prerogative**. In essence, this is the body of customary privileges and powers historically acquired by reigning monarchs (predominantly in the Middle Ages). Today, the majority of so-called 'prerogative powers' derived from this principle are exercised not by the Crown itself, but by Parliament.

The origins of the modern British monarchy

Although the present monarchy is also descended from several powerful families with roots outside the UK, Queen Elizabeth II is said to be able to trace her line on one side directly to King Egbert, the ruler who united England under one throne in AD 829. The position that she occupies is that of Britain's longest standing secular institution (its only interruption being the previously mentioned interregnum from 1649 to 1660).

Although it was short-lived, this period—sometimes referred to as the 'English Revolution'—marked a symbolic break with the past that was to change the role of the British monarchy forever. Beforehand, the prevailing 'rationale' for the existence of the sovereign derived from the 'Divine Right of Kings'. By propagating the idea that they could not be held answerable to 'manmade' institutions such as mere parliaments, European medieval monarchs sought to reign with the minimum of outside interference—with the possible exception of that of the Church, which, in some notable instances (such as Henry VIII's inability to obtain permission from the Pope to divorce his first wife, Catherine of Aragon) directly challenged their pre-eminence. Parliaments were generally regarded as tools to enable kings and queens to raise taxes, pass edicts, and declare wars with impunity (and a veneer of legitimacy).

In England, all of this was to change following the execution of Charles I. While his eldest son, Charles II, ultimately succeeded him following Cromwell's death, the concept that any monarch had a divine right to rule unchallenged had, by then, been all but rescinded. Through a succession of landmark constitutional statutes—most notably, the Bill of Rights and Act of Settlement (see pp. 8–12)—a newly liberated Parliament stamped its authority on the nation, and (in all but name) the monarch.

The role of the monarchy today

In *The English Constitution*, Bagehot (1826–77) argued that it was incumbent on monarchs to embody the following qualities:

"The right to be consulted, the right to encourage, the right to warn."

Specifically, the role and powers of the monarch are best explained by splitting them into two broad categories: *actual* and *notional*.

Actual prerogative powers—those exercised by the monarch

Despite the huge upheavals of recent centuries, the reigning sovereign still holds the following key constitutional offices:

- head of state;
- head of the executive, legislature, and judiciary;
- commander-in-chief of the armed forces;
- supreme governor of the established Church of England;

- head of the Commonwealth (and head of state of 15 of its 53 members);
- the authority from which the Royal Mint derives its licence to coin and print money (at present, in his or her image).

But so much for their official titles: what does the monarch actually *do*? And more specifically: which prerogative powers do monarchs personally still exercise in an age when the government holds sway over most key political decisions?

The core roles and duties fo the monarch—many of which are largely ceremonial—include:

- reading Her Majesty's Most Gracious Speech, or the 'Gracious Address'—better known as the **Queen's Speech**—at the annual State Opening of Parliament each October or November, or shortly after a general election;
- governing the Church of England;
- 'creating' peers, and conferring knighthoods and honours in person;
- meeting the prime minister once a week (usually on Tuesdays) to discuss Cabinet business and to offer advice on affairs of state;
- entertaining visiting heads of state at Buckingham Palace;
- visiting other nations on official state visits—including those of the Commonwealth—as Britain's premier overseas ambassador;
- chairing meetings of the **Privy Council** (a body of advisers made up of members of the current and previous Cabinets, plus other distinguished individuals, which issues Royal Charters and Orders in Council—see p. 73);
- attending, on horseback, the 'Trooping the Colour' (the monarch's annual birthday parade, led by regiments of HM Armed Forces).

Although this list of powers may seem feeble in the scheme of things, there is considerable anecdotal evidence to suggest that recent monarchs have discharged their duties with some rigour. Queen Elizabeth II is reputed to have given certain prime ministers a hard time in her weekly audiences by grilling them on specific details of Cabinet business. In her first audience with then newly elected Labour Prime Minister Harold Wilson, in 1964, she famously wrong-footed him by expressing interest in proposals for a 'new town' near Bletchley. Having not yet read his Cabinet papers, he clearly knew nothing of them. In his 1975 resignation speech, Wilson made a joke of the episode, saying that he would advise his successors to 'do their homework' before meeting the Queen.

In addition to the above prerogative powers retained by the monarch and his or her immediate family, the monarch has traditionally been called on to fulfil a unifying role as a national figurehead at times of crisis. The late HM Queen Elizabeth the Queen Mother famously toured bombsites in London's East End to provide comfort to dispossessed families during the Blitz, while the Queen's annual televised Christmas Day address is designed as much to 'sum up' the year past and look to the one ahead on behalf of the whole nation as to update her subjects on her own regal affairs. Such is the onus placed on the sovereign to 'speak for the nation' at times of tragedy or disaster, that the initial silence of Queen Elizabeth II following the death of Diana, Princess of Wales and lover Dodi Fayed in a Paris car crash in 1997 became a cause célèbre among her critics—and allegedly prompted newly elected premier Tony Blair to appeal to her to make a statement in tribute to her daughter-in-law (as dramatized in the Oscar-winning film *The Queen*).

Notional prerogative powers—those deferred to government

Most sovereign powers are exercised 'on the advice of ministers', which means that it is ministers—and the prime minister, in most cases—who take the necessary decisions. In practice, then, it is the monarch who offers the 'advice' to prime ministers, rather than the other way around, and prime ministers who discharge the following functions:

- dissolving and summoning Parliament—that is, calling elections and forming new parliaments after the results are in;
- giving the Royal Assent to Bills passed by Parliament;
- appointing ministers and other senior public officials, including judges, diplomats, governors, officers in the armed forces, police *chief constables*, and Church of England bishops and archbishops;
- devising the legislative *agenda* for each parliamentary session (year of Parliament) and writing the Queen's Speech, which will make these proposals public at the State Opening of Parliament;
- declaring war and peace;
- the *prorogation* of Parliament—that is, the suspending of the activities of Parliament (if not Parliament itself) for the duration of holiday periods, such as the Summer Recess, and the annual Christmas and Easter breaks;

- drawing up lists of nominations—in consultation with the leaders of opposition parties—for peerages, knighthoods, and other honours in the New Year *Honours List* and the Queen's Birthday Honours List.

In addition, the monarch may occasionally issue a 'Royal Pardon'—known formally as the 'Royal Prerogative of Mercy'—to convicted criminals. This tends to happen either when an individual found guilty of a crime is subsequently pardoned in light of new evidence, or (very rarely) when the actions and/or behaviour of a prisoner are deemed to warrant their early release from a sentence. Unlike all other sovereign powers exercised by the government on the monarch's behalf, pardons are issued on the advice not of the prime minister, but of the Home Secretary in England and Wales, and the First Minister in Scotland, following the introduction of *devolution* (see p. 31–40). A recent example of a Royal Pardon was the posthumous forgiveness offered to families of all British soldiers executed for cowardice during the Second World War.

How the monarchy is funded

The income of the reigning monarch and his or her immediate family—known as the 'Royal Household'—comes from four principal sources:

- the *Civil List*;
- grants-in-aid;
- the Privy Purse;
- personal income.

The Civil List

Often used by those in favour of abolishing the monarchy as a form of shorthand for the Royal Family as a whole, this core fund, financed by the British taxpayer, ultimately originated with the Bill of Rights.

With the accession to the throne of William and Mary, Parliament voted to give the Royal Household £600,000 to aid it in 'civil government'. The Civil List in its present form was set up in 1760, during the reign of George III. In return for the king's surrender to Parliament of his so-called 'hereditary revenues'—that is, the income generated by the Crown Lands (estates owned over a period of time by the monarchy)—MPs agreed to pledge a fixed annual income to the Royal Household. In practice, this exchange has reaped huge dividends for Parliament: in 2007–08, the income from the

Crown Lands (as administered by the Commissioners of Crown Lands) was £190.8m, compared to the £40m paid to the monarch.

Since 2001, the Civil List itself has been fixed at £7.9m a year for the Queen until 2011, with her husband, the Duke of Edinburgh (Prince Philip), receiving a separate annuity of £359,000. In a deal struck with the Royal Household by then Chancellor Gordon Brown, the Queen agreed to finance any increases in her outgoings from a 'reserve fund' worth up to £30m accumulated over the previous decade. In return, her own and her husband's 'fixed' incomes would rise by 7.5 per cent a year to keep them abreast of *inflation* (which, at 3 per cent in 2001, was less than half as high). As a result, by the end of 2007–08, the Civil List had actually swelled to £12.7m.

So for what does the Civil List *pay*? In broad terms, it funds the following expenses for both the reigning monarch and his or her spouse:

- around 70 per cent pays the salaries of the 645 servants, butlers, and other employees of the Royal Household;
- most of the remaining 30 per cent covers the costs of royal garden parties (attended by some 48,000 people each year) and hospitality during state visits.

In addition, a number of annual parliamentary allowances are issued each year to individual members of the Royal Family, including the Duke of York (Prince Andrew) and the Princess Royal (Princess Anne), under the auspices of the Civil List Acts. These amount to £2.5m extra in total. Since April 1993, however, the Queen has, in practice, refunded £1.5m of this money to Parliament, using her personal pot of money, the Privy Purse (see p. 28). The remaining £1m has been retained annually as income for the Duke of Edinburgh and, until her death in 2002, the Queen Mother (who received £643,000 a year). All other senior royals performing official duties are now paid annuities out of the Privy Purse, rather than the Civil List.

Perhaps surprisingly, one of the few key members of the Royal Household who derives no such annuity income is the present heir, the Prince of Wales (Prince Charles), who, as Duke of Cornwall, earns substantial income from his sprawling 130,000-acre Duchy of Cornwall estate. Originally bestowed on the Black Prince in 1337, despite its name, the Duchy actually extends over 23 counties. According to the Prince's official website, in 2007–08, his income from the Duchy was £16.3m, a year-on-year increase of £1m, or 7 per cent—twice the rate of inflation.

Grants-in-aid

Awarded to the Crown by the Department of Culture, Media and Sport (DCMS), grants totalling £15.3m a year (fixed until at least 2011) are bestowed on the so-called 'occupied royal palaces'. These are those in which members of the Royal Family still live, as distinct from the likes of Hampton Court Palace and the Tower of London, both of which are overseen by a separate organization, Historic Royal Palaces (also funded by DCMS).

The occupied palaces include the following:

- Buckingham Palace (home of the Queen and Prince Philip);
- St James's Palace (home of Prince Charles);
- Kensington Palace;
- Windsor Castle (second home of the Queen).

In addition to grants-in-aid, Buckingham Palace and Windsor Castle also help to maintain themselves by means of their summer public openings. Grants may not be used for the upkeep of the two royal estates—Sandringham in Norfolk and Balmoral in Scotland—which are the Queen's private property and not her legacy as head of state.

A further set of grants, meanwhile, are awarded by the Department for Transport (DfT), to the tune of £6.2m in 2007–08. These cover the cost of transporting members of the Royal Family to and from their three thousand annual engagements in the UK and overseas. Until she was decommissioned in 1997, the biggest grant was used to maintain the Royal Yacht *Britannia*, the Queen's official ship, which was launched in 1953. Now that *Britannia* is little more than a visitor attraction, royal transport consists of:

- the Royal Air Force (RAF) aircraft of the No. 32 (The Royal) Squadron;
- the Royal Train;
- other chartered and scheduled flights on official visits.

In 2007–08, disclosure of the Royal Family's movements in the preceding 12 months produced some typically eyebrow-raising details. The Queen and her husband—occasionally accompanied by one or two fellow family members—made journeys totalling £200,000 on the Royal Train during the year, including one from Windsor to Euston—via, of all places, Liverpool—to attend the Royal Variety Performance. This convoluted trip cost £23,750. But while £200,000 may sound a lot of money, it is half as much as the £400,000 that the royal couple spent on 11 train trips in 2006–07—including a return visit to Brighton, which set them back £19,271.

No such restraint was visible, however, in the royals' flying habits: security concerns have seen family members avoiding scheduled flights in certain parts of the world more than ever before, with the result that they spent £275,506 between them on chartered flights in 2007–08—£203,007 of it on helicopter trips. A further £143,461 was spent on scheduled flights and, on top of that, £692,790 on flights on various smaller commercial aircraft, including Sikorsky S-76 Spirit helicopters, BAe 146 light aeroplanes, and HS125 corporate jets. Not for the first time, the Duke of York was by far the most extravagant individual air traveller—notching up flights totalling £640,987 in the course of the year, including a £212,880 charter flight in the Far East, taking in stops including Singapore, Jakarta, Delhi, and Mumbai.

The most expensive single flight was the use of a chartered plane by the Queen and Duke of Edinburgh for a May 2007 round trip from London Heathrow via Richmond, Norfolk, Lexington, and St Andrews Airforce Base, which set the taxpayer back £381,813. Intriguingly, this cost even more than a chartered flight for the Prince of Wales and Duchess of Cornwall from Lyon to Uganda and Turkey as part of a Foreign Office visit, which totalled £327,801 (less £11,740 in reimbursements).

The remaining portion of the grants-in-aid budget (amounting to £500,000 in 2007–08) is spent on royal 'communications'—that is, letters, telephone bills, and other correspondences, including invitations to garden parties.

The Privy Purse

Dating back to 1399, the Privy Purse is derived largely from the income generated by the Duchy of Lancaster—a huge expanse of land covering 19,268 acres and the sole surviving Crown estate to remain in the hands of the monarch. It is kept under lock and key by the monarch's personal accountant and administered by the Chancellor of the Duchy of Lancaster—in recent years, almost always a senior Cabinet minister.

Personal income

Like anyone else, senior members of the Royal Family, despite deriving much of their income from the state, are free to generate their own earnings— provided that they pay Income Tax on them, like their subjects. Examples of the personal incomes earned by individual members of the Royal Household include the military salaries drawn by Prince Charles, who served for a time in the Royal Navy, Prince Andrew, who saw action during the Falklands

War, and Prince Harry, who is currently in the Household Cavalry (Blues and Royals). Other examples include the income earned by Prince Charles from his Duchy of Cornwall estate, in the form of land rent and the proceeds from goods produced there—for example, his 'Duchy Originals' products. His youngest brother, Prince Edward, Duke of Wessex, has a film and television company, Ardent Productions.

More sporadic sources of income might include everything from share dividends to windfalls from betting on the races (the Queen Mother famously liked a flutter). Perhaps the most controversial example, however, was that which emerged following the collapse of the trial of Paul Burrell, former butler of the late Diana, Princess of Wales, in 2003. During the hearings, it emerged that Prince Charles's household had been giving away—and, in some cases, selling off—unwanted official gifts bestowed on members of the Royal Household during state visits to foreign countries. Following a lengthy and controversial inquiry led by Sir Michael Peat, the Prince's private secretary, the future king was forced to dismiss his most trusted valet, Michael Fawcett—the servant who had disposed of many of the items. It was never established how much involvement in, or knowledge of, these practices the Prince himself had.

Taxation and the monarchy

It has long been argued by republicans that the Queen and Royal Family derive great dividends each year from the British taxpayer, while giving back little, or nothing, in return. In truth, this is not entirely true. Like everyone, the Queen has always paid *indirect taxes*—that is, Value-Added Tax (VAT), and other tariffs levied on consumer goods and services. She has also long paid, on a voluntary basis, local taxation—that is, *Council Tax* and, before that, the Community Charge (or 'Poll Tax') and rates. It was not until 1993, however, that she agreed to pay *direct taxes*—principally, Income Tax. This decision was taken in the wake of a mounting backlash over the revelation that much of the £60m cost of repairing Windsor Castle following a devastating fire in 1992 was funded by taxpayers, despite the fact that they already hugely subsidized the Royal Household.

The monarch and certain members of her immediate family do, however, continue to enjoy substantial tax breaks not granted to her subjects. In particular, while the Privy Purse pays tax and the Queen's personal estate is subject to Inheritance Tax, grants-in-aid are not regarded as taxable, and neither is any transfer of property 'from sovereign to sovereign'—that is, between the Queen and her successor.

The succession

For many centuries, as is commonly the case in other European nation states, the monarchy has tended to pass from father to son in Britain, through a process known as 'eldest male primogeniture'. Only when a male line (going through the eldest son) has been exhausted does the crown pass to the next eldest male sibling of the originator of that line, and only after that will it ever go to a female sibling. Therefore, as things stand, Prince Charles will inherit the throne from his mother on her death and, after he dies, it will pass to his eldest son, William, and from him to the eldest of his own sons. If William were to fail to have any sons, but have a daughter, it would eventually pass to her, but if he were to have no children and die before his brother, Harry, the crown would finally pass to him.

The other key 'rules' governing the succession—between them derived from the Bill of Rights and Act of Settlement—state that they must:

- be in communion with the Church of England;
- not marry a Roman Catholic;
- swear to preserve the Established Churches of England and Scotland;
- swear to uphold the Protestant succession.

Monarchy versus presidency—which way forward?

Although Britain has had a monarchy for the best part of 1,500 years, today it is one of only a handful of 'developed' nations to retain one—let alone to boast an extended Royal Family, funded largely by the taxpayer. Perhaps unsurprisingly, the past decade or more has witnessed growing calls from some quarters for the monarchy to be abolished and replaced by an elected head of state, in the guise of a president. These calls have been fuelled by a succession of controversies surrounding the Royal Household and, in particular, that relating to Prince Charles's divorce from the late Diana, Princess of Wales, and revelations about his long-standing relationship with Camilla Parker-Bowles (now his second wife). Further succour was given to those arguing for Britain's hereditary figurehead to be replaced by an elected one by the narrow decision of the Australian electorate to retain the Queen as their head of state in November 1999. In 2007, the country's Labour Prime Minister, Kevin Rudd, announced his intention to hold a further such *referendum* in the near future.

The argument for an elected head of state is fairly self-explanatory: in a modern democracy, so the republican case goes, it is surely only right that the state's ultimate ambassador—that is, the individual who most represents its interests on the international stage—should gain their 'mandate' to do so from their subjects. But what of the arguments for retaining a monarchy? Opinions differ among constitutional historians about the merits of the institution, but perhaps the most oft-cited argument in favour of the hereditary principle is that it produces heads of state who have the luxury of being able to maintain an objective, independent-minded *distance* from the day-to-day workings of the political process—rather than being hidebound by the narrow, short-term thinking that constrains politicians reliant on the votes of a fickle electorate. In addition, the presence of Queen Elizabeth II through fifty years of changing governments and shifting political priorities has provided, argue some, a welcome note of continuity that is absent from presidential states.

▌ Devolution—from union to government in the nations

The bulk of this chapter has focused on outlining the process by which the modern British state came into being, and the rules, customs, and laws that has evolved to determine the balance of powers between Parliament, the monarchy, and citizens.

The UK is a 'representative democracy'—that is, a state, the power of which is exercised through democratically elected representatives (in the UK's case, MPs in the Commons). Broadly speaking, there are two main types of democracy: *federal* and *unitary*. In federal democracies, countries are divided into separate political units, each of which has a large degree of autonomy over its own affairs. The USA is a good example of a federal democracy: major foreign and domestic policy decisions are taken by the national government—president and Congress—but many day-to-day matters are decided by individual federal administrations on a state-by-state basis. The most oft-cited example of *federalism* in action relates to the manner in which different states punish felons convicted of serious crimes such as murder and rape: while 14 of the states that make up the USA favour custodial sentences, such as life imprisonment, the remaining 36 still practise the death penalty.

Britain, in contrast to the USA, is a *unitary* democracy. This means that the bulk of power remains in the hand of central government and the Westminster Parliament. But while the constitutional story of Britain since the late medieval period has, for the most part, been one of the gradual consolidation of a single UK run from the centre, in recent years, this has been compromised by moves towards a more decentralized form of government, taking power closer to the people from whom it derives.

The story of the emergence of local government—that is, elected local authorities, funded by local taxpayers, which run services in individual areas of the UK—is told in detail in the second half of this book. But, at a higher level than the strictly 'local', there now exists in Scotland, Wales, and Northern Ireland a further tier of government to which significant powers have recently been devolved by Westminster, taking decision-making closer to the inhabitants of those countries. This statutory transfer of power from central government to the constituent nations that, alongside England, make up the UK is known as 'devolution'.

Before proceeding further, however, it is necessary to underline the important distinction between 'devolution' and 'independence'. Although the parties that most enthusiastically embraced devolution in Scotland, Wales, and Northern Ireland tend to be 'nationalist' ones—that is, those that would ultimately like to break away from the UK and become independent states—the policy does not amount to any form of independence in itself; neither does it inevitably follow that, having gained devolution, a country will one day become independent. Indeed, one of the principal arguments used by Labour to justify devolution was that, in granting it, they were trying to safeguard the union of Britain, by permitting a limited degree of autonomy that made practical sense and would answer many of the frustrations expressed by dissatisfied, but otherwise loyal, British subjects in those countries. Conversely, those in favour of independence have argued that, in the long term, it makes little sense for a national parliament in Scotland or Wales that takes most of its own day-to-day decisions without needing formal permission from Westminster to remain its vassals and that full self-government is the logical next step. Although an Act of Parliament would have to be passed at Westminster to pave the way for independence in practice, the clamour for a breakaway government has become even more acute since Alex Salmond, leader of the Scottish Nationalist Party, was elected First Minister in May 2007, eradicating Labour's majority share of the vote in Scotland for the first time in fifty years.

Mr Salmond has pledged to hold a referendum on the question within the next four years, although he has as yet failed to set a date—inviting speculation in some quarters that he might ultimately cry shy. In an apparent attempt to call his bluff, the former Scottish Labour Party leader, Wendy Alexander, incurred the wrath of Gordon Brown in May 2008 by publicly announcing that she favoured holding a referendum immediately to 'settle the issue'—and claiming that she had spoken to the prime minister on the phone before making her statement and that he had said he agreed with her.

The unification of Great Britain

Wales

Like much of the UK's constitutional heritage, the concept of devolution originated in the Middle Ages, when Wales and Scotland first began to demand the right to rule themselves independently of the English sovereign. Of the two countries, Wales has the longest formal association with England. The main stages in its moves towards incorporation into the UK are outlined in Table 1.6.

Scotland

Scotland's progress towards integration in the UK was a more complex one—due, at least in part, to the fact that it was never formally absorbed

Table 1.6 Timeline for the incorporation of Wales into the UK

Date	Event
Fifth century	Departure of the Romans and rise of Anglo-Saxon hegemony over much of Britain, despite attempts by a number of Welsh kingdoms—including Gwynedd, Powys, Dyfed, and Gwent—to unite in defiance of this latest invasion
Late thirteenth century	The Norman Conquest finally reaches south Wales
1093	By now, all of Wales has been subsumed under English rule
1707	The Acts of Union are passed, fusing England, Scotland, and Wales into a single 'United Kingdom of Great Britain'
1536 and 1543	Two Acts of Parliament formally incorporate Wales into a new Realm of England. Although English is the official language, Wales continues to exert its distinctive Celtic heritage into modern times—leading to the bilingualism of modern times
1925	The Welsh Nationalist Party, Plaid Cymru, is formed, and its first MPs are elected to Parliament in the 1960s

Table 1.7 Timeline for the incorporation of Scotland into the UK

Date	Event
Fifth century	Romans leave Britain, having failed to conquer Scotland fully
Ninth century	Individual Scottish kingdoms unite under a single Celtic monarchy, which goes on to rule for several hundred years
1296	Edward I tries to impose English rule; William Wallace leads Scots revolt
1328	Edward III is forced to recognize Robert Bruce as Robert I of Scotland—the first king of the House of Stuart, which went on initially to establish strong links with France, rather than England
1567	The English force Mary, Queen of Scots, to abdicate and hand the throne to her infant son, James VI (later James I of England). The Presbyterian Church usurps Catholicism to become the established church of Scotland
1603	James VI succeeds the childless Elizabeth I to the English throne
1707	The Acts of Union are passed. Scotland subsequently dissolves its own Parliament and sends its MPs to the English Parliament at Westminster

into the Roman Empire. It took centuries of conflict during the medieval period for it finally to succumb to the authority of the English Crown, a broad timeline of which is outlined in Table 1.7.

Northern Ireland

Northern Ireland's incorporation into the UK was more problematic, encompassing as it did its split from southern Ireland (Eire). The early stages of the process are outlined in Table 1.8.

The path to devolution in Scotland

The workings of the governing institutions set up under devolution in Scotland, Wales, and Northern Ireland are explored in more detail in the next chapter. What follows here is an outline of the process by which these institutions were put in place following the 1997 referenda and the levels of devolution granted in each case.

Of the three countries, Scotland has been granted the most extensive degree of devolved government, following the enabling legislation passed to formalize devolution in 1998. In part, this is a reflection of the fact that, for complex historical reasons, the country has long had certain devolved functions—most notably, a distinctive legal system. More significantly, however, it reflected the growing calls north of the border after 18 years of

Table 1.8 Timeline for the incorporation of Northern Ireland into the UK

Date	Event
1171	Henry II invades Ireland and proclaims himself overlord of five extant Irish provinces (each governed by 300-year-old clans)
Sixteenth and seventeenth centuries	Catholics flee Ireland, leaving land around Ulster to be occupied by Protestant Scottish and English migrants
1692	Protestants assume control of Ireland, spurred on by the victory of William of Orange (the first of the 'Orangemen') over deposed James II at the Battle of the Boyne a year earlier
Eighteenth century	Growing pressure for greater self-determination from England by controlling Protestant Irish minority
1886, 1893, and 1912–14	Successive Home Rule Bills introduced, unsuccessfully, to give Ireland a form of limited self-government
1916	Ireland declared a republic at Dublin's General Post Office after Easter Rising by Irish Volunteer rebels (forerunners of the IRA), who surrender five days later
1918	Sinn Féin (meaning 'Ourselves Alone'), the IRA's political wing, wins 73 Irish seats at the general election—more than twice as many as are won by the Unionist parties combined
1920	The IRA effectively rules large areas of Ireland as the country slips into civil disobedience. Parliament passes the Government Act of Ireland, which sets up two Home Rule parliaments: one in Belfast, covering six of Ulster's nine counties; the other in Dublin, covering the remaining 23 (the 'Republic of Ireland')
December 1921	Anglo-Irish Treaty passed, formalizing Northern Ireland's status as a sectarian society
1949	Republic names itself 'Eire' and pulls out of the Commonwealth

Conservative rule at Westminster for a greater degree of autonomy from a national Parliament that seemed increasingly remote—both politically and geographically—from Scottish interests.

The path to Scottish devolution began in the 1960s, when a previous Labour government established a Royal Commission to examine the arguments for some form of home rule in the country. The sequence of events leading to eventual devolution was as outlined in Table 1.9.

Unlike Wales and Northern Ireland, where (at present) the powers devolved are much the same, the *Scottish Parliament* has considerable authority, with only foreign affairs, defence policy, the welfare system, and the introduction

Table 1.9 Timeline for the introduction of devolution in Scotland

Date	Event
1973	Royal Commission on the Constitution, set up by Harold Wilson's Labour government in the late 1960s, recommends devolution to Edward Heath's Conservatives
1978	Re-elected Labour government passes the Scotland Act, paving the way for a referendum on Scottish self-government. Under its terms, 40 per cent of the entire Scottish electorate must vote for devolution for it to be granted
March 1979	Devolution is put on hold indefinitely because, although 52 per cent of those who turned out to vote supported the idea, this was equivalent to only 32 per cent of those *entitled* to vote
July 1997	Newly re-elected Labour government publishes Scotland's Parliament, a **White Paper** advocating devolution
11 September 1997	This time, the referendum attracts a 60 per cent turnout, with 74 per cent of voters voting for devolution and 64 per cent voting 'yes' in answer to a second question, asking if they want a Scottish Parliament to have *tax-varying* powers
1998	Government of Scotland Act is passed, conferring devolution
12 May 1999	Queen opens new Scottish Parliament after its precise powers are confirmed by a consultative steering group
7 September 2004	Grand opening of £420m purpose-built Scottish Parliament at Holyrood, by foot of Edinburgh's Royal Mile

of new taxes outside its remit. Its powers therefore include determining education, health, environment, and transport policy in Scotland, and, perhaps most significantly, being able to 'vary'—that is, raise or lower—Income Tax by up to three pence in the pound.

The 'West Lothian Question'

The growing assertiveness of the Scottish Parliament in light of these powers—for example, it voted to reject foundation hospitals and undergraduate top-up fees, two deeply unpopular Blair policies that were passed into law south of the border—has raised some significant constitutional questions. None is more explosive than the 'West Lothian Question': the argument that devolution allows Scottish MPs to continue to vote on issues that do not affect their own country, but directly affect England and Wales, while members with constituencies in those countries have no power to vote on issues specific to Scotland. Although devolution was only introduced a decade ago, this quandary was first raised in debate in the Commons by Labour **backbencher** Tam Dalyell in the 1970s. It was dubbed the 'West Lothian Question' by then Tory MP Enoch Powell after the name of Dalyell's then constituency.

Today, the West Lothian Question rages more than ever—not least because, on more than one occasion before he handed over to Gordon Brown, Mr Blair managed to bolster a shaky Commons majority in votes on controversial legislation with the help of Scottish MPs who had let it be known that they did not support the same policies in their own country. The fact that Brown is a Scottish MP himself, and represents a Scottish constituency to boot, has done little to dampen the issue.

The path to devolution in Wales

Welsh devolution was introduced as outlined in Table 1.10.

The rocky road to devolution in Northern Ireland

Due to the fallout from 'The Troubles', the devolution process in Northern Ireland has been characteristically problematic, with the various parties unable to agree a workable framework for devolved government until very recently. A landmark agreement signed in 2007 appeared finally, however, to bury the hatchet between the main Republican and Unionist parties, with the ruling Democratic Unionists accepting that the IRA had decommissioned its weapons, as it had long claimed and the Northern Ireland Assembly having power restored.

The saga that led to the granting of meaningful devolution to Northern Ireland lasted decades, as outlined in Table 1.11.

Table 1.10 Timeline for the introduction of devolution in Wales

Date	Event
July 1997	White Paper entitled *A Voice for Wales* introduced by the new government, outlining its proposals for Welsh devolution
18 September 1997	Referendum attracts low turnout of around 50 per cent, but 50.3 per cent vote in favour of devolved powers
1998	Government of Wales Act passed to lay out framework
1999	National Assembly for Wales (Transfer of Functions) Order introduced, to provide the legal and constitutional framework
6 May 1999	First election for National Assembly for Wales
12 May 1999	National Assembly for Wales meets for first time
1 March 2006	Queen officially opens new purpose-built £67m Welsh Assembly building in Cardiff

Table 1.11 Timeline for the introduction of devolution in Northern Ireland

Date	Event
1968	Civil Rights Movement starts in Ulster. Street violence erupts between Protestants and Catholics (dawn of 'The Troubles')
1972	Most notorious explosion of violence in the history of The Troubles, 'Bloody Sunday', takes place in Northern Ireland, culminating at the Bogside, a Catholic ghetto in Londonderry
1972	Northern Ireland constitution, prime minister and Parliament suspended for a year due to escalating violence
November 1985	The Anglo-Irish Agreement (officially, 'The Hillsborough Agreement') is signed by Britain and Ireland. It recognizes that any constitutional change in Northern Ireland can only come about with the agreement of its occupants through referendum.
November 1992	Inconclusive end to talks flowing from Anglo-Irish Agreement
December 1993	UK Prime Minister John Major and Irish Taoiseach, Albert Reynolds, issue a Joint Declaration from 10 Downing Street ('The Downing Street Declaration'), setting out constitutional principles and political realities to safeguard the interests of both Protestants and Catholics in Northern Ireland. Its key principle is that, in future, participation in discussions about the government of Northern Ireland should be restricted to parties committed to 'exclusively peaceful means'
31 August 1994	IRA announces its first ceasefire, describing it as a 'complete cessation of military operations'
13 October 1994	Combined Loyalist Military Command does likewise
February 1995	British and Irish governments launch *A New Framework for Accountable Government in Northern Ireland*, which outlines proposals for new democratic institutions
February 1996	The Docklands bomb brings the IRA ceasefire to an end
June 1996	Former US Senator George Mitchell convenes a Northern Ireland Forum at which he outlines six so-called 'Mitchell Principles' for moves towards peace. Sinn Féin excluded until the IRA formally readopts its ceasefire. The process wobbles again briefly, following two further IRA bomb explosions, in Manchester city centre and County Antrim
July 1997	Sinn Féin president Gerry Adams and vice-president Martin McGuinness elected as Westminster MPs, and IRA announces resumption of its ceasefire. An international commission on decommissioning is set up under the auspices of the Canadian General, John de Chastelain, to oversee the process
September 1997	Sinn Féin signs up to Mitchell Principles and multiparty talks start at Stormont. After being switched to Lancaster House in London, a deadline of 9 April 1998 is set for agreement
1998 (Good Friday)	The Good Friday Agreement published, as the basis for dual referenda on devolution in Northern and Southern Ireland. Constitutionally, the way was paved with the passage of the Northern Ireland (Elections) Act 1998 and a 19th Amendment to the Irish Constitution (renouncing Eire's claim on the north)

Date	Event
22 May 1998	Referendum of the whole of Ireland produces a 94 per cent majority in favour of devolved government among residents of Eire and a 71 per cent 'yes' vote in Northern Ireland
25 June 1998	First elections for Northern Ireland Assembly see the Ulster Unionist Party gaining the most seats (28), with the Social Democratic and Labour Party coming second (24)
1 July 1998	New assembly meets for the first time and Northern Ireland Secretary Mo Mowlam appoints Lord Alderdice as the country's first Presiding Officer. David Trimble, the leader of the Ulster Unionist Party, is elected as First Minister Designate and Seamus Mallon (deputy leader of the Party) becomes his designated deputy. At least three Nationalist and three designated Unionists are intended to be included in government under part of the devolution deal known as the 'd'Hondt procedure', a formula named after the Belgian, Victor d'Hondt, whereby each party is allocated seats on a 'largest average' basis relating to the number of votes that they receive
15 August 1998	Twenty-nine people die in Omagh bomb planted by IRA splinter group, the 'Real IRA'. New ceasefires announced 1998 (3 Sept); President Clinton delivers address in Belfast calling for peace
29 November 1999	The d'Hondt procedure is used to allocate seats in the Assembly, with the largest party given first ministerial nomination, followed by second largest, until all ten portfolios are filled
1 December 1999	Direct rule of Northern Ireland from Westminster formally comes to an end with the Queen's signing of the Northern Ireland Act 1998. New Northern Ireland Secretary Peter Mandelson remarks wryly that he is pleased to be losing his authority over the province so soon after taking the post
2 December 1999	Anglo-Irish Agreement is replaced by the British-Irish Agreement, which formally creates the North-South Ministerial Council and British-Irish Ministerial Council envisaged in the Good Friday Agreement. On the same day, the Irish Parliament replaces Arts 2 and 3 of the Irish Constitution, thereby formally abandoning Eire's historic claim to hegemony over Northern Ireland, and IRA appoints an 'interlocutor' to liaise with General de Chastelain and the recently created international decommissioning body
11 February 2000	Assembly is suspended over continuing disagreement over the pace of the terrorists' decommissioning of their weapons. UK government passes swift legislation to enable this to happen in effort to avoid Mr Trimble's tendering his resignation as First Minister (he had already handed over his post-dated resignation as a form of 'guarantee' to the Unionists of his determination to ensure full IRA decommissioning took place)
30 May 2000	Renewed period of direct rule from Westminster ends as gradual movement occurs on decommissioning and Unionists approve Mr Trimble's return to his chair on executive
2001	Mr Trimble finally resigns from executive, having failed to secure the tangible proof of IRA decommissioning on which the Unionists were insisting and following months of explosions in London. UK government gives the two sides until 6 August to respond to a new implementation plan

(continued)

Date	Event
6 August 2001	General de Chastelain announces his International Commission on Decommissioning is satisfied with new methods proposed by the IRA for verifying decommissioning
11 August 2001	After a further—one-day—suspension, the Assembly is finally restored and a deadline for the next election of the first minister and deputy first minister is set at 22 September
22 October 2001	Gerry Adams asks the IRA to begin decommissioning and the process finally begins the following day
6 November 2001	Mr Trimble is re-elected as first minister by a narrow majority from Unionists, but a decisive vote by Nationalists
14 October 2002	Northern Ireland Secretary again forced to suspend both the Assembly and the executive over renewed controversy surrounding the transparency of the decommissioning process
December 2003	New Assembly elections give largest number of seats (30) to the Reverend Ian Paisley's Democratic Unionist Party, followed by the Ulster Unionist Party (27) and, close behind, Sinn Féin (24), with only 18 for the moderate nationalist Social Democratic and Labour Party
August 2005	IRA announces final cessation of hostilities in its long-running armed conflict. Talks resume to reinstate devolution
March 2007	After further elections in Northern Ireland and power-sharing talks, an agreement is finally struck to restore devolution
April 2007	The Loyalist Volunteer Force announces that it is ceasing to be a paramilitary outfit and will commit to peace
May 2007	Power-sharing restarts in the Assembly

Ironically, the *level* of power devolved to the province is much more limited than that of Scotland. As is Wales, Northern Ireland is currently restricted to:

- determining some budgetary priorities in education, health, etc.;
- funding, directing, and appointing managers of its National Health Service (NHS) bodies;
- administering any EU structural funds;
- determining the content of its version of the **National Curriculum**.

As with the **Welsh Executive**, however, the Northern Ireland administration is in discussions with the government about the possibility of extending its devolved powers to other, as yet unspecified, areas in the near future.

Moves towards devolution in England

The increasing autonomy given to Scotland, Wales, and Northern Ireland has led to growing demands from some quarters for the major English regions outside London to be given similar powers to determine their own affairs.

Oddly enough, tentative moves towards an embryonic English regional devolution actually emerged under the Tories, when John Major set up a series of regional offices manned by civil servants seconded from the main spending departments at Whitehall. As befitted these nine 'Government Offices of the Regions', however, their role was largely administrative and there were no moves to extend the remit of this 'devolved' power to embrace any form of elected government.

When Labour returned to power in 1997, however, steps were taken to introduce the idea of some form of elected regional authorities by then Deputy Prime Minister John Prescott's so-called 'super-ministry': the (in the end) short-lived Department for the Environment, Local Government and the Regions. The path towards regional devolution took the course outlined in Table 1.12, while that of the eight appointed 'regional assemblies' introduced to pave the way for elections is outlined in Table 1.13.

In the event, in November 2004, the North East Regional Assembly was the only one actually to hold its local referendum on the designated date—a postal-only ballot that proved hugely controversial, in the wake of allegations of corruption in similar-style votes for Birmingham City Council in the months preceding it. The region voted decisively against the introduction of an elected assembly—by a margin of 78 to 22 per cent—throwing regional devolution into turmoil. Local people appeared not to want yet another tier of government, and to be unclear about the tangible benefits and powers that would have derived from such a body. Although chastened at the time, Mr Prescott vowed to resurrect the regional plan at a later date and it was recently mooted again by Hazel Blears, when Gordon Brown made her Secretary of State for Communities in his first Cabinet.

Public affairs for journalists

Table 1.12 Timeline for the establishment of English regional assemblies

Date	Event
1 April 1999	**Regional development agencies** (RDAs) are created as a result of the passage of the White Paper *Building Partnerships for Prosperity* and the Regional Development Agencies Act 1998 in the following eight English regions: the East Midlands; East of England; North East; North West; South East; South West; West Midlands; Yorkshire and Humber. They are statutory organizations responsible for promoting economic development and regeneration, business efficiency, employment, and sustainable development. Regional chambers are also established, which the RDAs are to consult when they draw up strategies covering their areas. Despite their titles, members are not directly elected, but appointed by John Prescott, with 70 per cent of their members drawn from local authorities, and 30 per cent from bodies such as the Confederation of British Industry (CBI), the Trades Union Congress (TUC), and the *Learning and Skills Council (LSC)*
May 2002	Government publishes its long-awaited regional government White Paper, entitled *Your Region, Your Choice—Revitalizing the English Regions*. It outlines proposals for directly elected regional assemblies, but immediately provokes criticism from various interest groups, because analysis of its small print suggests that the public will not be consulted on whether there should be regional assemblies to represent them 'full stop'—but merely on whether or not their members should be elected. Some are suspicious that the government wants to undermine the authority of local councils by setting up more easily controlled assemblies
May 2002–8 May 2003	Subsequent Regional Assemblies (Preparations) Bill receives Royal Assent. This enables designated English regions to hold referenda to allow them to adopt elected assemblies.
22 July 2004	Government publishes Draft Regional Assemblies Bill, explaining the proposed roles and powers of the new regional assemblies. Initial referendum date set for each region of 4 November. It outlines a tripartite role for these assemblies. They are given responsibility to promote economic and social development, and to protect the environment. To this end, they will be allowed to form their own companies, foster public–private partnerships, and acquire and dispose of land, buildings, and other property

Table 1.13 The regional assemblies set up by the Labour government

Assembly	Website
East Midlands Regional Assembly	www.eastmidlandsassembly.org.uk
East of England Regional Assembly	www.eelgc.gov.uk
North East Assembly	www.northeastassembly.org.uk
North West Regional Assembly	www.nwra.gov.uk
South East England Regional Assembly	www.southeast-ra.gov.uk
South West Regional Assembly	www.southwest-ra.gov.uk
West Midlands Regional Assembly	www.wmra.gov.uk
Yorkshire and Humber Assembly	www.yhassembly.gov.uk

→ Further reading

Cannon, J. and Griffiths, R. (1998) *The Oxford Illustrated History of the British Monarchy*, Oxford: Oxford Paperbacks. **Full-colour history of the British monarchy, from King Egbert to Elizabeth Windsor, including an examination of the social and cultural roles of the monarchy in modern Britain.**

Hardman, R. (2007) *Monarchy: The Royal Family at Work*, London: Ebury Press. **Populist, but informative, companion book to the BBC series of the same name, giving insights into the day-to-day reality of how the monarchy works—covering everything from Privy Council meetings, to how the Queen pays her bills.**

Harrison, K. and Boyd, T. (2006) *The Changing Constitution*, Edinburgh: Edinburgh University Press. **Comprehensive examination of the origins and history of the British constitution, with particular emphasis placed on recent and upcoming reforms, including devolution and the introduction of a new independent Supreme Court.**

Hazell, R. and Rawlings, R. (2007) *Devolution, Law Making and the Constitution*, Exeter: Imprint Academic. **Detailed look at the mechanics of lawmaking through the devolved administrations in Scotland, Wales, and Northern Ireland.**

Leach, R., Coxall, B., and Robins, L. (2006) *British Politics*, London: Palgrave Macmillan. **Excellent guide to the nuts and bolts of contemporary British political institutions and processes at local, regional, national, and international levels.**

Moran, M. (2006) *Politics and Governance in the UK*, London: Palgrave Macmillan. **Forward-looking textbook focusing on British politics in the early years of the twenty-first century, and the new and evolving forces at work in local, regional, national, and international governance in an increasingly globalized world.**

? Review questions

1. Outline the main sources and principles of the British constitution. What are the advantages and disadvantages of an unwritten constitution?

2. What is meant by the principle of 'separation of powers' and to what extent does it work in practice in the UK?

3. What are the main roles and powers of the British monarch—notional and actual—and how is the Royal Family funded?

4. Given that royal sovereignty has been superseded by parliamentary sovereignty, what are the arguments for retaining the British monarchy?

5. Is there an 'answer' to the West Lothian Question?

Online resource centre

www.oxfordtextbooks.co.uk/orc/Morrison
Visit the Online Resource Centre that accompanies this book for web links and regular updates.

2

Parliamentary democracy in the UK

▌ The origins of the British Parliament

As Chapter 1 explained, the reins of power in Britain no longer lie with the sovereign. Rather, they are vested primarily in the Houses of Parliament, and specifically in the elected members of Parliament (MPs) who sit in the primary legislative chamber: the House of Commons.

But how did today's 'bicameral legislature'—that is, a Parliament comprising twin chambers, each with its own distinct constitutional role—originate? How does it discharge its functions, and exercise the prerogative powers vested in it by the Crown? And what are the implications for it of recent moves towards *devolution* in the provinces?

The UK Parliament has its roots in a succession of bodies that emerged in the medieval period—initially to bolster, but ultimately to counteract, the power of the reigning monarch. The most significant of these institutions originated in Norman times, in the era of root-and-branch constitutional upheaval that also witnessed the publication of the Domesday Book—England's first great population census—for William I in 1086. To provide mechanisms through which the sovereign could tax and rule over his subjects on a practical basis, a succession of bodies was established, one or two of which survive, notionally, to this day. These included the **Privy Council**, a group of personal confidantes of the sovereign at whose meetings they continue to officiate (see p. 47), and two other bodies—*Magnum Concilium* and *Curia Regis*—the history, roles, and composition of which are outlined in Table 2.1.

Parliament today

As the previous chapter illustrated, Parliament long ago took precedence over the sovereign in the day-to-day exercise of constitutional power in the UK. As early as the fourteenth century, monarchs were increasingly forced to recognize that the earls and barons on whom they depended to maintain their authority must, for that reason, be consulted (and listened to) on major affairs of state. It was during this tumultuous century that kings first came to accept, reluctantly, the need to gain consent from their landed supporters to raise or levy taxes and, in the following century, that a newly assertive Parliament of 'Commoners' secured the right to play an active part in converting royal petitions (or Bills, as they are known today) into statutes (Acts).

Then came the English Civil War of the seventeenth century, and with it the series of decisive breaks with tradition outlined in Chapter 1 that were to usher in a new order. But it was a further two hundred years or more (despite the lofty ambitions of the more revolutionary Parliamentarians— notably, the Levellers and the Diggers) before most people were granted the vote and, with it, a true stake in parliamentary democracy.

The above developments are discussed in detail in Chapter 4, which explores the British electoral system. But what exactly is this Parliament— this great organ of government and citizenship—in which UK citizens are expected to invest such faith? This chapter explores two key aspects of parliamentary democracy in Britain: the nature and composition of the various institutions of Parliament, and the range of roles, duties, and responsibilities that its members discharge on the country's behalf.

Hansard

Before examining the workings of Parliament, it is worth pausing to mention how its practices are recorded. Since 1909, all debates, votes, and other

Table 2.1 The role and composition of the forerunners to the Houses of Parliament

Body	Role and composition
The *Curia Regis* (King's Court)	Formed in 1066, to replace the pre-existing Anglo-Saxon body the *Witenagemot*, this was a council of 'tenants-in-chief' and senior clergymen established to advise the sovereign on prospective new laws. Although, at the time, it was composed entirely of wealthy, landed individuals (or their representatives), the *Curia Regis* was the forerunner of the *Commune Concilium* (Common Council), as today's Houses of Parliament are collectively known. It was set up on a semi-professional basis and upheld a formal legislative framework. Arguably, the first meeting of a bona fide English parliament was convened by Simon de Montfort, sixth Earl of Leicester, during the reign of John's successor, Henry III. In 1265, in an act of defiance against the Crown, he summoned a gathering of his supporters without seeking the king's permission. By the end of Henry's reign, an embryonic parliament, comprising two houses, was meeting on a regular basis. Edward II (1307–27), although derided for ignoring the views of his barons, further formalized England's parliamentary arrangements with the construction of the Star Chamber (or Starred Chamber) for the *Curia Regis*.
The *Magnum Concilium* (Great Council)	Although its existence was only formalized in the reign of Henry III (1216–72), this body had effectively begun in the reign of William I. A putative House of Lords in all but name, it was a gathering of landowners, barons, and church leaders, who would meet the sovereign to discuss affairs of state (and their own interests) on a twice-yearly basis. Although technically still in existence, the Great Council has not been summoned since 1640.
The Privy Council	With the law courts and the two other councils mentioned above, this is the fourth principal council of state. It was once a hugely influential body, made up of carefully chosen aristocrats who were trusted allies of the monarch of the day and convened to provide them with sound, confidential advice. The Council still exists, in diminished form (although it numbers more than five hundred members). Whereas once it helped the sovereign to exercise prerogative powers, its functions have largely been delegated to the most important of its committees, the prime minister's Cabinet (see p. 103). Neither are its principal members today the landed gentry of old: it is composed of members and former members of the Cabinet (i.e. senior ministers in the elected government of the day), whose status as Privy Counsellors/Councillors is recognized by the title 'Right Honourable' with which they are addressed in Parliament. The Leader of the Opposition and heads of other major parties are honorary members, and places are also reserved for other senior public figures, including archbishops and judges—although only serving ministers take part in its actual decision-making. Barring expulsion for a serious offence, membership is for life. The Council has a range of responsibilities—principally, agreeing Orders in Council with the monarch, advising him or her on the use of the Privy Purse, and formally sanctioning the introduction of new public holidays.

proceedings have been written up in a sprawling record known as **Hansard**. With the exception of the words of the serving prime minister, it may not be a verbatim account—it deliberately seeks to edit out *'repetitions, redundancies, and obvious errors'*—but it is the nearest that we have to a definitive account of Parliament's business.

Although Hansard has only been published by Parliament itself for about a hundred years, it has existed for far longer. As early as 1771, a printer called Miller was hauled up before the Lord Mayor of London for producing illicit reports of parliamentary debates, while radical free speech campaigners John Wilkes and William Cobbett fought for the right to publish their own versions. The latter's *Parliamentary Debates* first appeared in 1802, courtesy of one Thomas Curson 'TC' Hansard, the printer after whom the 'official' record is now named.

▌ The House of Commons

The linchpin of modern constitutional government in the UK is the 'lower house': the House of Commons. It is currently made up of 646 members of Parliament (MPs), each representing a seat—or **constituency** (electoral district)—averaging 65,000 inhabitants. By 2010, the number of seats will have increased to 650 (see p. 139).

Unlike many other parliaments, including that of the European Union (EU), the Commons chamber is ranged along two sets of opposing benches, presided over by its chairperson, the **Speaker** of the House of Commons (usually known simply as the 'Speaker' and referred to by members as 'Mr Speaker' or 'Madam Speaker'). To the right of the Speaker's chair are the government benches—those occupied by the governing party of the day and its allies—while to their left are the Opposition benches, home of 'Her Majesty's Loyal Opposition' (the Opposition)—generally the second biggest party after a general election. All other MPs not allied to the government of the day also sit along this side.

The adversarial layout of the Commons chamber is a reflection of the so-called 'two-party politics' that have dominated the British parliamentary scene, for complex historical reasons, almost since its inception. Since the later medieval period, debate has tended to be divided broadly along conservative versus radical/reformist lines, with, at various times: Royalists ranged against Parliamentarians; landowning Whigs battling to preserve the status quo against progressive Tories during the Industrial Revolution; and latterly Liberal, then Labour, MPs championing the rights of the common man against the forces of a more establishment 'big C' Conservatism.

In modern times, two-party politics has been largely preserved, due in no small part to the quirks of the UK's electoral system. As we will see in Chapter 4, the so-called 'first past the post' (FPTP) process sees only the candidates who win the most votes in their constituencies elected to the Commons—meaning that all of those votes cast in favour of anyone else are effectively 'wasted'. As a result, the electoral process favours parties that can muster sufficient concentrations of support in enough constituencies to stand a chance of winning the number of seats needed to form a government. With the Conservatives traditionally representing the more affluent classes and Labour supplanting the Liberals in the early twentieth century as the party of ordinary working people (the recent realignment under Tony Blair notwithstanding), elections have ended up being a straight fight, for the most part, between these two parties. The FPTP system does not favour minority parties or independent candidates.

While Commons debates are chaired by the Speaker, its business time-table is set by a *Cabinet* minister: the *Leader of the House*. The typical Commons year is outlined in Table 2.2, while its usual weekly sittings are set out in Table 2.3.

Table 2.2 The annual timetable for the House of Commons

Date	Event
October/November	State opening of Parliament
December–January (for four weeks)	Christmas recess
February (one week)	Half-term recess
March/April (two weeks)	Easter recess
May (one week over Spring Bank Holiday)	Whit recess
July–September (two months)	Summer recess
September/October (three weeks)	Party conference season
October/November	*Prorogation*

Table 2.3 The weekly timetable for the House of Commons

Day	Time of sitting
Monday	2.30–10.30 p.m.
Tuesday	2.30–10.30 p.m.
Wednesday	11.30 a.m.–7.30 p.m.
Thursday	10.30 a.m.–6.30 p.m.
Friday (13 days a year, for private members' business, including PMBs)	9.30 a.m.–3 p.m.

The role of the MP in relation to constituents

Ordinary MPs currently receive a salary of over £61,000 a year, as well as generous personal allowances to enable them to employ their own personal secretaries or researchers. In return, they are expected to represent the concerns and interests of *all* of their constituents—regardless of individual voters' political affiliations.

At any time, the serving government has anything between 80 and 100 MPs in its ranks. All other MPs—save the 'shadow ministers' on the Opposition frontbench—are known as 'backbench MPs', or *backbenchers*.

The principal ways in which MPs discharge their responsibilities to their constituents include:

- holding weekly 'surgeries' in their constituencies;

- writing to the ministers responsible for relevant government departments to try to resolve grievances voiced by constituents;

- asking written or oral questions in the House of Commons at 'Question Time'—both 'Prime Minister's Questions' on a Wednesday, and other regular slots during which senior departmental ministers answer for their ministries;

- canvassing support among fellow MPs for 'early day motions' (EDMs)—that is, formal parliamentary records expressing strong views on an issue;

- requesting leave from the Speaker for 'adjournment debates'—that is, those held in the half-hour adjournment at the end of a day's sitting;

- tabling urgent debates (with the Speaker's consent) on '*specific and important matters that should have urgent consideration*'—to a maximum of once or twice a year;

- introducing *private member's Bills (PMBs)*—that is, a form of potential legislation that, if passed, would change the law of the land (see p. 71).

The three main forms of debate that may be tabled by backbenchers are explained in Table 2.4, but certain of their roles justify more detailed explanation.

Table 2.4 Types of House of Commons debate that may be tabled by backbenchers

Name	How it works	Example
Early day motions (EDMs)	Despite their title, these rarely result in actual 'motions' (votes) and seldom win sufficient signatures to warrant full debate on the floor of the House. This only usually happens when at least half of the sitting MPs support the motion. Nevertheless, as they become part of the official record of the Commons immediately they are tabled, they have an official status over and above that accorded to more minor procedures. In practice, they often provide journalists with considerable fodder for stories—meaning that, in this age of media-driven policy initiatives, they can wield considerable influence on governments. Perhaps the most important function of EDMs is to enable backbenchers to highlight issues of concern to them and to gauge support among their colleagues for a more definite attempt to initiate change by introducing a PMB (see pp. 71–2).	The most significant EDM of recent times was that tabled by then Leader of the Opposition Margaret Thatcher in 1979, censuring Jim Callaghan's incumbent Labour government. Mr Callaghan's administration had arguably been on its last legs since the collapse of the Lib–Lab Pact that he had negotiated with David Steel's Liberal Party the previous August and, in time, Mrs Thatcher's motion precipitated the vote of no confidence that brought it to an end. What followed for Labour, on 4 May 1979, was a landslide election defeat to the Tories.

Others have included the hugely influential EDM signed by 412 of the 646 MPs days after the 2005 election, calling for a Climate Change Bill, which duly followed in 2006. Only three other EDMs have ever been signed by more than 400 MPs. |
| Adjournment debates | A half-hour debate on the motion that 'this House do now adjourn' held either on the floor of the Commons or in neighbouring Westminster Hall at the end of a day's business. It is an opportunity for a backbench MP to raise an issue of concern to his or her constituents—and, more importantly, to 'summon' a minister to respond to it. Although, as with EDMs, it is highly unusual for an | Conservative Prime Minister Neville Chamberlain, signatory to the ill-fated Munich Agreement with Nazi Germany, was effectively brought down by a motion flowing from an adjournment debate: while the government won the vote—effectively a motion of confidence in his leadership in the wake of Adolf Hitler's breach of the agreement by invading |

(continued)

Name	How it works	Example
	adjournment debate to result in an actual vote, on rare occasions, this has happened, when the debate has raised a nationally significant issue over which there are strong differences of opinion between opposing sides.	Poland—it was by such a narrow margin that his credibility was left in tatters. He was swiftly replaced by Winston Churchill.
Urgent debates	Any MP may apply to the Speaker for an urgent debate—formerly an 'emergency debate'—'on a specific and important matter that should have urgent consideration' under Standing Order No. 24. In practice, far more MPs apply for these than are granted and the Speaker will only allow one or two per session. If granted, the debate will take place within 24 hours.	Recent urgent debates have included a three-hour session on the future of British troop deployments in Afghanistan, forced by then Shadow Defence Minister Bernard Jenkin on 20 March 2002.

Surgeries

Also known as 'clinics', these weekly drop-in sessions may be attended by any constituent who wishes to voice a concern. They are normally held on Fridays (when little parliamentary business is timetabled), or Saturdays in the case of MPs whose constituencies are a long way from London. Although many MPs hold surgeries in the offices of their constituency party, they frequently take place in more informal surroundings—church halls, community centres, and even pubs.

Question Time

This opportunity to quiz senior departmental ministers directly about their policy decisions and the day-to-day workings of their ministries is held for at least one hour a day whenever the Commons is sitting. On Mondays and Tuesdays, it takes place between 2.30 p.m. and 3.30 p.m.; on Wednesdays, from 11.30 a.m. to 12.30 p.m.; on Thursdays, from 10.30 a.m. to 12.30 p.m. (the two-hour slot on this day is intended to make up for the fact that Parliament rarely sits on a Friday).

Each department takes its turn to answer questions from the floor of the House on a fortnightly rota. In addition to the departmental question times, questions can be put to the prime minister on Wednesday lunchtimes, between 12 noon and 12.30 p.m. Until Tony Blair's election in 1997, 'Prime Minister's Questions' (PMQs, as it is commonly known), occupied a twice-weekly 15-minute slot: on Tuesdays and Thursdays, between 3 p.m. and

3.15 p.m. Mr Blair's decision to combine the two into a single session was widely criticized at the time as a high-handed presidential-style gesture calculated to limit opportunities for Parliament and his own party to scrutinize him publicly. Nonetheless, the advent of a bumper Wednesday PMQ slot—combined with the fact that, since 1989, it and other key Commons proceedings, such as the Budget Speech, have been televised live on BBC2—has become a knockabout media highlight of the weekly Commons timetable.

Questions posed at departmental question-time sessions tend to be for a verbal (oral) response. They are answered by ministers according to a rota called the 'Order of Oral Questions'. Prime Minister's Questions, in contrast, takes one of two forms:

- oral;
- written (otherwise known as 'questions for a written answer').

For obvious reasons (in that they are posed in front of television cameras), oral questions attract the most media attention—although more often for the 'Punch and Judy' nature of the proceedings, rather than the substance of what they contain. Because PMQs can be very oversubscribed, MPs keen to ask a question are advised to give the Speaker three days' advance notice of their intentions, to ensure that their name appears sufficiently early on the order paper for them to be called in the allotted time. Giving such notice in advance does *not*, however, mean that MPs must specify the *exact wording* of their questions at that stage; merely that they should let it be known that they wish to ask one.

PMQs follows several curious conventions. The first question faced by the prime minister is always one asking him or her about the other engagements that they have scheduled for the same day. This will usually be immediately tailed by a 'follow-up' question tabled by whichever MP posed the initial procedural one. This is the *real* question and, while the prime minister may have prior notice of to what it relates, he or she rarely knows exactly how it is going to be phrased. The prime minister's hope is that he or she will have been sufficiently well briefed by civil servants on the issue concerned to be able to ad-lib a convincing answer (or at least to sidestep it effectively). When, later in the session, the prime minister refers before taking a question to 'the reply I gave some moments ago', he or she is alluding to the fact that the MP about to ask him or her a question has used the same procedural nicety about his or her engagements to get their name on the order paper.

Despite being the most talked-about parliamentary activity, Question Time is often criticized by serious-minded observers for being superficial and insincere, and playing to the cameras. And it is not only ministers and their would-be replacements on the Opposition frontbench who are accused of this: the most derided questions are often those asked by jobbing back-benchers seen to be using the session either as an opportunity to curry favour with the media in their own constituencies (and by extension their electorates) by focusing on the minutiae of extraordinarily specific local issues, or to massage ministers' egos in the hope of gaining promotion.

In general, MPs genuinely seeking to hold ministers to account for their actions and to influence decision-making on behalf of their constituents will pose *written questions* (which are not only written themselves, but are in-tended for written answers). This enables them to be more forensic and to seek more detailed replies than are likely to be delivered during the theatri-cal point-scoring exercise that Question Time often resembles. An alterna-tive is to table what, until recently, were known as 'private notice questions' (now 'urgent questions'). These are questions on issues that have suddenly come to light and do not require the MP to give the usual three days' notice.

Although ministers invariably try to put a positive gloss on their poli-cies—and the luxury of being able to map out a considered written answer gives them ample scope to do so—they are under a constitutional obligation to reply to written questions thoroughly and accurately. From a journalis-tic point of view, while snappy sound bites offered up in the heat of battle between harassed ministers and their counterparts on the Opposition benches may generate easy headlines, stories that emerge from skilfully worded written questions can be more newsworthy in the long run.

None of this is meant to downplay the importance of oral questions, or PMQs in particular. As a weekly barometer of how the political wind is swaying, there is nothing to rival it. While ordinary backbench MPs may ask only one question, the Leader of the Opposition is allowed to pose six supplementary questions and the leader of the third largest party, the Lib-eral Democrats, two. As a result, PMQs provides a lively, sometimes heated, exchange between the serving prime minister and the pretender who would dethrone him or her—and it has often been said to make or break party lead-ers. Despite a shaky start, Mr Blair became an adept operator at the Dis-patch Box in his decade in power. Nonetheless, on handing over to Mr Brown in summer 2007, he admitted that, whatever his apparent bravado, he had always dreaded the weekly ordeal. For his part, there has been criticism of Mr Brown's more stilted performances at PMQs (despite the experience that he gained handling tricky exchanges over the Budget during ten years as Chancellor of the Exchequer).

The role of the MP in relation to Parliament and party

As stated earlier, MPs' primary duty of care lies, constitutionally, with their constituents. In addition to this, elected members have a responsibility to Parliament and, through it, to the British people as a whole to participate in debate, and to scrutinize and hold to account the executive (the government and Cabinet). One of the chief ways in which they discharge this responsibility is through the committee system—one of several key 'checks and balances' built into the workings of the legislature to ensure the transparency and accountability of government.

In practice, however, the nature of Britain's party system means that these constitutional responsibilities can conflict with the pressure that most MPs are under to act in accordance with the official policies of the parties of which they are members. This sense of instilled discipline—increasingly enforced by a strict party *whip* system—is known as 'toeing the party line'. The idiomatic expression refers to the clearly delineated lines drawn along the length of the Commons in front of each set of benches, behind which members sitting on either side are required to stand while debating. It relates to the somewhat arcane principle that opposing MPs should be made to stand sufficiently far apart to ensure that, if they were to draw their swords in the heat of debate, they would be able to hold their arms fully outstretched without their weapons clashing.

Parliamentary scrutiny and the committee system

The majority of backbench MPs at any one time—and, indeed, peers, who have an equivalent, if smaller scale, system in the Lords—will be members of at least one committee. Each is made up of between 12 and 15 members, and chaired by a sitting member. The proportion of committees chaired by an MP or peer drawn from one party or another broadly reflects the distribution of seats in the House. In recent years, therefore, Labour has had proportionately more chairpersons than all of the other parties put together, reflecting its majority in the Commons.

Although committees have become more 'fluid' in the forms that they take in recent years—a parliamentary committee against anti-Semitism was formed in 2005—they can generally be divided into four broad types:

- *select committees*;
- *public Bill committees*;

- ad hoc committees;
- joint committees.

Select committees

The most frequently publicized type of committee is the select committee. These are formed to scrutinize the workings of individual government departments and Parliament itself, and, as such, are permanent (at least, until the department to which they relate is renamed or disbanded). At present, there are 15 select committees covering departmental issues and several others focusing on internal parliamentary matters—for example, catering and administration. Departmental committees include the Children, Schools and Families Committee—which scrutinizes the recently formed Department for Children, Schools and Families (DCSF)—chaired by Labour backbencher Barry Sheerman, and the Culture, Media and Sport Select Committee—relating to the Department of Culture, Media and Sport (DCMS)—chaired by Conservative MP John Whittingdale, a former Shadow Culture Secretary. There is also a Commons Liaison Committee, which is made up of the chairpersons of all of the other select committees, to which the prime minister submits him or herself for questioning once a month. This was established by Mr Blair, in a rare example of making himself *more* open to parliamentary scrutiny than his predecessors, and meets the prime minister twice a year for up to three hours in order to question him or her on government policy.

Select committees have the power to call MPs, senior civil servants, and other public officials as witnesses, and to publish reports on their findings. Recent reports have included one by the then Education and Skills Committee into the future of higher education funding in July 2003, which was highly critical of the potential deterrent presented by university top-up fees to applicants from poorer families.

One of the more explosive hearings of the past few years occurred around the same time, when, on 15 July 2003, the late Dr David Kelly was grilled by members of the Foreign Affairs Select Committee in the wake of the controversy over a dossier compiled by the government to justify its case for war against Saddam Hussein's Iraq. Dr Kelly, who was found dead near his Gloucestershire home two days later, was subjected to intense questioning about whether he was the source of a story on Radio 4's *Today* programme by BBC defence correspondent Andrew Gilligan, which claimed that senior intelligence sources were concerned that ministers had 'sexed up' the dossier by exaggerating the likelihood that Saddam's forces could unleash weapons of mass destruction (WMDs) within 45 minutes of being ordered to do so.

Public Bill committees

The other most widely publicized type of committee is what is now known as the 'public Bill committee', which was formerly known as the 'standing committee'—the term 'standing' being an archaic reference to the fact that its members do not remain in post for long enough to warrant permanent seats. Its new name better reflects its function: to scrutinize, comment on, amend, and/or *refer back* to the Commons for further consideration Bills as they pass along the route to becoming Acts of Parliament.

As the work of public Bill committees can take some time, in recent years, governments have increasingly tried to bypass them when rushing to pass legislation that they deem urgent. Under these circumstances, if agreed by the Speaker, the Commons itself can take on the role of a public Bill committee, as a 'Committee of the Whole House'. The *committee stage* of Bills is explored in more detail below.

Ad hoc committees

As their name suggests, ad hoc committees are also temporary in nature, but, unlike public Bill committees, are formed to focus on specific topical issues of wide public concern, rather than prospective legislation. The most recent ad hoc committee to be set up was the House of Lords Ad Hoc Committee on Intergovernmental Organisations, formed in December 2007 to examine how cross-border policy issues (such as the spread of communicable diseases) are being addressed through the UK's membership of intergovernmental bodies such as the European Union.

Joint committees

So-called because they are composed jointly of MPs and peers, joint committees include the Joint Committee on Human Rights and the Joint Committee on House of Lords Reform, formed in 2002 to consider a range of alternative options for the composition of the Upper House in the wake of the, as yet incomplete, reforms introduced by Labour in 1999 (see pp. 66–70). Since 1894, there has been a joint committee devoted to assisting the swift passage of laws designed to rationalize the number of Acts on the statute book (the record of all parliamentary legislation in place at any one time).

These 'consolidation Bills', normally introduced in the Lords rather than the Commons, seek to bring together a number of different Acts on the same or similar subjects in a single, all-encompassing Act.

Party loyalty and the whip system

As discussed earlier, British MPs tend to be affiliated to political parties. There have been a few notable exceptions, such as Martin Bell, the one-time BBC foreign correspondent who overturned disgraced former Conservative minister Neil Hamilton's huge majority in Tatton in 1997, standing as an independent candidate on an 'anti-sleaze' ticket. But, in most cases, the nature of Britain's electoral system tends to guarantee candidates backed by the full force of their party machines—and particularly those representing the three main sides: Labour; the Conservatives; the Liberal Democrats—the best chance of election.

Party membership is a double-edged sword. On the one hand, being selected as an official candidate for any of the main parties gives you access to a huge support network, including significant financial backing in the run-up to an election. Independents, in contrast, must largely use their own money to finance their campaigns, or canvas for donations. But being a partisan MP comes at a price. Parties in Britain have traditionally painted themselves as 'broad churches' representing people united by certain common ideals, but who may otherwise hold a variety of shades of opinion on some issues. In recent times, however, party leaders (particularly serving prime ministers) have been criticized for stifling dissent within their ranks and for using the party whip system to force their MPs to back the official line when voting.

There are three broad definitions of the term 'whip':

- whips;
- the party whip;
- three-line whips.

Whips are actual MPs (or peers in the Lords) assigned the task of 'whipping into line' backbenchers when a debate or vote regarded as important by the leadership is pending. It is the job of the whips, led by a chief whip, to try to persuade MPs whose views are known to differ to those of the party's leadership to 'toe the party line'—that is, to attend the debate and to vote with the party when the time comes.

Whips have frequently been accused of, at best, cajoling and, at worst, bullying MPs into doing their leaders' bidding. When John Major was struggling to pass a Bill incorporating the Maastricht Treaty into British law in May 1992 in the face of a backbench rebellion by Euro-sceptic Tories, ailing loyalists including one who had just had brain surgery—known as the 'stretcher vote'—were taxied to the Commons to act as 'lobby fodder' for the government. Under Labour, whips are notorious for bombarding MPs with pager alerts urging them to turn up and vote along party lines, and to stay 'on message' when making speeches and giving interviews.

Mr Blair's prolonged honeymoon with both the voters and his own MPs after his 1997 election victory ended with a bump in his second term, when he faced a succession of knife-edge Commons votes, despite retaining a landslide majority in the House. He squeezed through some of his more controversial reforms, such as foundation hospitals and university top-up fees, by the smallest of margins. In his third term, he actually lost the vote to extend the length of time for which terrorist suspects may be questioned by police without charge from 14 to 90 days, in spite of rigorous arm-twisting by the Labour Chief Whip Jacqui Smith (the future Home Secretary).

In addition to being fixers, the whips also play a more 'constructive', less intimidating role. Crucially, they act as unofficial personnel officers for the party leadership, talent-spotting potential future ministers and frontbench spokespeople, and providing important lines of communication between leader and party.

The term 'party whip' effectively refers to an MP or peer's 'membership' of his or her parliamentary party. Like any such affiliation, this can be withdrawn if the member in question is felt to have broken the 'rules' attached to membership. Mr Major temporarily withdrew the whip from the 22 Maastricht rebels—including future party leader Iain Duncan Smith—as a punishment for their disloyalty. More recently, Labour backbencher George Galloway, MP for Glasgow Kelvin, had the whip removed in October 2003 following repeated public attacks on his leader, Mr Blair, over the invasion of Iraq. In 2005, he was re-elected to the Commons in a different constituency, Bethnal Green and Bow, as an MP for Respect, the anti-war party.

Votes judged by party leaders to be of the greatest importance are highlighted—and underlined three times—in a weekly circular sent to their MPs and peers, called *The Whip*. These votes are referred to as 'three-line whips', and attendance and voting along party lines is regarded by party leaders as compulsory. There are two lower levels of voting.

- 'One-line whips' (or 'free votes') tend to be called on so-called 'matters of conscience'—that is, non-party-political issues, such as foxhunting or euthanasia.

- With 'two-line whips', MPs are advised that they 'must attend' unless they have made legitimate arrangements to be absent under the *pairing* system.

Pairing is a parliamentary convention that allows an MP sitting on one side of the House to miss a vote on which they would have voted one way at the same time as an MP with opposing views on the other side of the chamber. Although regarded as acceptable, leaders would obviously prefer all of their MPs to attend and vote along party lines, regardless of whether members on the other side are absent, to increase their chances of winning votes and of doing so decisively. In turn, certain 'tribal' MPs, such as Labour's Tony Benn, have refused on principle ever to participate in pairing.

Although, technically, pairing is still possible, it was last used in 1996. At that time, the Labour and Lib Dem Chief Whips—Donald Dewar and Archy Kirkwood, respectively—suspended the arrangement indefinitely in protest at an incident in which, encouraged by their 'pairing whip', Derek Conway, three Conservative MPs cheated the system by each pairing up with a member from both of the other parties—thereby cancelling out six, rather than three, votes.

MPs and conflicts of interest—and how to avoid them

In addition to their responsibilities to their constituents, Parliament, and their parties, recent years have seen MPs accused of compromising their integrity by affiliating themselves to 'outside interests' over and above those to which they have constitutional obligations. To promote greater openness about such outside interests—and to avoid charges of corruption or deceit about their motives—MPs have, since 1974, been expected to declare any and all gifts or income received over and above their parliamentary salaries on a *register of members' interests*.

On the face of it, the idea that an MP might have a financial or non-pecuniary interest in an organization other than the House of Commons is hardly new. When the Labour Party was formed, at the tail end of the nineteenth century, one of its aims was to get working-class candidates elected to the Commons, to counter the long-standing dominance of the middle and upper classes. To enable people from poorer backgrounds to fight elections, the trade union movement (one of several bodies that came together to form the party) offered to 'sponsor' them—a traditional source of funding that continued for more than a century, but has recently been switched from MPs themselves to their constituencies. Despite his repeated pledges to end direct trade union sponsorship, Mr Blair was himself sponsored by the now-defunct Transport and General Workers' Union (TGWU, later T&G) for much of his time as an MP. The Hull East constituency of his deputy, John Prescott, a former merchant seaman, was sponsored for many years by the Rail and Maritime Union (RMT) and its precursor, the Seaman's Union, until it withdrew its support in protest at his backing Blairite industrial policies in June 2002.

While Labour—and some of its individual MPs—have long been accused of being in the pockets of the unions, similar charges have traditionally been levelled at the Conservatives in relation to big business. When Kenneth Clarke, a former Tory Health Secretary and Chancellor, retired to the backbenches in 1997, after losing his bid to lead his party to the more youthful William Hague, he took on several company directorships, as well as the chairmanship of British American Tobacco. But the outside interests of some of his erstwhile frontbench colleagues were far more controversial. Jonathan Aitken, Minister for Defence Procurement in Mr Major's government, notoriously signed a 'gagging order' during the so-called 'Iraqi Supergun' affair, preventing it being disclosed that a British arms company of which he was a non-executive director, BMARC, had sold weapons to Saddam's regime. It was controversies such as the latter and the 'cash for questions' scandal involving Trade Minister Neil Hamilton that led Mr Major to order a wholesale tightening up of the way in which MPs—and, in turn, peers and local councillors—declared their interests.

The 'cash for questions' saga had erupted when Hamilton and a colleague, Tim Smith, were accused in *The Guardian* of receiving money in brown paper envelopes from Harrods owner Mohamed Al Fayed in exchange for asking parliamentary questions on his behalf—a flagrant breach of House of Commons rules. Both were forced to resign and, although Hamilton was granted immunity from *parliamentary privilege* to sue both the paper and Al Fayed (see pp. 10–11), he was unsuccessful.

Following the Hamilton debacle and a series of personal scandals involving other members of his government, Mr Major lost little time in setting up a new Committee for Standards in Public Life (now known as the 'Committee on Standards and Privileges', or simply the 'Standards Committee'), under the distinguished judge Lord Nolan. After six months of deliberation, the Nolan Committee published *Seven Principles of Public Life* (see Table 2.5),

Table 2.5 Lord Nolan's 'Seven Principles of Public Life'

Principle	Meaning
Selflessness	A duty to act solely in terms of the public interest (i.e. not for financial gain for himself or herself, or his or her family and friends)
Integrity	A duty not to sustain any financial obligation to outside individuals or organizations that might seek to influence him or her in the performance of his or her duties
Objectivity	The principle that appointment to his or her position be based purely on merit
Accountability	A duty to be accountable for his or her actions to the public and to submit him or herself to 'whatever scrutiny is appropriate' to his or her office
Openness	A duty to be open about his or her actions and decisions in office
Honesty	A duty to declare any private interests relating to his or her public duties and to take steps to resolve any conflicts of interest
Leadership	A duty to promote all principles by leadership and by example

to which it stated MPs and other senior public officials should be expected to adhere.

In recent years, it has become increasingly common for MPs of one party to report to the Standards Committee those from another whenever they encounter the slightest whiff of 'abuse' of the parliamentary rules governing openness and accountability. In 2008, the Conservative backbencher Derek Conway had his whip withdrawn by Mr Cameron after Labour MP John Mann reported him for using his parliamentary allowance to pay his younger son, Freddie, £40,000 over three years and his eldest, Henry, a further £32,000, for allegedly working as his parliamentary researchers. The scandal did not so much centre around the idea of their being employed at all—it emerged at the time that such nepotism is not uncommon at Westminster—but over the question of whether they actually carried out the duties, of which no records were kept. As well as being suspended from his party, Mr Conway was asked to repay £13,161 by the Committee. The three main parties swiftly ordered all of their MPs to make full declarations about any relatives whom they were employing, the nature of their engagement, and details of their remuneration.

The ensuing controversy led to further disclosures about the rather arcane allowances regime governing MPs. It soon emerged that many MPs—including the Speaker, Mr Martin—were claiming allowances of up to £22,000 to help with mortgage repayments on their second homes (those in their constituencies), despite the fact that some had long since paid off the loans. Embarrassingly, Mr Martin, who was chairing a committee tasked with reviewing the expenses system, was exposed to personal criticism after it emerged that his wife, Mary, had claimed £4,000 for taxi fares while out shopping to buy food for official functions.

The expenses furore deepened further when it was revealed that MPs were not expected even to enter receipts in respect of claims of less than £250—unlike virtually any other employee. Mr Brown ordered a further review of the system and swiftly announced that this level would be slashed to require members to provide receipts for any expense over £25. But no such measures were sufficient to stem the media furore over a further revelation, in March 2008, of a so-called 'John Lewis list' of perks for which MPs are eligible in relation to their second homes. Details obtained under a Freedom of Information (FoI) Act 2000 request disclosed that members were able to claim (at the taxpayers' expense) up to £22,000 to furnish the properties—including around £10,000 for a new kitchen, £300 for air-conditioning units, £35 per square metre for new carpets or wooden flooring, and £750 apiece for television sets.

From this point on, the stories kept coming. Two months after details of the John Lewis list first emerged, the High Court ruled that a request made more than two years earlier under FoI for full disclosure of MPs' expenses should be granted. Under intense media pressure, the custodian of this information, Mr Martin, reluctantly agreed to publish a receipt-by-receipt breakdown—in so doing, revealing that Mr Brown had claimed £4,471 to modernize his kitchen in 2005, while his predecessor at Number 10, Mr Blair, had been reimbursed to the tune of £10,600 for a new kitchen at his former constituency home in Sedgefield. Perhaps most bizarrely, between 2001 and 2003 Cabinet Minister Margaret Beckett had claimed £12,170.67 on household repairs—including those necessitated by a smelly manhole—and a further £190 on building a rockery for her back garden. Only weeks after these disclosures, husband and wife Tory MPs Nicholas and Ann Winterton were found guilty by the parliamentary commissioner, John Lyon, of breaching rules introduced two years earlier to stop MPs claiming back rent on properties owned by family members. Having paid off the mortgage on their £700,000 London flat in the early 1990s, the couple had placed it in a family trust to avoid Inheritance Tax. But since 2002, they had occupied it again as tenants, paying the trust £21,600 a year out of their joint Commons second-home allowances—known as the 'additional costs allowance' (ACA). The couple, who denied any intentional wrongdoing, were given a grace period up until September 2008, during which they were permitted to continue using their ACAs to pay rent while they made alternative arrangements.

The Parliamentary Commissioner for Standards

To reinforce his determination to stamp out the perceived culture of 'sleaze' among certain members of his party, Mr Major had a formal code of conduct for MPs drawn up and appointed Sir Gordon Downey the first **Parliamentary Commissioner for Standards** in 1995. The new Commissioner's job was to oversee personally the register of interests, and to summon and hold to account any member felt to be in breach of the code. He was later replaced by Elizabeth Filkin, but, controversially, in late 2001, her job was advertised while she was still in office. Many argued that this was because she had been too robust in holding MPs and government to account, but, whatever the reason, she wrote to the Speaker in November of that year declaring that she would not be reapplying for the post. She has subsequently become a vocal critic of what she sees as Parliament's unwillingness to move with the times. Her successor, Sir Philip Mawer, was replaced by Mr Lyon in summer 2008.

The ongoing controversies over the lobby system and party funding are explored in more detail in Chapter 5.

▌ The House of Lords

Before describing the means by which Parliament introduces new legislation, it is necessary to take a look at the nature and composition of the second chamber: the House of Lords. Since the passage of the House of Lords Act 1999, which Labour introduced to start the process of reforming or replacing this institution, it has been in a state of effective limbo—and is currently described as a 'transitional' House.

What is the point of the Lords?

Even among those who dispute the current makeup of the Lords, few believers in parliamentary democracy argue against the principle that it is important for the main lawmaking chamber in a bicameral legislature to be held to account by a second one of some description. The arguments that have raged for the past few decades over whether the Lords should be reformed or abolished have been less about any real desire to get rid of the Upper House altogether than a growing recognition that, in a modern democratic state, a second chamber composed primarily of political appointees and people entitled to sit there by birthright alone is fundamentally undemocratic. Few, however, dispute the need for some form of 'check and balance'.

The question of how, and to what extent, the Lords needs reforming is far from a new one. As long ago as the early twentieth century, it had begun to seem outmoded, as its staunchly establishment outlook came increasingly into conflict with the reformist governments of the likes of Herbert Asquith and James Ramsay Macdonald. It was the former's Chancellor, David Lloyd George, who brought the matter of Lords reform to a head, when he introduced his seminal 'People's Budget' in 1909, which sought to raise taxes to fund social reform. The budget was rejected by the disproportionately Conservative Lords, so after Asquith narrowly won a further election the following year, he made it his mission once and for all to prevent the Lords being able to reject legislation outright. The 1911 Parliament Act replaced its power of veto with a right merely to *delay* bills—and for a maximum of two calendar years (or three parliamentary sessions). This delaying period was subsequently truncated, by the Parliament Act 1949, to two sessions over 13 months. Any attempt to delay further, in defiance of the will of the Commons, has since seen governments 'invoke' the Parliament Acts. This happened most recently when the Lords' repeated attempts to thwart Labour's ban on hunting with dogs was finally defeated.

Since Asquith's run-in with the Lords, and despite repeated promises to further curtail its powers and change its composition by Labour, nothing decisive has so far happened. Nothing, that is, apart from the House of Lords Act 1999, which finally sounded the starting pistol for reform of the chamber by abolishing all but a handful of the remaining hereditary peers at the time still sitting in the House. Its long-term aim, as yet unrealized, was to replace the hereditary principle with some form of membership entitlement based on individuals' contribution to society through public service or other major achievement.

The composition of the Lords prior to the 1999 Act was as follows.

(a) *The **Lords Spiritual**—26 peers comprising:

- the Archbishops of Canterbury and York;
- the Bishops of London, Durham, and Winchester;
- the 21 next most senior Church of England diocesan bishops.

(b) *The Lords Temporal*—1,263 peers comprising:

- all 759 *hereditary peers* of England, Scotland, Great Britain, and the United Kingdom (but not including Northern Ireland);

- *The Lords of Appeal (the Law Lords)*—27 peers 'created' by successive governments under the Appellate Jurisdiction Act 1876 to help the Lords fulfil its role as the UK's final court of appeal;
- the 477 other *life peers* who had been created in *honours lists* under the terms of the Life Peerages Act 1958.

Hereditary peers have long been permitted to disclaim their peerage rights to enable them to contribute to public life by standing as MPs and this has happened on several occasions over the past fifty years. Former Labour MP Tony Benn inherited the hereditary title Viscount Stansgate while sitting in the Commons—thereby finding himself banned by law from retaining his seat. After several years of campaigning for the right to renounce his peerage and resume his seat as an MP, he persuaded Harold Macmillan's Conservative government to set up a joint committee to examine the issue and, ultimately, to change the law through the Peerage Act 1963.

Others have since followed his lead. Quintin Hogg (Lord Hailsham) disclaimed his family seat to fight a by-election in, ironically, his father's old constituency of St Marylebone. He ultimately changed his mind, however, reverting to his inherited title to become a Tory **Lord Chancellor**. Most peculiarly, in 1963, Lord Home performed a double-flip by giving up an inherited title that had earlier forced him to resign a Commons seat to return to the Lower House as prime minister. His action—prompted by his election to replace Mr Macmillan as Conservative leader—had the unique consequence of creating a two-week interval between his 'resignation' as a peer and re-election as an MP, during which Britain's prime minister was neither a member of the Commons nor of the Lords.

The House of Lords Act 1999

The House of Lords Act 1999 contained five key clauses that were designed to pave the way for an, at least partially, elected second chamber. After a series of run-ins between Mr Blair, his own backbenchers, the Tories, and the Lords itself, however, it was decided to move towards reform gradually by setting up a *transitional* chamber, which would remove the automatic membership rights of all but 92 hereditary peers. In the meantime, the thorny question of exactly what the final composition of a new Upper House should be was handed to a Royal Commission headed by former Tory minister Lord Wakeham.

Of the 92 hereditary peers allowed to remain in the House during the hazily defined transition period, 90 were to be elected—but by their fellow peers, not the public. The aim was to single out individuals with a history of making valuable contributions to Lords debates, rather than the majority who rarely, if ever, attended proceedings in practice. As well as the 90 lords with *elected hereditary peerages*, however, a further two hereditary peers were permitted to remain as *ex officio* members, on the basis of their ceremonial significance to the chamber. These were the Earl Marshal, the Duke of Norfolk, and the Lord Great Chamberlain, the Marquess of Cholmondeley. In addition, ten new life peerages were controversially created to enable several hereditary peers who were *not* elected to remain. These included former Tory Leader of the House Lord Cranborne, ex-Foreign Secretary Lord Carrington, and the Earl of Longford. More contentious still was the decision to retain Lord Snowdon, Princess Margaret's ex-husband, who was widely felt to have demonstrated little interest in the chamber. The process by which the transitional House was set up was brokered as a compromise amendment to the Bill by Lord Weatherill, the former Speaker of the Commons.

After the internal election that followed the passing of the 'Weatherill Amendment', the composition of the Lords was as follows:

- 26 Lords Spiritual;
- 598 Lords Temporal, comprising: 27 Law Lords, two non-elected hereditary peers, 90 elected hereditary peers, and 477 life peers.

Since then, life peers have continued to be appointed at a prodigious rate and the balance of power between parties has fluctuated wildly. The political composition of the Lords as of July 2008 is as outlined in Table 2.6.

Table 2.6 The composition of the House of Lords (July 2008)

Party	Life peers	Hereditary (elected) by party	Hereditary (elected) office-holders	Hereditary (royal office-holders)	Bishops	Total
Conservative	154	39	9	0	0	**202**
Labour	211	2	2	0	0	**215**
Liberal Democrat	71	3	2	0	0	**76**
Crossbench	170	29	2	2	0	**203**
Bishops	0	0	0	0	26	**26**
Other	11	2	0	0	0	**13**
Total	**617**	**75**	**15**	**2**	**26**	**735**

 NOTE: A regularly updated version of this table can be found on the Online Resource Centre that accompanies this book.

The Wakeham Commission and the 2001 White Paper

The Wakeham Commission was set up to address the following questions.

- What is to the role of the second chamber?
- How is the second chamber to be composed in future (appointed or elected)?
- Is an entirely appointed second chamber the best option?
- Is an entirely elected second chamber the best option?

Its report, *A House for the Future*, was finally published at the end of January 2000. It made a series of recommendations, subsequently crystallized in a 2001 House of Lords **White Paper** that, to date, has yet to be acted on. The latter, *A Chamber Fit for the 21 Century*, outlined the more modest proposals summarized in Table 2.7.

The years since have seen plenty of talk, but little action. By the time that Mr Blair stepped down as prime minister, ten years after initiating reform, he had veered away personally from wanting a wholly elected second chamber, via advocating one made up partly of appointed members and partly of elected ones, to favouring an entirely appointed Upper House. Mr Blair's argument—one frequently rehearsed by previous governments—was that to replace the existing Lords with a wholly elected Upper House might provoke a constitutional crisis. By introducing a second chamber made up of members elected by the public, he argued, the Commons risked lending it the same legitimacy as itself, undermining its own supremacy in the process.

Table 2.7 The main recommendations of the 2001 House of Lords White Paper

Recommended reform	Resulting effect
Hereditary peers axed	All 92 remaining hereditary peers would lose their seats
Life peers phased out	Existing life peers would remain, but only 'transitionally'—their exact tenure would be decided only with the length of transition period to a fully reformed House
Concept of 'House of Lords' to go	All link between peerages and membership of the House finally removed
Cap to number of members	The size of the second chamber would be capped at 600 after an initial transition period of ten years—to avoid the House outgrowing the Commons
Mix of appointed and elected members	Most members of the new chamber would be nominees of main parties. About 120 would be independent and appointed by a new **quango**, the Appointments Commission, with a further 120 elected to represent the nations and regions
Other faiths and denominations to be represented	An as-yet-unspecified continuing role for the senior Church of England bishops

To some, however, his position represented the worst of both worlds. An all-party motion signed by 131 MPs (including 60 Labour rebels) as far back as March 1999 demanded that the new Lords be entirely elected—a stance that accorded with earlier Labour proposals. Since then, the Tories, although long opposed to the abolition of the Lords, have seized the opportunity to take the moral high ground by calling for a wholly elected second chamber and branding Mr Blair's alternative idea an attempt to shore up his power base by appointing 'Tony's Cronies'. Memories were evoked of the 'Lavender List'—the notorious string of honours for trusted allies and confidantes that another waning Labour Prime Minister, Harold Wilson, patronized on retiring in 1975.

The government disputes this, however, pointing out that, under its various recent proposals, a great many appointed members of any new second chamber would be chosen by the independent Appointments Commission, rather than by the serving prime minister and Opposition leaders, as has long been the case with life peers.

Despite the fact that MPs have voted several times since 1999 for a fully elected second chamber, a White Paper published in 2006, by then Leader of the House of Commons Jack Straw, proposed a 50–50 split between elected and appointed members as its preferred compromise solution. Controversially, only 20 per cent of appointees would be chosen by the Commission, however, with the remaining 30 per cent nominated by their own parties—making it likely that the chamber would end up biased politically in favour of serving governments. Members would be entitled to a full-time salary of £50,000 a year, to encourage them to participate fully in proceedings, or a pro rata sum if they were to continue working part-time in other employment.

In July 2008, Mr Straw published a further set of proposals, this time suggesting that the new-look House should be 80–100 per cent elected and members be paid salaries of £55–60,000. The number of members would be reduced from around 700 at the time to 400–450 maximum and anyone found guilty of being 'lazy' or 'corrupt' would be expelled. Had this rule existed years earlier, Lord Archer—the Tory peer jailed for perjury in 2000—and Dame Shirley Porter—surcharged by Westminster City Council for the 'homes for votes' scandal (see pp. 443–4)—would surely have been out on their ears!

One factor that appears to be pushing the government towards swifter reform of the Lords is its continuing opposition to more controversial legislation, including former Home Secretary David Blunkett's bid to remove the automatic right of defendants to elect trial by jury and the swingeing measures introduced following 11 September 2001 in the form of the Anti-terrorism, Crime and Security Bill. In the months leading up to his departure,

Mr Blair threatened to remove all hereditary peers from the House following their renewed opposition to his asylum policies.

▌ Types of legislation

As Britain's legislature, the primary purpose of Parliament is to legislate. So
how exactly does it do this and what forms can legislation take?

Laws in the UK are divided into two broad types: *primary* and *secondary*.
Primary legislation is the umbrella term for all Bills passed by both Houses
of Parliament and given the **Royal Assent** to become Acts. It is also known
sometimes as 'enabling legislation', in that Acts must be passed to 'enable'
the government and Parliament to issue the various rules, regulations, and
instructions needed to implement changes in the law on the ground.

Primary legislation

The four main categories of primary Bill are as follows:

- public Bills;
- private Bills;
- hybrid Bills;
- private member's Bills.

Public, private, and hybrid Bills

Public, private, and hybrid Bills all have one thing in common: they are all
initiated at the behest of the government. But that is where their similarities end. Whereas a public Bill will set out to change 'the law of the land', a
private Bill seeks only to affect a specific individual or organization—for
example, a company or a local authority.

Briefly, the majority of new laws that gain media attention—and about
which journalists normally find themselves reporting—are public Bills. The
Health and Social Care Bill 2003, which, controversially, introduced foundation hospitals, the Higher Education Bill 2004 introducing university top-up
fees, and the numerous 'anti-terror' Bills of recent years all are, or were, public Bills affecting the entire population of England, if not the UK as a whole.
Private Bills, in contrast, are usually introduced at the request of a specific

individual or body, either to exempt them from a law otherwise affecting the whole country, or to grant them some other discrete privilege. The **Highways Agency**—the **executive agency** of the Department for Transport responsible for building and maintaining major **trunk roads**, A-roads, and motorways—has often been granted private Bills to enable it to extend, or introduce, roads in new areas. Another recent example is the London Local Authorities Bill 2007, which invited complaints from the British Beer and Pub Association over the fact that it required pub landlords to submit any plans to extend or otherwise alter their licences to the authorities responsible for local litter policy—in addition to the eight other bodies that they were already expected to inform.

Hybrid Bills are, as their name suggests, a mix of the other two. On the one hand, like public Bills, they affect the whole population, but on the other, they resemble private Bills, in that they impinge on some of us more than others. Examples of hybrid Bills include the one passed to sanction construction of the Channel Tunnel. As residents living along the length of the tunnel were affected by the work taking place there significantly more than those who might occasionally use it, the government granted it hybrid Bill status—thereby giving those residents the right to be formally consulted on the legislation over and above the extent to which the rest of us were. The prospective Bill to enable work to begin on the long-delayed Crossrail project in London, finally confirmed by ministers and then London Mayor Ken Livingstone in 2008, is another example of hybrid legislation.

Private member's Bills

Private member's Bills (PMBs) warrant a separate category because, unlike all of the above types of legislation, they are introduced not by governments, but by backbench MPs. PMBs may be introduced in one of three ways listed in Table 2.8.

The primary purpose of **ten-minute rule** Bills is to enable MPs to raise issues that they deem important—rather than actually to get their measures onto the Statute Book. In practice, it is unlikely that the MP will be able to persuade their party, or the government, to allocate sufficient parliamentary time to take the Bill any further (although there have been some celebrated cases in which this has occurred—see p. 72).

To qualify to introduce a ten-minute rule Bill, an MP must be 'the first member through the door' to the Public Bill Office on the Tuesday or Wednesday 15 working days prior to the date when they wish to introduce it. They must

Table 2.8 The three ways of introducing private member's Bills (PMBs)

Method	Procedure
PMB Fridays	Early in each parliamentary session, MPs can take part in a so-called 'ballot' for the opportunity to introduce their own Bill on one of 13 'PMB Fridays'. On these days, PMBs take precedence over government and Opposition business. The first 20 names drawn in the ballot—effectively, a 'hat' from which the lucky few are plucked—are allowed to introduce their Bills. The six or seven at the top of the list are likely to have their proposals discussed in some detail in the Commons.
The ten-minute rule	MPs may instead choose to use the 'ten-minute rule' (officially, Standing Order No. 23), which applies on most Tuesdays and Wednesdays at the very start of public business in the Commons. This entitles them to make a 10-minute speech outlining their proposals, with the support of at least ten other members. An opponent may make a 10-minute speech in reply.
Presentation Bills	MPs may introduce a presentation Bill (under Standing Order No. 57). This is simply a means of drawing limited attention to a particular issue of concern to the MP, because—unlike the other two methods—it does not allow him or her to make a speech outlining the Bill's details in the House.

also have the Bill proposed and seconded, and receive written backing from ten colleagues.

A number of significant issues have been raised as a result of the introduction of private member's Bills. In 1997, after initial indications that he would receive government backing, Labour backbencher Michael Foster introduced his own Bill proposing a ban on hunting with dogs (a measure proposed in the Labour Party's manifesto). He later withdrew it when it became clear that ministers were not going to accord it sufficient parliamentary time to see it through all of its stages in the face of mounting opposition from the Conservative Party and the Lords. In 2001, another Labour MP, Kevin McNamara, in collusion with *The Guardian*, introduced a Bill designed to repeal the 1701 Act of Settlement—the law that first banned Catholics being able to succeed to the throne. It also sought to repeal the Treason and Felony Act 1848, to end the arcane criminal offence of advocating the abolition of the monarchy.

Perhaps the most famously successful PMB was former Liberal leader David Steel's Abortion Bill 1967, which legalized terminations of unwanted pregnancy for the first time in Britain, albeit under strict conditions and only up to 24 weeks after conception. Touching on an issue of huge public concern at the time as it did, it was allotted ample time for full debate and scrutiny, and duly passed into law.

Secondary legislation

It has increasingly been the convention for primary legislation to cover only the fundamental *principles* underpinning a change in the law of the land. In contrast, **secondary legislation**—otherwise known as 'subordinate legislation', or **delegated legislation**—is the term used to refer to powers 'flowing from' the Acts themselves, and the rules, regulations, and guidelines drawn up to implement them. For primary legislation to be put into practice, ministers need the authority to introduce the measures that it contains on the ground. For this reason, they require secondary—or 'delegated'—legislative powers, the main types of which are listed in Table 2.9.

Table 2.9 The main types of secondary legislation

Name	Definition	Example
Statutory instrument	The main form of delegated legislation, this is the system of rules, regulations, and guidelines issued by ministers to flesh out the detail of newly passed Acts or to update detail in existing ones. Although no further Act is required to implement the measures, they still technically require the formal agreement of Parliament. The 'parent' Act will usually specify whether an affirmative or negative agreement is required (the former means that a statutory instrument will not come into play unless Parliament formally approves a resolution, while the latter means it will automatically do so if, after 40 days, no motion has been passed objecting to it).	A series of complex instructions issued by the Department for Culture, Media and Sport to enable local authorities and the police to take over responsibility for issuing liquor and public entertainment licences under the Licensing Act 2003 (see p. 604). These took so long to come into force that '24-hour drinking' was only introduced in pubs in November 2005—two years after the Act received Royal Assent.
By-law	Localized laws passed on the approval of the relevant government minister, the scope for which is enshrined in an existing Act.	City-centre street drinking bans introduced by local authorities in problem areas.
Order in Council	Submitted by ministers for approval by the sovereign at a meeting of the Privy Council. A draft is normally agreed by Parliament before being submitted by ministers.	Orders in Council were used to introduce much delegated anti-terror legislation relating to Northern Ireland in the 1960s and 1970s.

▶ The passage of a Bill

Before it can be introduced into Parliament as a fully fledged Bill, the detail of prospective government legislation is initially publicly aired in two early draft forms: a **Green Paper** and a White Paper. The former is a sketchy consultation document outlining the *broad spirit* of a proposed Bill. It is open to significant redefinition depending on the response that it elicits from the public and other interested parties. The latter is a more *crystallized outline* of a proposed law—again issued for consultation purposes—that normally prefigures a Bill to be introduced in the next session.

Bills can be introduced in either the Commons or the Lords, although they are normally instigated in the former. The process is as outlined in Table 2.10.

Speeding up the legislative process

As illustrated above, the legislative process can be a very involved one and over the decades, perhaps unsurprisingly, MPs of all parties have become increasingly adept at delaying the passage of Bills to which they object. Traditionally, they have conspired to do so by making excessively long speeches designed to frustrate the government's attempts ever to get through the various stages that are needed for the Bill to become law. If strategically timed, 'filibustering' (as it is known) at one time proved sufficiently obstructive to delay indefinitely and, in some cases, totally 'kill off' prospective Acts. If a Bill were to be delayed by time wasters long enough for the government that was trying to pass it to be voted out of office in an election, that might well spell the end of it, because the Opposition waiting to take over would be unlikely to resurrect it.

The term 'filibustering' was first coined in reference to pro-independence Irish MPs in the nineteenth century, who, in an effort to force the Westminster government's hand over 'home rule' for the province, would deliberately hold up Bills on other issues. Today, filibustering and other forms of time wasting, repetition, and drawn-out debate can be countered in one of the four ways outlined in Table 2.11.

Table 2.10 The passage of a Bill through Parliament

Stage	Process
First reading	When Bills are first presented, the only thing that actually happens is that their titles are read out in the Commons. Although this may sound like a short procedure, in practice, it can take several minutes, because the full titles of Bills tend to sum up the substance of their proposals and can be lengthy.
Second reading	The general principles of the Bill are read out, debated, and voted on for the first time. This normally happens in 'an afternoon' between 4 p.m. and 10 p.m. (barring a recent experiment, when late Leader of the House Robin Cook introduced a new 'family friendly' parliamentary timetable more in keeping with the rest of the working population). The second reading can, however, run over several days if the Bill has major implications (as with the Foundation Hospitals Bill).
Committee stage	A public Bill committee set up especially for the purpose undertakes detailed consideration of the main clauses in the Bill. Sometimes, this stage is carried out by the Commons itself, sitting as a Committee of the Whole House (this normally happens when a treaty is being ratified, or when a Bill needs to be passed urgently—e.g. the recent anti-terror legislation). This also happens automatically following the annual Budget Speech, when aspects of the Finance Act flowing from it are fast-tracked—the thinking being that government would grind to a halt if this 'money Bill' were not passed swiftly.
Report stage	The committee's recommendations are referred to the Commons in a written report and further amendments can follow before the Bill proceeds to a third reading. This stage often involves late sittings.
Third reading	The Bill is reviewed and debated in its final intended form. At this stage, all opportunities for the Commons to make amendments to it have passed (although the Lords can still do so).

The Bill is now formally referred to the Lords (or 'another place' in parliamentary parlance). Here, it follows much the same sequence of stages as those of the Commons, but this time, its committee stage will usually be taken on the floor of the House.

The House of Lords and the Lords' report to the Commons	Amendments made by the second chamber must be agreed by the first chamber before it can proceed to the Statute Book. Should there be significant differences of opinion between the two (e.g. over recent asylum legislation, foxhunting, or top-up fees), a joint committee will usually be set up to resolve them. Under the successive Parliament Acts, the Lords cannot delay a money bill, and can only delay other Bills by up to 13 months, after which they are automatically given Royal Assent.
Royal Assent	The final seal of approval for a Bill, which turns it into an Act, is notionally still given by the monarch, but the last time this formally happened was in 1854. It is conferred in Norman French, *La Reine le Veult*, and has not been refused since 1707, when Queen Anne declined to grant it for a Bill to settle the militia in Scotland. The sentence preceding every Act reads: '*Be it enacted by the Queen's Most Excellent Majesty, by and with the advice and consent of the Lords Spiritual and Temporal, and Commons, in this Parliament assembled, and by authority of the same, as follows...*'

Table 2.11 Devices used to speed up debate in the House of Commons

Device	Definition
Allocation of time motion (the 'guillotine')	A device used by the Leader of the House to limit formally the amount of time that can be taken by specific stages of a Bill (i.e. to set a deadline). This was first used in 1887 to push through the Criminal Law Amendment (Ireland) Bill following a mammoth debate that lasted 35 days (including some all-night sittings), largely because of the obstructive actions of Irish MPs. Six years earlier, the Commons had sustained its single longest ever sitting: a debate over the Protection of Person and Property (Ireland) Bill 1881, lasting 41 hours and 31 minutes. Most recently, the guillotine was used in June 1997 to force through the Referendums (Scotland and Wales) Bill, when opponents had tabled 250 amendments.
A motion of closure	Requires a petition of 100-plus MPs to be submitted to the Speaker calling for a vote to be swiftly taken.
The 'kangaroo'	The Speaker chooses to combine, in one hit for one vote, a number of virtually identical motions or suggested amendments tabled by different MPs.
Programme orders	A relatively new device that replaces the guillotine in many cases, this allows the Leader of the House to set a fixed number of sittings for the passage of a Bill or a fixed date for its completion. Programme orders may be moved after the second reading stage.

▌ The role of the Commons Speaker

The most important officer of the Commons, the Speaker is effectively the chair of all business in the chamber. As such, he or she must preside over votes and debates, intervene to restore 'order' when members become too rowdy, and choose which member should be next to speak when confronted by MPs waving their order papers in a bid to 'catch the Speaker's eye'.

The Speaker's main roles today are as follows:

- controlling debates, including deciding when those on specific subjects should end and be voted on, and suspending or adjourning sittings if they get out of hand. Debate over the Hutton Report published into the death of Dr Kelly (see p. 56) was suspended by the Speaker after protesters invaded the public gallery in the Commons. He was forced to take similar action during two other protests in the House: on one occasion, in May 2004, when activists from Fathers4Justice, a pressure group campaigning for equal access rights to children for fathers separated from their partners, threw a missile containing purple powder from the guests' gallery at Mr Blair while he was addressing MPs, and again, in September of that year, when pro-hunt protestors led by Otis Ferry, son of singer Bryan Ferry, invaded the floor of the chamber;

- ordering MPs who have broken the rules of the Commons to leave the chamber. This happened on several occasions to the former Democratic Unionist Party leader, Reverend Ian Paisley, when he accused fellow MPs of 'lying'—that is, using 'unparliamentary language', which is expressly banned from the chamber by convention. More recently, in July 2007, Mr Galloway was suspended from the Commons for 18 days for failing to declare his links to the **United Nations (UN)** 'Oil for Food' programme—a charitable appeal allegedly partly funded by a supporter involved in the sale of oil under Saddam Hussein;
- certifying some Bills as 'money Bills' to give them swift approval;
- signing warrants to send members to jail for contempt of the House;
- chairing the House of Commons Commission—that is, the main body that administers the procedures of the Commons;
- chairing the **Boundary Commission for England**, and those for Wales, Scotland, and Northern Ireland—which, until now, have been charged with reviewing general election constituency boundaries. This function will be transferred to the **Electoral Commission** with effect from the next boundary review (due to be completed between 2014 and 2018). This Commission also oversees the free and fair operation of the British election process, and investigates alleged breaches of party political funding rules.

Traditionally, the Speaker (the first of whom, Peter de Montfort, was appointed as Parlour of the Commons in 1258) is chosen by an election of MPs called by the 'Father of the House'—that is, the MP with the longest unbroken membership of the Commons, who is not a minister. For the past thirty-plus years, it has also been customary for the two main political parties to alternate in providing Speakers. On the most recent occasion when the post became vacant, with the retirement of Betty (now Baroness) Boothroyd, however, backbenchers became so annoyed by the government's insistence that the custom be upheld that they defied it by voting in another Labour MP, Michael Martin, instead of Mr Blair's preferred candidate, former Tory minister Sir George Young. On taking office, the Speaker must discard any previous party allegiance for the duration of his or her time in the post. After the 2005 election, however, then Father of the House, Labour backbencher Tam Dalyell, was faced with the prospect of Mr Martin's re-election as Speaker being contested amid criticisms from the Tories that his independence of government was questionable.

◗ The changing role of the Lord Chancellor

Officially the 'Lord High Chancellor of Great Britain', this ancient post—dating back at least as far as the 1066 Norman Conquest—has seen a momentous (if not always smooth) transition over the past five years. The office of Lord Chancellor is the second most senior of the so-called 'Great Officers of State of the UK' (the highest ranking being the Lord High Steward—a post that is generally kept vacant, except during coronations, when it is filled on a temporary basis). As explained in Chapter 1, the Lord Chancellor was, for centuries, a bastion of all three branches of the British constitution, being head of the judiciary, Speaker of the House of Lords (legislature), and, as Cabinet minister responsible for what until recently was known as the 'Lord Chancellor's Department', a member of the executive.

The Lord Chancellor still retains many of the key ceremonial roles that the title has held for time immemorial. As 'Custodian of The Great Seal of the Realm', or 'The Great Seal of the United Kingdom', he or she has the ability to authorize the reigning sovereign's documents (most notably the Royal Assent) on his or her behalf—thereby preventing the monarch having to sign each one personally. The Lord Chancellor also remains a minister.

Since 2003, however, the Lord Chancellor has ceased to retain quite the authority that the title possessed previously—to the annoyance of the Lords, which sought initially to prevent Mr Blair from denuding its powers. In a notoriously botched Cabinet reshuffle, precipitated by the sudden resignation of Health Secretary Alan Milburn, Mr Blair replaced outgoing Lord Chancellor Derry Irvine with Lord Falconer of Thoroton. In doing so, however, he sought to rename the post 'Secretary of State for Constitutional Affairs'—effectively *abolishing* a constitutional role that had existed, more or less uninterrupted, since the Middle Ages.

In the event, he was forced to take a step back from scrapping the post outright and, although he did get rid of the Lord Chancellor's Department, Lord Falconer retained the dual titles of Constitutional Affairs Secretary and Lord Chancellor throughout his four years in office. Further changes did, however, come about after the 2005 election, when the Constitutional Affairs Act 2005 created a new post of **Lords' Speaker** to assume the Lord Chancellor's role as chair of the Lords and handed responsibility for running the judiciary to the Lord Chief Justice.

More recently, Jack Straw was named Lord Falconer's successor in Gordon Brown's first Cabinet and, although he retained responsibility for a department, it became the Ministry of Justice (MoJ), rather than the Department of Constitutional Affairs. Mr Straw was also the first Lord Chancellor since that of Henry VIII, Cardinal Wolsey, gave way to several laymen in the sixteenth century to be an MP—*not* a lord.

▌ The Opposition

The largest party other than the governing one (in terms of the number of seats that it has in the Commons) is known as 'Her Majesty's Loyal Opposition'. In recognition of its official status, the Leader of the Opposition, the Opposition Chief Whip, and the Opposition Deputy Chief Whip each receive allowances over and above their normal parliamentary ones to aid with their responsibilities.

The Opposition is charged with:

- holding the government to account for its actions by appointing a 'Shadow Cabinet' covering the main departmental briefs;
- contributing to the legislative process by proposing amendments;
- setting out its policies as an alternative government using designated 'Opposition Days', which are schemed into the parliamentary timetable to allow it, rather than the government, to dictate the flow of Commons business. In each parliamentary session, there are 20 Opposition Days in total (17 of which go to the largest Opposition party and three to the second largest).

▌ Devolution in practice—parliaments in the provinces

The first chapter laid out the overall constitutional framework governing the UK, while introducing the concept of devolution and how it has recently been introduced in the constituent countries of the UK outside England. There follows an explanation of how devolution has come to work in practice in Scotland, Wales, and Northern Ireland, through the aegis of the new institutions created to implement it.

The Scottish Parliament

Comprising 129 members of the *Scottish Parliament* (MSPs), the Scottish Parliament is, unlike the Westminster Parliament, a 'unicameral' legislature—that is, it only has one House. Again unlike the Commons, which can be elected anything up to every five years after the date of the previous election, the Scottish Parliament is elected *every four years* exactly, in the manner of councillors in UK local authorities.

During the initial transition stage flowing from the establishment of the Scottish Parliament in 1998, some of the existing MSPs elected to represent their country in the new Scottish Parliament were permitted to remain as members of the House of Commons as well (a similar arrangement is currently under way in relation to Northern Ireland Assembly members, following the recent restoration of devolved government in that province). This swiftly changed, however, when they assumed their place as MSPs full-time and by-elections were held to find replacements for them in their previous Commons constituencies.

Long before Scottish devolution was established, concerns were raised about the iniquity of allowing MSPs to sit and vote on English issues in the London Parliament while their Westminster equivalents would be barred from doing so in Scotland. One of the most vocal advocates of this view—dubbed the 'West Lothian Question' after the name of his Scottish constituency—was Labour backbencher Mr Dalyell. Indeed, since devolution was introduced, the arrangement has proved incendiary: in November 2003, the votes of Scottish Labour backbenchers secured a knife-edge victory for the most controversial clauses of the government's Bill to introduce foundation hospitals in England—legislation with no bearing on their own constituencies. The Scottish Parliament—buoyed by the votes of Labour MSPs—had previously voted *against* the imposition of foundation hospitals north of the border.

In terms of the make-up of the Scottish Parliament, initially 73 MSPs were elected using the UK's traditional first past the post (FPTP) electoral system and the other 56 were elected under a regional list form of *proportional representation* (see Chapter 4). Each elector was given two votes: one for their constituency, and the other for a political party the names of which appeared on their regional list.

Initially, MSPs met in a temporary chamber at Edinburgh's Church of Scotland Assembly Hall on The Mound. This was belatedly replaced by a purpose-built Parliament at Holyrood, at the foot of the Royal Mile, in 2004.

One MSP is elected to be 'Presiding Officer' (equivalent to the Commons Speaker), supported by two deputies. The terms of Parliament last for four years from the date of an election and each year is divided into a parliamentary session, which is further split into 'sitting days' and 'recess periods'. On sitting days, Parliament tries to finish its business at 5.30 p.m., except on Fridays, which tend to wrap up at 12.30 p.m.

MSPs can raise issues in one of several ways:

- by asking oral questions during parliamentary sittings;
- by submitting written questions;
- by giving notice of, or moving, a motion.

Scottish parliamentary committees

Unlike at Westminster, much of the nitty-gritty work of the Scottish Parliament is done through its 18 committees—a system that is intended to make it easier for individual members to hold the devolved government to account. Each committee is made up of 5–15 MSPs and chaired by a 'convener'. Meetings are held in public and can be convened anywhere in Scotland. This is meant to provide more direct access for ordinary people to the democratic process. A member of each committee is appointed as a 'reporter' and MSPs are allowed to take part in meetings of committees of which they are not members (although they cannot vote).

Committees are charged with examining the following:

- the policy, administration, and financial arrangements of the *Scottish Government*, or *Scottish Executive* (see p. 120);
- proposed legislation in the Scottish and Westminster Parliaments;
- the application of EU and international laws or conventions in Scotland.

The role and responsibilities of the Scottish Parliament

The Scottish Parliament has responsibility for *domestic* issues that are specifically relevant to Scotland, but not foreign policy. The roles retained by the Commons include:

- foreign and defence policy;
- most economic policy;
- social security;
- medical ethics.

The legislative process in Scotland

The four main types of Bill that can be introduced into the Scottish Parliament are as follows:

- *executive*—introduced by a minister;
- *committee*—introduced by the convener (chair) of a committee;
- *members'*—introduced by individual MSPs, like private member's Bills at Westminster, with the support of 11 fellow members;
- *private*—introduced by private individuals or promoters.

When introduced in the Scottish Parliament, Bills must be accompanied by the documents listed in Table 2.12. To become law, they must pass through the four key stages outlined in Table 2.13, in a streamlined version of the Westminster process.

The National Assembly for Wales

Elected every four years, the Cardiff-based *National Assembly for Wales* has 60 members—40 elected for constituencies and 20 on the basis of four for each of five larger regions. An Assembly Member (AM) can be an MP at the same time, as is also the case in Northern Ireland, but it is proposed that, as in Scotland, joint membership will soon cease, as progressively more power is devolved to the Welsh administration.

Each elector in Wales has two votes: one for a constituency member and the other for a name from the relevant regional list. The Secretary of State for Wales retains a degree of responsibility for the province and, unlike in Scotland, the Assembly does not yet have tax-varying powers. He or she is charged with ensuring that devolution is working effectively, by chairing a joint ministerial committee between the UK and the devolved governments.

The Assembly's responsibilities include:

- determining budgetary priorities;
- funding, directing, and appointing managers of NHS bodies in Wales;
- administering EU structural funds aimed at Wales;
- determining the content of the *National Curriculum* in Wales.

The legislative process in Wales

The legislative process in Wales resembles that of Scotland, in that it is overseen by a presiding officer and his or her deputy, elected by other members

Table 2.12 The documents required to accompany different types
of Scottish Bill

Document	Definition
All Bills	
A written statement from the Presiding Officer	Confirming that the provisions of a prospective Bill come within the legislative remit of the Parliament, highlighting any provisions judged to be outside its authority
A financial memorandum	An estimate of the administrative, compliance, and other costs to be incurred by the Scottish Executive, local authorities, other bodies, and businesses and individuals in meeting the Bill's provisions
An Auditor General's report	Confirmation of the appropriateness of any charges to be incurred during legislative process by Scottish Consolidated Fund
Executive Bills only	
A written statement from a departmental minister	Confirming that the proposed Bill falls within the remit of the Scottish Parliament
Explanatory notes	A fair and thorough summary of the Bill's proposals
A policy memorandum	Setting out the Bill's objectives and any possible alternative proposals

Table 2.13 The passage of a Bill through the Scottish Parliament

Stage	Process
Stage one	An examination of the Bill's general principles, normally handled by a lead committee (i.e. a committee specializing in the relevant subject area)
Stage two	A more detailed, line-by-line examination of the Bill, either by the lead committee, another committee, or the whole Parliament. Amendments can be made and debated at this stage
Stage three	Final consideration of the Bill by the full Parliament. Amendments can be made and debated, and Parliament will decide whether it should be passed in this form. More than 25 per cent of all MSPs must vote on the issue one way or another, if it is to be passed
Final stage	The Parliament decides, finally, whether to approve the Bill when it is referred back to a meeting of the full House. It is then automatically submitted by the Presiding Officer for Royal Assent (there is no House of Lords stage)

of the Assembly. Again, executive functions are wielded by a First Minister at the head of a devolved government (see p. 119). This was initially called the **Welsh Executive,** but is now referred to as the **Welsh Assembly Government.**

The Assembly meets in public in plenary sessions in Cardiff and business is directed by the presiding officer through a business secretary and business committee. Each session allows at least 15 minutes for oral questions of the First Minister and, each four weeks, similar sessions are held to allow AMs to question their departmental ministers. In addition, any member can propose a specific motion once a week, before the conclusion of a plenary session, and there are two forms of committees to consider matters in plenary session: 'subject committees' and 'regional committees', which cover specific areas of the country.

The Northern Ireland Assembly

Due to the ongoing fallout from 'The Troubles', the devolution process in Ireland has been a rocky ride and it was only in 2007 that devolved government finally came into effect properly, with the signing of a landmark power-sharing agreement between the two biggest parties following the then most recent elections in the province: Rev. Paisley's Democratic Unionist Party (DUP) and Gerry Adams's Sinn Féin. In April 2008, Rev. Paisley (a stalwart of Northern Irish politics for more than four decades) retired as First Minister and DUP leader, to be replaced by East Belfast MP Peter Robinson. Deputy First Minister was Sinn Féin chief negotiator Martin McGuinness.

Areas of responsibility retained over Northern Ireland by the UK

The Secretary of State for Northern Ireland remains responsible for the following:

- international relations;
- defence;
- taxation;
- law and order (including security);
- police and criminal justice policy.

Several agencies remain at Whitehall with responsibility for overseeing specific areas, including the Northern Ireland Prison Service, the Compensation Agency, and the Forensic Agency of Northern Ireland. All other legislative and executive power was transferred to the Northern Ireland Assembly at Stormont.

The legislative process in Northern Ireland

The remit of the Northern Ireland Assembly, the nature and titles of senior politicians and officers, and the legislative process are all virtually identical to those in Wales.

→ Further reading

Jones, B. (2004) *Dictionary of British Politics,* Manchester: Manchester University Press. **Does exactly what it says on the cover: a thorough, accessible A–Z of terms and of recent developments on the British political scene.**

Jones, B., Kavanagh, D., Moran, M., and Norton, P. (2006) *Politics UK,* 6th edn, London: Longman. **Full-colour edition of established core text giving a comprehensive overview of the structure and workings of the British political system. Updated to reflect results of the 2005 general election.**

Norton, P. (2005) *Parliament in British Politics,* London: Palgrave Macmillan. **A thoughtful evaluation of the changing significance of the British Parliament in light of recent constitutional developments, such as the establishment of devolved assemblies and the partial reform of the House of Lords.**

Rogers, R. and Walters, R. (2006) *How Parliament Works,* 6th edn, London: Longman. **Sixth edition of this indispensable layman's guide to the often complex, and sometimes archaic, workings of the British Houses of Parliament.**

? Review questions

1. Outline the role of backbench MPs. To whom do MPs owe primary responsibility—Parliament, party, or public?

2. What is meant by the terms 'party whip', the 'whip', and 'three-line whip'?

3. What are the arguments for and against an elected second chamber?

4. What is the role of private member's Bills and what do they actually achieve?

5. Has the creation of the Lords' Speaker and the removal of the condition that the Lord Chancellor must be a peer rendered the position redundant?

Online resource centre

www.oxfordtextbooks.co.uk/orc/Morrison
Visit the Online Resource Centre that accompanies this book for web links and regular updates.

3

The prime minister, Cabinet, and government

Having examined the competing seats of constitutional power in Britain—the sovereign and Parliament—it is now necessary to look in detail at the means by which, in practice, most of that power is exercised. This chapter focuses on the make-up and workings of the executive branch of the UK constitution—the government—and, in particular, on the role of the inner circle of ministers known as the *Cabinet,* and the most senior of these, the prime minister.

▌ The origins of the role of prime minister

Compared to ancient posts like that of *Lord Chancellor,* the role of prime minister emerged surprisingly recently, and owes its origins to historical accident. When German-born George I succeeded to the British throne in 1714, he could speak little English. Traditionally, the Cabinet had always been chaired by the monarch (albeit in an increasingly notional way since the passage of the Bill of Rights 25 years earlier), but with the newly crowned king literally incapable of understanding the language of UK government—and displaying little interest in it—a practical need arose for a senior minister to perform this duty in his place. Thus was born the idea of a post that became that of de facto head of government in Britain—or 'prime' minister.

But which of the existing government ministers should assume this privileged position? After some debate, the honour fell to Sir Robert Walpole, holder of the extant post of 'First Lord of the Treasury' (in effect, the Lord High Treasurer, or official head of HM Treasury—the department of state responsible for raising taxes to finance government policy). His previous duties were generally assumed from this date by the Lord High Commissioners of the Treasury.

Despite assuming the day-to-day role of prime minister, however, Walpole retained the official title 'First Lord of the Treasury', as did his successors for the best part of a century afterwards. In fact, although the term 'prime minister' was used informally within government from 1714 onwards and started appearing on government documents in the 1860s, under Benjamin Disraeli, it was only coined publicly during the term of Liberal premier Sir Henry Campbell-Bannerman (1905–08).

Given the disproportionate degree of power wielded by the prime minister, since the position arose, it has been contentious constitutionally. Prior to its introduction, all ministers of the Crown were regarded as equals, with shared responsibility for governing the nation. The emergence of a Cabinet chairperson from within its own ranks made an immediate mockery of this idea, by implicitly elevating that minister to a level *more equal* than that of the others. This curious, somewhat contradictory, position spawned a Latin phrase that has been associated with the post of prime minister ever since: *primus inter pares*—or 'first among equals'. The notion is that prime ministers are 'equal' to their peers in the Cabinet—and, indeed, the House of Commons (the legislature)—in that, as elected members of Parliament (the last peer to have been prime minister was Lord Salisbury, who left office in 1902), they must be voted in to represent *constituencies* and can be removed by local people if they become unpopular. To this extent, they are ordinary MPs like any other. In contrast, they are 'first among' those notional 'equals' by dint of being not only senior ministers in the government (the executive), but also presiding over Cabinet meetings.

The role of prime minister today

Today, there are many established traditions and conventions surrounding the office of prime minister, almost all of which have grown up since the time of Walpole. The prime minister—or 'premier'—tends to be the leader of the party that wins the most seats in the Commons at a general election. To this extent, although British voters are theoretically turning out to elect their local MP on polling day (not to mention the small matter of a national government for their country), the emphasis of elections is inherently 'presidential'. Everyone knows that if X party gets in, Y leader will become prime minister. Historically, the majority of premiers have hailed from either of the two biggest parliamentary parties at any one time. In the twentieth century, only four prime ministers were Labour, compared to 12 Conservatives. The Tories' dominance of the office, until recently, saw them regarded as the 'natural party of government'.

Although many of the prerogative powers exercised on behalf of the sovereign by government are discharged collectively at Cabinet meetings (at least notionally), by custom the prime minister remains the only minister ever granted a private audience with the reigning monarch. Incoming prime ministers first meet the Queen in this capacity when they visit her at Buckingham Palace to be offered the post formally after their election. This behind-the-scenes ritual is known as the 'kissing of the hands'. According to the 2006 film *The Queen*, Tony Blair actually did kiss the Queen's hands, although this has not generally been the practice for generations.

Despite widespread belief to the contrary, Mr Blair was not always so deferential in his handling of the Queen, however. Another long-standing tradition surrounding the relationship between the prime minister and the monarch is that they will meet to discuss government business in person once a week (normally on a Tuesday). At the height of the Iraq War, Mr Blair was reported to have cancelled or cut short his weekly audiences on more than one occasion.

The prime minister's official London residence is at 10 Downing Street and he or she also has the use, throughout his or her tenure, of a sprawling country estate at Chequers in the Chilterns. Like many conventions, of course, such rules are there to be bent when circumstances dictate: when Mr Blair came to power, he struck a deal with his Chancellor of the Exchequer, Gordon Brown, whose official residence was next door at Number 11, to swap domestic quarters. Mr Blair had a growing family of three children, while at the time Mr Brown was a childless bachelor.

By far the most important convention relating to the prime minister, however, is the fact that whoever holds the office has the authority to exercise, on behalf of the sovereign, the majority of the powers entrusted to him or her by the *Royal Prerogative*.

The principal prerogative powers discharged by the premier are to:

- appoint fellow ministers of the Crown;
- chair meetings of the Cabinet at least once a week;
- appoint members of *Cabinet committees*;
- keep the sovereign informed of government business on a weekly basis;
- declare war and peace;
- recommend the passage of government Bills to *Royal Assent*;
- recommend the *dissolution* of Parliament for a general election;
- recommend the *prorogation* of Parliament for the summer recess;
- draw up his or her party's manifesto at election time and write the *Queen's Speech*—the annual announcement of proposed government legislation;
- recommend for the sovereign's approval appointees to senior positions in the clergy, including the Church of England bishops and deans;
- recommend the appointment of senior judges;
- recommend appointees for senior positions in public corporations, including the posts of director-general and chairman of the British Broadcasting Corporation (BBC);
- recommend prospective recipients of honours and peerages in the Queen's Birthday *Honours List* and the New Year Honours List;
- answer for his or her government's policies and actions at Prime Minister's Questions (PMQs) every Wednesday lunchtime.

In addition to the above, the prime minister—like the monarch, in relation to his or her oversight of the Church of England and the Armed Forces—has an additional, distinct title: that of Minister for the Civil Service. The department that he or she oversees in this capacity is the Cabinet Office (effectively the 'Ministry for the Civil Service') and his or her *permanent secretary* (the most senior civil servant) is the Cabinet Secretary.

Towards 'elective dictatorship'—are prime ministers now too presidential?

The British prime minister may not be the country's head of state, but to pedantic observers, he or she appears to be such in all but name. No monarch has had the temerity to challenge the passage of a government Bill since Queen Anne did so three hundred years ago. And the notion that a king or queen would defy the will of the electorate to block the appointment of a premier whose policies they opposed is the stuff of establishment conspiracy theories (although, for a time, more pessimistic Labour **backbenchers** are said to have envisaged such action in the 1980s, when the party was lurching to the far Left and seemed incapable of convincing the public it was a credible alternative to Margaret Thatcher's all-conquering Tories).

Perhaps unsurprisingly, therefore, power has been known to go to some prime ministers' heads. As long ago as 1976, Quintin Hogg—who, as Baron Hailsham, twice served as Conservative Lord Chancellor—used his Richard Dimbleby Lecture to criticize what he described as the 'elective dictatorship' of British governments. The thrust of his argument was that successive prime ministers had accrued substantial additional power over and above that invested in them constitutionally, and were increasingly using their parliamentary colleagues to steamroller their policies through Parliament. Moreover, he argued, those same policies were often thought up, and effectively decided upon, behind closed doors—long before they were ever put before Parliament for debate. At best, this backstage policymaking would take place around the Cabinet table, among premiers and their ministerial colleagues; at worst, it might be dreamt up more informally between the prime minister and a close-knit inner circle of trusted confidantes, not all of whom were even ministers. This mode of governing has often been referred to as 'prime ministerial government'—or, more recently, 'sofa government'—as opposed to the collective decision-making embodied by traditional 'Cabinet government'.

Indeed, it was often said that the governments of the late 1960s and 1970s were prone to thinking up policies and striking deals in 'smoke-filled rooms', with business leaders, trade union bosses, and other interest groups invited to have a direct input into policymaking. In the case of Labour governments, the phrase 'beer and sandwiches' was coined to refer to the cosy chats that the likes of Harold Wilson and James Callaghan would reportedly have with the leaders of unions that helped bankroll the party prior to announcing new wage and industrial policies.

But these tactics—increasingly common to governments of both main parties—are far from the only examples of perceived presidential behaviour by modern prime ministers. Sometimes, slips of the tongue by prime ministers under pressure have spoken volumes about their apparent sense of superiority or infallibility. In 1989, in one of her more notorious remarks in the later stages of her decade in power, Mrs Thatcher referred to herself using the royal 'we' when she spoke to the media outside Downing Street to express her delight at news that the wife of her son, Mark, had given birth. Her exact words were: 'We are a grandmother.'

Mr Blair—of all recent prime ministers other than Mrs Thatcher, the one most frequently described as presidential—was also prone to such lapses towards the end of his term in office. In an interview on the ITV1 chat show *Parkinson* in March 2006, it was put to him by host Michael Parkinson that his job brought with it a huge amount of responsibility, in light of his status as commander-in-chief of the British Armed Forces. Mr Blair failed to challenge this assertion, despite the fact that, constitutionally, the office of commander-in-chief still resides with the Queen. In the same interview, he controversially intimated that God had guided his actions over Iraq (an echo of words used by President George Bush several years earlier).

So much for the sound bites, however: in what ways do our prime ministers' actions amount to high-handed behaviour in ways that *matter*? Broadly, the examples of such presidential actions can be broken down into four major categories:

- bypassing and/or downgrading the role of the Cabinet in devising policy;
- announcing policies to the media before announcing them to Parliament/the Cabinet;
- ignoring popular opinion and protest;
- grandstanding on the international stage.

Bypassing and/or downgrading the role of the Cabinet in devising policy

Prime ministers are charged with chairing meetings of the Cabinet. It is here that policies are traditionally first debated in detail and fine-tuned, before being announced to the press and public. In recent decades, however, there has been a growing tendency for premiers to downgrade the role of Cabinet in policymaking—and, in some cases, to bypass it entirely, in favour of taking advice primarily from a small posse of trusted friends and colleagues known as a 'kitchen Cabinet'.

'Kitchen Cabinets' in Britain have taken various forms and have been dependent, to a large extent, on the politics and personal leadership styles of individual prime ministers. One of the first manifestations of a UK kitchen Cabinet was Conservative Prime Minister Ted Heath's Central Policy Review Staff (CPRS), a group of advisers within the Cabinet Office (including some senior civil servants—see p. 112) entrusted with streamlining the formulation of government policy across departments. The formation of the CPRS had been recommended by the Fulton Committee, set up by his predecessor, Labour Prime Minister Harold Wilson, in 1966 to review the workings of the Civil Service. The Committee had also suggested that there should be a separate 'policy unit' set up to coordinate long-term strategic planning in each individual ministry and, when Mr Wilson was duly returned to power in 1974, he swiftly acted on this suggestion by forming the Downing Street Policy Unit (effectively his own kitchen Cabinet), chaired by Sir Bernard Donoghue.

Indeed, Mr Wilson (more than any prime minister before him) had long had a reputation for valuing the views of personal friends over those of Cabinet colleagues when it came to devising policy. Among his closest confidantes were his private secretary, Marcia Williams, and his trusted press secretary, Joe Haines. This fashion for consulting close allies—elected or otherwise—before presenting one's ideas to Cabinet, let alone Parliament, was also favoured by his successor-but-one, Mrs Thatcher, whose closest aides included her press secretary, Sir Bernard Ingham, and her private secretary, the former businessman Charles Powell.

More recently, the plotting and ruminations of the kitchen Cabinet have become increasingly associated with the work of so-called 'special advisers' and, in particular, the **spin doctors** employed by the Blair and (to a lesser extent) Brown administrations to put a positive gloss on government policy. This development will be discussed more fully later in this chapter, but it is worth reflecting on briefly here in relation to one particular casualty of the so-called 'sofa government' favoured by Mr Blair: Cabinet decision-making. As with his weekly meetings with the Queen, when the Iraq War was in full swing, Mr Blair reportedly downgraded formal Cabinet meetings for a time, to such an extent that deliberations that would traditionally take up to two or three hours were often reduced to 30 minutes or less. In addition, he is said to have left many detailed policy debates customarily held in full Cabinet session to be discussed by Cabinet committees, ensuring that those hearings were chaired by his most loyal colleagues, to reduce the likelihood that his own ideas would be questioned or rejected. It was for this and other tendencies that she saw as fundamentally undemocratic that former Cabinet minister Clare Short publicly dubbed Mr Blair a 'control freak' after resigning from the government over its handling of the post-invasion reconstruction of Iraq in 2003.

Recent prime ministers—in particular, Mrs Thatcher and Mr Blair—have also been accused of trying to bypass, or downgrade, the role of Parliament in the legislative process. The most common way in which this is seen to happen is through the heavy-handed use of the party *whip* system to coerce MPs and peers to attend votes, and to back the party line. Mr Blair was frequently accused of using his large Commons majority to 'steamroller' through Parliament policies that were unpopular with the public (and often with many of his own backbenchers). Examples include the various anti-terror measures introduced in the wake of the attacks on the Twin Towers in New York and, more recently, the 7 July 2005 bombings in London—many of which were rushed through in a matter of days, with the *committee stages* taking place on the floor of the Commons. Other examples include the knife-edge votes on foundation hospitals, university top-up fees, and enabling police to detain terrorist suspects for up to 90 days without charge—which actually failed, in spite of the inordinate pressure put on backbench Labour MPs by party whips.

Announcing policies to the media before announcing them to Parliament/the Cabinet

Briefing the media (or targeted sections of the media sympathetic to the government) on policy proposals ahead of formal announcements to Parliament and the public has become a growing—and, to many, deeply worrying—trend under recent administrations. Indeed, in some instances under Mr Blair, this secondary form of bypassing the normal machinery of government has seen ministers close to the prime minister spoon-feeding policy details to favoured journalists before even the Cabinet (let alone the House of Commons) has had a chance to discuss them. Arrangements for the briefings invariably involved the spin doctors and/or special advisers with which Mr Blair surrounded himself—principally, his official spokesman and long-time director of communications, Alastair Campbell, and/or Downing Street chief of staff Jonathan Powell. A fuller discussion of the roles of these two follows later this chapter.

So what forms do these 'off-the-record' briefings actually take and how often have they involved policy announcements yet to be debated in Cabinet? The most widely used form of policy briefing by ministers, special advisers, or government press officers acting on behalf of their superiors are explained in Table 3.1.

From a policy point of view, one of the most infamous examples of serious proposals being released to the press in advance of even full Cabinet discussion occurred in 2002, when Alan Milburn, then Secretary of State for Health and a close political ally of Mr Blair, gave an interviewer from *The Times* a detailed explanation of his so-called 'Ten-Year Plan for the National Health Service' (NHS). Among the more controversial policy ideas that he mooted (which have since come to fruition) was the introduction of foundation hospitals—a new type of **NHS trust** with far greater control over its own finances and management than had ever previously been the case (see p. 191).

Ignoring popular opinion and protest

During his first four years in office, Mr Blair was notorious for consulting opinion pollsters and focus groups before taking any remotely radical policy decision. His critics (including many within his own party) argued that this was, at best, a waste of the mandate that he had achieved by winning such a large parliamentary majority in the 1997 election and, at worst, a betrayal of promises made in the Labour Party's manifesto, which were often watered down to the point at which they no longer resembled the original pledges.

In his second term, however, Mr Blair developed a tendency to do precisely the opposite—becoming increasingly bold and risky in his political judgements. Perhaps the most notorious example of this headstrong approach was the messianic zeal with which he pushed the case for war with Iraq, citing supposed evidence (which turned out to be deeply flawed, and remains unsubstantiated) that Saddam Hussein was stockpiling weapons of mass destruction (WMDs). Defying huge opposition in the country at large—most symbolically articulated by the biggest peacetime demonstration in Britain's history, when up to 500,000 protestors marched through central London and converged on Trafalgar Square just days before the war—he persuaded a reluctant Commons to vote for the invasion.

Mr Blair's new appetite for defying public opposition owed much to the approach taken by Mrs Thatcher, particularly in her third and final term. The policy that most clearly demonstrated her stubbornness in the teeth of

Table 3.1 Types of media briefing used by ministers and special advisers

Name	Definition
Kite-flying	A recently coined term referring to the government practice of releasing details through the media of potential policy initiatives, to gauge the public's reaction before committing itself to them. Ideas mooted in this way have included extending the right to vote to 16-year-olds, banning teenagers from wearing 'hoodies' (hooded tops), and allowing the police to march those guilty of anti-social behaviour to cash points to pay on-the-spot fines. None of these policies has so far been implemented (although some local authorities and commercial companies, including Kent's Bluewater shopping centre, have banned hoodies).
Leak	Traditionally, the term 'leak' has been associated with the release of confidential and/or advance information of a controversial nature, often by someone 'in the know' who is unhappy about what is going on behind the scenes. Perhaps the most famous leak in recent British history was by civil servant Clive Ponting, who passed details of the sinking of the Argentinian warship *The General Belgrano* during the Falklands War to a journalist. More recently, leaking has become an even murkier affair and there have been accusations of complicity by ministers in releasing potentially controversial information prematurely, in the hope that a gradual 'drip, drip' of information will lessen the impact of a later announcement. The Hutton Report into the circumstances leading to the apparent suicide of government scientist Dr David Kelly was leaked to *The Sun* the night before its publication. Although no one admitted culpability, it is widely believed that the leak was a form of attempted damage limitation by a government source.
Rebuttal	The practice of issuing swift denials to criticisms, accusations, and announcements made by political foes (e.g. rebutting claims of wartime casualties by the enemy). Occasionally, these have pre-empted the pronouncements they are meant to be 'rebutting', in an effort by the rebutter to neutralize the impact of those criticisms by 'getting in first'.
Trail	Similar to kite-flying, these are frequently offered to Sunday newspapers. Because they are published only once a week and there is generally less diary-based news (e.g. court hearings, parliamentary proceedings) around when they go to press than in the case of daily papers, the Sundays rely more than any other kind of publication on exclusive stories. The more certain they can be that they have a story that no other media organization has yet run, the more likely they are to 'run it big'. Government press officers and special advisers are usually keen to offer such 'scoops' to Sundays with which they have good working relationships, because a large spread in a paper aimed at their target audience on a day of the week when more people read papers than at any other time will have the effect of generating significant publicity. It is also customary for the following day's papers to follow up big stories of interest to their readers—particularly if they have only previously appeared in one of the Sundays. To aid them in deciding when to 'trail' a policy in the press, government spin doctors and press officers work to a schedule known as 'The Grid'. This maps out, for their own reference, a putative timetable of when policy announcements, Cabinet and Commons debates, publication of reports, etc., are due, so that press officers can release 'sneak preview' information strategically to ensure the maximum—or minimum—publicity. Occasionally, the aim is to suppress information by going through the motions of announcing it, but doing so in such a way or at such a time that it is likely to attract little coverage. The most notorious recent example of this was when, on 11 September 2001, Jo Moore—a spin doctor in the then Department for Transport, Local Government and the Regions (DTLR)—sent an email to all

(continued)

Name	Definition
	press office staff containing the following instruction: *'It is now a very good day to get out anything we want to bury. Councillors' expenses?'* After issuing a grovelling televised apology to relatives of the victims of the World Trade Center terrorist attacks, she saved her job—but only for a short time. Five months later, in February 2002, she was sacked after being accused by a colleague, Martin Sixsmith, of trying to use another occasion for mourning (the funeral of Princess Margaret) as an opportunity to release embarrassing information—relating to poor train performance data (see p. 118).

huge public opposition was ultimately—like the Iraq War, arguably, in relation to Mr Blair—to hasten her downfall: the introduction of the Community Charge, or 'Poll Tax' (see p. 130). This deeply unpopular local 'head tax'—a replacement for the property-based rates system—provoked some of the largest-scale public protests in British history. Mrs Thatcher remained resolute, however, and it was only when her successor, John Major, came to power a year or so after the demonstrations that the tax was finally abandoned.

Grandstanding on the international stage

As Britain's de facto head of state, the prime minister inevitably has the biggest global profile of any individual UK politician. Nonetheless, some prime ministers take to the role of international statesperson more than others. In the nineteenth century, the Liberal William Gladstone and Tory Benjamin Disraeli were the two most accomplished and successful British premiers, but of the two, it was arguably the latter—famous, like Mrs Thatcher and Mr Blair after him, for his interventionist foreign policy—who really impressed on the international stage. Of twentieth-century prime ministers, Winston Churchill was widely regarded as the most accomplished statesman—principally because of the leadership he gave to Europe during the Second World War.

Examples of 'presidential-style' political grandstanding on the global stage in recent times have included Mrs Thatcher's decisive handling of the Falklands War and high-profile 'love-ins'—frequently caught on camera at the White House and broadcast globally—with US president Ronald Reagan. Her implacable opposition to communism and her determined negotiation of various British opt-outs from European Union (EU) legislation, also helped to maintain her high international profile.

Mr Blair, meanwhile, waged at least four wars during his ten years in Downing Street. During his first term, he was a party to the launch of two military campaigns: the *North Atlantic Treaty Organization (NATO)* intervention over alleged 'ethnic cleansing' of Albanians by Slobodan Milošović's Serbs in Kosovo, and a decisive move to halt the civil war in the former British colony of Sierra Leone. In his second term, he became forever wedded in the public eye to George Bush's US administration through his pledge to 'stand shoulder to shoulder' with the country following the 11 September terrorist attacks, and through the subsequent invasions of, first, Afghanistan, then Iraq.

Mr Blair's exhausting schedule of shuttle diplomacy in the run-up to the Iraq War—flying across Africa to persuade smaller *United Nations (UN)* member states to support Britain and the USA's calls for a second UN resolution to justify military action—buoyed up his profile still further. So too did his earlier, and later, missions to tackle poverty in Africa, to forge peace in Northern Ireland, and to promote a decisive 'two-state solution' to the long-running stand-off between Israel and Palestine in the Middle East. His involvement in brokering the latter saw him rewarded after stepping down as prime minister with a new diplomatic role as Middle East peace envoy for 'the Quartet'—a loose international body representing the EU, UN, USA, and Russia.

Finally, although the Queen is still charged constitutionally with entertaining visiting heads of state on official visits (which she did for President Bush in 2004 and France's President Sarcozy in 2008), Mr Blair would also get in on the action even here, often inviting world leaders to stay at his Chequers estate after they had left her.

Holding the prime minister to account

Given the extraordinary degree of power accrued by the office of prime minister, what mechanisms exist to hold him or her to account? As we know from our earlier discussions on the subject, monarchs have long since lost their inclination (if not their ability) to challenge their most senior elected officials, with Queen Anne's notable stand against a government Bill in 1707 being the last to date. Notwithstanding Queen Elizabeth II's reported predilection for wrong-footing Harold Wilson and her frosty relationship with Mrs Thatcher, there has been little evidence in modern times of reigning monarchs displaying an appetite for confrontation. Nonetheless, there remain significant means by which the actions of the prime minister can be influenced, if not actually controlled. For reasons of simplicity, these can be divided into four broad areas:

- public;
- press;
- Parliament;
- party.

Public

The primary way in which prime ministers can be held to account by the public goes right back to that first principle—namely, that prime ministers are ultimately MPs like any other and, as such, have to stand for re-election in their constituencies come polling day. The party that they represent is similarly dependent on a public mandate for its Commons majority: if enough of its MPs lose their constituencies' support at an election, another party will emerge with more seats and take over in government.

The resounding defeat of John Major's Conservative government in 1997 by Mr Blair's 'New Labour' was the clearest example in recent times of an ailing administration being unceremoniously ejected by an electorate that had decided it wanted change. Not only did the Tories suffer a landslide defeat, but many of their most prominent MPs—including Defence Secretary Michael Portillo—lost their seats. Although Mr Major managed to escape this ignominy himself, it has been known for prime ministers in some countries to lose their own constituency seats, as well as their parliamentary majorities. Such a fate befell Australian premier John Howard, in the 2007 election, which booted him out of office after more than a decade in power.

Prime ministers can also be held to account by the public in other ways. It has long been the practice, for example, for by-elections, and local and European elections, to be treated as 'protest votes' by voters disgruntled with the serving government—that is, as occasions on which they choose to vote for a candidate or party other than that of the prime minister to give him or her a 'bloody nose'. Others prefer to withhold their support from a governing party that they might still back at a general election by abstaining from voting altogether. There is significant anecdotal evidence that protest votes and abstentions have risen in Britain in recent years, especially among traditional Labour voters disillusioned by the government's centrist policies and the invasion of Iraq. The combined effect of protest votes and abstentions on the one side, and renewed determination to harness support on the other, can lead to situations such as that witnessed in the 2007 and 2008 local elections, and the by-election in the previously solid Labour parliamentary seat of Crewe and Nantwich following the death of veteran backbencher Gwyneth Dunwoody, both of which were 'won' by David Cameron's resurgent Conservatives.

Other forms of public pressure that can be put on prime ministers include demonstrations (such as the Stop the War Coalition marches over Iraq and the Countryside Alliance's over the hunting ban), industrial action by public sector employees—for example, the recent strikes by firefighters, postal workers, and local government employees—and the rejections of key policies in national *referenda*. Although British governments rarely put individual questions to the public vote in this way—preferring to invoke the constitutional principle of **parliamentary sovereignty**, which upholds the supremacy of Parliament—both Mr Blair and Mr Brown were accused of avoiding referenda on the EU's 2007 Lisbon Treaty (described by its opponents as an 'EU constitution' in all but name) for fear of losing it.

Press

If there's one thing guaranteed to worry a prime minister silly—and to send him or her scurrying in pursuit of all manner of populist policy ideas to regain public support—it is a negative headline in one of Britain's major tabloid newspapers. Not for nothing is the press frequently described as the 'Fourth Estate' of government.

In recent years, the national press—particularly the biggest-selling daily papers, *The Sun* and the *Daily Mail*—has been seen to wield disproportionately more influence than other media on the actions of successive governments. Mrs Thatcher's hat-trick of election wins in the late 1970s and 1980s were put down, in no small part, to the support of 'white van man' or 'Essex man'—terms used to denote a new breed of aspirational working-class voter who had become weary of the 'class warfare' espoused by old-school Labour politicians, and who were attracted by the doctrines of self-help and share and home ownership ushered in by Thatcherite ideology. Although formerly a red-blooded Labour paper (*The Daily Herald*), *The Sun* under Rupert Murdoch came to epitomize this new spirit of entrepreneurship, just as the high moral tone of the *Daily Mail* appealed to 'traditional' Conservatives.

Throughout the 1980s, *The Sun* remained one of the staunchest advocates of Thatcherism, using many memorable front-page headlines to bolster support for her peculiarly tough-talking and resolutely patriotic brand of politics. Among its most controversial splashes was its celebration of the sinking of the Argentine warship *General Belgrano* with the headline 'Gotcha!' and the one with which it urged voters to support Mr Major rather than Labour leader Neil Kinnock in the 1992 election: 'If Neil Kinnock wins today would the last person to leave Britain please turn out the lights.' After more than a decade of supporting the Conservatives, Britain's biggest-selling paper switched horses in the run-up to the 1997 election, backing Mr Blair, but it remains to be seen how Labour will fare come the next poll (especially given Mr Brown's decision to sign the 2007 Lisbon Treaty without a referendum—something for which *The Sun* had tirelessly campaigned).

Although this has been strenuously denied by both Mr Blair and Mr Brown, a recent liberalization of media ownership laws in the UK that enabled Mr Murdoch—despite his significant share of the national newspaper market—to buy a stake in ITV is said by some to have come as a direct result of his behind-the-scenes lobbying (and, it is rumoured, a threatened switch of support away from the government if it failed to oblige). Mr Blair is reported to have frequently invited Mr Murdoch to private talks at Downing Street and Chequers, and to have visited him in Australia—often at times when he was otherwise preoccupied with major concerns, such as Iraq.

Mr Brown, meanwhile, is known to have been friendly with Paul Dacre, editor of the *Daily Mail*, and—significantly, for such a stalwart Tory paper—it avoided criticizing him in the months after he became prime minister, despite a series of major policy blunders that saw even loyal papers, such as the *Daily Mirror*, question his judgement.

Parliament

Prime ministers are held to account by Parliament in a number of ways, the most demonstrable of which is Prime Minister's Questions (PMQs)—the weekly half-hour session in which he or she is taken to task for his or her actions (see pp. 52–4).

Most MPs also sit on committees. Through participating in the work of *select committees*, they examine in detail the workings of individual government departments—and, indirectly, those of the Cabinet over which the prime minister presides. Standing committees, meanwhile, are there to scrutinize the wording of prospective legislation, the bulk of which will have originated in the in-trays of the prime minister and his or her most senior ministerial colleagues. Prime ministers also now subject themselves to twice-yearly scrutiny by the Commons Liaison Committee (see p. 56).

MPs can also use a variety of other parliamentary procedures outlined in the last chapter—including early day motions (EDMs), urgent debates, and adjournment debates—to influence and/or criticize prime ministers and their policies. In January 2008, Shadow Universities Secretary, David Willetts, led a half-day Commons debate designed to embarrass the government—and, by implication, the prime minister—arising from an EDM signed by 211 MPs, including 86 Labour backbenchers. It criticized plans to remove £100m from the budget set aside to help people study for qualifications at the same, or a lower, level than those that they already had.

Perhaps the single most powerful way in which MPs—and, to a lesser extent, peers—conspire to embarrass, and occasionally humiliate, serving prime ministers is to vote down their policies in Parliament. Because most British governments tend to have a working majority in the Commons and can usually martial sufficient support from their own party MPs in votes, historically government legislation has rarely been defeated in its entirety. On some significant occasions, however, prime ministers have found themselves so out of step with their own parliamentary parties that (whatever their nominal majority) they have struggled to get their proposals passed.

Mr Blair generally managed to squeak through most of his more controversial legislation—barring his attempt to allow anti-terror police to continue questioning suspects without charge for up to 90 days, which was defeated by one such backbench rebellion. But there have been times when the extent, and frequency, of indiscipline in a governing party's ranks has become so serious that it has had long-lasting, if not fatal, consequences for prime ministers and for their governments.

Party

When Parliament conspires to censure prime ministers, derail their legislative programmes, or otherwise undermine their authority, it usually succeeds in doing so only with the complicity of government backbenchers who have become so dismayed with their leadership's direction that they are prepared to vote against it en masse. In Mr Blair's second and third terms, backbench rebellions became so frequent at times that Labour MPs were increasingly described as the 'unofficial Opposition' (particularly when the *real* Opposition, the Tories, were still under the stuttering leadership of William Hague, Iain Duncan Smith, and Michael Howard).

The most serious form this censure of serving prime ministers by their own backbenchers can take is through the aegis of a 'motion of no confidence' (also known as a 'vote of no confidence', or a 'censure motion'). This is when a device such as an EDM is put before the Commons—customarily by the Leader of the Opposition—inviting MPs to pass a motion (vote) expressing a loss of 'confidence' in the serving prime minister. If the prime minister loses the motion, it will normally mean that even his or her own MPs have signalled their withdrawal of support and an election will be called.

The election that saw the end of Mr Callaghan's Labour government in May 1979 was ultimately precipitated by a confidence vote tabled by Opposition leader Mrs Thatcher. Because Mr Callaghan was reliant for his continuation in power on a coalition with the Liberal Party—the 'Lib–Lab Pact'—it was the loss of support of the latter, rather than his own backbenchers, which brought down his administration.

More unusually, prime ministers in desperate strait have been known to call their own votes of confidence, in an effort to instil discipline in their party ranks and to force through legislation that they are determined to pursue. In 1993, Mr Major tabled such a high-risk 'back me or sack me' motion, to force the hand of the so-called 'Maastricht rebels' (Euro-sceptic Conservative backbenchers who had repeatedly voted against the Treaty on the European Union—popularly known as the 'Maastricht Treaty'—that his government was struggling to ratify). In the event, he won the vote—not least because most of the rebels represented marginal seats—that is, those that could easily be lost to another candidate or party in the event of an election—so were understandably wary of the prospect of an imminent poll.

There are, of course, various other ways in which governing parties can hold their leaders to account—and even dispose of them, if the mood takes them. Once a week, when Labour is in government, leaders subject themselves to a lengthy meeting of the *Parliamentary Labour Party (PLP)*—essentially the 'body' representing all elected Labour MPs. Although Mr Blair was given a famously easy ride for his first few years in power, in the aftermath of the Iraq debacle, PLP meetings are said to have become increasingly strained, with the prime minister fielding harder questions, and occasionally even being booed and jeered.

Conservative MPs have an even more ferocious means of grilling—and occasionally deposing—their leaders. The *1922 Committee* is a body made up of all backbench Tory members (although, when in Opposition, as at present, frontbench MPs other than the party leader may also attend its meetings). Actually formed in 1923 (but taking its name from the 1922 election), this influential committee has an 18-strong executive committee, charged with overseeing the election of new party leaders, and has, at times, acted to remove existing ones. As the 'voice' of the majority of Tory MPs, the 1922

Committee is seen to represent the collective 'mood' of the party at large. If it passes a vote of no confidence in its leadership, therefore, it is normally only a matter of time before he or she will jump (that is, assuming that he or she is not pushed first).

The role of the 1922 Committee is examined in more detail in Chapter 5, but it is relevant here in relation to its involvement in the removal of a recent Tory premier: Mrs Thatcher. Her downfall was effectively instigated by her former Cabinet colleague, Michael Heseltine, when he challenged her for the party leadership in November 1990. Although she won the first round of voting in the election that followed, she did so by too small a margin to win the contest outright. To do so, she had to secure the backing of an absolute majority of Tory MPs and to achieve 15 per cent more votes than her nearest rival—a target that she narrowly missed. Despite initially announcing her intention to continue fighting for her position through the second round, in the interim Mrs Thatcher was visited by a deputation of backbenchers, who made it clear to her she had lost the backing of much of her parliamentary party. After taking counsel from fellow ministers, she withdrew her candidacy—paving the way for Mr Major's election soon afterwards.

▶ Cabinet versus government—what is the difference?

Despite the clear moves towards a more presidential—or, at least, 'prime ministerial'—form of government, constitutionally speaking, the role of the Cabinet remains of paramount importance in the exercise of elected power in Britain. So what exactly is the 'Cabinet', and how does it differ from—and relate to—the 'government'?

Perhaps the simplest way to explain the relationship between the two is to view the Cabinet as a 'subset' of the government. The government is made up of *all* ministers appointed by the prime minister, while the Cabinet is composed of only the most senior ones. Governments and Cabinets have been known to vary wildly in size from one administration to another, with some favouring a more compact, rationalized approach and others an all-encompassing one.

Historically, the average size of a Cabinet has been 20—although, at times, it has been, by turns, significantly larger and significantly smaller. For much of the Second World War, Winston Churchill ran a Cabinet numbering a mere

68 ministers, while in 1922, Andrew Bonar Law formed a peacetime Cabinet of only 16. In contrast, Labour prime ministers in particular have tended to appoint larger Cabinets—at least in part as a bulwark against what the party for many years saw as the intransigence of senior civil servants when presented with its policies in government. Harold Wilson had one Cabinet comprising 24 members and Mr Blair raised the bar to 26. Mr Brown, meanwhile, appointed an enlarged 'hybrid' first Cabinet, effectively numbering 29. While only 22 of these were permanent members, an additional seven (including Olympics Minister Tessa Jowell and Attorney General Baroness Scotland) were permitted to attend its meetings on a de facto basis.

In his October 2008 reshuffle, Mr Brown expanded the Cabinet even further, to 34 (including the 'occasional' members). Its numbers were boosted, in part, by his decision to create a new Department for Energy and Climate Change (DECC), and to reinstate two distinct offices for Defence and Scotland, in response to criticisms from military chiefs and the devolved *Scottish Government* respectively of his earlier decision to combine the two under one Secretary of State, Des Browne. Mr Browne left the government voluntarily at this time, after being offered a post overseeing a combined department covering Scotland, Wales, and Northern Ireland. His resignation prompted Mr Brown to revert to the old model of a separate ministry for each country.

Cabinet ministers have, until recently, always been either MPs or peers. For some time, the idea of even a peer—a lord or lady who has not stood for election for public office—being entrusted with a ministerial brief was viewed as highly contentious. Nevertheless, there have been many high-profile examples of such appointments, including Lord Young of Graffham (Trade and Industry Secretary under Mrs Thatcher), Lord Carrington (Foreign Secretary at the time of the Falklands War), and Lord Sainsbury (a science minister under Mr Blair). Today, the appointment of a peer to high government office would scarcely raise an eyebrow.

Mr Brown arguably took the prime minister's discretion to choose ministers from outside the Commons to a new level, with his declaration on entering office that he wanted a 'government of all the talents'. This assertion—an extension of the 'big tent' politics for which Mr Blair was so often criticized by Labour traditionalists—has seen a number of individuals from outside his own party's ranks appointed to senior advisory positions in government. Perhaps most controversially, Baron Jones of Birmingham, former director-general of the Confederation of British Industry, was appointed a minister at the newly created Department of Business, Enterprise and Regulatory

Reform (BERR)—despite making it clear that he had no intention of join-ing the Labour Party. Equally unprecedented was the decision to appoint Sir Mark Malloch Brown, former UN deputy secretary-general and neither a peer nor an MP, as Minister for Africa, Asia and the UN. Mr Brown also dispensed with another Cabinet tradition: since 1963, its meetings have gen-erally been held on Thursdays, but he switched them to Tuesdays.

The majority of Cabinet ministers have the title *secretary of state*, rather than *minister of state*, denoting their senior status. This normally means that they are the head of a major government spending department, such as health—and often have several junior ministers—that is, members of the government, but not of the Cabinet—answerable to them. In terms of the choice of ministerial posts included in the Cabinet, this can vary greatly, depending on the political priorities of the day. For example, until Mr Blair's election win in 1997, overseas aid and development was treated as a rela-tively minor ministerial area and was the responsibility of a non-Cabinet minister within the Foreign Office. When Labour was re-elected, the post was promoted to become that of 'International Development Secretary'. Its first incumbent, Clare Short, was put in charge of her own dedicated depart-ment and promoted to the Cabinet.

In addition to the more obvious senior departmental posts, traditionally, the Cabinet also contains one or two honorary posts that are awarded to loyal lieutenants of the prime minister of the day whom they would like to retain close at hand, but for more general duties than overseeing a specific portfo-lio. One such post is that of 'Chancellor of the Duchy of Lancaster'—a sine-cure deriving from an office once involved in the daily management of the sovereign's one significant surviving estate following the handover of the Crown Lands to the state (see p. 25). When veteran Labour MP Jack Cunning-ham was appointed to this post by Mr Blair in 1998, the media swiftly dubbed him variously 'Cabinet enforcer' and 'Cabinet fixer', because his brief was said to be to take charge of coordinating the government's message in its dealings with press and public. Another such post is the recent addition of 'Minister without Portfolio', an office briefly occupied after the 1997 election by Mr Blair's close ally Peter Mandelson (who made a surprise return to the Cabinet in Mr Brown's second reshuffle). As of 3 October 2008, the Cabinet was as listed in Table 3.2.

So much for the Cabinet: what of the government as a whole? Its size can also vary, but in modern times, it has become customary for it to number anything up to a hundred ministers at a time. The most junior ministerial post is that of *parliamentary under-secretary*, who ranks beneath both a

Table 3.2 The composition of the UK Cabinet (October 2008)

Title	Name
Prime Minister/First Lord of the Treasury/Minister for the Civil Service	Gordon Brown
Chancellor of the Exchequer	Alistair Darling
Secretary of State for Foreign and Commonwealth Affairs (Foreign Secretary)	David Miliband
Secretary of State for Justice/Lord Chancellor	Jack Straw
Secretary of State for the Home Department (Home Secretary)	Jacqui Smith
Secretary of State for Defence	John Hutton
Secretary of State for Health	Alan Johnson
Secretary of State for Energy and Climate Change	Ed Miliband
Secretary of State for the Environment, Food and Rural Affairs	Hilary Benn
Secretary of State for International Development	Douglas Alexander
Secretary of State for Business, Enterprise and Regulatory Reform	Baron Mandelson of Foy and Hartlepod
Leader of the House of Commons/Lord Privy Seal/Minister for Women/Labour Party Chair	Harriet Harman
Secretary of State for Work and Pensions	James Purnell
Secretary of State for Transport	Geoff Hoon
Secretary of State for Communities and Local Government	Hazel Blears
Parliamentary Secretary to the Treasury and Chief Whip	Nick Brown
Secretary of State for Children, Schools and Families	Ed Balls
Minister for the Cabinet Office/Chancellor of the Duchy of Lancaster	Liam Byrne
Secretary of State for Culture, Media and Sport	Andy Burnham
Secretary of State for Northern Ireland	Shaun Woodward
Secretary of State for Wales	Paul Murphy
Secretary of State for Scotland	Jim Murphy
Leader of the House of Lords/Lord President of the Council	Baroness Royall of Blaisdon
Chief Secretary to the Treasury	Yvette Cooper
Secretary of State for Innovation, Universities and Skills	John Denham
In addition, the following senior ministers are also allowed to attend Cabinet:	
Minister for the Olympics and Paymaster General	Tessa Jowell
Attorney General	Baroness Scotland of Asthal
Minister for Housing	Margaret Beckett
Minister for Employment and Minister for London	Tony McNulty
Minister for Children, Schools and Families	Beverley Hughes
Minister for Innovation, Universities and Skills	Lord Drayson

Title	Name
Minister for Europe	Caroline Flint
Minister for Africa, Asia and the UN	Lord Malloch Brown
Parliamentary Private Secretary to the Prime Minister	Ian Austin
Parliamentary Private Secretary to the Prime Minister	Angela E. Smith

 NOTE: A regularly updated version of this table can be found on the Online Resource Centre that accompanies this book.

minister of state and secretary of state. Also usually included in this over-all tally are government whips and MPs given the role of *parliamentary private secretary (PPS)*. These are junior posts ascribed to ambitious MPs who aspire to become ministers. They serve as a point of contact or liaison in Parliament (or, as some would have it, 'spy') for serving ministers and, as such, are informally connected to those ministers' departments. The prime minister tends to have two PPSs at any one time.

Ministerial salaries

In recognition of their higher levels of responsibility, ministers who are elected MPs receive substantially higher salaries than their backbench col-leagues. The precise levels of ministerial salaries, however, can vary sig-nificantly, depending on the degree of that additional responsibility and the overall complexity of their jobs. According to figures published in May 2007, the prime minister was paid £128,174 on top of his basic MP salary—taking his total income to £188,849. Cabinet ministers and the government chief whip, meanwhile, were paid a total of £137,579, while ministers of state outside the Cabinet generally received £100,568, and parliamentary under-secretaries, £90,955. Ordinary government whips were paid £86,348. In a symbolic ges-ture of solidarity with public sector workers whose pay rises were being limited because of what Mr Brown described as the 'economic uncertainty' of the time, ministers declined their annual 1.5 per cent pay rise in 2008.

Although peers are not paid as yet (see p. 69), those occupying positions in government do receive parliamentary remuneration. Cabinet ministers drawn from the House of Lords are paid £104,386 by the taxpayer, while ministers of state get £81,504. Indeed, the highest-paid minister of all is not the prime minister, but the Lord Chancellor, who is entitled to the princely sum of £232,900 (although the incumbent at the time of the report, Jack Straw, actually only drew £104,386).

Inflated salaries are also paid to the most senior members of the Opposition frontbench, although at a substantially lower level than their government counterparts. As leader of the Opposition, David Cameron currently earns £131,172 a year.

Collective responsibility versus ministerial responsibility

The actions of ministers, especially those in Cabinet, are governed by two constitutional conventions: *collective responsibility* and *individual ministerial responsibility*. While one of these relates to their role as part of a collective decision-making body, the other concerns their duty to manage the day-to-day running of their individual portfolio (department) and to 'take the rap' if mistakes are made.

Collective responsibility

Cabinet ministers are expected to endorse and support publicly the actions of the government of which they are a part, even if they do not agree with them in private. This doctrine—known as 'collective responsibility'—rests on the assumption that individual ministers are broadly in favour of the policy programme adopted by their government, but may occasionally disagree with a specific proposal. It has long been the custom, under these circumstances, for ministers to bite their tongues rather than speak out. On many notable occasions, however, individuals have found themselves increasingly out of step with the views of their Cabinet colleagues over time and have ultimately resigned as a result—freeing themselves to speak their minds.

In 1986, Defence Secretary Michael Heseltine quit the Cabinet over the controversy surrounding the proposed merger of Westland, Britain's last surviving helicopter manufacturer, with the American company Sikorsky. He dramatically stormed out of a Cabinet meeting in full view of waiting television cameras, making it clear that he had had enough of Mrs Thatcher's dictatorial decision-making style. In 2003, the late Robin Cook, then Leader of the Commons, resigned from government in protest at what he saw as Mr Blair's belligerent stance over Iraq. He was followed, some time after the invasion, by International Development Secretary Clare Short, who blamed the chaotic reconstruction of the country in the aftermath of Saddam Hussein's defeat for her decision. John Denham, reappointed to the Cabinet under Mr Brown, also resigned from a junior post over Iraq.

In a risky, but ultimately shrewd, tactical manoeuvre, in 1975, Labour Prime Minister Harold Wilson took the, so far unique, step of temporarily suspending collective responsibility, in relation to a debate over an issue that he feared would otherwise create potentially fatal Cabinet divisions. Having called a national referendum on Britain's continued membership of the European Community, which he subsequently won, he allowed members of his Cabinet with strong views either way to campaign for or against the 'yes' vote. Among the strong Euro-sceptics in his Cabinet was left-winger Tony Benn, who argued that the 'Common Market', as it was widely known, would destroy British jobs by preventing the country from using protectionism—or customs duties—to inflate the price of imports of manufactured goods, in the interests of persuading people to 'buy British'. Asked about his similarly inclusive policy towards troublesome colleagues, US President Lyndon B. Johnson once said of FBI director J. Edgar Hoover:

   ❝ It's probably better to have him inside the tent pissing out than outside the tent pissing in. **❞**

Individual ministerial responsibility

The other principal convention relating to the work of a Cabinet minister is that of individual ministerial responsibility. This is the doctrine that, should a serious error or scandal occur 'on the watch' of a departmental minister—for example, a huge blunder costing millions of pounds of taxpayers' money—that minister should do the honourable thing and resign. Lord Carrington, for example, stepped down as Foreign Secretary over the Argentine invasion of the Falkland Islands in 1982.

But he was something of an exception. In contrast to the position in relation to collective responsibility, recent history is littered with examples of significant departmental errors for which ministers have been reluctant to take the blame. The fiasco over Britain's sudden withdrawal from the European exchange rate mechanism (ERM) in 1992 would, on many other occasions, have seen the immediate departure of the Chancellor of the Exchequer—the minister in charge of the economy. In fact, then Chancellor Norman Lamont stayed on for several months before belatedly being sacked by Prime Minister John Major.

More recently, as Labour's Defence Secretary Geoff Hoon survived a series of explosive controversies surrounding everything from the non-discovery of Saddam's alleged WMDs to a scandal over the inadequate military equipment with which British soldiers were revealed to be fighting in both the conflicts in Iraq and Afghanistan. Jacqui Smith later weathered a series of crises as Home Secretary, involving asylum seekers, prison over-crowding, and a potential strike by police officers over pay, while Alistair Darling saw out the collapse of the Northern Rock and Bradford & Bingley banks, the market turmoil caused by the global financial crisis that broke out in September 2008, and the loss of 15 million UK taxpayers' bank details on a data disc mislaid by HM Revenue and Customs (see pp. 252-4).

But there have been nobler examples. Estelle Morris quit her job as Education Secretary in 2002 over a controversy surrounding the inaccurate marking of thousands of A-level exam papers, saying that she did not feel that she was 'up to the job'. Ironically, many people—including some poli-tical opponents, teachers, and union leaders—felt that she was premature in taking this decision and was not personally to blame. The controversy had erupted when it emerged that a large number of A-level students whose papers were marked by certain exam boards had received grades substan-tially lower than those they were predicted. Headteacher unions accused the boards of unfairly penalizing students because of pressure from Britain's main examinations body, the *Qualifications and Curriculum Authority (QCA)*, to limit the number of A and A* grades in the wake of past controversy over so-called 'grade inflation'. In the end, a mass remarking took place and a number of students' grades were revised. Although Ms Morris arguably had nothing directly to do with the marking procedure and had acted promptly, she decided to 'fall on her sword'. In 2006, meanwhile, Ms Smith's predeces-sor-but-one as Home Secretary, Charles Clarke, resigned voluntarily after a succession of controversies on his watch—including the revelation that more than a thousand foreign nationals convicted of criminal offences in the UK had been freed from prison without being considered for deportation.

In practice, ministers are often sacked by their prime minister before they have a chance to quit. The prime minister's ability to remove colleagues unceremoniously dates back to a convention initiated by William Pitt in the early nineteenth century. It almost always precipitates a process known as a 'Cabinet reshuffle', during which several other ministers will have to be moved from one job to another to fill gaps created by the removal of their errant colleague and whoever has replaced them.

The Cabinet Office and Cabinet committees

The Cabinet Office is effectively the 'Civil Service of the Cabinet'—that is, the administrative staff and machinery that organizes its meetings and keeps its business running on a day-to-day basis. It comprises a Cabinet Secretariat—responsible for organizing the *minutes* of Cabinet meetings— and the Office of Public Service—which oversees government business as a whole—and is headed by the Cabinet Secretary, or Head of the Home Civil Service.

In turn, the Secretariat is made up of six separate departmental secretariats:

- the Economic and Domestic Affairs Secretariat;
- the Defence and Overseas Affairs Secretariat;
- the European Secretariat;
- the Constitution Secretariat;
- the Central Secretariat;
- the Intelligence Support Secretariat.

In addition, Cabinet committees have increasingly been set up to deal with the finer points of policymaking. They tend, in practice, to be chaired by ministers whose personal views are close to those of the prime minister. When Mr Blair was prime minister, a significant number were chaired by his loyal deputy, John Prescott—who was said by critics to require this role 'to give him something to do'. As with parliamentary committees, there are several types of Cabinet committee, as outlined in Table 3.3.

Table 3.3 Types of Cabinet committee

Name	Role and composition
Standing committees	Unlike Commons committees of the same name, these are permanent (at least for the duration of a Parliament). They focus on broad-ranging policy areas (e.g. transport or health), in an effort to encourage more coordinated policymaking and to avoid duplication. They tend to be composed of the most relevant senior departmental ministers—e.g. a health standing committee would almost certainly involve the Health Secretary, the Social Security Secretary, and, say, the Education Secretary.
Ad hoc committees	Like parliamentary standing committees, these are formed to look at temporary issues and disbanded when they are resolved.
Ministerial committees	Formed to consider the work of specific government departments. Despite their title, they are made up solely of civil servants.

▶ The Civil Service

If ministers are the engine of government—brainstorming and formulating policies in Cabinet—then civil servants are the stolid engineers on the factory floor, responsible for oiling the machinery of state that puts these ideas into practice. The 'Civil Service' is the collective term for the administrative structure that underpins and carries out the work of the various government departments, and many of the numerous agencies and other bodies that implement policies on their behalf.

Dating back to the secretariats that first emerged, piecemeal, in the latter years of the British Empire in the eighteenth century, the Civil Service has become the one true constant in the UK system of government. The fact that this government—in broad terms—continues to operate uninterrupted even after the governing party has changed at an election (and, indeed, while the country is without any MPs—although not without ministers—during election campaigns) is largely down to the continuity guaranteed by the professionals responsible for 'keeping things running'.

The foundations of today's Civil Service were first laid down in the Northcote–Trevelyan Report 1854, which stipulated the following:

- all appointments should be made on *merit*;
- there should be *fair and open competition* for advertised posts.

Efforts were quickly made to establish a professional structure for the Civil Service and successive governments have made this progressively more rigorous. Senior civil servants—known colloquially within the profession as 'mandarins'—are recruited by independent Civil Service commissioners through the auspices of the Civil Service Board. Some recruits manage to rise to senior ranks very quickly, via the Fast Stream development programme, which admits around three hundred graduates a year.

Altogether, Her Majesty's Civil Service comprises some 480,000 officials working across anything up to sixty departments of state and a hundred associated bodies—that is, *executive agencies* and *quangos* (see pp. 115–17)—based principally at Whitehall and Millbank, only a stone's throw from Parliament. Each department is headed by a senior civil servant known as a 'permanent secretary'. As with civil servants of lower ranks, they are employed because of their expertise in the particular areas overseen by their departments. They are not to be confused with secretaries of state (senior departmental ministers) and, indeed, often have a far longer record of service to their departments than such individuals, given that they are paid employees of the Crown and, as such, will remain in post indefinitely—irrespective of whether the government changes at an election. Although they come into close daily contact with ministers and often advise them on policy, as paid officials, rather than elected politicians, permanent secretaries are expected to be politically neutral at all times.

Political neutrality in practice

Although the doctrine of 'political neutrality' is held sacrosanct in the upper echelons, in particular, of the Civil Service, in recent times there have been several controversies concerning civil servants who have acted in an apparently politically motivated way. The machinations of Sir Humphrey Appleby—the odious permanent secretary for the Ministry for Administrative Affairs in the classic 1980s BBC1 sitcom *Yes, Minister*—is said to have taken its inspiration, at least in part, from real-life shenanigans in certain Whitehall circles. But perhaps the most significant Civil Service scandal of modern times occurred in 1985, when Clive Ponting, a civil servant in the Ministry of Defence, was tried under the Official Secrets Act 1911 for passing classified details to an unauthorized person about the sinking during the Falklands War of the Argentine ship the *General Belgrano*—allegedly while it was both retreating and outside the 'exclusion zone' declared by the British government around the islands. Although Ponting, who has gone on to be a successful writer, was acquitted of breaching s. 2 of the Act, the case prompted then Cabinet Secretary Sir Robin Butler to issue the following 'Note'—by way of an addendum to the code of conduct earlier drafted for the Civil Service:

> The determination of policy is the responsibility of the minister . . . When, having been given all the relevant information and advice, the minister has taken the decision, it is the duty of civil servants loyally to carry out that decision . . . Civil servants are under an obligation to keep the confidences to which they become privy in the course of their official duties.

In the aftermath of the Ponting affair and a series of smaller-scale 'leaks' by similarly ethically motivated officials, new stipulations were drawn up to clarify the *levels* of political neutrality expected of civil servants on different rungs of the professional ladder. While all civil servants—whatever their rank—were expected to remain politically impartial in their day-to-day behaviour in the workplace, it was decided that the extent to which they had to be entirely neutral *outside* work would depend on their seniority (see Table 3.4).

Table 3.4 Levels of political impartiality in the Civil Service

Level	Degree of neutrality	Definition
'Industrial' and 'non-office' grades	Politically free	Low-level clerks and non-office civil servants are allowed to engage freely in political activity, even standing as MPs, **members of the European Parliament (MEPs)**, or councillors. But once their nomination papers were formally submitted to the **returning officer** (see p. 135), they would still need to resign.
Intermediate grades	Case-by-case consideration	Medium-level civil servants who may *apply* to their managers for permission to engage in political activity at national or local level.
Senior ranks, including 'mandarins'	Politically restricted	Forbidden from taking part in national political activities. Should they choose to stand as prospective MPs or MEPs, they must resign as soon as adopted as candidates—irrespective of their eventual success.

In running their departments on a day-to-day basis, civil servants are expected to abide by the 'three Es'—'economy, efficiency, and effectiveness'. This maxim has been underlined by two key milestones: the Efficiency Strategy published in 1979 by Sir Derek (now Lord) Rayner and the 1982 Financial Management Initiative, which sought to provide departmental managers with 'a clear view of objectives and performance' in the context of the responsibilities of their individual ministries.

Civil Service accountability

A number of recent government initiatives have attempted to give the Civil Service a better name by making it appear more efficient. In 1991, Mr Major launched his much-vaunted Citizen's Charter, which called for a 'revolution in public services' and, at least in theory, gave the public recourse to complain about everything from lack of information, through waste, to discourtesy in their dealings with government departments. In January 2002, Charter Mark services were extended to cover the conduct of purely *internal* departmental divisions that do not come into direct contact with the public. New Labour also coined the buzzwords 'joined-up government' to refer to its attempts to encourage individual government departments to work closer together.

Executive agencies

The work of the Civil Service is necessarily so all-consuming and involved that, from time to time, governments have tried to rationalize departments, or break them down into smaller, more manageable units. These units—effectively *subsets* of their parent departments—focus exclusively on the *delivery*, rather than the *formulation*, of policy. Today they are generally known as 'executive agencies'.

Initially established in 1988 by Mrs Thatcher—who had determined to move away from what she saw as an over-centralized, monolithic Civil Service structure—in terms of their 'office culture', these smaller scale, breakaway departmental bodies were designed to resemble commercial companies, rather than traditional organs of government. As such, they were each given their own *chief executive*, who presided over a board of directors—at the time, a hugely radical departure from the more bureaucratic way in which the Civil Service had previously been run. Unlike commercial companies, executive agencies had no shareholders (and therefore no profit motive) and were staffed by civil servants seconded from their parent departments. But as time went on, their managers were increasingly drafted in from industry, rather than graduating from the ranks of the Civil Service itself (the theory being that importing talent from the private sector would reduce bureaucracy and increase efficiency). This approach was ultimately to have a sweeping impact across the public sector that continues to be felt to this day, with everything from local NHS trusts to *further education* colleges adopting the chief executive and board model at their helm.

Initially, there were only a handful of executive agencies, the first of which, the Vehicle Inspectorate—now the Vehicle and Operator Services Agency (VOSA)—was established in August 1988. Since then, the number has mushroomed, particularly under Labour, with some 130 in total—90-plus reporting to government departments at Whitehall, with the remaining 40-odd answering to the three devolved administrations in Scotland, Wales, and Northern Ireland. While some smaller spending departments have only one or two agencies working under them, bigger ones like the Home Office and Department for Work and Pensions (DWP) allocate much of their day-to-day work to agencies. The single biggest agency, in terms of staffing and budget, is *Jobcentre Plus*, which employs 100,000 people and spends £4bn a year of taxpayers' money. With 36 agencies, the Ministry of Defence (MoD) has more than any other ministry.

One of the major criticisms of executive agencies is that they are used by ministers as a means of absolving themselves from individual ministerial responsibility. By devolving power to a 'breakaway' section of his or her department, a minister might disclaim personal liability for its mistakes. This arguably happened in November 2007 when Chancellor Alistair Darling refused to accept culpability for the loss of two unencrypted computer discs containing the names, addresses, dates of birth, *National Insurance (NI)* numbers, and bank details of 25 million families by HM Revenue and Customs (HMRC), an executive agency of the Treasury (see pp. 252–4). The Child Benefit-related data had been on its way to the National Audit Office (NAO) when it was mislaid. In the ensuing furore, it was HMRC's chief executive, Paul Gray, who resigned—not Mr Darling.

Quangos

When executive agencies were still a twinkle in a Tory policy adviser's eye, there were already a large number of taxpayer-funded organizations carrying out work on behalf of government departments. But until the advent of executive agencies, these non-departmental public bodies (NDPBs) tended to be staffed not by seconded civil servants from specific departments of state, but by their own staffs, which they recruited and employed as discrete entities, notionally independent of government. Over time, an umbrella term was coined for these bodies: 'quasi-autonomous non-governmental organizations', or 'quangos'.

Quangos are often confused with executive agencies and, on the face of the matter, it is easy to see why. Like agencies, they have their own management boards—although these are headed by honorary chairpersons, rather than salaried chief executives. They also have control of significant budgets, largely funded by the taxpayer.

Perhaps unsurprisingly, therefore, quangos frequently come under fire from the media—and, to a lesser extent, the public—for their lack of accountability. Whereas agencies are at least answerable to ministers whose government can be booted out at an election if the electorate is unhappy with its actions, quangos have traditionally had a degree of autonomy that puts them beyond such nominal 'control'. Yet, like agencies, they receive the bulk of their funding from taxpayers—through the aegis of related departments. Much of the budget for Arts Council England, for example, comes from the Department for Culture, Media and Sport (DCMS).

Lack of accountability might be the main criticism levelled at quangos; another is nepotism. Because they, like executive agencies, are run by boards, the members of which have customarily been nominated (for which, read 'selected') by relevant ministers, how can we be certain that individuals are genuinely being chosen on merit, rather than because they are friends and/or political allies of the government? The recently disbanded BBC board of governors—charged with holding the Corporation to account for its public service broadcasting responsibilities—was a quango in all but name. The oft-repeated phrase 'Tony's Cronies' was coined when Mr Blair chose veteran television producer Greg Dyke, a Labour donor, to become the BBC's new director-general in 2000 and Gavyn Davies, another party supporter, as its chairman.

Sustained criticism of the so-called 'quangocracy' has led to several recent moves to address the nepotism question, if not that of accountability. In 2000, the government introduced an Appointments Commission to appoint chairpersons and non-executive directors of NHS bodies, including hospitals, *primary care trusts*, and *strategic health authorities* (see Chapter 6). The body also has powers to vet appointees to other quangos at local, regional, and national levels. Its own appointments are regulated by an Office of the Commissioner for Public Appointments (OCPA).

In July 1996, a democratic audit identified 6,224 executive and advisory quangos, run by 66,000–73,500 people and responsible for spending £60.4bn. On coming to power, Mr Blair vowed to scrap 'unaccountable quangos' and Mr Brown spoke of a 'bonfire of the quangos'. But figures from the Cabinet Office published in August 2007 revealed that quangos had spent £167.5bn in the previous year.

Taskforces

A new form of non-elected body created by New Labour, particularly during its first term, the number of taskforces in place by 2000 was already 44. They were generally set up to deal with short-term issues of public concern and were headed by senior public figures dubbed 'tsars' (effectively, hired trouble-shooters). Examples include the Rough Sleepers' Unit, led by 'Homelessness Tsar' Louise Casey, which set out to tackle street homelessness, and a short-lived drugs taskforce run by 'Drugs Tsar' Keith Hellawell.

Spin doctors and special advisers

The number of special advisers and, in particular, spin doctors—that is, those largely concerned with the effective presentation of policy to the electorate through the media—has hugely multiplied in recent years. By the end of Mr Major's reign, they had increased to 38, but under Mr Blair, there were as many as 74 at any one time. At its peak, the advisers' salary bill topped £3.6m, but their number has since declined.

In recognition of their overtly political role, unlike civil servants special advisers and spin doctors tend to be *party*, rather than government, employees. This was the case with both of the big hitters at Downing Street of the Blair years: Alastair Campbell, the prime minister's official spokesman, and Jonathan Powell, his chief of staff. Sometimes, the edges are more blurred, however: Sir Bernard Ingham, Mrs Thatcher's bullish and highly political press secretary, started out as a civil servant, before switching to the Conservative Party's payroll while Mrs Thatcher was in government.

In 2000, the Neill Committee on Standards in Public Life published a report entitled *Reinforcing Standards*, which recommended that Westminster, like Scotland and Wales, should place an upper limit of a hundred on its tally of advisers. Yet their number has continued to be high and their actions to become more controversial.

Under Mr Blair, some special advisers have become bywords for cold-hearted manipulation. Jo Moore, an adviser at the Department of Transport, Local Government and the Regions (DTLR), was forced to resign in February 2002 following a series of controversies about her management style and, in particular, the publication of an explosive email she sent on 11 September the previous year—the date of the terrorist attacks on the Twin Towers—describing it as a 'very good day' to 'bury' bad news (see p.96).

Mr Blair's reliance on advice from spin doctors and party appointees over senior civil servants frequently saw him accused of 'politicizing' the Civil Service by the back door (an accusation levelled at more than one previous government). One of his first actions on taking office in 1997 was to pass an executive order allowing senior advisers such as Mr Campbell and Mr Powell to issue orders to civil servants. Mr Brown revoked this, symbolically, within hours of replacing Mr Blair at Number 10, but cynics have since dismissed even this gesture as spin, in light of recent statistics indicating that the number of special advisers, spin doctors, and press and marketing staff employed by the government actually continued to climb during his first few months in power. A Whitehall audit found that 68 additional special advisers were employed by ministers during 2007, all of them still in post at the end of the year—six months after Mr Brown took over. The overall number of press office staff (many of them civil servants, but nonetheless employed to put a positive gloss on government policy) had risen to 3,250. Between 1997 and 2007, Labour increased the annual cost of 'government PR' (public relations) to £338m—with a £15m rise in 2007 alone.

In July 2001, following years of controversy about Labour's reliance on special advisers and spin doctors, a Code of Conduct for Special Advisers was published. It defined them as 'temporary civil servants' who did not necessarily have to be appointed 'on merit', but were nonetheless expected to comply with the Civil Service Code governing all other departmental civil servants. If they wished to campaign on behalf of their ministers during the lead-up to a general, once the election was called, they must first stand down from their posts, in recognition of their political affiliation. Mr Campbell did just that in 2005.

The Parliamentary Ombudsman

Despite the title, the *Parliamentary Ombudsman* (or *Parliamentary Commissioner for Administration*) is charged with investigating complaints from the public not about the operation of Parliament itself, but about government departments and other public bodies, such as quangos. The basis of an individual's complaint has to be that he or she has suffered an injustice due to maladministration arising from delay, faulty procedures, errors, unfairness, and/or bias. Complaints against judges, police officers, and local authorities are not investigated by the Ombudsman, but by separate bodies and procedures.

The Ombudsman is sometimes derided as 'a watchdog without teeth' because, even though it can recommend that a department or body found to be at fault provide a 'remedy' to its mistakes, its findings of maladministration cannot be *enforced*.

Since *devolution*, there have been separate Ombudsmen for Scotland and Wales.

▌ Devolved government—executive decision-making in the regions

Chapters 1 and 2 laid out, first, the manner in which devolution came about in the UK and, then, the forms of government subsequently settled on in each of the three countries outside England. There follows a brief overview of the manner in which *government* is constituted in those countries.

The Scottish Government/Executive

Just as the legislative process prevailing in Scotland is distinct from that which applies in Wales and Northern Ireland, so too is its executive framework. Scotland now boasts its own official Scottish Government. Until recently, this was known as the *Scottish Executive*, but when the Scottish Nationalist Party (SNP) became the largest party in the Holyrood Parliament in May 2007 and its leader, Alex Salmond, replaced Labour's Jack McConnell as First Minister (effectively Scotland's prime minister), he renamed it. The Scottish Government is much more fully formed than either of its cousins in Cardiff or Stormont. Like the British government, it has its own Cabinet (currently an SNP–Green coalition). It meets on Tuesday mornings at Bute House in Edinburgh's Charlotte Square, the First Minister's official residence. The administration itself is based at St Andrew's House, along with its own secretariat, and has two subcommittees: a Cabinet subcommittee on legislation and a Scottish Executive emergency room Cabinet subcommittee.

The Welsh Assembly Government/Welsh Executive

Like the Scottish Executive, the *Welsh Executive* recently changed its name to the *Welsh Assembly Government* to reflect the increasing autonomy granted to it since devolution. It, too, is led by a First Minister—in Wales's case, the Labour leader Rhodri Morgan, who, after the 2007 Welsh Assembly election, headed a coalition with Welsh nationalist party Plaid Cymru. His deputy first minister under the new arrangements is Plaid Cymru leader Ieuan Wyn Jones. Mr Morgan recently confirmed that he would be stepping down in 2009, around the time of his 70th birthday in September.

The Northern Ireland Executive

The so-called 'power-sharing executive' in Northern Ireland has been a coalition since its rocky inception more than five years ago—and only recently began to function properly, following the conclusion of a substantive peace agreement in spring 2007.

→ Further reading

Budge, I., Crewe, I., McKay, D., and Newton, K. (2007) *The New British Politics*, 4th edn, London: Longman. **Fourth edition of highly acclaimed critical introduction to British parliamentary and governmental politics at the dawn of the twenty-first century, updated to cover the Brown administration.**

Burnham, J. and Pyper, R. (2008) *Britain's Modernised Civil Service*, London: Palgrave Macmillan. **Thorough examination of the evolution of the British Civil Service in recent decades, incorporating analysis of the impact of changes introduced by the Thatcher, Major, Blair, and Brown governments.**

Campbell, A. (2007) *The Blair Years: Extracts from the Alastair Campbell Diaries*, London: Hutchinson. **Candid, if at times restrained, personal diaries of Tony Blair's chief spin doctor, charting the period from his employer's election as Labour leader in 1994 to his resignation as prime minister in 2007.**

Crossman, R. (1979) *The Crossman Diaries: Selections from the Diaries of a Cabinet Minister, 1964–1970*, London: Book Club Associates. **Widely regarded as among the most incisive and revealing political diaries to have been written by a British Cabinet minister, these highlights are edited by one of Britain's foremost contemporary political biographers.**

Hennessey, P. (2001) *The Prime Minister: The Job and Its Holders Since 1945*, London: Penguin. **Colourful run-down and evaluation of British premiers in the post-war period, balancing serious academic discourse with story and anecdote.**

Jones, N. (2002) *The Control Freaks: How New Labour Gets Its Way*, London: Politico's Publishing. **Detailed, blow-by-blow unpicking of the 'New Labour' government's media strategy by a former BBC political correspondent.**

? Review questions

1. Outline the role and powers of the prime minister. To what extent, in practice, does his or her position differ from that of a head of state?

2. To what extent can recent prime ministers be accused of being 'presidential'—and can they still claim to adhere to the maxim of 'first among equals'?

3. What is the distinction between 'collective' and 'individual ministerial' responsibility, and do Cabinet ministers always abide by either, or both?

4. What is the difference between the Cabinet and the government, and is there an optimum size and composition for either, or both?

5. To what extent can the use of 'kitchen Cabinets', special advisers, and spin doctors be said to have 'politicized' the Civil Service?

Online resource centre

www.oxfordtextbooks.co.uk/orc/Morrison

Visit the Online Resource Centre that accompanies this book for web links and regular updates.

4

The electoral system

Chapters 1–3 examined the constitutional framework governing the UK and the gradual shift from royal to *parliamentary sovereignty* that has taken place over the past four hundred years or so. But the legitimacy of the UK legislature—and the executive, the members of which are drawn from it—today derives from more than mere historical precedent: it stems from the system of democratic elections that is the bedrock of modern British government.

▌ The origins of the British franchise

British social reformers were demanding the vote for their fellow citizens for centuries before it was finally granted. For the rank and file who made up the New Model Army, the Levellers and their offshoot, the Diggers, and propelled Oliver Cromwell to power, the English Civil War was about far more than a tussle for constitutional supremacy between Parliament and Crown. To John Lilburne, radical leader of the Levellers, parliamentary sovereignty meant nothing if it was not exercised by ordinary people. For this to happen, he argued, all 'free-born Englishmen' must be given a direct say in how Parliament is run: in other words, a vote.

Lilburne's arguments were to echo down the decades for some two hundred years before being answered, even in part—through the writings of Thomas Paine, the marches of the nineteenth-century Chartists, the speeches of the Labour Party's firebrand first member of Parliament, James Keir Hardie, and the campaigns of the Suffragettes. But it was to be a further century or more before every adult (regardless of class or gender) was granted a say in the running of his or her country's affairs. The slow extension of the UK 'franchise'—that is, the number and range of people entitled to vote in parliamentary elections—is charted in the timeline in Table 4.1.

While the primary significance of the above acts was to extend the voting entitlement to more people, the most radical of them went further. To ensure parliamentary democracy operates in as fair and equitable a way as

Table 4.1 Acts of Parliament that extended the UK franchise

Year	Act	Effect
1432	Electors of Knights of the Shire Act	Voting rights restricted to men living in county areas. All men who own freehold property or land worth 40 shillings in a county may vote in that county.
1832	Representation of the People Act ('Great Reform Act')	Huge extension of the franchise—by 50–80 per cent, with one in five men (653,000) now allowed to vote—but women explicitly excluded. In counties, vote given to all owners of land worth £10 or more in 'copyhold' (a medieval form of title deed), all owners of land worth £10 on long-term leases (60 years or more), and holders of land on medium-term leases (20–60 years) worth £50. In boroughs, all men with property worth £10 given vote, except in 'freeman boroughs', where it went only to those with 'freedom of the borough'.
1867	Representation of the People Act ('Second Reform Act')	All male urban householders given vote, along with all male lodgers paying £10 or more a year for unfurnished rooms. Electorate nearly doubled as a result, with a further 1.5 million men added.
1884	Representation of the People Act	Electorate increased to around 5.5 million through the extension of voting rights given to boroughs in 1867 to the countryside. All men owning property worth £10—or renting it to that value—now had vote.
1918	Representation of the People Act	Franchise extended to all men over the age of 21 and to women for the first time—although only those aged over 30. Voting still subject to minimum property qualifications, but less strict than in past. The electorate tripled from 7.7 million to 21.4 million.
1928	Representation of the People Act	Universal suffrage extended to all adults over the age of 21.
1969	Representation of the People Act	Voting age lowered to 18 years for all adults.

possible, it has been necessary for governments periodically to introduce additional structural and procedural reforms.

The Great Reform Act 1832, as it was popularly known, owes its place in history less to a wholesale extension of the franchise and more to its abolition of the so-called 'rotten boroughs', which, by that point, had become an anachronistic and, in some cases, shameful hangover from medieval times. The term 'rotten borough' was used to refer to areas of the country in which *constituency* boundaries ought to have been altered to reflect dwindling population numbers, but had not. In other words, there existed (prior to the Act) boroughs in which MPs were dependent for their election on a fraction of the number of adults whose votes had to be sought by their parliamentary colleagues.

In some cases, the number of local electors was so minimal that it was, quite literally, possible for a parliamentary candidate to win his seat by bribing voters. In 1831, the year before the Act was passed, the constituency of Old Sarum in Wiltshire had just three houses and 11 registered voters. Glatton in Surrey, meanwhile, had 23 houses, but only seven voters. As a result, rotten boroughs had become a byword for corruption, with some constituency seats effectively being bought and sold, and others passed from father to son like an inheritance. Before being awarded a peerage (and eventually becoming prime minister), Arthur Wellesley, the Duke of Wellington, once served as MP for the rotten borough of Trim in County Meath. Rotten boroughs were memorably satirized in the BBC1 sitcom *Blackadder the Third*, in which a dog won the fictitious seat of 'Dunny-on-the-Wold'.

Another significant reform—but one that took a lot longer coming—was the abolition of so-called 'plural voting'. This was the tradition that allowed individuals who owned properties in two or more areas—or those attending university in one area when their family home was in another—to have a multiple say in the outcome of a general election, by voting in each constituency. This practice—not to be confused with that, still common today, which allows individuals in these positions to choose in which constituency they would like to vote—was ended by the Representation of the People Act 1948.

The British franchise today—who can vote?

Elections to the House of Commons are known as 'general elections'. They take place up to five years to the day after the previous Parliament has been assembled following a poll and, for convoluted historical reasons, tend to be held on Thursdays (see p. 143).

As its name implies, at a general election, all sitting MPs will formally resign to contest their seats on the coming polling day. This means that elections are held simultaneously in all 646 House of Commons constituencies, and a new Parliament is summoned by the sovereign as soon as all the votes are counted and seats allocated. After the 2005 election, the distribution of seats in the House of Commons was as outlined in Table 4.2.

Whereas in local and European elections, the franchise has gradually been extended to include European Union (EU) citizens resident in Britain at the time of a poll, voting remains more restricted in general elections. Currently, it is open to citizens of Britain, the Irish Republic, and the Commonwealth who are normally resident in the UK, subject to the following criteria:

- the citizen's name must be on the *electoral register* for the constituency in which he or she lives;
- he or she must be over 18 years of age at the time of the election—while he or she may enter his or her name on the electoral register when aged 17, he or she can only vote once aged 18.

Despite these broad qualification criteria, the following individuals are barred from voting:

- peers still entitled to sit in the Lords under the House of Lords Act 1999 (but *not* those excluded after this date);
- foreign nationals (including citizens of other EU states);
- patients detained under mental health legislation in relation to criminal activities;
- convicted people detained in prison (but not those awaiting trial in custody);
- people convicted during the preceding five years of 'corrupt' or 'illegal election practices'.

The rules governing eligibility to vote in general elections also have the following quirks:

- members of the armed forces, and Crown servants of British embassies, the Diplomatic Service, and the British Council employed overseas (along with their partners and other relevant family members), may register to vote in the constituencies '*where they would normally live*';
- UK citizens living abroad ('ex-pats'), but resident in Britain and registered as electors *within the previous 15 years*, can make annual

Table 4.2 The distribution of seats in the House of Commons following the 2005 election

Party	Seats	Gains	Losses	Net gain/loss	Seats (%)	Votes (%)	Votes	Swing
Labour	356	0	47	−47	55.2	35.3	9,562,122	−5.4%
Conservative	198	36	3	+33	30.7	32.3	8,772,598	+0.6%
Liberal Democrat	62	16	5	+11	9.6	22.1	5,981,874	+3.7%
UK Independence	0	0	0	0	0	2.2	603,298	+0.8%
Scottish National Party	6	2	0	+2	0.9	1.5	412,267	−0.3%
Green	0	0	0	0	0	1.0	257,758	+0.4%
Democratic Unionist	9	4	0	+4	1.4	0.9	241,856	+0.2%
British National Party	0	0	0	0	0	0.7	192,746	+0.5%
Plaid Cymru	3	0	1	−1	0.5	0.6	174,838	−0.1%
Sinn Féin	5	1	0	+1	0.8	0.6	174,530	−0.1%
Ulster Unionist	1	0	5	−5	0.2	0.5	127,414	−0.3%
Social Democratic and Labour	3	1	1	0	0.5	0.5	125,626	−0.1%
Independent	1	1	0	0	0.2	0.5	122,000	+0.1%
Respect	1	1	0	+1	0.2	0.3	68,094	N/A
Scottish Socialist	0	0	0	0	0	0.2	43,514	−0.1%
Veritas	0	0	0	0	0	0.1	40,481	N/A
Alliance	0	0	0	0	0	0.1	28,291	0.0%
Scottish Green	0	0	0	0	0	0.1	25,760	+0.1%
Socialist Labour	0	0	0	0	0	0.1	20,192	0.0%

(continued)

Table 4.2 The distribution of seats in the House of Commons following the 2005 election

Party							Votes	%
Liberal	0	0	0	0	0	0.1	19,068	0.0%
Health Concern	1	0	0	0	0.2	0.1	18,739	0.0%
English Democrats	0	0	0	0	0	0.1	14,506	N/A
Socialist Alternative	0	0	0	0	0	0.0	9,398	N/A
National Front	0	0	0	0	0	0.0	8,029	N/A
Legalise Cannabis	0	0	0	0	0	0.0	6,985	0.0%
Community Action	0	0	0	0	0	0.0	6,557	N/A
Monster Raving Loony	0	0	0	0	0	0.0	6,311	0.0%
Christian Vote	0	0	0	0	0	0.0	4,004	N/A
Mebyon Kernow	0	0	0	0	0	0.0	3,552	0.0%
Forward Wales	0	0	0	0	0	0.0	3,461	N/A
Christian Peoples	0	0	0	0	0	0.0	3,291	N/A
Rainbow Dream Ticket	0	0	0	0	0	0.0	2,463	N/A
Community Group	0	0	0	0	0	0.0	2,365	N/A
Ashfield Independents	0	0	0	0	0	0.0	2,292	N/A
Alliance for Green Socialism	0	0	0	0	0	0.0	1,978	N/A
Residents' Association of London	0	0	0	0	0	0.0	1,850	N/A
Workers' Party	0	0	0	0	0	0.0	1,669	0.0%
Socialist Environmental	0	0	0	0	0	0.0	1,649	N/A
Scottish Unionist	0	0	0	0	0	0.0	1,266	0.0%
Workers' Revolutionary	0	0	0	0	0	0.0	1,143	0.0%
New England	0	0	0	0	0	0.0	1,224	N/A
Communist	0	0	0	0	0	0.0	1,124	0.0%

The Community (Hounslow)	1,118	0.0	0	0	N/A
Peace and Progress	1,036	0.0	0	0	N/A
Scottish Senior Citizens	1,017	0.0	0	0	N/A
Your Party	1,006	0.0	0	0	N/A
SOS! Northampton	932	0.0	0	0	N/A
Independent Working Class	892	0.0	0	0	N/A
Democratic Labour	770	0.0	0	0	N/A
British Public Party	763	0.0	0	0	N/A
Free Scotland Party	743	0.0	0	0	N/A
Pensioners Party Scotland	716	0.0	0	0	N/A
Publican Party	678	0.0	0	0	N/A
English Independence Party	654	0.0	0	0	N/A
Socialist Unity	581	0.0	0	0	N/A
Local Community Party	570	0.0	0	0	N/A
Clause 28	516	0.0	0	0	N/A
UK Community Issues Party	502	0.0	0	0	N/A

NOTE: A regularly updated version of this table can be found on the Online Resource Centre that accompanies this book.

declarations allowing their names to be included in the register for constituencies *'where they were living before they went abroad'*. They can then vote by proxy—that is, they can appoint a friend or family member to vote on their behalf—at any Westminster, **Scottish Parliament**, Welsh Assembly, and **European Parliament** (but not local) election;

- holidaymakers are allowed 'absent votes' in national elections under the Representation of the People Act 1985—provided that the electoral registration officer is *'satisfied that the applicant's circumstances on the date of the poll will be or are likely to be such that he cannot reasonably be expected to vote in person'*;

- although there is nothing stopping reigning monarchs and their immediate heirs from voting in theory, were they to do so in practice, this would be seen as unconstitutional.

Registers of electors are compiled by local electoral registration officers and completion of electoral registration forms is compulsory—although, unlike in countries such as Australia, it is *not* compulsory to vote. Many people technically broke the law when local taxpayers were charged the Community Charge ('Poll Tax')—which was a head tax payable by each individual, rather than household—by deliberately not filling in forms to avoid being billed.

The Representation of the People Act 2000 has changed the precise way in which registration is carried out in the following respects:

- prior to the Act, electors were registered to vote wherever they were resident on 10 October each year. Although an annual canvass is still carried out—now on 15 October—a new rolling registration system has also been introduced, enabling electors to register themselves at a new address at the beginning of any month;

- draft registers used to be open for inspection until 16 December. This date has now been brought forward to 1 December. The register cannot (except as the result of a formal appeal) be altered once the final date for registration has passed.

The Labour government has also liberalized some pre-existing voting disqualifications, while remaining strict about others. Until recently, many people detained under mental health legislation in a hospital or other mental institution (as opposed to being there on a voluntary basis) were barred from voting, on the grounds that they were not of 'sound mind'. This is no longer the case (unless they are there after being convicted of a crime). Homeless people were also enfranchised formally for the first time with the passage of the 2000 Act. People with no permanent address may now vote subject to a 'declaration of local connection'. Despite repeated appeals by convicted prisoners against their prohibition from voting, however, the government defiantly cites a ruling by the **European Court of Human Rights (ECtHR)** that this ban does not infringe the European Convention (see p. 13).

Although its stance has been more liberal than those of previous governments in some ways, Labour has tightened up certain qualifications. The Representation of the People Act 1989 made it easier for ex-pats to vote in UK general elections, by allowing them to do so up to 20 years after emigrating. At the time, this was viewed by critics of the then Conservative government as a cynical manoeuvre designed to boost its vote (the assumption being that many people who had retired abroad were likely to be wealthy and therefore inclined to vote Tory). After the 2001 election, Labour reduced this entitlement period to 15 years.

▌ General elections and candidacy—who can stand?

As of June 2007, any citizen of the UK, the Irish Republic, or a Commonwealth country resident in Britain and aged over 18 on the day on which he or she is nominated (the age qualification was previously 21) may stand for election as an MP—provided that he or she is not disqualified from sitting in the House of Commons. Such disqualification might arise because he or she is:

- a peer retained in the House of Lords under the 1999 Act;

- a bishop currently sitting in the Lords;

- an undischarged bankrupt subject to a bankruptcy restriction order under the Enterprise Act 2002 in England and Wales. These are made by the Insolvency Service—an *executive agency* of the Department of Business, Enterprise and Regulatory Reform (BERR)—if a bankrupt individual is found to have acted dishonestly, or in an otherwise 'blameworthy' way. In Northern Ireland, anyone adjudged bankrupt is barred from standing, while in Scotland, anyone whose estate has been sequestered is banned;

- a patient detained for criminal activities under mental health legislation;
- someone sentenced to, and currently serving, more than one year's imprisonment;
- a person found personally guilty of *corrupt* election practices during the preceding ten years (if in the same constituency) or in the last five years (if in a different one);
- someone found personally guilty of *illegal* election practices in the last seven years (if in his or her constituency) or five years (if elsewhere);
- a holder of the offices listed in the House of Commons Disqualification Act 1975:

  - *politically restricted posts* within the Civil Service—that is, senior civil servants in close day-to-day contact with government ministers or elected councillors;
  - members of the regular armed forces or the Ulster Defence Regiment;
  - serving police officers;
  - holders of judicial office;
  - members of specified commissions—for example, the **Commission for Equality and Human Rights (CEHR)**, the **Independent Police Complaints Commission (IPCC)**, and the Lands Tribunal.

Some disqualifications are more liberal than others. While convicted prisoners are not entitled to vote in a general election, they may stand as candidates—provided that they are serving 12 months or less for their crimes. This 'loophole' was once even more open-minded: Provisional Irish Republican Army (IRA) member Bobby Sands was imprisoned for 14 years for possessing firearms in 1977, yet managed to get himself elected as MP for Fermanagh and South Tyrone in April 1981, after standing on a so-called 'Anti-H Block/Armagh Political Prisoner' ticket. He was on hunger strike at the time, however, and died a few weeks later. After his death, Margaret Thatcher's government hastily passed the Representation of the People Act 1981, which introduced the current 'maximum 12-month sentence' qualification for serving prisoners with parliamentary ambitions. The swiftness with which it did so stopped any of Sands's fellow hunger strikers standing for election in his stead.

How the British electoral system works

The system used to elect MPs in British general elections is known as 'first past the post' (FPTP). Essentially, this means that, in each of the 646 constituencies, the candidate with the highest number of votes—known as a 'simple majority'—will automatically be elected as its MP. Similarly, the political party that gains the most seats in the House of Commons once all constituency votes are counted nationwide will normally form the government—except in rare circumstances, when it has only a handful more than its nearest rival (allowing it to form only a *minority* administration, as Labour did in February 1974). This type of result is known as a 'hung Parliament'. In such cases, in theory one or two other parties might strike a deal to form a coalition, enabling them to muster between them significantly more seats than the biggest individual party. More usually, one party will win an 'overall majority'—that is, more seats than all of the other parties and independents put together.

The British electoral system has long been controversial, because of the frequent imbalance between the number of votes cast for a particular party and the quantity of seats into which they translate. Because only the first-placed candidate in a given constituency is elected, all other votes cast (often numbering tens of thousands) are effectively 'wasted'. In practice, it is only the Conservatives and Labour who stand a realistic chance of forming a government, because in order to win sufficient seats to do so, a party has to rely on *concentrations* of support. Traditional heartlands—for the Tories, the affluent south-east; for Labour, the post-industrial north and Scotland—have tended to swing the pendulum from one to the other.

General elections have also produced governments in which the number of seats has vastly outstripped their share of the vote. Recent examples include the 1997 election, which saw not one Conservative MP elected in Scotland—despite the fact that a number of Scots still voted for the party. The 2005 poll saw Labour win well over half of the available seats, despite only gaining 35 per cent of the vote (equivalent to 21 per cent of registered voters, given the low turnout on the day). In contrast, the Lib Dems, who won more than 22 per cent of votes cast, gained only one in ten seats. Subsequent analysis found that the average Labour MP re-elected in 2005 needed only 26,858 votes, while Tories required 44,241, and Lib Dems, 98,484.

Some election results have been even more unfair. In February 1974, incumbent Prime Minister Ted Heath's Tories won 200,000 more votes than Labour, but the inequity of the UK FPTP system meant that they secured four fewer seats. Wilson consolidated his victory in October that year, securing a small working majority of three and one million more votes than the Tories, but that did little to defuse the initial sense of injustice. It has not always been this way around: in 1951, Labour Prime Minister Clement Attlee was beaten by Winston Churchill's Tories, who won seven more seats despite polling more than a million fewer votes.

Tactical voting

In recent elections, it has become increasingly common for people in certain constituencies to vote *strategically*—that is, to back candidates other than those that they would most like to see elected, in the hope of preventing the election of those they like least. This method of casting votes—rejecting one's 'sincere preference' in favour of a compromise choice who is more likely to win—is known as **tactical voting**.

There are many types of tactical voting, but because this book is about British public affairs, we will look at how it works in UK elections. An oft-cited example is of a voter who strongly identifies with Labour, but lives in a constituency in which the sitting MP is Conservative. At the last election, the Labour candidate came third, behind not only the Tories, but also the Lib Dems—so, on that basis, a vote for Labour this time would be 'wasted'. Because the Lib Dems were only a few thousand votes behind the Conservative candidate last time, they have a chance of beating them and, because opinion polls suggest that they are gaining ground, it is worth the Labour supporter voting tactically, backing his or her 'least worst option' over the one that they most favour.

Examples of MPs elected by tactical voting in recent years abound. Lib Dem Mark Oaten's decisive 1997 victory in the Winchester by-election prompted by an electoral petition from Tory Gerry Malone, described later in this chapter, is believed to have been due, in large part, to a wholesale tactical switch by Labour supporters to the Lib Dems. Indeed, by 1997, the Conservatives had become so unpopular generally, after 18 years in power, that widespread tactical voting was used to get them out—whatever the cost—across the UK. In 2001, the protest singer Billy Bragg organized a national campaign designed to prevent the Tories winning seats by getting fellow opponents of the party to 'trade' their tactical votes with electors living elsewhere in Britain. A Lib Dem voter living in a Labour/Tory marginal constituency, for example, might 'vote by remote' for his or her party of choice in a distant Lib Dem/Tory marginal—trading his or her own constituency vote with a Labour supporter whose home was in that area.

▶ The election process

The sequence of events leading to a general election is as outlined in Table 4.3.

Each candidate must put down an *election deposit* of £500, which will be returned provided that he or she receives at least 5 per cent of the votes cast in the relevant constituency. The deposit was introduced in 1918 as a means of discouraging 'frivolous' candidatures—and, cynics suggest, boosting the Treasury's coffers (it made £800,000 from forfeited deposits in 2001).

Voting procedure on the day—the role of the returning officer

The administration of voting in general elections at a local level follows a tightly regulated procedure. After polling closes, it culminates in an election-night 'count' at a chosen venue—normally, a large local authority building somewhere near the constituency's geographical centre—which is overseen

Table 4.3 The general election process in Britain

Event	Condition
Election date announced	Elections must be called *at least 17 working days* before polling day
Nominations for candidates—until recently prospective parliamentary candidates (PPCs)—entered	The nomination process closes at 12 p.m. on the nineteenth day before the election (excluding Sundays and Bank Holidays)
Checking that nomination meets basic conditions for eligibility and registration	Each candidate must have his or her nomination proposed and seconded by two 'subscribing' electors, and signed by eight other 'assenting' electors—all registered in the constituency. Nominations include a brief description of the candidate (up to six words covering his or her name and political affiliation) to identify them on the ballot paper. Candidates do not have to be backed by political parties (i.e. can be 'independent', as in the case of former BBC foreign correspondent Martin Bell, who beat former Tory minister Neil Hamilton in his previously safe Tatton seat in 1997). Each candidate allowed to post one 'election communication' to registered voters
Disqualification of invalid nominations	Returning officers may reject any nomination paper that they deem 'out of order' on the day of voting

by a *returning officer*. In practice, the role of returning officer has tended to be discharged by a senior officer in the local authority containing, coterminous with, or neighbouring the constituency—often its *chief executive*—but, in theory, it is the responsibility of the council's chairperson or *mayor*. In 2007, Justice Secretary Jack Straw issued a *statutory instrument* clarifying the position, in which he stipulated that the role should be taken by chairpersons or mayors, except in 'county constituencies' (rural ones). In those areas, it should fall to an 'acting returning officer'—that is, the electoral registration officer employed by a specified nearby district council. Electoral procedure on the day is outlined in Table 4.4.

Should results be especially close and if it is felt that disallowed ballot papers might have produced a different result had they been included, dissatisfied candidates can apply to the High Court for an 'election petition' against the returning officer. This happened in 1997, when sitting Conservative MP Gerry Malone lost his Winchester seat by a mere two votes to Liberal Democrat candidate Mark Oaten—the closest result since 1945. Mr Malone's petition succeeded, but when the election was rerun in November of the same year, he lost by a 21,566-vote landslide—suggesting that there's more than a little truth to the adage that nobody likes a bad loser! The by-election result is almost certain to have been nearer the electorate's original wishes than the knife-edge outcome of the general election poll, given that, on the earlier occasion, many voters had been confused by the candidacy of Richard Huggett, who listed himself on the official ballot paper as 'Liberal Democrat Top Choice for Parliament' (forcing Mr Oaten to have the words 'Liberal Democrat Leader Paddy Ashdown' written alongside his name). Mr Huggett stood again in the ensuing by-election—this time under the label 'Literal Democrat'—but, this time, the adverse publicity generated by his first campaign blunted his vote. The use of such deliberately confusing labels was subsequently made illegal by the Registration of Political Parties Act 1998, which set up the *Electoral Commission*.

Limits on election spending

Election spending is closely controlled by the Electoral Commission to stop any one candidate or party having a significant advantage over his or her/its competitors. Each candidate must appoint an election agent with an office in the constituency. The maximum sum that candidates may spend on campaigning in their seats is fixed by law. At the time of publication,

Table 4.4 The electoral process on the day of voting

Event	Conditions
Polling stations open at 7 a.m. and close at 10 p.m.	Registered electors who have not chosen to use some other means (e.g. post, email, or proxy) cast their votes at these stations, usually based at schools and community centres.
Absent votes may be cast in advance	Those who cannot reasonably be expected to vote in person (e.g. are on holiday) can apply for 'absent votes', while the physically incapacitated or those who cannot vote because of the nature of their work or because they have moved to a new area since the electoral roll was last compiled can apply for 'indefinite absent votes'. Anyone entitled to an absent vote can either vote by post or have someone else do so in person at a polling station on his or her behalf (a 'proxy vote'); postal ballot papers *cannot*, however, be sent to addresses outside the UK. Assuming that electors follow the normal process, ballot papers are issued to them at the polling station by election staff (with official marks impressed on the papers at this stage).
Secrecy of ballot preserved—no interference with ballot boxes	Ballot boxes are sealed at the close of poll, before being taken to the counting place to be counted either straightaway or the next day.
Official count starts after close of poll—only valid papers counted	The count is supervised by the returning officer—observed by the candidates, their agents, the media, and a small number of 'scrutineers'. Any 'spoilt' ballot papers—i.e. those with a cross placed beside the name of more than one candidate or on which the choice of candidate is unclear—are disallowed.
Recount if result is too close to call	If the winner's victory is marginal, the candidates can demand a recount (and, on occasion, more than one, until the returning officer decides that the result is clear). In the event of a dead heat, the returning officer is required by law to settle victory by intervening more directly. He or she will normally do so by resorting to a game of chance—either by tossing a coin, or by asking the two neck-and-neck candidates to write their names on slips of paper and drawing the winner out of a hat.

it was just under £7,150, plus five pence per voter in urban constituencies and seven pence in rural ones. At a national level, however, parties may also spend £30,000 fielding each candidate.

In addition, so-called 'recognized third parties' may separately spend money campaigning in support of, or against, a candidate—up to £500 apiece. They are, however, permitted to spend considerably more in support of a party as a whole. *UNISON* is registered as a 'recognized third party' supporter of Labour. It is allowed to spend up to £793,000 on the party's behalf at a general election, or £30,000 in elections to devolved assemblies. Other organizations or individuals who wish to campaign on behalf of a political party as a whole (rather than an individual candidate)—but are 'unregistered'—are legally limited to spending £10,000 in England, or £5,000 in the other UK countries.

In *referenda*, meanwhile, 'permitted participants'—that is, those registered to campaign for a 'yes' or 'no' vote—may spend up to £500,000 on a UK-wide poll, but only £10,000 may be spent by anyone who is *not* so permitted. The Commission may 'designate' specific permitted participants to campaign for a 'yes' or 'no' vote to ensure order. Such bodies may claim up to £600,000 to finance their campaigns and spend up to £5m.

▶ Before the event—how constituency boundaries are decided

As explained earlier this chapter, there are currently 646 Commons constituencies in England, Wales, Scotland, and Northern Ireland. Until recently, however, there were as many as 659 and, from time to time, the number rises or falls in line with population changes. Variations in population do not only have an impact on the number of constituencies, however: they can also influence the size and shape of individual constituencies in areas of the country especially affected by those changes. In some cases, constituencies the populations of which have fallen significantly might cease to exist entirely, or be merged with neighbouring ones, while large localized increases in population can lead to the introduction of additional constituencies, or existing ones being split into two or more.

Parliamentary electoral boundaries are reviewed on an 8–12-year cycle, to ensure that they keep pace with demographic fluctuations in the UK. The task of conducting these reviews currently falls to four independent 'boundary commissions'—the ***Boundary Commission for England***, and those for Scotland, Wales, and Northern Ireland.

Boundary changes are often controversial. The act of abolishing constituencies, creating new ones, subdividing them, and/or merging two or more can often have a significant impact on the ability of a particular political party to win seats at subsequent elections. Although the commissions are required to operate on a strictly non-partisan basis, successive governments have been accused of trying to influence their decisions, to ensure that any proposed changes are favourable to their own parties at election time. The most recent boundary review, completed under Labour, has, however, been widely interpreted as a boost to the Tories. According to an analysis of the proposed changes by Electoral Reform Society researcher Lewis Baston and politics lecturer Simon Henig, published in June 2006, of the 13 additional constituencies created, ten are likely to go to the Conservatives (on the basis of voting patterns in the 2005 election), while the Lib Dems would win two, and Labour only one. Six of the nine seats to be abolished at the next election are currently Labour-held, while former Labour strongholds such as Enfield North and Sittingbourne could be vulnerable to the Tories because of large movements of voters from urban areas into the suburbs.

The most recent boundary review was completed by the English and Welsh Commissions in April 2007, with new boundaries for Assembly member (AM) constituencies in place for the National Assembly of Wales elections in May that year. At the next general election, the number of Westminster constituencies will increase to 650, with 500 having their boundaries at least partly redrawn. The change is likely to prove controversial in some parts of the north and in Labour heartlands, because all four new constituencies are in the south. They will include Meon Valley, a new seat north of Fareham in Hampshire.

The next boundary review will be carried out by the Electoral Commission, a ***quango*** established by the Political Parties, Elections and Referendums Act 2000 to provide comprehensive oversight of the election process in Britain. Its other responsibilities include:

- registering political parties (and preventing their names being used by others);
- ensuring that people understand and follow the rules on party and election finance;
- setting standards for running elections and reporting on how well this is done;

- ensuring people understand that it is important to register to vote and know how to do so;
- making sure that the funding of candidates' election campaigns is legal and transparent.

In addition to overseeing election-related funding, the Commission was also given responsibility for policing party finance as a whole—that is, for vetting how political parties raise money and declare their donations. This area is examined in greater detail in Chapter 5.

How parties select their candidates

Just as different political parties have their own membership policies, so too do they have their own preferences about how to select the candidates that they wish to field at general elections. Because the primary purpose of the next chapter is to examine the workings of Britain's main political parties, and the internal structures and procedures that distinguish one from the other, discussion of individual parties will be kept to a minimum here. It is, however, worth briefly looking at significant trends and developments in candidate selection procedures.

The Conservative Party

Historically, the Conservatives have favoured a centrally controlled selection procedure, which sees a list of 'approved candidates' compiled by *Conservative Campaign Headquarters*. This initially involves staff from the party's candidates' department sifting through CVs and letters from applicants, and inviting a selection of them to attend a 'candidates' weekend', at which they will face aptitude tests to ascertain their suitability. A central list is then drawn up and distributed to local Conservative constituency associations, who will advertise vacancies for prospective candidates in their areas as and when they arise (sitting MPs who wish to run again are normally automatically reselected, as in the other main parties). After a series of public meetings, at which 3-5 competing applicants will have a chance to prove their mettle in debates with rivals, a vote on which individual should be adopted to fight the seat will be held among local party members.

While this broad process remains in place, David Cameron's tenure as party leader has already seen several significant moves towards an even greater level of centralization. Perhaps the most controversial aspect of this has been the drawing up of the so-called 'A list' of aspiring Tory MPs, including a number of celebrity supporters: former *Coronation Street* star Adam Rickitt; 'chic lit' author Louise Bagshawe; and Zac Goldsmith, editor of *The Ecologist* magazine and son of late Tory defector Sir James Goldsmith, whose Referendum Party stood against Europhile Tory MPs in the 1997 election. Local parties in some areas have been dismayed at the leadership's apparent intention to parachute in cherry-picked individuals, often with little or no history of involvement in the party, in place of loyal members who have lived and worked locally for much of their lives.

Another recent development (equally contentious in some quarters) has been the introduction of 'open primaries' modelled on the US voting system. This unprecedented move gives everyone on the electoral register in a given constituency a chance to vote on which prospective candidate should stand for the Conservative Party at the next election—irrespective of whether they are Tory members, or even supporters.

The Labour Party

Labour's selection process for candidates has traditionally been more democratic than that used by the Conservatives. In recent years, however, it has become increasingly centralized and, given recent moves by the Tories to encourage greater public involvement in their internal party procedures, Labour can no longer so easily claim to be more transparent.

Up to 31 January 2001, constituency Labour parties (equivalent to the Tories' constituency associations) and affiliated organizations, such as trades unions, could each nominate up to two candidates from a list approved by local party leadership. The general council of the Constituency Labour Party (CLP) then drew up a shortlist, which was circulated to local party members who could vote by either postal ballot, or at a 'hustings'—that is, a public meeting involving a debate between the rival candidates, as described above.

On the pretext of speeding up this time-consuming process, Mr Blair introduced a streamlined (some would argue 'control-freakish') version of it after 31 January 2001. To reduce the time taken up with initial vetting procedures, future lists of candidates would be centrally approved by the party's ruling National Executive Committee (NEC). CLPs in need of a new candidate would be presented with this list and asked to vote for one of the approved names. Critics of Mr Blair saw this as a clear attempt to weed out left-wing candidates and to impose a more Blairite/New Labour agenda on the party's grass roots.

An earlier example of the centralizing tendency among recent Labour leaders was the party's adoption of all-women shortlists for parliamentary candidates in 1993. The positive discrimination policy was brought in to increase the number of women MPs to reflect better the gender balance in the British population (51 per cent of which is female). In 1996, Labour's stand was judged unlawful, in a case brought under the Sex Discrimination Act 1975, but once in power, Labour introduced the Sex Discrimination (Election Candidates) Act 2002, which guaranteed the legality of all-women shortlists until 2015. Since then, successive Conservative leaders have mooted using the policy, in an effort to make their party appear less male and middle-aged, and the proportion of women MPs has more than doubled from 9 per cent in 1997 to 20 per cent after the 2005 election. Nonetheless, the policy still has its critics—most notably, some groups representing ethnic minorities, who argue that white women may get selected in some areas known for their racial diversity at the expense of strong potential candidates from minority communities.

The Liberal Democrat Party

Although they often claim to be more democratic than their bigger Westminster rivals, the Liberal Democrats use a similarly centralized selection system. A list of approved names is drawn up centrally. Constituencies looking for a new candidate must first advertise this fact in *Liberal Democrat News*, the party's main publication, and individuals whose names are on that list may apply for the vacancy. A selection committee will then interview them and a shortlist will be put before the local party membership.

Quirks of the British electoral system

Parliamentary candidates may stand, and even be elected, in more than one constituency. If elected in both, however, they must immediately decide which constituency they would like to represent and stand down from the other. The seat forgone will pass to the second-choice candidate in that constituency. This follows rules set out in Erskine May (see p. 18) and laid down in House of Commons procedures.

Candidates may withdraw their nominations for election—provided that this is done in writing by the candidate (with one witness attesting) and reaches the returning officer by noon on the sixteenth day before polling day. This throws up the intriguing possibility that an individual might one day be elected to serve as an MP, despite having decided against standing at the last minute—but this is not thought to have happened so far.

Since 1935, elections have generally been held on Thursdays. The precise historical reasons for this are obscure, but the day is thought to have been arrived at through a process of elimination. As the traditional Christian day of worship, Sundays are out, and weekends, as a whole, are seen to present too many leisure options to ensure that voters will discipline themselves to turn out and vote. Mondays have the highest employee absence record of any working day—making it difficult to be sure of a solid turnout—while Tuesdays and Wednesdays are the main working days (thereby providing few opportunities for people to escape the workplace to vote). As the traditional market day in many towns and cities, Thursday has traditionally been favoured. In addition, holding elections before a weekend is seen to have advantages if there is a change of government, because it allows the new administration to use Saturday and Sunday to prepare itself to start work in earnest the following week.

The British electoral system produces a clear divide between 'marginal constituencies' (or 'marginals'), on the one hand, and 'safe seats' on the other. In marginals—normally seen as the key battlegrounds on election-day—incumbent MPs have small majorities (in some cases, having won only a handful more votes than their nearest rivals at the previous election), so their seat is considered vulnerable and a key target for competing candidates. Candidates tend to concentrate their energies on attracting the support of so-called 'swing voters'—that is, individuals with no firm historical loyalty to one party or another. Safe seats, in contrast, are those in which sitting MPs have large majorities that (barring a huge upset) are unlikely to be lost at the next election. These tend to be located in party political heartlands—for example, the north for Labour and the home counties for the Tories. Such seats would require huge 'swings'—switches of support from one candidate or party to another—if they were to change hands.

Other than local and European elections, one of the biggest litmus tests of British public opinion has traditionally been the by-election—a vote in a single constituency to replace a sitting MP who has usually either retired or died between general elections. Towards the end of Mrs Thatcher's reign in the late 1980s and in the early 1990s, under Mr Major, by-elections frequently produced bruising results for the Tories, seen as indicative of their growing unpopularity in the country at large. By 2008, it was Labour's turn to suffer in by-elections and, over a three-month period before the summer recess, the party sustained a series of humiliating defeats, including two in previously safe seats. The first of these was in the Crewe and Nantwich constituency of veteran *backbencher* Gwyneth Dunwoody, whose 7,000–strong majority was overturned by the Conservatives, in their first by-election victory over

Labour for thirty years, despite the fact that her daughter, Tamsin, stood to replace her. The second was in Glasgow East, a dyed-in-the-wool Labour seat on Mr Brown's own doorstep, where the Scottish Nationalists achieved a 22.5 per cent swing to snatch the seat. The most peculiar by-election of modern times, however, was held the same summer in Haltemprice and Howden, the constituency of former Tory Home Affairs spokesman David Davis. In an unprecedented move, Mr Davis resigned his safe seat to contest a symbolic contest over his opposition to the government's then recently passed Bill to give police powers to detain terrorist suspects for up to 42 days (see p. 264). Neither Labour nor the Lib Dems contested the seat—each arguing that his move was a vanity exercise—but he was faced by a record 26 minority candidates. Of these, 23 lost their deposits and Mr Davis was duly re-elected with 72 per cent of the vote.

▌ Proportional representation (PR) and other voting systems

Such are the inequities of the British electoral system that pro-democracy campaigners have long argued for its replacement by one the outcomes of which more accurately reflect the distribution of votes between rival candidates or parties. Pressure groups such as the Electoral Reform Society and Charter 88 advocate *proportional representation (PR)*—an umbrella term referring to a variety of alternative models that they judge to be fairer. Such a switch has, for many years, been official policy for the Lib Dems, who suffer more than any other party from the current FPTP system, due to the wide dispersal of their vote across the country. Ironically, they would need to get into power to be able to introduce it—something of a catch-22 situation, given that, without it, this is unlikely to happen (other than in a hung Parliament).

Unsure that it would win a working majority at the upcoming election, in its 1997 manifesto, Labour committed itself to re-examining voting in general elections. To this end, the late Robin Cook, a long-time supporter of PR and a signatory to Charter 88, and the Lib Dems' Robert Maclennan drafted a joint agreement outlining a tentative timetable. In December of that year, an Independent Commission on the Voting System was set up under the chairmanship of the late Lord Jenkins of Hillhead, a Lib Dem peer and former

Labour Chancellor. He reported in 1998, advocating either a hybrid system modelled on that to be used in Scotland and Wales (see pp. 80 and 82) or a new system called 'alternative vote plus' (AV+).

AV+ would have involved a reduction in the number of constituencies, but with the number of MPs remaining the same as at present. Between 80 and 85 per cent of MPs would continue to be elected on a constituency basis, with the rest voted in via a 'top-up process'. This would work 'correctively'—that is, on the basis of electors' second votes, to give a better reflection of the electorate's overall preferences. His advice has yet to be acted on.

Table 4.5 gives a run-down of the most common PR systems used in other countries, together with explanations of how they work. Some of the key arguments used by advocates and opponents of the introduction of PR in the UK are outlined in Table 4.6.

▶ Elections under devolution

The devolved parliaments in Scotland, Wales, and Northern Ireland are elected on a set timetable every four years—an electoral cycle that bears more of a resemblance to those of local authorities than the House of Commons. But this is not the only point of difference from Westminster: more significantly, the voting systems used to elect members of the Scottish Parliament (MSPs), AMs, and members of the Northern Ireland Assembly use elements of PR.

In Northern Ireland, the single transferable vote (STV) system is now used, in line with the system used in southern Ireland since 1919. Both Scotland and Wales have adopted the 'additional member' system (see p. 148) to introduce an element of proportionality alongside FPTP.

▶ The future of voting

Electoral turnout in recent British general elections has been consistently lower than at any other time since the Second World War. In the 2005, it was just 61.3 per cent—2 per cent up on 2001, but only thanks to a small surge in voting in certain marginal seats where voters disenchanted with Mr Blair's

Table 4.5 Different types of proportional representation (PR) and how they work

Name	How it works	Where used
The single transferable vote (STV)	The system favoured by the Liberal Democrats. Unlike in UK general elections, in which each constituency has only one MP, STV states have multi-member constituencies—making it more likely that a voter will end up with at least one local representative from a party that they support. Electors mark each candidate on their ballot paper in order of preference (1, 2, 3, etc.) and, once a candidate has achieved a predetermined quota (e.g. one-fifth of all votes cast if there are five seats available), he or she will be elected. The second choices listed on all 'surplus' papers that named that candidate as 'first choice' will then be treated as first choices and distributed accordingly among the remaining candidates. The means by which some ballot papers are chosen to be the 'surplus' (rather than primary) ones varies: in some countries, 'surplus' papers are selected randomly from all of those with the initial winning candidate as first choice, while elsewhere papers are accorded primacy on a 'first come, first served' basis (i.e. ones submitted later become 'surplus'). The process of reallocating second choices, third choices, etc., as 'first choices' continues until the required number of candidates is elected.	The Irish Dáil; Scottish local authorities; local and European elections in Northern Ireland
Party list systems	Seats are allocated to parties in direct proportion to the number of votes that they receive. Candidates are chosen by voters from lists supplied by their parties—meaning that, in theory, they can opt	European elections in most member states; regional and national parliamentary elections in European states, including Sweden and the Netherlands; Israel's Knesset

Name	How it works	Where used
	for someone with a local connection to their area, even if the 'constituency link' preserved by UK elections is more remote. Where the system can prove controversial is in the degree to which electors are able to vote for individual candidates (rather than simply their parties) in practice. In an *open*-list system, they will be able to do this: parties supply a list of candidates; electors choose the individuals that they would most like to represent them; the party will then allocate the seats that it wins to named candidates, according to those expressed preferences. In *closed*-list systems, voters have less say, because parties have already decided which of their candidates they wish to take seats in parliament, assuming that they win enough votes. Although Britain has yet to adopt PR for general elections, like all other EU member states, it now uses the party list system as its main means of electing **members of the European Parliament (MEPs)**. In the 2004 European Parliament elections, the UK Independence Party controversially used a closed-list system to cherry-pick the candidates that it wanted to represent it as MEPs—regardless of preferences expressed by its voters. This ensured that former BBC talk show presenter and ex-Labour MP Robert Kilroy-Silk made it into the Parliament.	
Alternative vote (AV)	Similar to STV, except only one MP is elected per constituency—meaning that the extent to which the outcome of the election will please all or most voters is much more limited. AV is, however, widely	Australia's House of Representatives

(continued)

Name	How it works	Where used
	seen as producing a more accurate reflection of voters' preferences than FPTP. It works as follows: if, after votes are counted, one candidate is found to have an *absolute majority*—i.e. more than half the votes cast—he or she is immediately elected. Where this is not the case, the candidate who received the least 'first choice' votes is struck out and the 'second choices' on all of the papers that put them top are distributed among the other candidates as if they were first choices. This process continues until, eventually, one candidate has more than half the votes cast. In theory, by using first and second preferences in this way, even though only one candidate is elected, he or she is likely to be someone with whom the majority of voters are comfortable.	
The supplementary vote (SV)	A modified version of AV. The only real difference is that, if no candidate initially obtains an absolute majority, all but the top two are eliminated and their 'second choices' reallocated to produce a winner.	English mayoral elections, including that for London mayor
The additional member system (AMS)	A hybrid of different systems, this sees a proportion of candidates elected in single-member constituencies (normally on a FPTP basis) and a second—'additional'—vote used to select from a regional list, which introduces a measure of 'proportionality' between votes and parties in parliament. As with the party list system, lists can be either open or closed.	Elections for the Scottish Parliament, Welsh Assembly, and London Assembly; parliaments in Germany, Italy, Mexico, New Zealand, and Venezuela

Table 4.6 The pros and cons of PR

For	Against
Governments elected under FPTP are often parties that win a majority of seats despite only securing a minority of the votes cast	PR produces more coalition governments—fragile alliances of minority parties with differing views. These can be less decisive and coordinated in their policymaking. Extremist parties (e.g. the National Front in France) can sometimes hold the balance of power, because their support is vital to enable mainstream ones to remain in government.
Many votes are wasted because a numerous electors are denied representation by MPs of their persuasion	PR means that voters are less able to hold a particular government responsible for its actions by decisively voting it out at a general election.
Changes in government between Left and Right can bring abrupt changes of policy and direction—leading to a lack of long-term continuity	Some PR systems break the constituency link between individual voters and their MPs—a cornerstone of Britain's democracy.
FPTP denies a voice in Parliament to minority parties, such as the Green Party, which have significant support in the country at large, but no elected MPs	PR can lead to more frequent elections and big compromises on policy, because many coalitions are inherently unstable. Sometimes, leadership and firmer action are needed.

government rallied to kick out sitting Labour MPs. This has prompted an ongoing debate about the perceived disengagement of voters—whether due to the increasingly indistinguishable nature of many Labour and Conservative policies, or the perception that politicians say one thing in their manifestos and do another once elected.

In addition to the deeper philosophical debates taking place in and around the main parties, there is a growing consensus that more needs to be done to encourage people to vote. One approach to this quandary—in recognition of the increasingly hectic lifestyles led by many British adults—is to make voting *easier*. The Representation of the People Act 2000 authorized various pilot schemes to see which worked best, including:

- electronic voting—via email, text messaging, the Internet;
- global postal voting;
- voting spread over a number of days;
- voting on Saturdays;
- taking polling stations to the voter—for example, to supermarkets, GP surgeries, etc.

Although the government has reiterated its commitment to postal voting as a universal option, there have been huge controversies over its vulnerability to fraud—particularly in multi-occupancy households, where, theoretically, one resident could vote multiple times by completing and sending off his or her housemates' forms as well as his or her own. In elections for Birmingham City Council in 2004, systematic corruption was exposed after a number of Labour Party workers were implicated in fraudulently submitting forms in support of Labour.

→ Further reading

Crewe, I. (ed) (1998) *Why Labour Won the General Election of 1997*, London: Frank Cass. **Illuminating critique of techniques of media management and triangulation used by 'New Labour' to improve its standing with the middle classes and to regain power after 18 years.**

Denver, D. (2006) *Elections and Voters in Britain*, 2nd edn, London: Palgrave Macmillan. **Second edition of authoritative text focusing on voting patterns in the UK, with particular emphasis on recent general elections. Includes data from British Electoral Study (BES) surveys.**

Gallagher, M. and Mitchell, P. (2008) *The Politics of Electoral Systems*, Oxford: Oxford University Press. **Comprehensive examination of the different electoral systems used in 22 countries, including Britain, incorporating comparative data and examples.**

Johnston, R. and Pattie, C. (2006) *Putting Voters in Their Place: Geography and Elections in Great Britain*, Oxford: Oxford University Press. **Thoughtful examination of geographical differences in voting and turnout patterns in local, national, and European elections around the UK. Examines issues including the emergence of safe seats, and the roles of marginal *wards* and constituencies in winning polls.**

? Review questions

1. What are the arguments for lowering the voting age in the UK to 16 years?

2. Given the imbalance between votes cast and seats won under the first past the post (FPTP) system, what are the arguments for and against proportional representation (PR)? Give an explanation of two or more different types of PR.

3. What are the qualifications for electors and candidates in UK parliamentary elections, and how can people be barred from standing for the Commons?

4. How are constituency boundaries determined, how many constituencies are there at present, and what role does the Electoral Commission play at general elections?

5. How is the government trying to increase turnout at general elections and can you think of any additional or alternative ways of improving voter engagement?

Online resource centre

www.oxfordtextbooks.co.uk/orc/Morrison
Visit the Online Resource Centre that accompanies this book for web links and regular updates.

5

Political parties, party funding, and lobbying

The 'party system' has long been one of the cornerstones of Britain's brand of representative democracy. It derives from a series of works of early political science penned in the nineteenth and early twentieth centuries, most notably *American Commonwealth* (1885) by English scholar James Bryce, and later writings (again focusing on the emergence of what was seen as a model democratic system in the USA) by the likes of Charles Merriam and William Nisbet Chambers. The notion of groups of like-minded individuals banding together to form 'parties' that would campaign collectively to win power might well have been relatively new across the Atlantic. But in the UK, the party was already a long-established tradition, as was the country's own peculiar version of party politics—the 'two-party system'.

As discussed in Chapter 4, Britain's 'first past the post' (FPTP) electoral system has always favoured candidates—and voters—representing the two or three most popular shades of opinion. Given the fact that British general elections produce a 'winner takes all' outcome at *constituency* level—with a single representative returned from each one—it has tended to be those candidates most closely identified with the (frequently polarized) concerns of each area who have been elected (historically, social reformers in the industrial north and conservatives in the wealthier south). The formation of a coherent nationwide government is only really possible if a number of elected representatives agree to share power and ascribe particular responsibilities to individuals from among their number. For both of these reasons, the emergence of a party system in Britain was logical, pragmatic, and, arguably, inevitable.

From the point at which Parliament first wrested sovereignty from the monarch, in 1689, up to the emergence of the Liberal Party nearly two hundred years later, the British two-party system revolved around two political groupings: the Whigs and the Tories. While the former are often crudely identified with the progressive tendencies later embodied by the nineteenth-century Liberals of William Gladstone and the latter with the modern-day Conservative Party (the term 'Tory' is still often used as shorthand for 'Conservative'), in truth, the distinction between the two was much more nebulous. Both were associated, to a greater or lesser degree, with the moneyed classes and, in particular, with the aristocracy. What differences there were initially rested largely on Christian denominational grounds, with the Whigs identifying more with the non-Anglican believers ('dissenters' such as the evolving Presbyterian Church in Scotland) and the Tories with the Church of England 'establishment'.

By the late eighteenth century, however, clearer party lines had become visible, with the ascendancy of Charles James Fox and William Pitt the Younger, as Whig leader and Tory prime minister, respectively. Within a few short decades, the Whigs would be advocating the abolition of slavery, the introduction of overseas free trade, and wider voting rights.

Although the purpose of this book is to give journalists a clear understanding of the present-day political framework governing the UK, no explanation of the British two-party system would be complete without a brief summary of how today's main parties came about.

▌The Conservative Party—a potted history

For much of the period from the 1950s to the 1990s, the Conservative and Unionist Party, to use its full title, was viewed as the 'natural party of government'. Of the 21 prime ministers who served in the twentieth century, 13 were Conservative, compared to three Liberals and five from Labour. The Tories were in power for 55 years, the Liberals for 17, Labour for 28.

Although William Pitt the Younger is widely regarded as the first 'Conservative' prime minister, in all but name, he was really the last of a long line of political leaders whose affiliation was rooted in that looser, more general Tory persuasion spawned in the seventeenth century. It was only after his death, in 1812, that a cohesive Tory Party organization began to emerge, initially under Lord Liverpool (who, as prime minister for 15 years, remains the longest-serving premier to date). Not until a decade later, however, was the term 'Conservative' tentatively coined, by his short-lived successor, George Canning.

The title 'Conservative Party' was officially adopted in 1834 by Sir Robert Peel, now widely credited as its true founder, who formalized it in a paper viewed as the blueprint for its later constitution, *The Tamworth Manifesto*. Ironically, he later all but destroyed the party, splitting it down the middle over his decision to repeal the 'corn laws'—tariffs protecting the profits of British landowners and farmers by artificially inflating the prices of imported foreign crops—to allay the suffering caused by the Irish potato famine of 1845–06. After being deposed as party leader, Peel formed his own faction in Parliament—the 'Peelites'—and was briefly courted by a coalition of Whigs and Radicals (later to form the Liberal Party) in 1849.

The late nineteenth century was notable for the emergence of two progressive political giants in the Conservative Party: Benjamin Disraeli, who served twice as prime minister between 1868 and 1880, and his successor, Lord Salisbury. Despite his imperialistic approach to foreign policy, Disraeli marked a break with tradition in the Tory ranks, extending the right to vote and embodying a more paternalistic attitude towards the poor. He even introduced a right to peaceful picketing in industrial disputes.

Disraeli's brand of moderate conservatism foreshadowed the so-called 'One Nation Toryism' that would characterize the terms of post-war twentieth-century premiers such as Harold Macmillan and Sir Alec Douglas-Home. Only with the emergence of Thatcherism—and its adherents' derogatory labelling of their ilk as 'Wets'—did the pendulum within the party swing decisively back to the Right, while adopting a more solidly free market approach to its handling of the economy and social welfare than ever before.

The last Conservative prime minister to date was John Major, who served from 1990 to 1997. Today, the party is still associated with certain core Tory values—privatization, low taxes, tough anti-crime measures, and a free market approach to the economy—but its latest leader, David Cameron, has also taken steps to 'modernize' its approach to issues that have traditionally been associated more with Labour, the Lib Dems, and even the Green Party. A series of recent policy reviews included those focusing on renewable energy, and on the widening gap between rich and poor. The author of the latter report, former leader Iain Duncan Smith, coined the term 'broken society' to describe Labour's legacy after ten years in power.

▌ The Labour Party—a potted history

Despite having long since supplanted the Liberal Party as the second of Britain's two main political parties—and the 'Tweedledum' to the Conservatives' 'Tweedledee'—Labour is little more than a hundred years old. For much of the nineteenth century, the Liberals were the progressive party—advocating what later came to be seen as core Labour values, such as social reform, a widening of democracy, and a foreign policy founded on tolerance and co-operation rather than imperialism. It was only when the vote was finally extended to men on more modest incomes—ironically, a policy ushered in by both Disraeli's Tories and Gladstone's Liberals—that rumbling calls for a voice in Parliament for the working classes, to counter that of the middle and upper echelons who had so far dominated, became a clamour.

Unlike the Conservative Party, which emerged organically out of the ranks of the propertied classes over a period of decades, Labour was formed through the coordinated amalgamation of a number of organizations founded to safeguard the interests of ordinary working people and united by a shared belief in its founding philosophy of democratic socialism. The first of these were the trades unions, which had evolved out of the aftermath of the Industrial Revolution to provide protection and representation for employees in the workplace. Having tried, but failed, to persuade the Liberals to sponsor sufficient numbers of its working-class candidates to stand in general elections in the later nineteenth century, the unions turned their attentions towards establishing their own political party.

Shortly before the turn of the century, several like-minded organizations began to talk seriously about the prospect of forming a new party: notably, two early think tanks, the Fabian Society and the Marxist Social Democratic Federation, and a body of aspiring parliamentary candidates and their supporters calling itself the Independent Labour Party (ILP). In 1900, at a special conference convened by the Trade Union Congress (TUC) in Farringdon, London, they formed between them the Labour Representation Committee (LRC). With future Labour Prime Minister James Ramsay Macdonald as its secretary, the LRC set about sponsoring candidates to fight the coming election. In the event, the so-called 'khaki election', which returned the Tories under Arthur Balfour that October following his perceived success in the Boer War, delivered the first two Labour MPs: Richard Bell, for Derby, and James Keir Hardie, for Merthyr Tydfil, who was to become its first leader.

Although hardly meteoric, the party's progress in Parliament was steady from now on. The 1906 election ushered in 17 years of reforming Liberal government, but a combination of factional infighting and growing Labour momentum during its later years ensured that this was its last term as a majority administration. Labour had gained 27 additional seats in 1906—thanks, in part, to a secret pact between Macdonald and Liberal Chief Whip Herbert Gladstone designed to stop Labour and Liberal candidates cancelling out each other's votes by contesting the same seats—but by 1910, it was up to 42. In 1924, aided by the Liberals' divisions, it won 191—enough to form its first government, under Macdonald.

From this point on, Labour was the second party. It secured its first decisive election victory in the wake of the end of the Second World War, in 1945—a landslide win for Clement Attlee and a radical team of ministers who went on to form the National Health Service (NHS), introduce free state education, and consolidate earlier moves towards establishing a welfare state to provide benefits for the unemployed, the low-paid, and the elderly. Three further periods of government followed: under Harold Wilson (1966–70); Wilson and James Callaghan (1975–79); Tony Blair and Gordon Brown (from 1997).

▌ The Liberal Democrat Party—a potted history

Although technically the youngest of the three main UK political parties, the Liberal Democrats—or 'Lib Dems', as they are commonly known—are essentially the successors to the Liberal Party. As discussed previously, the Liberals were a dominant force in British politics until a combination of the erosion of their grass-roots support by Labour and internal divisions caused by the bitter rivalry between the last Liberal Prime Minister David Lloyd George and his predecessor, Herbert Asquith, led to their sharp decline in the late 1920s.

Between the 1920s and 1980s, the Liberals consolidated their status as Britain's 'third party', with modest parliamentary gains that were never again sufficient to propel them to power in their own right, but at times gave them a toehold in government. In 1977, buffeted by rising *inflation* and wildcat union strikes, Mr Callaghan kept himself in Number 10 by negotiating a Lib–Lab Pact with Liberal leader David Steel. The Liberals effectively held the balance of power for a year, but the alliance soon broke up, and Labour were brought down on a Tory-instigated confidence vote in March 1979 (see p. 102).

In 1981, as Labour swung back towards hard-Left policies following its election defeat, four of its most senior moderates—former Chancellor Roy Jenkins, Foreign Secretary David Owen, Science Minister Shirley Williams, and Transport Secretary Bill Rodgers—quit to form the Social Democratic Party (SDP). By 1983, the so-called 'Gang of Four' had recruited enough supporters to form a credible new party and joined with Mr Steel's Liberals to form the SDP–Liberal Alliance. Such was the state of the UK economy in the early 1980s that the Tories began flatlining in opinion polls—with the Alliance reaping the benefit, given the continued infighting within Labour. At one point in 1982, it reached a rating of 50 per cent, with the Tories and Labour more or less neck and neck on around 25 apiece. But for the Falklands War, it is possible that the next election would have produced a hung Parliament, with the Alliance as the biggest party. In the event, buoyed by victory in the South Atlantic, Mrs Thatcher increased her majority and the Alliance went on to perform modestly in both the 1983 and 1987 polls, before disbanding.

In 1988, more than two-thirds of existing Liberal and SDP members—and all of their serving MPs—combined forces to form a new party: the Liberal Democrats. Initially led jointly, like the Alliance, by Mr Steel and Robert Maclennan, Mr Owen's successor as SDP leader, it soon elected Paddy Ashdown as their single replacement. He was succeeded by Charles Kennedy, Sir Menzies 'Ming' Campbell, and Nick Clegg.

▶ The structure and constitution of the modern Conservative Party

Many aspects of the internal organization of the Conservative Party remain the same today as they were a hundred years ago. It has, however, introduced significant changes in the past decade, most notably democratizing its leadership elections.

As with any organization, the lifeblood of the party is its grass-roots membership. It is ordinary members who swell the party's coffers by paying their annual subscriptions, fund-raising, and making donations; it is they who troop out, unpaid, on cold winter evenings to canvas in the run-up to elections; it is they who can usually be relied on to vote loyally for it come polling day. In return, it is incumbent on the party's leadership to give something back to members—policies that they can support and also a sense of involvement. This can come through everything from participating in fund-raising events to attending the annual party conference—which, like those of Labour and the Lib Dems, are held at the end of the summer recess, traditionally in large coastal towns such as Brighton, Bournemouth, or Blackpool.

Notwithstanding Labour's close ties with the unions, traditionally, the Conservatives have had the largest individual subscribing membership of any British party. Although recent years have seen a noticeable decline in party membership across the board, the Tories remain the biggest at grass-roots level, with some 290,000 members at present. These members have customarily been connected to the party at national level through local constituency associations, which began springing up around the UK in the wake of the Reform Act 1832. Unlike in the Labour Party, in which membership activities have always been directed from the centre, these associations initially sprouted independently. They could, however, wield considerable clout: in affluent areas, the associations would recruit candidates and finance their campaigns.

Despite being gradually incorporated into the overall party structure, in de facto terms, constituency associations retained a large degree of notional independence until 1998, when then newly elected leader William Hague formalized their party status, in an effort to impose discipline on what he perceived as errant elements (some of whom he controversially labelled 'out of touch' and 'racist'), and kick-start a grass-roots Tory revival following years of declining popularity under Mr Major. To this end, he introduced the party's first codified constitutional document, *Fresh Future*. This imposed new conditions on associations, but gave them significant new rights. Their position in the modern Tory Party's internal hierarchy—beneath its constitutional college and **Conservative Campaign Headquarters** (formerly known as 'Conservative Central Office')—is explained in Table 5.1, while the way in which the various components of the party's central organization fit together is shown in Table 5.2.

Although the Tories usually take a drubbing in both general and devolved elections in Scotland and Wales—they currently do not have a single Scottish MP—unlike Labour, they still contest some seats in Northern Ireland. This is a hangover from the party's strong historical ties to the province, as evidenced by its official 'Conservative and Unionist Party' title. In July 2008,

Table 5.1 The internal structure of the modern Conservative Party

Level	Party in the country	Party in Parliament
Top table	**Chairman of the Conservative Party** (head of Conservative Campaign Headquarters) and Conservative Party Board	Party leader
Middle tier	Constitutional college, incorporating National Conservative Convention (made up of MPs **members of the European Parliament (MEPs)**, and other senior activists)	1922 Backbench Committee
Grass roots	Constituency associations	Individual backbenchers

Table 5.2 The main components of central Conservative Party organization

Body	Role and composition
Conservative Party Board	Ultimate decision-making body, comprising 18 members, including the chairman of the Conservative Party and deputy chairman. The Tories' equivalent to the National Executive Committee (NEC) of the Labour Party.
Conservative Campaign Headquarters	Main fund-raising, campaigning, and recruitment body, which coordinates its electioneering and marketing. Headed by the party chairman.
Constitutional college	Body comprising representatives from all levels of the party, including constituency associations and ordinary rank-and-file members, which has a say in questions of reform and long-term policy strategy. Incorporates the National Conservative Convention— made up of MPs, MEPs, and senior party activists.
Constituency associations	Grass-roots member organizations, originally only loosely affiliated to the party, but now formally incorporated. Now permitted to play significant role in selecting prospective candidates for Parliament, **European Parliament**, and elections for the devolved assemblies.

Mr Cameron and the leader of the Ulster Unionists, Sir Reg Empey, published a joint letter in the *Daily Telegraph* pledging to revive their parties' historic electoral alliance, dating back to the 1880s, which had been severed some thirty years earlier due to infighting.

How the Conservatives choose their leader

From the mid-1960s until the adoption of *Fresh Future* in March 1998, Conservative leaders had always been elected by their parliamentary colleagues— that is, with no formal input from rank-and-file party members. From that point onwards, however, only the first stage of this election process was to be handled exclusively by MPs and peers. Once two frontrunners had been produced by this means, their names would be put forward to ordinary members around the country—on a 'one member, one vote' basis—and the final say would rest with them.

While the introduction of this huge extension of party democracy signalled that the new, young Tory leader (Hague was only 36 years old at the time) was serious about modernizing his party, it was not long before his fellow MPs were ruing the day that they voted for it. When Hague was defeated by Mr Blair at the 2001 election, he swiftly resigned, in time-honoured tradition, only to be replaced by the little-known Duncan Smith. Although he was widely perceived by both his colleagues in Parliament and political commentators as uncharismatic, Iain Duncan Smith beat his more dynamic challengers, Kenneth Clarke and Michael Portillo, because of his solid support among grass-roots Tories. A former army officer, devoted family man, and staunch Euro-sceptic, he chimed far more than his rivals with typical Tory members—the average age of whom, despite Hague's reforms, was still 64. In contrast, Clarke's Europhile views and Portillo's admission of a previous homosexual relationship did little to endear them.

Duncan Smith's later removal in a vote of no confidence instigated by a group of Tory MPs paved the way for a new leader before the following election, in former Home Secretary Michael Howard. Recognizing the need to ensure that the party elected leaders more in touch with the wider public in future, after losing the May 2005 election, he tried to reverse Mr Hague's reforms in his remaining months in office. In September of that year, Howard's proposals were defeated, however, after failing to win the required two-thirds majority among Tory MPs and activists in the party's 1,141-strong constitutional college.

The 1922 Committee

Also known as the '1922 Backbench Committee', the *1922 Committee* is made up of all backbench Conservative MPs at any time and can therefore number in the hundreds. The Committee is often referred to as 'influential'—something of an understatement, given that it represents all elected Tory members and is therefore in a position to articulate the 'mood' of the parliamentary party like no other organization. Leaders ignore its views at their peril.

Far from being a mere 'talking shop', the Committee retains huge constitutional clout within the party. It is headed by an 18-member executive committee, the chairperson of which is often referred to as the party's 'shop steward', charged as he or she is with overseeing elections for its leadership (even under the new rules). He or she also oversees votes of confidence called to dismiss leaders with whom the party has become disgruntled. Such a vote can be triggered by a letter to the chairperson signed by 15 per cent of Tory MPs. The last time that this happened was in 2003, when Mr Duncan Smith was deposed. The Committee is also believed to have instigated the final twist of the knife that unseated Margaret Thatcher following Michael Heseltine's 1990 leadership challenge (see p. 103).

The Committee meets every week when Parliament is in session and is governed by some curious conventions. When the Tories are in Opposition, frontbench spokespeople other than the leader may attend its meetings—acting as intermediaries between them and their parliamentary party. When in government, neither leader nor *Cabinet* colleagues may attend.

Although the 1922 Committee is by far the largest and most powerful subgroup of the Conservative Party, there are several smaller such 'clubs' that MPs and peers may choose to join, depending on where their views fall on the wide political spectrum that unites members of the party. These associations of like-minded left or right-wingers—or members united in their views on a particular issue, such as Europe—have traditionally been known as 'ginger groups', although, in recent times, many have morphed into semi-professional think tanks. Among the most active today are the Bow Group, which describes itself as Britain's 'oldest centre-right think tank', and the Thatcherite group Conservative Way Forward. In addition, the Conservative Party has a long tradition of support from certain upmarket gentlemen's clubs, the most famous being the Carlton Club.

▶ The structure and constitution of the modern Labour Party

Unlike the Conservative Party, which emerged in a 'top-down' way from one of the two principal parliamentary factions that evolved in the late seventeenth and early eighteenth centuries, the Labour Party came into being in 'bottom-up' fashion—as a membership-led organization formed by establishment outsiders to campaign for election. Its creation was also more *deliberate*, with several groupings coming together to establish it formally in 1900. As such, it has had a codified constitution since its inception.

In addition to its de facto union members, the Labour Party today is made up of some 200,000 subscribing individuals. For a brief period under Tony Blair, its membership reached an all-time peak—at 400,000 overtaking that of the Conservative Party, many of whose older subscribers were, quite literally, dying off—but this later fell due to growing disenchantment with his leadership. Although it has had traditional strongholds in Scotland, Wales, and northern England, Labour does not organize in Northern Ireland. In that province, its closest equivalent is the centre-Left Social Democratic and Labour Party (SDLP).

The main constituent elements of the Labour Party today are as outlined in Table 5.3. Of its main leadership bodies, by far the most significant is the **National Executive Committee of the Labour Party (NEC)**. Its role in relation to two other organizations, the National Policy Forum (NPF) and the Labour Party Conference, is explained in Table 5.4.

Clause 4 and the birth of 'New Labour'

The most significant internal victory for Mr Blair's leadership came not in his frequent run-ins with his own **backbenchers** after being elected prime minister, but in his first year as leader, with the party still in opposition. At its 1995 Easter conference, bolstered by his rabble-rousing deputy, John Prescott (whose similarly tub-thumping speech had helped John Smith, his predecessor, to win the 'one member, one vote' debate—see Table 5.3), Mr Blair successfully passed a motion to reword one of the most sensitive and symbolic sentences in the Labour Party's constitution.

'Clause 4' had been written in the context of a pre-war British society in which ownership of the country's assets and wealth was concentrated in the hands of very few individuals, and, in the absence of any state provision, 'public services' such as free health care and education were largely reliant on charity. As a result, its wording bore the strong imprint of the Marxist ideology on which the party's original values were based—focusing on the need to take into public ownership the 'means of production' (industry and agriculture) and give workers a greater share in their fruits. The clause,

Table 5.3 Member organizations of the Labour Party

Organization	Role and functions
Constituency Labour Parties (CLPs)	Equivalent to the Conservatives' constituency associations, these represent the voice of ordinary party members and activists. Although a key component of the party's internal decision-making structure, their influence has diminished in recent years, as party leadership has exerted greater control over their activities—in particular, the selection of candidates for parliamentary elections. The CLP still technically has the final say over who represents its constituency, but it must choose from a centrally vetted list of applicants. In addition, the party's central National Executive Committee (NEC) may overrule the decisions of CLP selection panels, parachuting in favoured candidates over the heads of those chosen locally. This was especially the case during the earlier years of Mr Blair's era, when he was determined to ensure that centrist candidates stood wherever possible, to prevent the Tories and media accusing the party of still being in thrall to the Left.
	CLPs are normally run by two committees: a general management committee (GC), and an executive committee (EC). The former are made up of delegates from branch Labour parties (smaller-scale ones in individual towns), local socialist societies, Co-operative Party branches, and unions. In addition, each CLP has several elected officers to discharge specific membership functions, including a chair, two vice-chairs, a secretary, a treasurer, a women's officer, a youth and student officer, and, increasingly, a black and ethnic minority officer. Each CLP elects representatives to national party policymaking entities, including the Labour Party Conference, and nominates candidates for election to its other two ruling bodies: the National Policy Forum and the NEC.
Affiliated trades unions	Certain trades unions are formally affiliated to the party—many of them 'sponsoring' individual MPs. These include **UNISON**—representing local authority and healthcare workers—and Unite—formed in 2006 from the amalgamation of technical union Amicus and the Transport and General Workers' Union (T&G). Among those that have disaffiliated in recent years, in protest at Labour's policies in government, are the Rail and Maritime Union (RMT) and the Fire Brigades Union. If an employee is a member of an affiliated union, he or she automatically becomes a de facto Labour member, although he or she may opt out of the party.

(continued)

Organization	Role and functions
	Between them, affiliated unions wield considerable influence on party decision-making, selecting 12 of the 32 members of the NEC and electing half of the delegates to the party conference. In voting at the party conference, however, their wings have been clipped in recent years. Until the early 1990s, despite significant reforms introduced in the 1980s under Neil Kinnock, unions still wielded a so-called 'block vote' at party conferences—allowing them to deliver votes for or against particular policy proposals en masse on behalf of their memberships, regardless of individual members' views. This led to numerous run-ins between a leadership intent on pursuing more modest social and economic goals through its policies, in an effort to appear more 'voter-friendly' in future elections, and unions determined to stick to a more socialist agenda. In 1993, Mr Kinnock's successor, John Smith, finally abolished the block vote, in favour of 'one member, one vote'.
Socialist societies	An umbrella term referring to various smaller associations that are instrumental in the party's foundation. Like unions, they pay an affiliation fee to the party and may elect one delegate between them to sit on its ruling NEC. The most famous socialist society is the Fabian Society, the early members of which included a number of writers, intellectuals, and campaigners, among them George Bernard Shaw, H. G. Wells, and Emmeline Pankhurst, one of the founders of the British suffragette movement. Other societies include the Christian Socialist Movement and the Society of Labour Lawyers.
The Co-operative Party	A small socialist party formed in 1881 through the establishment of a joint parliamentary committee to act as a watchdog on activities at Westminster from the point of view of under-represented working people, this has a long-standing arrangement with Labour not to contest the same seats separately at elections. Instead, in areas in which it is established, it fields joint candidates with Labour under the banner 'Labour and Co-operative Party'.

penned by Marxist intellectual Sidney Webb in 1917 and formally adopted by the party a year later, vowed:

❝ To secure for the workers by hand or by brain the full fruits of their industry and the most equitable distribution thereof that may be possible upon the basis of the common ownership of the means of production, distribution and exchange, and the best obtainable system of popular administration and control of each industry or service. ❞

Table 5.4 The main constitutional bodies of the Labour Party

Body	Role and composition	Notes
National Executive Committee of the Labour Party (NEC)	Often described as its 'ruling' body, the National Executive Committee of the Labour Party (NEC) is meant to represent all wings at a national policymaking level, taking delegates from all affiliated groupings (see Table 5.2). It has traditionally acted as a counterweight to the power of the party leadership, although its influence declined under the more presidential stewardship of Tony Blair and with the formation of the National Policy Forum. As of August 2008, the NEC had 31 members—not counting its two *ex officio* ones: the party leader and deputy leader. These included former *EastEnders* actor Michael Cashman, party treasurer Jack Dromey, and stalwart backbencher Dennis Skinner. In addition to its policymaking role, the NEC also enforces party discipline. It was recently asked to consider the case of George Galloway, former Labour MP for Glasgow Kelvin, who was accused of bringing the party into disrepute in a series of inflammatory speeches that he made criticizing Mr Blair's actions in Iraq, accusing him and US president George Bush of having *'lied to the British Air Force and Navy, when they said the battle of Iraq would be very quick and easy'*. Labour's constitutional committee (made up largely of NEC members) expelled him after a hearing that Galloway described as 'a kangaroo court'.	Mr Blair's neutering of the NEC was partly a response to the frequent run-ins that his predecessors had had in the 1980s and early 1990s with it over proposed policy changes, such as the party's abandonment of its long-standing commitment to scrap Britain's nuclear weapons after the 1987 election. Equally humiliating was the repeated election to its membership of vocal critics of the leadership, such as veteran left-wingers Tony Benn and Ken Livingstone, and the failure of 'placemen' such as ex-minister Peter Mandelson to secure a place.
National Policy Forum (NPF)	Set up by Mr Blair in 1997, under his 'Partnership in Power' initiative, this has some 184 members, drawn from all levels of the party. It meets over 2–3 weekends a year to examine in detail policy proposal documents generated by six policy commissions, the members of which include representatives of	Introduced ostensibly as a means of widening party democracy in Labour's ranks, but often perceived as the leadership's instrument for quelling dissent.

(continued)

Body	Role and composition	Notes
	the leadership, NEC, and NPF. Its ruminations are then passed to the annual Labour Party Conference for debate and ratification.	
Labour Party Conference	Unlike the Conservative and Lib Dem conferences—which are more about political grandstanding by their leaders, and opportunities for ordinary members to air their views and meet senior figures—the Labour Conference has traditionally been viewed as less an event than it is the party's supreme decision-making body. Presiding over the Conference is one of the Labour Party's most senior officers: its general secretary (a title reflecting the party's union roots).	Theoretically, it is still the Conference that has the final say on major policy and constitutional changes. In practice, however, since returning to government in 1997, the party's leadership has made it clear that it is willing to overrule Conference decisions about which it is unhappy. Mr Blair also reduced the weight of the vote by affiliated organizations at conference from 80 to 50 per cent (four-fifths of which are still wielded by union members).

Basing his version on a pamphlet that he had written for the Fabian Society, Mr Blair reworded it:

" The Labour Party is a democratic socialist party. It believes that by the strength of our common endeavour we achieve more than we achieve alone, so as to create for each of us the means to realise our true potential and for all of us a community in which power, wealth and opportunity are in the hands of the many, not the few, where the rights we enjoy reflect the duties we owe, and where we live together, freely, in a spirit of solidarity, tolerance and respect. "

The rewriting of Clause 4 was a defining moment in the creation of the 'New Labour' brand—a project initiated years earlier, under Neil Kinnock, who had moved to soften the party's image by replacing its Soviet-style, Red Flag-inspired logo (and conference anthem) with the now familiar 'red rose' motif. Under Mr Blair, this process was accelerated, as the party embraced more mainstream policies, the language and aspirations of business, and an affinity with media management—or 'spin'—designed to improve its public image after years in the political wilderness (see p. 117). Soon terms such as 'third way', 'big tent politics', and 'triangulation' had entered the political vernacular to explain the tactics used by Mr Blair and his apparatchiks to neutralize their opponents, by bringing together people from a variety of shades of 'liberal' opinion in a new coalition against what he would describe in a later conference speech as 'the forces of conservatism'.

How Labour chooses its leader

Labour's leadership election procedure has trodden a long, slow road towards democratization over recent decades—beginning the process well in advance of more recent Tory moves to involve ordinary party members. From 1922 to 1981, leaders were elected solely by the party's MPs. Annual contests were held at the party conference, but, in practice, leaders were normally re-elected unopposed, so these were little more than formalities.

In 1981, although it was to be some years before any wholesale reform of the party's constitution, Labour established an electoral college: in future, only 30 per cent of votes in leadership elections would be cast by Labour MPs, with another 30 per cent going to Constituency Labour Parties (CLPs) and 40 per cent to the unions. Further reform followed in 1993, when the union block vote was scrapped and the weighting equalized to give each grouping a one-third share of the vote. There remain some inequities, however: individuals who are members of two or more affiliated organizations— for example, a union and a CLP—may vote more than once. Other anomalies abound: although Labour has so far balked at introducing **proportional representation (PR)** for parliamentary elections when in office (see p. 144), it uses the single transferable vote (STV) for its own leadership elections.

The Parliamentary Labour Party (PLP)

Like the Conservative Party, Labour has a body that represents the views of rank-and-file MPs—known as the **Parliamentary Labour Party (PLP)**. It too meets in a room in the Palace of Westminster on a weekly basis and it too has a chairperson elected from among its number annually, normally at the start of the parliamentary session.

Between 1921 and 1970, the chair of the PLP was the party leader. But since 1970, the two posts have been permanently split and the PLP has become (like the 1922 Committee) largely a means for backbenchers to hold their leaders to account. Unlike the 1922 Committee, however, the PLP may be attended by leaders themselves, even when in government. In his last months in office, Mr Blair endured hostile receptions from the PLP on more than one occasion (although, intriguingly, he received a standing ovation at the meeting following his resignation). Like the 1922 Committee, the PLP has the power to instigate a vote of no confidence in its leadership, but, in practice, Labour has refrained from dumping unpopular leaders, who have generally jumped before being pushed despite murmurings of rebellion.

As well as the PLP, Labour has within it a number of ginger groups and is associated with various think tanks. One of the most famous, the Left-leaning Tribune Group, was wound up some years ago, but revived in 2005 by backbencher Clive Efford as a direct challenge to the leadership's perceived move to the Right. More Blairite examples include the Institute of Public Policy Research (IPPR).

▶ The structure and constitution of the Liberal Democrat Party

As the youngest of Britain's major political parties, the Liberal Democrat Party also has the newest constitution. Unlike either Labour or Conservatives, the party has a *federal* organization, comprising separate, but conjoined, parties for England, Scotland, and Wales. It currently has some 72,000 paying members and, like Labour, encompasses several affiliated groupings, known as 'specified associated organizations' (SAOs). These each represent particular sections of the membership, such as women, ethnic minorities, lesbian, gay, bisexual and transgender (LGBT) members, trades unionists, and youths and students.

Like Labour and the Tories, the Lib Dems have a parliamentary party to act as a voice for ordinary MPs: in fact, they have three, in recognition of their federal structure. The party also organizes in Northern Ireland, but, rather than contesting elections under its own banner, has a semi-official arrangement to support the Alliance Party of Northern Ireland.

The question of where the Lib Dems fall on the Left–Right political spectrum has long been open to debate. Traditionally, like the Liberals before them, they have been seen as centrists—that is, pro-welfare state, on the one hand, but in favour of the free market (subject to effective regulation), on the other. It is this that has arguably been their great electoral asset—enabling them to appeal to Labour voters in Tory-held marginals, on the one hand, and Conservatives in Labour ones, on the other. In recent years, however, the Lib Dems have often appeared more conventionally left-wing in their policy ideas than Labour—thanks, in large part, to Labour's rhetorical embrace of many Thatcherite economic reforms, the encroachment of market forces into public services, and its increasingly interventionist foreign policy. For many years, the Lib Dems advocated a 50 per cent upper rate of Income Tax (something that Labour has long since abandoned) and they still support a local income tax to replace the *Council Tax*, arguing that it would take more account of individuals' ability to pay.

Under Nick Clegg, the party has reasserted many centre-Left tendencies, but there are also signs of a more market-friendly approach—including a commitment (first floated by Mr Campbell) to reduce the Income Tax burden on middle-income families. In 2004, Mr Clegg, along with several fellow leading lights, including recent caretaker leader Vince Cable, co-authored the *Orange Book*, a collection of essays advocating more free market policies.

▶ The deselection process

Once a parliamentary candidate has been selected by his or her constituency party or association and elected to Parliament, he or she will usually serve until voted out at another election, or until he or she decides to retire. Under certain circumstances, however, it is possible for a candidate to be 'deselected'—that is, sacked—by either his or her local party or that party's leadership. The process by which this can happen varies from party to party, but, in general terms, follows much the same pattern.

The most recent deselection (and the first for ten years) was that of Jane Griffiths, Labour MP for Reading East, who was removed by her local party for what it described as 'personality issues'. Derek Conway, the Tory backbencher who had the *whip* withdrawn by Mr Cameron over his misuse of his parliamentary allowance, announced his intention to stand down at the next election before his local party had a chance to deselect him.

Notable examples of MPs who have avoided deselection included the succession of Conservatives who defected to other parties in the last years of Mr Major's leadership. Emma Nicholson, MP for Torridge and West Devon, switched to the Lib Dems in 1995, but continued serving her constituency (despite quitting her local Conservative Party) until the 1997 election. Fellow former Tories Alan Howarth and Shaun Woodward both jumped ship to Labour, but retained their seats after the election and went on to serve as ministers under Mr Blair (indeed, the latter was appointed Northern Ireland Secretary in Mr Brown's first Cabinet).

Deselection of sitting MPs normally leads to a by-election—an election in his or her constituency alone—giving the local party that he or she previously represented a chance to field a replacement candidate and retain the seat, and its opponents an opportunity to win.

▌ Party funding now and in future

One endlessly debated issue surrounding the party system is that of funding. Because political parties are intrinsic to British parliamentary democracy, there has long been a vocal lobby calling for their work to be financed, at least in part, by the state. At present, only Opposition parties receive any state subsidies in Britain—a privilege that is designed to counteract the perceived advantage that governing parties have, because of the resources that can be marshalled by their sitting MPs. Introducing wholesale state funding of parties would signal a major change. But the idea of using taxpayers' money to fund the activities of political organizations the beliefs of which many of them are unlikely to share could be deeply problematic. Given the ever-escalating costs of Britain's existing public services, without significantly increasing the tax burden, where would 'the state' find the extra cash needed to fund parties? And, if state funding were to become an entitlement for registered political parties, would it only be the larger and/or more mainstream ones that benefited, or could taxpayers expect some of their money to go to minority extremist parties, such as the British National Party (BNP)?

For these and other reasons, successive governments have sidestepped the question of state funding. But in the absence of such grants, how do political parties fund their campaigns? Because membership subscriptions provide only a modest, if regular, source of revenue, parties have come to rely increasingly on bequests, loans, and donations from wealthy supporters. Naturally, this has given rise to charges of inequity—if one party attracts higher donations than another it can mount a bigger campaign—and suspicions that rich donors are using their money to buy levels of influence that are denied to ordinary supporters.

The 1990s was marked by various controversies over party finance. In the later years of the Tory government, there was growing unease about the party's use of anonymous multimillionaire donors and money originating in offshore tax havens, not least the so-called 'Ashcroft millions' funnelled away by the party's ex-pat treasurer, Lord Ashcroft. Labour promised to deal with these issues by limiting the ability of non-domiciles to finance parties and making the source of donations transparent, but within months of its election, it was embroiled in its own controversy when Formula One boss Sir Bernie Ecclestone was identified as the source of a £1m donation to its campaign. The fact that Formula One had just been granted a temporary exemption from an impending ban on tobacco sponsorship fuelled suspicions that he had used money to buy influence.

To wrest back the moral high ground, the party subsequently returned the donation and set about reforming the rules governing party funding in two ways: by introducing a new statutory register of all significant donations, and by creating new criminal offences relating to false and late declarations. But, with near-Shakespearian inevitability, 11 years after he thought he had laid it to rest, the Ecclestone affair returned to haunt Mr Blair in October 2008, when the Commons Speaker announced that he would be investigating claims that the former prime minister had deliberately misled Parliament at the time of the original controversy. Newly released papers suggested that, contrary to Mr Blair's protestations that he was a 'pretty straight kind of guy', within hours of holding a meeting with Ecclestone, he had begun frantically looking for ways of exempting Formula One from the advertising ban. Because Mr Blair had ceased to be an MP more than a year earlier, however, it was far from clear what sanctions, if any, Mr Martin would be able to bring even if Blair were to be found 'guilty' of the deception.

Under the Political Parties, Elections and Referendums Act 2000, registration of donations now rests with the newly established **Electoral Commission**, which, in addition to overseeing election procedures, has the responsibilities laid out in Table 5.5.

Table 5.5 The role of the Electoral Commission in relation to donations and loans

Role	Process
Registers donations and loans	Established a statutory register of donations, requiring all political parties and affiliated organizations to declare any donation, loan, or benefit in kind of more than £1,000 made to a constituency or local party office in a single year, and all donations or loans of £5,000-plus paid to central offices. Parties must detail them in quarterly reports.
Defines 'permissible donors'	Clamps down on anonymous donors. Anyone donating more than £200 to a party will be named on the register and such donations will only be accepted from 'permissible donors'— individuals on the UK *electoral register*, or organizations registered in the EU and carrying out business in the UK. 'Donations in kind' (e.g. office space, printing of campaign literature) will be treated as donations.
Limits spending	Monitors compliance with spending controls during election campaigns (see p. 136).
Refers abuses to Crown Prosecution Service (CPS)	There are now three levels of offence relating to false or late declarations: (a) failure to submit a return in time—a civil offence by the party and a criminal offence by the treasurer; (b) submitting a return that fails to comply with the Act—a criminal offence by the treasurer; (c) making false declarations on a return—a criminal offence by the treasurer.

▌ 'Lobbygate', 'cash for honours', and Labour's deputy leadership row

Despite Labour's professed determination to 'clean up' party funding, since 1997, it has frequently been embroiled in controversies concerning alleged lack of financial transparency on the one hand, and underhand links with business on the other. By the time that Mr Brown succeeded Mr Blair in Downing Street, the tension between the government's pledge to be 'whiter than white' financially while still raising enough money to keep the Labour Party machine afloat had reached breaking point. Successive scandals about undeclared—or, at best, underdeclared—donations and loans had forced ministers into embarrassing admissions; as a consequence, the political initiative was handed to Mr Cameron, who demanded a cap of £50,000 on all individual payments—including its main lifeline, donations from trades unions. Whatever his political instincts, Mr Brown was hardly in a position to comply, arguing instead that trade union contributions should be viewed as comprising a number of smaller individual donations. With 'Middle England' deserting the party in favour of the resurgent Conservatives, disclosure of Labour's annual accounts in July 2008 revealed the full extent of the party's mounting debt—some £24m was owed to various creditors, including a number of individual donors whose money was due back that year. At the time of writing, the party was in the midst of trying to negotiate extended repayment terms.

'Lobbygate'

Political lobbying is nothing new. The Conservatives have never been shy about their links to big business, while Labour MPs in certain constituencies have been sponsored by unions for decades. But the emergence of specialist lobbying companies purposely set up to help individuals and interest groups gain access to ministers, in the hope of influencing government policy, is a phenomenon that was not widely exposed until the early 1990s.

The involvement of one such company, Ian Greer Associates, as an alleged intermediary in the 'cash for questions' affair (see pp. 11 and 61) was, for many, the first time that they had heard of such practices. Labour promised to stamp out such activities, but, within a year of regaining power, senior ministers—including Mr Blair's right-hand man, Peter Mandelson—were being linked to lobbying firms boasting of their ability to buy access to those in power. One such firm was Lawson Lucas Mendelsohn, run by former Labour campaign strategy adviser Neal Lawson, business intermediary Jon Mendelsohn, and Ben Lucas, one of Mr Blair's political briefers. Another, GPC Market Access, employed one of Mr Mandelson's ex-special advisers, Derek Draper, who is alleged to have bragged to clients that he could buy them tea with Geoffrey Robinson, Labour's then Paymaster General, or dinner with Mr Blair. While investigating the simmering controversy, journalist Greg Palast said that Draper told him:

“ There are 17 people that count. To say that I am intimate with every one of them is the understatement of the century. ”

'Cash for honours'

If 'Lobbygate' and the Ecclestone affair were early shots across the bows for Labour, then the various 'cash for honours' rows that followed provided the smoking gun that proved for many that the party had succumbed to the advances of big business by selling its soul for cash.

Of these, by far the most damaging was the so-called 'loans for peerages' scandal. Exposed by the *Independent on Sunday* in October 2005, the controversy erupted in earnest in March the following year, when the then recently formed **House of Lords Appointments Commission** rejected several nominees that Mr Blair had put forward for **life peerages**. It quickly emerged that each of the men concerned had recently loaned the Labour Party substantial sums of money on an anonymous basis. A loophole in the 2000 Act meant that, although all *donations* of £200 or more had to be properly declared, the same rule did not apply to loans—provided that they were taken out on normal commercial terms.

In light of the fact that the party was in huge debt in the run-up to the 2005 election, Mr Blair and his advisers appeared to have deliberately sidestepped a law that they themselves had introduced on the pretext of wanting to make party funding more transparent by courting loans, rather than actual handouts. Although the revelation that the party had gone 'cap in hand' to anonymous lenders was embarrassing enough for the government, there was no suggestion that the letter of election law had been breached (even if its spirit might have been). What led to the subsequent criminal investigation—and the ignominious spectacle of Mr Blair becoming the first serving prime minister to be questioned by police, albeit as a witness—was the allegation, levelled by Scottish Nationalist MP Angus McNeil, that attempts had been made by some of his aides to 'sell' honours (an offence under the Sale of Peerages Act 1925).

In the ensuing months, the spotlight came to focus on Lord Levy, Labour's chief fundraiser (and Mr Blair's tennis partner), who was alleged to have asked one of the lenders, Dr Chai Patel, director of the Priory healthcare group, to change a gift that he planned to offer the party into an unsecured loan for £1.5m, to sidestep the new donation rules. As the controversy escalated, Lord Levy—known as 'Lord Cashpoint' in some Labour circles—briefly faced the prospect of being charged with conspiracy to pervert the cause of justice, while Downing Street adviser Ruth Turner was subjected to a dramatic dawn raid by the Metropolitan Police amid rumours that she was facing similar charges.

No charges were ultimately brought, but the year-long investigation, which ended weeks before Mr Blair left Downing Street, cast a long shadow over his final year in office. To regain the political initiative at the height of the controversy, Mr Blair launched a cross-party review of party funding, chaired by Sir Hayden Phillips, chairman of the National Theatre and a senior partner with corporate financiers Hanson Westhouse. But in October 2007, the talks were suspended amid scenes of dissent between Labour and the Tories. This did not stop Sir Hayden making his own recommendations public. They included a proposal to cap individual donations after a transitional period at a maximum of £50,000.

The Labour deputy leadership donations

If Mr Brown had hoped to close the lid on allegations of financial sleaze on entering Downing Street, his dream was swiftly dashed. Within months of joining his new Cabinet, several of his colleagues were immersed in a new funding controversy, this time surrounding donations made to their individual campaigns for the party's deputy leadership post.

In November 2007, it emerged that David Abrahams, a property magnate and one-time Labour parliamentary candidate, had bypassed the new law on donations by hiding behind a third party when he paid £5,000 into Harriet Harman's winning campaign. The money had been passed to Ms Harman's team by a friend of Mr Abraham, Janet Kidd. Apparently accepting the gift at face value, Ms Harman wrote to Mrs Kidd to thank her.

Ms Harman denied any wrongdoing, stressing that she had registered the donation with the Electoral Commission (albeit under Mrs Kidd's name). But eyebrows were raised about her apparent ignorance of the party's own rules on donations, let alone the wider law. It emerged that both Hilary Benn, a fellow deputy leadership candidate, and Mr Brown had turned down offers of donations by Mrs Kidd—the latter because she was 'not known' to his team. Despite also being unfamiliar with Mrs Kidd, Ms Harman, married to then Party Treasurer Jack Dromey, appeared to have been less scrupulous about checking her out.

With the prospect of yet another police investigation into his party's finances, Mr Brown entered the New Year with a further scandal looming. In January 2008, it emerged that Peter Hain, then Work and Pensions Secretary and Welsh Secretary, had failed to declare 17 donations to his deputy leadership bid, together worth £103,000, until four months after the contest ended. Mr Hain blamed his ministerial workload for the poor organization of his campaign, but when his case was referred to the Met, he said that he had 'no choice' but to resign.

Mr Hain's case was not the last to tarnish Mr Brown's premiership. In July 2008, after months of sustained political pressure from the Scottish Nationalists, the Lib Dems, and the Tories, Wendy Alexander, Leader of the Scottish Labour Party, resigned over an undeclared £950 donation to her 1997 campaign to succeed Jack McConnell.

→ Further reading

Marr, A. (2008) *A History of Modern Britain*, London: Pan Books. **Critically acclaimed tie-in to the 2007 BBC2 documentary series of the same name, chronicling British social and political history from the post-war period to the present day.**

Roy, D. (2005) *Liberals: A History of the Liberal and Liberal Democratic Parties*, London: Hambledon Continuum. **Overview of the complex history of the Liberal Party and its successors, starting with the origins of liberalism in the eighteenth and nineteenth centuries; following the party's decline in the early twentieth century; and its resurgence in the 1970s and 1980s.**

Seldon, A. and Snowdon, P. (2004) *The Conservative Party*, Stroud: The History Press. **Colourful history of the Conservative Party from the late eighteenth century to the present day, including a thoughtful examination of the party's recent troubles over Europe.**

Thorpe, A. (2001) *A History of the British Labour Party*, 2nd edn, London: Palgrave Macmillan. **Second edition of this comprehensive history of the Labour Party, which chronicles the evolution of its policies and institutions, from its late nineteenth-century origins, up to the election of the second 'New Labour' administration in 2001.**

? Review questions

1. Which is the oldest UK political party—Conservative, Labour, or Liberal Democrat?

2. To what extent has Labour stayed true to its democratic socialist roots, and are traditional labels such as 'left-wing', 'right-wing', and 'centrist' still relevant today?

3. Outline the similarities and differences between the role of the 1922 Committee in the Conservative Party and the Parliamentary Labour Party.

4. How is party funding regulated in the UK, and what is the difference between a donation and a loan in the eyes of the law?

5. What are the arguments for and against state funding of political parties in Britain?

Online resource centre

www.oxfordtextbooks.co.uk/orc/Morrison

Visit the Online Resource Centre that accompanies this book for web links and regular updates.

6

The National Health Service (NHS)

If there is a single British institution beside Parliament with the capacity to dictate the country's news agenda, it is the National Health Service (NHS). For many journalists, however, the newsworthiness of the NHS is matched only by its ability to perplex them.

When it was founded in 1948, three years into the life of Clement Attlee's reforming post-war Labour government, the NHS was designed to be exactly what it said on the tin: a *national* health service providing high-quality medical treatment, 'free at the point of need', on a uniform basis wherever one lived in the UK. But the story of subsequent decades—in particular, the past twenty years—has been of the gradual fragmentation of this idealized model of social health care. What was once a single, monolithic health service, run directly by central government, is now more an umbrella organization encompassing a series of connected, but increasingly autonomous, units. Much like individual companies in the commercial marketplace, most of these units have their own boards of directors and delegated budgets. Again like companies, they 'commission services from' and 'sell services to' one another. And, with the recent introduction of the concept of 'patient choice'—allowing those in need of operations and other treatment to shop around between hospitals, like customers looking for a new MP3 player—they have even begun to compete.

This chapter charts how the NHS in its current form came about and tries to explain how these many disparate strands link together.

▌ The origins of the NHS

Although not formally established until the passage of the National Health Service Act 1946, the NHS emerged from mounting concern over a period of decades about the ever starker inequalities in personal well-being between the richest and poorest Britons. At heart, it had its roots in two key developments. These were the so-called Beveridge Report (of which more in a moment) and the introduction by Liberal Chancellor David Lloyd George, as far back as 1911, of a *National Insurance (NI)* scheme—which, in exchange for docking 4d a week from their wages, insured low-paid workers against sickness and unemployment.

At the time that this modest measure was introduced, the concept of an NHS offering a comprehensive range of treatments was still some way off. It was not until Labour ministers were invited into Winston Churchill's wartime national government in 1940 that the idea of a system of universal, needs-based health care was born. Arthur Greenwood, then Minister without Portfolio, commissioned Liberal economist William Beveridge to head up an interdepartmental committee on social insurance and allied services in 1941. Its report, published a year later, was to form the blueprint for not only the NHS, but for the all-encompassing 'welfare state' of which it became part—leading to Attlee's famous pledge, on entering Downing Street, to harness the spirit of collectivism born out of the war effort to look after the poor, sick, and vulnerable 'from the cradle to the grave' during peacetime.

The Health Minister entrusted with launching the embryonic NHS was Aneurin 'Nye' Bevan, whose vision was inspired by his memories of witnessing the suffering of steelworkers and miners in his native Tredegar, south-east Wales, as a younger man, and the work that voluntary societies and charity-funded cottage hospitals had done, in the absence of government funding, to care for such people. He reputedly modelled the NHS on the Tredegar Medical Aid Society, a community-run healthcare collective set up in 1874.

Because there was no national template for the NHS, Bevan initially had something of a fight on his hands persuading family doctors and consultants—most of whom, up to now, had been able to dictate their own working conditions and pay—to sign up to his new project. In the end, he did so by offering them generous contracts that, by his own admission, 'stuffed their mouths with gold'. When he triumphantly unveiled the new NHS at its inaugural outlet, Park Hospital in Manchester, on 5 July 1948, Bevan declared:

❝ We now have the moral leadership of the world. ❞

Although Bevan's vision of a health service for all was arguably largely fulfilled, it was not long before the sheer economics of providing universal health care on such a massive scale began to chip away at some of its guiding principles—notably, that of universal free access to treatment, regardless of ability to pay. In May 1951, buffeted by global economic turbulence and its dependence on US loans to continue financing its social welfare programme, the Labour government reluctantly introduced the first NHS charges: £1 for spectacles prescribed by an optician and a half-cost price for dentures. A year later, a flat rate £1 fee for visiting the dentist was introduced, along with a 5p generic prescription charge. In what was to be a mortal blow for Attlee, Bevan—the architect of his greatest achievement—resigned from the government even before the first of these new charges had taken effect. Among those who joined him was a young Harold Wilson, a future prime minister.

How the NHS is funded

Although the proportion of Britain's **gross domestic product (GDP)** ploughed into the NHS each year has varied wildly from one government to another—with Labour administrations traditionally investing more, even if not always wisely—the general breakdown of sources from which this investment derives remains broadly the same as it was in the early 1950s. Around 80 per cent comes from general taxation (Income Tax, VAT, duties on tobacco and alcohol). The remaining 20 per cent stems from:

- the NHS element of National Insurance contributions;
- charges to patients for drugs (prescriptions) and treatment;
- income from land sales and income-generation schemes;
- funds raised from voluntary sources—for example, local hospital appeals.

▌ The end of the post-war consensus and the birth of the NHS internal market

For forty years or more after its foundation, the NHS retained largely the same structure: it was funded centrally through taxation, with ministers and civil servants filtering the money down to hospitals, surgeries, and ambulance services. Of the tens of thousands of nurses, doctors, and paramedics (not to mention catering and cleaning staff) working in the health service at one time, most were effectively on the government's—and, by extension, the taxpayers'—payroll.

Today, this is no longer the case. A series of institutional reforms since the late 1980s have transformed the NHS into a different kind of organization entirely. Nowadays, the bulk of family doctors, or 'general practitioners' (GPs), are self-employed; many specialists work as freelance locums, moving from hospital to hospital, or clinic to clinic, as demand arises; junior doctors, nurses, and care workers are increasingly employed through agencies, rather than as full-time members of staff. Catering, cleaning, and security workers are routinely supplied by outside contractors, rather than being employed in-house, and even treatment itself is sometimes contracted out to providers in the private and voluntary sectors.

So how and why did this apparent sea change in the day-to-day running of the NHS come about, and who is responsible for running the modern-day health service?

It is impossible to understand the shape of the NHS today without first examining the emergence of the so-called 'internal market'. As long ago as 1973, the National Health Service Reorganisation Act spearheaded by then Conservative Health and Social Security Secretary Keith Joseph (in time, one of the architects of Thatcherism) aimed to shake up the NHS by introducing a more efficient management structure, with more 'generalist' managers joining existing clinical experts on hospital boards and incentives to generate revenue by letting out unused wards for the use of private patients. These themes were revisited a decade later, in 1983, when alarmed at the escalating cost of NHS treatment and wage bills, another Tory Health Secretary, Norman Fowler, commissioned then deputy chairman and managing director of Sainsburys, Sir Roy Griffiths, to chair an inquiry into making the health service more efficient. His specific remit was to recommend an alternative management structure, and to find ways of cutting running costs by using staff and other resources more economically.

The resulting Griffiths Report proposed a wholesale restructuring of the health service, putting the onus on two key recommendations:

- the introduction of *general managers* to run the existing district health authorities (DHAs)—essentially the administrative presence on the ground in each area of the then Department of Health and Social Security (DHSS), directing funding to local hospitals and surgeries—who would oversee the efficient use of NHS budgets at local level. This would replace the so-called 'management by consensus' philosophy (under which medical practitioners had effectively been their own managers) used since previous, smaller-scale, reforms had occurred in 1974, an approach that Griffiths felt provided little more than crisis management;

- a greater focus on *community-based* health care—with GPs, dentists, and other primary care providers given control of their own budgets, along with the freedom to commission services on behalf of their patients without the need to go through the government, or even their local health authorities. The aim was to make the allocation of finite NHS funds more efficient by replacing the 'one size fits all' approach to funding GP surgeries of old with a more targeted allocation of resources tailored to the particular needs of the individuals on their books.

Amid criticisms from the Labour Party that they were primarily motivated by a desire to save money (and accusations from some quarters that they were conspiring to privatize the health service by stealth), the Tories initially took only tentative steps towards implementing the report's findings. But a series of **White Papers** that flowed from the inquiry in ensuing years eventually paved the way for an internal market that was, if anything, *more* radical and far-reaching.

The Act that finally established this internal market (in so doing, defining the term for the first time) flowed from a further review of the NHS announced by Prime Minister Margaret Thatcher in 1988. At about the same time, she decided to split the mammoth DHSS in two, in recognition of its burgeoning workload: creating the Department of Social Security (DSS) to run the benefits system and a separate Department of Health (DH).

The National Health Service and Community Care Act 1990 implemented two of the previous White Papers: *Caring for People* and *Working for Patients*. It ushered in a phased reorganization with the following key features:

- hospitals, mental health units, ambulance services, and other NHS bodies directly involved in patient care became **NHS trusts**—with their own management boards, incorporating both practitioners (consultants and other senior clinical staff) and general managers charged with improving their efficiency;

- GPs were offered the opportunity to become 'fundholders'—that is, to 'opt out' of district health authority control and take charge of their own budgetary decisions;

- GP fundholding practices, DHAs, and family health service authorities (FHSAs) were redefined as 'purchasers' of NHS care on behalf of their patients. While GPs would now focus on *primary care*—providing 'first port of call' treatments such as diagnoses, vaccinations, and referrals for X-rays and tests—FHSAs would purchase other community-based services, and DHAs would purchase acute hospital services such as accident and emergency (A&E) facilities;

- NHS trusts were defined as 'providers' of services under the new internal market.

In theory, the new internal market would operate as illustrated in Figure 6.1 below.

In practice, the implementation of the internal market was far from smooth. For a start, as independent contractors, GPs had to *want* to be integrated into it in the first place. While some relished the opportunity to control their own budgets and to direct spending towards areas that they felt to be in need of cash, others were alarmed at the prospect of an increased workload and, potentially, making the wrong decisions about how to spend their money—only to face tricky dilemmas should unforeseen needs arise during a financial year. Only family practices with more than 5,000 patients on their books in England and Northern Ireland (4,000 in Wales and Scotland) were allowed to apply for fundholder status. By the time that Labour came to power in 1997, some 3,500 practices had signed up, involving 15,000 GPs—fewer than half of the estimated 40,000 practising across the UK. By mid-1996, there were more than 520 NHS trusts in place, but mergers had reduced this tally to 450 by 1999.

The internal market was also criticized for placing too much emphasis on management and recruiting suited senior staff, with clipboards and flow

Figure 6.1 How the Conservatives' NHS internal market was structured

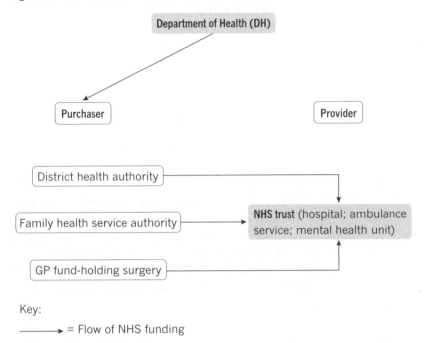

Key:

⟶ = Flow of NHS funding

charts, and on high salaries, at the expense of adequate numbers of front-line workers such as nurses. Managers were increasingly headhunted from the private sector—a reflection of the Conservatives' belief that individuals with business expertise were likely to be better at running the organization itself than medical practitioners whose skills lay primarily in patient care. This trend has continued to this day, with chief executives of most NHS trust boards taking home six-figure salaries. In 2005, a survey by Incomes Data Services identified Derek Smith, chief executive of Hammersmith Hospitals, as the first NHS manager to top the £200,000 mark. It also found that chief executive salaries across the board had risen 70 per cent in the previous decade. At the same time, the average starting salary for a newly qualified nurse was around £17,000.

The emergence of the 'postcode lottery'

There was widespread agreement before the introduction of the internal market that the original 'one size fits all' NHS model needed adapting to the changing needs of a British society on the cusp of a new century—not least because of the widening disparities between different areas in terms of average income, age, healthcare needs, and other demographic factors. Nonetheless, the decision to grant increased autonomy to DHAs and individual GPs was to have one unintended consequence: the steady emergence of significant variations in the level and nature of treatment available to people with the same conditions living in different parts of the country. This increasing trend—dubbed the 'postcode lottery' by critics of the Thatcher and Major governments—led many to question whether the NHS could any longer seriously be described as a 'national' health service.

One of the most famous cause célèbres for those arguing against the delegation of funding decisions to local level was the case of 'beta interferon'—an expensive drug that, according to some experts, dramatically decreases the number of relapses suffered by people with multiple sclerosis (MS). In the early 1990s, it emerged that a number of DHAs were refusing to fund beta interferon on the NHS—arguing that the £10,000 a year per patient needed to buy in the drug would be better spent on other treatments, such as physiotherapy. Its supporters argued that prescribing the medicine early could save the NHS money in the long run, by delaying the need for residential and/or palliative care.

Another early example of the postcode lottery (which remains the case to this day) was the differential availability of fertility treatment for childless couples and, in particular, in vitro-fertilization (IVF)—the process by which egg cells are fertilized by a man's sperm outside a woman's womb before being transferred back to stimulate pregnancy. Despite recent efforts by Labour to end the postcode lottery by establishing national service frameworks (NSFs) designed to harmonize provision of essential health services across the country (see p. 188), wide disparities remain. In November 2005, it emerged that Ipswich Hospital NHS Trust and a number of Suffolk *primary care trusts (PCTs)*—that is, the bodies that now run the healthcare commissioning process (see later this chapter)—had decided to ration hip and knee replacement operations by refusing to offer them to patients judged obese, other than in exceptional circumstances. At the time, Dr Brian Keeble, director of public health for Ipswich PCT, justified the decision by telling the press that it was for patients' own good, because overweight people 'do worse after operations' and hip replacements might fail.

But critics of the move—since emulated by several other trusts—condemned it as discrimination against patients whose conditions were judged to be self-inflicted. Their concerns were compounded when, just days later, a leaked paper from the *National Institute for Health and Clinical Excellence (NICE)*—an agency that vets potential new treatments and makes recommendations to the government on whether they should be funded on the NHS—indicated that plans were afoot to ration treatment for heavy smokers and drinkers.

The World Health Organization (WHO) defines anyone with a body mass index (BMI) of 30 as clinically obese. Those critical of the Suffolk trust's decision argued that it gave the impression that anyone falling into this category only had themselves to blame. Several studies, however—including one published in January 2008 in the *American Journal of Clinical Nutrition* by University College London researchers—have since suggested that numerous other factors may be involved besides poor diet and lack of exercise, including genetic ones.

The postcode lottery has become such a political 'hot potato' in recent years that ministers have increasingly found themselves drawn into disputes over individual cases of patients denied treatment by their local PCTs. So potentially damaging has the issue become that, in June 2008, Health Secretary Mr Johnson pledged publicly to end it once and for all—by banning PCTs from denying patients costly treatments approved by NICE for NHS use.

NHS waiting lists and the origins of Blair's health reforms

Perhaps more controversial still, in light of escalating criticisms of the Conservative government's concentration on spending NHS money more efficiently rather than pouring more of it in, was the 'waiting list' crisis that emerged in the late 1980s and early 1990s. By the time that Labour were elected in May 1997, some 1.3 million people were listed as awaiting operations or other inpatient treatments, with 'guaranteed maximum waits' from initial GP referral to actual treatment being 18 months. In the final years and months of Mr Major's government, the tabloids were filled with stories about elderly and vulnerable patients falling seriously ill, or even dying, while awaiting surgery. Equally alarming were the numerous stories printed about the lengthy queues that people had to endure in A&E units—and the often overcrowded and undignified conditions in which they were forced to do so.

Such was the public outcry that one of Tony Blair's central election pledges in the campaign leading to his 1997 landslide was to cut waiting lists by 100,000 by releasing £100m from so-called 'NHS red tape'. Despite a sluggish start, by November 2004, official figures suggested that waiting lists had hit a 17-year low: although 857,000 people were still listed, this was down 300,000 on 1997. Perhaps more importantly for the individuals concerned, waiting *times* were found to have fallen, with only 19 patients having waited longer than a year for treatment and 122 for more than nine months. Health Minister John Hutton declared at the time that, by the end of 2008, no patient should be waiting longer than 18 weeks.

New Labour's restructuring of the NHS

The story of the Blair government's blizzard of NHS reforms is a confusing one. Significant achievements in some areas—bolstered by unprecedented public investment—have been marred by inconsistent, sometimes down-right contradictory, policymaking in others.

When Labour returned to power after 18 years in opposition, it inherited a health service that was widely seen as being in a state of crisis. After an initial period of caution, during which the new government pledged to stick to public spending limits stipulated by the Tories before leaving office, then Chancellor of the Exchequer Gordon Brown announced a huge increase in funding for the NHS—taking it above and beyond the average annual invest-ment of other European countries in public health care. In 1997, the propor-tion of Britain's GDP spent annually on the NHS was 6.7 per cent, but in his 2002 Budget, Mr Brown used his first tax rise (a 1 per cent increase in National Insurance) to raise it to 7.4 per cent a year. By 2007–08, it was due to have risen to 9.4 per cent—more than a percentage point higher than the European average.

Mr Blair quickly decided that pouring more money into the NHS was not enough. To ensure this investment was spent wisely, like Mrs Thatcher before him, he set about restructuring the health service. Having promised to dis-mantle the 'wasteful' internal market while in opposition (and initially doing so under his 'Old Labour' Health Secretary Frank Dobson), he appeared to begin reinventing the wheel, by introducing a new form of localized manage-ment and budgetary control seen by many as his own version of the internal market.

The New Labour model for the NHS originated in the Health Act 1999 and the White Paper that preceded it, entitled *The New NHS: Modern and Dependable*. Its main emphasis was on the primacy of community-based health care—steering patients, wherever possible, away from hospital, and giving GPs and other primary care providers the money and autonomy needed to offer a wider range of treatments through their practices.

On the face of it, the resulting reforms were initially modest. In place of fundholding, which had effectively fostered an element of 'competition' between GP surgeries, Mr Blair sought to introduce greater cooperation between practices, by establishing primary care groups (PCGs). These collaborative bodies brought together GPs, community nurses, and other related practitioners in a given geographical area to promote closer liaison and, ultimately, a more coordinated use of NHS resources. The idea was that, as PCGs grew in confidence and evolved, they would have increasing levels of responsibility delegated to them. In the end, like fundholding GP practices, they would also assume control of their own budgets, establishing NHS trust-style boards to take their financial decisions for them.

By 2002, the bones of today's NHS structure were established, as follows:

- PCGs have been replaced by 'primary care trusts' (PCTs), each covering populations of more than 100,000 people. Like fundholding GP practices, these effectively purchase clinical services from NHS trusts on behalf of their patients—except that, rather than calling this 'purchasing', Labour prefers the term 'commissioning'. PCTs are collectively responsible for spending 80 per cent of the overall NHS budget, having taken over virtually all local commissioning;

- after initially being replaced by 96 health authorities (HAs), DHAs have since given way to much more arms-length administrative bodies called *strategic health authorities (SHAs)*, of which there were initially 28—a number further reduced to a mere ten in July 2006. As the population covered by each authority has increased, its level of direct involvement in patient care has dwindled. SHAs are primarily responsible for monitoring local healthcare provision to ensure that there is fair access to services such as GP surgeries and dentists. They also publish health improvement plans (HIPs) every three years, designed to identify local health concerns, such as rates of heart disease or diabetes, and to promote healthier lifestyles and disease prevention;

- NHS trusts continue to be classed as service 'providers', but with the prospect of greater autonomy over their budgets being granted if they performed well in future NHS 'league tables'. Ultimately, many of them have been granted the 'self-governing' status of *foundation trusts* (see p. 192);

- county councils and unitary authorities have established *local involvement networks (LINks)* to act as the voice of local service users. Run directly by local taxpayers, LINks have the authority to demand specific changes to health and social care in their areas. They replaced a prior Labour invention, 'patients' forums', which were staffed by volunteers from the local community formally appointed by an *executive agency* of the DH, the now-defunct Commission for Patient and Public Involvement in Health (CPPIH). The forums, which had to be formally consulted on major structural changes in their areas and allowed to view related documentation, had in turn replaced 'community health councils' (CHCs), run by paid officers, which had existed for the previous 25 years.

Labour's revamped internal market therefore works as outlined in Figure 6.2.

Since the introduction of the new structure, it has been rationalized more than once. On 1 October 2006, the number of PCTs was reduced by nearly half, dropping from 303 to 152. The mergers that enabled this to happen were intended to promote efficiency savings, by preventing duplication between trusts in neighbouring areas with broadly similar needs. As a result, many PCTs now cover up to 600,000 inhabitants. There are now fewer hospital trusts, too (partly as a result of the closure and merger of hospitals in some areas). At the time of writing, there were 290 trusts covering 1,600 hospitals.

In addition to the above reform at local level, Labour strengthened the hand of the DH and the Secretary of State for Health, by giving them the power to set nationwide targets and standards of care in priority areas to which all SHAs, PCTs, and NHS trusts must adhere. These 'national service frameworks' (NSFs), established in 1998, were described as 'long-term strategies' designed to provide consistency of care across the UK, reducing the impact of the postcode lottery. In effect, they amounted to a set of 'rules',

Figure 6.2 How Labour's version of the internal market is structured

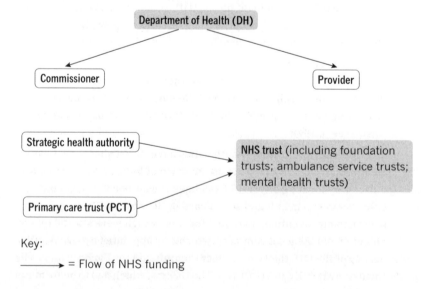

Department of Health (DH)

Commissioner

Provider

Strategic health authority

NHS trust (including foundation trusts; ambulance service trusts; mental health trusts)

Primary care trust (PCT)

Key:

⟶ = Flow of NHS funding

similar to the *National Curriculum* used to enforce uniformity of teaching in core subjects such as English and maths in schools. At present, NSFs cover 11 areas, as outlined in Table 6.1.

Table 6.1 NHS national service frameworks (NSFs) (August 2008)

Condition/ Service area	Target/Aim
Blood pressure	To reduce coronary heart disease and kidney disease by working with the Blood Pressure Association (BPA) to raise awareness about the risks of hypertension (high blood pressure) through initiatives such as National Blood Pressure Testing Week
Cancer	To improve preventative measures, such as vaccination and screening, for cervical, breast, and bowel cancer, as part of the DH's wider Cancer Reform Strategy
Children	Covers specific aims for improving treatment for children with disabilities and implementation of the 'Every Child Matters' agenda through children's services departments (see p. 475)
Chronic obstructive pulmonary disease (COPD)	Improving drug therapy for a wide range of respiratory illnesses, such as bronchitis and emphysema
Coronary heart disease	Specific target of a 40 per cent cut in the death rate for people under the age of 75 from heart disease and strokes by 2010
Diabetes	A ten-year programme of improvements to all aspects of diabetes treatment, set out in 2003
Long-term conditions	Five outcomes to improve treatment and quality of life for people with long-term conditions, through measures designed to reduce dependency and improve choice—including the introduction of direct payments (see p. 545)
Long-term neurological conditions	As above
Mental health	Specific focus on the disproportionate number of people from black and minority ethnic (BME) backgrounds with diagnosed mental health issues—one in five, compared to one in ten of the general UK population
Renal	Raising the quality of care available to people with kidney conditions, especially in the last days or weeks of their lives
Strokes	Target to reduce the under-75 death rate from this condition—the third biggest killer in the UK—by 40 per cent by 2010
Vascular	Commitment to reduce the number of deaths from this disease, which causes 39 per cent of all deaths in Britain each year, and disproportionately affects people from deprived backgrounds and specific ethnic groups, such as South Asians

 NOTE: A regularly updated version of this table can be found on the Online Resource Centre that accompanies this book.

The use of NSFs to impose uniformity of health care for priority conditions was strengthened in the first few years of the Labour government by the introduction of 'health action zones' (HAZs) in deprived areas. These were used to address 'health inequalities' between rich and poor districts by targeting additional resources at communities with high rates of unemployment, poverty, and poor housing, to ensure that public health—and quality of health care—in those areas kept pace with that in more affluent ones.

A further attempt to tackle the postcode lottery came with the formation of the National Institute for Clinical Excellence (NICE) in 1999. Since renamed the National Institute for Health and Clinical Excellence, this executive agency of the DH is charged with promoting improved public health, and ensuring that consistent, high-quality healthcare provision is available across the country, by:

- offering guidance on the prevention of ill health to NHS workers, local authorities, and the wider public and voluntary sectors;

- advising the government on whether new and existing clinical treatments, medicines, and procedures should be made, or remain, available on the NHS;

- giving advice to ministers and the public on the most appropriate treatment for individuals with specific ailments and diseases.

NICE's decisions have often been controversial. Campaigners representing sufferers from specific conditions frequently accuse it of simply trying to save money by failing to endorse new drugs, or recommending the abandonment of others—for example, in a preliminary ruling in 2001, it ruled that beta interferon should no longer be available on the NHS. On other occasions, its intervention has taken a more positive approach to countering the postcode lottery. In June 2006, NICE issued draft guidance to PCTs recommending the use of the then recently licensed drug Herceptin® for early-stage breast cancer. Its decision followed the case of Barbara Clark, a 49-year-old nurse who persuaded Somerset Coast PCT to pay for the £20,000-a-year drug by threatening it with litigation in the *European Court of Human Rights (ECtHR)*.

The DH's other key roles under the New Labour NHS model include:

- setting the *direction* of health policy—by outlining an overall strategy for the NHS, formulating policies, passing legislation and setting regulations, allocating resources, setting the overall NHS operating framework, and putting in place local area agreements between partner organizations to implement DH policy on the ground;

- supporting the *delivery* of NHS services—by monitoring and evaluating the performance of health service bodies and professionals, increasing capacity and improving the NHS skills base, and ensuring value for money for service users;
- promoting health and well-being among the population—by working with public, private, and voluntary sectors to encourage healthier lifestyle choices, and liaising with international bodies such as the European Union (EU), WHO, and the Organisation for Economic Co-operation and Development (OECD);
- accounting to Parliament and the public for the performance of the NHS—by answering parliamentary questions, responding to correspondences from the public, and communicating through speeches and public events.

In addition, the DH today has three overarching 'objectives', as set out in Table 6.2.

The 'Ten-Year NHS Plan', foundation hospitals, and 'patient choice'

If health professionals had hoped that the Blair government would call a halt to reform after the second wholesale restructuring of the NHS in less than a decade, they were to be disappointed. Even before the new Blairite version of the internal market had fully come into force, his ministers were signalling plans for a more fundamental revolution. This Labour administration was about to take the Thatcher reforms to their logical conclusion—by freely introducing free market terms such as 'choice' and 'competition' into the health service lexicon, and effectively redefining patients and service users as 'consumers'.

Table 6.2 The three key objectives for the Department of Health (DH) under Labour

Objective	Meaning
Better health and well-being for all	Helping people to stay healthy and well Empowering people to live independently Tackling health inequalities
Better care for all	Providing the best possible health and social care that offers safe and effective care, when and where people need it Empowering people in their choices
Better value for all	Delivering affordable, efficient, and sustainable services Contributing to the wider economy and the nation

The blueprint for this revolution first appeared in the so-called 'Ten-Year NHS Plan' unveiled to the public in 2000. Pledging to 'give the people of Britain a health service fit for the twenty-first century', it initially set eyes glazing over with its use of technical jargon: a 'Modernization Board' would be formed, chaired by the Health Secretary, to judge if change was happening fast enough, while NHS 'taskforces' would be set up to 'drive' that change 'at the coalface'. But it was not until the flesh was put on the bones with a series of stage-managed announcements by ministers that the true scale of the overhaul became apparent. At carefully timed intervals between early 2001 and 2003, the architect of the plan, Mr Dobson's archly 'New Labour' successor, Alan Milburn, outlined the plans listed in Table 6.3.

Back-door privatization? Criticisms of the New Labour reforms

Perhaps unsurprisingly, not everyone welcomed such a far-reaching reinvention of the NHS. For some long-serving Labour **backbenchers** and loyal party supporters, the idea of *any* private sector involvement in the NHS—direct or indirect—was too much to stomach.

Facing accusations that allowing NHS patients to be treated in private clinics and hospitals, and using private money to pay for new hospitals, was tantamount to privatizing the health service 'by the back door', the government argued forcefully that it was no such thing. Mr Blair retorted that it was the ends, not the means, that mattered—and that if using a spare BUPA ward meant that great-uncle Harold would have to wait 18 months less for his hip replacement than would otherwise be the case, neither he nor his family were likely to be fussed about outdated ideological objections. Yet the media was quick to pick up on the incongruous spectacle of the first NHS patients being flown overseas for surgery—and to criticize the principle that anyone should be expected to travel hundreds of miles for an operation that, by rights, ought to be available equally soon in their own area.

Among the most vocal critics of the latest wave of reforms was Mr Dobson, who accused his party's leadership of being 'elitist' and 'following a Tory consensus'. He and others argued that, by naming and shaming 'failing' hospitals in league tables and allowing 'successful' ones (foundation trusts) to offer inflated salaries for the most qualified and experienced staff, Labour was creating a 'two-tier health service'. Higher performing trusts would inevitably become yet more successful, gaining even greater freedoms in the process, while those stuck at the bottom of the ladder would continue to

Table 6.3 Key aspects of Alan Milburn's 'Ten-Year NHS Plan'

Reform	Detail
Pragmatic approach to cutting waiting times	To speed up the process of cutting waiting times, a 'concordat' was to be negotiated with private healthcare providers such as BUPA. Anyone who had spent six months on a waiting list could have his or her operations in a private hospital—or elsewhere in the EU. Special terms were negotiated with private providers allowing the NHS to buy the use of their spare capacity at a reduced rate broadly equivalent to the cost of standard NHS treatment.
'Patient choice' extended to surgery	People waiting for operations given the option of having their surgery fast-tracked by travelling elsewhere in the country—or even abroad—to a hospital with shorter waiting times. Future league tables would offer detailed information on waiting times of individual trusts to enable patients to choose between hospitals in an informed way. In time, star ratings would be awarded for everything from hospital cleanliness, to the standard of its food.
More and better hospitals	A huge hospital building programme was to begin, fast-tracked with the help of up-front investment from the private sector. These have been financed through so-called 'public–private partnerships' (PPPs)—Labour's version of the Tories' controversial **private finance initiative (PFI)** (see p. 238–9). In addition to offering commercial companies a chance to profit from lucrative leaseback arrangements on these projects, ministers were prepared to offer them stakes in the day-to-day running of some NHS hospitals.
More independence for hospitals	Successful hospital trusts to be given greater autonomy, in a similar way to PCTs. These 'foundation hospitals' are allowed to manage their own budgets without government interference, and to set their own pay scales for certain key staff over and above national wage agreements negotiated with unions. The aim is for all hospitals to gain foundation status over time.
Division between general and specialist hospitals	Increased emphasis on hospital 'specialization', with trusts renowned for their treatment of specific conditions, such as cancer, becoming specialist hubs and the highest performing trusts given 'super-hospital' status. Lower performing hospitals and those in less populated areas might be merged or closed, while still others stood to lose costly, underused departments—including maternity and A&E units.
High-street NHS treatment	A network of NHS 'treatment centres' was to be opened on high streets. These would focus on routine diagnostic procedures, such as blood and allergy tests, to relieve pressure on overstretched GP surgeries and hospitals. By 2005, at least 25 had already been opened and plans have since been announced to open them in branches of chain stores such as Boots.

spiral downhill, devoid of the reputation, resources, and autonomy needed to improve their performance.

Others argued that the 'patient choice' agenda was counter-intuitive. Given the option of going to a poor-performing hospital in one area or a better one in another, few patients would choose the former, so, in reality, the so-called 'choice' was academic. And like the most popular schools, the best-performing hospitals ultimately had a finite capacity—meaning that it would only be so long before they became oversubscribed and incapable of dealing with demand. The waiting time and waiting list spiral would then start all over again.

As if deliberately antagonizing his critics, Mr Milburn went further in an interview with *The Times* in January 2002, when he not only dispensed with constitutional etiquette by unveiling policy to the media before consulting either **Cabinet** or Parliament (see pp. 93–4), but also enraged Labour traditionalists by describing the NHS as 'Britain's last great nationalized industry'. He went on to suggest that it represented a model unsuitable for the twenty-first century.

Despite Mr Milburn's triumphalism, he was not to get his way entirely. A behind-the-scenes spat with then Chancellor Mr Brown saw him forced to rein back on one of his most radical proposals for foundation trust autonomy—allowing them to borrow on the open market. Mr Brown's objection to this move was attributed to two things. On the one hand, he was said to oppose the principle of opening the NHS up to the vicissitudes of profit-driven banks and stock markets. Perhaps more tellingly, however, he disliked any idea of losing control of government spending—and allowing individual parts of the NHS to borrow money as and when they needed to, on commercial terms, would inevitably weaken the Treasury's grip on the public finances. Nonetheless, the Tories have subsequently adopted the same policy as that advocated by Mr Milburn—pledging to make every hospital a foundation trust on regaining power and allowing them to borrow freely without government interference.

For Labour opponents of the changes, the final insult came at the hands of some of their fellow backbenchers, on a glacial November evening in 2003. With the help of a handful of Scottish MPs—many of whom had personally opposed the imposition of foundation hospitals in their home country, where members of the **Scottish Parliament** (MSPs) had only recently rejected the proposal—the government scored its lowest Commons victory to date, squeezing the Health and Social Care Bill through on a majority of only 17.

New Labour's version of the internal market has had an even bumpier ride in the provinces. Scotland rejected the idea of foundation hospitals at the outset and the overall structure of the NHS north of the border still bears a strong resemblance to the way that it looked nationwide before Mrs Thatcher's time. Meanwhile in Wales, a year after Labour was forced into an uneasy coalition with Plaid Cymru in the Welsh government, the country began systematically abandoning the internal market in time to mark the sixtieth birthday of the health service—returning to an old-style model that saw funding channelled directly from the health department down to trusts and 'health boards' (the Welsh equivalent of STAs).

More recent controversies and the future of the NHS

The NHS is never off the political agenda—or out of the media—for long. Although new reforming ideas have been kept to a minimum by ministers since 2003, a succession of issues has arisen in relation to those introduced in previous years under New Labour.

Among the more potentially damaging controversies for the government was the revelation in 2006 that huge deficits had been accumulated by some NHS trusts—at least partly in the act of paying off long-term leases to private sector companies in lieu of their investment in hospitals funded by *public–private partnership (PPP)*. Then Health Secretary Patricia Hewitt responded to this crisis by giving debt-ridden trusts permission to borrow money from other—'better performing'—trusts, the finances of which were in surplus. Critics argued that, because they were supposedly part of one united NHS, the very idea of some trusts being in 'in the red' while others were 'in the black' was absurd.

A further controversy emerged later over the government's apparently 'botched' 2004 contract negotiation with GPs. Family doctors had been offered 'bonuses' for providing certain services—for example, flu vaccinations for asthmatics and the elderly—over and above their general practice. As a result, many had ended up effectively earning huge salaries (the national average was found to be around £100,000), while not necessarily providing many of the services that their patients craved—such as emergency out-of-hours cover. Rumbling controversy over this perceived injustice led eventually to a new agreement between the government and the British Medical Association (BMA) in February 2008, with GPs reluctantly agreeing to renegotiate their collective contract, and offer weekend and evening services.

It did not take long for the BMA to get its own back on the government. In June 2008, as Mr Brown was still reeling from a succession of major political blows including a pasting at the May local elections and a high-profile row over the abolition of the 10p starting rate of Income Tax, it seized the opportunity to declare war publicly over ministers' plans to establish a new England-wide network of 150 Continental-style 'polyclinics'—that is, multidisciplinary one-stop shops for NHS treatment, where patients would be able to drop in to see GPs, district nurses, and specialist practitioners under one roof. Health Minister Lord Darzi argued that the launch of these 'super-surgeries', which would open from 8 a.m. to 8 p.m. seven days a week, could only benefit the public. But the BMA claimed that they would undermine existing GP services, by poaching their patients and depriving them of funds, and that the involvement of private firms in running the clinics amounted to backdoor privatization of NHS primary care—making patients subservient to shareholders. Although furiously denied by Mr Brown, the claims enabled GP leaders to collect a 1.2 million-strong petition opposing the policy.

Indeed, summer 2008 saw a frenzy of activity from ministers keen to wrest back the political initiative over the future of the NHS. First, Health Secretary Mr Johnson appeared on BBC1's *Andrew Marr Show* announcing plans to end the postcode lottery by forcing all PCTs to provide the same treatments throughout the country (see pp. 183–5). Within 48 hours of his announcement, Lord Darzi, the experienced surgeon appointed a health minister in Mr Brown's first ministerial reshuffle, published the recommendations of a year-long review into the next ten years of NHS funding, in which he unveiled plans to award hospitals multimillion-pound bonuses for demonstrating top-quality clinical performance. Assessments of their success in this area would be based both on hard data—covering everything from waiting times for operations, to the death rates of individual surgeons—and views of patients on the quality of treatment that they receive at hospitals. Also proposed was a new 'NHS constitution' outlining what patients have a right to expect from the health service, including dignity, privacy, and confidentiality (an echo of the 'Patients' Charter', an earlier statement of rights introduced by John Major and updated by Mr Blair's government when it first came to power). In addition, 15 million people with long-term health conditions, such as asthma and diabetes, will be given new personalized care plans, with 5,000 taking part in a pilot scheme to give them greater control over their treatment through a 'personal health budget'—a reform already in place in relation to domiciliary care provided by council social services departments for the elderly and mentally ill (see pp. 561–2).

No sooner had Parliament reconvened after the 2008 summer recess than the NHS was starting to make headlines again—even when almost everything else had been forced off the news agenda by the global financial crisis. The cause of the latest controversy was the revelation by a commercial drugs company that it had signed contracts with some thirty hospital trusts to provide private 'top-up' treatment not available on the NHS to cancer patients in their own homes. At the time, ministers' official position was that private top-ups to NHS treatment were banned. But in November 2008, Mr Johnson over-turned the top-up ban—in response to recommendations by 'Cancer Tsar' for England Mike Richards—saying they would be permitted, on condition that they were acquired at a 'different time and in a different place' to where the NHS treatment was provided.

▌ Making complaints about the NHS

As things stand, anyone dissatisfied with the quality of his or her NHS treat-ment may make a formal complaint, initially at local level, and his or her case may be referred to one of three Health Service Commissioners—cov-ering England, Scotland and Wales. In practice, these posts are held collec-tively by a single official, dubbed the 'Health Service Ombudsman', who is also *Parliamentary Commissioner for Administration*, or the *Parliamentary Ombudsman*. A separate office exists in Northern Ireland.

The Commissioner, who produces an annual report for consideration by Parliament, handles complaints from patients in relation to:

- failure in service standards from an NHS body;
- failure to provide a service to which a person is entitled;
- maladministration by an NHS body;
- failure in the exercise of clinical judgement by hospitals or GPs.

Complaints are handled in according to the sequence outlined in Table 6.4.

Table 6.4 The complaints process to the Health Service Commissioner (Health Service Ombudsman)

Stage	Process
Stage 1 (Local resolution)	The complainant and the 'complaints manager' (an official appointed by the trust, GP, or other respondent) try to resolve the dispute between them at local level.
Stage 2 (Independent review)	A specially trained member of the trust or health authority, known as a 'convener', asks an independent layperson to arbitrate between the complainant and the respondent.
Stage 3 (Intervention by Ombudsman)	As a last resort, the Ombudsman intervenes directly. He or she is interested not only in the substance of a complaint, but in how it has been handled before reaching him or her.

In addition, the Social Care (Community Standards) Act 2003 set up the Commission for Healthcare, Audit and Inspection (or **Healthcare Commission**), a self-styled 'independent watchdog' charged with promoting ongoing improvements in the health service and reviewing complaints by service users unhappy with the local resolution of their cases. Individuals must, however, have gone through the full NHS complaints procedure before their cases can be referred to this **quango**. As of April 2008, its functions were due to be combined with those of the **Commission for Social Care Inspection (CSCI)** (see p. 569) under a new joint body, the Care Quality Commission (CQC), authorized to issue trusts with fines, fixed penalties, and enforcement notices for breaking the terms of their registrations—and even withdraw NHS licences from acute hospitals that persistently fail cleanliness inspections.

Oversight of the performance of the NHS at local level is also now carried out by **health service scrutiny committees** set up by county councils and unitary authorities. These tend to be made up of around 15 members, including a chairperson and vice-chairperson. Membership is drawn not only from the county or unitary authority, but also for local district or **borough councils**, and relevant voluntary organizations, such as Age Concern, the National Society for the Prevention of Cruelty to Children (NSPCC), and the National Association for Mental Health (Mind). Finally, the NHS is also held accountable in England and Wales by the **Audit Commission**, which scrutinizes the accounts of each and every trust, PCT, and STA. Its Scottish equivalent is Audit Scotland, while the Northern Ireland Audit Office (NIAO) performs this role in that province.

→ Further reading

Ham, C. (2004) *Health Policy in Britain: The Politics and Organisation of The National Health Service*, 5th edn, London: Palgrave Macmillan. **Fifth edition of leading text on the history and evolution of the health service, including updates on the reforms of the Blair government, and developments in health policy in Scotland, Wales, and Northern Ireland since devolution.**

Klein, R. (2006) *The New Politics of the NHS: From Creation to Reinvention*, Abingdon: Radcliffe Publishing. **Comprehensive overview of the history of the health service, starting with its creation in the post-war period and charting its evolution up to the present day.**

Pollock, A. M. (2006) *NHS plc: The Privatisation of Our Health Care*, London: Verso Books. **Thoughtful critique of the growing involvement of the private sector in running the NHS by Allyson M. Pollock, professor of health policy and health services research at University College London.**

Pollock, A. M. and Talbot-Smith, A. (2006) *The New NHS: A Guide to Its Funding, Organisation and Accountability*, London: Routledge. **Indispensable guide to the changing internal structure and practices of the NHS since the introduction of the internal market, including overviews of New Labour's patient choice agenda and the Ten-Year NHS Plan.**

? Review questions

1. What were the founding NHS principles? To what extent were they ever achieved?

2. Labour pledged to scrap the Conservatives' internal market when it returned to power, but many argue that it actually consolidated the Tory model. Who is right and why?

3. Can the NHS still be described as a 'national' health service? If not, why not?

4. Given the variable needs and demands of different areas of the UK, what are the arguments for and against pursuing the NHS ideal?

5. Outline what is meant by the concept of 'patient choice'. What measures have been introduced so far to put this idea into practice—and how successful have they been?

Online resource centre

www.oxfordtextbooks.co.uk/orc/Morrison

Visit the Online Resource Centre that accompanies this book for web links and regular updates.

7

The Treasury, industry, and the utilities

During the 2002 US presidential election race, James Carville, campaign strategist for then aspiring Democratic nominee Bill Clinton, coined a phrase that was to go down in political (and journalistic) folklore. Commenting on the issue that he felt was most important in persuading the US electorate to back a candidate, he said simply 'the economy, stupid'. So it is, arguably, in Britain. Although historians and political scientists have observed that UK voters do not always switch horses at times of economic crisis (the deep *recession* of the early 1990s saw John Major return the Conservatives to power, albeit with a drastically reduced majority), perceived economic competence has proved the making of certain prime ministers (Margaret Thatcher; Tony Blair), and the downfall of others (Ted Heath; James Callaghan).

This chapter explores the work of the two principal government departments charged with overseeing the British economy: HM Treasury and the Department for Business, Enterprise, and Regulatory Reform (BERR)—which was, until recently, the Department for Trade and Industry (DTI). It will examines the remit and composition of the main non-departmental bodies charged with managing specific areas of economic performance, such as the *Bank of England*'s *Monetary Policy Committee (MPC)* and the *Office of Fair Trading (OFT)*.

▌ The role of the Treasury and the Chancellor of the Exchequer

In recent years, it has become customary for prime ministers to appoint deputy prime ministers to stand in for them when they are absent on foreign business or on holiday. If there can be said to be a 'true' deputy prime minister, however, it is the Chancellor of the Exchequer. Charged with controlling the government's purse strings, the Chancellor is indisputably the most powerful minister in *Cabinet*, beside the premier. The workings of government would quite simply grind to a halt if it were not for taxes and loans, and it is the Chancellor's job to raise this money. Even the name of the department that he or she heads—the Treasury—testifies to his or her authority: not for nothing is the prime ministers's official title 'First Lord of the Treasury'.

The Chancellor has the following key responsibilities:

- overseeing the government's public spending commitments by managing fiscal policy—that is, the raising or lowering of taxes and/or duties, and their investment in public services (schools, hospitals, prisons);
- managing the national debt—that is, the level of borrowing needed to top up taxation revenues in order to finance the government's spending programme;
- promoting economic growth in the UK economy and encouraging British exports;
- controlling domestic *inflation* and unemployment.

In recognition of the huge degree of responsibility that comes with the post of Chancellor, he or she is assisted by one of the largest ministerial teams of any Whitehall department. Unlike most other ministries, the Treasury boasts at least three secretaries of state in addition to the Chancellor: the Chief Secretary to the Treasury, the Financial Secretary to the Treasury, and the Economic Secretary to the Treasury.

Fiscal policy and taxation

One of the principal means by which British governments have traditionally attempted to control the economy is through so-called 'tax and spend' tactics—more formally known as 'fiscal policy'. Based on the writings of

Liberal economist John Maynard Keynes, fiscal policy rests on the raising or lowering of taxation to influence the consumer behaviour—and/or to improve the health of the government's finances. By raising Income Tax rates, for example, the Chancellor effectively cuts individuals' take-home pay and, by extension, spending power—which should have the knock-on effect of reducing demand for goods and services, thereby curbing inflation. At the same time, raising taxes will increase government revenue for public spending on schools, hospitals, etc., and reduce the need for the Chancellor to *borrow* money (increasing the size of the 'national debt' into the bargain).

Until the 1980s, there was a broad post-war consensus in favour of managing the economy via fiscal policy (although, on balance, it tended to be favoured more by Labour governments than by Conservative ones). Labour's enthusiasm arose largely out of its traditional emphasis on taxation as an instrument for redistributing income from higher to lower earners through the benefits system. From the advent of the National Health Service (NHS) onwards, Labour also gained a reputation as the 'high tax party' on account of its ideological commitment to strong investment in state health care and education (all of which required high tax revenues). Prior to the Thatcher years, the party also favoured the public ownership of many industries and these, too, required huge injections of money to keep them maintained.

There are two broad types of taxation: **direct taxes** and **indirect taxes**. Direct taxes are those that are 'up front'—that is, those explicitly taken from individuals or businesses as deductions from their basic earnings—and the main types are outlined in Table 7.1.

The fact that direct taxation is charged at different rates, according to an individual's or company's income, means that it is often also referred to as 'progressive taxation'. By taking into account people's 'ability to pay', it is seen as fairer than a simple flat rate charge—such as a water bill, for example, or a television licence—which costs the same to everyone, regardless of their earnings.

By contrast, indirect taxes do the opposite and, as a result, are often described as 'regressive'. Unlike income or corporation taxes, they are 'built in' to the prices of goods and services that consumers buy (including basic utilities such as gas and electricity, without which it is hard to live). Because these 'pay as you spend' charges—often described as 'hidden' or 'stealth taxes'—are levied at across-the-board rates, they take no account of individuals' ability to pay. The two most familiar—VAT and tobacco/alcohol duties—are set out in Table 7.2.

Table 7.1 Types of direct taxation in the UK—and how they work

Tax	How administered	Rates (2008–09)	Notes
Income	Paid by working people through either Pay As You Earn (PAYE) contributions deducted from their gross salaries by their employers, or as retrospective payments to HM Revenue and Customs (HMRC) by self-employed	Personal allowance— £ 6035 Standard rate— 20% (20p in £) Higher rate— 40% (40p in £) Top rate—45% (45p in £) to come in for those earning £150,000 or more from 2011	As of the 2008–09 tax year (4 April–3 April), the 10% starting rate introduced by Gordon Brown as Chancellor for those earning less than £2,230 above their £5,225 'personal allowance' (the amount that they can earn before paying tax) has been scrapped. But the standard rate—for those earning up to around £35,000—has been cut from 22% to 20%. The upper rate of 40% remains, although the level at which this kicks in was reduced by Mr Darling (from £41,435 to £40,835) in May 2008, as part of a package of measures designed to compensate low-paid workers who had lost out because of the abolition of the 10p rate. At the same time, everyone benefited from a £600 increase in their personal allowances, to £6,035. The November 2008 pre-Budget Report raised it further for basic rate taxpayers, to £6,475 for 2009–10.
Corporation	Paid by companies on their profits—an 'income tax for companies'	Small companies' rate—22% (22p in £) Main rate—28% (28p in £)	As with Income Tax, the standard rate (known as the 'main rate') was reduced in 2008–09, from 30% to 28%. The main rate applies to any company whose profits in a given tax year are £1.5m or more. But the small companies' rate is due to be raised in 2009 from 19% to 22%. The government has moved to counter criticisms of this by offering small businesses a 100% relief on any capital investment up to £50,000, and a 175% tax credit to encourage research and development.
Capital gains (CGT)	Paid by the owners of financial assets, property, and other items, such as expensive jewellery or sports cars, sold by them for personal gain	Entrepreneurs' rate—10% (10p in £) General rate— 18% (18p in £)	There has been huge controversy about capital gains in the British media recently, in light of the mammoth profits made by 'private equity firms'—groups of wealthy speculators who club together to buy underperforming companies, turn their fortunes around, and sell them on for profit. Amid mounting criticism of the sector (some directors are reputed to pay less Income Tax than their cleaners), the UK government recently introduced a new 18% flat rate for CGT for anyone whose gain exceeds £1m—although Mr Darling later watered down this reform by bowing to pressure for a 10% rate (dubbed 'entrepreneurs' relief') for gains of less than £1m.

(continued)

Tax	How administered	Rates (2008–09)	Notes
Inheritance (IHT)	A 'death duty' paid in respect of value of estates (including financial assets, property, and other valuable items) handed down from the deceased to friends or family members by the executors of their wills	40% (40p in £) for legacies of over £600,000	Until recently, it was charged at 40% on all estates worth £300,000-plus, but mounting controversy over the low level of this threshold (average house prices were near that level by 2007) prompted Mr Darling to use his first Pre-Budget Report to double it with immediate effect for married couples and those in civil partnerships seeking to bequeath their estates to their children. He was widely criticized, however, for 'stealing' a Conservative policy: only weeks earlier, Shadow Chancellor George Osborne had pledged to raise the threshold to £1m.

 NOTE: A regularly updated version of this table can be found on the Online Resource Centre that accompanies this book.

Major public spending announcements have historically been reserved for the Budget (see p. 212), but in 1997, Mr Brown introduced a new innovation designed to set out publicly his spending plans for three years at a time. The idea was partly motivated by a desire to create the appearance of greater financial transparency; it was also intended to encourage individual spending departments dependent on Mr Brown's handouts to plan in a more long-term way, rather than from year to year as previously. Spending reviews are generally held on a three-yearly basis, but two of them—in 1998 and 2007, respectively—were termed *Comprehensive Spending Reviews (CSRs)*, in recognition of their more wide-ranging outlooks.

Managing national debt

Other than raising taxes, the principal way in which governments fund public spending is through borrowing. Chancellors run what is known as the *public sector net cash requirement (PSNCR)*. Formerly the 'public sector borrowing requirement' (PSBR), this is effectively the difference between the total that the government intends to spend on public services and the amount that is available to it through taxation revenue. To avoid unpopular tax rises, governments have historically favoured loans as a means of financing costly public expenditure. Usually, this is done by selling bonds (known as 'gilt-edged securities', or 'gilts') to the public. Government borrowing is projected to sour to record levels of £118bn in 2009-10 following the announcement of emergency measures designed to limit the impact of recession in the 2008 Pre-Budget Report (see p.221).

Table 7.2 Types of indirect taxation in the UK—and how they work

Name	How administered	Rates (2008–09)	Notes
Value-added tax (VAT)	A 'hidden tax' embedded in the retail prices of items that consumers buy in supermarkets, high street stores, and online	17.5% (17.5p in the £) ; cut to 15% for 13 months from December 2008	For essential items like domestic fuel and power there is a reduced rate of 5%, while certain items are exempt—including food, children's clothes, books, newspapers and magazines, and some equipment for the disabled
Tobacco products duty and alcohol excise duties	Embedded in the retail price of items that are subject to excise duty	22% (22p in £) on packet of 20 cigarettes, plus £108.65 per thousand cigarettes 21.35% (21.35p in £) per litre of spirits and wine exceeding 22% ABV 248.85p in £ per hectolitre of wine and sparkling wine of 8.5–15% alcohol by volume (ABV) 14.96% (14.96p in £) per hectolitre of beer	Always controversial among smokers and drinkers, these are significantly higher in Britain than elsewhere in the European Union. Duties on alcohol products range widely from one to another: the 2007 Budget saw the tenth consecutive freeze in duty on spirits, but that on beer rose by 1p a pint. Petrol duties have also been a source of unrest in recent years, in light of the increasing underlying price of car fuel caused by the ongoing global oil crisis.
Fuel tax escalator	Additional tax added to VAT on motor fuel	50% (50p in £) per litre for unleaded petrol and diesel 30% (30p in £) per litre for biodiesel and bio-ethanol	In 2000, Mr Brown was reviled by farmers and long-distance hauliers for raising fuel duty—known as the 'fuel tax escalator'—at a time of already rising prices. His action led to the first large-scale protest of the Blair era, as convoys of angry fuel protestors clogged the M1 and M6. More recently, Mr Darling delayed a planned 2p rise in recognition of similar oil price hikes, at a time of more general rises in consumer prices. The AA had argued that the average monthly bill of filling up a car with unleaded petrol had topped £100.

 NOTE: A regularly updated version of this table can be found on the Online Resource Centre that accompanies this book.

At times of acute economic crisis, it has also been necessary for governments to approach global financial institutions. In the mid-1970s, then Labour Prime Minister James Callaghan was forced to borrow money from the International Monetary Fund (IMF)—a crisis bank that Britain had helped to

found in the wake of the Second World War (see p. 333)—to stabilize the UK economy as it was buffeted by stagflation—that is, rising inflation and unemployment at the same time. The IMF only agreed on condition that the government made substantial public spending cuts to save money. Documents released by the National Archive in December 2006 under the '30-Year Rule'—a convention stipulating that all but the most sensitive government papers should be made public 30 years after being written (a gift for journalists!)—revealed that the country nearly had to scrap its nuclear deterrent simply to balance the books.

More recently, it emerged that the huge injections of extra funding into the NHS and state education system under New Labour have been financed largely by borrowing. According to figures released in early 2008, having initially dropped sharply after the party returned to power in 1997, the national debt more than doubled between 2001–02 and 2007–08, leaping from £315.5bn to £650bn. It rose by £100bn in one stroke at the height of the Northern Rock crisis, when the government bailed out the Northern Rock bank in an effort to save the deposits of its customers and restore confidence in the UK financial sector following the bank's near-collapse at the end of 2007. Northern Rock—which had overstretched itself by making high-risk home loans to customers without the guaranteed means of repaying them—initially made an emergency plea for support to the Bank of England (reflecting trends in the so-called US 'sub-prime market'). It was eventually nationalized by the government, as a 'temporary measure', after months of talks to find a suitable private buyer failed.

By this time, however, the bill for propping up the beleaguered bank had already topped £100bn (more than the total annual spend on the NHS). Britain's national debt currently costs UK taxpayers £31bn a year in interest—marginally less than the country's defence budget. In a further sign that the government's grip on public finances was slipping, in July 2008, Mr Darling revealed that he was reviewing Mr Brown's so-called 'Golden Rule' governing fiscal policy: the principle, adhered to for more than a decade, that the government should only borrow for public *investment*, rather than *current spending*. In a swift move designed to signify that ministers had learned lessons from the Northern Rock debacle, in September 2008, Mr Darling wasted little time nationalizing the assets of another bank, the Bradford and Bingley, to prevent its collapse. While some media critics immediately accused him and Mr Brown of again using taxpayers' money to secure irresponsible loans made by a reckless bank at the height of the credit boom, they were widely praised for avoiding spending much more than £3bn of public money in the end, by instigating a new Financial Services Compensation Scheme (FSCS) introduced in response to the Northern Rock crisis. This mechanism, triggered by the Financial Services Authority (FSA), forced the banking sector as a whole to absorb Bradford and Bingley's losses, while still guaranteeing protection to those with savings in the bank of initially up to £35,000 (see p. 222).

Controlling inflation and unemployment

Inflation and employment have a complex relationship. Historically, when the cost of living—inflation—is rising, unemployment tends to be low, and vice versa. Only at certain crisis points—the Depression; the late 1970s oil crash—have both risen sharply at the same time.

The reasons for this trade-off relate to basic economics. When the prices of goods and services rise, this tends to mean one of two things: either demand for them is high—that is, shops and manufacturers can get away with charging more, because people are willing and able to pay—or the cost of producing them is rising. If the cost of producing goods is rising, this will often be down to rising wage bills—in other words, the fact(s) that more workers have been taken on to produce and deliver those goods or services, and/or that their salaries have risen.

Conversely, at times when demand for goods is falling, the first casualties tend to be at least some of the workers employed to produce them. Employers will lay off workers to reduce their running costs and to enable them to continue in business on a more manageable scale, cutting prices to attract more custom if necessary. If such redundancies become more widespread in the economy, overall unemployment will rise. And, of course, at times of high unemployment, people have less money to spend on goods and services—so prices will have to fall further if consumer demand is to be sustained.

Therefore, rising unemployment tends to lead to falling inflation. A knock-on effect of this is a reduction in economic growth—that is, the expansion of the economy through rising demand for goods and services, and increased private sector investment, job creation, and exports. Theoretically, growth can be an ever-increasing circle: more jobs should mean more people with money to buy things, more companies manufacturing goods, and higher employment. In practice, the promotion of free trade has meant that many of the products that British people are now buying are cheap imports from the

Far East and elsewhere—which means that they no longer necessarily lead to industrial expansion and job creation in the UK.

Given the tensile nature of this relationship between inflation and unemployment—referred to by economists as the 'inflation–unemployment see-saw'—governments find it difficult to keep a grip on both for any length of time. When New Labour was elected in 1997, Mr Brown pledged to put an end to the 'boom-and-bust economy' of previous decades by doing just this, but despite the fact that Britain enjoyed a decade of sustained growth afterwards, and that both inflation and unemployment were kept at reasonable levels, signs of an economic slowdown are becoming ever more obvious.

The role of the Bank of England in monetary policy

If fiscal policy was the favoured approach to keeping the British economy afloat in the 1950s and 1960s, *monetary policy* was the vogue throughout the 1980s and 1990s. Widely credited as the 'invention' of free market US economist Milton Friedman (a hero of Mrs Thatcher's), this contrasting approach to economic management involves **interest rates**—that is, the cost of borrowing money—being used to direct consumer behaviour and control inflation. The theory is that if rates rise, people will be more likely to *save* money (banks and building societies should theoretically be offering them a profitable return for their investment) and less likely to *spend or borrow* it (credit cards and loans will cost more).

In Britain, inflation figures are calculated on a monthly basis. The government uses two tools for measuring them: the **retail prices index (RPI)** and the **consumer prices index (CPI)**. Both track movements in the prices of notional 'baskets' of goods bought regularly by a 'typical' household—including food, clothes, household products, tobacco, and motoring costs. The difference between the two is that the CPI—the measure preferred by governments—*excludes* more volatile items, such as energy bills and mortgage payments, and places more emphasis on items that people buy only occasionally, such as DVD players and other electronic goods, than day-to-day expenses. Given that these are the costs that most burden households, critics view the CPI as highly misleading. Nonetheless, the use of these statistics has enabled Labour to maintain low 'headline inflation' figures on the whole since regaining power, even if the 'underlying inflation' cited by the Opposition and some economists has begun to rise.

Until 1997, responsibility for reviewing interest rates each month rested with the Chancellor. Within days of taking on that job, however, Mr Brown made the Bank of England independent—in so doing, handing it the task of controlling inflation on his behalf. In practice, decisions about interest rates would in future rest with a new Monetary Policy Committee (MPC), made up of nine members, including the bank's chief economist, and chaired by its governor. The government would set an inflationary target—currently, 2 per cent—and if this were missed, according to CPI figures, the governor would have to write formally to the Chancellor to explain why and to lay out the action that the MPC intended to take to lower it. In April 2007, Mervyn King became the first incumbent to have to do this, when headline inflation hit 3.1 per cent.

The quest for full employment

Successive Labour Chancellors, in particular, have long dreamt of the holy grail of 'full employment'—an ideal state in which everyone capable of working can find a job suited to their abilities and aspirations. In practice, full employment remains elusive.

At certain times, unemployment rates in Britain have reached levels that have been politically damaging for the government of the day. In the early 1980s, Mrs Thatcher's mass closure of coal pits, steelworks, and shipyards in northern England and Wales, combined with her crackdown on trade union power (see p. 225), saw the national jobless total rise to around four million. While Labour has largely maintained a much lower official unemployment rate than this—using a combination of 'carrot' and 'stick' policies, such as tax credits and its so-called 'New Deal', to entice people off benefits and back to work—nationwide unemployment still hovers around 1.5 million-plus. Moreover, there has been huge criticism of the increasing 'casualiza-tion' now widespread in the British working environment—with many of the new jobs created over the past decade taking the form of part-time and/or short-term contracts devoid of the entitlements (for example, pensions, holi-day pay) that are available to full-time, permanent staff.

Some of these themes are discussed in more detail in the next chapter.

Promoting economic growth and UK exports

A word that strikes fear and terror into the hearts of prime ministers and Chancellors is 'recession'—a term describing a rapid economic slowdown. Technically speaking, a recession is signalled by a period of two succes-sive economic quarters during which the economy 'shrinks'—that is, during which less money is being borrowed and spent by consumers, leading to lower sales and profits for businesses, the scaling back of production, and redundancies. Britain has lived through two recent recessions—in the early 1980s and 1990s—both associated with prolonged high unemployment. At the time of writing, Mr. Darling had recently confirmed that the economy was about to sink into a new recession.

Little wonder that governments have become so obsessed with achieving growth. There are two engines of this growth: rising employment and prosperity among a country's citizens, leading to increasing domestic demand and the development of overseas export markets for products manufactured at home. In theory, each of these should lead to wealth creation.

We have already examined the inflation–unemployment quandary and how British governments have tried to boost the economy by juggling these 'twin evils'. But how do they go about promoting the UK's exports abroad—and measuring their success or failure in doing so? Taking the latter question first, there are two measures:

- the *balance of trade*—that is, the difference in value between the total of all goods and services bought by British residents from overseas (imports) and that of all British-made goods and services sold abroad (exports) in a given year. This includes both visible products (physical goods, such as food, clothes, and television sets) and invisible ones (virtual goods, such as information technology and financial services);

- the *balance of payments*—that is, the difference in value between the total of *all* payments of every kind flowing between the UK and other countries, including imports and exports, but also financial transfers and debt payments to foreigners. The balance of trade is therefore a 'subset' of the balance of payments.

If, in a given financial year, either of these two measures indicates that Britain is buying more foreign imports than it is selling exports overseas, its current account will be in *deficit*. This means that (like individuals whose monthly outgoings exceed their wages) the country is 'in the red'. In contrast, if the UK sells more abroad than it buys in, it is in *surplus*.

Recent decades—particularly since the advent of Britain's membership of the European Union (EU) (see p. 281)—have seen the UK importing disproportionate quantities of cheap foreign clothing, toys, electrical items, and motor vehicles. The slow decline of indigenous industries such as shipbuilding and coalmining, meanwhile, has seen the emphasis of the country's economic output switch to services such as telecommunications, information technology (IT), and the stock market (see p. 219). As a result, while the UK has historically had a significant balance of trade deficit in terms of visible items, its service sector has often generated a surplus. The UK's overall deficit in trade on goods and services was £4.7bn in December 2007, according to the Office of National Statistics (ONS), but, when broken down into the two categories, it showed a £2.9bn surplus in the service sector, compared to a £7.6bn deficit in goods.

In view of the high importance attached to the balance of trade, successive Chancellors have tried to incentivise people to 'buy British', both at home and abroad. Prior to its entry into the then European Economic Community (EEC) in 1975, Britain had a history of doing this through 'protectionism'. It would levy customs duties (or tariffs) on companies seeking to import foreign goods into the UK—a tactic designed to inflate their prices artificially and to encourage consumers to 'buy British' (saving jobs as a consequence).

An alternative approach is to try to influence international exchange rates for the British currency, the pound sterling. Both Labour and Tory Chancellors have, in the past, 'devalued' the pound—for example, by issuing more banknotes to increase the overall money supply in the economy. The idea was that, by reducing sterling's value, they would be cutting the price of British goods abroad—making them more attractive to foreign buyers and boosting the country's exports. But the relative value of the pound is affected by other factors, too—including the 'demand' for sterling at any one time in world money markets. Fear of *undermining* the value of the pound was at the heart of Tory Chancellor Norman Lamont's decision to pull Britain out of the European exchange rate mechanism (ERM)—which was designed to harmonize the exchange rates of all EU member states. (This is explored in detail in Chapter 9.)

In addition to the balance of trade and balance of payments, there are two other 'litmus tests' of the current state of economic growth in the economy:

- *gross domestic product (GDP)*—the total profit from all goods and services produced in Britain in a given year, irrespective of which country derives income from them;
- *gross national product (GNP)*—the total profit from all goods and services produced by British companies in a given year, irrespective of where they are produced.

It has become customary for governments to cite favourable GDPs as evidence of the strong performance of their economies. In reality, however, while a high GDP should bring down unemployment (a foreign-owned company on UK soil is as likely to generate jobs as a British one), and to contribute to increased spending and investment in the local economy where a factory or call centre is based, for example, this is only part of the picture. The bulk of the income generated by foreign-owned companies will flow back to the countries in which they are based, limiting the longer-term benefits to the British economy brought by those that choose to relocate to the country. Conversely, GNP may often give a truer indication of levels of wealth generation for the UK economy: the numerous British-based telecoms firms that have recently outsourced their call centres to the Far East, where labour costs are cheaper, may have done little to help Britain's employment figures, but most of the income that they generate will go to the Treasury.

▶ The Budget process

The highlight of the Treasury's calendar is the annual Budget Speech and accompanying Finance Act. This used to take place in the autumn, but is now held in spring. Since Mr Brown became Chancellor, the Budget itself has been preceded by an annual Pre-Budget Report (or 'Pre-Budget Statement'), released during the previous autumn. Initially, this was intended simply to set the scene for prospective tax and spending plans to be announced in the Budget, acting as a 'health check' on the performance of the British economy over the preceding 12 months. More recently, the Pre-Budget Report has become almost as much of a news story as the Budget itself—with Chancellors going into increasing detail about their plans and using it as an opportunity to test public opinion on changes that they are considering.

In his inaugural Pre-Budget Report, Mr Darling signalled several head-line-grabbing changes—including his intention to introduce a flat rate tax of 18 per cent on all capital gains over £1m. After several months of sustained lobbying on behalf of small businesses, led by the Confederation of British Industry (CBI), he performed a U-turn, announcing that upcoming 'entrepreneurs' would qualify for an 8 per cent reduction (see p. 203). Fearing further reprisals from within the business community—which Labour had assiduously courted since winning power—he also backtracked on plans to tighten up tax regulations relating to wealthy UK-based 'non-domiciles' (or 'non-doms')—that is, individuals living and working in Britain, but registered for tax in another country. Mr Darling had been expected to force them to disclose details of offshore financial holdings, but instead limited his actions in the subsequent Budget to introducing the promised £30,000 a year 'wealth tax' for non-doms. Beyond this, they would continue to pay only tax related to their UK-based earnings in Britain.

The Budget itself, generally held in early March, has two elements:

- the Budget Speech;
- the Finance Act.

The Budget Speech

The Budget Speech is designed to:

- forecast short to medium-term movements in the economy (1–3 years), and review how it has performed in the preceding 12 months;
- announce rises and/or cuts in direct and indirect taxation, and public spending, and the prioritization of particular areas over others (for example, health, education, defence);
- announce new taxes, tax breaks, and/or benefits to finance investment and/or help low-income groups (for example, tax credits, cold weather payments for the elderly);
- give the Chancellor a platform for political grandstanding—allowing him or her to boast about the country's economic performance.

The speech—which occasionally runs for more than an hour—is immediately followed by a similarly lengthy retort from the Shadow Chancellor or Leader of the Opposition and a debate on the floor of the Commons. More than 150 years after the event, William Gladstone holds the dubious honour of having delivered the longest ever continuous Budget Speech. His 1853 address lasted four hours and 45 minutes.

The Finance Act

For measures announced in the Budget to take effect, the Commons must legislate to implement them. Unlike most legislation, however, the Bill needed to carry through the proposals is given swift passage and substantially passed on the same day as the Speech. Dubbed the 'Finance Bill', it is designated a 'money Bill' by the *Speaker*—enabling it to bypass the usual stages that Bills must negotiate before receiving the *Royal Assent*. The initial 'stages' are effectively gone through in one fell swoop, with the Speech itself being treated as the *first reading* and the rest of the process fast-tracked. The Commons must pass individual resolutions to approve each specific tax or duty change within ten sitting days, but, under the Collection of Taxes Act 1968, minor changes can be agreed immediately—to enable the business of government to continue in the interim. The Bill's *second reading* must be heard within 30 days, but the *committee stage* may be split, with more important resolutions heard by a committee of the whole house and the remaining ones considered by a standing committee of 30–40 MPs. Following this arduous process, the *third reading* will be steamrollered through, usually on the second day of the *report stage*.

Since the confrontation between the Commons and the House of Lords over David Lloyd George's 1909 'People's Budget', there has been no Lords stage to the Finance Bill (see p. 75). Nonetheless, even today, there is potential scope for Budgets to fall at a late hurdle. The row over Labour's abolition of the 10p starting rate of Income Tax so raised the hackles of backbench rebels led by former Welfare Minister Frank Field that, prior to the announcement of a compensation package for low earners penalized by the change, it looked as if Mr Darling's first Budget might be defeated—inevitably forcing his resignation. In the event, he staved off this prospect by issuing an 'emergency Budget' designed to compensate the losers—some of whom stood to be left £230 a year worse off. This raised the Income Tax threshold—that is, the minimum income above which the tax must be paid—by £600, lifting 600,000 people out of tax altogether. The move was backdated to 1 April—meaning that everyone paying the new 20 per cent basic tax rate, but not earning enough to pay it at 40 per cent, gained a staggered 'rebate', through their pay packets, of £120. In the November 2008 Pre-Budget Report, this 'bonus' was made permanent—and raised to £145 from 2009–10.

Public spending outside England—the Barnett Formula

To ensure that the three UK countries outside England—Scotland, Wales, and Northern Ireland—benefit fairly out of central government tax revenues, public spending is allocated on a per capita basis across Britain using a system called the 'Barnett Formula'. In theory, the formula—devised in the late 1970s by then Labour Chief Secretary to the Treasury Joel Barnett—ensures that the amount given to each country corresponds to its population size (and, by definition, the extent to which its inhabitants have contributed to taxes).

In practice, the formula has proved highly controversial—successive recalculations have benefited Scotland, in particular, relatively more than the rest of the UK. Resentment between it and the other countries has escalated since *devolution* was introduced in 1998, because not only has Holyrood continued to do disproportionately well out of taxes, but the *Scottish Parliament* has used the freedom granted to it to spend its share of the money as it chooses to subsidize its public sector in ways unseen elsewhere. Barnett has, among other things, enabled Scotland to reject university top-up fees and to begin phasing out NHS prescription charges—two highly controversial levies that remain elsewhere.

▌ The government's role in promoting British industry and commerce

Other than their tax and spend policies, for the past thirty years British governments have taken an increasingly laissez-faire approach to running the economy. The mass privatization programme of the 1980s saw a swathe of industries sold into private ownership, from motor manufacturer British Leyland to British Airways, British Steel, all of the major utilities (gas, electricity, water), and, ultimately, the railways. In the decades since, the mantra has been one of 'consumer choice', with successive governments promoting the idea of competition between rival private-sector providers over any state monopoly. In theory, this allows people to shop around for the best deals on virtually any product—with market forces (supply and demand) ensuring that they are high quality and competitively priced.

In practice, however, the government continues to play an interventionist role in promoting the interests of British industry and protecting it from the worst ravages of *globalization*—the process by which national economies are becoming absorbed by a greater international whole. The decision by ministers to step in to save a succession of banks and earlier attempts to broker a rescue package for the Rover car company—the last surviving British-owned motor manufacturer until its collapse in 2005—demonstrate this. Moreover, the free market ideal of a private sector that, left alone, will 'regulate itself' efficiently and fairly has proved elusive—forcing the state to introduce greater regulation.

The Department for Business, Enterprise and Regulatory Reform (BERR)

The department responsible for promoting British industry and commerce, and overseeing regulation of the free market within the UK, is the

Department for Business, Enterprise and Regulatory Reform (BERR). Until summer 2007, it was known as the Department of Trade and Industry (DTI) and, before that, simply the Department of Trade.

Led by the Secretary of State for Business, Enterprise and Regulatory Reform, the Department's website describes it as '*the voice for business across government*'.

It has the following specific responsibilities:

- creating conditions for business success and raising productivity in the UK economy;
- championing the interests of employees and employers;
- promoting consumer interests;
- encouraging sustainable business development.

Although formal regulation of the business environment is delegated to a series of non-departmental bodies, there have been signs, since BERR replaced the DTI, that the Secretary of State for BERR may play a more hands-on role in future than in the recent past. Early in 2008, Mr Hutton publicly ordered BSkyB, the satellite broadcaster owned by Rupert Murdoch's multinational media company News Corp, to sell more than half its shares in rival company ITV. He was endorsing a ruling by the **Competition Commission** (see p. 218) that the shareholding represented 'a substantial lessening of competition' in the television market.

As well as overseeing the regulatory framework, it is the job of the Secretary of State for BERR to liaise regularly with the main bodies representing employees and employers: the Trades Union Congress (TUC) (see p. 226) and the CBI, respectively.

The roles of the regulatory authorities

While it is BERR's responsibility to draft the laws governing fair competition, consumer protection, and sustainable business, these are administered on the ground by two principal regulatory authorities: the Office of Fair Trading (OFT) and the Competition Commission.

The Office of Fair Trading (OFT)

Established in 1973, this *quango* is charged with ensuring that the 'rules' of fair play—in other words, genuine choice and competition—are actually applied in practice. Its remit is to protect both consumers and companies, ensuring that small businesses in particular are protected from anti-competitive practices by larger, more established rivals. Until 2003, the OFT was headed by a Director General of Fair Trading, but it is now run by a board, headed by a chairperson.

According to its current statement of aims, the OFT's duties are to:

- encourage businesses to comply with competition and consumer law, and to improve their trading practices through self-regulation;
- act decisively to stop hardcore or flagrant offenders;
- study markets and recommend action where required;
- empower consumers to make informed choices and get the best value from markets, and to help them to resolve problems with suppliers through Consumer Direct—a regionally based, government-funded advice service established in 2000.

It is the OFT that launches investigations into allegations of so-called 're-strictive practices'. These can take various forms, but, most commonly, a small or medium-sized business will complain that its attempt to break into an established market (for example, telecoms) is being frustrated by the fact that larger-scale, more-established companies are offering dis-counts on their wares that it cannot hope to match as it struggles with initial overheads. To some extent, being initially 'out-competed' by the big boys is inevitable as one tries to set oneself up in a new marketplace, but history is littered with examples of competition being deliberately stifled by established players using underhand means. The most notorious examples have occurred when rival companies have colluded to peg their prices at the same level and/or undercut potential new competitors by of-fering 'loss leaders' (cheap deals at below-cost price) to lure customers. These unofficial alliances—known as 'cartels'—can effectively stop new competitors getting established, by using economies of scale achieved through years of trading in the sector to sell certain items at unrealisti-cally low prices.

Companies have also been accused of unfair trading in relation to the prices that they pay their suppliers—that is, the businesses that make their prod-ucts. In recent years, there has been concern about the below-cost prices al-legedly offered by supermarket chains such as Tesco and Asda to producers in developing countries for everything from bananas to coffee, while British farmers have consistently complained of being offered unsustainably low prices for meat and dairy products. The appalling press generated by such controversies has prompted retailers to embrace 'fair trade' goods and to invest millions in corporate social responsibility (CSR).

Of course, it is not only other businesses that are hurt by restrictive practices: price-fixing can work upwards, as well as downwards, and, at times, consumers get the worst deal. In December 2007, Asda and Sainsbury's were among several companies forced to admit to having conspired to fix the price of milk between 2002 and 2003, following an OFT investigation. The supermarkets charged inflated prices for the product—despite offering farmers minimal payment for it at the other end of the food chain—and, as a result, the British consumer was left £270m out of pocket.

A separate regulator oversees the financial services sector—that is, banks, building societies, and insurance companies. This is the Financial Services Authority (FSA), the conduct of which was called into question following its failure to act on the banking sector's increasingly cavalier mortgage lending policies prior to the collapse of Northern Rock in late 2007 and the subsequent onset of the so-called 'credit crunch'—a crackdown on poorly secured mortgages and loans caused by a dramatic fall in confidence and liquidity in the banking sector (see p. 221).

The Competition Commission

Formerly known as the 'Monopolies and Mergers Commission', the Competition Commission is less concerned with the day-to-day market practices that preoccupy the OFT than with movements in company ownership that may potentially affect fair competition in future. Although most markets are now 'deregulated'—that is, open to full free market competition—in practice, there has been huge consolidation in many of them over the past decade, with larger, more profitable companies taking over or merging with smaller, less successful ones. As a result, markets that, at one time, offered dozens of alternatives from which consumers could choose are increasingly dominated by a handful of providers—and sometimes only one or two.

Nowhere is this lack of genuine competition more obvious than on supermarket shelves. While most stores offer myriad varieties of essentially the same products, many superficially different brands are actually made by a single company. Other than supermarkets' own-brand options, household cleaning products tend to be manufactured by Unilever, or Procter and Gamble; while many types of chocolate bar line the confectionary counter, most will somewhere bear the small print of Nestlé, Mars, or Cadbury.

It is the Commission's job to ensure that, wherever possible, choice is genuine. One way of doing this is to prevent mergers and takeovers that would otherwise restrict it—and avoid 'monopolies', which can be defined as a state in which one company has more than a 25 per cent market share in a particular product. Among the Commission's most high-profile recent rulings was its decision to approve supermarket chain Morrisons' takeover of rival Safeway in 2003—provided that it first agreed to sell off 53 stores in areas where local competition might suffer as a result of the acquisition. In February 2008, the Commission issued a much-anticipated report focusing on the question of whether the proliferation of out-of-town supermarkets was contributing to the decline of town centres and local grocery stores. It angered critics by finding no conclusive evidence to support this assertion—although it did argue that a new 'competition test' should in future be applied by local authorities when deciding whether to grant *planning permission* for superstores. In arguing for the test, it cited the example of the 'Tesco town' of Bicester in Oxfordshire, which is ringed by five branches of the supermarket chain. The report also disappointed campaigners by failing to compel major supermarket chains to dispose of so-called 'land banks'—areas of prime development land that they have acquired to prevent rivals building there.

Types of company

There are three main types of corporate structure in the UK:

- limited liability companies ('Ltds');
- private limited companies;
- public limited companies ('plcs').

The principal differences between the three are explained in Table 7.3.

The role of the Stock Exchange

Shares in plcs are traded on global stock markets, one of the biggest of which is the London Stock Exchange (LSE). Established in 1760, when 150 brokers expelled from the Royal Exchange for rowdiness formed a spontaneous share-trading club at Jonathan's Coffee House, it registered as a private limited company in 1986 and, finally, as a plc in 2000. Like all plcs, the LSE is susceptible to potential takeover bids. In 2004, it became the first stock market to be targeted by a prospective purchaser when it faced an £822m hostile takeover bid from little-known Swedish company the OM Group, a technology manufacturer that runs the Swedish Stock Exchange.

Table 7.3 Types of company in the UK

Type of company	Definition
Limited liability companies (Ltds)	One up from a sole trader, this is one of the most common forms of company, particularly in the small business arena. Introduced to provide some security for individuals or small companies that would otherwise have to shoulder all of the burdens of risk associated with borrowing money, investing, and conducting day-to-day business, it provides them with a guarantee that is not enjoyed by larger, more commercial companies with shareholders. Limited companies—which include enterprises such as theatres, charities, and voluntary trusts—instead only allocate 'liability' (risk) to their investors to the value of a nominal sum (usually £1). This will be agreed with them when they initially sign the company's 'original memorandum' and 'articles of association'.
Private limited companies	Again, usually small or medium-sized, these are not permitted to issue shares to the public via the stock market. The liability of individual investors for any shortfalls or debts incurred by the company is limited in this case to the nominal value of the shares with which they were initially issued (i.e. they could lose all of the money that they initially invested in it).
Public limited companies (plcs)	These have at least two shareholders and may offer shares to the public. Their owners will 'float' them and they will be listed on the LSE. They must have issued shares to the value of £50,000 before being allowed to trade. Larger plcs are often referred to as 'blue chip' companies, and include household names such as BP and Marks and Spencer.

Four years later, its shareholders rejected a £1.35bn offer by its German rival, Deutsche Börse.

Today, the LSE has regional bases in Belfast, Birmingham, Glasgow, Leeds, and Manchester. Some 2,600 UK and overseas companies are listed on it at any one time, and shares are traded electronically via a computerized system called 'CREST'. Minute-by-minute movements in share prices of listed companies are tracked by a series of nine indices collectively known as the 'Financial Times Stock Exchange' ('FTSE', or 'FOOTSIE'). The most famous of these indices is the **FT100 Share Index (FOOTSIE)**, which lists the hundred highest-valued companies at any one time, in order of value, and monitors the movements in share prices of these firms. The FT All-Share Index, meanwhile, lists all of the 2,500-plus companies on the stock market, again in order, and monitors daily movements.

All manner of factors can have an impact on company share prices. Mergers and takeovers—or the mere prospect of them—can send prices soaring or crashing, according to the market's assessment of how favourable such outcomes will be for its commercial fortunes. The hostile £79bn takeover of German company Mannesman by Vodafone in January 2000 initially sent its share price rocketing, and briefly saw BT, BP, and Vodafone together account for 30 per cent of the overall share value of the FT100, as the latter became Britain's single biggest company. More recently, the takeover of Hollinger International (the parent company of the *Telegraph* newspaper group) by American billionaires the Barclay brothers saw a sharp rise in its share price for a time, while shares in Marks and Spencer (M&S) are notoriously prone to fluctuations depending on the state of the company's profits.

Sometimes, companies' share prices suffer because of factors far beyond their control. Amid growing suspicions among share traders that the 1980s stock market bubble was about to burst, 'Black Monday' on 1 October 1987 saw the biggest one-day crash in history. By the end of the month, the value of LSE shares alone had plummeted by 26.4 per cent.

As well as the LSE, London also now boasts an Alternative Investment Market (AIM), launched in 1995, which provides a market for shares in smaller developing companies, ethical traders, and/or those whose value has fallen so low that they have decided to 'delist' from FTSE. Sometimes, the trend goes in reverse: when The Body Shop was acquired by French cosmetics giant L'Oréal in 2006, it moved from AIM to FTSE.

The 2008 global banking crisis

After years of unsustainable growth in the mortgage and banking sectors, and the credit market as a whole, September and October 2008 saw the onset of arguably the biggest global financial meltdown since the Wall Street Crash of 1929 and the ensuing Great Depression. Eighteen months after the term 'sub-prime' had first begun to seep into the mainstream media—in relation to the crisis of insecurity sparked by defaults on 'toxic' mortgage loans made by US banks to people without the means to pay them back—major financial institutions from Europe to the Far East were brought to their knees by the knock-on effects of these and similar practices elsewhere. In the end, the position of household-name banks, from Merrill Lynch to Barclays, became so perilous that governments in Britain, the USA, and across mainland Europe were forced into doing what the long-standing free market consensus would previously have deemed unthinkable: pouring vast sums of money into the banking sector to shore up savings and pensions, and to keep the system functioning. But even this was not enough in itself and, before long, Mr Brown's government led the way by going a stage further—taking controlling stakes in major high street banks and, in some cases, bringing them into wholesale public ownership. After decades of runaway privatization and deregulation, the term 'nationalization' (see p. 230) once more re-entered the political lexicon.

The culmination of the escalating financial crisis began unfolding in late September 2008, when, within the space of a week, investment bank Lehman Brothers filed for bankruptcy, Merrill Lynch was taken over by the Bank of America, and the US Federal Reserve Bank (the US equivalent to the Bank of England) announced an $85bn rescue package for the country's biggest insurance firm, AIG, in return for an 80 per cent stake in the business (thereby effectively nationalizing it). Within a fortnight, an even bigger collapse occurred, when Washington Mutual—the largest US mortgage lender—was shut down by regulators and sold to JP Morgan Chase. To prevent other financial giants facing a similar fate, the White House administration—in the shape of US Treasury Secretary Henry (Hank) Paulson—began drawing up a $700bn rescue package for the country's entire banking sector, which would involve the state bailing out the sector's bad debts with taxpayers' money. Such was the disdain of Congress—which had to approve the deal formally—towards the senior bankers and brokers whose reckless lending and speculating had fuelled the crisis that it took the best part of a week for it to be finalized, during which time the value of the US banking sector plunged to a record low as confidence drained from the stock market.

But more dramatic state interventions were to come. Barely a week after Lloyds TSB stepped in to announce a buyout of Halifax Bank of Scotland (HBOS), one of Britain's biggest mortgage lenders, following its near collapse, the government nationalized the bulk of Bradford and Bingley's assets, by taking control of the former building society's £50bn mortgage and loans business, while selling off its branches and savings operation to Spanish bank Santander. At around the same time, the Treasury moved to guarantee all savings deposits in UK banks of up to £35,000 (a limit later raised to £50,000), in an effort to prevent a 'run on the banks'—that is, the mass withdrawal of savings by panicked investors worried about losing their money if a bank were to collapse. Meanwhile, the FSA had announced a ban until at least January 2009 on 'short-selling'—a shady form of stock market speculation that entails gambling on a company's share price falling, and which had been blamed in some quarters for helping to undermine confidence in the banking system. Short-selling involves seasoned speculators 'borrowing' shares—the value of which they expect to fall—from a third party, selling them on, and then buying them back after their value has plummeted (before returning them to their original owner)—making a tidy profit in the process.

By far the most radical development of those seen anywhere in the world, however, was initiated by the British government on 8 October. Amid fever ish rumours and leaks, and jittery fluctuations on the stock market, Mr Brown and Mr Darling announced details of a £500bn bailout for the UK's banking sector, which would see up to eight high street banks and build ing societies part-nationalized in a last-ditch attempt to persuade financial institutions to resume lending to each other, and—more importantly for the 'real economy'—to small businesses and the public. An initial £25bn in tax-payer-backed loans was pledged, to help banks to 'recapitalize', along with a further £25bn capital injection, in return for which the state would be issued with 'preference shares' giving it partial control of the companies. Holders of preference shares (as their name suggests) take priority over normal shareholders when any dividends are paid out by a bank on the back of future profits, but, unlike ordinary shares, preference shares do not give their holders voting rights over company policies.

In addition to the above, a further £200bn would potentially be made available to banks in short-term loans, with £250bn more to underwrite lending between banks—effectively guaranteeing that one institution would be repaid should another default on a loan.

In the event, when confirmation of which banks would be taking the government up on its offer finally came, on Monday 13 October, it was by turns both more and less dramatic than had been expected. Only Lloyds TSB and HBOS and the Royal Bank of Scotland (shares in which had, by then, plummeted) initially accepted the government's offer, with the other major banks, including Barclays, opting to go it alone to try to raise capital on the open market. The price paid by the banks that went with the 'final' £37bn Treasury package, however, was significant. First, the FSA ordered the government to acquire not only preference shares, but also ordinary ones—thereby giving the government company voting rights. Secondly, it emerged that ministers would be appointing their own directors to the banks, giving them more direct control over boardroom decisions, and that no bonuses would be paid to senior staff for at least the first year. This latter measure went some way towards allaying mounting public outrage at the scale of the 'bonus culture' that had exploded during the boom years, with directors often taking home multimillion-pound perks—irrespective of how well their company was performing. Making good on Mr Brown's vow in a television interview to 'punish' those who had irresponsibly profited from the near-collapse of the banking sector, the government swiftly replaced several leading bankers at the helm of the semi-nationalized institutions, including the chief executive of RBS, Sir Fred Goodwin—known as 'Fred the Shred', as a result of his notoriously ruthless cost-cutting in a previous job at the Clydesdale Bank. RBS was 60 per cent nationalized, while the state took a 41 per cent stake in Lloyds TSB and HBOS.

In the same tumultous week, Mr Brown entered into a public row with Iceland, after a number of the country's leading banks fell like dominoes, and it emerged that dozens of British local authorities, charities, universities, and other bodies had substantial sums invested in them (see pp. 400-2). When Iceland's prime minister, Geir Haarde, announced that he was guaranteeing the safety of all Icelanders' deposits, but not those of Britons caught up in the collapse, Mr Brown used anti-terror legislation to freeze the £7bn in assets held in the UK by Landsbanki, the country's national bank, to recoup some of the costs.

After months of criticism of his leadership, and dissenting voices among senior bankers and Opposition MPs, Mr Brown was widely praised for his handling of the financial crisis in the British and international media. His model of state intervention was swiftly emulated by the USA and a number of mainland European countries. At a press conference in London with foreign journalists, he was asked by one if he considered himself a superhero like 1920s comic book space explorer Flash Gordon. With trademark seriousness, he replied: 'Just "Gordon", I can assure you.'

◗ The government's role in industrial relations

In the 1960s and 1970s, when many industries were still state-owned, battles between the government and trade unions over wages policy, working conditions, and their ability to take industrial action when relations broke down were seldom out of the news. After years of struggle between the unions and employers, and growing in-fighting within the Labour movement, tensions came to a head in 1978–79 with the so-called 'Winter of Discontent'—a prolonged period of strikes and wildcat action across the public services during which, at one point, the dead infamously 'went unburied' when even funerary workers joined the melee.

Hand in hand with its programme of mass privatization, Mrs Thatcher's government introduced swingeing clampdowns on the rights of workers to take industrial action. Legal barriers were introduced to block strikes wherever possible, while the new generation of private sector employers with whom unions were now confronted were no longer required by law even to 'recognize' their existence formally —let alone to negotiate with them over job cuts or changes in working practices. Mrs Thatcher also put an end to:

- the 'closed shop'—a rule that had forced employees working in specific trades or industries to join a specific trade union;
- 'secondary picketing'—the ability of workers in trades *related* to those the union members of which were in dispute with their employers to take 'sympathy action'.

Although both of the above remain illegal to this day, when Labour returned to power in 1997 certain workers' rights were restored. Many of these—such as the right to sick pay and paid leave, subject to certain conditions, and a maximum number of weekly working hours—were guaranteed under the terms of the European Social Chapter, belatedly signed by Mr Blair in 1998 (see p. 306). The new government introduced a national minimum wage (NMW). It also moved to extend some rights that were previously the preserve of full-time permanent employees to those on part-time and temporary contracts.

The role of trade unions

As discussed in Chapter 4, the unions initially emerged in the eighteenth and nineteenth centuries. They were formed to provide representation for the large groups of workers being recruited by the owners of Britain's emerging manufacturing industries. In time, dismayed by the lack of attention paid to their cause by politicians of their day, they began seeking their own stake in power and, to that end, joined with other bodies to form the Labour Party—with which many of them retain strong links to this day (see p. 155).

Unions use collective bargaining to:

- negotiate and protect a fair wage for given trades and professions;
- negotiate fair working conditions—that is, working hours, holiday entitlement, sick pay, compensation in the event of work-related injuries or illnesses, etc.;
- provide their members with training, educational and social opportunities, and a 'fighting fund' for living costs in the event of prolonged industrial disputes.

In addition, unions traditionally offer legal and financial support in the event of disputes between individual employees, or groups of employees, and their employers. Unions have historically achieved many favourable settlements for aggrieved workers unfairly dismissed from their jobs, or bullied at work by colleagues or bosses. Sometimes, this is done on an out-of-court basis, but on other occasions, unions represent employees at employment tribunals.

Over the past thirty years, the number of unions has declined by a third, with many pooling their resources to strengthen their voice at the negotiating table. The most recent amalgamation was that of the Transport and General Workers' Union (TGWU) and Amicus, Britain's biggest technical union, which together became Unite in 2007. The senior officer of a trade union is usually called the 'general secretary'. Like the Labour Party, it will also usually have an elected national executive committee that debates changes of policy and practice, and, beneath that, regional and district organizations. There will also be branch organizations, often based in individual workplaces, and houses or shop stewards' committees, which act as focal points for negotiations between employees and employers.

The 'big three' British unions as of 2008 are as set out in Table 7.4.

The majority of unions are affiliated to a single representative body, the Trades Union Congress (TUC), which holds an annual conference like those organized by the main political parties to rally opinion from members and to ratify changes in policy. The leader of the Labour Party is traditionally invited to give its keynote speech.

The TUC dates back to 1868 and its membership currently consists of 76 trade unions, representing some 6.8 million people (equivalent to 80 per cent of trade union members in the UK). It has six regional councils in England and a single one for Wales. Scotland has its own equivalent body: the Scottish Trades Union Congress (STUC).

Table 7.4 Britain's 'big three' trades unions (as of 2008)

Union	Trade represented	Membership
Unite	Formed from the merger of the Transport and General Workers' Union (T&G) and Amicus (the biggest technical and manufacturing union)	2 million
UNISON	Local government and health workers	1.3 million
General Municipal Boilermakers (GMB)	Britain's 'general union', representing workers from all sectors	600,000

NOTE: A regularly updated version of this table can be found on the Online Resource Centre that accompanies this book.

The path towards trade union recognition—and what it is worth

For unions to be able to negotiate with employers about working practices, pay, and conditions, they first need to be *recognized* by their members' employers. After years of having their power diluted, unions were given a new impetus to recruit in the Employment Relations Act 1999, which introduced a statutory process through which they could demand recognition on meeting specific criteria.

If claims for recognition cannot be satisfied bilaterally between a union and the relevant employers, it has the right to apply for help from a new Central Arbitration Committee (CAC), which assigns a three-person panel to each case. There are two main ways in which a union may achieve recognition with the help of the CAC—regardless of whether this is desired by the employers with which it is in dispute:

- *without* a ballot—a union is entitled in law to *automatic* recognition if *more than 50 per cent* of its 'bargaining unit' (that is, all of the employees entitled to join it) have done so;

- *with* a ballot—if *at least 40 per cent* of the bargaining unit vote in favour of recognition in a ballot called by the house or chapel *and* this number constitutes a majority of those who cast votes. It is not necessary in law for a worker in a bargaining unit to have joined a union to be able to vote in strike ballots.

Ironically, one of the most notorious industries for union recognition is print journalism. There have been many cases in which the managers of larger regional newspapers and some nationals (including Express Newspapers and Independent Newspapers) have fought hard to prevent it. In the run-up to the passage of the 1999 Act, some regional newspaper groups tried to argue that, to achieve recognition, the unions representing their journalists would need to obtain the support of 40 per cent of their *overall workforces*—that is, including their advertising and sales staff, etc.—rather than simply the writers and sub-editors who made up the bargaining unit.

Prior to 1999, unions were restricted from taking strike action in the sense that any withdrawal of their labour over a trade dispute constituted a breach of contract. Theoretically, this entitled bosses either to sack striking workers or to sue them for damages and loss of business. However, the 1999 Act has entitled 'recognized' unions to be consulted formally over any changes in working conditions for employees they represent—for example, the movement of a British-based call centre to the Far East or a proposed merger with a rival company. It has also given unions immunity from prosecution for industrial action provided that:

- action is 'wholly or mainly in contemplation or furtherance of a trade dispute between workers and their employer' (that is, it is not secondary picketing);
- the union has gone through the correct ballot procedures beforehand. This involves a secret postal ballot, followed by a letter giving the employer seven days' notice of the intended action and details of the ballot result.

Some restrictions remain, however. In addition to being barred from secondary action, unions must keep picket lines to a negotiated level, to avoid intimidating colleagues who opt not to take part. This latter clause was inserted to avoid the kinds of harassment to which 'strike-breaking' coalminers and other workers were allegedly subjected in the 1980s by picketers.

Interestingly, while secondary action is illegal, the definition of this term has been tested in recent years. In 2005, British Airways baggage handlers walked out in a two-day 'wildcat strike' in sympathy with employees of Gate Gourmet, a company that supplied BA's airline meals. The workers had been ordered to sign new contracts cutting their wages and benefits in the wake of the sudden sacking of 670 colleagues. Because Gate Gourmet had previously been owned by BA and was being subcontracted by BA management to produce meals for its passengers, it was a moot point whether the smaller company's workers were indirectly still 'employed' by the airline. If this were so, was this action really 'secondary'?

Avoiding a strike—the role of the Arbitration, Conciliation and Advisory Service (ACAS)

When negotiations between employers and employees break down, one or other party—or sometimes the government—may decide to seek impartial help in reaching a settlement from a quango: the *Advisory, Conciliation, and Arbitration Service (ACAS)*.

The role of ACAS is to:

- *advise* warring parties on how to avoid industrial action in the first place;

- *conciliate*—that is, intervene—in disputes when invited to do so and try to encourage the parties to reach their own agreement peacefully;
- *arbitrate* to restart negotiations in disputes that have resulted in industrial action;
- help out in instances of grievances between individual employees and their employers—notably, in relation to prospective employment tribunal cases (relating to unfair dismissal, gender, age, or racial discrimination, etc.).

There have been numerous recent examples of ACAS's involvement in industrial disputes. In July 2007, its chair was called in by ministers to report on the issues arising out of the strike by Royal Mail workers over the imposition of new modernization plans and a below-inflation 2.5 per cent pay deal. In May 2005, ACAS was called in by the National Union of Journalists (NUJ) to mediate in its dispute with British Broadcasting Corporation (BBC) director general Mark Thompson over his plans to slash four thousand jobs, many through compulsory redundancies. At time of writing, this dispute remains to be fully resolved and ACAS is still arbitrating.

Health and safety in the workplace

Health and safety in the workplace is regulated by the Health and Safety at Work Act 1974, which covers the operation of work-based equipment, and a number of subsequent regulations, including the Control of Substances Hazardous to Health (COSHH) Regulations 1999, relating to exposure to virtually all potentially dangerous substances.

Until April 2008, the job of developing policy guidelines on workplace health and safety fell to the Health and Safety Commission (HSC). It also had specific duties to safeguard the gas, petroleum, and railway industries. The job of *enforcing* its regulations through formal workplace inspections fell to the **Health and Safety Executive (HSE)**. From 2008, the two bodies were merged under the HSE banner.

The HSE's day-to-day work is carried out by its Field Operations Directorate (which incorporates separate factory, agriculture, and quarries inspectorates), and regional officers of the Employment Medical Advisory Service. Its powers are set out in Table 7.5.

In addition, some health and safety legislation (covering shops, offices, warehouses, restaurants, etc.) is enforced by local authority environmental health departments (see p. 598).

Table 7.5 The responsibilities of the Health and Safety Executive (HSE)

Role	Responsibilities
Inspection	Site visits, examination of written safety procedures, and staff interviews
Investigation	Formally investigating organizations against which an allegation of breach of health and safety procedure has been made
Enforcement	Serving notice on an employer or other health and safety 'duty-holder' ordering it to amend procedures. Inspectors may withdraw an organization's licence to carry out work
Prosecution	Working with the Crown Prosecution Service (CPS) to prosecute for serious breaches of health and safety procedures, particularly if they have resulted in severe injury or death

The utilities

In Britain, a 'utility' is an organization—whether publicly or privately owned—that is responsible for maintaining and delivering a reliable and affordable supply of a commodity that is essential to the lives of the country's citizens. The main utilities are those charged with providing so-called 'natural monopolies'—that is, the basic services needed to sustain a society, such as water and energy (gas and electricity). Traditionally, the railways, postal services, and telecommunications have also been grouped under the utilities umbrella in the UK.

In recognition of the vital nature of water and power—and the belief that everyone should have guaranteed, equitable access to reliable and affordable supplies of both—the post-war Labour government nationalized all of the utilities in 1948. Until that point, like schools and hospitals, they had been in the hands of an ad hoc medley of local corporations and charities, with the result that service standards varied wildly from place to place.

For forty years, the utilities remained in the public sector. While individuals still had to pay their own rail fares and electricity bills (according to how much of any service they individually used), the industries were hugely subsidized through general taxation. Despite the fact that there was no outside competition from other service suppliers to help to drive down prices, subsidies generally enabled utilities to keep their charges at reasonable levels.

The privatization of the utilities

In the 1980s, however, the ethos governing the way in which state-owned utilities were perceived began to change, as free market economics infiltrated the public services for the first time. Mrs Thatcher's government began a wholesale privatization of the utilities, believing that the monolithic state-owned industries were inefficient and bureaucratic, and offered the public too little 'choice'. Arguments for and against privatization are set out in Table 7.6.

The first utility to be privatized was British Telecom—a then state telecommunications provider that, at one time, had been owned and run by the General Post Office. The British Gas Board followed two years later, with electricity changing hands in 1990, and the railways two years after that. Each of these privatizations is explored in more detail below.

Privatization itself was to be only the first step in Mrs Thatcher's mission to 'liberalize' Britain's utility industries. Unusually for someone celebrated (and reviled in equal measure) for her radical handling of the economy, she initially moved tentatively—allowing only minimal competition in the

Table 7.6 Arguments for and against the privatization of the utilities

For	Against
Privatization makes utilities more efficient by introducing competition from rival suppliers (each competing for custom through competitive pricing) and enabling these suppliers to woo managers and directors with experience in the commercial sector.	The introduction of the profit motive—and private companies' reliance on shareholders to raise finance for investment—raised suspicions that their main priority was to boost revenue for their backers, rather than using cost and/or efficiency savings to lower prices and improve quality for the public.
It enables them to respond to the wishes of consumers by reacting to supply and demand with a wider choice of services—rather than assuming that 'the state knows best'.	In practice, periods of intense competition between rival gas and electricity suppliers, combined with ineffective regulation, has led to consolidation in the hands of a few large companies. The public monopolies of old could be replaced by private monopolies and, whereas unpopular governments can be removed at elections, the boards of private companies are not accountable to the public.
Privatization removes the old 'statist' philosophy imposed on the publicly owned utilities, allowing them to cut out waste and contract out ancillary services—such as cleaning, catering, and maintenance—to smaller companies that specialize in those areas. Doing so saves money on overheads, which can be ploughed into improving the product.	Some privatized utilities—particularly private monopolies, such as the water companies—have been accused of passing costs on to the consumer rather than bearing them internally, in an effort to placate their shareholders. The major infrastructural investment in the water industry required by recent EU Directives led to disproportionately high increases in water bills, while share dividends continued to rise.
It raises revenue for future government spending, while saving the state money in the long run by cutting the cost of maintaining huge infrastructures and workforces.	Privatization divests the country of significant assets built up through the investment of taxpayers' money over a long period of time and gives commercial companies 'something for nothing'. Former Tory Prime Minister Harold Macmillan described it as 'selling off the family silver'.

privatized utilities, to ensure that the transition from public to private sectors had time to bed down before being opened to the ravages of the free market. But by the early 1990s, the gas, electricity, and telecommunications industries had been almost totally deregulated—meaning that, for the first time, a variety of different companies were allowed to compete for business in each sector. On the railways, meanwhile, travellers were soon being referred to as 'customers' rather than 'passengers'.

The onward march of deregulation has continued to this day, even in the few sectors that are still dominated by major public sector providers. In January 2006, the Royal Mail was opened up to full free market competition for the first time in 350 years, as industry regulator the *Postal Services Commission (Postcomm)* gave the go-ahead for any licensed business to deliver letters in the UK.

Although British governments today favour a 'light touch' approach to regulation—preferring to let the free market determine prices and services—they continue to set certain minimum standards specific to each sector. For example, BT (the successor to British Telecom) is still required by the terms of its licence to maintain public telephone boxes to ensure that there is provision for people without mobile phones. In addition, each industry is overseen by at least one regulator with a statutory duty to ensure that customers are given value for money and appropriate access to essential services. The overall responsibilities of the regulators include:

- laying down limits on price increases;
- monitoring service quality;
- ensuring that true competition is maintained.

Over the years, however, there has been a great deal of criticism aimed at these regulators—often derided as 'watchdogs without teeth', in light of their perceived reluctance to interfere too forcefully in the way in which the utilities they oversee are managed. In April 2008, the chair of an all-party committee on fuel poverty, Labour *backbencher* John Battle, tabled a Commons motion publicly demanding that ministers force the gas and electricity regulator, the *Office of Gas and Electricity Markets (Ofgem)*, to crack down on energy companies charging higher unit rates to poor households reliant on prepayment meters than better-off customers paying by direct debit. Energy Minister Malcolm Wicks promptly intervened to urge the regulator to stop poorer people having to 'subsidize' the better off. The government recently set itself a new 'legally binding' target to end fuel poverty by 2010—a goal that it may struggle to meet.

Communications

British Telecom was privatized in 1984. Initially, only limited competition was allowed, with a single alternative provider, Mercury Communications Ltd—a digital phone network that was then part of the Cable and Wireless Group—allowed to enter the market.

After what was perceived as a successful trial, this so-called 'duopoly' ended in 1991. Some 150 licensed telecommunications companies, including 125 cable operators, and 19 regional and national public telecoms operators, soon sprung up, although the market has since radically rationalized through mergers and takeovers. Today, consumers can also choose from a range of mobile phone companies, the largest of which include Orange, O2 (previously BT Cellnet), Vodafone, and T-Mobile (formerly One2One), not to mention a growing number of Internet service providers, including AOL, Virgin, and Tiscali.

Confusingly for some, most telephone land lines are still provided by engineers from BT, but customers are billed by the suppliers that they pay to deliver services to them through those lines. A similar division between the companies that own the physical infrastructure and those who provide services via that infrastructure exists in most utilities.

Until 2003, the telecoms industry was regulated by the Office of Telecommunications (Oftel), under the Director General of Telecommunications. But in recognition of the increasing overlap between traditional telecommunications and television, radio, and other digital and interactive services, Oftel has since been replaced by the *Office of Communications (Ofcom)*, an all-encompassing 'super-regulator'.

Prior to Ofcom, the broadcast industry was overseen by a collection of disparate regulators, including the Independent Television Commission (ITC), the Broadcasting Standards Commission (BSC), the Radio Authority, and the Radiocommunications Agency. The BBC occupied an unusual position in that it had its own board of governors to monitor certain aspects of its performance (including its current affairs provision and editorial independence), but this was recently replaced by an independent BBC trust. In terms of taste and decency, it now falls under Ofcom's remit.

The postal industry is regulated by the Postal Services Commission (Postcomm), and there is also a consumer-run body that channels complaints and observations from the public to government: *Postwatch*.

Postcomm has the following principal responsibilities:

- protecting a universal postal service;
- licensing postal operators;

- introducing competition into mail services;
- regulating Royal Mail;
- advising the government on the Post Office network.

With more than 90 per cent of mail still delivered by Royal Mail, a former monopoly, it is perhaps unsurprising that Postcomm is most often in the news when it is pronouncing on that organization's performance. In May 2008, the regulator issued a report warning that, unless Royal Mail were partly privatized, allowing it to raise additional investment on the open market, it would face having to axe Saturday postal deliveries to save money. In the year to March 2008, the company made a loss of £10m.

Given its continued dominancy of postal services, Royal Mail is also unique in that it can be fined by Postcomm for failing to meet government-set targets (a threat used in 2002 to chivvy up Consignia—as it was then known—after it missed targets for speeding up the delivery of business mail).

The energy industry

In 1986, gas—then the preserve of the British Gas Board—was privatized. Although the newly rechristened 'British Gas' was initially a private monopoly, the industry swiftly became the first utility to be fully deregulated. At first, the emerging new generation of gas companies (like electricity suppliers later) tended to be regionally based—households and businesses in south-east England were given a choice of only one alternative to British Gas, the headquarters of which were located in the region. Today (as with electricity), it is possible for most people to buy their gas from suppliers based anywhere in the UK, or even abroad, and many companies, including British Gas, supply 'dual fuel' (both gas and electricity).

As with telecoms, there is a division between supply companies that bill customers and the single firm that owns the infrastructure used to 'transport' fuel to them. Both the network of pipes for gas, and the cables and pylons used to transmit electricity, are owned by National Grid plc, a monopoly. Suppliers pay the company for using the network.

When electricity was privatized in 1990, it was originally split into three generating companies and 12 supply companies. An example of a regional supply company was the South East Electricity Board (Seeboard), subsequently bought by French-owned company Électricité de France (EDF Energy) in 2002. Since then, the electricity supply chain has evolved into the three-stage process outlined in Table 7.7.

Table 7.7 The energy industry supply chain

Process	Supplier
Generation	Companies including National Power plc, PowerGen plc, British Energy, Magnox North, and independent generators using gas-fired and combined heat-and-power stations, such as US-owned companies Eastern and AES
Transmission	National Grid plc
Distribution	Regional electricity companies (RECs) formed after privatization and independent energy providers that have since emerged

While England and Wales is governed by this system, Scottish Power plc and Scottish Hydro-Electric between them generate, transmit, and distribute all of the electricity in Scotland.

The gas and electricity utilities used to have separate regulators, but are now overseen by the Office of Gas and Electricity Markets (Ofgem) and the Director General of Gas and Electricity Markets. Following a number of controversies over double-digit rises in energy bills (blamed by companies on the rising price of crude oil—despite the fact that most have continued to report substantial profits), a new consumer watchdog has also emerged. Unlike Ofgem, *Energywatch* has no statutory powers, but its recent campaigns have managed to capture numerous headlines in the media—including its online service directing customers to better deals with different suppliers according to their postcodes.

Water and sewerage

Perhaps the most controversial of all utility privatizations was that of the water industry, which was sold off in 1989. Given the essential nature of clean, safe water supplies, many critics of privatization (and some supporters) viewed the idea of opening it up to free market competition as a step too far. Some regarded the very notion of company shareholders being allowed to profit from such a fundamental life-giving commodity as amoral.

There were also practical objections. Given the peculiar difficulties of being able to 'subdivide' the industry's infrastructure—to take an extreme, of allocating one stretch of a reservoir to one company and the next to another—it quickly became clear that introducing conventional competition was going to be almost impossible. As a result, to this day, water continues to be supplied to British consumers by companies that are local monopolies—making a mockery, argue some, of the whole premise for privatizing the industry.

At the time of privatization, ten water and sewerage companies were set up. Each was given responsibility for supplying water, storing and recycling it, and treating and disposing of sewerage. Confusingly for journalists, the industry today is regulated by not one, but three bodies, the roles of which are outlined in Table 7.8.

Industrial and commercial water users are metered today, and domestic users may be charged on the basis of their *Council Tax* band—or opt to be metered—depending on where they live. Consumers with a record of unpaid bills are often forced to have such meters installed, to avoid them getting into arrears in future. As in the energy industry, there has been periodic controversy about meters, with campaigners arguing that they leave poor people particularly vulnerable: if they do not have the money to put into their meter, their water supply is effectively cut off. Moreover, companies have been criticized for charging higher rates per unit used to customers with meters than they do to those who pay by conventional bill. These and other concerns prompted the emergence of another watchdog: the *Consumer Council for Water*.

In Scotland, water effectively remains a nationalized utility. Three regional water authorities, covering the north, east, and west of the country, were merged in April 2002 to form a single state-owned company: Scottish Water. Scottish Water is overseen by the Water Industry Commission for Scotland (WICS) and its accounts are audited by Audit Scotland.

The railways

Privatization of the railways has taken a different route to that of the other utilities and today, albeit by default, the industry is effectively a *public–private partnership (PPP)* (see p. 238). In 1993, following years of negotiation with the private sector to sell off franchises covering marginal and unprofitable lines, the railway system was finally privatized. It was initially fragmented under more than a hundred separate private sector

Table 7.8 The regulation of the water industry

Regulator	Remit
The *Office of Water Regulation (Ofwat)* The *Water Services Regulatory Authority*	Regulates the structure of the industry and its financial transparency (examining annual accounts, and vetting proposed mergers and takeovers)
The Drinking Water Inspectorate	Regulates the quality of water supplies to customers
The *Environment Agency*	Monitors pollution, and regulates the water quality in inland, estuary, and coastal waters. It also has responsibility for flood protection

operators—that is, the companies that bought up engines, carriages, and other rolling stock to manage individual routes on renewable franchises. Meanwhile, as in the energy industry, ownership of the rail network (the tracks, signals, and stations) was transferred from the government to Railtrack, a private monopoly. Following a spate of controversies—including several major rail accidents, among them the 1999 Paddington train crash, in which 31 people died—ministers wound down Railtrack in 2002, replacing it with a not-for-dividend company called *Network Rail*. The infrastructure was therefore effectively taken back into a form of qualified public ownership.

Network Rail now charges the remaining 25 train operators to travel over its lines and to use its infrastructure, although, in practice, many operating companies run their local stations as subcontractors. Franchises are awarded by the government on the basis of a guaranteed 'minimum level of service' specific to each one and companies are invited to tender for renewable terms, which can be anything between seven and 20 years. The company that wins a franchise is likely to be that which is willing to run the service with the lowest government subsidy—giving rise to concerns about underinvestment and price rises. Current examples of franchisees include Southern (which runs the main London to Brighton line and manages stations for Network Rail along that route), Virgin (operator of the west coast mainline), and coach company National Express (which recently fought off competition from Virgin, Arriva, and First Group to secure the east coast mainline from London to Scotland).

In some areas, two or more companies operate services in competition with each other, but elsewhere, there are local monopolies. In practice, any competition that does exist is largely notional, because it is physically impossible for two companies to run directly competing services (no two trains can use the same track between the same stations at the same time).

Huge increases in the number of people commuting to work in Britain in recent years have put growing pressure on the rail network and fare prices have continued to rise well above inflation, even at times when service quality has appeared to deteriorate. Overcrowded carriages, broken-down engines, late arrivals, and cancellations—at a time when the annual government subsidy to the rail network remains significantly higher than that before privatization—have conspired to make the railways an enduring ministerial headache.

The regulation of the rail industry is currently split between two authorities. The Office of Rail Regulation (formerly the Office of the Rail Regulator) ensures that charges are fair and that there is equitable access to the tracks for operators. Meanwhile, the Department of Transport (DoT) itself recently took responsibility for awarding and reviewing franchises, and fining operators for repeated lateness, cancellations, and other aspects of poor performance back in house. Beforehand, this role had fallen to the Strategic Rail Authority (SRA).

As with the other utilities, there is also a watchdog representing the voice of consumers: ***Passenger Focus*** (or the ***Rail Passengers' Council***).

The private finance initiative (PFI) and public–private partnerships (PPP)

The pressing political 'need' for governments to get major utility projects up and running quickly—rather than having to wait until they have accumulated sufficient tax revenue—has fostered the development of a new type of capital initiative designed to harness the spending power of the private sector, while retaining a form of broad 'public ownership' of the resulting assets. The so-called ***private finance initiative (PFI)*** was introduced by John Major's Conservative government in 1992, initially to fund the building of new prisons at a time of acute overcrowding and repeated breakouts (see p. 273). The classic PFI model sees a private company financing the bulk of the initial capital investment (buildings and equipment), often along with some ancillary staff to man the facility, and effectively 'owning' it for a period of years or decades thereafter. The public sector will gradually buy it back by paying 'rent' and interest in a long-term leaseback arrangement.

Although initially opposed to taking major infrastructural investments off the public sector balance sheet, Labour has now wholeheartedly embraced the PFI concept, rechristening it 'public–private partnership' (PPP). Today, virtually all new schools, hospitals, and prisons are financed in this way—and so too are major capital projects related to the utilities, such as the proposed new generation of nuclear power stations approved in 2008.

One of the main advantages to governments of using private finance to fund capital projects is that the initial outlay does not appear on the Treasury's balance sheet—and therefore does not technically *count* as public expenditure. In contrast to the huge start-up costs of some of these projects, the face value of contracts awarded to private businesses as an incentive for them to carry out the building work is relatively low. Critics argue, however, that PPPs have notable disadvantages—as outlined in Table 7.9.

Table 7.9 Criticisms of the private finance initiative (PFI) and the public–private partnership (PPP)

Criticism	Explanation
Can only generally be financed through borrowing	Because the government's borrowing is better secured than that of the private sector, the interest rates faced by private companies investing in PPP projects will be higher than those offered to the state.
Companies put shareholders before the public (or 'customers')	Private companies have a legal responsibility to make profits for their shareholders—raising suspicions that their motives are not always noble and making it likely that, whatever the short-term savings to the government, the final cost to the public purse will, over time, be greater than that had the state financed the project itself from scratch.
PFI/PPP agreements are like credit card debt or 'hire purchase' agreements—money borrowed on the 'never never'	PFI/PPP can create confusion over who actually 'owns' the project. Some regard it as akin to hire purchase (HP) agreements entered into by governments in the 1960s. Questions over ownership also raise the question below.
Who is responsible if something goes wrong—the private investor or the taxpayer?	The closure of Railtrack by ministers has increased pressure on the state to provide guarantees underpinning the private sector's investment in prospective PPP projects, so as not to deter them.

→ Further reading

Edwards, P. (2003) *Industrial Relations: Theory and Practice in Britain*, 2nd edn, London: WileyBlackwell. **Second edition of acclaimed text focusing on recent developments in worker–employer relations in Britain, in light of the incorporation of European Union employment law, trade union recognition, and the growing casualization/flexibility of labour markets.**

Grimsey, D. and Lewis, M. (2007) *Public Private Partnerships: The Worldwide Revolution in Infrastructure Provision and Project Finance*, London: Edward Elgar. **Illuminating overview of the increasing role of private capital in major public sector infrastructural investment and the costs that this brings to the public purse. Includes comparative examples of PPP-style projects from a number of states outside the UK.**

Michie, R. C. (2001) *The London Stock Exchange: A History*, Oxford: Oxford University Press. **Acclaimed history of Britain's biggest money market—and one of the largest in the world—incorporating up-to-date explanations of the modern-day operation of the stock exchange and how the FTSE listings system works.**

Monbiot, G. (2001) *Captive State: The Corporate Takeover of Britain*, London: Pan Books. **Critically acclaimed exposé by one of Britain's leading campaigning journalists** of the creeping growth in the influence of commercial companies in British public affairs.

Swann, D. (1988) *Retreat of the State: Deregulation and Privatisation in the United Kingdom and the United States of America*, London: Prentice-Hall. **Accomplished exploration of the privatization revolution on both sides of the Atlantic, and the introduction of choice and competition into everything from formerly state-owned utilities to public services.**

Wrigley, C. (2002) *British Trade Unions Since 1933*, Cambridge: Cambridge University Press. **Textbook giving comprehensive overview of the evolution of trades union and industrial relations policy in Britain since the 1940s.**

? Review questions

1. What role does the Budget play in fiscal and monetary policymaking in Britain?

2. What was the thinking behind Gordon Brown's decision to make the Bank of England independent and to give it responsibility for setting interest rates?

3. Outline the present-day rights of trades unions and the process by which individual unions gain legal recognition. Who has the most power: employers or employees?

4. How effective has regulation of the privatized utilities proved in the UK?

5. What are the arguments for and against the privatization and deregulation of the utilities?

Online resource centre

www.oxfordtextbooks.co.uk/orc/Morrison

Visit the Online Resource Centre that accompanies this book for web links and regular updates.

8

Social welfare and home affairs

In Chapter 1, we explored the rights and responsibilities of British *subjects* in the rather abstract context of the country's constitution. This chapter focuses on the rights and responsibilities of UK *residents* in relation to the more tangible areas of social welfare, criminal justice, and that most contested and politically sensitive of terms: 'citizenship'.

From a journalistic point of view, it is no exaggeration to say that, along with the National Health Service (NHS) and education, the twin briefs of 'social affairs' and 'home affairs' occupy more newspaper column inches and minutes of current affairs airtime than almost any other areas of British life (save, perhaps, those heavyweight topics—sport and celebrity). From government crackdowns on 'benefit cheats' and the escalating cost of Incapacity Benefit to the taxpayer, to controversies about immigration, prison breakouts, or gun crime, barely a day goes by without at least one story generating screaming headlines. In the week that the bulk of this chapter was written, the government launched the following initiatives:

- a pledge to encourage GPs to issue patients 'well notes', rather than 'sick notes', to tackle the mounting cost of absenteeism to the British economy;

- a threat to withdraw benefits from claimants convicted of drug dealing;
- a toughening up, or weakening—depending on which paper you read—of immigration rules to force migrants from outside the European Union (EU) to go through a period of 'probationary citizenship' on top of an initial five years on work visas before being granted 'indefinite leave to remain'. (*'Migrants must earn citizenship, says Brown,'* wrote *The Guardian*; *'The great passport giveaway,'* claimed *The Daily Mail.*)

The story of British citizenship in the modern age is one of 'carrot' and 'stick': 'carrot', in terms of the rights, entitlements, and benefits to which UK citizens are eligible (subject to meeting the relevant criteria); 'stick', in terms of prosecution, punishment, and, ultimately, imprisonment for those who 'break the rules' by failing to meet the responsibilities expected of them as citizens.

We will start with the 'carrot'.

▌ The basis of the welfare state

Earlier, we outlined the origins of the welfare state in relation to the NHS (see pp. 178-9). Before exploring the ways in which social welfare is applied in Britain today, it is worth considering its underlying premise and the extent to which this has ever been fulfilled.

The primary purpose of the welfare state initiated by the Liberal government of Herbert Asquith and David Lloyd George, and solidified by the post-war reforms of Clement Attlee's Labour administration, was to provide a 'safety net' for members of society who fell on hard times, whether temporarily (through the loss of a job, or a period of sickness that prevented them working), or more indefinitely (as a result of the diagnosis of a serious injury or illness). Other than in exceptional situations, life 'on the social'—or, in the case of unemployment, 'on the dole'—was never envisaged as a permanent state of affairs for any individual; rather it was meant to prevent those who, through no fault of their own, found themselves unable to work, earning low wages, or in other economically straitened circumstances sinking into poverty. The concept of 'deserving' and 'undeserving' poor was arguably enshrined in the minds of the governing classes of Britain well before the Thatcher revolution.

According to eminent historian Asa Briggs, the term 'welfare state' was first coined by William Temple, Archbishop of Canterbury during the Second World War. It is widely recognized, however, that the practical foundations of a prototype welfare state had been laid during Lloyd George's time as first Chancellor of the Exchequer, then prime minister, two decades or more earlier. In his 1909 'People's Budget' (see p. 65), he introduced not only old-age pensions, but also *National Insurance (NI)*—the progressive tax that remains the bedrock of the benefits system to this day. From the outset, the welfare state was to be a safety net based on both *need* and *entitlement*: those in need would be looked after, but their entitlement to this support derived from the presumption that when they were able to work and pay their way, they would do so. Even today, a British citizen's ability to claim higher-rate benefits to help them through periods of sickness and/or unemployment is contingent on their having made sufficient NI contributions and having paid enough tax during periods of work.

Nonetheless, while a certain amount of 'responsibility' has always been expected of benefit claimants and those in receipt of other forms of welfare support, in return for their 'rights' to such help, there has been a marked hardening of attitude under recent governments. The early 1980s saw a huge increase in unemployment as entire industries were effectively closed down by the radical market reforms introduced by Margaret Thatcher. Few could argue at the time that the hundreds of thousands of workers made redundant had themselves to blame for their predicament. Yet it was not long before Mrs Thatcher's ministers were invoking the image of the jobless layabout. Shortly after the Handsworth and Brixton Riots of 1981, her Employment Secretary Norman Tebbit was asked by a journalist if he felt that rising unemployment had anything to do with these outbreaks of civil unrest. He replied:

❝ I grew up in the 1930s with an unemployed father. He did not riot. He got on his bike and looked for work, and he went on looking until he found it. ❞

Mr Tebbit's reply has gone down in British political folklore (although it is often misquoted as a more direct jibe than it actually was). In many ways, it was to set the tone for future policy by not only the Conservatives, but also

Labour. When Tony Blair was elected in 1997, his Chancellor, Gordon Brown, took little time initiating an ambitious plan to reduce unemployment under the 'Welfare to Work' banner. His so-called 'New Deal for the Unemployed' (based on a model adopted in some US states) aimed to provide a wider choice of work-related opportunities for the long-term unemployed, rewarding those who undertook specified training programmes and/or voluntary work with an initial £10 top-up to their weekly benefits. In return for these entitlements, however, it would demand ever more stringent demonstrations of their efforts to find work, organizing regular interviews with 'supervisors' in the then Employment Service to monitor their rate of applications and help them with job searches. This built on tough measures introduced in the later years of the Tory government, when high-profile crackdowns were introduced to target 'welfare scroungers'—particularly those who accepted 'cash in hand' work on top of their benefits, but failed to declare it.

Social welfare services today

The bill for social security represents the single largest area of government expenditure in the UK. Defined broadly as the welfare provision that is allocated to guarantee *a basic standard of living for those in financial need*, social security accounts for more than 30 per cent of Britain's overall public spending budget and 21 per cent of its ***gross domestic product (GDP)***. A comparison between Britain's level of social welfare spending and those of other major nations, as calculated by the Organisation for Economic Co-operation and Development (OECD), is outlined in Table 8.1.

Over the years, social welfare services have been administered by a succession of, often overlapping and sometimes conflicting, government departments and agencies. The landscape today is no less patchwork, as is shown by the breakdown in Table 8.2.

Because this chapter is primarily focused on the social security system—and, more specifically, the benefits and tax incentives introduced by governments to promote welfare and employment—it will concentrate on the work of the two biggest players: the Department for Work and Pensions (DWP) and HM Treasury.

Table 8.1 Comparisons of gross domestic product (GDP) expenditure on social welfare in OECD member states

Nation	Welfare expenditure (% of GDP)	GDP per capita (PPP US$)
Denmark	29.2	$29,000
Sweden	28.9	$24,180
France	28.5	$23,990
Germany	27.4	$25,350
Belgium	27.2	$25,520
Switzerland	26.4	$28,100
Austria	26.0	$26,730
Finland	24.8	$24,430
Netherlands	24.3	$27,190
Italy	24.4	$24,670
Greece	24.3	$17,440
Norway	23.9	$29,620
Poland	23.0	$9,450
United Kingdom	21.8	$24,160
Portugal	21.1	$18,150
Luxembourg	20.8	$53,780
Czech Republic	20.1	$14,720
Hungary	20.1	$12,340
Iceland	19.8	$29,990
Spain	19.6	$20,150
New Zealand	18.5	$19,160
Australia	18.0	$25,370
Slovak Republic	17.9	$11,960
Canada	17.8	$27,130
Japan	16.9	$25,130
USA	14.8	$34,320
Ireland	13.8	$32,410
Mexico	11.8	$8,430
South Korea	6.1	$15,090

Sources: Organisation for Economic Co-operation and Development (OECD) and United Nations Development Programme (UNDP)

Table 8.2 A breakdown of the main government departments involved in social welfare

Department	Role
Department for Work and Pensions (DWP)	Formerly the Department for Social Security (DSS), this is the ministry that oversees welfare benefits and job creation. It is led by the Secretary of State for Work and Pensions.
Department for Children, Schools and Families (DCSF)	The ministry that replaced the Department for Education and Skills (DfES) when Mr Brown became prime minister. It has a hand in welfare services in relation to its role in promoting affordable early-years childcare through tax credits and nursery vouchers. It is headed by the Secretary of State for Children, Schools and Families.
Department of Health (DH)	Under Labour, this department has played a greater role in promoting child welfare, and there have been attempts to involve both DH and DCSF (and its precursors) more directly in addressing inequalities in the distribution of high-quality health and education services. This has been done through such mechanisms as health and education action zones, patients' forums, and local involvement networks (LINks).
Department of Communities and Local Government (DCLG)	Responsible for various areas linked to social welfare, including the provision of low-cost affordable housing for key workers (nurses, teachers) and social housing for those on low incomes. (For more on housing policy, see Chapter 17.)
HM Treasury	The advent of the Labour government has also seen Chancellors play a much more hands-on role in providing welfare services. The New Deal programmes, cold-weather payments for pensioners, the tax credit system, and the child trust fund all derive from Treasury initiatives. Much of the Treasury's welfare-related work is carried out on its behalf by HM Revenue and Customs (HMRC)—the huge tax-gathering agency formed through the amalgamation of the Inland Revenue and Customs and Excise.

▌ The Department for Work and Pensions (DWP)

The DWP has overall responsibility for the Welfare to Work programme. When Labour first returned to power, its immediate concern was to tackle the perceived growing problem of intergenerational unemployment—that is, the increasing numbers of long-term unemployed (those who had been out of work for six months or more and, in many cases, for a number of years), on the one hand, and on the other, 18–25-year-olds with sporadic work or none at all (many of whom hailed from the same families as long-term claimants). The New Deal policies that followed were criticized as much for their narrow focus on these two target groups, to the exclusion of others such as under 16-year-olds and older unemployed people, as for the stiff conditions that they imposed on those they were meant to be helping.

Following the 2001 and 2005 Labour election wins, the New Deal was gradually extended to cater for various other target groups, including the over-25s, the over-50s, lone parents, people with disabilities, and even musicians—who are offered various forms of support in pursuing music careers, including government-funded open learning modules.

The vast and complex benefits system over which the DWP presides is administered in practice by a range of *executive agencies*, the roles of which are outlined in Table 8.3.

Types of benefit and their relationship to NI

There are two broad categories of benefit in the UK. Whether a particular benefit falls into one category or the other depends on the extent to which NI contributions have been made, as follows.

- *Contributory benefits* are benefits that are available to people subject to their prior payment of sufficient NI contributions. These include contributions-based *Jobseeker's Allowance* (the higher rate of JSA) and Incapacity Benefit.

Table 8.3 A breakdown of the executive agencies involved in social security

Agency	Role
Jobcentre Plus	Despite its title, this has a far wider remit than mere employment-related welfare—although that accounts for much of its work. Introduced as a replacement for the Benefits Agency (BA) in 2002, it administers most state benefits, ranging from Child Benefit, maternity benefits, and widows' pensions to Income Support, Incapacity Benefit, Disability Living Allowance (DLA), and Jobseeker's Allowance (JSA), the principle unemployment benefit. Local authority housing departments administer Housing Benefit on its behalf.
Child Support Agency (CSA)	Assesses and collects maintenance payments for children from parents under the terms of arrangements made in the family courts.
Pension Service	An agency set up to help people to navigate the complex web of alternative pension options and related state benefits.

- **Non-contributory benefits** are those benefits that bear no relationship to an individual's prior NI contributions. Most non-contributory benefits are basic 'needs-based' payments available to anyone whose income falls below a certain level and/or who meets certain other criteria (for example, for Disability Living Allowance). These include **Income Support** and the basic level of JSA. Some, however, are universal (such as Child Benefit).

There are five different classes of NI contribution. The one that affects the most people is Class 1, which is paid by both employers and employees in proportion to their levels of earnings. One oft-cited advantage of working for someone else (as opposed to being self-employed) is that for every pound invested into the NI 'pot' that entitles a person to future benefit, should they need it, a further pound at least is paid in by his or her employer. By contrast, self-employed people have sole responsibility for paying their own NI. To make matters more complicated, they are subject to two types: Class 2 (paid at a flat rate each week by those earning above a minimum threshold) and Class 4 (a profit-based rate for higher earners).

In addition to these main types of NI contribution, there are two other classes: Class 1A, which is paid by employers who operate company car and fuel schemes for their employees for their private use, and Class 3, which is paid voluntarily by those with the money to do so to safeguard their future eligibility to benefits, should they need them. By way of a long service award, those who continue working after pensionable age—presently, 65 for men and 60 for women, although the retirement age for women is due to rise gradually, from 2010, to 65 years old by 2020—are no longer required to pay NI, although their employers continue to do so on their behalf.

Jobseeker's Allowance (JSA)

JSA is paid to adults working fewer than 16 hours a week and 'actively seeking' full-time work. There are two levels of benefit: contributions-based (for those who have paid sufficient NI contributions in the past) and lower-rate income-based (for those who satisfy a financial means test, as well as the job-seeking criteria, regardless of prior NI contributions). People with savings of more than £16,000 are unlikely to be eligible for JSA, whatever their circumstances, while those with up to £6,000 in the bank will receive reduced payments.

As with other forms of unemployment benefit that preceded it, JSA has been the subject of periodic criticism from all sides over the perceived fairness or otherwise of the criteria used to award or refuse it, not to mention the level of the benefit itself. For decades, British governments have agonized over the benefits-related 'poverty trap'—put crudely, the fear that giving too much money to the unemployed will act as a disincentive for them to obtain work. In taking up a job, an unemployed person instantly loses any entitlement to unemployment benefit and, even if he or she continues to qualify for certain other payments—for example, *Housing Benefit*—he or she will instantly be paying Income Tax and NI contributions out of his or her wages. For some people, such as single parents, the option of taking up a low-paid job rather than remaining on JSA often seems almost impractical: the cost of childcare that they would otherwise not need, combined with loss of benefits, can make the prospect of remaining unemployed (however unpalatable) a more attractive option.

Few would dispute that benefit levels need to remain at least slightly lower than pay rates in order to encourage people to return to work when they find a suitable job. But for some campaigners, including trade unions and social policy think tanks such as the Joseph Rowntree Foundation, the poverty trap arises less out of overinflated benefits, than out of the fact that wages for many jobs are too low. As of the 2008–09 tax year, JSA stood at £46.85 for 18–25-year-olds and £59.15 for over-25s—hardly the stuff of which millionaires are made!

Labour tried to address the issue of low wages by introducing Britain's first national minimum wage (NMW) in 1997 (see p. 225), backed by a national hotline to help people to report employers who tried to sidestep the legislation. Yet many workers—particularly those in low-skilled jobs such as security and care work—continue to receive poverty wages that take little account of the cost of living where they are based. Employment agencies in cities such as Brighton and Hove—where costs are only marginally lower than those in London—still routinely offer £6–7/hr for basic catering and office-based work.

Concern about the poverty trap has led Labour to introduce a new form of payment for people on low incomes directed to them through their pay packets, rather than the traditional 'giro cheque'-based benefits system: tax credits. This is discussed further in the section below on HM Revenue and Customs (HMRC). Such measures have, however, been tempered by continuing threats to make life harder for the minority of people that successive governments have insinuated are 'refusing' to work, despite having the opportunity to do so. In February 2008, the government launched a major 'rethinking' of welfare, in which it announced plans to contract out *Jobcentre Plus*-style job search advice and support services to the private sector—paying companies who successfully found work for claimants and managed to keep them in those jobs for six months or more. Fees would be paid according to a sliding scale, with placements for the long-term unemployed netting companies the biggest bonuses. Claimants who did not turn up for interviews or appointments with their personal supervisors would have money docked from their benefits. And similar penalties would be faced by unemployed drug addicts who failed to attend rehab programmes.

Weeks earlier, then Housing Minister Caroline Flint had foreshadowed this new approach when she told the Fabian Society that new council tenants might be asked to sign 'commitment contracts', promising to look for work in return for being offered social housing. Although she said that she merely wanted to 'begin a debate' about whether the unemployed should have to prove that they were looking for work in order to remain in council or *housing association* accommodation, her championing of a 'something for something' culture was widely interpreted as a veiled threat to evict tenants who fail to take up those opportunities that are open to them.

Income Support

Income Support is a flexible non-contributory benefit that is available to people aged between 16 and 60 years who are on low incomes, not in full-time paid employment, and who satisfy various other criteria (for example, being single parents, full-time carers, or registered blind). As of summer 2008, there were three rates for single people:

- £35.65 for 16 and 17-year-olds;
- £46.85 for 18–25-year-olds;
- £59.15 for those aged over 25.

As with other types of benefit, payments to couples take account of their ability to cut costs by shopping and cooking together, and paying joint utility bills. These joint payments are relatively lower as a consequence. The standard rate for all couples in which both partners were aged 18 or over was £92.80.

Again there are restrictions on individuals' eligibility to claim if they have any form of personal savings.

Incapacity Benefit, Employment and Support Allowance (ESA), and Disability Living Allowance (DLA)

Just as there are different levels and types of JSA, so too there is more than one form of benefit for the sick and/or disabled. Incapacity Benefit is a contributions-based benefit that is paid to people judged incapable of working, who are under state pension age, and meet one or more of the following criteria:

- have received statutory sick pay through their employer that has ended, despite the fact that they remain incapable of working;
- are self-employed or unemployed;
- have been receiving Statutory Maternity Pay (SMP), but have not gone back to work for their employer because they are incapable of work.

There are three rates of weekly Incapacity Benefit for people of working age (as at summer 2008):

- short-term (lower)—£61.35;
- short-term (higher)—£72.55;
- long-term (which kicks in after someone has been claiming for 53 weeks)—£81.35.

Pensioners are eligible for short-term rates only, at £78.05 and £81.35, respectively.

Due to its relatively generous size and the sheer number of claimants (some 2.6 million as of January 2008, at an annual cost of £12bn), Incapacity Benefit has become a huge political issue. Labour announced a root-and-branch reform of the rules governing the benefit in 2005, vowing to reduce the number of recipients by one million. The resulting Welfare Reform Act 2007 introduced these changes, but only in relation to new incapacity claimants (as opposed to existing ones). As of October 2008, new claimants would potentially be entitled to a new Employment and Support Allowance (ESA). This ESA would be paid at one of two rates: a higher one for people with serious long-term conditions who remain unable to work, but a lower one for those considered capable of returning to work who fail to do so. Regular employment interviews would be arranged for the latter, while 'work capability assessments' would be introduced to put the accent on what jobs and activities claimants were capable of performing, rather than on their disabilities. Those judged to be capable of seeking work, but who fail to do so, would face benefit cuts.

Claimants hoping for salvation from David Cameron's new 'compassionate Conservatives' had better think again: the Tories have pledged to be even tougher, testing *all* claimants (including long-standing ones) to verify their inability to work.

The other principal sickness-related payment, Disability Living Allowance (DLA), is a non-contributory benefit based purely on an assessment of mental or physical need (usually regardless of an individual's income or savings, or ability to work). People under the age of 65 may claim DLA if they are physically or mentally disabled and need help caring for themselves or with walking. Because it covers both of these aspects, DLA is comprised of a *care component* and a *mobility component*. It is possible for an individual to qualify for one or the other, or both. As of August 2008, the higher rate of the care component was £64.50, the middle rate £43.15, and the lower rate £17.10. The mobility component has only a higher and a lower rate (£45 and £17.10, respectively).

▌ HM Revenue and Customs (HMRC)

HMRC plays an integral role in the welfare system in two key respects: it raises taxes to pay for benefits (known in economics as 'transfer payments'), but of more importance in this chapter, it also makes discreet payments to families, pensioners, and others on limited incomes through tax credits—a system designed to encourage low earners to stay in employment by rewarding them with modest rebates paid through their pay packets, in place of the old-style handouts designed to compensate them for being out of work. As the tax credit system has evolved, it has expanded to provide much needed 'minimum income guarantees' (MIGs) for other vulnerable groups, including pensioners. The main types are outlined in Table 8.4.

The elements that make up Disabled Persons' Tax Credits (DPTCs) are more or less the same as those that together compose Working Families Tax Credits (WFTCs)—that is, 'basic', 'child', 'childcare', 'extra 30 hours', etc. They also include elements for 'enhanced disabled child' (for each child receiving DLA, or registered blind) and 'enhanced disabled adult' (for high levels of disability). There is a new Fast-Track Gateway designed to enable people to start receiving DPTCs without having to prove first that they are eligible for disability benefits.

Table 8.4 A breakdown of the main tax credits available from HMRC

Name of credit	Purpose and scope
Working Families' Tax Credit (WFTC)	Formerly Family Credit, this is paid through low earners' pay packets, in addition to their official wages or salaries. Means-tested, it is seen as a way of topping up the earnings of employed or self-employed people on low or middle incomes. A single WFTC is paid to each eligible household, normally monthly, comprising several different elements—basic (i.e. one per family); extra 30-hour (if at least one family member works for 30 hours or more a week); disability (if either or both parents, or a child has one); child (an extra top-up for each dependant); childcare (up to 70 per cent of eligible approved costs). To be eligible, families must meet the following criteria: (a) be working for 16 hours or more a week; (b) have one or more dependent children under the age of 16 (or under the age of 19 in full-time education); (c) have savings of £8,000 or less.
Child Tax Credit (CTC)	Designed to encourage parents to return to work after having children, these means-tested credits are awarded on a sliding scale to families whose household incomes are £58,175 or less (£66,350 if they have a child under the age of 1).
Pension Credit	In recognition of the fact that a large number of elderly people in Britain did not have the income when still working to save for their retirements, the government introduced this additional tax credit to help poorer pensioners. As of August 2008, everyone over the age of 60 was guaranteed a minimum weekly income of £119.05 for single people or £181.70 for couples. This system is administered by the government's Pension Service.
Disabled Person's Tax Credit (DPTC)	Formerly Disability Working Allowance, this is designed to encourage people with disabilities to return to work. It includes an element covering childcare costs and is designed to top up the earnings of disabled people on low or middle incomes who: (a) work for 16-plus hours a week; (b) already receive disability or incapacity benefits; (c) have savings of £16,000 or less.

The other principal welfare innovation administered by HMRC is the child trust fund (CTF). All British babies born since September 2002 have been entitled to one-off payments by the government of between £250 and £500 (depending on parental income). While parents may decide where to invest the money on behalf of their offspring, only the child is entitled to withdraw it—and only then on his or her eighteenth birthday. In the meantime, parents are encouraged to top up their children's CTF accounts, to a maximum of £1,200 a year, either in one-off payments or instalments of as little as £10 a time. Estimates vary widely as to how much a fund might be worth by 2020, but according to the Nationwide Building Society's annual *Children's Savings Report*, published in 2006, if the initial £250 were to be invested in a share-based option, it could top £40,000 over 18 years (assuming a £1,200 annual top-up and annual growth of 7 per cent). Putting £43 a month away ought to cover the cost of a deposit on a first home (estimated at £15,200 on the basis of current trends).

The aim of the CTF is to foster a culture of saving among young people— particularly those from poorer backgrounds with less parental financial support or savings upon which to rely. The Treasury recently confirmed that a further one-off payment would be made into funds when children reach their seventh birthdays and there is talk of another at the age of 11.

▌ Other forms of welfare support

In addition to the needs-based benefits outlined above, there are a number of other sources of support that are available on a more 'universal' basis (subject to certain qualifying criteria).

Child Benefit is paid to mothers for each child under the age of 16, or under the age of 19, but still in full-time education, or under the age of 18 and registered for work or training through the government's careers service, Connexions. It has long been controversial, given that high-income households arguably have little need for it, while low-earning families receive no more per child.

Statutory maternity and paternity pay are paid via employers to parents of recently born children. Mothers are now entitled to up to a year's paid maternity leave, albeit at a rate of 90 per cent of their usual income for the first six weeks and only £112.75 per week thereafter. Fathers are currently only eligible for two weeks' paid paternity leave, at either 90 per cent of their normal earnings or the £112.75 rate (whichever is lower)—although the government has plans to allow a father to use the mother's maternity leave entitlement in future if she earns more than him and therefore decides to return to work earlier.

Other state entitlements include statutory sick pay, which is available for a maximum of 28 weeks to those in full-time employment unable to work through ill health, and widows' pensions, which are lump sums paid to women whose husbands were below retirement age when they died. Payments begin from the date at which they would have qualified for pensions had they lived.

A further type of welfare support specifically aimed at those on low incomes (whether employed or unemployed) is the one-off payment. This can take several forms, but the most common are crisis loans (lump sums to help out in the event of emergencies or disasters, such as floods or fires in the home), and the Social Fund, which offers either 'regulated'—that is, compulsory—help to those who meet the criteria (for example, one-off payments to help with funeral costs) or 'discretionary' awards, such as short-term budgeting loans to help people get over rocky patches while waiting for their next pay packets or benefit cheques.

The future of the state pension

Although there has been much debate in recent years about the size of the basic state pension—and, in particular, its decreasing value in relation to living costs and average earnings—Britons retain an automatic entitlement to a retirement pension funded out of general taxation.

At present, British men retire at the age of 65, while women can draw their pensions from the age of 60, but this is in the process of changing. Equalization of the retirement age for men and women is due to be phased in over ten years from 2010. Women born before April 1950 will still retire at 60, but those born between 1950 and 1955 will instead do so at 65. As a reflection of the demographic changes currently facing the country—a rapidly ageing population, with pensioners living longer and relatively few people of working age available to support them—the government recently approved plans to raise the age at which UK citizens become eligible for state pensions: to 66 years in 2024, 67 years in 2034, and 68 years in 2044.

The introduction of the basic state retirement pension was one of the founding initiatives of the welfare state in 1948. The basic provision—funded through NI contributions—was supplemented in 1978 with the introduction of the now contentious State Earnings-Related Pension Scheme (SERPS), championed by the bastions of 'Old Labour' (most famously, the late Baroness Castle, who, as then Health and Social Security Secretary, was its main architect). SERPS was seen by many as guaranteeing a civilized degree of comfort to people in their retirement because of the principle that underpinned it—namely, that the value of state pensions should keep pace with that of the average wage.

By the late 1970s, the majority of working people were required by their employers to contribute to a second, occupational, pension, normally through their wage packets. Nowadays, however, the framework of pension provision in the UK is a patchwork one, with many workers having neither the security of employment, nor the level of income needed to pay into a pension scheme over and above their state one.

Mrs Thatcher's government actively encouraged employees to opt out of SERPS and to use their money to invest instead in potentially more lucrative, if riskier, private or personal pensions. In recent years, the vulnerability of some personal pension schemes has been exposed by several major controversies—most notably, the mis-selling scandals that hit Royal and Sun Alliance and Standard Life, and the fraudulent misuse of the Mirror Group pension fund by the late newspaper tycoon Robert Maxwell.

Since the mid-1990s, the pensions issue has become an increasingly pressing one. There has been a growing awareness of the fact that, as the population is living longer, radical steps must be taken to ensure that everyone can retire on a comfortable—or at least liveable—income. As the proportion of the population of working age diminishes, the pressure for people to save for their own retirement is increasing: no longer is there a guarantee that there will be enough money in the public purse to pay for them when they reach retirement age.

The Welfare Reform and Pensions Act 1999 paved the way for potentially radical pension reform. But ministers' attempts to move from this to a definitive and coherent framework for state-funded pensions stuttered for the best part of a decade afterwards, and only after several high-profile reviews of the policy by independent commissions and numerous changes of Pensions Secretary was a conclusion of sorts reached. At time of writing, there are three types of government-backed pension, as outlined in Table 8.5.

Table 8.5 The three types of government-backed pension

Type of pension	How it works
State retirement pension	A contributory benefit, the 'real value' of which has been plummeting in recent years, as the cost of living has risen. It is currently linked to inflation, rather than to average earnings (as under SERPS). Those who do not pay enough NI contributions during their working lives qualify for Income Support on retirement.
Stakeholder pension	Introduced to help those without occupational pensions (e.g. the self-employed), but who earn enough money to save something for their retirement. They are distinct from most personal pension schemes operated by banks and building societies in that they are lower cost and more flexible (people can move them from job to job). The government puts in monthly contributions in place of the employers who do so for those with occupational pensions.
State second pension	Brought in as a replacement for SERPS in April 2002, this is aimed at providing a minimum income guarantee (MIG) for people who do not have the money to save much for their old age through NI credits. In practice, the main beneficiaries are carers and disabled people with sporadic work records.

Following a report by Lord Turner's Pensions Commission, in May 2006, then Work and Pensions Secretary John Hutton belatedly unveiled the most radical shake-up of state pensions for decades. Under his proposals, the following changes are now planned:

- all workers are to be co-opted into a new national pension savings scheme from 2012. Individuals may opt out, but those who do not do so will have to pay 3 per cent of their salaries into a top-up pension pot, with a further 3 per cent contributed by their employers and 1 per cent by the government through tax relief;

- in an echo of SERPS, the state pension will be linked to average earnings, rather than living costs, from as early as 2012;

- entitlement to the state pension is to be reduced to 30 years' worth of NI contributions.

▶ Reviews and appeals under the benefits system

If claimants are dissatisfied with the outcome of a decision on their eligibility for benefit, or a move to withdraw it from them, they may appeal against the decision. Before lodging an appeal, however, the claimant must first go through the full formal complaints process, which requires him or her to file a formal complaint with a so-called 'local decision-maker'. Should he or she be dissatisfied with the outcome, the complainant may apply for a 'review' by the decision maker.

Finally, the claimant has recourse to one last stab at 'justice': an appeal, handled by the *Appeals Service*, otherwise known as the Social Security and Child Support Appeals Tribunal (SSCSAT). Set up in 2006, this agency handles appeals about claims for all kinds of benefit—from DLA to SMP—and the appeals process is as outlined in Table 8.6.

Once the Tribunal has reached its decision, appeals can only ever be taken a further stage than this *on a point of law*. In such circumstances, they are dealt with by either the Social Security Commissioner or by the Child Support Commissioner (two independent ombudsmen).

Table 8.6 The benefit appeals process

Stage	Process
Appeal lodged	Claimant must give formal notice of an appeal, outlining the reasons and background to his or her complaint.
Initial response from benefits office	The office that made the decision sends the appellant and other people involved in the appeal a copy of the reasons for its decision. It also sends a copy of the reasons to the Tribunal.
Formal submission of reasons for appeal	The appellant sends the completed 'pre-hearing enquiry form' to the Tribunal, outlining its reasons for appealing and the details of the original decision.
Hearing of case for and against	A time and place is arranged for a hearing, and the Tribunal hears the appeal.
Decision publicized	Copies of the Tribunal's decision, together with notes explaining it, are sent to the appellant and other people involved in the appeal.

▌ The changing face of home affairs

One of the biggest offices of state, the Home Department (as it is officially known), was split in two in spring 2007 by Mr Blair's final Home Secretary John Reid. He had declared the unwieldy Home Office 'not fit for purpose' on taking over from his predecessor, Charles Clarke, in 2006. Mr Clarke had endured a succession of public embarrassments over the department's handling of security or anti-terrorism and asylum policy, as well as presiding over a ticking time bomb in a prison service creaking under the weight of too many inmates.

Mr Reid stepped down voluntarily when Gordon Brown replaced Mr Blair as prime minister, but not before instigating one of the biggest shake-ups of this sprawling department in its 225-year history. For some years, there had been something of an artificial 'Chinese Wall' between the responsibilities of the Home Office and those of the *Lord Chancellor*'s Department (renamed the 'Department for Constitutional Affairs' by Mr Blair in 2005) in relation to crime and disorder. With the emergence of a raft of new internal security issues in relation to the growing threat of Islamist terrorism, Mr Reid judged that the department needed to cede some of its criminal justice powers to enable it to focus more effectively on the various other policy areas for which it was responsible.

When Mr Brown arrived in Downing Street, he swiftly replaced the Department for Constitutional Affairs with a new 'Ministry of Justice' (MoJ), headed by Lord Falconer's replacement as Lord Chancellor, Jack Straw. Mr Straw became the first Lord Chancellor in more than three hundred years to be a member of Parliament (MP), rather than a peer. As a reflection of this, he was given the additional title 'Secretary of State for Justice'. This better described his powers, in light of the fact that his post had lost several of the Lord Chancellor's traditional roles—notably, that of chairing debate in the House of Lords, which went to the then newly appointed *Lords' Speaker*.

The division of responsibilities between the dual departments for internal affairs that have resulted from this series of recent reforms are now as outlined in Table 8.7.

To aid the Home Office in its new responsibilities for counter-terrorism policy, it was given a new 'subdepartment': the Office for Security and Counter-Terrorism. A 'National Security Board' (NSB)—a weekly forum chaired by the Home Secretary—has also been set up to discuss security threats when they occur. In addition, a National Criminal Justice Board (NCJB) was formed to promote 'joined-up government' between the two departments responsible for different aspects of criminal justice policy, chaired jointly by the Home Secretary, the Justice Secretary, and the Attorney General, Britain's most senior lawyer.

The new-look Home Office

In a symbolic break with generations of male dominancy at the top table in *Cabinet*, Mr Brown appointed former Chief Whip Jacqui Smith as Britain's first female Home Secretary in July 2007. The chief responsibilities of the Home Secretary are examined in the following sections.

Policing and crime prevention

The role of Her Majesty's Constabulary is explored in depth in Chapter 11. In examining the work of the Home Office, however, it is important to out-

Table 8.7 A breakdown of the responsibilities of the Home Office and Ministry for Justice (MoJ)

Home Office	Ministry of Justice (MoJ)
Policing and crime prevention	The court system and sentencing policy
Security and counter-terrorism	Prisons
Asylum, immigration, and citizenship	Probation
ID cards	Prevention of reoffending

line the extent to which police forces in England and Wales remain under the overall authority of this department.

The Home Office funds the police, and is responsible for overall recruitment, training, and pay. Responsibility for organizing policing on the ground, like so many areas of public policy, has long since been delegated from central to local government. In theory, it is down to individual local *police authorities* to appoint, hold to account, and—very occasionally—dismiss the *chief constables* responsible for running the police forces in their areas. In practice, even today, he or she must endorse the appointments and, if there is a perception of declining confidence in either the chief constable or the authority, the Home Secretary may intervene to remove either, or both, against their wishes. In June 2001, then Home Secretary David Blunkett publicly urged Sussex Police Authority to consider sacking its local chief constable, Paul Whitehouse, over his handling of an inquiry into the fatal shooting by a police marksman of an unarmed alleged drug dealer, James Ashley, in St Leonards three-and-a-half years earlier. Mr Whitehouse, who had recently promoted two of the officers involved in the incident, resigned before he could be forced out.

The traditional responsibility of the Home Secretary for overseeing policing in London, through the aegis of the Metropolitan Police Commissioner, was formally handed to a newly created police authority, under the auspices of the *Greater London Authority (GLA)*, in 2000. But even this is seen to wield considerable influence. The GLA passed a vote of no confidence in Sir Ian Blair, then Met Commissioner, in November 2007, following the Old Bailey's decision to convict his force for breaching health and safety legislation when anti-terror officers mistakenly shot dead Jean Charles De Menezes, an innocent Brazilian man, at Stockwell tube station in July 2005. Despite widespread calls for Sir Ian's dismissal, Ms Smith and London Mayor Ken Livingstone publicly defended him. The former's endorsement was seen as a decisive factor in Blair's ability to retain his job at the time, though critics of the shooting were ultimately vindicated when an inquest jury returned an open verdict into his death in December 2008—pointedly disbelieving testimony by police officers who insisted they had shouted a warning to him before opening fire.

It was to be only a matter of time before Sir Ian would finally be forced out, though. In October 2008, five months after Conservative Boris Johnson unseated Mr Livingstone as mayor, Mr Johnson publicly called for a change of leadership at the Met—leaving the Commissioner with little option but to resign. Mr Johnson's immediate criticisms of Sir Ian appeared to have been sparked by accusations of unfair treatment for black and Asian officers in the force. Two of Sir Ian's harshest critics, Assistant Commissioner Tarique Ghaffur (Britain's most senior Muslim officer) and Ali Dizaei, had only recently been suspended, with the former placed on 'gardening leave' in response to his public conduct on filing a £1.2m racial discrimination claim against the Met. The mayor, who was about to take over as chairman of the Metropolitan Police Authority, is believed effectively to have sacked Sir Ian by privately threatening him with non-cooperation if he remained in his £240,000-a-year post. Mr Johnson immediately launched a new inquiry into allegations of racism in the Met—as if to underline his insinuation that the former Commissioner had presided over a force that remained 'institutionally racist', despite its protestations to the contrary. (The term had been coined a decade earlier by Sir William Macpherson's report into the murder of the black teenager Stephen Lawrence. Police botched their investigation into the racially motivated crime, scuppering an initial trial, and Lawrence's killers have yet to be brought to justice.)

The timing of Mr Johnson's intervention coincided with the launch of an advertising campaign by the Met's Black Police Association to deter people from the black and Asian communities from joining the force. Despite this endorsement, the mayor's action brought him into a near head-on collision with Ms Smith, who—despite stopping short of reinstating Sir Ian—warned Mr Johnson that she would not be dictated to by him in relation to the Commissioner's replacement.

The Met aside, Labour's reign has been marked by periodic run-ins with the police as a whole—usually over issues relating to pay and recruitment. In December 2007, the Metropolitan Police Federation declared itself 'at war' with the government over its decision to stagger a 2.5 per cent pay rise, awarding increases only when it was satisfied that productivity targets were being met in relation to crime detection and prevention. While Ms Smith refused to buckle over the pay issue, she did signal a willingness to listen to other concerns—notably, the growing discontent among officers about increases in paperwork that they argued were preventing them from getting out onto the streets, where the public wanted to see them. Ms Smith agreed to start cutting red tape by simplifying an exhaustive form that officers were expected to fill in whenever they questioned a member of the public under 'stop and search' rules. The form had originally been introduced to allay concerns that black men were being searched disproportionately, compared to people from other ethnic backgrounds.

There has also been dismay over crime rates under Labour. In the decade from 1997 to 2007, police funding rose by 77 per cent in real terms (£4.8bn), yet statistics were far from conclusive about the extent to which crime was falling. According to British Crime Survey figures published in January 2008, the risk of becoming a crime victim in Britain had fallen to a 27-year low, with a year-on-year fall in reported crime of 9 per cent. But figures obtained from the police themselves showed that drug offences had soared by nearly a quarter in the previous 12 months. The number of firearms-related arrests had risen by 4 per cent.

When Mr Blair was still prime minister, his wackier policy proposals often received short shrift from the police. In 2002, he mooted the idea of imposing spot fines on people caught in the act of drink-related antisocial behaviour, suggesting that the miscreants could be frog-marched to the nearest cash point by officers and forced to withdraw the necessary money. The Police Federation dismissed the idea as unworkable.

Like hospitals, schools, and care homes, police forces have to submit themselves to regulation and inspection. The body responsible, Her Majesty's Inspectorate of Constabulary (HMIC), is actually the oldest organization of its kind—dating back more than 150 years, to the County and Borough Police Act 1856. Both the Prisons Service and the Probation Service also have their own inspectorates: the former coming under the Home Office, and the latter having recently switched from that department to the MoJ.

Security and counter-terrorism

When 52 commuters were killed in a succession of suicide bombings in central London on 7 July 2005, the British government decided at once that security policy would have to be at the heart of its future political agenda. Ever since the attacks on New York's World Trade Center on 11 September 2001, and the UK's subsequent support for US-led military action in Afghanistan and Iraq, the country had been periodically threatened with its own atrocity—both covertly, through tip-offs gathered by its intelligence services, and overtly, by the increasingly bellicose online proclamations of Osama bin Laden, his chief 'lieutenant' Ayman Al Zawahiri, and Abu Musab al-Zarqawi, late so-called leader of 'Al-Qaeda in Iraq'.

As a result of these threats—real and perceived—Mr Blair's government had already passed a succession of 'anti-terror' laws long before the 7 July bombings took place. In fact, so proactive had it been, that some critics of his policies (not to mention the Iraq invasion itself) argued that, far from preventing further attacks, they may actually have provoked them.

Of all anti-terror policies introduced in Britain in the wake of the 11 September attacks, the most controversial and far-reaching measures have been those relating to the detention of terrorist suspects. At the heart of the controversy has been ministers' cavalier willingness—in the eyes of their critics—to dispense with more than eight hundred years of due legal process by detaining people for prolonged periods without charge. Civil liberties campaigners saw moves such as the internment in Belmarsh Prison of individuals suspected of, but not yet tried for, terror offences as a clear breach of the sacrosanct constitutional principle of habeas corpus—essentially, the right to a fair trial before one's peers—first introduced under Magna Carta. Signed by King John in 1215 (see p. 7), this mammoth document stipulated:

❝ No free man shall be seized or imprisoned . . . except by the lawful judgement of his equals or by the law of the land. ❞

The policy of detaining so-called 'terror suspects' summarily (before trial) at Belmarsh began in late 2001, shortly after the 11 September attacks. It was not long before the government—which had opted out of the article of the Human Rights Act barring it from taking such action—was facing significant challenges to its authority. As early as July 2002, the Special Immigration Appeals Commission (SIAC)—a Home Office *quango*—ruled in response to an application by four of the detainees that the Anti-Terrorism, Crime and Security Act 2001—under which they had been imprisoned—unjustifiably discriminated against foreign nationals. Although this ruling was later overturned by the Court of Appeal, which argued that Britain was facing a state of emergency, worse was to come for the government. Most significantly, in December 2004, the Law Lords ruled by an eight-to-one majority that continued detention of the 12 individuals still in custody was incompatible with human rights legislation.

Despite an initial show of defiance, then Home Secretary Mr Clarke was forced to release the suspects early in 2005, replacing indefinite detention with new 'control orders'—sweeping powers to confine suspects in the community through the use of electronic tagging, curfews, and even house arrest. But these soon ran into trouble, too. Because an order could be introduced for between six and 12 months at the Home Secretary's behest, with little or no opposition, the policy again upset civil liberties campaigners. Neither was it an unqualified success on a purely practical level: in May 2007, it emerged that three men allegedly plotting to kill British troops abroad—Lamine Adam, aged 26, his brother Ibrahim, aged 20, and Cerie Bullivant, aged 24—had absconded while under control orders, prompting calls for the system to be tightened up by the independent reviewer of terrorism laws, Lib Dem peer Lord Carlile.

The most recent controversy concerning terror suspects relates to the period of time for which police are permitted to detain them for questioning without charge. In November 2005, Tony Blair suffered his first House of Commons defeat in eight years as prime minister by staking his authority on a vote to increase the period from an existing limit of 14 days to 90. Mr Blair—who claimed that senior police officers had told him that the case for extending their detention powers to nearly three months was 'compelling'—had to accept a compromise of 28 days.

Shortly after replacing Mr Blair, Mr Brown made clear his determination to revisit the issue by extending the time limit to up to 58 days. After months of wrangling with rebellious **backbenchers**, he finally settled on an upper limit of 42 days and offered a series of compromises to placate opponents, although it stopped short of including a 'sunset clause' requiring the Bill to be renewed every year, as some wanted. Even then, the measure had to be forced through the Commons on a three-line **whip**—with the government relying on support from the Democratic Unionists in an echo of the Tories' problems over the Maastricht Treaty (see p. 282). Because 36 Labour MPs broke ranks to vote against the extension with the Conservatives and Lib Dems, the reform was squeezed through by a majority of only nine.

But this was not to be the last word on the subject. On 13 October 2008—the day on which the British government announced the £37bn partial takeover of the Royal Bank of Scotland and the merged Lloyds TSB and HBOS (see p. 221)—Ms Smith formally shelved the 42-day detention plans after they were defeated in the House of Lords by a majority of 191 votes. Among those who voted against the measure were Mr Blair's former Attorney General Lord Goldsmith and ex-Lord Chancellor Lord Falconer, as well as erstwhile MI5 heads Dame Eliza Manningham-Buller and Dame Stella Rimington. Ms Smith insisted the following day that the government would revisit the proposal in the form of emergency legislation at a later date, should Britain face a further terrorist attack, but Opposition parties sought to portray Mr Brown's decision not to force it through the Lords using the Parliament Act (see p. 65) as a humiliating climbdown.

Asylum, immigration, and citizenship

Before terrorism shifted the goalposts in 2001, perhaps the single biggest home affairs issue of the past decade had been the dual question of asylum and immigration. The term 'asylum seeker' entered the media lexicon around the time that war broke out in the Balkans in the early 1990s. Tabloids and broadsheets alike were quick to focus on this new 'threat' to Britain's borders, and, by 2002, the red-tops were filled with scare stories about impending invasions of 'illegal immigrants' lured by the UK's 'soft touch' benefits system. Their agitated prose was fuelled by the initially laissez-faire attitude of the French government to a burgeoning refugee camp at Sangatte, near Calais, from which 1,600 asylum seekers from all around the world were apparently planning to sneak into southern England.

More recently, *enlargement* of the European Union (EU), first to 25, then 27, countries, has led to a significant 'influx' of economic migrants from other parts of Europe—and, in particular, from former Eastern Bloc countries such as Poland—in pursuit of paid work. This, too, has been controversial, with national newspapers such as the *Daily Mail* and the *Daily Express* pandering to the concerns of local communities in some areas of the country that foreign workers were 'stealing' job opportunities from long-standing residents and putting pressure on already overstretched public services, such as social housing, schools, and health care. There have also been numerous headlines blaming immigrants for rises in certain types of crime. In fact, according to two reports published in April 2008, immigrants have actually had little, or no, negative impact on either demand for public services or crime. The first, published by the Association of Chief Police Officers (ACPO), found that offending rates in the Polish, Romanian, and Bulgarian communities (the focus of the study, due to the influx of economic migrants from those countries following their accession to the EU) were broadly proportionate to that within the British population as a whole. The second, a joint study by the *Commission for Equality and Human Rights (CEHR)* and the Local Government Association (LGA), found little evidence (contrary to popular myth) that migrants were jumping the queue to obtain social housing before local people: in fact, it said 60 per cent of those who had moved to Britain in the previous five years were in private rented accommodation.

But not every survey paints a rosy picture of immigration: according to a report by the Lords Economic Affairs Committee, also published in April 2008, immigrants have had 'little or no impact' on the UK's economic well-being. The Committee, chaired by Lord Wakeham, recommended a formal 'cap' on immigration numbers (a position now supported by the Tories).

This was not the first such embarrassment for the government. In December 2007, analysis of employment data by the Statistics Commission found that 80 per cent of all new jobs created in Britain since 1997 had gone to foreign-born workers (1.4 million out of 1.7 million). Equally alarming was Ms Smith's admission around the same time that as many as 11,000 non-EU nationals licensed to work in the security industry might be illegal immigrants. One had been involved in repairing Mr Blair's car; another was found to be working as a cleaner in the House of Commons in February 2008.

Of course, asylum seekers, illegal immigrants, and economic migrants often have a far from cushy time when they arrive in Britain. In 1999, papers across southern England were filled with reports about the appalling housing conditions that some families were forced to endure while their asylum applications were processed and as they waited to be 'dispersed' to other parts of the country. Meanwhile, an emerging black market in cheap foreign labour (employed on rates well below the minimum wage) fostered by unscrupulous people traffickers has led to some high-profile tragedies. In February 2004, 21 Chinese refugees were drowned in Morecambe Bay, Lancashire, while illegally working as cockle pickers.

Sensationalism aside, the UK's population is undoubtedly rising fast: according to the Office for National Statistics (ONS), it has soared by 8 per cent since 1971 and is projected to increase by a further 4.4 per cent by 2016. In September 2007, the ONS predicted that the number of immigrants arriving in Britain would continue rising by up to 190,000 a year—three times higher than previous estimates—while, three months later, it was reporting the fact that the birth rate among foreign-born women living in the UK had overtaken that of British-born mothers. These and other demographic trends have turned immigration and asylum into the most problematic and divisive issue facing government.

The decision by aspiring immigrants and economic migrants to relocate to the UK can also have a negative knock-on effect on their countries of origin. The migration of large numbers of skilled Polish workers, such as plumbers and electricians, to the UK following the country's admission into the EU produced as many negative newspaper headlines in Poland as it did in Britain. In some media, whole towns were depicted as having been 'drained' of their most highly trained artisans by Britain and other west European countries. Meanwhile, the backlash among some sections of the electorate over the perceived impact of inward migration and immigration on the availability of job opportunities for native Britons led to the UK imposing restrictions on migration from the two newest member states, Bulgaria and Romania (both of which joined in January 2007), and to Mr Brown's controversial pledge to work towards a guarantee of a 'British job for every British worker'.

But what do terms such as 'asylum seeker' and 'illegal immigrant' actually *mean*—and what, if anything, is the difference between these categories of person? Put simply, the term 'asylum seeker' is generally used as a synonym for 'refugee', which the 1951 **United Nations (UN)** Convention Relating to the Status of Refugees described as follows:

> A person who owing to a well-founded fear of being persecuted for reasons of race, religion, nationality, membership of a particular social group, or political opinion, is outside the country of their nationality, and is unable to or, owing to such fear, is unwilling to avail him/herself of the protection of that country."

The term 'asylum' is also distinct from that of 'immigration', in that it is often used to describe a *temporary* state of affairs—an individual fleeing tyranny in his or her home country is not necessarily seeking to remain permanently in the land to which he or she has fled.

Immigration, in contrast, is used to describe the process of becoming a citizen of a different country. 'Illegal immigrant' is frequently used a pejorative term by right-wing politicians and newspapers. It refers to individuals who illegally cross borders to enter a country without following the official asylum procedure. Before the Sangatte camp was closed, there were several instances of refugees illicitly entering Britain through the Channel Tunnel.

Asylum policy is overseen by the Border and Immigration Agency (previously the Immigration and Nationality Directorate), a Home Office executive agency. The question of whether to grant asylum does not arise in the case of Irish Republic or Commonwealth citizens who had the right of abode in Britain before January 1983; neither does it apply to EU citizens. It applies only marginally to nationals of the European Economic Area (EEA), a region of *potential* EU countries, which encompasses the Union itself, plus neighbouring states such as Iceland, Liechtenstein, and Norway. Residents of these countries are already allowed (subject to certain limitations) to work in the UK and, if they can support themselves, live here too. But nationals of most countries outside these areas, including many African and Asian nations, require a visa before entering Britain. Some also require 'entry clearance'.

Other recent changes to asylum and immigration policy are outlined in Table 8.8.

In an effort to reassure UK taxpayers that the country is no 'free for all' for foreign immigrants, the Home Office has introduced a succession of measures designed to make 'successful' applicants 'earn' their status as putative UK citizens, as outlined in Table 8.9.

Table 8.8 Recent rule changes covering asylum and immigration policy

Rule	How it works
Redefinition of 'refugee' status	People fleeing persecution or refugees can seek asylum in Britain, in accordance with the United Nations Protocol on the Status of Refugees 1951. Under the Asylum and Immigration Act 1996, introduced by Mr Major's government in response to growing feelings that some asylum seekers were 'economic refugees' (i.e. people in search of more prosperous surroundings and state benefits, rather than those trying to escape tyranny), however, certain countries were designated as not begetting refugees.
'One-stop' appeal system	The Immigration and Asylum Act 1999 introduced a new appeal process for those applying for asylum or immigrant status whose applications are refused. The fast-track approach requires asylum seekers to declare immediately every reason for wanting to stay in the UK—meaning that, at the outset, all relevant circumstances are taken into account and the authorities cannot be accused of failing to consider his or her whole situation (i.e. it is a system designed to have 'one application, one decision, and one appeal'). Appeals must be formally lodged within ten days of receipt of a one-stop notice from the Home Secretary or Home Office officials.
'Before or after' appeals	Immigration appeals can be either on-entry or after-entry—depending on when, in a refugee's arrival process, the decision being appealed against was made. In rare situations, involving national security or the public interest, the Special Immigration Appeals Commission oversees the right of appeal.
Asylum or immigration— 'make your choice'	Asylum appeals rest on an individual's claim for only that—rather than for permanent immigrant status. If an appellant is involved in an immigration appeal process, he or she cannot later raise asylum grounds if he or she loses the former. It is sometimes possible, however, for an applicant to be given 'exceptional leave to remain' even though he or she does not strictly qualify for asylum status under the 1951 Refugee Convention. This happens when the Home Secretary decides that the applicant cannot be expected to return to his or her country of origin. There are around 5,000 'hard case' asylum seekers in Britain at any one time, hailing from countries such as Iraq, Zimbabwe, and Somalia. Unsuccessful applicants, meanwhile, are sometimes deported to a 'safe third country'.

Identity cards and the great DNA debate

If any issue raises the hackles of civil liberties campaigners almost as much as that of detention without trial it is that of identity (ID) cards. Similarly contentious is the related argument over proposals for a national DNA database to aid in the fight against crime.

As of 2009, British citizens applying for adult passports for the first time, or renewing existing ones, are now offered a choice between being issued with national identity cards containing both their specific personal details

Table 8.9 New 'rights and responsibilities' measures for 'successful' immigration applicants

Device	How it works
Vouchers	To avoid accusations that it was prepared to give asylum seekers cash handouts equivalent to the state benefits for which British citizens are eligible, the government introduced vouchers, which could be exchanged for food and toiletries by refugees in the process of applying for asylum. The scheme was scrapped by Mr Blunkett in 2002 following a riot at the Yarl's Wood detention centre, but reintroduced in 2006, following controversy about the cash payments system that replaced it. Under the scheme, 'failed' asylum seekers who cannot be deported to their home countries because of human rights concerns also qualify for the vouchers, worth £35 a week, in addition to a bed. Alternatively, they can claim three meals a day and no additional financial support.
Citizenship ceremonies	Intended to steady community relations between British residents and the perceived new 'waves' of foreign immigrants moving into their areas, these were introduced in 2004. On 26 February of that year and in the presence of the Prince of Wales, 19 people—including three children—swore allegiance to the Queen, sang the national anthem, and vowed to respect the rights and freedoms of British citizens. Since then, citizenship ceremonies have been held repeatedly across the UK. New immigrants are also given an 'immigration handbook', and are expected to attend classes in the English language, UK institutions and the law, to familiarize themselves with Britain's cultural heritage.
Points system	Introduced for *economic migrants* in early 2008, this five-tier system seeks to limit the ability of unskilled workers from non-EU countries to come to work in Britain, while welcoming skilled migrants as 'key contributors' to the UK economy. Introducing the measure, Immigration Minister Liam Byrne revealed points for 'highly skilled migrants' would be awarded on the basis of age, qualifications, and previous salary. Around 75 points are needed to guarantee entry.
Probationary citizenship	In a **Green Paper** published in February 2008, *The Path to Citizenship*, Ms Smith outlined plans to delay the granting of full citizenship to non-EU economic migrants who apply to settle in Britain permanently. Under the previous system, migrants could apply for a British passport after five years of living and working in the country. The new system now requires them to serve a probationary period of 'earned citizenship' following their initial five-year stay of between one and three years. Under the proposals, the prospect of someone being granted full citizenship increases if he or she takes part in voluntary work, but goes down if he or she commits a crime. In the meantime, benefit and social housing entitlement is limited.

(name, age, address, etc.) and biometric data (fingerprints, facial character-istics, irises), or a new-style 'biometric passport' containing more limited information. The aim of the 'biographical footprint' held on the ID card is to enable certain accredited organizations to use it—with the cardholder's permission—to confirm his or her identity. Students will be eligible to apply for them from 2010. Foreign nationals living and working in the UK have been issued with biometric ID cards since 2008. Although having a card is not currently compulsory, the government plans to make them so eventu-ally. There are, however, no firm plans to force people to carry their cards at all times.

Opponents of ID cards broadly fall into two camps: the pragmatists and the idealists. Pragmatists, such as former Conservative Shadow Home Sec-retary David Davis, have argued that questions over the reliability of the technology used to produce the cards, combined with the fact that owning one will not be compulsory for the foreseeable future, threaten to make the scheme an ineffective waste of taxpayers' money. Idealists, such as cam-paign group Liberty, and many Labour and Lib Dem MPs, see the cards as a dangerous next step on the road to turning Britain into a paranoid surveil-lance society. They also point to inconsistencies in the arguments that minis-ters have used to justify the measure: when first mooted, in the aftermath of 11 September, it appeared that they were primarily intended as a weapon in the 'war on terror', but towards the end of Mr Blair's premiership, he argued that the government's main intention was to protect people against the grow-ing threat of identity fraud.

Concerns about the 'Big Brother' aspects of the ID card scheme have been compounded by publicity surrounding the expansion of the national DNA database—a sprawling electronic record of DNA samples taken from crime scenes and individuals held in police custody. Originally set up in 1995, by 2008, it contained 4.5 million DNA samples (equivalent to 5.2 per cent of the population), according to Home Office figures. Since 2004, anyone penalized for an arrestable offence—even those given a simple police caution—have had their samples added to the database. To give some indication of how comprehensive the British system is compared to those adopted in other countries, the US database contains samples from a mere 0.5 per cent of its citizens. To ensure that the database is not misused, it is regulated by a board comprising members of the Home Office, ACPO, the Association of Police Authorities (APA), and the Human Genetics Commission (HGC).

A series of high-profile convictions of serial murderers and sex attackers in early 2008 led to calls from senior police officers in some areas for the government to extend the scope of the database to include the whole British population. But the Home Office has so far resisted these demands—despite suffering several embarrassments over revelations about the extent to which 'innocent' people are already being added to the database. In December 2006, then Home Secretary Mr Reid was forced to admit that more than a million of those whose details were on the database had been neither cautioned, nor convicted. One reason for the apparent anomaly was the fact that police had failed to remove the details of individuals arrested and charged with criminal offences, but subsequently acquitted.

As with ID cards, defenders of the database—including those who believe that it should be made universal—have argued that the innocent have nothing to fear from it. But its opponents say such views are counter-intuitive and that inclusion of non-offenders on a police record contradicts the basic tenet of British justice that individuals are 'innocent until proven guilty'. Not all critics of the policies have been Opposition MPs, disgruntled backbenchers, or people with other obvious agendas. In August 2004, the government's own *Information Commissioner*, Richard Thomas, told *The Times*:

> ❝ My anxiety is that we don't sleepwalk into a surveillance society where much more information is collected about people, accessible to far more people shared across many more boundaries, than British society would feel comfortable with. ❞

Three years later, one of Britain's most senior judges, Lord Justice Sedley, described the current DNA database as 'indefensible' and suggested that it be extended to cover the whole population as soon as possible—if only to address what he perceived as its intrinsic discrimination against people from ethnic minorities.

Safeguarding human rights for British citizens

The passage of the Human Rights Act in 1998 (see p. 13) marked the beginning of a sustained championing of equality of opportunity and basic freedoms by the Labour government, which has since led to everything from the equalization of the age of consent for gay and heterosexual sex, to the introduction of civil partnerships for gay couples.

To spearhead the government's drive to guarantee British citizens equal opportunities—regardless of age, gender, race, or disability—it established three new quangos on entering office in 1997:

- the Equal Opportunities Commission (EOC);
- the Commission for Racial Equality (CRE);
- the Disability Rights Commission (DRC).

Ten years later, on 1 October 2007, these bodies were merged to become the Commission for Equality and Human Rights (CEHR), also known as the 'Equality and Human Rights Commission'. The Commission's remit has been extended to cover sexual orientation and religious beliefs, in addition to the areas dealt with by the three former quangos.

In addition to investigating individual complaints about discrimination, the Commission:

- enforces the law in relation to equal opportunities and rights;
- influences the development of the law and government policy;
- promotes good practice;
- fosters better relations between communities.

▌ The Ministry of Justice (MoJ)

The British criminal justice system has two core elements—the court system and the treatment of offenders—both of which are now the responsibility of the Justice Secretary.

The court system and civil law

The day-to-day work business of running the British courts is carried out by Her Majesty's Courts Service, an executive agency of the MoJ. The Justice Secretary him or herself is responsible for promoting more general reforms of the civil law and the legal aid system.

The government's principal legal advisers are the Attorney General and Solicitor-General, both of whom are members of either the Lords or the Commons. In Scotland, their roles are performed by the Advocate General for Scotland (who has assumed the roles previously held by the Lord Advocate and the Solicitor General for Scotland).

Subordinate to the Attorney General are the Director of Public Prosecutions (DPP), who runs the Crown Prosecution Service (CPS)—that is, the state-owned legal service that brings prosecutions on behalf of the Crown—and the DPP for Northern Ireland, along with the Director of the Serious Fraud Office. At present, there are, as yet unfinalized, proposals to strip the Attorney General of certain powers that are seen to promote conflicts of interest between his or her judicial role and his or her partisan one as member of the government. Lord Goldsmith (the last Attorney General under Mr Blair) was seen to be torn between party loyalty and legal protocol in giving advice on the legitimacy of invading Iraq, and in relation to the more recent controversy not to press charges against BAE Systems over its alleged corrupt dealings with Saudi Arabia.

Criminal law

The Justice Secretary has overall responsibility for criminal law and the introduction of Bills needed to change it. In this respect, his or her work is delegated to the following two principal agencies:

- the *National Probation Service (NPS)*—which oversees the supervision of individuals serving community-based sentences for criminal offences, or periods in their prison terms during which they are permitted to live in the community. Each year, the NPS supervises 175,000 offenders (90 per cent of whom are male, 10 per cent of whom are female), a quarter of them 16–20-year-olds. There are 42 county-based probation services in England and Wales, the areas of supervision of which correspond with those of local police force boundaries. Since 2001, the NPS has come under a new National Probation Directorate in the Home Office and been supervised by an independent HM Inspectorate of Probation,

- the *National Offender Management Service (NOMS)*—with its own chief executive, NOMS has taken over the overall running of the 135 prisons in England and Wales from the Prisons Service (Scotland currently retains the old system). Formed in April 2008, NOMS oversees *all* prisons—whether publicly or privately funded and/or owned—and its chief executive office has been left with ultimate responsibility for administrative mistakes arising from its conduct. The prisons service still exists—but only as one 'unit' of NOMS, with responsibility for publicly funded jails.

Recent developments in the prison system

The Prisons Service employs the 48,000 wardens, officers, and governors who maintain and administer prisons on the ground on a day-to-day basis. Since the Criminal Justice Act 1991, the management of many prisons has been contracted out to the private sector—as has the transportation of defendants held in custody to and from court. The first four newly built prisons handed over to private managers were The Wolds (on Humberside), Blaken-hurst (in Worcestershire), Doncaster, and Buckley Hall (Rochdale).

In addition, all new jails built since the early 1990s have been funded through the **private finance initiative (PFI)** or the **public–private partnership (PPP)**, as New Labour renamed it (see pp. 238–9). The first four privately financed jails, opened in 1998–99, were on Merseyside, and in Nottinghamshire, South Wales, and Kilmarnock.

Complaints about the prison and probation services are handled by a single authority: the independent Prisons and Probation Ombudsman (PPO) for England and Wales. HM Prison Inspectorates—one for each of England, Scotland, and Wales—are charged with visiting prisons every three years to report on conditions and treatment, in much the same way that **Office for Standards in Education (Ofsted)** inspectors visit schools and *further education* colleges to observe teaching standards (see p. 480). Individual prisons and young offenders' institutions also have their own 'boards of visitors'—that is, groups of local people appointed by the Home Secretary to relay complaints from prisoners in the same way as **local involvement networks (LINks)** operate in the NHS (see p. 187).

Since the early 1990s, prisons have seldom been out of the news in Britain. Typically, stories about them tend to be negative, focusing on overcrowding, riots, and occasionally even breakouts. To try to provide spare capacity, successive governments have done everything from adapting military camps to act as temporary prisons to commissioning a 'prison ship', *HMP Weare*, moored off Portland, Dorset. During his time as a tough-talking Home Secretary in Mr Major's government, Michael Howard vowed to cut the number of community sentences and send more people to jail, particularly violent offenders. But his famous cry of 'Prison works!' set him on a collision course with then director-general of the Prison Service, Derek Lewis, who warned of dangerous levels of overcrowding. In January 1995, the simmering prisons crisis came to a head during a succession of riots and breakouts, first at Everthorpe Jail, Humberside, then at Parkhurst. A damning report into the state of the system saw Mr Howard sack Mr Lewis in October of that year—but not without facing tough questioning from Jeremy Paxman in a now legendary interview for BBC2's *Newsnight*, during which Mr Paxman asked Mr Howard 12 times if he had 'threatened to overrule' Mr Lewis.

Overcrowding remains a serious concern for the government to this day. In May 2007, the prison population reached 80,500—within a whisker of the total capacity in the system. At the time, a further three hundred prisoners were being held in police and court cells. Lord Falconer, then Lord Chancellor, issued an appeal to the courts to limit their use of prison sentences for people convicted of minor offences and it emerged that the government was considering the early release of 3,000 inmates to free up cells for more serious offenders. To add to ministers' blushes, Lord Phillips, the Lord Chief Justice, said in a public statement:

❝ The prisons are full and the predictions are that the rate of prison sentencing is bound to outstrip the capacity of the prisons, despite the plan to provide another 8,000 prison places. ❞

More recent controversies around the prison service have focused on the plight of staff themselves and, in particular, the poor pay and conditions of many prison officers. In August 2007, 20,000 members of the Prison Officers' Association (POA) threatened a 24-hour wildcat strike in protest over overcrowding and a below-*inflation* pay rise of 1.9 per cent.

The rehabilitation of offenders

Convicted offenders receive a sentence that is either *custodial*—that is, detention in a prison or young offenders' institution—or *non-custodial*—for example, conditional discharge, community service, probation, fines, compensation orders, etc. The latter are supervised in England and Wales by the NPS; in Scotland, they fall under the auspices of local authority social workers.

Other than in the exceptional cases when Royal Pardons are issued on the advice of the Home Secretary (see p. 25), prisoners are only generally granted early release from jail in recognition of 'good behaviour' in custody. This system is known as **parole**. Although the application process is relatively simple, parole itself is complex, in that prisoners' eligibility to apply for it will depend on a variety of factors—most notably, the nature and severity of their offences. Those eligible for parole may apply in the first instance six months before their earliest possible release date (normally specified at the time that they were sentenced). A file on the prisoner will be compiled and three members of the Parole Board—the body that advises the government on parole applications—will meet to decide whether to grant the prisoner's wishes.

A swift decision may be taken for more minor offenders to allow them parole 'on licence'—under which they may be released early subject to the condition that they do not reoffend. If they do so within the remaining period of their original sentence. they may end up having to serve the remainder of that term in jail after all, as well as any additional period relating to their latest conviction. A full Parole Board hearing tends to be called only for the most serious offenders.

Due, in part, to concerns about prison overcrowding, in practice, parole has become all but automatic for the great majority of offenders. In 1991, Mr Howard toughened up the procedure. The conditions that he introduced to guide future parole decisions included that:

- prisoners other than the most serious offenders (rapists and murderers) serving *four years or more* should be released on Parole Board recommendation after serving half of their sentence and will normally be automatically released after serving two-thirds of it;

- final decisions on the early release of prisoners serving *more than four, but less than seven years*, should be taken by the Parole Board;

- prisoners sentenced to life imprisonment for certain kinds of murder—for example, the murder of police officers, terrorism, and child killings—tended automatically to serve at least 20 years. The early release of such 'mandatory life prisoners' could only be authorized by the Home Secretary in consultation with the Parole Board and the judiciary;

- those sentenced to life for offences other than murder would normally be released by the Home Secretary after a period set by the judge at their trial. The Board still has the power, however, to direct that continued confinement beyond this period is necessary to protect the public. Such sentences—known as 'indeterminate sentences for public protection' (IPP)—have caused headaches for recent governments. In February 2008, three Court of Appeal judges and the Lord Chief Justice ruled that the board was not sufficiently independent of ministers to approve IPPs at their request, and that Mr Straw had acted 'unlawfully' in his prior treatment of such prisoners. Among the high-profile prisoners repeatedly refused release on grounds of public safety, as well the peculiar seriousness of their crimes, was the late Moors murderer Myra Hindley; Peter Sutcliffe, the 'Yorkshire Ripper', is another example.

In addition to the 1991 Act, the Crime (Sentences) Act 1997 (based on the preceding *Protecting the Public* **White Paper**) further toughened the sentencing regime by putting greater emphasis on the idea of prisoners *earning* their parole, by restyling them 'early release days', which could be gained and lost.

It also introduced the following:

- automatic life sentences for those convicted twice of serious sexual or violent crimes;
- mandatory minimum prison sentences for drug dealers and serial burglars.

Until 2006, Scottish parole policy was slightly more lenient:

- the Parole Board could release prisoners serving between four and ten years after they had served half their sentence—but the early release of anyone serving more than ten years needed the personal consent of the Home Secretary;
- those released early from sentences of four years or more were supervised to the end of their allotted terms, with the help of their local authority social work departments.

Under the Custodial Sentences and Weapons Act 2007, passed by the *Scottish Parliament*, conditions for early release were significantly toughened. Automatic early release without conditions for prisoners serving fewer than four years was replaced with a new licensing system. Anyone released early who breached his or her licence terms would be returned to jail. In addition, sentencing judges who considered a particular defendant to be of particular risk to the public could in future stipulate that the date after which parole applied to that individual was later in his or her sentence than the usual halfway mark. The Parole Board would also be given powers to increase this custodial period at a later date, should the circumstances arise. Two years earlier, the Management of Offenders (Scotland) Act 2005 had ended unconditional early release for sex offenders sentenced to between six months and four years, subjecting them to a new licence-and-supervision system.

In Northern Ireland, special circumstances apply in terrorism cases, in recognition of the unique nature of The Troubles. Until 1995, terrorists sentenced to five years or more were usually paroled only after serving two-thirds of their sentences, but this has since been brought in line with the rest of the UK—that is, eligibility after serving half a sentence. Terrorists convicted of another offence before the end of their original sentences have to complete their original sentence before the next one starts. In response to the positive progress of the Northern Ireland peace process, a one-off arrangement was made allowing inmates of the Maze Prison out on licence for Christmas 1999 and New Year 2000.

→ Further reading

Bartholomew, J. (2006) *The Welfare State We're In*, London: Politico's Publishing. **Critique of the welfare state, using examples of its failings in areas as diverse as state education and the pensions system to argue that Britain would have been better off without it.**

Glendinning, C. and Kemp, P. (2006) *Cash and Care: Policy Challenges in the Welfare State*, Bristol: Policy Press. **Comprehensive overview of recent trends in the provision of social security, including evaluations of the impact of policy initiatives such as tax credits and Welfare to Work, and the changing socio-economic profile of benefit recipients.**

Hansen, R. S. (2001) *Citizenship and Immigration in Post-war Britain: The Institutional Origins of a Multicultural Nation*, Oxford: Oxford University Press. **Accomplished evaluation of the socio-economic and cultural impact of immigration since 1945.**

Lowe, R. (2004) *Welfare State in Britain Since 1945*, 3rd edn, London: Palgrave Macmillan. **Third edition of standard work on the evolution of the welfare state, incorporating analysis of recent trends in social welfare provision, such as tax credits and Welfare to Work.**

Reiner, R. (2000) *The Politics of the Police*, 3rd edn, Oxford: Oxford University Press. **Fully revised third edition of standard text on the origins, history, and present-day makeup of the British police. Includes detailed analysis of current issues and updates on recent reforms, including those arising out of the Macpherson Report into the Stephen Lawrence case.**

Sanders, A. (2006) *Criminal Justice*, London: LexisNexis UK. **Critical analysis and explanation of the criminal justice system in Britain, focusing on all aspects of crime and punishment, including habeas corpus, the penal system, and sentencing procedures.**

? Review questions

1. What is the difference between a 'contributory' and a 'non-contributor' benefit?

2. Outline the history, aims, and responsibilities of the Home Office. To what extent have these changed and been extended since its inception?

3. To what extent has the welfare state remained true to its founding principle to look after British citizens—regardless of their means—from the cradle to the grave?

4. Outline the recent developments in UK pensions policy, explaining the main types of state-funded pension and some of the alternatives.

5. Which government department—the Home Office or the Ministry of Justice—has the greater jurisdiction over criminal justice matters in the UK? Outline the specific responsibilities in relation to crime, policing, and the courts of each department.

 Online resource centre

www.oxfordtextbooks.co.uk/orc/Morrison
Visit the Online Resource Centre that accompanies this book for web links and regular updates.

9

The European Union (EU)

The European Union (EU) is one of those subjects that divides politicians, the public, and, for that matter, the media in Britain into two more or less equal (and equally vociferous) camps. On the one side are 'Europhiles'—those who see closer economic and political integration as a no-brainer; embracing collaboration between neighbouring European states as a logical, common-sense, and desirable state of affairs that can only enhance mutual understanding and, ultimately, prosperity. On the other side stand the opponents of the EU—the 'Euro-sceptics'. Some are merely critical of its current composition, seeing it as overly bureaucratic, undemocratic, and lacking accountability; others still view the very idea of the union as an anathema, arguing that it threatens individual nations' rights to sovereignty and self-determination.

As befits such a contentious issue, Europe generates more than its fair share of coverage in the British press. Although EU press officers are forever complaining about how difficult it is to interest editors and reporters in writing meaningful news stories about its work, the number of column inches devoted to supposed pronouncements from 'Brussels' (to cite the commonly used shorthand) has been steadily increasing since the dramatic parliamentary scenes of the early 1990s surrounding the passage of the 'Maastricht Treaty' (see pp. 59 and 102). The furores have often verged on the ridiculous. In 1998, *Daily Mail* readers were greeted by near-hysterical headlines in response to the *European Commission*'s att-empt to force British chocolate manufacturers such as Cadbury to rede-fine their products as 'vegelate', reflecting the high percentage of vegetable fats contained in their products compared to cocoa butter. More recently, in 2005, *The Sun* launched a 'Save our Jugs' campaign in protest at a supposed attempt by 'EU killjoys' to force busty barmaids to cover up their cleav-ages. The actual proposal (dropped in light of the opposition) was a draft 'Optical Radiation Directive' designed to protect workers from builders to park-keepers from excessive exposure to the sun. It made no mention of barmaids' breasts.

So what *does* EU membership mean for Britain and how did it come about?

▶ Britain's twisty path to EU membership

The European 'Common Market' (as it was widely known in the UK until the 1970s) began its slow emergence in the post-war period, as the continent struggled to rebuild itself after six years of bruising conflict. But, although it shared many of the same economic interests as its neighbours, for a long time Britain's attitude towards it was lukewarm at best. Buffered by the existence of its Commonwealth of dependent nations on the one hand and its 'special relationship' with the USA on the other, it was reluctant to be too tied to the activities of its Continental cousins.

By 1961, however, the positive economic impact membership of the European Economic Community (EEC) appeared to be having for its mem-ber states encouraged the UK, under then Conservative Prime Minister Harold Macmillan, to apply for membership, alongside Denmark, Ireland, and Norway. But its application was blocked by France's then president, Charles de Gaulle, first in 1963 and subsequently in 1967.

De Gaulle precipitated one of the biggest constitutional crises in the hist-ory of the embryonic EU in 1965–66, by refusing to send representatives from France to meetings of any of the three Communities (this was known as the 'empty chairs crisis'). His action led, in 1966, to the passing of the Luxembourg Compromise—an informal understanding that agreements bet-ween member governments must, in future, be made *unanimously*, rather than by *majority vote*, as had been the case before.

Following the resignation of de Gaulle in 1969, negotiations began in earnest for Britain's accession to the new Community and the country was taken into it by Edward Heath's government in 1973. Ireland and Denmark joined at the same time.

But any hope that the country's accession would finally put an end to the years of squabbling between Britain and its European neighbours—not to mention the internecine fighting over the European Community (EC) within the UK's main political parties—were short-lived. By the time of the next general election in 1974, divisions were so marked within Harold Wilson's Labour Party and, according to opinion polls, in the country at large, that Labour pledged to hold a *referendum* on the issue if returned to power. This it did, on 5 June 1975, but only after Mr Wilson had waived the decades-old convention of *collective responsibility* (see p. 108) to allow members of his *Cabinet* who disagreed with his pro-European stance to campaign actively for 'no' votes. These included then Industry Secretary Tony Benn and Employment Secretary Michael Foot, who blamed rising unemployment figures on the UK's membership of the EC. He argued that free trade between Britain and its Continental neighbours was allowing cheap overseas imports to flood high street shops, undermining the profits of British-based manufacturers and leading to job cuts.

Despite the best efforts of the 'no' lobby, Mr Wilson got his way decisively enough to lay to rest the EC membership debate for the time being (although not, it transpired, forever). Two months after weathering a humiliating defeat on the issue by members of his own party at a one-day Labour conference, his 'yes' campaign clinched more than 67 per cent of the vote in the referendum, on a 64 per cent turnout.

Mr Wilson's triumph was ultimately a pyrrhic one: Britain's troubled admission into the EU marked the beginning of what has continued to be, at best, a love–hate relationship with the union. At various points during its membership, the country has stubbornly refused to toe the line—negotiating 'opt-outs' from clauses to treaties that bind most, if not all, of its peers (John Major's refusal to sign the Social Chapter of the 'Maastricht Treaty' being a famous example), and struggling to win parliamentary approval for various others. In 1992, Mr Major's government was almost brought down by its own *backbenchers* over Maastricht—an episode explored in depth later this chapter—while, more recently, Tony Blair and Gordon Brown both stoutly resisted the clamour for a referendum on the 'Lisbon Treaty', a similarly controversial agreement that many Euro-sceptics (and some Europhiles, such as the former Tory Chancellor Kenneth Clarke) argue is essentially the same document as the ill-fated 'EU Constitution' signed by all member states in 2004, but scrapped after both France and the Netherlands rejected it in national referenda.

Britain's intransigence over other aspects of EU integration continues to frustrate many of its own citizens. Aside from Sweden and Denmark, the UK is the only EU state to have held out against joining the euro, while its refusal to sign the ***Schengen Agreement*** (see Table 9.1, below) is the reason why Britons are still expected to show their national passports when crossing internal EU borders—including returning to their home country—while citizens of fellow member states are not.

The evolution of the EU

So how did today's EU come about? What happened to transform it from a loose confederation of states cooperating over trade in core post-war raw materials such as steel and coal into a sprawling supranational alliance exercising a degree of control—often contentiously—over everything from employment rights to economic migration?

Its growth and transformation can best be charted with reference to the succession of key treaties and summits that paved the way for it to become the hugely influential entity that it is now. Providing a detailed explanation of every agreement signed during the almost sixty years since the idea of a 'European Union' of sorts was first committed to paper would take up a chapter in itself. Instead, the most significant developments in the evolution of the EU are outlined in Table 9.1.

Of all of the treaties listed, the British government found it particularly difficult to ratify 'Maastricht' (see below), but it was not alone in encountering hurdles. In June 1992, the people of Denmark—who were given the chance to voice their views in a national referendum—voted against it. The Danish government finally squeaked it through 11 months later, after being forced to negotiate 'opt-outs' from two of its key provisions: the Economic and Monetary Union (EMU), and the move towards a common European defence policy.

Table 9.1 The chronology of the evolution of the European Union (EU)

Agreement	Year	Main provisions
The Treaty of Paris	1951	Coming into force on 23 July 1952, this established the earliest forerunner of the EU: the European Coal and Steel Community (ECSC). Membership was initially limited to France, Germany, Italy, Luxembourg, Belgium, and the Netherlands. The Treaty initiated the following two developments: (a) joint production of the two materials most central to the war effort—that is, coal and steel; (b) a fledgling European assembly, which met for the first time in Strasbourg in September 1952.
The Treaties of Rome	1957	Often erroneously referred to in the singular, these twin treaties spawned the two organizations that were ultimately to coalesce into the modern EU: the European Economic Community (EEC), and the European Atomic Energy Community (EURATOM). Its aim was to foster trading links between member nations by: (a) ending tariffs/customs duties imposed by one nation on imports from another; (b) removing other distortions in the operation of the market; (c) introducing the **Common Agricultural Policy (CAP)**—a means of encouraging free trade in agricultural products within the EEC, while guaranteeing EEC farmers' incomes in relation to competition from third-party countries through protectionism (tariffs and subsidies, as consolidated in 1962 by the formation of the European Agricultural Guidance and Guarantee Fund/EAGGF); (d) creating a 'common market' for the free movement of goods, services, and capital between member states (in practice, only free trade in goods followed, until the passage of the Single European Act 1986—see below).
Merger of the three European Unions	1965	With effect from 1967, the ECSC, EURATOM, and the EEC were merged into a single European Community (EC). From the outset, this consolidated alliance was to be framed around four core institutions: the European Commission (the EC's 'Civil Service'); the European Assembly (later renamed the European Parliament); the European Court of Justice; and what was to become the Council of the European Union—better known today as the EU Council of Ministers.
Launch of the European Monetary System (EMS)	1979	This initiative—designed to relax, if not abolish, exchange rates between individual member states—would eventually lead to the launch of a European single currency, the euro (see p. 301).
Enlargement	1981	Greece is admitted into the EC.
The Single European Act and further enlargement	1986	The first full-scale revision of the original 1957 European treaties, this encapsulated in one document the structure of the new-look EC and formally paved the way for the following extensions of the pan-European links: (a) greater economic integration;

Agreement	Year	Main provisions
		(b) strengthening of supranational institutions to speed up decision-making;
		(c) kickstarting practical moves towards a single European currency and linked exchange rates in the form of the European Monetary Union (EMU). In the same year, Spain and Portugal are admitted into the EC.
The Treaty on the European Union ('Maastricht Treaty')	1992	This formally renamed the EC the European Union (EU) and added new areas of responsibility for the Community. Although signed in February 1992, it had to be formally ratified by each member state and its passage was far from smooth—notably in Britain (see pp. 59 and 102). Its main provisions were to: (a) introduce a new EU-wide commitment to move towards full economic and monetary union (EMU) in three stages—the ultimate end being either a single European currency, or a 'common' one (native currencies retained, but in parallel with an EU one); (b) establish a single European Union from existing communities; (c) set up the framework for a potential common foreign and security policy; (d) increase cooperation on domestic issues, particularly criminal justice; (e) define the principle of 'subsidiarity'—a system that (theoretically) safeguards the ability of individual states to run their own internal affairs without consulting the EU unless they cannot achieve their objectives unilaterally; (f) introduce the concept of 'EU citizenship' for the first time.
The Corfu Treaty	1994	This allowed Austria, Finland, and Sweden to join the EU in January 1995, and paved the way for Norway also to be admitted (although it subsequently declined to join).
The Amsterdam Treaty	1997	This arose out of the 1996 Inter-Governmental Conference convened by the heads of the EU states. It provided for the EU to extend protection of its citizens in the following areas: (a) consumer protection; (b) extending the fight against crime and drugs; (c) improving environmental protection; (d) recognizing a Charter on Fundamental Workers' Rights. The Summit attempted—but failed—to persuade all member states to agree an EU-wide immigration and asylum policy. Britain, Ireland, and Denmark opted out of these plans, leaving the rest to form the so-called Schengen Group, which the UK declined to join at the 2000 Nice Summit. Its name referred to the Schengen Agreement—signed in two stages, in 1985 and 1990, respectively—which had abolished border controls between participating nations.

(continued)

Agreement	Year	Main provisions
The Helsinki Summit	1999	This removed a pre-existing system under which notional target dates had been set for the accession of specific countries to EU membership. From now on, any country that met qualifying conditions would be eligible for swift entry. Entry talks quickly began with Slovakia, Malta, Lithuania, Bulgaria, Latvia, and Romania. Turkey also entered talks soon after, despite having previously been rejected in 1997. It remains outside the Union.
Agenda 2000, *For a Stronger and Wider Europe*	2000	This European Commission discussion document set out a blueprint for onward development of the Community in the twenty-first century. Many of its provisions were intended to prevent future disagreements between member states such as those provoked by discussion of EMU, the proposed common defence policy, and CAP. It also signalled an attempt to set firm ground rules for the acceptance of any new countries intent on joining the EU. Among its stipulations were:

    (a) any country that now wished to join the EU must meet the economic and political criteria for membership and adopt the acquis communitaire—that is, the laws and policies of the EU—before being accepted (as Cyprus had just been admitted, the new regulations kicked in with accession negotiations for the ten additional states that entered in 2004);

    (b) to redefine CAP and the 'structural funds' used to ensure an equitable socio-economic infrastructure across Europe;

    (c) to express the then European Commission's view on the proposed accession to the EU of countries in Central and Eastern Europe;

    (d) to propose a new budgetary framework for the EU, with initial proposals for a Community-wide budget 'not exceeding 1.27 per cent of the EU's GNP'.

| The Nice Treaty | 2000 | Notorious for a public stand-off between French President Jacques Chirac and Chancellor Gerhard Schroeder of Germany, this Treaty 'proclaimed' the so-called EU Charter of Fundamental Rights (a conflation of principles outlined in the preceding European Convention on Human Rights, devised in 1950 by the **Council of Europe**– not the EU). The Charter's 53 'Articles' were not legally binding at the time, but expressed a shared set of principled aims, including: |

    (a) equality between men and women;

    (b) fair and just working conditions;

    (c) workers' rights to collective bargaining and industrial action;

    (d) public rights to access EU documents;

    (e) the right of elderly people to a life of 'dignity'.

The Nice Summit also aired many of the concerns that have since come to dominate political discussion about the EU— including the implications of accepting the 12 prospective additional members of the community who have since joined.

A consensus emerged that the main governing institutions set up when the EU was formed would have to be changed over a

Agreement	Year	Main provisions
		period of time for the following reasons:

(a) the arrival of 12 potential new member countries would mean that they too would need to be given votes at the negotiating table in the Council of Ministers, and allocated EU commissioners, seats in the European Parliament, and judges;

(b) the reunification of Germany, following the fall of the Berlin Wall in 1990;

(c) the impact of EU enlargement on asylum, immigration, and economic migration.

Agreement	Year	Main provisions
The Goteburg Summit	2001	Due to focus on EU enlargement, this proved disappointing for its Swedish hosts. One sticking point was the perceived conflict between EU membership and the Irish Constitution, particularly in relation to the province's neutrality. At around the same time as the Summit, Ireland narrowly voted 'no' in a referendum on EU membership. Another controversy that arose stemmed from the growing realization of larger member states that enlargement might result in a reduction in the monetary benefits they received as individual nations from the EU. With admission into the Community of smaller nations, France, for example, was likely to lose out in its share of agricultural subsidies from the CAP.
White Paper on *EU Governance*	2001	Produced in response to mounting distrust of un-elected EU policymaking institutions (as exemplified by Ireland's rejection of EU membership), this sought to pave the way for a more democratic and accountable approach to EU governance by:

(a) involving individual states, especially smaller ones, more openly in decisions;

(b) introducing 'better policies and regulations';

(c) moving towards a system of 'global governance';

(d) 'refocusing' the EU's core institutions.

These rather hazy ideas were underpinned by a clearer list of principles that the EU pledged to embody in future:

(a) openness—encouraging its institutions to work together more openly;

(b) participation—encouraging all members actively to take part in decision-making;

(c) accountability—giving clearer definitions of the roles of EU institutions;

(d) effectiveness—ensuring policies are appropriate to the current socio-economic climate, and are promptly implemented once decided upon;

(e) coherence—making sure that policies can be easily understood;

(f) proportionality;

(continued)

Agreement	Year	Main provisions
		(g) subsidiarity—ensuring 'action' by the EU in relation to a member state's affairs is only taken when strictly necessary.
Enlargement of the Union	2004	Czech Republic, Estonia, Hungary, Latvia, Lithuania, Poland, Slovakia, and Slovenia, Malta, and Greek Cyprus join the EU.
Enlargement of the Union	2007	Romania and Bulgaria join the EU.
The European Union Reform Treaty ('Lisbon Treaty')	2007	Almost as contentious as 'Maastricht', this followed hot on the tails of an abortive 'EU Constitution'—which had been subject to individual ratification by member states, and was abandoned after being rejected in referenda in France and the Netherlands. The 'Lisbon Treaty' was also rejected—this time, by Ireland— but, at time of writing, the EU officially remains committed to adopting it. The main provisions of the Treaty are to: (a) make the Charter of Fundamental Rights legally binding; (b) extend the role of the directly elected European Parliament; (c) introduce a permanent president of the Council of Ministers in place of the current 'rotating presidency', which sees each member state take it in turns to hold the post on a six-monthly basis; (d) give the EU as a whole the legal status of a single entity capable of signing international treaties with other institutions or bodies.

▶ The 'three pillars' of today's EU

One of the key sticking points of the Maastricht Treaty for individual member states was its underlying emphasis on fostering a 'supranational' approach to major policy areas over and above the EU's traditional drive towards Europe-wide free trade. Where several countries—notably Britain, Sweden, and Denmark—were keen to limit the EU's influence to the economic sphere (ideally preferring an 'intergovernmental' approach even to that—that is, bilateral negotiated agreements between independent member states), others such as France and Germany were keen to roll out the Union's responsibilities to encompass everything from criminal justice and drugs policy, to defence and security. In so doing, they also appeared willing to surrender varying degrees of national sovereignty—giving EU institutions the power to determine policies governing these areas with limited input from national parliaments.

The process of negotiating the Maastricht settlement led to the emergence of three broad areas of policy to be overseen in future, to a greater or lesser degree, by the *European Parliament (EP)*, the European Commission (EC), and

Table 9.2 A breakdown of the EU's 'three pillars' structure

First Pillar	Second Pillar	Third Pillar
European Communities (EC)	Common Foreign and Security Policy (CFSP)	Police and Judicial Cooperation in Criminal Matters (PJCC)
Customs union and single market	Human rights	Drug trafficking
Common Agricultural Policy (CAP)	Democracy	Weapons smuggling
Common Fisheries Policy (CFP)	Foreign aid	People trafficking
Competition law	European security and defence	Terrorism
Economic and Monetary Union (EMU)	Battle groups (small EU military units)	Organized crime
EU citizenship	Peacekeeping	Bribery and fraud
Education and culture		
Consumer protection		
Health care		
Research (e.g. technology)		
Environmental law		
Social policy		
Asylum policy		
Schengen Agreement		
Immigration policy		

the Council of the European Union (Council of Ministers). The remit of each of these areas—known as the three 'pillars' of the EU—is outlined in Table 9.2.

The main EU institutions

Journalistically, the best EU stories invariably arise out of conflict and confrontation. Notwithstanding ongoing wrangles over the Union's future direction and scope, many contentious issues emerge from the day-to-day deliberations of the EU's four principal governing institutions:

- the *Commission of the European Union*;
- the European Parliament (EP);

- the *Council of Ministers of the European Union*;
- the *European Court of Justice (ECJ)*.

Each of these institutions is chaired by a president, whose method of election or appointment varies from one to the other.

The powers and remits of these four institutions are described in the following sections. In addition, there is one further body that asserts a significant influence on the direction of EU policy (although, unlike the above, it wields no formal executive or legislative powers). This is the European Council—more commonly referred to as the 'European Summit', to avoid confusion with the Council of Ministers. Composed of the heads of state or most senior politicians (presidents and prime ministers) from the individual member states of the EU, it meets up to four times a year and is chaired by whichever country is in possession of the rotating presidency at the time.

The Commission of the European Union (the European Commission)

Often mistakenly cited as the most powerful of the EU's governing institutions, the European Commission, formed in 1951 and based in Brussels, is nonetheless hugely influential. Effectively the Civil Service and executive arm (government) of the EU rolled into one, it employs 25,000 staff working at various levels across more than thirty internal and external policy departments, known as 'directorates-general' and 'services'.

Each of the major directorates-general is headed by one of 27 commissioners—one from each member state, appointed for a five-year period. Meetings are chaired by one of their number, elected president by the European Parliament (on the recommendation of the European Council/Summit). The president chairs meetings of the Commission in much the same way as a prime minister sitting in Cabinet. Although the Council of Ministers (composed of elected representatives from each member state's government) takes the final decisions on major political developments and structural changes within the EU, the Commission is unique in being the only institution permitted to *initiate* policy. It does this in much the same way as national policy is originated through cabinet government, with the commissioners sitting around a long table devising and debating ideas for prospective legislation.

What makes this process so much more controversial in relation to the European Commission compared to, say, the workings of the British Cabinet is that none of the commissioners is elected: all are 'proposed' (nominated) by the governments of their native countries. The fact that they are chosen by democratically elected politicians arguably gives them some degree of legitimacy. Nevertheless, they are not elected themselves and, as such, are not directly accountable to the European citizens whose lives their proposals affect. This perceived lack of transparency and electoral accountability has been described by critics of the EU's existing structure as a 'democratic deficit'—a term attributed to the British Liberal Democrat MEP Bill Newton Dunn, who coined it in a 1980s pamphlet.

The Commission issues its policy pronouncements in the form of Directives. More minor decisions—such as issuing new guidelines to local authorities on kerbside recycling—may be implemented without having to be formally approved by the Council of Ministers; major policy proposals may not and must go through the Council.

Not that policymaking is the Commission's only role: although it has far greater political clout than the British Civil Service—the job of which is merely to implement the government's policies 'on the ground' once Parliament has approved them (see p. 112)—the Commission also fulfils this basic administrative function. Moreover, proposals put forward by the Commission are rarely a 'done deal': the elected *members of the European Parliament (MEPs)* have the opportunity to scrutinize them at length and the authority to reject them.

The European Parliament may also dismiss the Commission in exceptional circumstances (although, curiously, it is prevented from taking action against an individual commissioner and must instead sack all of them at once). This scenario has arisen at least once in recent years. In March 1999, the Commission under then president Jacques Santer resigned en masse following the publication of a damning report into its alleged corruption and nepotism. Although it stopped short of suggesting that any commissioner was directly involved in corrupt practices, the 144-page report, by five independent 'wise persons', singled out former French Prime Minister Edith Cresson for her 'dysfunctional' organization and favouritism in staff appointments.

A similar crisis was narrowly averted in October 2004, when MEPs rejected the appointment of incoming Italian Commissioner for Justice, Freedom and Security Rocco Buttiglione, a devout Roman Catholic, who had made inflammatory speeches about homosexuality and the role of women in society. In the event, the Italian government withdrew Mr Buttiglione's nomination at the last minute, thereby preventing the newly appointed Commission under its then new president, Jose Manuel Barroso, from being dismissed.

Although not elected to their EU posts, most commissioners tend to be experienced politicians and/or public figures who have previously served in senior positions in their home countries. Until the EU's membership expanded from 15 to 25 states in the 2004 *enlargement*, the countries with the biggest populations—Britain, Germany, France, and Italy—had two commissioners each, rather than only the standard one. Among those who served in this capacity were Neil Kinnock, the former Labour leader, who was Commissioner for Transport, and ex-Conservative Home Secretary Sir Leon Brittan, who was Commissioner for External Trade Relations. Peter Mandelson, the former Northern Ireland Secretary, became Britain's first single Commissioner in 2004 (overseeing trade), but he was replaced by Baroness Ashton of Upholland in October 2008 after being recalled to the British Cabinet in Gordon Brown's second reshuffle.

Enduring controversy over the composition, powers, and privileges of the Commission has led to repeated attempts to reform it. For many years, its mammoth expenses bill was cited as one of the main causes of concern for EU taxpayers, and terms such as 'Brussels bureaucrats', 'free-loading', and 'gravy train' were frequently seen alongside each other in the British tabloids. This particular issue has been somewhat addressed in the wake of the 1999 report and subsequent reforms—some instigated by Lord Kinnock, who, in his role as vice-president of the Commission, tried to clean up its act by establishing an internal audit service and ethics committee. But concerns about the inordinate amount of power wielded by the Commission—and the apparent dominance of certain countries in its decision-making process—led to several further reforms being proposed in the 'Lisbon Treaty', including:

- reducing the number of commissioners, with only two-thirds of member states represented at any one time, but seats to be distributed fairly on a rotating basis;

- formalizing the status of the European Council/Summit as an EU governmental institution and giving it the power to nominate commissioners (with the European Parliament then 'electing' them, rather than simply 'approving' them as at present).

The composition of the current Commission is outlined in Table 9.3, which can be found on the Online Resource Centre that accompanies this book.

The European Parliament (EP)

Despite its title, when originally christened in 1958, the EP's representatives were not elected at all, but were appointed delegates from each of the member countries. Today, in contrast, the European Parliament is a fully elected institution and has been since 1979. By that time, the number of representatives—that is, members of the European Parliament (MEPs)—had increased from 142 to 410.

The current membership numbers 732. Elections are held every five years and, prior to 1999, were conducted on a 'first past the post' (FPTP) system analogous to that used in UK general elections (see p. 133). The European Parliament Act 1999 changed this by introducing *proportional representation (PR)*, generally based on the party list system. Parties are awarded a number of seats proportional to their share of the vote.

The UK is currently divided into 12 electoral regions (including Northern Ireland, which uses its own version of PR). Each region returns between three and ten MEPs, depending on its population size. There are 78 British MEPs altogether: 64 elected in England, seven in Scotland, four in Wales, and three in Northern Ireland.

Like the Commission, the EP has its principal base in Brussels and, for three weeks of every month, its members sit in the parliament building there. For the other week, they travel to Strasbourg in neighbouring France, convening in an identical chamber.

As at the British Parliament at Westminster, members of the EP sit in political groupings reflecting their ideological affiliations, rather than regional or national delegations. The minimum number of MEPs needed to form a group is as follows:

- 29 if they all hail from a single member state;
- 23 if they come from two member states;
- 14 if they come from four or more member states.

There are currently seven political groupings in the EP, although some MEPs remain 'non-attached' (independent). The groupings sit at designated points around the semi-circular (or 'hemispherical') parliamentary chamber, according to their notional position on the Left–Right political spectrum. For example, communist MEPs will sit to the far left of the central seat occupied by the EP president, while fascists and extreme right parties such as France's National Front will occupy the seats, appropriately enough, on the far right.

The current breakdown of political groupings is as follows:

- Group of the Party of European Socialists (PSE);
- Group of the European People's Party and European Democrats (PPE-DE);
- Group of the European Liberal, Democratic, and Reform Party (ELDR);
- Confederal Group of the European United Left/Nordic Green Left (GUE/NGL);
- Group of the Greens/European Free Alliance (Verts/ALE);
- Union for Europe of the Nations Group (UEN);
- Group for a Europe of Democracies and Diversities (EDD).

While the British Labour Party remains part of the Socialist Group, despite its recent drift to the political centre ground, there has been much debate about the future place of the Conservatives, whose increasingly Euro-sceptic stance during the 1990s put them out of kilter with the views of most of their colleagues in the European People's Party (EPP). In an effort to win support from right-wing rank-and-file party supporters in the 2006 Tory leadership contest, David Cameron pledged to withdraw from the EPP. He has yet to make good on his promise—at least partly due to resistance from some of his own MEPs to the move. Because the Conservatives currently have only 27 MEPs, they would need to form an alliance with at least two other members to form a legitimate political grouping, but, in practice, they would probably need more than this, because some centrist Tory MEPs have indicated that they might defy the party *whip* to remain within the EPP, irrespective of their leader's wishes.

So much for the political composition of the EP: what are its actual powers? Although the EP has the appearance of a legislature, in practice it is less significant in proposing or deciding policy than either the European Commission or the Council of Ministers. Ultimately, it is there to be *consulted* on decisions, rather than to take them itself. Although Maastricht gave it the ability to *reject* legislation that it disliked for the first time—a process known as 'codecision'—it is more akin to a giant UK-style Commons committee (see p. 57) than a parliament, per se. The EP does, however, share power with the Council of Ministers over the EU budget and was recently given extra clout to influence the Council's direction through a so-called 'cooperation procedure'. A breakdown of the proposed 2009 EU Budget is given in Figure 9.1.

The administration of the EP's functions is overseen by yet another layer of EU bureaucracy: a 'bureau' run by the president, no fewer than 14 vice-presidents, and five so-called 'quaestors' (civil servants with responsibility for administrative and financial matters directly affecting the MEPs themselves).

The Council of Ministers of the European Union

The Council of Ministers of the European Union—often simply referred to as the Council of Ministers—is the single most powerful EU institution. Comprised of departmental ministers from each of the 27 member states, its precise composition varies according to the particular issue being debated on

Figure 9.1 A breakdown of the proposed €14.4bn EU budget for 2009

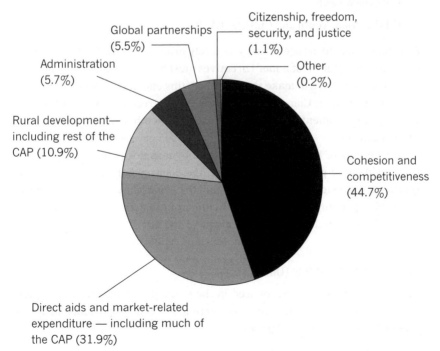

Global partnerships (5.5%)

Citizenship, freedom, security, and justice (1.1%)

Administration (5.7%)

Other (0.2%)

Rural development— including rest of the CAP (10.9%)

Cohesion and competitiveness (44.7%)

Direct aids and market-related expenditure — including much of the CAP (31.9%)

Source: European Union

a given day. If, for example, the Council is debating health policy, a health minister from each member state will attend, while discussions about crime, policing, and security issues will involve interior ministers (in Britain's case, the Home Secretary or a Home Office minister).

The Council has nine so-called 'configurations', reflecting the broad policy areas under its jurisdiction:

- General Affairs and External Relations (GAERC)—composed of foreign ministers;
- Economic and Financial Affairs (Ecofin);
- Agriculture and Fisheries;
- Justice and Home Affairs Council (JHA);
- Employment, Social Policy, Health and Consumer Affairs Council (EPSCO);
- Competitiveness—European Affairs, Industry, Tourism and Scientific Research;
- Transport, Telecommunications and Energy;
- Environment;
- Education, Youth and Culture (EYC).

Although policy ideas are often proactively proposed in the EU by the Commission, all but the most minor Directives must be formally approved by the Council of Ministers to make them 'law'. To this end, it is supported by a related institution, the Committee of Permanent Representatives (COREPER), made up of permanent civil servants from each member state or each state's EU ambassador.

All meetings of the Council are chaired by a senior politician (normally the president or prime minister) from the country currently holding the rotating EU presidency. The UK last held the presidency in 2005. In view of the need for continuity emphasised by this rota system, the Council has its own dedicated civil service in the shape of the General Secretariat of the Council.

Qualified majority voting (QMV)

The decision-making process used in the Council of Ministers is complex and, as such, warrants its own small section, given its importance in determining the direction of EU policy.

The unanimous approval of member states is normally required to pass major decisions with implications for the future of the EU—such as whether to admit additional countries into the Union. The annual confirmation of the EU's Budget also traditionally requires unanimity. Since Maastricht, however, an increasing number of (often significant) decisions have been agreed through a process known as *qualified majority voting (QMV)*. As its name suggests, the premise of QMV is for agreement on a policy to be reached without the need for every member state to approve it—that is, on a majority basis. This majority system is 'qualified', however, in two key respects:

- a simple majority system (like that which determines whether policies are passed in the British Parliament) would require only one more 'yes' vote than the total number of 'no' votes—QMV often requires a bigger majority than this;
- the way in which a majority of votes is obtained is *not* on the basis of an equal say for each member state—rather, the number of votes per state is weighted to reflect the size of its population, giving some countries a bigger say than others.

Of the bigger EU countries, France, Britain, Germany, and Italy have the most votes, with 29 apiece. The smallest populated country, Malta, has just three. The overall breakdown of vote allocations under QMV is spelt out in Table 9.4.

Under the terms of the Nice Treaty (at time of writing, the prevailing system), a vote is passed by the QMV process if *all* of the following conditions are met:

- it is backed by *either* at least half of the member states (if a simple majority method of voting is agreed) *or* at least two-thirds of member states;
- the number of votes cast in favour is equivalent to 74 per cent of those cast;
- the countries supporting the proposal represent 62 per cent of the EU population.

Perhaps unsurprisingly, QMV has its critics. Some smaller EU member states argue that, at times, they are having policies imposed on them—regardless of their views—by more heavily populated ones. Euro-sceptics, meanwhile, see the absence of a 'one member, one vote' system in the Council as

Table 9.4 The allocation of voting power under qualified majority voting (QMV)

Country	Population (% of EU population)		Number of votes (% of total)		Proposed vote weighting (Penrose)	
Germany	82m	16.7%	29	8.4%	9	9.3%
France	63m	12.8%	29	8.4%	8	8.2%
UK	60m	12.3%	29	8.4%	8	8.2%
Italy	59m	11.9%	29	8.4%	8	8.2%
Spain	44m	8.9%	27	7.8%	7	7.2%
Poland	38m	7.7%	27	7.8%	6	6.2%
Romania	22m	4.4%	14	4.1%	5	5.2%
Netherlands	16m	3.3%	13	3.8%	4	4.1%
Greece	11m	2.3%	12	3.5%	3	3.1%
Portugal	11m	2.1%	12	3.5%	3	3.1%
Belgium	11m	2.1%	12	3.5%	3	3.1%
Czech Republic	10m	2.1%	12	3.5%	3	3.1%
Hungary	10m	2.0%	12	3.5%	3	3.1%
Sweden	9.0m	1.8%	10	2.9%	3	3.1%
Austria	8.3m	1.7%	10	2.9%	3	3.1%
Bulgaria	7.7m	1.6%	10	2.9%	3	3.1%
Denmark	5.4m	1.1%	7	2.0%	2	2.1%
Slovakia	5.4m	1.1%	7	2.0%	2	2.1%
Finland	5.3m	1.1%	7	2.0%	2	2.1%
Ireland	4.2m	0.9%	7	2.0%	2	2.1%
Lithuania	3.4m	0.7%	7	2.0%	2	2.1%
Latvia	2.3m	0.5%	4	1.2%	2	2.1%
Slovenia	2.0m	0.4%	4	1.2%	2	2.1%
Estonia	1.3m	0.3%	4	1.2%	1	1.0%
Cyprus	0.77m	0.2%	4	1.2%	1	1.0%
Luxembourg	0.46m	0.1%	4	1.2%	1	1.0%
Malta	0.40m	0.1%	3	0.9%	1	1.0%
EU	493m	100%	345	100%	97	100%

evidence that individual countries are increasingly being subsumed within an embryonic 'European super-state', rather than treated as a confederation of independent—and equal—countries.

Given the inequitable allocation of votes between member states, the fact that some decisions need only obtain a simple majority to be passed can prove especially controversial. In the past, it has been possible, on occasion, for a handful of the most populated countries to muster sufficient votes to approve a policy by rallying support from a bare 50 per cent of the member states.

The 'Lisbon Treaty' proposes several modifications to the current QMV weighting—largely designed to redress the balance of power in favour of smaller countries and some of those that have only recently joined. Most significantly, it increases the size of majority needed to approve a proposal and states that 'final' decisions will also require a 'double majority' to be passed—that is, that they must achieve majorities according to not one, but two sets of criteria. The proposed majorities needed will be both of the following:

- *either* at least 55 per cent *or* 72 per cent of all member states (depending on vote);
- at least 64 per cent of the overall EU population.

In addition, Poland, one of the most populous of the newly admitted member states, has proposed a further reform, in the guise of the so-called 'Penrose Method' (also known as the 'square-root system'). This would scrap the requirement for there to be a majority of states in favour of a proposal entirely, replacing it with the need for a 61.4 per cent share of all of the votes cast—however that total is achieved.

The European Court of Justice (ECJ)

Set up in 1952, the European Court of Justice (ECJ)—officially titled the 'Court of Justice of the European Communities'—is the EU's supreme legal institution. Unlike other bodies, it is based in Luxembourg City, but like them, it has its own president. Presidents are elected by their fellow judges on renewable three-year terms.

Again like the other key EU institutions, the Court has one judge per member state—that is, 27 in total. For practical reasons, however, only 13 of these will hear a case at any one time, sitting in the Court's so-called Grand Chamber. Since the signing of the 'Lisbon Treaty', they have been assisted by 11 'advocates-general'—that is, lawyers tasked with presenting to the judges impartial 'opinions' on cases assigned to them. Judgments are made in a collegiate way and must, in the end, be unanimous.

Judges are nominated by the member states from which they hail on renewable six-year terms. Until 2008, there were only eight advocates-general, five of whom were nominated by the biggest EU member states—Britain,

France, Germany, Italy, and Spain—with the other three rotating in alpha-betical order between the remaining 22 states. During negotiations over Lisbon, Poland successfully argued that, because its population is only mar-ginally smaller than that of Spain (and its representation under the QMV voting system in the Council of Ministers is the same), it, too, should have an automatic right to nominate an advocate-general. As a result, six are now nominated by the bigger nations. The remaining five are chosen on rotation by other countries.

The Court may be required to pass judgment in a variety of circum-stances—for example, if there is evidence that a member state has not implemented a treaty signed by the EU, or a complainant alleges that a gov-ernmental institution, non-government organization (NGO), or commercial business has, in some other way, broken EU law.

Areas of EU law covered by the Court include:

- free trade and the free movement of goods and services in the EU single market;
- employment law and the European Social Chapter (see p. 306);
- competition law (cartels, monopolies, mergers and acquisitions);
- public sector regulation.

In practice, it is fairly unusual for a case involving an individual or small group of individuals to go before the ECJ itself. And even when a case *is* heard by the Court, it may only go before three or five judges, rather than the Grand Chamber of 13. Only in the most exceptional, large-scale cases (such as when an EU commissioner is alleged to have seriously failed to fulfil his or her obligations) will it ever sit as a 'full court'. Even then only a quorum of 15 judges—rather than the full complement of 27—are needed.

In the majority of lesser cases, hearings will be convened by a junior body established in 1989 to deal with the growing number of routine com-plaints being generated as the EU extended its influence: the General Court (until Lisbon, known as the 'Court of the First Instance'). Like its more illustrious counterpart, this Court also boasts 27 judges, one from each member state. Unlike the ECJ, however, it has no advocates-general of its own to speak of, so a judge from among its own number is sometimes nominated to fulfil this role. A 'judge-rapporteur' will also be appointed to oversee proceedings and to draft a provisional judgment—to be deliber-ated on by the judges—after hearing representations from complainant and respondent.

The General Court's responsibilities encompass the following policy areas:

- agriculture;
- state aid;
- competition;
- commercial policy;
- regional policy;
- social policy;
- institutional law;
- trade mark law;
- transport.

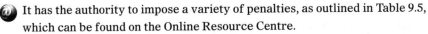 It has the authority to impose a variety of penalties, as outlined in Table 9.5, which can be found on the Online Resource Centre.

Judgments by the General Court are subject to a right to appeal to the ECJ. In addition to the General Court, meanwhile, two further courts have been created in recent years to deal with more specific cases: the Civil Service Tribunal, which handles complaints about maladministration by employees of EU institutions, and the Court of Auditors (responsible for overseeing the EU's accounts).

▌ The evolution of the euro

As discussed earlier this chapter, the concept of moving towards some form of single European currency has been quietly fermenting for decades. But what started out as the seed of an idea in the minds of European commissioners in the late 1960s took the best part of thirty years to reach fruition. The following section focuses on the more decisive stages in the development of the *euro* project.

The exchange rate mechanism (ERM) debacle and 'Black Wednesday'

In an effort to control *inflation*, encourage trade, and stabilize exchange rates between individual EU member states' currencies—in doing so kickstarting the process of introducing a single European currency—in 1979, the EU introduced the exchange rate mechanism (ERM). The ERM was based on the idea of fixing narrower margins between which member states' currencies would be permitted to fluctuate in value in relation to those of other members—effectively 'pegging' one country's exchange rate to another's. Prior to the introduction of the ERM, bilateral exchange rates between EU states were based on the European currency unit (ECU)—a form of 'virtual' European currency traded in stock markets—the value of which was equivalent to a weighted average of those of the individual EU members' currencies. As a condition of EU membership, states were required to contain fluctuations in the value of their currencies within a margin of 2.25 per cent on either side of their bilateral exchange rates (with the exception of Italy, which was allowed a variance of up to 6 per cent).

The Maastricht Treaty envisaged the European monetary system (EMS) moving towards full monetary union in three stages, as set out in Table 9.6, which can be found on the Online Resource Centre.

As ever reluctant to take a lead in furthering EU integration, Britain was slow to sign up to the ERM. It finally did so in 1990, when John Major was Chancellor, but pulled out dramatically on 16 September 1992 after a panic-stricken day of stock market speculation and *interest rate* hikes by his successor, Norman Lamont.

'Black Wednesday'—as this day came to be known—arose out of the unsustainable position in which the British currency (the pound sterling) had found itself in during the months after the country signed up to the ERM. Throughout much of the 1980s, Margaret Thatcher's Chancellor Nigel Lawson had 'shadowed' the German Deutschmark in his decisions on whether to raise or lower interest rates in an effort to maintain sterling's value. By September 2002, this had had the effect of valuing sterling unsustainably high compared to the US dollar. Because many British exports were valued in dollars—not sterling—the UK was potentially losing significant income from overseas markets by allowing the gap between the dollar and the pound to widen. But with Britain pegged to the ECU in the ERM, there was limited room for the Chancellor to devalue sterling in the way that he otherwise might have done to remedy this.

The approaching crisis reached its tipping point when US currency speculators, including billionaire George Soros, began frenziedly borrowing pounds and selling them for Deutschmarks in mid-September, in the belief that sterling was about to be devalued and that they could therefore make profits by repaying their loans at a deflated price. This prompted Mr Lamont to raise interest rates from 10 to 12 per cent on 16 September (with the promise of a further increase, to 15 per cent, later the same day), in an effort to steady the ship and stop sterling's value falling too far by tempting speculators to buy pounds. But, apparently disbelieving him, speculators instead began selling pounds, in anticipation of a slump in its value.

With sterling's value plummeting as a result, at 7 p.m. that day, Mr Lamont took the decision to pull Britain out of the ERM—freezing interest rates for the time being at 12 per cent, rather than raising them to the promised 15 per cent. During the course of the day, he had spent £27bn of Britain's gold reserves propping up the pound. By the time that the Conservatives lost to Labour five years later, in the 1997 election, official Treasury estimates calculated that the ultimate cost to the taxpayer of 'Black Wednesday' was £3.4bn. The Tories' previous reputation for economic competence was dealt a body blow by the events of that day, from which it took years to recover.

The launch of the euro and the growth of the eurozone

The euro has been in existence in a 'non-physical' form—that is, in the guise of travellers' cheques, electronic transfers, etc.—since 1 January 1999, but it officially came into being on 1 January 2002, when the *European Central Bank (ECB)* in Frankfurt began issuing notes and coins in the 12 EU member states that had signed up to join. At the time, there were only 15 EU states and membership of the euro has since been extended to include two of the additional 12 countries admitted through enlargement: Malta and Slovenia. Of the 'original' 15 EU members, Britain, Sweden, and Denmark are the only three so far to have resisted joining. Both the Swedish and Danish populations have rejected the single currency in national referenda (the latter twice), and the former has since circumvented any pressure from the so-called 'eurozone' states to make a fresh attempt to join them by failing to adhere to the 'convergence criteria' that countries are expected to meet before being accepted into the euro.

The main convergence criteria, designed to promote price stability across the participating states, require applicant countries to achieve the following:

- an inflation rate that is no more than 1.5 per cent higher than that of the three lowest-inflation member states of the EU;
- a ratio of no more than 3 per cent between their annual government deficit and *gross domestic product (GDP)* at the end of the preceding tax year;

- a ratio of gross government debt to GDP no greater than 60 per cent at the end of the preceding tax year (it is sometimes acceptable to be approaching this target);

- membership of the successor to the original ERM—ERM II—for at least two consecutive years without at any point simultaneously devaluing their currencies;

- a nominal long-term interest rate no more than 2 per cent higher than that of the three lowest-inflation EU member states.

At time of writing, the 15 countries in the eurozone were (in alphabetical order): Austria; Belgium; Cyprus; Finland; France; Germany; Greece; Ireland; Italy; Luxembourg; Malta; the Netherlands; Portugal; Slovenia; Spain. In addition, Denmark has recently made tentative steps towards joining the euro by becoming a member of ERM II in preparation and there is talk of a further referendum.

For its part, Britain remains a stubborn refusenik. Mr Major's government negotiated an 'opt-out protocol' before belatedly signing the Maastricht Treaty, removing any *obligation* on its part to move from stage two to stage three of EMU. On entering office, Mr Blair (widely seen as a Europhile, compared to his more cautious Chancellor, Mr Brown) promised to hold a referendum before committing the UK to the single currency. He repeated this pledge at various points during his ten years in power and is thought always to have been broadly supportive of the idea of one day joining. But Mr Brown, now installed at Number 10, remains sceptical. In 1997, he announced that, before surrendering the strength of sterling to the untested vagaries of the euro, he would need to be convinced that Britain had met what he described as 'five economic tests'. These 'tests'—actually questions to determine whether the UK economy would benefit from entry—are outlined in Table 9.7.

Critics have argued that these questions are, at best, susceptible to obfuscation and, at worst, unanswerable. In reality, many argue, they are there to enable Mr Brown to place continual delays in the way of any referendum on euro entry—arguing, at any moment in time, that one or the other of them has yet to be answered to his satisfaction.

Because not all EU member states have opted thus far to join the single currency, the Union is currently often described a 'two-speed' Europe. Some observers argue that a time will come when Britain and all other EU member states outside the euro will be forced to join, if only to retain their influence at the negotiating table over other issues affecting the Union. Former

Table 9.7 Gordon Brown's 'five economic tests' for Britain's entry to the euro

Test 1	Would joining the euro create better conditions for firms making long-term decisions to invest in the UK?
Test 2	How would adopting the euro affect the UK's financial services?
Test 3	Are business cycles and economic structures compatible to the extent that the UK and other EU countries could live comfortably with euro interest rates on a permanent basis?
Test 4	If problems emerge, is there sufficient flexibility for them to be dealt with?
Test 5	Will joining the euro help to promote higher growth, stability, and a lasting increasing in jobs?

French President Jacques Chirac and German Chancellor Gerhard Schroeder each made several speeches when in office emphasizing the need for Britain to commit more fully to the EU by entering the euro.

▶ Towards an EU 'super-state' and constitution

Of all of the issues to divide the main British political parties in recent years, none has been more damaging than what many see as the gradual shift from an EU based on mutual cooperation between sovereign nations to the idea of a 'federal' union more akin to the United States of America. As early as the late 1980s, the perception that many mainland European countries (in particular France and Germany) were intent on creating a 'United States of Europe'—or 'European super-state'—saw staunch resistance by Mrs Thatcher and her more Euro-sceptic ministers to almost any prospect of further UK involvement. Perhaps most symbolically, during a Commons debate on proposals by charismatic European Commission president Jacques Delores to accelerate the pace of EU integration, she declared 'no, no, no' to his vision.

Although, as Leader of the Opposition, Mrs Thatcher had been a steadfast supporter of the 'yes' campaign for Britain to remain in the then EEC, a decade into her premiership, she saw things differently. By then, the pace of integration had stepped up a gear, and the likes of Delores and German Chancellor Helmut Kohl were championing ever-closer ties between member states, with the contents of the Maastricht Treaty a particular bone of contention. High-profile resignations by pro-European Cabinet colleagues, such as Chancellor Nigel Lawson and Foreign Secretary Sir Geoffrey Howe, did little to dampen her resolve. It was the Tories' growing internal rift over Europe as much as the Poll Tax riots that led to her being challenged for the party's leadership by a 'stalking horse' candidate, the obscure backbencher Sir Anthony Meyer, in 1989, and her ultimate downfall in her ill-fated defence against the 1990 challenge by Michael Heseltine (see p. 103).

Despite ushering in a more mild-mannered replacement, the ensuing leadership election did little to heal the party's wounds. Mr Major did much to placate his Euro-sceptic colleagues in his first months in Downing Street. Among other things, he negotiated British opt-outs to various clauses in the Maastricht Treaty—notably, the Social Chapter (the section later signed by Mr Blair's government, which enshrined new rights for EU workers, including the Working Time Directive barring employers from forcing their staff to work more than 48 hours a week, and recognition of their right to trade union membership and collective bargaining).

But such fillips to the right of the party could only delay an inevitable confrontation over Maastricht (which effectively *had* to be signed if Britain were to remain in the EU) for so long. By May 1992, having secured a narrow fourth successive Tory victory in an election earlier that month with a majority of only 18 MPs, Mr Major found himself being held to ransom by a hardcore of Euro-sceptic backbenchers, known collectively as the 'Maastricht rebels' (see p. 59). Only by temporarily withdrawing the whip from these MPs, building a fractious alliance with the Ulster Unionists and Democratic Unionists, and threatening his party with a further election, which it would almost certainly have lost, did Mr Major finally force through the European Communities (Amendment) Bill on a wafer-thin majority. Among those actively rebelling from the backbenches were bullish former Employment Secretary Lord Tebbit and a certain Mrs Thatcher. In addition to the usual suspects, such as stalwart right-wingers Bill Cash and Teddy Taylor, the rebels included no fewer than three present-day frontbenchers: David Willetts, Dr Liam Fox, and Alan Duncan. One of their number, Iain Duncan Smith, later became leader.

Throughout its time in opposition, the Conservative Party has remained divided over Europe, although it has appeared more unified under David Cameron than under any of his recent predecessors. At the time of writing, it remains broadly the most Euro-sceptic of the three main political parties. But it is far from the only one split over the most recent moves by the EU to extend its reach.

Old divisions resurfaced in the Labour Party in 2004 when a draft 'EU Constitution' was published. The Constitutional Treaty—or the Treaty Establishing a Constitution for Europe (to give it its full name)—ostensibly did little more than drawing together in a single, if mammoth, document a number of earlier agreements, such as the 1986 Single European Act and Maastricht. But those already wary of earlier shifts towards a more centralized EU power structure saw in it a clear attempt to consolidate the Union, leading to greater *federalism*—a reduction in status of the sovereign governments of member states akin to the limited *devolution* accorded to individual states in the USA. Ironically, the Treaty emphasized the concept of *subsidiarity*—the antithesis of federalism, which defines member states as being paramount and the EU as only a 'last port of call' should individual countries' self-determination falter. It also, for the first time, set out the practical steps to be taken by a state that wished to withdraw from the EU altogether. Nonetheless, under mounting pressure from the Tories and his own backbenchers, Mr Blair promised a referendum on the constitution if he were to win a third term in the 2005 election. In the event, he was let off the hook by two earlier polls—in France and the Netherlands, respectively—in which the 'no vote' triumphed. Because each member state needed to ratify the treaty individually, these put paid to the constitution as it stood.

But then came the 'Lisbon Treaty'. Having promised a referendum in its 2005 election manifesto, Labour declined to offer one when Lisbon produced an agreement that, in the eyes of many, was the same document in all but name. After months of pressure from his own backbenchers and a Commons debate lasting 12 days, Mr Brown formally settled the referendum issue in February 2008 with a slim victory in a three-line whip vote (to the fury of Euro-sceptic papers such as *The Sun* and the *Daily Mail*, whose front-page headline described the outcome as '*The Day They Betrayed British Democracy*'). Some 29 Labour MPs defied the party whip by backing a referendum and it was the only decision of Lib Dem leader Nick Clegg to whip his MPs into abstaining (rather than voting against the government) that carried the day for the prime minister. In doing so, Mr Clegg opened a potentially damaging rift in his own ranks: three frontbenchers resigned and 15 voted for a referendum, despite his using a three-line whip to discipline them. Oddly, the Lib Dems had spent much of the previous week in Parliament demanding a referendum on Europe—but on Britain's ongoing membership of the EU, rather than the constitutional issue in particular.

Disagreement in the British Parliament and internal wrangles within Labour's ranks began to appear academic when, on 13 June 2008, the only EU state to hold a referendum on the issue, Ireland, voted against it by a margin of 53.4 to 46.6 per cent. Despite the question marks raised over the future of the Treaty following Ireland's rejection, within days of the 'no' vote, Britain ploughed on with formally incorporating it into UK law. A last-ditch attempt by Tory peers to delay its passage through the Lords for four months fell on 18 June, when this motion was defeated by 93 votes. Even at this eleventh-hour stage it was unclear whether the government's ratification would be entirely successful, after a senior British judge warned Mr Brown that he would have to wait for the outcome of a legal hurdle threatening to derail the process in the Czech Republic before finally being signing off the Treaty. With recriminations between pro-Lisbon EU leaders and Ireland continuing to fly in the wake of these developments, and some suggesting that the country be asked to leave the Union rather than obstruct further integration, a firm decision on how to address the new 'Irish question' was put off until at least October 2008.

It was not long before the question of EU solidarity was rearing its head again—with Ireland once more singled out for criticism. As European leaders and finance ministers frantically tried to reach a consensus on how to deal collectively with the global banking crisis, in October 2008, the Irish government pledged to offer unlimited guarantees on all deposits held by the country's banks. Neelie Kroes, the EU's Commissioner for Competition, condemned the action, arguing that—due to the global nature of modern banking—it potentially contravened the Union's competition law. No sooner had she spoken than Ireland's actions were being replicated by several of the other member states that had initially been quick to criticize it. On the same day, German Chancellor Angela Merkel and the country's finance ministry broke ranks by issuing a unilateral statement promising blanket protection for all private savings accounts. Twenty-four hours later, Denmark followed suit.

▌ Other issues facing the EU

Although the twin issues of the euro and further EU integration are undoubtedly still the biggest sticking points for Euro-sceptics and Europhiles alike, there remain a number of other thorny issues surrounding Britain's membership of the EU. It would be impossible to give an exhaustive list of these areas—which range from fears about security and terrorism, to more traditional concerns such as economic growth and free trade—but some of the more potentially explosive are explained in Table 9.8.

Table 9.8 Major issues facing Britain's membership of the EU

Issue	Explanation
Common Agricultural Policy (CAP) and the British rebate	More than fifty years after it was first devised, the CAP still takes a bigger annual chunk out of the EU's budget than any other area—equivalent to 44 per cent of spending in any given year. Mrs Thatcher negotiated a generous annual rebate for Britain from the CAP and other EU subsidies in the late 1980s, in recognition of the fact that Britain did less well out of them than other states that rely more on agriculture, such as France. But in December 2005, Mr Blair was forced to climb down after a row with outgoing French president Mr Chirac. Because unanimity in the Council of Ministers is required for the EU Budget to be passed, the stalemate between the two countries had to be resolved, so, in the end, Mr Blair reluctantly accepted a £1bn a year cut in Britain's £3.6bn annual rebate. His opponents had argued that increased subsidies from richer western European countries were needed to assist some then new member states—particularly former Soviet countries such as Poland and the Czech Republic.
Enlargement of the EU	The most heated debate around further expansion surrounds the question of whether Turkey should be admitted into the EU. The country, on the Europe–Asia border, has long expressed a desire to join the Union, but several existing member states appear implacably opposed, citing the country's disputed human rights record as their main concern. Despite the secular nature of the Turkish government, others are concerned about the prospect of accepting the first majority Muslim country into a community that, despite the increasingly multicultural nature of individual states' populations, has until now displayed a broadly Christian bias. The fact that Turkey has a bigger population than any other EU state is also an issue because, under QMV, it would potentially end up with more say in the Council of Ministers than any other.
Common Fisheries Policy (CFP)	This long-standing policy is designed to protect fish and seafood stocks in European seas by using a 'quota' system for fishing rights, supposedly fairly allocated among relevant member states. In the mid-1990s, there were frequent confrontations between Britain and Spain over accusations of 'quota-hopping'—the alleged practice by Spanish trawlers fishing in British waters of registering boats under a third county's flag of convenience to enable them to exceed their country's quota. In the early 1990s, the British government was often accused of being ineffective in negotiating a better deal for lifelong UK trawler men forced to scrap their boats and change jobs because of the swingeing nature of quotas introduced in the waters that they fished.
Common defence policy	The concept of greater cooperation over defence was formally introduced in the Maastricht Treaty. In Britain, Euro-sceptics saw this as another step too far in terms of loss of sovereignty, but then Defence Secretary Michael Portillo (a Euro-sceptic) tried to reassure them in a patriotic speech at the Conservative Party Conference that Britain would never surrender the right to maintain its own independent armed forces. His headline-grabbing tirade ended with him quoting the motto of the SAS: 'Who dares, wins.' It remains unclear to what extent the EU will ever try to develop its own 'European army', but talk of an EU 'Rapid Reaction Force' designed to intervene swiftly in the event of a member state being threatened or invaded, or war breaking out between two or more members, remains on the table (see p. 330).

(continued)

Issue	Explanation
Economic migration	Expansion of the EU to encompass former Eastern Bloc countries has seen an increase in economic migration from poorer to richer countries, fostered by recent moves to allow free movement of labour (as well as goods, services, and capital) between member states. In some regions, this has put strain on community relations and public services—creating tensions between migrants and indigenous peoples. Britain recently took the unilateral step of introducing new restrictions on migrant workers from the two newest EU states, Bulgaria and Romania. It remains to be seen if this will be allowed to continue. If so, it is likely that other countries, such as France, Germany, and Italy, may well imitate.

→ Further reading

Bomberg, E. and Stubb, A. (eds) (2008) *The European Union: How Does it Work?*, Oxford: Oxford University Press. **Concise introductory text focusing on demystifying the key institutions of the EU and their sometimes arcane governing procedures.**

Daniels, P. and Ritchie, E. (1996) *EU: Britain and the European Union*, London: Palgrave Macmillan. **Analytical examination of the relationship of Britain and its main governmental institutions with those of the EU.**

Jones, A. (2007) *Britain and the European Union*, Edinburgh: Edinburgh University Press. **Invaluable introduction to the EU, its history, and its institutions, with particular emphasis placed on the changing relationship between the EU and UK.**

McCormick, J. (2008) *Understanding the European Union: A Concise Introduction*, London: Palgrave Macmillan. **Leading introductory text to the history, institutions, and treaties of the EU. The latest edition includes a comprehensive assessment of the Lisbon Treaty and the impact of EU enlargement.**

? Review questions

1. Outline the roles, structures, and composition of the main European Union institutions. Which is the most powerful and why?

2. How does qualified majority voting (QMV) work, where and how often is it used, and can it be described as fair and democratic? If not, why not?

3. What were the main stages leading up to full Economic and Monetary Union (EMU)? What are the arguments for and against Britain joining the euro?

4. Is the EU a federal super-state in the making, or one that has stayed true to its stated aim of preserving subsidiarity? To what extent, if any, is national sovereignty threatened by recent developments in European integration?

5. List some of the main issues affecting the future of the EU, explaining why they are significant to the UK's membership of the Union.

Online Resource Centre

www.oxfordtextbooks.co.uk/orc/Morrison
Visit the Online Resource Centre that accompanies this book for web links and regular updates.

10

International relations

We live in an era when terms such as *globalization*, 'development', 'fair trade'—and, regrettably, 'rogue state' and 'regime change'—are becoming part of our everyday cultural vocabulary. More than at any other time in its history, Britain's fortunes are tied to those of its neighbours in Europe. But its involvement in international affairs stretches well beyond the European Union (EU). The country is involved in at least two ongoing conflicts, in Afghanistan and Iraq. UK-based multinationals such as Shell and BP retain oil and mineral interests across Africa, Latin America, and the Middle East. And then there are those last vestiges of the once sprawling British Empire, in the guise of Northern Ireland, the 53-nation Commonwealth, and a handful of island protectorates, such as Gibraltar, the Falklands, and Diego Garcia.

At the same time as Britain is flexing its military and economic muscle, it has become one of the biggest players in the fight to eradicate global poverty, contributing nearly £7bn a year in overseas aid to developing countries in Africa, Asia, and South America, and leading the way at recent *G8* summits for binding multilateral agreements on debt relief. The country has also played a significant—if so far limited—role in brokering international agreements on issues ranging from climate change to human rights abuse.

Any attempt by a textbook of this nature to examine the UK's role in global politics and economy needs to be selective. The purpose of this chapter is to outline the work of the principal government departments and agencies involved in international relations, and the most significant institutions and issues with which they are engaged.

The Foreign and Commonwealth Office (FCO)

The Foreign and Commonwealth Office (FCO)—commonly known as the 'Foreign Office'—is the government department in charge of Britain's overall foreign policy. It was formed in 1968 from the merger of the existing Foreign Office (dating from 1782) and the then separate Commonwealth Office. At its head are several ministers, the most senior of whom is the Foreign and Commonwealth Secretary, or 'Foreign Secretary'.

The main roles of the FCO are to:

- maintain diplomatic and/or consular relations with 188 different countries;
- maintain diplomatic missions with a further nine countries;
- act as the UK's main broker in the drawing up of international treaties, common defence policies, and economic sanctions;
- use its overseas embassies to act as local focal points for diplomatic relations between Britain and the countries concerned;
- help to promote the UK as a trading partner with countries through its embassies.

When Labour regained power in 1997, its newly installed Foreign Secretary, the late Robin Cook, vowed to pursue an 'ethical foreign policy', which would put diplomacy and campaigning on human rights ahead of narrow national interests and warfare. But, in 2001, he was replaced by Jack Straw, who had earned a reputation as a tough-talking Home Secretary in the government's first term. Within months, the FCO was dealing with the fallout from the 11 September terrorist attacks on New York. In 2006, under then Foreign Secretary Margaret Beckett (the first woman to hold the post), the FCO announced ten new 'strategic priorities' for the next five to ten years (as outlined in Table 10.1).

Unlike most government departments, the FCO has only one *executive agency*: Wilton Park International Conference Centre organizes summits on international social problems attended by academics, business people, and other relevant professionals. Although staffed by FCO civil servants, Wilton Park prides itself on its academic independence. This is assured by the fact that its members are selected by an advisory council—not by ministers. Nonetheless, because this council is appointed by the Foreign Secretary, it is a moot point as to whether its independence is largely notional. There are

Table 10.1 The ten-year strategic objectives of the Foreign and Commonwealth Office (FCO)

	Objective
1	Making the world safer from terrorism and weapons of mass destruction (WMDs)
2	Reducing the harm to the UK from international crime, including drug trafficking, people smuggling, and money laundering
3	Preventing and resolving conflict through a strong international system
4	Building an effective and globally competitive EU in a secure neighbourhood
5	Supporting the UK economy and business through an open and expanding global economy, science and innovation, and secure energy supplies
6	Achieving climate security by promoting a faster transition to a sustainable, low-carbon global economy
7	Promoting sustainable development and poverty reduction, underpinned by human rights, democracy, good governance, and protection of the environment
8	Managing migration and combating illegal immigration
9	Delivering high-quality support for UK nationals abroad—in 'normal times' and crises
10	Ensuring the security and good governance of the UK's overseas territories

also several independent think tanks with close links to the FCO, the most famous of which is the Royal Institute of International Affairs, founded in 1920 and based at Chatham House, St James's Square, London (commonly known simply as 'Chatham House'). It is from Chatham House that the so-called 'Chatham House Rule'—beloved of, and cursed by, journalists in equal measure—originates. This is a 'gentleman's agreement' that allows the media access to candid discussions and debates held by private or public organizations in return for their agreement to respect the anonymity of participants. Reporters are normally permitted to make use of some, or all, information gained from such meetings, but on the strict condition that they do not attribute it to named individuals. The precise original wording of the 'Chatham House Rule' is as follows:

" When a meeting, or part thereof, is held under the Chatham House Rule, participants are free to use the information received, but neither the identity nor the affiliation of the speaker(s), nor that of any other participant, may be revealed. "

The civilized, but rather quaint, rule is reflective of the culture of the Foreign Office as a whole. The FCO is often criticized for its antediluvian procedures, maintaining a cosy 'old boy' approach to doing business more redolent of a Graham Greene novel than the harsh realities of twenty-first century *Weltpolitik*. In August 2005, Andrew Mackinlay, a Labour member of the Commons Foreign Affairs Select Committee, leaked details of a report by management consultancy Collinson Grant, which suggested that it was hugely overmanned and needed reform to address the following weaknesses:

- the fact it was often too 'slow to act';
- delegation was lacking within the management structure;
- accountability was poor;
- the need to cut 1,200 jobs and save at least £48m annually.

Of the high-profile recent controversies involving the Foreign Office, none has been more damaging than the debacle over Iraq. There is insufficient space here to go into detail about the circumstances leading to the US-led invasion of the country over Saddam Hussein's alleged stockpiling of weapons of mass destruction (WMDs), or the subsequent failure to locate any such arms—let alone the ongoing saga over when British and US troops will finally be pulled out of the war-ravaged country. It is fair to say, however, that the spectre of this ongoing conflict—not to mention the threat of terrorism, as brought home to the UK in the multiple bombings on 7 July 2005—is reflected in the wording of the FCO's new statement of 'priorities'.

Many other recent issues faced by the FCO—and played out in the media—have also stemmed in large part from Britain's involvement in the so-called 'War on Terror' (although Gordon Brown's **Cabinet** pointedly dropped this expression when he took office). These have included the UK government's belated intervention to secure the release of British-based terrorist suspects held in the US Guantanamo Bay detention camp on Cuba, which finally saw four returned to their families in 2007—five years after being captured by the US military in Afghanistan. More recently, a row broke out over Foreign Secretary David Miliband's admission—contrary to previous assurances by ministers—that a British territory had been used for so-called 'extraordinary rendition' by the USA. This is the process by which suspected terrorists are flown to a third-party country to be interrogated by agents working on behalf of the Central Intelligence Agency (CIA). The process has been criticized as 'torture by proxy' by human rights organizations, which argue that, by allowing prisoners to be questioned in countries known for their strong-arm tactics, the USA is giving tacit approval interrogation practices banned in its own country. In a speech to the Commons in February 2008, Mr Miliband revealed that he had been told by US Secretary of State Condoleezza Rice only after the event that US planes, each carrying a single suspect, had stopped on the British island of Diego Garcia in the Indian Ocean. One had been en route to Guantanamo Bay; the other to Morocco.

The Diplomatic Service

A 'sub-department' of the FCO is the Diplomatic Service. Staffed by seconded FCO administrators, and responsible for manning the embassies and consulates through which Britain discharges its diplomatic relations with their host countries, this employs up to 20,000 officials at one time and is headed not by a government minister, but by a career civil servant. Despite the fact that he or she is a salaried official, rather than an elected member of Parliament (MP), this civil servant has a title similar to a certain type of minister: 'Permanent Under-Secretary of State at the FCO'.

Personnel employed by the service at all levels enjoy 'diplomatic immunity'—that is, freedom from prosecution under the laws of the countries in which they are based. They may, however, be expelled for committing an offence—and could well be tried back in Britain.

▌ The Ministry of Defence (MoD)

What with the continuing military operations in Iraq and Afghanistan, controversies over the treatment of service personnel at home and abroad, and periodic outbursts about both these and other issues by retired senior officers, the Ministry of Defence (MoD) has grabbed more recent headlines than virtually any other government department. When Tony Blair was first elected, he made a famous speech in which he declared himself part of the 'first generation' able to '*contemplate that we may live our entire lives without going to war or sending our children to war*'. Yet, by the time he stepped down ten years later, he had taken Britain into no fewer than four wars: to prevent ethnic cleansing by Serbia's Slobodan Milošević in Kosovo (1999), to intervene in the civil war in Sierra Leone (2000), to support the US-led invasion of Afghanistan (2001), and to 'liberate' Saddam Hussein's Iraq and root out his supposed WMDs (2003). In addition, UK planes were heavily involved in the sustained bombing of Iraq by Bill Clinton's US administration in 1998.

Mr Blair's last Defence Secretary and Mr Brown's first, Des Browne, became the subject of unwitting controversy after being given two ministerial briefs (he remained Scottish Secretary after his appointment). In November 2007, a sustained attack was mounted by five retired chiefs of staff (heads of the Armed Forces) over his dual role and other cutbacks in the defence budget at a time when British troops were stretched to the limit in the Middle East. Former Royal Navy chief Admiral Lord Boyce accused the government of leaving 'blood on the floor' of the MoD by failing to resource the department adequately. Mr Brown went some way towards addressing this concern with his second reshuffle, in October 2008, when he replaced Mr Browne with former Business Secretary John Hutton—in so doing, stripping his role of responsibility for overseeing Scotland.

Formed in 1964 from the amalgamation of four other departments of state—the War Office, the Admiralty, the Air Ministry, and the Ministry of Aviation—the MoD is, perhaps ironically, most often in the news in times of conflict. Once diplomacy has broken down and Britain has decided to declare war on another nation, the FCO tends to fade out of the picture, to give way to the department charged with coordinating the military. Although its original aim was, as its name suggested, to provide a first line of 'defence' for Britain against foreign aggressors, in practice, it is as likely to see action at times when the UK is doing the attacking.

The principal roles of the MoD in its present form are as outlined in Table 10.2.

In recent years, the *raison d'être* of the MoD has changed in light of developments on the global stage, principally the end of the Cold War, on the one hand, and the rise of the terrorist threat, on the other. Current operations in

Table 10.2 The principal roles of the Ministry of Defence (MoD)

	Role
1	To deter threats to and, if necessary, defend the freedom and territorial integrity of, the UK and its dependent territories (e.g. the Falkland Islands)
2	To contribute to the promotion of the UK's wider security interests, including the protection of freedom, democratic institutions, and free trade
3	To promote peace and help to maximize the UK's international influence
4	To act as an international headquarters for the British Armed Forces—wherever they are in the world
5	To finance, provide, and maintain a permanent army, navy, and air force, as well as weaponry, uniforms, and other military equipment
6	To finance, provide, and maintain accommodation for the UK Armed Forces at home and overseas (barracks), as well as land and facilities for training and equipment

Iraq and Afghanistan notwithstanding, so-called 'conventional warfare'—involving ground troops, tanks, helicopters, planes, and ships—is becoming less commonplace. For a time during the 1980s—prior to the collapse of the Berlin Wall and the ensuing demise of the Soviet Union—the consensus view was that future wars would generally be fought 'by remote', with computerized systems and nuclear missiles replacing traditional armaments. While nuclear strikes have yet to occur, today's field weapons are increasingly sophisticated and the number of soldiers required to fight conflicts continues to diminish as their equipment becomes capable of doing more of the work for them. In response to the new challenges, and opportunities, presented by modern warfare, the UK government has published two major reviews of defence expenditure in the past decade. The 1998 Strategic Defence Review and the 2003 **White Paper** *Delivering Security in a Changing World* both envisaged the following approach for the Armed Forces:

- the ability to support three simultaneous small to medium-scale operations, with at least one as an enduring peacekeeping mission—for example, Kosovo. These forces must be capable of representing the UK as lead nation in any coalition operations;
- the ability, at longer notice, to deploy forces in a large-scale operation while running a concurrent small-scale operation.

Unlike the FCO, the MoD contains numerous executive agencies responsible for specific areas of its operation. These include a British Forces Post Office (in charge, as its name suggests, of all postal communications for the military), Defence Estates (responsible for maintaining MoD barracks and land), and such specific agencies as the Defence Storage and Distribution Agency, and the Defence Aviation Repair Agency.

The Chief of the Defence Staff—effectively, the **permanent secretary** of the Armed Forces as a whole—is supported by a Vice-Chief of the Defence Staff and the following heads of three individual Armed Forces:

- First Sea Lord/Chief of the Naval Staff;
- Chief of the General Staff;
- Chief of the Air Staff.

Aside from the ongoing criticisms of levels of defence expenditure—the MoD's annual budget is said to be less than the £100bn spent by the Treasury on 'rescuing' the Northern Rock bank from collapse (see p. 206)—the ministry has weathered numerous other storms in recent years. At the height of the

Iraq War, then Defence Secretary Geoff Hoon was accused of failing to provide adequate equipment in sufficient quantities for British troops engaged in the conflict. Mr Hoon, like Mr Blair, had also been repeatedly criticized for his apparent eagerness to invade Iraq on the basis of questionable intelligence about Saddam's WMD threat—and his unwillingness to apologize for the ensuing loss of life when it later emerged that no such weapons existed.

More recently, the MoD has been castigated in the press for failing to maintain barracks and domestic quarters for service personnel to a civilized standard, and for selling off large amounts of military accommodation to private landlords—only to end up renting it back from them. In March 2008, it emerged that British taxpayers were paying a private housing company £29m a year through the MoD for the privilege of renting 8,200 marital homes that were lying empty in lieu of any Forces families to move into them.

▌ The Department for International Development (DfID)

Until the 1997 election, the fields of humanitarian aid and investment in developing countries were the responsibility of a minister in the Foreign Office, the Minister for Overseas Development. When Mr Blair was elected, however, this post was incorporated into the Cabinet. Its first incumbent was Clare Short, a passionate advocate of overseas aid and sustainable development, who belatedly resigned from the Cabinet over the invasion of Iraq. After a period in which the Department for International Development (DfID) was run by Hilary Benn, he was replaced by a close ally of Mr Brown's, Douglas Alexander.

Today, DfID works directly with some 150 countries in the developing world—principally, in Africa, parts of Asia, Latin America, and the Far East. Its annual budget is in excess of £4bn and it has two headquarters: in London and East Kilbride, near Glasgow.

DfID initially stipulated a time frame within which it hoped to achieve key goals designed to tackle child poverty, and to improve the welfare and rights of children and women worldwide. In its 1997 White Paper, *Eliminating World Poverty: A Challenge for the 21st Century*, it outlined the key objectives for Britain's overseas aid policy listed in Table 10.3.

Table 10.3 Key Department for International Development objectives

By 2005	By 2015
Achieving gender equality and empowerment of women, as agreed by the Fourth World Conference on Women in 1995	Cutting by 50 per cent the number of people living in extreme poverty
Ensuring that national strategies for sustainable development are implemented in all countries	Ensuring that there is universal primary education in all countries
	Cutting by two-thirds the mortality rate of infants and children aged under 5
	Reducing by three-quarters the level of maternal mortality
	Providing access to reproductive services through primary health care by 2015, as agreed by the 1994 International Conference on Population and Development
	Ensuring trends towards environmental overdevelopment are halted and/or reversed. This was prefigured by:
	(a) the Convention on Climate Change at the 1992 Earth Summit, which limited the number of greenhouse gases; (b) the Montreal Protocol Multilateral Fund, which focused on the phasing out of ozone-depleting substances; (c) the Rio Biodiversity Convention, which pledged to halt the loss of animal and plant species, and the preservation of genetic resources.

The Department's stated objectives have become more modest—and decidedly less time-specific—in recent times. Its so-called 'Millennium Goals' are listed in Table 10.4.

Table 10.4 Department for International Development 'Millennium Goals'

	Goal
1	Halving the number of people living in extreme poverty and hunger
2	Ensuring that all children receive primary education
3	Promoting sexual equality and giving women a stronger voice
4	Reducing child death rates
5	Improving the health of mothers
6	Combating HIV and AIDS, malaria, and other diseases
7	Making sure that the environment is protected
8	Building a global partnership for those working in development

▶ Britain's role in the United Nations (UN)

In addition to the EU, Britain is a participating member of several major international organizations with differing, if sometimes overlapping, remits. Of these, perhaps the most significant is the *United Nations (UN)*—a global body set up after the Second World War with the stated aim of promoting peace, preventing future conflicts, and achieving international cooperation on economic, social, cultural, and humanitarian issues. From the outset, the UN has been committed to solving dispute between nations by peaceful means, wherever possible, and when it sends troops into a country, this tends to be in a *peacekeeping* capacity—that is, to police borders, protect aid routes, etc.—rather than with the intention of engaging in active hostilities against any party.

Formally established in October 1945, the UN set out to avoid the perceived errors of its precursor, the League of Nations. Born in the wake of the First World War, the League had imposed crippling reparations on Germany, in so doing contributing to the dire economic woes that were to foster the rise of Nazism. While the UN was pointedly to exclude Germany from the top table in its main governing institutions (a state of affairs that, to a large extent, remains the case to this day), it was determined not to make the mistake of isolating the country entirely, let alone financially penalizing it, as it struggled to rebuild its shattered infrastructure (and reputation) following Hitler's defeat.

Initially founded by 51 states, today the UN embraces some 192 participating nations. The most senior UN official is its secretary-general. In theory, UN membership is open to every recognized state in the world, but, in practice, individual countries have been periodically excluded—or have chosen to exclude themselves—in disputes over their legitimacy (or, occasionally, that of the UN).

The UN is based in New York—a fact that has given rise to periodic controversy. Some member states (particularly those with a history of disagreement with the USA) have argued that the American government wields a disproportionate influence on its decisions, although this charge has been harder to sustain in light of the difficulties that President George W. Bush faced when trying to win UN backing for the Iraq invasion. In October 2006, deputy leader of Somalia's Islamic Courts, Hassan Turki, one of several parties wrestling for control of the war-ravaged country, declared that he did not recognize the UN—dismissing it as an 'American interest group'.

The UN Security Council

The term 'United Nations' was first coined during the Second World War itself, when Winston Churchill and US president Franklin D. Roosevelt began using it in speeches to refer to the Allies—that is, the countries opposing Hitler. But it was only born in earnest after the UN Conference on International Organization was convened in April 1945, and a formal UN Charter was drafted and signed by the majority of its founding states on 24 October. Giving substance to Churchill's famous remark that '*history is written by the victors*', of these 51 nations, the five who had played arguably the most significant role in defeating Hitler were awarded permanent seats on a newly formed UN Security Council—the body charged with allocating peacekeeping forces around the world, ratifying economic sanctions, and, in extreme cases, authorizing military action.

According to the UN Charter, its role is to:

- investigate any situation threatening international peace;
- recommend procedures for peaceful resolution of a dispute;
- call on other member nations to completely or partially interrupt economic relations as well as sea, air, postal, and radio communications, or to sever diplomatic relations;
- enforce its decisions militarily, or by any means necessary.

The five permanent members of the UN Security Council are as follows: the USA; the UK; France; the Republic of China (later to be renamed the People's Republic of China); the Soviet Union (now the Russian Federation). They are joined at any one time by a further ten members, elected by the UN's 'parliament', the General Assembly, for two-year terms. These are chosen from among the remaining 187 UN countries on a rotational basis. For the two-year period commencing 1 January 2008, the temporary members of the UN Security Council were as outlined in Table 10.5, which can be found on the Online Resource Centre that accompanies this book.

As a mark of their seniority, each permanent member has the right to exercise a *veto* in votes on prospective UN action. It was this fact that presented the single biggest stumbling block to Britain and the USA's campaign to win support for a 'second resolution' authorizing a military strike on Iraq that they relentlessly pursued in the run-up to their joint 2003 invasion. Both the French president, Jacques Chirac, and his Russian counterpart, Vladimir Putin, made it clear that they had no intention of supporting such a resolution without conclusive proof that Saddam was stockpiling WMDs. Their intransigence blocked the passage of any such resolution, forcing the UK and US governments to abandon their pursuit of it and go it alone.

In recent years, there has been some discussion about the possibility of increasing the number of permanent members on the Security Council. Representations have been made not only by Germany (now a key player in the international community), but also by Japan, Brazil, and India. In 2004, then Secretary-General Kofi Anan proposed doubling the number of permanent members, to include each of the aforementioned states as well as one from Africa and/or one from the Arab League (a regional organization of Arab nations in the Middle East and North Africa, the members of which include Egypt, Iraq, Saudi Arabia, and Libya). A two-thirds vote in favour by UN General Assembly is needed before this can come into effect.

The UN General Assembly

The primary purpose of the other main governing body, the UN General Assembly, is to approve the UN's annual budget and appoint non-permanent representatives to the UN Security Council. It also receives reports from the UN's various other subsidiary bodies, and wields considerable influence over such policy areas as international aid and climate change.

Unlike the Security Council, the Assembly gives each UN member state an equal say at meetings. It convenes for regular annual sessions, lasting for the three months from September to December, but can be assembled for emergency meetings at other times. Meetings are chaired either by the serving secretary-general, or by a president, elected by Assembly members on a yearly basis. Votes are passed if a two-thirds majority of those present at a given meeting is achieved.

Like Britain's Parliament at Westminster, the Assembly has various committees charged with overseeing specific policy areas, in addition to some seven commissions, six boards, five panels, and numerous working groups. Of the 30 committees, the most influential are numbered one to six and focus on the following issues:

1. Disarmament and International Security (DISEC)
2. Economic and Finance (ECOFIN)
3. Social, Humanitarian and Cultural (SOCHUM)
4. Special Political and Decolonization (SPECPOL)
5. Administrative and Budgetary
6. Legal.

Other UN bodies and agencies

Like every major organization, national or international, the UN requires a bureaucracy. This role falls to the UN Secretariat, which employs 8,900 staff. The majority are based at the UN headquarters in New York, but others are stationed in its regional headquarters in Addis Ababa, Bangkok, Beirut, Geneva, Nairobi, Santiago, and Vienna. The Secretariat's responsibilities are divided, like those of the British Civil Service and the *European Commission*, into separate departments overseeing discreet policy areas:

- the Division for the Advancement of Women (DAW);
- the Department of Disarmament Affairs (DDA);
- the Department of Economic and Social Affairs (DESA);
- the Department of Political Affairs (DPA);
- the Department of Peacekeeping Operations (DPKO);
- the Office for the Coordination of Humanitarian Affairs (OCHA);
- the Office of the High Commissioner for Human Rights (OHCHR);
- the United Nations High Commissioner for Refugees (UNHCR);
- the United Nations Development Fund for Women (UNIFEM).

Other significant agencies of the UN and their responsibilities are outlined in Table 10.6.

 The present composition of the International Court of Justice is laid out in Table 10.7, which can be found on the Online Resource Centre.

▶ Life after the Cold War—Britain's ongoing role in NATO

Founded in 1949, the *North Atlantic Treaty Organization (NATO)* is, unlike the UN, a *military* alliance established against the backdrop of the emerging Cold War between East and West, and the ensuring nuclear arms race, to protect the security of Western powers. NATO is made up of 26 member states—principally, the USA, Canada, and a collection of west European countries, although in the wake of the collapse of the Soviet Union, it has also embraced a number of former Eastern Bloc nations.

Table 10.6 The subordinate bodies of the UN and their responsibilities

Body	Role and remit
The International Court of Justice (ICJ)	Made up of 15 judges elected for nine years at a time, this sits in the Peace Palace in The Hague, the Netherlands. Its purpose is to hear cases referred to it by member states and adjudicate between the warring parties. Several countries—among them, the USA, France, Germany, and China—have, however, refused to be bound by its rulings. Among its most famous recent cases was the protracted trial of the late Serbian dictator, Slobodan Milošević, on 66 charges of genocide and 'crimes against humanity', and the recently opened hearings into the similar charges brought against Bosnian Serb leader Radovan Karadžić. (Membership of the Court for the nine years beginning March 2007 can be found in Table 10.7.)
The United Nations Economic and Social Council (ESOCOC)	Formed to promote cooperation between UN states on economic and social policy, this has 54 participating members, all elected at the same time by the General Assembly for a three-year term. It has a president, elected for a one-year term from among the smaller and 'middle-ranking' states represented on the ESOCOC. Historically, it meets once a year, in July, for four weeks, but, since 1998, has also met in April to liaise with finance ministers who head the key committees of the World Bank and International Monetary Fund (IMF). The ESOCOC works in close consultation with some 2,000 non-government organizations (NGOs) and oversees a large number of agencies, including UNESCO, UNICEF, WHO, UNDP, ILO, and UNHCR (see next entries).
The United Nations Educational, Scientific and Cultural Organization (UNESCO)	With 193 member states and six associate members, this was formed to promote cultural understanding through education, science, and the arts. It has more notional participants than the UN itself, with a base in Paris and 30 other offices.
The United Nations Children's Fund (UNICEF)	Formerly the 'United Nations International Children's Emergency Fund', this was set up to provide urgent food and health care to children whose countries had been devastated in the Second World War. Based in New York, it is a voluntary agency that relies for income on governments and private donations.
The World Health Organization (WHO)	Established on the first World Health Day, on 7 April 1948, this body is charged with coordinating international efforts to monitor outbreaks of deadly diseases such as malaria, cholera, typhoid, and AIDS, as well as sponsoring vaccination programmes and medical research. Among its more famous pronouncements is its widely publicized 'Breast is Best' advice to mothers in developing countries, designed to encourage the use of breast milk to rear infants, rather than formula, which relies on clean water supplies to make it safe. UN-affiliated NGOs such as the UK-based Baby Milk Action have repeatedly come into conflict with the multinational Nestlé over its alleged promotion of powdered milk.

(continued)

Body	Role and remit
The United Nations Development Programme (UNDP)	An executive board within the Assembly, but funded by voluntary donations, this is the world's largest international source of aid for investment in industrial and agricultural development.
The International Labour Organization (ILO)	Based in Geneva, Switzerland, this body aims to promote opportunities for both men and women to *'obtain decent and productive work, in conditions of freedom, equity, security, and human dignity'*. As with many UN bodies, in recent years, its focus has been increasingly on the unequal plight of women in developing countries. It meets three times a year—in March, June, and November—and holds an International Labour Conference in Geneva each June. The ILO boasts a governing body comprising representatives from 28 member governments, 14 workers' groups, and 14 employers' groups. Ten seats are held permanently by the USA, UK, Brazil, China, France, Germany, India, Italy, Japan, and the Russian Federation; the remaining ones are elected by member states on a three-year basis.
The Office of the United Nations High Commissioner for Refugees (UNHCR)/The United Nations Refugee Agency	Established in 1950, this aims to coordinate international efforts to protect refugees and relieve situations that might lead to indigenous peoples fleeing their countries. It employs 6,300 staff in 110 countries.

NATO's origins lay in an earlier agreement, the 1948 Treaty of Brussels, which founded the Western European Union, a smaller-scale forerunner of the alliance composed entirely (as its name suggests) of west European countries. In fact, its only signatories were Britain, France, and the Benelux countries: Belgium, the Netherlands, and Luxembourg. As the Western Union began deliberating, its members concluded that, for any military counterweight to the Soviet Union to be truly effective, it would need to include the USA. Hence the decision was taken to open its doors to the USA and, in due course, on 4 April 1949 NATO was formed with the signing of the North Atlantic Treaty in Washington DC. Along with the USA and Canada, Portugal, Italy, Norway, Denmark, and Iceland were admitted at the same time. Greece and Turkey joined in 1952. Perhaps unsurprisingly, given the nature of the global political climate at the time, West Germany had to wait longer to join, but it finally did so on 9 May 1955. East Germany was effectively absorbed into the alliance in 1990, following the reunification of Germany a year earlier.

Given the rapid expansion of NATO and its open hostility to Stalin's growing empire in the East, it was only a matter of time before the Soviet Union retaliated by establishing its own equivalent organization. It did so with the signing, on 14 May 1955, of the Warsaw Treaty of Friendship, Cooperation and Mutual Assistance—better known as the 'Warsaw Pact'. In time, it came to encompass all of the Soviet countries, with the exception of Yugoslavia. But, in belated recognition of the redundancy of the Warsaw Pact following the collapse of Communism in the East, on 12 March 1999 the following former members joined NATO: Hungary, Poland, and the Czech Republic. Bulgaria, Estonia, Latvia, Lithuania, Romania, and Slovakia followed suit in March 2004.

NATO remains based in Brussels, but, as with the UN, this has not stopped some countries accusing it of being in the USA's pocket. In 1958, French president Charles de Gaulle provoked its first constitutional crisis by proposing a new tripartite 'directorate' of NATO, headed jointly by the USA, Britain, and France. Writing to US President Dwight D. Eisenhower and then British Prime Minister Harold Macmillan, he accused them of undermining NATO's collective decision-making process through their cosy 'special arrangement'.

The North Atlantic Treaty

As stated above, the foundation stone of NATO was the North Atlantic Treaty. Perhaps its most defining (and oft-cited) clause is Art. V, which sets down the principle of 'collective defence'. Essentially, this describes the notion that an attack on one or more members of the alliance should be regarded as an attack on all of them, thereby warranting a collective response from its members. The precise wording of Art. V is as follows:

> The Parties of NATO agreed that an armed attack against one or more of them in Europe or North America shall be considered an attack against them all. Consequently they agree that, if such an armed attack occurs, each of them, in exercise of the right of individual or collective self-defence will assist the Party or Parties being attacked, individually and in concert with the other Parties, such action as it deems necessary, including the use of armed force, to restore and maintain the security of the North Atlantic area.

The most recent invocation of Art. V came in the aftermath of the 11 September attacks on New York, when the USA argued that the terrorist strikes on the World Trade Center effectively amounted to a military attack on the country and therefore required a joint response from NATO members. There was some dispute about whether the usual rules applied, given that the precise identities and nationalities of all of the terrorists were not immediately known, making any decision to target a specific country in retaliation problematic. Having asserted an Al-Qaeda link, the USA argued that the Taliban in Afghanistan was principally answerable, since its then leader, Mullah Omar, was believed to be harbouring leaders of the Al-Qaeda movement, including Osama bin Laden.

In the event, action in defence of the USA was authorized on 4 October 2001 (despite rowdy scenes in some NATO meetings leading up to the agreement) and the alliance participated in two subsequent operations: Operation Eagle Assist and Operation Active Endeavour. The former was a series of precautionary sorties over US skies performed by planes from 13 NATO states. The latter was to become an ongoing naval operation in the Mediterranean Sea designed to intercept the passage of WMDs. Since Operation Active Endeavour commenced, it has involved 12 NATO members and five partner countries (Russia, Egypt, Tunisia, Morocco, and Ukraine). Some 79,000 ships have been monitored and a hundred boarded.

Previous attempts to invoke Art. V have not always met with success. In 1982, Margaret Thatcher's government attempted to persuade NATO to do so in response to the Argentine invasion of the Falklands, but because those islands are located thousands of miles from the UK, in the South Atlantic, the invasion was not deemed to be an attack on Britain.

The North Atlantic Council (NAC)

NATO's principal governing body, the North Atlantic Council (NAC), meets twice a week: once on a Tuesday, for an informal lunch meeting, and then again on Wednesdays, for a formal decision-making session. Its composition varies in terms of the officials who actually attend its meetings: on some occasions, so-called 'permanent representatives' (PermReps)—salaried career diplomats from each state—will do so; on other occasions—particularly when major issues are due to be debated—member states tend to send their foreign or defence ministers.

The most senior official in NATO, as with the UN, is its civilian secretary-general, whose job it is to chair meetings of the NAC and to act as the alliance's public figurehead.

The secretary-general is supported by a deputy secretary-general.

The Military Committee

NATO's status as an alliance focusing on security and defence-related issues means that some of its operational decisions require a more direct input than might otherwise be the case from military personnel. To facilitate this process, the Organization has its own Military Committee, which (unlike the NAC) is composed of professional members of the armed forces rather than civil servants. Each member state sends to its meetings a military representative (normally a chief of staff). The Committee has its own permanent chairman.

The Committee also has several subsets: an Allied Command Europe, Allied Command Atlantic, Allied Command Channel, and Regional Planning Group (for North America), each under its own 'supreme commander'.

The NATO Parliamentary Assembly

Not actually part of NATO's official structure—but created in 1955 to complement and liaise with it—the NATO Parliamentary Assembly is a fairly informal annual convention of parliamentarians/legislators (that is, MPs) from each member state of the alliance, which meets to discuss common policy issues.

The future of NATO

There has been much debate in the media about whether NATO remains 'relevant' in a post-Cold War environment. Leaving aside the recent diplomatic contretemps between Russia and the USA, over the latter's decision to expand its new Missile Defence Shield to cover former Soviet states such as Poland and the Czech Republic, and the stand-off between Mr Putin and Britain (of which more later), few observers argue that we are about to be plunged back into a new East–West arms race. Nevertheless, the Western world can hardly be described as being safe from outside attack, given the events of 11 September 2001 and 7 July 2005 (not to mention the 2004 Madrid bombing). While terrorist attacks of this kind may be harder to defend—let alone to retaliate against—than conventional invasions or missile strikes, recent secretary-generals have argued that the alliance has a clear role to play in devising strategies to counter them. Its ongoing presence in Afghanistan is a symbol of this resolve.

Then there are the flashpoints of more conventional conflict that continue to erupt periodically on European soil. In the 1990s, NATO did a good job redefining itself as a proactive third-party fighting force in the Balkans, first during the Bosnian War, then during the Serbian assaults on Albania and Kosovo. Recent events in Serbia, leading to the unilateral declaration of independence by Kosovo and rumblings of discontent in Belgrade, have led some to question whether the alliance's work in the region has yet been concluded.

All of these developments aside, NATO is facing an emerging challenge from the European Union. As the threat of terrorist attacks on European soil becomes ever more real, EU leaders have placed the development of their embryonic 'Rapid Reaction Force' squarely on the agenda for the next few years (see p. 309). The 'Force', as it stands, is little more than a notional one—the term refers to the EU's ability to mobilize up to 60,000 troops, 400 combat aircraft, and 200 ships drawn from member states at short notice to defend its borders; there is no talk yet of formally establishing a collective 'European army'. Nonetheless, in the eyes of some Western governments, the threat to NATO's hegemony remains a potent one.

▌ The Council of Europe

Founded in 1949, the *Council of Europe* pre-dates by two years the European Union (with the institutions of which it is often confused). As such, it has the status of being the longest-running organization dedicated to promoting European integration and cooperation. Recognized under international law, it has 47 member states (20 more than the EU to date).

Its prime purpose is to promote the adoption of common legal standards and human rights among its members. To this end, its most famous institution is the *European Court of Human Rights (ECtHR)* at Strasbourg, and by far its most celebrated achievement is the European Convention on Human Rights (ECHR), which the Court is charged with upholding. (The Convention is discussed in detail in relation to its relationship to the British constitution in Chapter 1.)

Moves to establish some form of European political and social confederation, of which the Council of Europe was to be the first expression, arose out of the alliance forged in the Second World War. In a famous speech at the University of Zurich in 1946, Winston Churchill (at the time Britain's Leader of the Opposition, following his defeat by Labour in the 1945 election) called for the formation of a 'United States of Europe', with France and Germany at its head. Although he pointedly stopped short of suggesting that Britain should be a part of this alliance—instead saying that it should join with the

USA in embracing it—his coining of the term is conveniently forgotten by many of his fans on the right of the Conservative Party today. In due course, the Council of Europe was established by the Treaty of London, on 5 May 1949, and a 'Statute' outlining its statement of principles was signed by the following ten countries: Belgium, Denmark, France, Ireland, Italy, Luxembourg, the Netherlands, Norway, Sweden, and the UK.

Article 1 of this Statute declared:

❝ The aim of the Council of Europe is to achieve a greater unity between its members for the purpose of safeguarding and realising the ideals and principles which are their common heritage and facilitating their economic and social progress. ❞

Its overall list of aims and objectives are as set out in Table 10.8, which can be found on the Online Resource Centre.

The governing institutions of the Council of Europe

The main decision-making bodies within the Council are the Parliamentary Assembly (PACE)—comprising parliamentarians (MPs) from each of the 47 member states—and the Committee of Ministers, made up notionally of foreign ministers from each participating country (but, in fact, by permanent representatives, as on NATO's General Assembly). As with both NATO and the UN, its most senior official is the secretary-general, who is elected for five years at a time by PACE. The secretary-general is head of the Council of Europe Secretariat (its civil service).

In addition to these core institutions, the Council also has a number of *quango*-style semi-autonomous structures, known as 'partial agreements', to which member states may send representatives. It also set up a Congress of the Council of Europe in 1994, to draw together representatives from local and regional government in the Council's member states.

▶ International trade and economy

Averting war and promoting peace is one key area of international cooperation in the modern world; the other is fostering free trade and financial investment between nations. Over and above the EU, the UN, and the Council of Europe, several key bodies were founded in the second half of the twentieth century to achieve these and related goals.

The evolution of the Group of Eight (G8)

The G8—or Group of Eight, to use its full title—is not a formal body like many of the others in this list, but rather a forum comprising the world's biggest leading industrialized nations and military superpowers. Its membership is as follows: Canada, France, Germany, Italy, Japan, the Russian Federation, the UK, and the USA. The most recent country to join was Russia and, even today, the group sometimes convenes in its absence. On such occasions, it reverts temporarily to its former title: the Group of Seven (G7).

The G8 has its origins in the seismic economic turmoil created in Europe by the 1973 oil crisis involving the USA, Japan, Britain, and other west European countries, on the one hand, and, on the other, the Arab members of the Organization of Petroleum Exporting Countries (OPEC), plus two of their allies, Egypt, and Syria. At the time, these countries were refusing to ship oil to the West in protest over its support for Israel in the Yom Kippur War. In response, the USA convened the so-called 'Library Group'—an informal meeting of financial experts from the USA, Britain, France, Japan, and West Germany—and, a year later in 1975, then French President Valéry Giscard d'Estaing called a summit in Rambouillet that led to the formation of a Group of Six (G6), comprising the future members of the G8 minus Canada and, obviously, Russia. Canada joined the following year.

Since then, the G6 and its successors have held annual meetings at different locations within participating member states, under a rotating presidency. Although the group has no economic or constitutional powers per se, it is seen as one of the most influential talking shops in global politics. At the G8 Summit in Gleneagles in July 2005, Mr Blair used his chairmanship to push through a pledge for a further £29bn boost to international aid and to cancel the debt of the 18 poorest African nations. Despite criticisms from some campaigners, Sir Bob Geldof and Bono described the date of the agreement as 'a great day'.

More recently, controversy has surrounded Russia's ongoing membership of the G8, in light of its increasingly belligerent foreign policy under newly installed president Dmitry Medvedev. When the country invaded Georgia in August 2008—ostensibly to protect the neighbouring territory of South

Ossetia in the Caucuses from Georgian aggression—it invited widespread condemnation. There were calls from some quarters for its G8 membership to be suspended.

The International Monetary Fund (IMF)

The International Monetary Fund (IMF) was, like many other supranational organizations, formed in response to the Second World War. It was founded in July 1944, when the representatives of 45 governments met at Bretton Woods, New Hampshire, and its remit from the outset was an intrinsically economic one—namely, to restore and maintain stability in the world's financial sector and to prevent widespread *recessions* through such mechanisms as exchange rate agreements and short-term monetary aid packages. Indeed, one of its key roles in the ensuing decades was to provide loans to countries experiencing temporary financial blips. This money is borrowed from a pool contributed to on a rolling basis by member states.

The IMF today counts some 185 countries among its members. All UN states, apart from North Korea, Cuba, Andorra, Monaco, Liechtenstein, Nauru, and Tuvalu, are included. Its headquarters is in Washington DC—a fact that has led to repeated accusations by some countries that it is effectively a puppet of the USA (a similar charge is often levelled against the World Bank and, indeed, certain institutions of the UN).

As with most banks, including the **Bank of England**, the IMF has its own ruling board of governors. While every member state has a presence on the board and may vote on resolutions, as with the EU Council of Ministers, some countries wield more power than others. The extent of an individual state's say on the board is governed by its 'quota' of the votes available. This relates as much to the amount of money that it has contributed to the running of the IMF in the past, as to the size of its population. Each state also has a corresponding right in relation to how much it is permitted to borrow, should it need to, from the bank's pool of finance. These entitlements are known as 'special drawing rights' (SDRs).

Both Britain and the USA do relatively well out of the IMF on paper. Britain wields nearly a 5 per cent quota of the available votes, while the USA can count on 17 per cent. In terms of borrowing ability, the USA has access to 37,149 million SDRs, and Britain to 10,739—compared to just 2,396 for Sweden. It is just as well that Britain has this help at hand: in 1976, Prime Minister James Callaghan had to approach the Fund to ask for an emergency loan to enable his government to plug a huge hole in the public finances (see pp. 205–6).

The IMF has seen its fair share of controversy since its inception. Perhaps giving succour to criticisms that the USA and certain European countries wield a disproportionate influence on its policy decisions, the governing board has in the past approved significant loans to dictatorships friendly to the West. Pinochet's Chile and Musharaf's Pakistan are only two of the states helped out by the fund, despite being boycotted by other organizations and non-government organizations (NGOs) in relation to their alleged human rights abuses. The Fund has also been heavily criticized for imposing strict 'conditionalities' on developing countries that approach it for assistance. The most frequently cited conditionality is a so-called 'structural adjustment programme', which essentially obliges the country seeking aid to privatize state-owned utilities and other industries as a prerequisite for its loan. Similarly contentious is the IMF's habit of charging high interest to countries judged at risk of defaulting and recalling loans at short notice—practices that precipitated severe financial crises in Argentina and Bolivia in the 1990s.

The World Bank

Also based in Washington DC, the World Bank was formally established on 27 December 1945. A sister organization of the IMF, its remit has evolved over the decades and now revolves, principally, around a set of so-called 'Millennium Development Goals' designed to eliminate child poverty and promote sustainable development in Third World countries. The Bank comprises five constituent parts, the most powerful of which are:

- the *International Bank for Reconstruction and Development (IBRD)*—originally formed to fund the rebuilding of countries devastated by the Second World War, but now primarily devoted to providing loans through secure bonds to developing countries to relieve poverty and build infrastructure to improve self-reliance. The bonds that it issues are rated 'AAA' (indicating that they are as secure as is possible). This is guaranteed by the fact that they are backed by member states' share capital;

- the *International Development Association (IDA)*—provides long-term, interest-free loans to the world's 81 poorest countries for help with education, health care, sanitation, clean water, and environmental protection. Since its inception, it has made loans totalling nearly £80bn (on average, £4–14bn a year).

The World Bank, like the IMF, has encountered increasing hostility from some development charities and NGOs, not to mention certain countries, on account of the stringent conditionalities that it requires of states before agreeing to grant assistance. Some see the criteria that it expects them to meet before recognizing them as a stable business environment as an attempt to impose an imperialistic, Western capitalist model on nations the indigenous institutions and sociocultural makeup of which do not sit easily with it. The 'five key factors' stipulated by the bank as necessary to promote economic growth are listed in Table 10.9, which can be found on the Online Resource Centre.

In terms of the USA's influence on the Bank, a high-profile row occurred in March 2005 when President Bush nominated his erstwhile Deputy Secretary for Defense, the ardent 'neo-Conservative' Republican Paul Wolfowitz, to the then soon-to-be-vacated post of World Bank Group president. Wolfowitz was criticized during his short-lived tenure (including by his own colleagues) for trying to skew the bank's policies on issues such as family planning and climate change towards a right-wing agenda. But by far the most significant controversy arose when it emerged that he had abused his position to award a disproportionate pay rise and promotion to Shaha Riza, a former bank employee with whom he had been having an affair. Mr Wolfowitz resigned in June 2007 after admitting his actions to the board of governors—although he maintained that he had 'acted ethically and in good faith'. He was replaced by another White House nominee and Republican ally of Mr Bush, Robert Zoellick.

The World Trade Organization (WTO)

Established on 1 January 1995, the World Trade Organization (WTO) replaced the General Agreement on Tariffs and Trade (GATT) originally set up after the Second World War to foster free trade and industrial harmony between member states. It is based in Geneva.

Although it theoretically promotes fairness of trade between different nations, the USA, in particular, has often been accused of ignoring or bypassing its rulings: the UK/EU tried to protect the Caribbean states by supporting the price of their banana exports recently, but the USA complained about this. In the end, the WTO found in favour of the USA.

More recently, the USA itself has tried to impose tariffs on its imports of foreign steel, thereby inflating their market price relative to domestically produced steel. Other UN nations have complained that this amounts to protectionism—a claim that the WTO is investigating.

The WTO is governed by:

- a Ministerial Conference, composed of finance ministers from all of the member states, which meets every two years;
- a General Council, which takes day-to-day decisions and runs its administration;
- a director-general appointed by the Council.

Originally, the *agenda* for WTO meetings revolved around the so-called 'Uruguay Round'—a set of concerns agreed by member states on its formation—but this has since been replaced by the 'Doha Development Agenda', which has focused on liberalizing trade between developed and developing countries, with the specific aim of removing all remaining customs barriers. Kickstarted in 2001, discussions reached an extremely rocky phase in July 2008, with the USA and EU refusing to give ground on free trade terms that some negotiators, including then EU Trade Commissioner Peter Mandelson, argued were vital to protect developing countries' interests as they prepared to open their markets up to global competition.

The Organisation for Economic Co-operation and Development (OECD)

Based in Paris and formally called the 'Organisation for European Economic Co-operation' (OEEC), the Organisation for Economic Co-operation and Development (OECD) is made up of 29 industrialized member countries. It was formed in 1948, initially to help to implement the Marshall Plan for the reconstruction of war-ravaged Europe, but changed its name in 1961 when the decision was taken to admit its first non-European member states.

The OECD's primary aims are to promote the spread of global free trade, hand in hand with representative democracy, and to this end (along with the G8, and the World Economic Forum) its primary focus is the encroachment of globalization—the term used to denote the increasingly interdependent nature of the global economy.

As with most supranational organizations, the OECD is run by a ruling council, and has a secretary-general and its own secretariat (civil service), which is divided into the following 15 directorates:

- the Centre for Entrepreneurship, SMEs [small to medium-sized enterprises] and Local Development;
- the Centre for Tax Policy and Administration;
- the Development Co-operation Directorate;
- the Directorate for Education;
- the Directorate for Employment, Labour and Social Affairs;
- the Directorate for Financial and Enterprise Affairs;
- the Directorate for Science, Technology and Industry;
- the Economics Department;
- the Environment Directorate;
- the Public Governance and Territorial Development Directorate;
- the Statistics Directorate;
- the Trade and Agriculture Directorate;
- the General Secretariat;
- the Executive Directorate;
- the Public Affairs and Communication Directorate.

The World Economic Forum (WEF)

The World Economic Forum (WEF) is a not-for-profit foundation based in Geneva, the aim of which is to improve the distribution of economic opportunity throughout the world by fostering interaction between governments, businesses, academic institutions, and the arts. Its members meet each year at the Davos Symposium in Switzerland. Some two hundred government leaders, eight hundred chief executives, and three hundred assorted experts, scientists, artists and media representatives take part in its summits.

▌ The end of empire—the Commonwealth and the British Council

The British Empire may have long since collapsed, but two more benign aspects of its legacy continue, in the institutional guises of the Commonwealth and the British Council.

The Commonwealth of Nations (the Commonwealth)

The Commonwealth today is comprised of 53 countries, most—but not all—of which are former British colonies. It takes its name from a remark by Lord Rosebery, the then Foreign Secretary (and a future prime minister), who, on visiting Adelaide in 1884, described what remained of the UK's then crumbling empire as 'the Commonwealth of nations'. The current membership of the Commonwealth is as outlined below in Table 10.10.

The principal purpose of the Commonwealth is to foster cross-cultural understanding and collaboration between some of the world's developed economies and the large number of developing states that are also members. The broad policy areas over which it seeks to reach agreement, by consensus are:

- democracy;
- economics;
- education;
- gender;
- governance;
- human rights;
- law;
- the treatment of small states;
- sport;
- sustainability;
- youth.

In addition, in 1971, the Commonwealth formally committed itself to upholding the following list of core values, by signing the Singapore Declaration,

Table 10.10 The current membership of the Commonwealth

Country	Year joined	Capital	Population	Land area (km²)
Antigua and Barbuda	1981	St John's	81,000	442
Australia	1931	Canberra	21,134,563	7,741,220
Bahamas	1973	Nassau	319,000	13,878
Bangladesh	1972	Dhaka	139,215,000	143,998
Barbados	1966	Bridgetown	269,000	430
Belize	1981	Belmopan	264,000	22,966
Botswana	1966	Gaborone	1,769,000	581,730
Brunei	1984	Bandar Seri Begawan	366,000	5,765
Cameroon	1995	Yaounde (constitutional) Douala (economic)	16,038,000	475,442
Canada	1931	Ottawa	33,039,367	9,970,610
Cyprus	1961	Nicosia	826,000	9,251
Dominica	1978	Roseau	79,000	751
Fiji	1970 1997	Suva	841,000	18,274
Gambia	1965	Banjul	1,478,000	11,295
Ghana	1957	Accra	21,664,000	238,533
Grenada	1974	St George's	102,000	344
Guyana	1966	Georgetown	750,000	214,969
India	1949	New Delhi	1,087,124,000	3,166,414
Jamaica	1962	Kingston	2,639,000	10,991
Kenya	1963	Nairobi	33,467,000	580,367
Kiribati	1979	Tarawa	97,000	726
Lesotho	1966	Maseru	1,798,000	30,355
Malawi	1964	Lilongwe	12,608,000	118,484
Malaysia	1957	Kuala Lumpur	27,356,000	329,847
Maldives	1982	Malé	321,000	298
Malta	1964	Valletta	400,000	316
Mauritius	1968	Port Louis	1,233,000	2,040
Mozambique	1995	Maputo	19,424,000	801,590
Namibia	1990	Windhoek	2,009,000	824,292
Nauru	1968	Yaren (unofficial)	13,000	21
New Zealand	1931	Wellington	4,109,000	270,534
Nigeria	1960 1999	Abuja	128,709,000	923,768

(continued)

Country	Year joined	Capital	Population	Land area (km²)
Pakistan	1949 1989 2004	Islamabad	161,488,000	880,940
Papua New Guinea	1975	Port Moresby	5,772,000	462,840
Saint Kitts and Nevis	1983	Basseterre	42,000	261
Saint Lucia	1979	Castries	159,000	539
Saint Vincent and the Grenadines	1979	Kingstown	118,000	388
Samoa	1970	Apia	184,000	2,831
Seychelles	1976	Victoria	80,000	455
Sierra Leone	1961	Freetown	5,336,000	71,740
Singapore	1965	Singapore	4,680,600	704
Solomon Islands	1978	Honiara	466,000	28,896
South Africa	1931 1994	Pretoria (executive) Bloemfontein (judicial) Cape Town (legislative)	47,208,000	1,221,037
Sri Lanka	1948	Sri Jayawardhanapura Kotte	20,570,000	65,610
Swaziland	1968	Mbabane	1,034,000	17,364
Tanzania	1961	Dodoma	37,627,000	945,087
Tonga	1970	Nuku'alofa	102,000	747
Trinidad and Tobago	1962	Port of Spain	1,301,000	5,130
Tuvalu	1978	Funafuti	10,000	26
Uganda	1962	Kampala	25,827,000	241,038
United Kingdom	1931	London	60,609,155	242,900
Vanuatu	1980	Port Vila	207,000	12,189
Zambia	1964	Lusaka	11,479,000	752,618
Total			**1,921,974,000**	**31,462,574**

which was further cemented twenty years later, in 1991, with the drafting of the Harare Declaration:

- world peace and support for the United Nations;
- individual liberty and egalitarianism;

- opposition to racism;
- opposition to colonialism;
- eradication of poverty, ignorance, disease, and economic inequality;
- free trade;
- institutional cooperation;
- multilateralism;
- rejection of international coercion.

While the Queen remains head of the Commonwealth as a whole, she is now head of state of only 16 of its member states (together known as the 'Commonwealth realms'): Antigua and Barbuda; Australia; the Bahamas; Barbados; Belize; Canada; Grenada; Jamaica; New Zealand; Papua New Guinea; Saint Kitts and Nevis; Saint Lucia; Saint Vincent and the Grenadines; the Solomon Islands; Tuvalu; the UK itself. Australia narrowly voted to retain the Queen as head of state in a *referendum* in 1999, but in 2007, Labour Prime Minister Kevin Rudd pledged a further vote in the near future.

There have been other significant ructions in the Commonwealth in recent times. South Africa rejoined in 1994, after a 33-year absence, following the election as president of Nelson Mandela. In contrast, Pakistan was expelled in 1999, following the military coup of President Pervez Musharaf. Zimbabwe, meanwhile, withdrew voluntarily after previously having been suspended in light of President Robert Mugabe's dubious human rights record.

Like most other supranational organizations, the Commonwealth has its own governing and administrative institutions, as listed in Table 10.11.

The British Council

The British Council is a registered charity that receives core grant aid from the FCO, but earns half of its total income from teaching English, run-

Table 10.11 Commonwealth institutions and their functions

Institution	Function
Meeting of Heads of Government	Held every other year in member states on rotation
The Commonwealth Secretariat	Based in London, this administers Commonwealth institution meetings
The Commonwealth Fund for Technical Co-operation	Arranges consultancy services and training awards for developing states
The Commonwealth Games	Held every four years, this has become as much a symbolic event designed to cement cultural links as a serious sporting contest

ning British exams, and managing training and development contracts. It is the UK's main agency for maintaining cordial, mutually beneficial cultural relations with other nations and, to aid it in this role, it has some 254 offices and teaching centres in 110-plus countries.

Among the technological, scientific, and artistic initiatives sponsored by the British Council is the British entry to the prestigious Venice Biennale, which showcases the work of a leading contemporary visual artist every two years. In recent years, Britain has been represented by such 'Brit Art' luminaries as Chris Ofili, Gilbert and George, and Tracey Emin. The British Council supports student exchange programmes between the UK and numerous other nations through its Central Bureau for Educational Visits and Exchanges.

Although generally perceived as a benign organization, the British Council has encountered notable diplomatic difficulties in recent months, most significantly in Russia. Since 1994, the British Council has been operating in Russia under the terms of an interim intergovernmental agreement focusing on the fields of education, science, and culture. But the cordial relations between the charity and the Russian authorities were abruptly cooled when, in May 2007, the British government demanded the extradition by Russia of Andrei Lugovi. Mr Lugovi had been identified as the prime suspect in the murder of Alexander Litvinenko, a former lieutenant-colonel in the Russian Federal Security Service, who was poisoned with the radioactive chemical polonium-210 while staying in London in November 2006.

Having already closed all of its branches in Russia, other than those in Moscow, St Petersburg, and Ekaterinburg, the British Council was ordered to shut up shop everywhere except the capital in December 2007. Justifying its actions, the Russian Foreign Ministry alleged that the Council was 'operating illegally' and had 'violated tax regulations, among other laws'.

→ Further reading

Brown, C. and Ainley, K. (2005) *Understanding International Relations*, London: Palgrave Macmillan. **Useful introduction to the discipline of international relations and diplomacy.**

Evans. G. and Newnham, R. (1998) *The Penguin Dictionary of International Relations*, London: Penguin. **An indispensable A–Z of international relations jargon, covering terms ranging from 'ambassador', to 'weapons of mass destruction.'**

Jackson, R. and Sorensen, G. (2003) *An Introduction to International Relations: Theories and Approaches*, Oxford: Oxford University Press. **A succinct introduction to the main political theories surrounding the study of international relations.**

Young, J. and Kent, J. (2003) *International Relations Since 1945: A Global History*, Oxford: Oxford University Press. **A concise single-volume analysis of international relations on the global stage during, and in the aftermath of, the Cold War, including an overview of topics ranging from conflict in the Middle East to the evolution of the European Union.**

? Review questions

1. What are the main government departments with responsibility for overseeing Britain's participation in international affairs? Which of these is the most significant?

2. Outline the founding principles of the UN, and give details of the specific roles and responsibilities of its main institutions. How true would it be to say that the UN is in the pocket of the USA?

3. Outline the founding principles of NATO, and the roles and responsibilities of its main institutions. How has NATO adapted in the post-Cold War era?

4. What are the main supranational bodies responsible for overseeing the world economy and the promotion of free trade? Which of these are the most influential?

5. What are the modern-day roles of the Commonwealth and the British Council? To what extent can they be said to be anachronisms?

Online resource centre

www.oxfordtextbooks.co.uk/orc/Morrison
Visit the Online Resource Centre that accompanies this book for web links and regular updates.

11

The origins and structure of local government

The history of government in Britain can be rationalized into two phases: the gradual unification of the UK beneath first a single monarch and then a centralized Parliament, and the more recent trend towards handing back much of the sovereign power accrued by the centre to regional and local administrations.

When the process of nation-building first began in the UK, competing kings vied with each other to extend their realms to encompass first England, then Wales, Scotland, and, in due course, Ireland. Ironically, by the time that these countries were formally consolidated into a single UK, in the 1707 Acts of Union (see p. 11), the power of the monarchy was already waning and it was not long either before Parliament would begin ceding a significant amount of self-rule to 'the provinces'.

That said, the evolution of local government in Britain has been as much a bottom-up process as it has been top-down. Medieval monarchs had a vested interest in appointing locally based courts and creating titled landowners to maintain loyalty and public order among their subjects. Conversely, pressure for jurisdiction over issues as diverse as public health, road maintenance, and refuse collection to be handed to locally based individuals, guilds, and, in due course, elected councils came from the artisans and merchants whose trade and enterprise fostered the emergence of the first towns. Their motives were those of pure self-interest: without adequate sanitation, water supplies, and housing, they would have no peasants to till the land or textile workers to spin their yarn; devoid of well-kept highways, they would have no trade routes through which to export their wares to ports and markets; without local law courts to assert their ownership rights, guarding them against theft and robbery, they would have no protection for their property or wealth. Over time, these early moves towards local government were to become increasingly sophisticated and multifaceted. Today, there are 465 UK local authorities—388 in England, 22 in Wales, 29 in Scotland, and 26 in Northern Ireland. What follows is the story of how this highly developed local government network came about.

The first 'British' local authorities

Long before the emergence of anything that could be described as a 'council'—that is, the term by which we refer to local authorities today—it suited those in power at the top of British society to maintain a rudimentary form of 'local government'. Even the absolutist monarchs of the early Medieval period promoted this—if only to maintain a stable administration of land ownership, to collect taxes to fund wars and public building works (and food surpluses and tributes to sustain their luxury lifestyles), and to prevent anarchy at grass-roots level by upholding the ***rule of law*** (see pp. 7–8). To this end, the Saxon kings set up 'shire courts' across the countryside—local bodies with executive, legislative, and judicial powers rolled into one—and their Norman successors established a feudal system based on this, with vassals (peasants) kept in check by lords of the manor who, in time, became the squires of the seventeenth, eighteenth, and nineteenth centuries. By the twelfth century, demographic changes had led to the emergence of the first true towns, as the population began to cluster around the newly flourishing markets and ports. With urbanization taking root, the individuals and groups whose activities provided the bedrock of their local economies—artisans, merchants, and guilds—began to see the virtue of establishing a strengthened form of local autonomy, to protect their rights to land, property, and free-flowing trade routes. Their pleas were rewarded with the granting of the first 'letters patent' and 'Royal Charters'—special privileges, approved on the advice of the **Privy Council**, conferring the status of an 'incorporated body' (a self-governing entity) on first cities, then 'municipal boroughs' (smaller towns recognized as having legitimate claims to run their own affairs on a commercial and legal basis). These areas were run by nominally elected 'municipal corporations'.

Both cities and boroughs continue to exist to this day, albeit largely in name, as their powers have been brought in line with those of other forms of local council. In rural areas, however, the shire courts were more short-lived. Struggling to maintain the same degree of order over local subjects as their urban equivalents—notably in the aftermath of the Black Death, which killed up to 60 per cent of the British population in the 1340s—they were eventually replaced by a new, solidified local regime: the Justices of the Peace (JPs). Unlike the shire courts, JPs' authority arose out of Acts of Parliament rather than common law and, over time, they were assisted in their work by their local 'parishes'. These bodies—comprising representatives of the local community elected by their propertied peers—were a form of embryonic local government structure based initially around ecclesiastical parish boundaries, but they ultimately evolved into the civil parish council structure that remains in place, in diluted form, today. This is further discussed later in this chapter.

The emergence of the modern idea of local authorities

It was in the early nineteenth century, at the height of the Industrial Revolution, that a combination of commercial, political, and simple logistical pressures combined to foster the emergence of the first true local authorities.

By the close of the eighteenth century, there were some eight hundred boroughs, most governed by a local major (mayor) and council. Unlike today's elected **mayors** and councillors who (theoretically) can hail from any background, class, or occupation, these were elected exclusively from among the wealthiest local merchants, industrialists, and landowners. The electorate, such that it was, was limited to other equally moneyed individuals and a handful of marginally less affluent tradesmen. Such public services as were performed—street lighting and road maintenance, for example—tended to be done largely to make conditions better for commerce.

In the eighteenth century, no new charters were granted, so major emerging industrial towns and cities such as Manchester and Birmingham had to make do with more limited autonomy, in the form of 'improvement commissioners' approved by Parliament. In rural areas, meanwhile, the by-then-established

JP/parish combination continued to hold sway. JPs and parish councils met four times a year in so-called 'quarter sessions', which tended to take place in public houses. They collected 'rates'—a form of local taxation based on the 'rateable' (or rental) value of land and property, which continued in one form or another until the late twentieth century—from local households to pay for the following core officials:

- parish constables;
- surveyors of the highways;
- overseers of the poor.

The origins of today's local government system lie in the key Acts listed in Table 11.1.

By 1894, the following five types of local authority—which have continued in more or less the same form for the best part of eighty years—were established outside London:

- county councils;
- county *borough councils*;
- municipal borough councils;
- urban district councils;
- rural district councils.

▐ The rolling reorganization of local government

Since the 1970s, there have been four significant reorganizations of local government:

- the 1974 introduction of the *two-tier structure* in England and Wales;
- the 1986 abolition of metropolitan counties in major urban areas;
- the 1990s phased introduction of unitary authorities;
- the gradual introduction of *directly elected mayors* in major towns and cities.

The following section examines each of these developments in more detail.

Table 11.1 A chronology of the main Acts instrumental in the emergence
of local government

Act	Effect
Great Reform Act 1832	Extended the right to vote in parliamentary elections to all 'ten-pound households' (i.e. those with property worth £10 or more). Abolished the majority of the 'rotten boroughs' (see p. 125).
Municipal Corporations Act 1835	Abolished the pre-existing government structure in urban areas, reforming constitutions of existing municipal boroughs to standardize their election methods and modus operandi. Extended the right to vote in municipal elections to *all* local ratepayers—regardless of the value of their properties—in an effort to prevent the corporations that ran them from effectively acting as self-perpetuating oligarchies. Some 178 boroughs were reformed in this way, with a further 62 towns incorporated under the Act, after petitioning the Crown for borough status.
Public Health Acts 1848, 1872, and 1875	The first of these reforms was prompted by the sweeping cholera epidemics of the 1840s. Under it, central government began to allocate more money to local areas for building houses and improving sanitation—that is, domestic hygiene and sewage disposal—in an effort to combat the spread of disease. What emerged were two new forms of local authority, with responsibility for promoting sanitation in towns and country areas respectively: *urban sanitary districts* and *rural sanitary districts*. They were administered in towns by boroughs, new local boards of health and improvement commissioners. In rural areas, they were overseen by voluntary Poor Law unions (charities, often run with Church involvement).
Local Government Act 1888	Set up a more formal system of county councils to take over the roles previously undertaken by Justices of the Peace (JPs) in their quarter sessions. County (rural) areas with populations of more than 50,000 were given county borough status, which meant that they could continue to run their own affairs, retaining the privileges granted to the extant municipal boroughs. Other rural areas were dubbed county councils. Some towns with smaller populations, such as Worthing in West Sussex, were granted municipal borough status, giving them the same powers of self-government as larger towns.
Local Government Act 1894	This renamed the sanitary districts in towns and country areas that had not been granted borough status by the Crown urban and rural district councils (forerunners of today's district councils).

Because the evolution of local government in both London and Scotland has followed different trajectories to the rest of the UK, however, they will be looked at separately.

The 1974 reorganization

Perhaps the largest scale restructure of the local authority framework in England and Wales (excluding London), the so-called '1974 reorganization' has its origins in the conclusions of a Royal Commission on Local Government set up in 1965 by Richard Crossman, then Minister for Housing in Harold Wilson's Labour government.

When it reported in 1969, the Commission (chaired by Lord Redcliffe-Maude) recommended that the thousand existing local authorities should be replaced by a rationalized system of 61 'local authority areas', of which 58 would be 'all-purpose authorities'. These would effectively be unitary authorities, which would take responsibility for all areas of local service provision—from sanitary issues, through waste collection, to education and local transport—while conurbations (major urban centres where two or more towns and cities have merged to form a single built-up area) such as Manchester and Birmingham would have their own two-tier *metropolitan* authorities, in recognition of their larger populations and community needs.

Labour lost the subsequent 1970 general election and the Commission's recommendations were deemed too revolutionary by the incoming Conservative administration of Ted Heath. In the event, it was not until John Major's time as prime minister in the early 1990s that unitary authorities finally began to appear.

Despite his reluctance to adopt many of the Redcliffe-Maude proposals, Mr Heath's government recognized the need for reform. It instituted this in the guise of the Local Government Act 1972, which took effect in 1974 and introduced:

- a new two-tier structure of county councils and district councils, which remained more or less intact until the mid-1990s and still exists in many areas today. Many of the new districts applied for Royal Charters subsequently to enable them to be called 'borough councils' or *city councils* (like the boroughs and cities of old). This move led to the amalgamation of some district and county councils, and reduced the overall number of local authorities to 39 counties and 296 districts in England, with an 8:37 split in Wales;

- an alternative two-tier 'metropolitan county' local authority structure in six pilot areas, covering the following conurbations: the West Midlands; Merseyside; Greater Manchester; West Yorkshire; South

Table 11.2 The composition of metropolitan county/borough areas

Metropolitan county	Metropolitan boroughs
Greater Manchester	City of Manchester; City of Salford; Bolton; Bury; Oldham; Rochdale; Stockport; Tameside; Trafford; Wigan
Merseyside	City of Liverpool; Knowsley; Sefton; St Helens; Wirral
South Yorkshire	City of Sheffield; Barnsley; Doncaster; Rotherham
Tyne and Wear	City of Newcastle upon Tyne; City of Sunderland; Gateshead; South Tyneside; North Tyneside
West Midlands	City of Birmingham; City of Coventry; City of Wolverhampton; Dudley; Sandwell; Solihull; Walsall
West Yorkshire	City of Leeds; City of Bradford; City of Wakefield; Calderdale; Kirklees

Yorkshire; Tyne and Wear. A breakdown of the towns and cities encompassed by each of these conurbations is contained in Table 11.2. This saw each conurbation split for administrative purposes into a number of 'metropolitan borough councils', which would take charge of financing and running most day-to-day local services—for example, rubbish collection, housing, and environmental health. The conurbations would each be overseen by a single 'metropolitan county council', in charge of services affecting the area as a whole, such as strategic town and country planning, main roads linking neighbouring towns, public transport, emergency services, and civil protection.

The new two-tier structure saw the end of some long-standing counties such as Cumberland, Westmorland, and the three different parts of Lincolnshire, and the introduction of new counties such as Avon, Cleveland, Cumbria, Humberside, Clwyd, Dyfed, and Gwent. Some of these were never wholly accepted by local people and have subsequently vanished. (Avon was merged with neighbouring Somerset as part of the post-1992 unitary authority settlement.) The reorganization also saw certain cities stripped of their pre-existent 'municipal borough' status. These included Nottingham, Bristol, Leicester, and Norwich—although, by way of compensation, they were allowed to retain their city status, not to mention their 'lord mayors' (senior officials who perform ceremonial duties and in other towns are called simply 'mayors').

Under the new rationalized two-tier structure, district councils, borough councils (districts with a historic Royal Charter status), and the new metropolitan borough councils were equivalent to each other, and, as such, were each given the same responsibilities—largely providing the most localized, 'door-to-door' services, such as rubbish collection. Likewise, county councils and metropolitan county councils became responsible for providing the remaining—'county-wide'—services, with social care and education being the biggest spending areas. A full breakdown of the responsibilities of the current types of local authority is outlined in Table 11.3. A breakdown of the central government departments at Whitehall responsible for overseeing each local authority service area is given in Table 11.4.

In Northern Ireland, the reorganization of local government took a different form and happened at a different pace. In 1973, 26 district councils emerged, but many functions were transferred from local to central government at Westminster. A wide-ranging Review of Public Administration (RPA) in the province recently recommended that its number of councils be cut to 11 in 2011.

The 1986 reorganization

The Tory Party's 1983 election manifesto described the six metropolitan county councils that it inherited on regaining power in 1979—together with the then Greater London Council (GLC), under the leadership of Ken Livingstone—as a 'wasteful and unnecessary tier of government'. It promised to abolish them and to return their functions to the second-tier metropolitan

Table 11.3 A breakdown of council services offered by different types of local authority

District councils, borough councils, metropolitan borough councils, and unitary authorities	County councils and unitary authorities
Environmental health (sanitation, drainage, pollution, food hygiene)	Education (schools and **further education**)
Development control (**planning permission**)	Social services (care for the elderly, mentally ill, and vulnerable children)
Housing and the homeless	Highways (road-building and maintenance, and on-street parking)
Refuse collection (now incorporating recycled waste)	Refuse disposal (landfill sites)
Car parks	Emergency planning
Council Tax and **uniform business rate (UBR)** collection	Cultural and leisure services (libraries, museums, sports centres)
Local strategic planning	County-wide strategic planning
Licensing	Passenger transport (buses, trams)

Table 11.4 Links between local authority service areas and Whitehall departments

Service area	Department responsible
Antisocial behaviour	Home Office; Department for Communities and Local Government (DCLG)
Car parks	Department for Transport (DfT)
Children's services (schools, child protection)	Department for Children, Schools and Families (DCSF); Department of Health (DH); DCLG
Council Tax and uniform business rates (UBR) collection	DCLG; HM Treasury
Cultural and leisure services	Department of Culture, Media and Sport (DCMS)
Education (further education)	Department for Innovation, Universities and Skills (DIUS)
Emergency planning	Department for the Environment, Food and Rural Affairs (DEFRA)
Environmental health (sanitation, drainage, pollution, food hygiene, waste management)	DEFRA; Home Office; Ministry of Defence (MoD)
Highways (road-building and maintenance)	DfT
Housing and the homeless	DCLG
Licensing	DCMS
Passenger transport (buses, trams)	DfT
Police	Home Office
Social services (care for the elderly, mentally ill, and vulnerable children)	DH
Town and country planning	DEFRA

borough councils (or, as they were redesignated in law, 'metropolitan district councils') that still existed 'beneath' them.

To this end, it passed the Local Government Act 1985, which had a rocky ride through Parliament before finally receiving *Royal Assent* on 31 March 1986. In the metropolitan areas outside London, one of its main effects was to set up new *police authorities*. Tyne and Wear was unusual, in that its police provision came under the auspices of the Northumbria Police Authority. The metropolitan areas also gained their own fire and civil defence authorities, and passenger transport authorities, and some also acquired joint boards responsible for handling their waste disposal services. This happened in Merseyside and Greater Manchester (except Wigan), although in the West Midlands, for example, joint arrangements set up between neighbouring boroughs were established on an ad hoc and purely voluntary basis. In other areas, in contrast, the commissioning and/or running of public transport services and waste disposal services continued to fall under the auspices of county councils.

Other than the introduction of these new, service-specific types of local authority, in all other respects the effect of the 1986 changes was to replace the pre-existing metropolitan two-tier structure with what were effectively the first unitary authorities—that is, all-purpose councils responsible for fulfilling the roles split in other areas between districts/boroughs and counties. Opponents of the move saw in it a clear attempt by the Conservatives to diminish the authority of metropolitan councils, by reducing them to lower-level, more localized administrations, on the one hand, and hiving off some of the responsibilities formerly overseen by the scrapped metropolitan counties to new bodies with clearly defined and limited scope, on the other. Mr Livingstone and other left-wing council leaders, such as Sheffield City Council and South Yorkshire County Council's David Blunkett (a future Labour Home Secretary), saw the dilution of their powers as an assault on their socialist policies by a right-wing government fearful of major populated areas becoming 'states within states'. Referring to this notion explicitly at one point in the late 1980s, Sir Cyril Irvine Patnick, Tory MP for Sheffield Hallam, famously described Mr Blunkett's fiefdom as 'the People's Republic of South Yorkshire'.

The 1990s introduction of unitary authorities

The most significant restructuring of local authorities since the 1974 reorganization was instituted in 1992, with the start of a process of phased change designed to rationalize local government across the bulk of England and Wales. The aim of introducing a *unitary structure* was to improve the efficiency and transparency of local administration by reducing the scope for duplication of services, slashing bureaucracy, and establishing a simplified, uniform council structure across the country. Unitary authorities are defined in law as being '*any authority which is the sole principal council for its local government area*'.

Despite the bold claims made in favour of the new unitary system, critics argue that it has only added to the confusion, by ushering in a patchwork landscape of local government, with unitary authorities in many areas sitting directly alongside councils that have retained the existing two-tier structure. Counties in which both unitary and two-tier authorities coexist are described as having a *hybrid structure*. Examples include Lincolnshire, where Lincoln City Council (a unitary authority) sits beside Lincolnshire County Council and borough/district councils in nearby towns such as Grantham and Gainsborough. In East Sussex, Brighton and Hove Council is a unitary authority, while down the road, Lewes District Council and Eastbourne Borough Council retain the classic borough/district responsibilities, with East Sussex County Council providing other services. The chronology of the phased introduction of unitary authorities followed is outlined in Table 11.5.

Table 11.5 A chronology of the phased introduction of unitary authorities

Year	Phase
1992	Local Government Act replaced the English Boundary Commission with a new Local Government Commission for England, under the chairmanship of Sir John Banham and answerable to the government. In Wales, the process was overseen instead by the Welsh Secretary and this led to some discord, as the existing system there was swiftly replaced by a framework of 37 new district councils and 22 unitary authorities.
1994 (December)	The first of a series of periodic reviews of local authorities coinciding with an initial tranche of conversions to unitary status. A 'Big Bang' approach à la 1974 was avoided in favour of a gradual reorganization. Subsequent reviews were due every 16 months. The phased approach took some surprising turns—when detailed guidelines were formulated, it emerged that the government was not going to stipulate that each unitary authority area should cover a minimum or maximum population size. This was a major departure from previous reviews, although, in practice, only one authority emerged to govern an area of fewer than 100,000 inhabitants: Rutland, which had a population of only 33,700. Tensions soon emerged between rural areas and urban areas, with the former accusing ministers of elevating the latter in importance by granting them unitary status. Fierce rival publicity campaigns were launched by the Association of District Councils (ADC) and the Association of County Councils (ACC).
1995 (1 April)	Following the detailed area-by-area reviews, four maiden unitary authorities emerged: the Isle of Wight, and unitary councils for each of Avon, Cleveland, and Humberside (the so-called 'unpopular' or 'unofficial' counties created in 1974).
	In the following counties, the Commission initially recommended no change: Cornwall; Cumbria; Hertfordshire; Lincolnshire; Northumberland; Oxfordshire; Suffolk; Surrey; Warwickshire; West Sussex.
1995 (July)	A new Commission chairman, Sir David Cooksey, replaces Sir John Banham, following his resignation. This leads to no fewer than 21 district councils being reviewed with a view potentially to becoming unitary authorities. Sir David's inquiry focuses on preserving the 'stability, viability, and identity' of these areas.
1995 (September)	The new-look Commission produces its first set of recommendations: the creation of ten new unitary authorities, eight being existing districts and two, in the 'Thames Gateway', created from the merger of two districts each.
2009 (1 April)	Cornwall and Northumberland became unitary authorities after all, alongside fellow newcomers Wiltshire, Shropshire, and County Durham.

In addition to the emergence of hybrid counties, the unitary authority system has produced other quirks. A growing number of unitary authorities encompass entire counties—notably, the Isle of Wight, Rutland, County Durham, and Cornwall. The Isles of Scilly, meanwhile, have their own unique form of council that, although not officially designated as such, is a *sui generis* ('in a class of their own') form of unitary authority.

▶ City councils and the meaning of city status

Between the reign of Henry VIII and the end of the nineteenth century, cities were generally synonymous with ecclesiastical seats of power and, more specifically, the presence of Church of England cathedrals and diocesan bishops. But even in the Tudor period, this was not always the case: in practice, city status could be conferred by the sovereign through letters patent (a legal instrument issued by a monarch), the granting of a town's Royal Charter, or even, over time, through accepted custom and practice.

In the nineteenth century, the Church of England sought actively to increase the number of its urban dioceses, creating more cities in the process. These included Ripon, Liverpool, St Albans, and Britain's south-western most city: Truro. But not all towns designated cities had prior royal borough status: Ely, for example, was a humble urban district when recognized as a city. In addition, by the close of the nineteenth century, cities had begun to spring up in places that did not have their own cathedrals—for example, Birmingham, which successfully petitioned Queen Victoria in 1889 on the basis of its large population and history of effective local government under its charismatic mayor, Joseph Chamberlain. It was around this time that Scotland gained its first cities by letters patent and Royal Charter—prior to 1889, major medieval towns such as Edinburgh and Perth were often referred to by the term 'civitas' and, although the word 'city' had been coined for them by the eighteenth century, their status remained unofficial.

Today, city status is no longer dependent on the presence of a cathedral, or any significant ecclesiastical presence. Neither are cities always major population centres: with a mere two thousand inhabitants, Britain's smallest city, St David's in Pembrokeshire, has a population that is significantly smaller than most towns.

For most of the twentieth century, it was the Home Secretary's job to advise the monarch on which towns should be made into cities. This happened to Lancaster in 1937, Swansea in 1969 (to mark the investiture of the Prince of Wales), and Sunderland in 1992 (to mark the fortieth anniversary of the Queen's accession to the throne). More recently, however, the rules have been bent somewhat. In December 2000, three new cities were created, in the form of Brighton and Hove, Wolverhampton, and Inverness, as part of a 'Millennium City' competition launched by the Labour government. The Queen created a further five in 2002 to mark her Golden Jubilee—Stirling, Preston, Newport, Lisburn and Newry—bringing the overall number of cities in the UK today to 66.

Just as the criteria used to determine whether a town qualifies for city status are nebulous, so too is the degree to which becoming a city has any tangible effect. A city council—the moniker adopted by local authorities with an official city designation—is not a type of council or administration in itself: rather, the term is really no more than an honorary title. In terms of their functions, city councils are actually other, standard types of local authority in all but name. Some operate as unitary authorities (Brighton and Hove, York, and Stoke-on-Trent are examples). The majority, however, are actually district or borough councils in a two-tier structure.

Confusingly, seven English cities—Chichester, Ely, Hereford, Lichfield, Ripon, Truro, and Wells—are actually no more than civil parishes—meaning that they technically fall within the remit of parish councils, the lowest tier of local government (see the next section). Even more confusingly, while the term 'city council' is used to denote the parish council in some of these places (Chichester and Hereford), in others (Truro and Ely) this is the title used by the principal service-providing local authority. In addition to these unconventional examples, in two English cities (Bath and Salisbury), city status is the preserve of so-called 'charter trustees'—an arcane form of local administration intended to be a temporary stopgap for towns the borough status of which has been removed by the Crown, prior to the formation of a parish council. Meanwhile, in two Welsh cities (Bangor and St David's), city status is possessed by local community councils (the equivalent of parish councils in Wales and Scotland).

A full rundown of designated cities, together with details of the type of local authority to which the designation applies in each place, is listed in Table 11.6.

Table 11.6 A list of cities with the types of local authority to which city status applies

City	Year granted	Cathedral (Y/N)	Type of local authority
England			
Bath	1590	Y	Charter trustees (unitary)
Birmingham	1889	N	Metropolitan borough
Bradford	1897	N	Metropolitan borough
Brighton and Hove	2000	N	Unitary authority
Bristol	1542	Y	Unitary
Cambridge	1951	N	District
Canterbury	No record	Y	District
Carlisle	No record	Y	District
Chester	1541	Y	District
Chichester	No record	Y	Civil parish (district)
Coventry	1345	Y	Metropolitan borough
Derby	1977	N	Unitary
Durham	No record	Y	District
Ely	No record	Y	Civil parish (district)
Exeter	No record	Y	District
Gloucester	1541	Y	District
Hereford	1189	Y	Civil parish (part of wider unitary authority)
Kingston upon Hull	1897	N	Unitary
Lancaster	1937	N	District
Leeds	1893	N	Metropolitan borough
Leicester	1919	N	Unitary
Lichfield	No record	Y	Civil parish
Lincoln	No record	Y	District
Liverpool	1880	Y	Metropolitan borough
City of London	No record	Y	City of London Corporation
Manchester	1853	Y	Metropolitan borough

(continued)

City	Year granted	Cathedral (Y/N)	Type of local authority
Newcastle upon Tyne	1882	Y	Metropolitan borough
Norwich	1195	Y	District
Nottingham	1897	N	Unitary
Oxford	1542	Y	District
Peterborough	1541	Y	Unitary
Plymouth	1928	N	Unitary
Portsmouth	1925	N	Unitary
Preston	2002	N	District
Ripon	1836	Y	Civil parish
Salford	1926	N	Metropolitan borough
Salisbury	No record	Y	Charter trustees (district)
Sheffield	1893	N	Metropolitan borough
Southampton	1954	N	Unitary
St Albans	1877	Y	District
Stoke-on-Trent	1925	N	Unitary
Sunderland	1992	N	Metropolitan borough
Truro	1877	Y	Civil parish (district)
Wakefield	1888	Y	Metropolitan borough
Wells	1205	Y	Civil parish (district)
Westminster	1540	Y	London borough
Winchester	No record	Y	District
Wolverhampton	2000	N	Metropolitan borough
Worcester	1189	Y	District
York	No record	Y	Unitary
Scotland			
Aberdeen	1891	N	Unitary
Dundee	1889	N	Unitary
Edinburgh	1329 (as royal burgh)	Y	Unitary
Glasgow	1492 (as royal burgh)	Y	Unitary
Inverness	2000	N	None
Stirling	2002	N	Former royal burgh within unitary council area

City	Year granted	Cathedral (Y/N)	Type of local authority
Wales			
Bangor	No record	Y	Community (district)
Cardiff	1905	N	Unitary
Newport	2002	N	Unitary
St David's	1995	N	Community (within a county council)
Swansea	1969	N	Swansea
Northern Ireland			
Armagh	1994	N	Unitary
Belfast	1888	N	Unitary
Derry	1604	N	Unitary
Lisburn	2002	N	Unitary
Newry	2002	N	None

▌ Parish councils, town councils, and community councils

The lowest tier of local government is represented by elected parish councils in England, and community councils in Wales and (as of 1973) Scotland. Civil parish councils—not to be confused with pre-existing ecclesiastical parishes established by the Church—were set up under the Local Government Act 1894 to oversee social welfare and basic civic duties in villages and small towns, and to act as the collective 'voices' of their local communities. Historically, some parish and community councils in larger villagers and small towns have chosen to define themselves as town councils. Those that do so tend to have their own town mayors—not to be confused with the more official (if also largely ceremonial) mayors of borough and city councils, or the directly elected mayors now found in some cities (see p. 427). Councillors take it in turns to spend a year as mayor, on rotation, with a formal 'mayor-making ceremony' often held in the town hall to mark the handover from one to another. The role of mayor is largely ceremonial (opening church fetes, switching on Christmas lights), although he or she also tends to chair full council meetings during his or her year in office.

Under the 1972 Act, all parishes with more than 150 inhabitants were compelled to have their own parish council—a stipulation that has significantly increased their number. Those with smaller populations are only required to hold *parish meetings*—regular gatherings that all local registered electors are permitted to attend. Unlike the meetings that might be held in towns and villages with formal parish councils, those convened in lesser populated parishes have statutory powers to act as de facto parish councils. In such circumstances, a clerk and chairman are elected to preside over business.

Today, many of the limited day-to-day powers once exercised by parish, community, and town councils are carried out by higher-level local authorities: county and district/borough councils, or unitary authorities. But parish councils are still allocated budgets by those authorities—dubbed 'parish precepts'—which, unlike revenue raised by higher level councils, cannot be capped by central government (see p. 396). Therefore, in areas where parish councils are more proactive, parish precepts can be high: Thurston Parish Council in Suffolk, for example, put its share of the *Council Tax* up by 214 per cent in 2008–09. In most areas, however, the precept is usually only sufficient to finance its rent of the town council buildings in which it holds its monthly meetings, and minor local improvements such as replacement street lights, park benches, or new goalposts for the village football pitch.

Parish councils do, however, play a significant advisory role. For example, they have a statutory right to be consulted formally by, and represent on, public inquiries into major planning applications affecting their localities. In fact, often the first that a reporter—and, by extension, his or her newspaper or other medium—will hear of a potentially controversial planning proposal or other council-related issue will be through attending a meeting at which it is thrashed out by his or her local parish council. And far from being mere talking shops, in truth, the importance of the parish council has been increasing again in recent years, as the Labour government has experimented with new models of service delivery, involving partnerships between neighbouring authorities and delegation of certain responsibilities to voluntary and lower level statutory bodies, including parish councils.

The two most influential partnership initiatives are as follows:

- local area management (LAM);
- *quality parish councils*.

Local area management (LAM)

LAM refers to the promotion of 'joined-up' service delivery and the sharing of 'best practice' between neighbouring local authorities, including parish, community, and town councils. Some parish, town, and community councils have joined forces with their local district/borough, county, or unitary authorities in recent years to form 'local strategic partnerships' (LSPs). These are semi-formal alliances designed to streamline services within individual local authority boundaries by drawing together public, private, and voluntary sector organizations in those areas to pool their resources, reduce their collective costs, and improve their efficiency. LSPs are set up under the terms of local area agreements (LAAs), approved by the Department for Communities and Local Government (DCLG).

Quality parish councils

Introduced by Labour in 2003, in a Rural **White Paper** published by then Minister for Rural Affairs and Urban Quality of Life Alun Michael, quality parish councils are parish, community, and town councils that have been granted 'quality' status in recognition of their efficiency in overseeing the limited local services that they have up to now provided. Their 'reward' is to be given additional responsibilities (matched by a variable rise in budget) commensurate with the following DCLG guidelines:

- to be representative of, and actively engage with, all parts of its community, providing vision, identity and a sense of belonging;
- to be effectively and properly managed;
- to articulate the needs and wishes of its community;
- to uphold high standards of conduct;
- to be committed to work in partnership with principal local authorities and other public service agencies;
- in proportion to its size and skills, to deliver services on behalf of principal local authorities when this represents the best deal for the local community;
- to work closely with voluntary groups in its community;
- to provide leadership to the community through its work on parish plans;
- working with its partners, to act as an information point for local services.

In practice, quality parish councils have, as a bare minimum, tended to play a greater role than previously in organizing community-based activities, such as youth activities, childcare, home support, and transport for the elderly and disabled. The more proactive ones have gone further, however, by taking on responsibility for delivering on the ground many of the services funded by their principal local authority, or authorities, such as libraries or buses. They are also expected to draw up and publish a parish plan, outlining medium and long-term proposals for their areas.

▶ The evolution of local government in London

The autonomy of London has always been exercised in a distinct way from the rest of the UK, although, at times, its local government structure has resembled that of the major English conurbations described earlier this chapter. Today, London operates under a unique two-tier system, with responsibilities for service provision split between the *Greater London Authority (GLA)*, headed by the capital's elected mayor, and 33 second-tier councils (a system akin to the pre-1986 metropolitan county/borough structure abolished by Mrs Thatcher's government).

Of these 33 councils, 32 are London boroughs, elected in similar fashion to the metropolitan boroughs that continue to operate in the other conurbations, but the last is a unique entity run by an unreformed medieval-style city corporation. The City of London Corporation—officially, the 'Mayor and Commonalty and Citizens of the City of London'—is Britain's oldest surviving local authority. It covers the so-called 'Square Mile' containing the capital's central commercial district and, although democratically accountable like other local authorities, it has long attracted criticism for the anachronistic nature of its electoral processes and its peculiar customs.

The City of London was the only corporation to escape the axe when the Municipal Corporations Act 1835 abolished all others and it continues to be presided over by a non-partisan administration of a kind that prevailed more widely before the emergence of formal political parties (see Chapter 5). At its head is the Lord Mayor of London, his attendant aldermen, and a Court of Common Council, beneath which are a range of committees responsible for specific areas of local policy. Again uniquely, the City of London Corporation was allowed to retain a system of *non-residential voting* (often referred to as the 'business vote') following its abolition elsewhere in 1969. This concession was, in part, in recognition of its tiny resident population (some nine thousand at the time of the 2001 census). (A fuller explanation of the voting system used here and elsewhere in London is given in Chapter 14.)

Among the most vocal critics of the corporation—which many see as a self-perpetuating, privileged old boy network—is Labour **backbencher** John McDonnell (an unsuccessful rival candidate for the party's leadership following Tony Blair's resignation). In the debate over the City of London (Ward Elections) Act 2002, which significantly increased the size of the business franchise in the capital, he said of it:

" The corporation is a group of hangers-on, who create what is known as the best dining club in the City . . . a rotten borough. "

A timeline of the evolution of local government in London is presented in Table 11.7.

The modern-day local government structure in London

As with **devolution** for Scotland, Wales, and Northern Ireland, Labour had advocated the re-establishment of a single overarching local authority for London long before it won the 1997 election. The abolition of the Greater London Council (GLC), under its then leader Ken Livingstone, in 1986 had been seen by some in the party as an act of war by the Conservative government. Others had viewed it as an error of judgement that needed redressing for more pragmatic reasons should their party regain power.

In its 1997 manifesto, Labour pledged to introduce a new form of 'elected city government', topped by an EU-style elected mayor. A year after the party regained power, the promised vote was held, and 72 per cent of London's electorate voted in favour of the proposed GLA. A year later, the Greater London Authority Act 1999 formally paved the way for the establishment of the new authority and, with more than a hint of déjà vu, Mr Livingstone was duly elected London mayor in March 2000.

Mr Livingstone's return to power in the capital was hardly smooth. As had happened (with varying degrees of success) in Wales and Scotland, the Labour leadership attempted to parachute in a cherry-picked candidate, in defiance of his support among the party rank and file. But its official choice, former Health Secretary Frank Dobson, was to be no match for the former GLC leader, who resigned his parliamentary seat and the Labour **whip** to fight for the mayoralty as an independent. In the event, he returned to the party fold prior to his 2004 re-election, by which time Mr Blair had reluctantly endorsed him as the prospective Labour candidate.

Table 11.7 A timeline of the evolution of local government in London

From	Legislation	System
1835	Municipal Corporations Act 1835	The small, ancient, and self-governing City of London is unreformed by legislation covering the other major city corporations and does not expand into the growing metropolitan area surrounding it. The area that is currently Greater London is administered by parishes and hundreds in the counties of Middlesex, Essex, Kent, Surrey, and Hertfordshire, with very little coordination between them. Special areas, such as the Liberty of Westminster, are exempt from county administration. In other areas, ad hoc single-purpose boards are set up.
1855	Metropolis Management Act 1855	The Metropolitan Board of Works is created to provide the infrastructure needed in the area now known as Inner London. Its members are nominated by the vestries and boards.
1889	Local Government Act 1888	The County of London is created from the area of responsibility of the Metropolitan Board of Works. A London County Council shares power with the boards and vestries. The City of London is outside of its scope. Croydon and West Ham (and, later, East Ham) become county boroughs outside the County of London, but also outside the control of the newly formed Surrey and Essex county councils.
1894	Local Government Act 1894	The rest of England, including the area around the County of London and the county boroughs (but not within it), is divided into urban districts and rural districts. In the Greater London area, they become consolidated over the next seventy years into municipal boroughs and urban districts with no rural districts remaining. Many districts later become populous enough to apply for county boroughs status, but are rejected. A Royal Commission on the Amalgamation of the City and County of London attempts to facilitate the merger of the City and County of London, but fails.
1900	London Government Act 1899	Metropolitan boroughs are created within the County of London and functions are shared with the London County Council. The vestries, boards, and liberties in the area are abolished.
1965	London Government Act 1963	An enlarged Greater London replaces the County of London, the county boroughs, and all local government districts within around a 12-mile radius. The mostly strategic Greater London Council shares power with the 32 London boroughs and the City of London.
1986	Local Government Act 1985	The Greater London Council is abolished and the London boroughs work as unitary authorities with strategic functions organized by joint boards and *quangos*. A residual Inner London Education Authority remains for the inner area, but is abolished during a national reform of education.
2000	Greater London Authority Act 1999	The regional Greater London Authority, consisting of the Mayor of London and the London Assembly, assumes a strategic function, sharing power with the London boroughs and the City of London.

Although the GLA was to become a model for certain other towns and cities that went on to adopt an elected mayor model (see Chapter 13), at the time its method of conducting business was unique among British local authorities. In a manner akin to the way in which the US President shares power with that country's parliament (Congress), the London mayor is elected separately to the 25-strong London Assembly with which he shares power over the GLA. As with the president, it is the mayor's job to propose policy and to set out a prospective annual budget to cover the cost of the services that he or she proposes to provide in the coming financial year. The Assembly must then approve or amend these proposals, in the manner of Congress, and its committees and subcommittees (like their congressional equivalents) may scrutinize the mayor's actions in office and the performance of the local services provided by the GLA. The parallels between the London mayoral and US parliamentary systems have gone further in recent years, in light of changes to the political composition of both. Just as President George Bush (a Republican) was forced to share power in his last two years in the White House with a Democrat-dominated Congress, Mr Livingstone found himself having to work with an Assembly, the biggest party presence in which was Conservative following the 2004 elections (nine members to Labour's seven). With the election of Conservative Boris Johnson as his successor, alongside a largely unchanged allocation of seats on the Assembly, the capital reverted to a period of Tory hegemony in May 2008.

The GLA is the top tier of local government in London, with individual boroughs continuing to provide day-to-day services for Londoners. The division between GLA and borough roles is explained in Table 11.8; of the major roles fulfilled by the GLA, the majority are overseen by the agencies listed in Table 11.9.

Table 11.8 A breakdown of local authority responsibilities in London

Greater London Authority (GLA)	London boroughs
Transport	Schools and further education (FE)
Policing	Social services
Fire and rescue	Waste collection
Congestion charging	Highways repair and maintenance
Environmental policy	Libraries, and local leisure and cultural services (museums, theatres)
Strategic development and planning	Development control

Table 11.9 The main agencies of the Greater London Authority (GLA)

Agency	Responsibilities
Transport for London (TfL)	Manages most aspects of London's transport system, including public transport (London Underground, the Docklands Light Railway, London Buses), main roads, and traffic management (including the congestion charge zone)
Metropolitan Police Authority (MPA)	Responsible for overseeing Metropolitan Police Service, which polices Greater London
London Fire and Emergency Planning Authority (LFEPA)	Administers the London Fire Brigade and coordinates emergency planning
London Development Agency (LDA)	Responsible for strategic development planning across London, focusing on the rejuvenation of deprived areas

▌ Local government in Scotland

As with several other aspects of public affairs—notably, its legal and education systems, the latter of which is explored in Chapter 15—Scotland does things differently to the UK when it comes to its basic local government framework.

Until the 1974 reorganization, Scotland effectively had a single-tier form of local administration. The Local Government (Scotland) Act 1929 had replaced the pre-existing parish councils with a nationwide network of district councils with significantly increased autonomy and budgets. This structure—refined by the Local Government (Scotland) Act 1947—created a distinction between smaller and larger 'burghs', which were a form of local unit derived from medieval administrative boundaries. The latter—that is, burghs with populations greater than 20,000—were given more power.

All of this changed with the passage of the Local Government (Scotland) Act 1973, which ushered in a two-tier system along the lines of that implemented in England and Wales. The district councils remained—albeit with slightly refined borders and some variation in their levels of responsibility—but the first tier authorities introduced were named 'regional councils', as opposed to county councils. Three notable exceptions—the Western Isles, Shetland, and Orkney—were, however, effectively given unitary status even at this early stage, on account of their perceived homogeneity.

When John Major's government began its phased reorganization of local authorities in the early 1990s, Scotland was again treated as an exception. In a 'Big Bang' approach that ministers avoided elsewhere, unitary authorities were introduced across the country in one fell swoop. While rationalizing a patchwork system, this 'one size fits all' approach was to cause controversy in some areas—not least because of the wildly varying population sizes covered by individual councils. The unitary authority for Inverclyde (an area with relatively few inhabitants) followed the same boundaries as the extant district council, while that of Clackmannanshire embraced the whole of that county, and that of Highland, a sprawling 30,650 km swathe of north-west Scotland, encompassing chunks of the former counties of Inverness-shire, Ross and Cromarty, Caithness and Nairnshire, as well as the whole of Sutherland.

Today, there are 32 such unitary authorities in place across the country.

▶ Emergency services at local level

While ambulance services are today part of the National Health Service (NHS) (see p. 182), with trust status akin to that accorded to hospitals, the other core emergency services are overseen by discrete forms of authority, as explained in the following section.

The origins of the British police force

Until the early nineteenth century, there was no such thing as a countrywide police force. Instead, local law and order fell to town magistrates to maintain, and before then, ad hoc arrangements had existed. Perhaps unsurprisingly, London was the first UK city to adopt its own police force. In 1749, the author Henry Fielding and his brother, Sir John, set up a group of semi-professional law enforcers known as 'The Bow Street Runners'. Operating out of Henry's house at 4 Bow Street, these early police officers wore civilian clothes and did not patrol like their modern-day equivalents. Instead, they acted to intercept criminals and bring them before the courts on the authority of local magistrates, who had become increasingly frustrated at their inability to prevent offenders absconding and enforce punishment without the help of an arresting force.

Shortly afterwards, an embryonic Thames Police was formed, partly based on the model established by the Fielding brothers. It was not until some eighty years later, however, when Sir Robert Peel was Home Secretary, that the first true police constabulary was set up, in the guise of the Metropolitan Police, based at Scotland Yard. Established in 1829 and variously dubbed the 'Bobbies' and the 'Peelers' after their founder, the 'Met' were funded by a local tax—known as 'the police rate'—which citizens were obliged to pay in addition to the 'poor rate' (used to fund limited handouts for the poorest members of society and to finance workhouses).

In due course, similar innovations followed in the emerging borough council areas and the introduction of a new breed of county magistrates.

Today, the UK Police Service, although notionally a nationwide organization, is actually divided into 43 local forces in England and Wales, and a further eight in Scotland. Northern Ireland has its own dedicated police force, dubbed the Police Service of Northern Ireland, which replaced the erstwhile Royal Ulster Constabulary (RUC) in November 2001. Most of the individual police forces in England, Scotland, and Wales have historically respected county boundaries, although there have long been some exceptions: for example, a single force, Sussex Police, covers both East Sussex and West Sussex, while the south-westernmost force is Devon and Cornwall Police. In 2006, then Home Secretary Charles Clarke proposed merging a number of forces (among them the five existing East Midlands forces, which would be turned into a single 'super-force'), bringing down the total number in England and Wales to just 24, in an effort to streamline the Service and better equip the country to fight terrorism. His plans—heavily criticized by both the Police Federation (the union representing police officers) and the Association of Chief Police Officers (ACPO)—were shelved by his successor, John Reid, later that year.

The role and powers of local police authorities

Other than in London, where the Metropolitan Police Authority was recently handed executive control over the Met by the government, UK police forces all come under the overarching control of the Home Secretary (or, in Scotland, the Deputy First Minister). Until 1995, the local force was regulated by a police committee that was answerable to the county council or unitary authority, but the advent of the Police and Magistrates' Court Act 1994 saw their abolition and replacement with a new second tier: the police authority. The change, consolidated by the Police Act 1996, has reduced the involvement of councillors from relevant local authorities, in favour of a mixed membership that is intended to represent local residents and the business community better.

Police committees were made up entirely of officials—usually, two-thirds councillors and one-third magistrates; the typical composition of a modern police authority is outlined in Table 11.10.

Police authorities raise their revenue by levying precepts—that is, annual budget requests—on their local **billing authorities**, which are then included—and normally made explicit—in local Council Tax bills (see p. 388).

Their responsibilities are to:

- maintain an effective and efficient force for their areas—and if they fail, the Home Secretary and/or Home Office Inspectorate have powers to 'act in default';
- publish an annual policing/Best Value performance plan, in consultation with the **chief constable** (appointed by the Home Secretary);
- publish their own local policing objectives, which must be consistent with the spirit of national objectives and ministerial priorities laid down by the Home Secretary;
- appoint assistant chief constables, one of whom will be designated by the chief constable to act as his or her deputy;
- hold open public meetings along the lines of those held by local authorities, at which their members are expected to answer questions on their activities;
- oversee the management of their land and buildings by the chief constable.

Northern Ireland's Police Service is overseen by an independent Police Board.

Table 11.10 The typical composition of a local policy authority

Members	How chosen
Nine councillors	Appointed from relevant councils covered by police authority area, including county and metropolitan borough councils, and unitary authorities. Where there is more than one relevant local authority, appointments are made by a special joint selection committee on which each one is represented.
Three magistrates	Chosen by a selection panel answerable to the local magistrates' courts committee.
Five independent members	Co-opted from among local electors and the business community by the councillor and magistrate members, following a complex selection process. Shortlists must be approved by the Home Secretary.

The role of chief constables

Chief constables have always had statutory responsibilities separate from those of their governing committee or authority. It is their role to deliver the policies agreed by their police authority on the ground. This entails appointing all officers in their force below the rank of assistant chief constable, producing an annual report on their performance in the preceding 12 months (covering specific categories of offence, along with other areas highlighted as being of local concern, such as violent crime), and disciplining officers for misconduct.

In operational terms, it is the job of the chief constable and his or her assistants to manage the force's budget, hire and fire other officers, and ensure that personnel are suitably distributed to maintain adequate patrols across the force area. But over the past twenty years, as both population levels and the range of responsibilities faced by the police have increased out of all proportion with the increases in the number of officers, successive governments have tried to remove some of the burden of more mundane police patrol duties from the professionals by bolstering them with semi-trained back-up officers recruited from the local community. Until recently, these were known as special constables—or 'specials'—but they are now called *police community support officers (PCSOs)*.

There are currently 16,000 PCSOs in England and Wales. In November 2007, they were given significantly greater powers—at least partly in response to complaints by senior police officers that their trained staff were overstretched, as a result of increased paperwork generated by recent legislation designed to make the stop-and-search and arrest procedures more transparent. Although they are entitled to paid overtime, a minimum of 21 days' annual leave, and various other benefits, PCSOs earn significantly less than fully trained officers. Starting salaries for professional police constables (PCs), the lowest rank, are around £22,000; in contrast, a PCSO will start on about £16,000. This fact—combined with evidence that police recruitment has been failing to keep pace with government targets in recent years—has led to many critical newspaper headlines about perceived underfunding of the Police Service.

In addition to PCSOs, Labour has introduced another layer of partially trained, community-based officials over the past five years, in the guise of *neighbourhood wardens*. A type of glorified Neighbourhood Watch coordinator, these uniformed individuals are an initiative of the DCLG's Neighbourhood Renewal Unit. They are meant to patrol, and be otherwise readily available in, those areas of the community with large numbers of elderly and/or vulnerable residents—particularly those with a reputation for property crime, graffiti, and antisocial behaviour. They currently have limited powers of intervention (reflected in their modest £15–19,000 salaries), but there are tentative government plans to extend their authority, giving them a semi-official 'assistant constable' status. Since 2005, both PCSOs and wardens have been working alongside fully qualified police officers, on the one hand, and groups of volunteers, on the other, in a new breed of de facto police force called a *neighbourhood policing team* (also known as a 'safer neighbourhood team' or 'safer, stronger community team'). Some 3,600 have been set up across England and Wales.

Today's PCSOs have considerably more clout than the specials of old. They are authorized to issue summary fixed-penalty notices on members of the public for offences ranging from littering and cycling on footpaths, to failing to keep their dogs under control. Under the authority vested in them by the government's 'Respect' agenda, they may also require names and addresses from people they apprehend for 'antisocial behaviour'—for example, fighting or swearing in the street. These details may subsequently be used by the police or local authority to apply to a magistrates' court for permission to impose an *antisocial behaviour order (ASBO)* on an individual. Given their proto-legal status, more detail on ASBOs—the subject of huge controversy on their initial introduction in Labour's second term—can be found in *McNae's Essential Law for Journalists*. They are civil penalties in the first instance, but breaching their conditions—for example, by failing to respect a curfew, or remain resident at a specified address—may see an individual prosecuted for a criminal offence. The Crime and Disorder Act 1998, which introduced ASBOs, defines antisocial behaviour as conduct that has:

> ❝ caused or was likely to cause alarm, harassment or distress to one or more persons not of the same household as him or herself and where an ASBO is seen as necessary to protect relevant persons from further anti-social acts by the defendant. ❞

The ASBO concept was recently extended to tackle lower-level problematic behaviour, with the advent of *acceptable behaviour contracts (ABCs)*. These are agreements that young people identified as having previously acted in an antisocial way may be asked to sign, with input from their parents or guardians, pledging to change their ways and/or to take specified action to make amends.

In addition to being able to impose orders and contracts on named individuals, both neighbourhood wardens and PCSOs have the power (like ordinary police officers) to apply to the local authority for *dispersal orders* to cover locations judged to be antisocial behaviour 'black spots'. Groups of two or more people alleged to be causing 'harassment, alarm, or distress' may be forcibly broken up and/or moved on from a location under the terms of such orders. Failure to comply can lead to fines of up to £2,500. As with ASBOs, the breach of the terms of a dispersal order may lead to prosecution.

Police can also obtain and enforce **designated public places orders (DPPOs)**—a variation on the dispersal order concept that is designed to clear specific streets, squares, or alleyways of drink-related antisocial behaviour. Anyone caught drinking in such locations who refuses to hand over his or her alcohol is liable for a £50 fixed penalty, or to be arrested and fined up to £500.

Despite the widespread ridicule with which news of some ASBOs was greeted in the media (a man was banned from his own home after being given one for playing his music too loud, while several have been imposed on grumpy pensioners for relatively minor 'offences' such as cursing at their neighbours), they have proved hugely popular among law enforcement agencies and many local communities blighted by unruly behaviour in the past. In the year to October 2004, 2,633 ASBOs were issued, with 418 dispersal orders imposed in the same period, according to an official press release from Mr Blair and then Home Secretary David Blunkett. The government used the growth in popularity of the orders as a springboard to expand the scope of its antisocial behaviour crackdown, by increasing the range of 'offences' for which summary penalties could be issued by the police and local authorities, and giving parish and community councils powers to impose them.

The police complaints process

Allegations of misconduct initially follow the same process as other complaints about the local police force. This process is as outlined in Figure 11.1.

In general, all cases involving a death in police custody or at the hands of an officer in the community—for example, the shooting of a drug dealer—will be automatically passed to the **Independent Police Complaints Commission (IPCC)**. Even when matters are handled locally by the chief constable or the police authority, the IPCC may intervene if dissatisfied with the choice of investigating officer. Alternatively, it will approve his or her appointment by issuing an 'appropriate statement'.

Taking disciplinary action is a matter for the police authority in relation to the most senior officers, or the chief constable in relation to all other officers. The authority has to follow a formal disciplinary procedure and can

Figure 11.1 A flow chart outlining the police complaints process

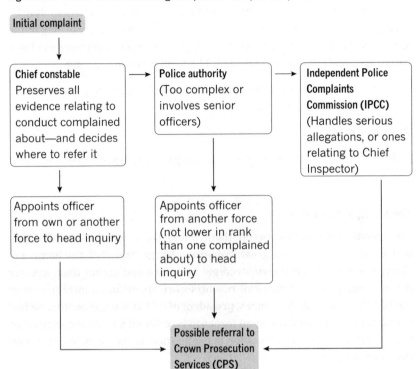

impose disciplinary sanctions on the senior officer (including the chief constable). If a chief constable indicates that he or she is *unwilling* to take action where the IPCC has become involved, the commission can *direct* him or her to do so. Disciplinary charges imposed on officers are heard by the chief constable (unless it is the chief constable him or herself, or an assistant chief constable, that is accused) and punishment can include a caution, reduction in rank, or, in certain cases, dismissal. There is a right of appeal from the chief constable's decision—and this must go to a police disciplinary appeals tribunal. In the last resort, members of the public left unhappy by the way in which a complaint has been dealt with may apply to the courts for a private summons to prosecute the police officers concerned (as was attempted unsuccessfully by the family of Mr De Menezes, prior to their successful private prosecution of the Met for breaching health and safety legislation).

In recent years, there has been some controversy over the extremely stringent 'standard of proof' required before disciplinary charges may be brought. This is illustrated by the stark contrast between the wording of the 'civil' standard—that is, that which is applied in most employment-related situations—and the 'police' standard. The former is worded thus:

> Is it more likely than not, on the balance of probabilities, that the police officer committed the disciplinary offence?

The latter reads:

> Did the police officer commit the disciplinary offence, beyond all reasonable doubt?

The future of the police

Like hospitals and schools before them, it may not be long before individual police forces are given a greater degree of organizational autonomy, enabling them to set their own strategic priorities and giving them greater control over how their financial resources are spent. In an interview with the BBC in June 2008, Ken Jones, president of ACPO, announced that he had submitted the proposal for some forces to be granted *foundation* status (see pp. 192–5) to the Home Office for consideration in its forthcoming **Green Paper** on police reform.

Mr Jones, who qualified his statement by saying that major policy areas such as counter-terrorism should be kept within the centralized remit of Whitehall, revealed that four forces were already piloting a 'common-sense' approach to policing, using their own discretion about whether to arrest certain kinds of minor offender. Others, including the Durham force, were keen to experiment with formal foundation status.

Fire and rescue authorities

Unlike the police (which, although divided into local forces, all comes under the umbrella of one national Police Service), technically speaking, fire and rescue services—or 'fire brigades' as they once were—are entirely locally based. In common with the police, they are managed by a separate authority, but unlike the police, they do not have their own discrete body. Instead, in two-tier areas, the 'fire and rescue authorities' are usually county councils, except should a fire service be based in a unitary area, in which case, a 'combined' fire authority is established. In metropolitan areas, fire services are overseen by separate fire and civil defence authorities (as in London). Table 11.11 is a timeline outlining the history of Britain's fire services.

An important distinction between fire services that fall under county councils and combined fire authorities, or fire and civil defence authorities, is that the former are supervised by county council committees and have their budgets managed by them, while the latter two determine their own budgets like police authorities. They are, however, answerable to the Secretary of State for Communities and Local Government.

It is the Communities Secretary's role to check, each year, the establishment schemes in place in each fire service area—that is, the level and precise nature of provision that it makes available to local people. In law, all fire services must:

- equip and train a firefighting force;
- make arrangements for dealing with calls for help;

Table 11.11 A timeline for the emergence of UK fire services

Year	Event
Before 1938	Volunteer fire brigades set up on ad hoc basis by local parish and town councils, and fire insurance companies (the latter only fought fires in houses belonging to their policyholders, however—indicated by a 'fire mark' plaque fixed to the exteriors of a home).
1938	The Fire Brigades Act makes it compulsory for county borough councils, non-county borough councils, and urban district councils to provide a fire brigade.
1939–45	All fire brigades combined for the duration of the Second World War as part of a National Fire Service.
1947	The Fire Services Act returns all fire brigades to local authority control, this time under the auspices of county councils (designated 'fire authorities').
1963	The London Government Act updates the above by creating the GLC in London.
1972	Metropolitan county councils are designated as fire authorities in the relevant areas by the Local Government Act.
1985	The Local Government Act abolishes the GLC and the metropolitan counties, and creates seven new 'fire and civil defence authorities'. In the six metropolitan areas, these were made up of councillors nominated by each new metropolitan borough council, and numbers were based on the size of each authority and the political balance of the councils. In London, one councillor was nominated from each of the 32 boroughs, plus one from the City of London.
1992	The rolling reorganization of local government ushers in new combined fire service authorities in unitary areas.
2000	The formation of the Greater London Authority has seen the pre-existing fire and civil defence authority replaced by a new London Fire and Emergency Planning Authority (LFEPA).

- gather information about local 'risk' buildings—for example, high-rises, timber-framed structures, or ones housing large numbers of elderly or disabled people;
- give advice on fire protection to the business community, local schools, etc.;
- make sure any local water companies maintain an adequate supply of water at a pressure suitable for firefighting;
- draw up mutually beneficial 'reinforcement schemes'—that is, pool their resources—with neighbouring fire services to help them deal with major fires.

Fire services are also called on to deal with other emergencies in addition to blazes. These so-called 'special services' are divided into two broad categories: humanitarian—for example, serious road accidents and floods—and non-humanitarian—that is, less urgent calls, such as a request to help a resident gain access to their home after leaving their keys inside. Whereas firefighters would once willingly answer calls to scale trees in pursuit of errant cats, it has become increasingly commonplace for today's fire services to charge for such 'non-essential' operations.

Under the Fire Precautions Act 1971, various types of premises are now barred from operating without an official fire service seal of approval in the form of a fire certificate. These are issued, after an inspection, by the fire authorities. The types of premises affected include:

- offices;
- sports grounds;
- hotels;
- theatres.

Other Acts passed to increase fire safety include:

- the Public Health Act 1936—which stipulated that fire escapes must be provided in buildings such as hotels and theatres;
- the Fire Safety and Safety of Places of Sport Act 1987—which introduced tough new seating standards in the aftermath of the 1985 Bradford City Football Club tragedy (including a cut in attendance limits at UK football grounds).

Emergency planning and civil defence

The aspect of 'emergency services' provision in which local authorities have historically had the most direct involvement is the broader category of emergency planning and civil defence. The notion of 'civil defence' in particular—namely, the idea that councils might be expected to help to protect citizens against enemy attack or any other form of security emergency— arose in the context of the Second World War. As a policy, it was initiated by the post-war Labour government, but has remained largely a notional responsibility for the most part in 'peacetime'—perhaps its most tangible application being the plans for an hypothetical nuclear attack expected to be updated by local authorities at various junctures during the Cold War. Notable exceptions included the strategies employed to safeguard's London population from terrorist bombs during The Troubles and the measures that had to be implemented following the Real IRA's attack on a Manchester shopping centre in 1996. In this age of increased security threats, however, it is not hard to imagine a time when renewed importance may be attached to civil defence departments.

As recently as 2004, a new Civil Contingencies Act effectively replaced the entire body of existing emergency planning legislation on the statute book. The most significant aspect of the shake-up, ordered by then Secretary of State for Transport, Local Government and the Regions John Prescott, was the new requirement placed on so-called 'responder' organizations in each local area to appoint a full-time *emergency planning officer* (sometimes known as a 'civil contingencies officer', 'civil protection officer', or 'resilience officer') to coordinate the measures that would be implemented in the event of a civil emergency. As well as security threats, such civil emergencies might include any number of natural or manmade disasters: for example, floods, major fires, landslides, or nuclear accidents. Responder organizations are divided under the Act into 'Category 1' and 'Category 2'. The list of bodies in each category is outlined in Table 11.12, which can be found on the Online Resource Centre that accompanies this book.

The history of local government's involvement with civil defence began with the passage of the Civil Defence Act 1948, under which the Home Secretary was empowered to direct local authorities to take 'appropriate measures' to ensure that the civil defence requirements for their populations were met. These were further defined by the Civil Defence (Planning) Regulations 1974, which gave county councils the power to 'make plans to deal with hostile attacks' and, in certain circumstances, to prepare for war, in consultation with boroughs/districts. It was only in the 1990s, in the wake of the end of the Cold War, that the term 'emergency' was explicitly redefined to cover peacetime disasters such as floods. Finally, in 2001, responsibility for civil defence shifted from the Home Secretary to a new *Cabinet Office Coordination Unit*.

A further type of agency involved in preparing for the event of civil emergencies is the newly formed 'regional resilience boards'. Sometimes referred to as 'regional control and resilience boards', these are joint bodies drawing together representatives from local police forces, fire service authorities, and council civil defence departments to oversee overall emergency planning for entire regions. The 2004 Act also required responder organizations to set up collaboratively more localized versions of the regional boards—'local resilience forums' (LRFs)—based in each police area. All are expected to produce a community risk register that is specific to their areas, outlining particular localities, buildings, businesses, or residential areas that are seen to be particularly vulnerable. They are overseen at national level by a new *executive agency* within the Cabinet Office: the Civil Contingencies Secretariat.

The government's much-vaunted new 'resilience' strategy for the country was prompted, in large part, by the 11 September 2001 terrorist attacks and the 2004 Madrid bombings (not to mention persistent fears of an avian flu pandemic, which have been periodically played up by the media since 2003). But this new state of preparedness failed to prevent the 7 July 2005 attacks on London. And more embarrassing still for ministers was the organizational chaos and buck-passing between local authorities, the *Environment Agency*, and central government that greeted the widespread winter floods that devastated parts of Britain in 2007.

At the very top of the chain of command for emergency planning is an ad hoc government committee, codenamed 'Cobra' and headed by the prime minister, which meets in a Cabinet Office briefing room whenever necessary. (Despite its James Bond-style title, the acronym actually stands for something rather mundane and unexciting: 'Cabinet Office Briefing Room A'.) Among the emergencies for which Cobra most recently convened were the 2007 foot-and-mouth outbreaks and the terrorist attack on Glasgow Airport—all of which occurred within weeks of Gordon Brown's becoming prime minister. When the premier is unavailable, his or her place is taken by the Home Secretary. This happened at the time of the 7 July bombings, because then Prime Minister Tony Blair was at a *G8* Summit in Gleneagles when the news broke.

Table 11.13 Local Government Association (LGA) strategic objectives

	Objective
1	Deepen and strengthen relationships with member councils
2	Deepen and strengthen relationships with our partners
3	Maintain its capacity to influence government
4	Strengthen its capability to influence the public
5	Develop capacity to initiate policy and initiate debate about policy
6	Adopt an intelligent, proactive approach to generating interest in the sector
7	Develop the LGA as an exemplar organization providing value for money and high-quality services to its customers

▌ Local government associations

The Local Government Association (LGA) was established in 1997 to give a collective voice in Whitehall policymaking to all 388 English local authorities. Describing itself as a 'voluntary lobbying organization' (as opposed to a trade union or association), it is based in Westminster offices close to Parliament, at John Smith Square, in the building that was formerly Transport House: the historic headquarters of the Labour Party. In addition to representing district/borough councils, county councils, metropolitan borough councils, and unitary authorities, the LGA also speaks on behalf of subscribing police authorities, fire authorities, *national park authorities*, and passenger transport authorities. Local authorities in Wales are represented by a Welsh Local Government Association (WLGA), which is a subset of the LGA.

In 2007–08, the LGA published the strategic objectives summarized in Table 11.13.

In addition to the central LGA, there are 13 regional *local government associations*, the remits of which broadly follow the boundaries of the government's English regions.

→ Further reading

Atkinson, H. and Wilks-Heeg, S. (2000) *Local Government from Thatcher to Blair*, Cambridge: Polity Press. **Comprehensive account of the succession of local government reforms passed by the Thatcher, Major, Blair, and Brown administrations.**

Stallion, M. and Wall, D. S. (2000) *The British Police: Police Forces and Chief Officers 1829–2000*, London: M. R. Stallion. **Exhaustive handbook to the UK Police Service from its inception to the new millennium, including a profile of every force past and present, and introductory essays.**

Stevens, A. (2006) *Politico's Guide to Local Government*, 2nd edn, London: Politico's Publishing. **Fully updated second edition of comprehensive guide to every aspect of local government, including the interplay between local and central administrations.**

Stewart, J. (2003) *Modernising British Local Government: An Assessment of Labour's Reform Programme*, London: Palgrave Macmillan. **A meditative examination of the impact of the Local Government Act 2000, focusing on the tension between the idea of increasing localism and complaints of diminishing council accountability.**

Wilson, D. and Game, C. (2006) *Local Government in the United Kingdom*, London: Palgrave Macmillan. **Revised fourth edition of what has become the standard text on contemporary local government in Britain. This covers all of the major recent developments, including the introduction of unitary authorities and elected mayors.**

Wilson, D., Ashton, J., and Sharpe, D. (2001) *What Everyone in Britain Should Know about the Police*, London: Blackstone Press. **Fully revised second edition of this informative core text charting developments in the UK Police Service from its origins in the early nineteenth century up to the present day, with a focus on recent changes from the idea of the traditional 'Bobby on the beat' to today's target-led—and frequently armed—officers.**

? Review questions

1. When did the first local authorities emerge, and what were their initial role and purpose?

2. What were the main reforms instigated in the 1974 reorganization of local government?

3. Outline the current local government framework in England and Wales. What are 'two-tier areas', 'unitary authorities', and 'hybrid councils'?

4. In two-tier areas, what is the division of responsibilities between district/borough and county councils?

5. How is the UK police force structured, and how and by whom can local chief constables be held to account?

Online resource centre

www.oxfordtextbooks.co.uk/orc/Morrison

Visit the Online Resource Centre that accompanies this book for web links and regular updates.

12

Financing local government

One of the most newsworthy and politically contentious local government issues is that of finance. News editors on the hunt for stories guaranteed to catch the eyes of local people as they scurry past newsstands could do a lot worse than set their reporters to work scouring the annual accounts of their local authorities—or plying them with requests under the Freedom of Information Act (FoIA) 2000 to find out exactly how they spent that 10 per cent hike in *Council Tax* last year. Above-*inflation* rises in councillor allowances, cutbacks in funding for local schools, all-expenses-paid 'fact-finding' junkets for the council leader and his mistress, and the question of how much tax-payers and businesses are being charged for their local services (and where that money is actually going) are rarely far from the local news agenda.

▶ Revenue versus capital finance

Local authorities need money for two types of spending: to build infrastructure—that is, offices, roads, traffic crossings, schools, and housing—and to operate and maintain that infrastructure on a day-to-day basis. The cost of building things is known as *capital expenditure*. Cash spent staffing, lighting, heating, and repairing them is called *revenue expenditure*.

▌ Revenue expenditure and how it is financed

Revenue spending is financed through the council's *income*: the grants that it receives from central government; the taxes that it raises and/or has allocated to it locally; and any up-front fees or penalties that it charges for local services—for example, parking permits and library fines. Each of these key income streams is examined in detail below, starting with the source of funds that underpins all others—the government grant system.

The reformed government grant system

The overwhelming majority (74 per cent as of 2008–09) of local authority revenue finance derives from government grants. Of this, until recently, the bulk came in the form of the **revenue support grant (RSG)**—also known as the **general block grant**—which individual local authorities were left to spend at their discretion, focusing on particular local funding needs. Since Labour returned to power in 1997, the process by which central government grants are allocated to local authorities has become ever more baffling. At the same time, the importance of the RSG has hugely diminished as more and more government money has become 'ring-fenced' and directed at specified areas of spending—notably, schools. This process—known as 'passporting'—has seen a steady decline in the size of the RSG, to the extent that it now represents only *3 per cent* of local authorities' annual revenue budget. By far the biggest portion—67 per cent—is allotted to councils in the form of discrete, and increasingly sizeable chunks, many of which must be spent in prescribed ways dictated by central government. Local authorities' own reserves and the annual grant given to the police between them make up a further 5 per cent. Perhaps surprisingly, given the controversy that it generates in the media, the Council Tax accounts for a mere quarter of revenue income. Figure 12.1 gives a full breakdown of the sources of local government revenue funding in 2008–09. Figure 12.2 summarizes the percentage of local authority revenue spending in each service area.

These are the facts and figures—but how exactly are the various types of grant defined and allocated in practice? It is probably easiest to explain the patchwork government grant system by splitting the payments into two broad categories: *formula grants* and *non-formula grants*.

Figure 12.1 A breakdown of regular local authority revenue income for 2008–09

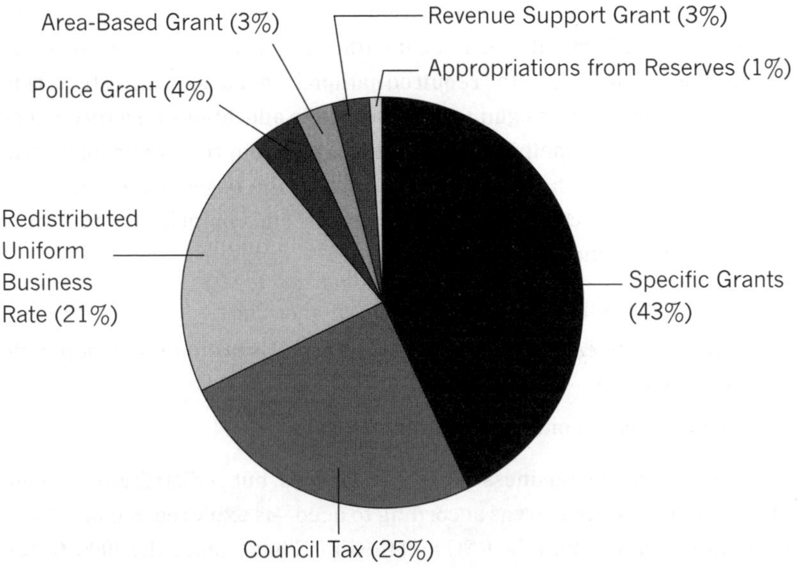

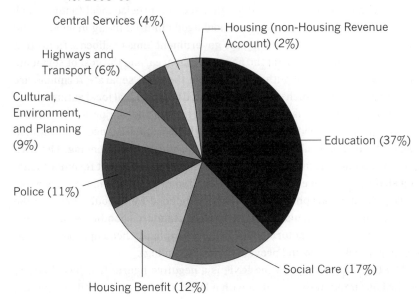

Area-Based Grant (3%)   Revenue Support Grant (3%)

Police Grant (4%)   Appropriations from Reserves (1%)

Redistributed
Uniform
Business
Rate (21%)   Specific Grants
(43%)

Council Tax (25%)

Source: Department of Communities and Local Government (DCLG)

Figure 12.2 A breakdown of annual local authority revenue spending patterns
for 2008–09

Central Services (4%)   Housing (non-Housing Revenue
Account) (2%)

Highways and
Transport (6%)

Cultural,
Environment,
and Planning
(9%)   Education (37%)

Police (11%)

Social Care (17%)

Housing Benefit (12%)

Source: Department of Communities and Local Government (DCLG)

Formula grants

Central government makes a calculation—traditionally, each year—of how much money it thinks individual local authorities need to provide services for their communities up to the required national standards. With effect from 2008–09, ministers have begun to calculate their allocations on a three-year basis, with the aim of helping local authorities to improve their long-term planning. The grants that ministers allocate on the basis of these calculations are known collectively as 'formula grants' and comprise the following three types of funding:

- the revenue support grant (RSG);
- *uniform business rates (UBR)*—also known as *national non-domestic rates (NNDR)*;
- the principal formula police grant (PFPG).

UBR—a tax levied on businesses based in an area, but redistributed by central government to local areas according to need—is explored in more detail later in this chapter. Both the RSG and the PFPG have, since the 2006–07 tax year, been worked out on the basis of a two new calculations: the relative needs formula (RNF) and the relative resource amount (RRA).

The RNF, as its title suggests, is a kind of formula based on detailed information about the population size, social structure, and other characteristics of a local authority area. By taking into account precise local factors, such as the number of pensioners and school-aged children living in an area and its relative economic prosperity, the government aims to allocate funds that fairly and accurately reflect the needs of that area, and the cost of servicing those needs to its local authorities. Within the RNF, separate formulae are used to decide how much should be allocated to individual local authorities to cover the likely expenses associated with each of the 'major service areas': education; social services; police; fire; highways maintenance; environmental; protective and cultural services (EPCS); and capital financing. The RNF plays the same role in the current system as the now defunct formula spending share (FSS)—an earlier attempt at making the system more responsive to specific demographic factors (also introduced by Labour). Prior to the FSS, grants were calculated on the basis of standard spending assessments (SSAs)—which were notorious for using a simple per head approach (relating to population size and previous years' spending).

The RRA, in contrast to the RNF, is a *negative* figure. It is based on the logical assumption that an area with a large number of Council Tax-paying households—particularly those in higher tax bands, indicative of a relatively affluent population—needs less financial help from central government than one in a poorer area. The RRA is essentially subtracted from the previously calculated RNF to give a figure that more accurately reflects what an individual area should be allocated in government formula grants. The resulting grant is shared between local authorities in that area in proportion to the level of responsibility that each has—with 'upper-tier' county councils and unitary authorities gaining more than 'lower-tier' district or *borough councils*, and police and fire authorities.

Over and above the core chunk of formula grants allocated in this way, there remains a small percentage in the overall 'formula pot' to be distributed between local authority areas on a purely per head basis. This is the same for all local authorities that deliver the same services—that is, all district/borough councils receive an identical per capita amount. This is known as 'central allocation'. In addition, the government uses a procedure known as 'floor-damping' to ensure that every local authority—no matter how poorly it has done out of a grant settlement relative to others—receives at least a *minimum* year-on-year increase in its formula grant. Four different 'floor levels' are set (one for each of the aforementioned types of authority). To cite a current example, for the year 2009–10, education and social services authorities (the upper-tier counties and unitaries) are guaranteed a 1.75 per cent increase in grant, whatever their perceived 'relative needs' and 'relative resource amounts'. The following year, their formula grants will grow by at least 1.5 per cent.

The total value of formula grants allocated by the British government to England for 2009–10 is £28bn. This will rise to £29bn in 2010–11.

Non-formula grants

Alongside formula grants, Labour has introduced a welter of other types of central government handout for local authorities—a growing number of which are 'passported' to be spent in specific areas. The main categories of *non-formula* grants are:

- *specific grants*;
- area-based grants (ABGs).

Despite their name, not all specific grants have to be spent by councils in strictly defined areas. In fact, there are two types of specific grant: *ring-fenced grants* and *unfenced grants* (sometimes also called *targeted grants*).

Ring-fenced grants—as their name suggests—are tied to spending in a particular area. One of the most famous is the **Dedicated Schools Grant (DSG)**, which councils may not spend on anything other than staffing and maintaining schools, or providing related services such as special needs teaching. As well as having to be spent on schools generally, the DSG is sometimes prescribed further still, with ministers stipulating that it goes towards particular running costs, such as buying more textbooks or improving extracurricular activities (the ministerial priority for 2006–07 and 2007–08 was personalized learning). But such passporting can prove a source of conflict between central and local government. In 2005, there was a high-profile contretemps between a number of local authorities and then Education Secretary Alan Johnson after it emerged that they had spent part of their schools grant on improving less generously funded local services.

Mr Johnson was also in charge when another ring-fenced school grant was introduced by the government, in the shape of the extra £627m payment that it pledged, in two stages, to roll out healthier school meals between 2005 and 2011. The initiative followed the high-profile 'Feed Me Better' media campaign fronted by television chef Jamie Oliver.

The other form of specific grant—the unfenced grant—is allocated to councils to spend however they see fit. Confusingly, this makes it superficially resemble the revenue support grant. Unlike the RSG, however, unfenced grants are not calculated on the basis of a formula related to local demographic and socio-economic factors; rather, they are residual pots of money to be spent on services judged to be equally worthy of central government funding across the country. An example of an unfenced specific grant is the Housing and Planning Delivery Grant (HPDG), which, although it may only be spent on services related to housing and/or planning, may be used in any number of ways by individual local authorities.

The government's stated aims for specific grants is to:

- help local authorities to achieve a specific purpose—for example, reducing Council Tax, or bringing in uniform standards of domestic upkeep or disabled access provision;
- help poorer areas in which the Council Tax base—that is, the number households eligible to pay Council Tax—is too low to meet the costs of local needs;
- cut the cost of a service that is either spread unevenly across the country—for example, the maintenance of a flood barrier—or is of benefit to the nation as a whole—for example, roads;

- fund services for which the government has laid down statutory requirements—for example, the Mental Illness Specific Grant (MISG), introduced under the Community Care Act 1990 to provide community-based support for people with mental health problems.

The final type of revenue grant—the area-based grant (ABG)—is a new addition to local authorities' financial armouries. Introduced in 2008–09, it is designed to encourage them to work with 'partners'—that is, other organizations, such as charities, local businesses, and even neighbouring authorities—to improve local services across the shared localities in which they operate. The idea is that, by forming partnerships, authorities will achieve efficiency savings and avoid duplicating or overlapping with other service providers.

The total value of specific and area-based grants combined for 2009–10 is £45bn, while £47bn will be allotted for 2010–11. A summary of the main types of central government-directed revenue grant is given in Table 12.1.

Passporting grants for specified purposes is seen by some as a means by which the government gets away with massaging public spending figures. In February 1999, a £50m additional grant for schools was very publicly allocated by ministers as an 'increase' in the value of the revenue support grant. In reality, however, this money was provided by taking it away from other local government services—a sleight of hand derided by Sir Jeremy Beecham, then leader of the Local Government Association (LGA), who accused ministers of 'holding local authorities to ransom' by a 'smoke and mirrors trick'.

Government efforts to constrain local authorities' abilities to spend their revenue income where they please do not stop with ring-fenced and area-based grants. It was once commonplace for councils that found themselves with unexpected shortfalls in one spending department during a financial year to transfer money over from the budget of a different one that was in surplus—a process known as *virement*. Today, this is becoming all but

Table 12.1 The different types of government revenue grant (2009–10)

Formula grants	Non-formula grants
Revenue support grant (RSG)	Specific ring-fenced grant
Uniform business rates (UBR)	Specific unfenced grant
Principal formula police grant (PFPG)	Area-based grant (ABG)
Floor-damping grant	

impossible for anything other than the most modest shuffling of books, because of the severe restrictions placed on authorities' ability to use money allocated for a specific purpose elsewhere.

Local taxation and the evolution of the Council Tax

The idea of local taxation ultimately goes back to a time when medieval churches charged 'tithes' to parishioners renting land from them and lords of the manor used bailiffs to extract land taxes from peasant farmers. But as early as 1601, it began to become a more systematic affair, with the emergence of the 'rates'—a property-based tax based on the *rateable value* of an individual's home, which was to remain in place (with some modifications) for four centuries.

The rates were a tax levied on domestic properties, rather than the individual citizens who occupied them. The broad assumption was that the bigger a property and the higher its rateable—or rental—value, the better off its occupants were likely to be. But over time, the rating system (to use its full title) produced some peculiar anomalies that led to growing calls for reform. Prior to its eventual abolition, by Margaret Thatcher's Conservative government in 1990 (1989 in Scotland), the most oft-cited illustration of its unfairness was that of the elderly pensioner living alone, on a fixed income, in a house for which he or she had spent their lifetime paying—next door to several sharing professionals whose combined incomes were far higher. Because rates were property-based, both 'households' might be charged exactly the same, meaning that each professional would be paying significantly less than the pensioner.

Although there was widespread agreement that rates needed reforming, their immediate successor was to be short-lived. Ushered in by the Local Government Finance Act 1988, the so-called Community Charge—dubbed the 'Poll Tax' by opponents—sought to address the grievances of ratepayers 'punished' for living alone by shifting the onus away from property and onto people. In future, individual residents would be billed for their use of local services—forcing everyone to 'pay their way'. But, while it may have seemed fairer in theory, in practice this new 'head tax' soon became even more unpopular than the rates. While various rebates and exemptions were introduced to take account of the inability of certain groups—for example, the unemployed—to afford it, working people living in the same area ended up paying identical amounts—regardless of any differences in their incomes: a multimillionaire tycoon might be charged exactly the same as his or her cleaner. In addition, some low-income groups previously excluded from local taxation altogether were suddenly included for the first time. Full-time students, for example, became liable (albeit with a 75 per cent reduction).

Such was the furore that greeted the introduction of the Community Charge that it has been widely viewed as the tipping point in the loss of confidence in Mrs Thatcher among Conservative members of Parliament (MPs) that ultimately led to her resignation partway through a leadership contest in 1990 (see p. 103). The tax also proved extremely costly to administer, due in part to the fact that many of its opponents seemed prepared to forgo their right to vote, by dropping off the electoral roll, rather than allowing themselves to be tracked down by the **billing authorities**. Others openly refused to pay, leading to costly litigation by councils (much of which never bore fruit). In the end, the government was forced to increase its grants considerably temporarily to allow for a gross reduction in Community Charge bills of £140 a person, funded by a 2.5 per cent increase in VAT. In 1990–91, the Poll Tax paid for 44 per cent of local expenditure, but this was halved to 22 per cent following the cut (compared to 25 per cent for today's Council Tax).

Following the biggest peacetime protests ever seen in Britain to date, Mrs Thatcher's successor, John Major, wasted no time abandoning the charge—replacing it with the Council Tax. This new 'hybrid' tax reinstated the property link, but, unlike the rates, related it to market or *capital* values, rather than rateable ones. To placate critics of the rates, it also retained an element of the 'individual' liability introduced by the Community Charge. Each household was billed on the assumption that it comprised two adults (meaning that bills did not increase for three or more). But to avoid returning to a time when households occupying identical properties paid exactly the same—regardless of how many working adults lived in each—a range of reductions and exemptions for single people and low-income groups were introduced to make the system fairer—as outlined in Table 12.2.

Although designed to deal with many of the anomalies and inequities preserved by previous local tax regimes, the Council Tax benefits and exemptions system inevitably ushered in its own. Full-time students may have been exempt from the Council Tax in theory, but, in practice, those renting from private landlords invariably found themselves having to pay it on the

Table 12.2 A list of Council Tax exemptions and reductions

Exemption/reduction	How it works
Single person discount	25 per cent off a full Council Tax bill
'Reductions for Disabilities' scheme	Lowers bills of homes in Bands B–H if they have been adapted to meet the needs of disabled people. It exists to ensure that a house is not unfairly overvalued because it has had expensive modifications
Exemptions	Applies to the severely mentally impaired, carers, and full-time students, as well as certain categories of dwelling, such as student halls of residence
Unoccupied dwelling discount	Discount of up to 50 per cent—although councils now have discretion to charge more in 'ghost towns'
Council Tax Benefit	Writes off Council Tax bills for the unemployed, and certain other people on low incomes and other benefits
'Transitional relief'	Provided during transition from Community Charge to Council Tax for those whose local tax bills suddenly leapt as a result

homeowner's behalf—or having their rent artificially inflated to cover the cost. Students sharing houses with one or more adults in employment also lost their exemptions, by default, because the household automatically became liable for Council Tax as a result.

Perhaps most controversial has been the 50 per cent reduction traditionally available to households with two or more properties whose additional homes are generally unoccupied. In Wales and south-west England, in particular, the 'ghost towns' created in picturesque areas favoured by wealthy city dwellers as the locations for their holiday homes have been exacerbated by the relative cheapness of keeping such properties empty for large parts of the year, in light of the Council Tax discounts that they receive. In certain areas blighted by this trend, councils have been given limited discretion by government to charge more than the standard 50 per cent, to deter property owners from leaving them unoccupied. A recent *statutory instrument*— the Council Tax (Prescribed Classes of Dwellings) (England) Regulations 2003—gave individual billing authorities the power to determine classes of discount in their areas for the first time, in recognition of the 'ghost town' issue (not to mention the risk of such properties being broken into). Unoccupied, but furnished, properties—those most likely to be used as second homes—became liable for a reduced discount of 10 per cent, while some long-term empty homes faced losing their reduction altogether. In April 2008, Newcastle City Council used this new power to scrap its 50 per cent reduction for unfurnished and uninhabitable homes—charging them the full Council Tax for the first time.

Table 12.3 Arguments for and against property-based and people-based local taxes

Property-based tax	People-based tax
Cheap to administer and collect, and provides a predictable source of income	Provides a boost to local finances, because the number of bills sent out hugely increases to reflect the fact that all adults—rather than households—are being charged
Difficult for people to avoid paying rates because property, unlike people, is immobile	Some argue that it is fairer in principle, because the burden of paying for local services is spread across all adults—including those who might otherwise be 'invisible' to a tax based on property values. A 'head tax' does not need to be 'one size fits all': a local income tax would reflect individuals' ability to pay
Simple, clearly understood system	Fosters greater local authority accountability, because all adults are charged and can voice their views on use of their money at local elections
Fair in theory, in that people occupying larger dwellings are likely to be better off	Because individuals have to fill in forms accepting liability for taxes such as the Community Charge, there is a huge disincentive for them to register. When it was introduced in the UK, many councils ended up collecting barely half of what they were owed—and those unable or unwilling to pay lost their right to vote by dropping off the electoral roll
Property taxes can be a disincentive to home improvement, because any major refurbishment or extension is likely to hike bills	Straight head taxes such as the Community Charge also mean that low-income groups such as students, pensioners, and working people on modest wages will be charged the same as vastly richer ones—unless explicit exemptions and reductions are introduced

Council Tax remains highly controversial to this day, however, and is seen by many as far being from perfect. Newspapers have frequently featured stories about the financial problems that it has caused for pensioners and other people on modest fixed incomes who do not fall into a category that makes them eligible for a reduction. Some have even been fined or jailed for 'refusing' to pay. In September 2005, Sylvia Hardy, a 73-year-old retired social worker from Exeter, was sent to prison for refusing to pay £53.71 in Council Tax arrears on time. She told Exeter magistrates' court defiantly that she was following the example of other individuals in history who had fought to change 'unjust laws'.

Such is the ongoing concern about the unfair impact of Council Tax on low-income households that the Liberal Democrats favour replacing it with a 'local income tax'—a system, based on the calculations used to determine national Income Tax bands, that should more closely match a household's Council Tax bill with its ability to pay. In Scotland, where the *Scottish Parliament* has the power to make changes to local taxation, the incumbent Scottish Nationalist-led administration was in the process of introducing a local Income Tax when this book went to press.

Table 12.3 outlines some arguments for and against a property-based—rather than people-based—local tax system.

Council Tax banding

But enough about those who do not pay the Council Tax—or at least do not pay the full amount: how does the system work for the overwhelming majority who do?

Council Tax bills in England, Scotland, and Wales are based on a *banding* system that divides domestic properties into one of eight bands (nine in Wales)—A–H (A–I), respectively—according to their notional capital values. In Wales, these bandings were most recently revised in 2005, to take account of changes in property prices in the 14 years that had elapsed since the original bands were set on 1 April 1991. Controversially, however, neither England nor Scotland has had its bandings changed since they were originally set—meaning that they remain exactly the same as on 1 April 1993 (by which time even the original valuations were out of date). Despite pledging in its 2005 election manifesto to revise the bands across the UK if re-elected, Labour dropped the policy on returning to power. Cynics saw its reluctance to tackle the issue anywhere but in Wales as an example of political back-pedalling motivated by a fear that it would lose future votes in marginal *constituencies* where people whose house prices had significantly increased in the previous decade might find themselves moving into higher bands. In fact, according to research by the Local Government Association (LGA), the number of households likely to lose out in a revaluation is the same as the number that would benefit (around four million).

Whatever the merits of the argument for retaining existing bandings, it is undeniable that the property values to which they relate are anachronistic today, in light of the substantial rises in house prices seen across most of the UK since the early 1990s. The highest Council Tax band (H) currently applies to all homes valued at more than £320,000 in 1991 (in Scotland, the top rate starts at just over the £212,000 mark). Homes built since that date are given nominal values based on what they would have been worth had they existed in 1991. The lowest Council Tax band was set for homes worth £40,000 or less in England and £27,000 or less in Scotland, while the 'average band' (B and D) covered those worth between £68,000 and £88,000 (£45–58,000 in Scotland).

The introduction of a revised banding system in Wales has led to complaints that the country is no longer on an equal footing with the rest of Britain. Since 2005, when a new system based on 1 April 2003 values was introduced there, the new Welsh Band A has covered properties worth £44,000 or less, with D encompassing those valued at £91–123,000, and the new band I (previously Wales, too, only had A–H) all dwellings over £424,000. Prior to the revaluation, Band A related to homes worth £30,000 or less, and D to those worth between £51,000 and £66,000.

Despite the fact that the price ranges covered by each of the bands in Wales were all adjusted upwards to reflect the general surge in property values since 1993, the revaluation was not simply a question of mapping properties in the old Band A over into the new one. Instead, it produced clear winners and losers. Because house prices in some areas had risen significantly further than in others—with some previously cheaper homes overtaking in value those that were once more expensive—many households found themselves moving into a higher band than before. Most went up at least one band, while some jumped two or more. Only 8 per cent of homes moved down.

At present, around 25 per cent of homes fall in the lowest band in England and Scotland as a whole, although in north-east England this proportion rises to 60 per cent. The current Council Tax bandings in England, Scotland, and Wales are outlined in Table 12.4.

Table 12.4 Current Council Tax bands and values in England, Scotland, and Wales

Band	England	Scotland	Wales
A	Up to £40,000	Up to £27,000	Up to £44,000
B	£40,001–£52,000	£27,001–£35,000	£44,001–£65,000
C	£52,001–£68,000	£35,001–£45,000	£65,001–£91,000
D	£68,001–£88,000	£45,001–£58,000	£91,001–£123,000
E	£88,001–£120,000	£58,001–£80,000	£123,001–£162,000
F	£120,001–£160,000	£80,001–£106,000	£162,001–£223,000
G	£160,001–£320,000	£106,001–£212,000	£223,001–£324,000
H	£320,001 and above	£212,001 and above	£324,001–£424,000
I	N/a	N/a	£424,001 and above

How individual bills are calculated—and who collects the money

As explained above, domestic properties are charged Council Tax in line with the bands into which they are placed based on their capital values in April 1991 (2003 in Wales). But who actually puts them in these bands and determines the nominal 1991/2003 value of a home built in the years since the bands were originally set?

Responsibility for valuing homes rests with the Valuation Office Agency (VOA), an *executive agency* of HM Revenue and Customs (and, ultimately, the Treasury), but it is for individual billing authorities to maintain lists of valuations. Based in 85 regional offices, the VAO's day-to-day work is undertaken by a team of *listing officers*, who compile and update lists of the properties grouped in each band in their area. Overall responsibility for running each district office falls on the local *valuation officer* (also sometimes known as the *district valuer*). It is his or her job to hear any formal appeals initiated by households unhappy with their property valuations.

Although the Council Tax banding system has never been reset in England and Scotland since the government's original mass valuation (and has only changed once in Wales), homes originally placed in one band can still be moved into a different one under certain circumstances. A property might go up or down for any of the reasons outlined in Table 12.5.

Over the years, considerable vitriol has been aimed at the VOA, not least by those whose homes are in higher bands. When they were initially set in 1991, it became an urban myth that the agents employed by the VOA to help valuation officers in the mammoth task of valuing millions of homes for Council Tax purposes for the first time did so simply by driving past houses and awarding them a notional market value purely based on their location and outer appearance. These were jokingly dubbed 'second-gear valuations'.

Local authorities that charge Council Tax to help to finance their services fall into two broad categories, depending on their degree of involvement in actually collecting the money:

- *billing authorities* (or *collection authorities*)—that is, councils that actually send out bills to households, and collect the proceeds to be distributed between themselves and other authorities in their area. In two-tier areas, the billing authority is the district or borough council, while in unitary areas, it is the unitary authority;

Table 12.5 Ways in which properties can change Council Tax bands between revaluations

Band change	How it happens
Neighbourhood changes or alterations to buildings	The property has fallen in value because part of it has been demolished, or the state of its locality has changed significantly (e.g. a sewerage works has been built)
Non-domestic use of property	A householder has started—or stopped—using his or her home for business purposes
Rise in value due to material change to property	A home can increase in value because of an extension or other major alteration—although an increase in band will not occur unless or until the property is sold
Home adaptations	Changes have been made to a home to adapt it for a person with a disability (e.g. disabled ramps, stair lifts, etc.)
Incorrect original valuation	A mistake was made with the original valuation. To determine this, the new occupants of the property must lodge an appeal with the listing officer within six months of moving in

- *precepting authorities*—that is, all types of authority entitled to issue a 'precept' (instruction or order) to their local billing authority asking for a share of local Council Tax proceeds. In two-tier areas, this applies to the billing authority itself, the county council (in its role as both top-tier council and local fire authority), and the local *police authority*, while in unitary areas, there are still three precepting authorities: the unitary, police, and county council fire authorities. Every annual Council Tax bill received by a paying household should include a breakdown of the proportions of Council Tax to be allocated to each precepting authority over the financial year. The largest portion goes to the local top-tier council (unitary or county). Parish councils also issue precepts for the modest local services they provide, so precepting authorities are grouped into 'major' (county/district/unitary) and 'minor' (parish).

When Council Tax bills for each band for the coming tax year have been determined by local precepting authorities, they will express their precepts publicly in terms of an 'average rate' of Council Tax and the 'average rise' in the value of this rate faced by local taxpayers in comparison to the previous year. As indicated earlier, the 'average rate' is that which applies to a Band D property. It is determined by the following formula:

Total amount the authority intends to spend − total non-Council Tax revenue

---

Council Tax base (number of eligible households)

How central government 'controls' Council Tax bills

The government has powers to prevent local authorities charging excessive Council Tax by introducing formal ceilings to stop bills rising above specified levels. This process—known as *capping*—was introduced by the Tories in the Rates Act 1984, and used with increased frequency during the 1980s and 1990s to restrict bill increases by supposed high-spending councils (often Labour ones in poorer areas, which argued that they faced above-average costs in housing, education, and social care). Labour has generally been reluctant to cap authorities, although it retains reserve powers allowing it to do so under certain circumstances. In 2008–09, the government announced its intention to cap Portsmouth City Council and seven police authorities—Bedfordshire, Cheshire, Leicestershire, Lincolnshire, Norfolk, Surrey, and Warwickshire—after each announced Council Tax rises above the 5 per cent ceiling beneath which it had urged them to remain. David Williams, Portsmouth's *chief executive*, criticized ministers, saying that the cost of rebilling taxpayers in his area would cost them £90,000, while only £40,000 would be refunded to 'overcharged' households—causing a deficit of £50,000. Ultimately, only Lincolnshire—which increased its precept by 78.9 per cent—was capped, although the other authorities face limits on precept increases in future.

Such examples aside, Labour's approach to holding down Council Tax bills has largely remained that of using its reserve powers to target specific authorities, rather than favouring the across-the-board capping occasionally used by the Conservatives. In November 2007, Tory leader David Cameron revealed that his party was considering readopting a version of this 'universal' approach if returned to power. Under his proposals, a so-called 'trigger threshold' would be introduced to limit bill rises. This would essentially be a government-dictated level above which authorities would not be allowed to raise Council Tax without first obtaining the permission of local people in a *referendum*. Critics argued that requiring the public to approve rises in Council Tax bills was tantamount to asking turkeys to vote for Christmas and was therefore capping in all but name.

A further way in which governments have sought to keep Council Tax at reasonable levels is by banning authorities from issuing supplementary precepts—that is, last-minute increases to the sums that they request from their local billing authorities, because of previously unforeseen changes to their budgetary predictions for the next financial year. This was outlawed under the Local Government Finance Act 1982.

The 'gearing' effect

Notwithstanding central government's ability to 'cap' bills, Council Tax is the one device available to local authorities to generate significant income over and above their annual grants to finance costly expenditure. Therefore, any decision by the government to *reduce* its contribution to a local authority (either by cutting or freezing the level of grants) is likely to force that authority to increase bills significantly to make up for the resulting shortfall. Similarly, if a council suddenly faces unforeseen revenue demands, but its contribution from government is already set, it will again have to turn to the Council Tax. The disproportionate rise in bills that can result in such circumstances is known as the 'gearing' effect.

To cite a theoretical example, if a council raises a total revenue income for the coming year of £100m—approximately £25m from the Council Tax—but ends up needing £101m to meet its final spending demands, it will need to raise Council Tax by significantly more than the 1 per cent shortfall to achieve this. In fact, its average Council Tax bills would have to rise by 4 per cent:

$$\text{Projected Council Tax increase} = £1m/£25m = 4 \text{ per cent}$$

Uniform business rates (UBR)

In addition to their responsibilities for valuing domestic properties, listing officers and valuation officers are also charged with administering the 'equivalent' tax for occupiers of local business premises. While this may sound straightforward enough, uniform business rates (UBR)—otherwise known as 'national non-domestic rates' (NNDR)—have proved almost as controversial as the Council Tax. Introduced alongside the Community Charge in 1990, its initial tax bands were based on a revaluation instigated at the time (based on *rateable* values in 1991), but it has since been revalued every five years. The next revaluation is due in 2010.

How UBR works and why it is so unpopular

Like both the long-standing domestic rates system and the previous local business tax before it, UBR is based not on a property's capital value, but on its *rateable* one. Local listing officers keep a rating list covering all business premises in their area. When first introduced in 1990, UBR caused uproar among many occupants of commercial and industrial land and buildings because of the huge increases in the values of those premises that had occurred since 1973, when the previous business tax—the 'general rate'— had been set.

UBR works as follows. Business premises are valued by the local listing officer (in Scotland, 'assessors'), based on how much they could have been let for in 1991. The amount that they are actually charged in UBR annually will then depend on a centrally determined calculation made by the Secretary of State for Communities and Local Government, known as the 'national multiplier' ('poundage' in Scotland). The multiplier is the number of pence in each pound of the value ascribed to a given business premises that its owner is liable to pay for that year. It is set at two levels: a 'standard' rate for middle-range and bigger companies, and a 'small business' rate for those that meet the necessary criteria to be defined as such by the Department for Business, Enterprise and Regulatory Reform (BERR) and the Treasury. Whichever category it fall into, the multiplier is normally held below the level of inflation for business properties with 'average' values.

UBR is therefore determined by the following formula:

$$\text{Rateable value of property} \times \text{National multiplier}$$

To cite a hypothetical example, a business, the premises of which have a rateable value of £50,000, would be expected to pay £25,000 in a year when the multiplier was set at 50p.

As of April 2008, empty business premises became liable for UBR for the first time—although, as with all bills, companies may challenge their ratings through a formal appeals process.

Separate multipliers are currently set for England and Wales. Scotland, in contrast, retains a different system of business rates, which is largely the same as that which first came into existence there in 1854. Although the 1988 Act amended the existing Scottish system as it did elsewhere in the UK, it remains distinct to this day. Until recently, when the *Scottish Government* began to 'pool' the revenue culled from business rates and redistribute it from the centre, one of its primary differences to the English and Welsh

UBR was the fact that it was still a 'local tax'—that is, one both collected and spent in each area.

And this is the single most contentious aspect of UBR. As with Council Tax, UBR bills are sent out to businesses by local billing authorities and revenue generated is initially collected by them—but that is where the similarities end. Having been raised locally, UBR revenue is gathered up by central government, which redistributes it to councils according to a population-based formula, taking into account variations in local socio-economic factors, such as unemployment levels (in a similar way to the RSG). In effect, this means that certain areas of the UK are 'subsidizing' others: the City of London, which is home to thousands of businesses—often occupying salubrious, and therefore highly rated, premises—will see millions of pounds raised through its UBR contribution siphoned off to poorer areas, such as the north-east, Devon and Cornwall, and parts of Wales.

Another controversial aspect of the UBR is the emphasis that it places on charging businesses according to the rateable values of the physical premises that they occupy, rather than their profit levels. A company operating a large factory on an out-of-town industrial estate, for example, will be charged significantly more than a neighbouring business based in a single office—irrespective of which earns the most money. Changes in the British economy over the past 15–20 years have seen many businesses that offer IT services, or legal and financial advice (the 'service sector'), generate huge profits—despite the fact that they often run their affairs from modest premises. In contrast, the decline of the manufacturing sector has seen the turnovers of old-style industries producing large consumer goods from expensive plants, using equally costly machinery, plummet.

These examples aside, like the Council Tax, UBR does offer reductions and exemptions for certain kinds of business property. In addition to those left unoccupied for large parts of the year, the exemptions include the following:

- agricultural land and buildings;
- place of public worship—for example, churches and mosques;
- property used by the disabled;
- fish farms;
- sewers;
- public parks;
- road crossings over watercourses—that is, traffic bridges;

- properties built in specified 'enterprise zones'—designations intended to rejuvenate deprived areas;
- property occupied by visiting armed forces.

Other sources of local authority revenue income

In addition to the Council Tax and grants, local authorities derive income from the following:

- council house rents;
- leisure service use—for example, swimming pools, sports centres, library fines, etc.;
- the collection of trade refuse;
- car parking tickets, fines, etc.;
- income from private contractors;
- the *European Social Fund (ESF)*, which provides grants to companies, voluntary groups, and communities in deprived areas to improve training and employment prospects.

The annual budget timetable at local level

As with most other organizations, the financial year for local authorities runs from 1 April to 31 March. While capital expenditure (to be dealt with next) has traditionally been planned on 3–5-year cycles, only in the past two years has the government sought to move revenue expenditure onto the same footing by introducing three-year grant settlements for authorities.

The basic process by which local spending is decided and provided for is outlined in Table 12.6.

Stories about local authorities being forced to make redundancies and/or slash their budgets for essential services as a result of real-term reductions in government grants have long been a staple of British newspapers. But in October 2008, as the full impact of the global banking crisis unfolded, it emerged that at least a hundred councils were facing a highly unusual threat to their solvency. The Local Government Association (LGA) revealed that up to £1bn of taxpayers' money had been collectively invested by councils and police authorities in collapsed Icelandic banks—notably, the

Table 12.6 The local authority budget-setting timetable

Time	Stage
April	The council holds a provisional meeting early in a given financial year to draw up an overall 'budget strategy' for the next one.
Late April/early May	A separate follow-up meeting is held to decide the levels of Council Tax needed to help to finance expenditure for the coming year.
Late May/early June	A full council meeting follows on from earlier meetings of the main financial committee. Until recently, this was normally known as the **policy and resources committee**; in new-style local authorities, it is the cabinet that fulfils the role of primary budget-setter (see p. 425). The council leader or elected **mayor** in charge of the council has to obtain the formal endorsement of their cabinet for major budgetary decisions.
July–September	Once an overall budget strategy has been decided on, broad revenue estimates for the following years must be ironed out.
October–December	The government will normally announce the following year's formula grant allocations around this time, forcing authorities to make significant adjustments to their budgeting for the coming financial year. This is usually the last stage at which it is possible for individual departments to increase their requests for revenue funding from the authority's 'pot' for the coming year. To do so, they must submit a **supplementary estimate**, outlining reasons for their increased outgoings.
January–February	The council is usually in a position to confirm and publish its final draft estimates for revenue spending.
February	The full council will have its say formally at a special meeting, deciding definitively on the levels of spending and Council Tax for the next financial year (budgets are normally approved in broad terms, but often with some modifications).

high-interest online institution Icesave. One authority alone, Kent County Council, had invested £50m, while *Transport for London (TfL)* had deposited £40m and the Metropolitan Police, £30m. Some of the news led to a media backlash against individual councils for their naivety in putting so much faith—and, more particularly, local taxpayers' money—in commercial institutions offering unrealistically generous rates. While a few had been remarkably canny (Brighton and Hove Council deciding not to trust the banks' promises), others were named and shamed for their foolhardiness. For example, Winchester City Council had invested £1m in Heritable, a subsidiary of Iceland's national bank Landsbanki, barely a fortnight before its parent company's collapse—apparently ignoring early warning signs that the country's institutions were on the brink.

At the time of writing, a final aid package had yet to be agreed by the UK Treasury and negotiations were ongoing with the Icelandic government, which (like Britain) nationalized several of its banks at the height of the stock market crash, including Kaupthing and Glitnir (see p. 224).

▌ The local authority capital budget

Spending on infrastructural improvements—such as land, roads, libraries, and other buildings and major items of equipment—is known as 'capital expenditure'. This is financed in a completely different way to the day-to-day running costs serviced by the revenue budget. The main sources of local government capital finance are as outlined in Table 12.7.

Capital borrowing

Although capital projects are funded in discrete ways that are significantly different from those that are used to finance revenue spending, they do incur a financial cost to local payers of the Council Tax. One regular outgoing that local authorities are compelled by central government to factor into their annual revenue budgets is a 'minimum revenue provision' to cover the systematic repayment of any outstanding debt. This is usually equivalent to 2 per cent of housing debt and 4 per cent of that incurred for other capital purposes in a given year. In addition to paying back the debit itself, it must also make provision for any interest on its long-term capital borrowing—that is, the so-called 'revenue implications of the capital programme'. These repayments of capital interest from the revenue account are known as the *debt charge*.

Despite the fact that it incurs interest and can take years to pay off, borrowing money to finance capital investment is often seen as politically desirable by both central and local government. The rationale is that, by taking out loans, authorities are *spreading the costs* of their spending over a number of years—meaning that it is not only local taxpayers living in the area at the time that a decision is taken to invest in a project who shoulder the costs, but anyone living in the area during its lifetime. In addition, borrowing avoids authorities having to fund an expensive project entirely up front, enabling them to fast-track the construction of schools, libraries, and other amenities that it would otherwise take them decades to afford.

Table 12.7 The main sources of capital finance available to local authorities

Source	How it works
Supported borrowing	Borrowing within credit approvals—i.e. limits agreed by the government—was introduced in 1990 to switch emphasis from controlling council *spending* to limiting *borrowing*. It is determined in three ways:
	(a) each council is allowed to borrow up to an 'affordable' figure in line with the Prudential Code endorsed by the Chartered Institute of Public Finance and Accountancy. Up to 2004, authorities were allocated an annual basic credit approval (BCA) - an aggregate figure decided by government departments in relation to the areas of activity that they covered (e.g. education), against which they issued annual capital guidelines (ACGs) relevant to these areas. This system was criticised for penalizing councils that did not spend their entire allocation in a given year. Councils could also apply for supplementary credit approvals, which were sometimes agreed late in the day in relation to specific projects (e.g. the allocation of revenues from the one-off 'windfall tax' on the profits of privatized utilities which funded the 1997 New Deal for Schools programme);
	(b) low-interest loans for specific projects from central government, through the **Public Works Loan Board (PWLB)**, a public body that operates within the UK Debt Management Office, an executive agency of the Treasury.
Prudential borrowing	Councils borrow money and repay it from their own resources without government support. They calculate how much they can afford to borrow according to a code drawn up a public sector consultancy, the Chartered Institute of Public Finance and Accountancy (CIPFA).
Capital receipts	The money raised through a local authority's sale of capital assets such as land or buildings, these are divided into two parts:
	(a) the *usable* part;
	(b) the *reserve* part.
	The council must set the latter aside for use in specified ways, such as paying back any existing debts. The former can be used to supplement BCAs to invest in new buildings, land, etc. The Secretary of State determines the percentage of usable capital receipts at any given time. In 1998, the agreed percentage was 50 per cent—except, controversially, for the receipts from the sale of council houses, only 25 per cent of which could be used for capital spending.
Capital grants	In addition to their RSGs, local authorities are sometimes allocated grants to help to finance specific projects. These can come from government departments, public bodies that distribute National Lottery money, or through hybrid arrangements that combine SCAs with grants (e.g. the Transport Supplementary Grant, Single Regeneration Budget, etc.).
European Union grants and loans	Money from EU pots, including: the **European Regional Development Fund** (for specific infrastructure projects and industrial development, usually in deprived areas); the European Social Fund (for training and employment initiatives aimed at young people); and structural funds covering a variety of 'objectives' (among them Objective 5b, which helped to fund socio-economic spending in deprived areas such as North Devon).

(continued)

Source	How it works
Private sector investment	This has often taken the form of an offer of development land and/or funding for capital works such as road access or traffic management from a private company, in exchange for its ability to recoup its investment at a later date by running a profit-based business related to the land in question (so-called **planning gain**—see also Chapter 16). The most favoured means of encouraging private capital investment today is through private finance initiative (PFI)—or public–private partnership (PPP)—arrangements for building new schools, care homes, etc. (see also pp. 238–9). These see private companies footing much of the initial construction cost, enabling the project to go ahead quicker than if it were to rely solely on public funds. In return, the companies will be paid back—with interest—over a period of years, in an arrangement that is similar to a mortgage. This means that the final cost to the public purse will be significantly higher than if the project had been paid for up front by the council. Recent examples of PFI-funded projects include Brighton and Hove's award-winning £14m 'eco' Jubilee Library, which is powered by solar energy.
Local lotteries	Local authorities are permitted to run their own lotteries under strict conditions outlined in the terms of the National Lottery Act 1993.
Local strategic partnerships	In January 2001, the government launched a new £36m Community Empowerment Fund designed to encourage community and voluntary organizations to cooperate in LSPs designed to tackle social deprivation. It aims to give £300,000-plus to each of the designated LSP areas through the government offices for the regions.

Similar arguments have been made by recent governments in favour of local authorities forming cofunding alliances with the private sector—so-called *public–private partnerships (PPPs)*, or *private finance initiatives (PFIs)*—to pay for capital projects that would otherwise take years to finance through public funds alone (see pp. 469 and 590).

▶ The future of local government finance

In the Local Government Act 2000, which introduced many sweeping changes to the governance of local authorities, Mr Blair outlined a view of their financial future free of significant shake-ups (the subsequently shelved nationwide review of Council Tax bands notwithstanding). Under pressure to address the continuing anomalies and anachronisms prevalent in the existing funding framework for councils, however, the government appointed Sir Michael Lyons to lead a full-blown inquiry into local government finance. In March 2007, he issued a wide-ranging series of recommendations for short-term, medium-term, and long-term reform. His suggested changes are listed in Table 12.8.

Table 12.8 Sir Michael Lyons' recommendations for the reform of local government finance

Short term	Medium term	Long term
More flexibility for councils to respond to local needs, by reducing the emphasis on specific and ring-fenced grants	Revalue Council Tax to update the tax base and improve fairness for households	Consider introducing a local income tax to make domestic taxation fairer
New powers to levy supplementary business rates, in consultation with business (legislation is expected in 2009, with the power due to come into effect in April 2010)	Reform Council Tax by adding new bands to reduce bills for those in the lowest value properties, paid for by increased bills for those in higher value properties—meaning that there should be no increase in average Council Tax bills as a result	Relocalizing business rates
A new power to introduce 'incentive charging' in relation to the disposal of domestic waste to help to manage pressures on Council Tax and to encourage recycling. The government is piloting schemes in five local authority areas.	Consider assigning a fixed proportion of Income Tax to local government	
An end to Council Tax capping	Find ways to improve incentives for focusing spending on priority areas within the grant system	
Changes to improve the fairness of Council Tax: recognizing that Council Tax Benefit is a rebate; automating the system to ensure the £1.8bn in unclaimed benefit helps the poorest households; raising the savings limit for pensioners to £50,000	Consider introducing the power to levy a 'tourist tax' if local government makes a strong case based on local public support	
Improving incentives for councils to promote economic growth		

→ Further reading

Challis, P. (2003) *Local Government Finance*, London: Local Government Information Unit. **Primarily aimed at local government professionals, this is nonetheless a thorough, detailed, but generally accessible guide to the complexities of revenue and capital budgeting.**

Fischel, W. A. (2005) *The Homevoter Hypothesis: How Home Values Influence Local Government Taxation, School Finance and Land-Use Policies*, Cambridge, MA: Harvard University Press. **Globe-spanning sociological text examining the impact of homeowners on the concentration and quality of local services, and the emergence of stakeholder-led localism.**

Hollis, G., Davies, H., Plokker, K., and Sutherland, M. (1994) *Local Government Finance: An International Comparative Study*, London: LGcommunication. **Again targeted at local government professionals, this offers useful comparisons between Britain's system of local government finance and those applied elsewhere, primarily in mainland Europe.**

Midwinter, A. F. and Monaghan, C. (1993) *From Rates to the Poll Tax: Local Government Finance in the Thatcher Era*, Edinburgh: Edinburgh University Press. **Thoughtful exploration of the turbulent Thatcherite reforms of local government finance, focusing on the replacement of the property-based rating system with the 'head tax' Community Charge.**

? Review questions

1. What is the difference between 'revenue' and 'capital' expenditure? Outline the main sources of each available to local councils.

2. How does the government determine how much money to give an individual local authority in grants each year, and how does it attempt to control how and where that money is spent?

3. How is the Council Tax calculated generally and how does this translate into the bills sent to households? List some of the exemptions and reductions.

4. What are the arguments for and against a property-based local tax?

5. Who sets and collects the uniform business rate (national non-domestic rate) and why is it so controversial?

Online resource centre

www.oxfordtextbooks.co.uk/orc/Morrison
Visit the Online Resource Centre that accompanies this book for web links and regular updates.

13

Local government decision-making

In the previous two chapters, we examined the nature of local authorities, how they evolved, and the funding systems underpinning them today. But how are councils structured *internally*? What form does their chain of command take, and how do they make decisions?

▌ Councillors and officers—who's who?

The work of local authorities is divided between two sets of individuals: *councillors* and *officers*.

Perhaps the best way to understand the distinction between the two is to draw an analogy between the work of councils and that of central government. Like central government, local authorities are composed of a series of spending departments the duties of which spread across the range of services for which they are responsible. These departments—covering areas such as education, housing, and social services—are each administered by paid civil servants who are expected to be politically neutral. *Appointed* to their posts on merit, like anyone else given a job, these are the *officers*.

At the same time, decisions to put money into one service area rather than another—and precise choices about how those services are run—are based on political judgements taken by elected members, whose role is to 'govern' the authority in a manner similar to the way in which members of Parliament (MPs) determine how Britain is ruled as a whole. Again like MPs, they each represent their own equivalent of a constituency. In the case of county councillors, these are known as electoral divisions (or 'county divisions'), while in unitary authorities, and district and borough councils, they are usually called wards (see p. 450). These *elected* officials are the *councillors*.

What kind of person becomes a councillor?

The 1972 Bains Report defined the duties of local councillors as to:

- direct and control the affairs of the local authority;
- take key policy decisions defining the objectives of the council and allocating the resources required to attain them;
- keep under review the progress and performance of local services.

This vision of the operation of local government was echoed 14 years later by the 1986 Widdecombe Report, which stressed the importance of the 'complementary relationship' between 'part-time councillors' and 'full-time officers with professional expertise'. The issue was also tackled by a 1990 Audit Commission discussion paper, entitled *We Can't Go on Meeting Like This*, which outlined a threefold role for councillors. Four years later, a report by Robert Gifford, then leader of Milton Keynes District Council, identified four 'typical' profiles for councillors. The main conclusions of the latter two papers are listed in Table 13.1.

Although councillors may be likened to MPs in that they are elected (and therefore accountable to voters), there is one fundamental difference between the two: unlike MPs, councillors do not receive a salary. The work that they do on behalf of local people is therefore essentially voluntary and, for those trying to juggle it with their day jobs, necessarily 'part-time'.

The fact that councillors are unsalaried has given rise to considerable controversy over the decades, not least because it leads to many councils being dominated politically by the retired and wealthy—that is, those with the time and money to devote themselves to unpaid work for their local communities. Because most councils and their committees have traditionally met for business during the normal working day, any employed person able to stand as a councillor has tended to be in a managerial post or running his

Table 13.1 Two models for effective councillors

What all councillors should aspire to be*	The four different types of councillor**
Politician—an agent of both policy and social change	*Strategists*—those driven to initiate change in a particular policy area
Representative—a guarantor that the local authority is held to account for prioritizing services, allocating resources, and its overall performance	*Community activists*—those keen to combat a particular local problem
Board member—willing to share collective responsibility for the organization and activities of the local authority, accountable to the dual threat of: (a) being *voted out* at an election, once every four years; (b) being personally *surcharged* for making serious mistakes in major decisions involving public expenditure and/or other responsibilities	*The conscientious*—those eager to repay society for advantages that they have enjoyed
	Stragglers—those who are 'last in the room when nominations are handed out'

* Audit Commission (1990) *We Can't Go On Meeting Like This: The Changing Role of Local Authority Members*, Management Paper No. 8, September, London: HMSO.

** Robert Gifford (1994) in *Municipal Journal*, June, London: Institute for Fiscal Studies.

or her own company—in other words, someone who is free to set his or her own hours, or to negotiate time off to attend meetings.

This combination of militating factors has also tended to discriminate against women, fewer of whom have historically been in such senior posts and many of whom have been housewives, with all the attendant childcare responsibilities. Ethnic minorities are also under-represented—even in areas of the country with large immigrant populations. Not for nothing does the media so often portray town halls as the preserve of pushy pensioners and white, middle-aged, middle-class men. Recent moves to introduce more evening sittings in some areas—particularly around London, where many people work long hours and commute long distances—have done something to address these issues, but not enough to satisfy critics.

In 1986, a now-famous survey of the makeup of UK local authorities by the government-appointed Widdecombe Committee found that 81 per cent of councillors were male and 59 per cent hailed from one of three socio-economic groups: professionals, employers and managers, and 'intermediate non-manual' jobs—together representative of only 23 per cent of the overall population. The average councillor at the time was aged 45, with none under the age of 24. The oldest was aged 85. The Committee made 88 recommendations for reform—although most concerned moves to democratize the *political* composition of councils and their committees. Many were implemented by the Local Government and Housing Act 1989.

According to recent research, little has improved. A report by the Employers' Organisation (EO) and the Improvement and Development Agency (IDeA), published in July 2005, found that while the proportion of women councillors had risen by half—from 19 per cent in 1986 to 29 per cent two decades later—the average age of councillors had *increased*, to 58 years old. Just under 87 per cent of all councillors were over the age of 45. Ethnic minorities also continued to fare poorly: only 3.5 per cent were non-white (compared to 8.4 per cent of the UK population). The findings prompted a belated call in a speech to the Labour Party Conference in September 2007 from newly appointed Communities and Local Government Secretary Hazel Blears for more younger people, women, and people from immigrant communities to stand (and be encouraged to stand) as councillors.

Almost as contentious as the question of how to make councillors more representative of multicultural twenty-first-century Britain is the issue of how much work should be expected of them, given their as yet 'unpaid' status. Various attempts have been made to find out exactly how much time is spent by the average member on council duties both inside and outside official hours—that is, meetings. Widdecombe compared his own research with that contained in an earlier study, published in 1964. At that time, the average number of hours that councillors spent on their duties was 52 a month; by 1986, this had risen to 74. According to a 1998 *Green Paper,* this figure had increased to 97 by 1992.

Perhaps the most comprehensive survey of councillors' hours to date, however, was undertaken by Ken Young and Nirmala Rao on behalf of the Joseph Rowntree Foundation, and published in 1994. Carried out among a large sample of 1,682 councillors in 53 local authority areas, *The Role of Local Government Councillors in 1993* found that:

- councillors spent 74 hours a month on average on council business— exactly the same as the number of hours found by the 1986 Widdecombe Report;
- a fifth of councillors felt that the hours were 'about right';
- most felt that their most rewarding duty was 'representing' their wards, with only a small minority preferring policymaking, or 'carrying out their party's programme';
- councillors spent most of their time (56 per cent) in council itself, whether attending meetings or liaising with council officers;

- most councillors were happy with the existing system of decision-making (rather than craving a *cabinet*-based system like that used at Westminster);

- there was widespread scepticism about the idea of adopting a Westminster-style cabinet model, but wide support for introducing Commons-style scrutiny committees.

The last two of these observations were ultimately to feed into a root-and-branch reorganization of the internal chains of command within councils, instigated by Labour in the Local Government Act (LGA) 2000 (examined in detail later this chapter).

Councillors' allowances and expenses

Introducing more 'flexible' working hours is not the only way in which local authorities have sought to increase participation by younger working people, women, and those from less affluent backgrounds. In a radical attempt to widen participation, some councils are increasingly bending the rules to offer more generous allowances in lieu of a formal 'wage'.

Although councillors are unsalaried, there has been a recognized system of allowances and expenses in place for some time. Allowances are designed to give elected members a modest payment for their time spent attending meetings, while they may claim expenses to reimburse themselves for the cost of return travel to meetings by car, bicycle, or public transport. Expenses are also available to cover other outgoings that may arise out of their official duties, such as paying for overnight accommodation, meals bought during the course of such business, and subsidizing domestic telephone bills for phone calls related to their pastoral work with local electors. Councillors under the age of 70 are also now eligible to join the generous Local Government Pension Scheme.

The two main types of allowance are:

- the *basic allowance*—a flat-rate annual payment, which is usually paid—like a salary—on a monthly basis, for *all* councillors representing a specific authority, to which they each become entitled from the moment they are elected as members;

- the *special responsibility allowance*—an additional payment received by councillors who, as well as representing their electors, hold posts within the council carrying extra responsibility. The size of allowances varies according to how much responsibility they have: a council leader (the most senior councillor) will receive the biggest special responsibility allowance, while members of subcommittees and committees, other than their chairpersons, will be paid much smaller ones.

Each council is free to set its own allowance levels, subject to certain restrictions. Since the LGA 2000, every council has been required by law to establish an *independent remuneration panel* comprising at least three individuals—none of whom are themselves councillors. It is the panel's task to review, and adjudicate on, any application by the authority to increase or otherwise amend its allowances.

Recent surveys point towards a wide disparity in the sizes of member allowances paid by different local authorities—with certain councils offering payments at a level comparable to full-time salaries. According to a 2006 survey by Local Government Analysis and Research, the data arm of the Local Government Association (LGA), the average basic allowance paid by British local authorities was £5,648, rising to £9,512 for metropolitan district councillors. Special responsibility allowances averaged £16,356 for council leaders across the UK, with those in London boroughs receiving an average of £31,784. In general, councils that pay more argue that they are trying to encourage a more representative cross-section of the community to stand. Others, such as Plymouth City Council, have argued that, to perform their council work properly, members need to treat it as a full-time job—and to be able to do this those without independent means require allowances that are equivalent to a liveable wage.

Expenses are also becoming more generous. In 2006–07, as well as offering its members a basic allowance of £9,381 (£8,447 for those newly elected), and its leader a special responsibility allowance rising to £35,000 by 2009–10, Richmond Borough Council in Surrey was offering 'subsistence' expenses of more than £6 for lunch and nearly £8 for dinner, car mileage at 38p a mile, and (in a nod to the green lobby perhaps) 50p a mile expenses for those travelling by bicycle.

Arguments for and against the idea of paying councillors more money are outlined in Table 13.2.

Meet the experts—the role of local government officers

The number of officers employed by councils varies widely and is ultimately decided by how many resources councillors allocate to finance them. In broad terms, however, every council is obliged to provide certain statutory services and its administration is therefore split, like Whitehall, into

Table 13.2   Arguments for and against higher remuneration for councillors

For	Against
Councillors need to work full-time hours to do their jobs properly. Without pay, this means that councils will inevitably be dominated by the affluent, the middle-aged, and the retired.	Standing as a councillor should be seen as a vocation, or a call to public duty. If councillors were paid salaries, they would just become like any other employee.
Low allowances foster cultures of 'enthusiastic amateurism', on the one hand, and world-weary time serving, on the other. Proper pay is needed to make sure that all councillors are well-informed, motivated, and put in sufficient hours to give adequate representation to their local electorate.	Research has shown that the role of the councillor is essentially a 'part-time' commitment. Councillors can perform their duties to a high standard by attending a few monthly meetings and being occasionally available by phone, so holding down a paid job as well should be no problem.
Relying on modest allowances skews council membership towards the management classes and the independently wealthy, and bars many women and younger people reliant on working for a living (especially those with families) from standing as local authority candidates.	The public finances are already very tight at local level, with costly services in education, social services, and other areas forever overstretched. Paying councillors would divert Council Tax revenue and other funding away from vital local services.
No one else—even in the public or voluntary sectors—would be expected to work the hours that councillors need to in order to get their job done properly with so little recompense. The most qualified councillors could earn more working fewer hours in the private sector.	Paying councillors too much money would run the risk of attracting the 'wrong people'. Councillors should be people motivated to 'give something back' to their local communities out of a sense of public service—not because of the high financial rewards.

a number of different departments. Each of these departments tends to be run by a qualified professional with expertise in the relevant area.

There are two main types of council spending department: *service* and *central*. As the term suggests, the former are concerned with delivering services to the public—that is, housing, education, social services, etc. Central departments are those concerned with the *administration* of the council's functions—principally, its legal and financial departments, and those devoted to corporate activities, such as public relations (PR) and marketing.

Officers, like Whitehall civil servants, must be *politically neutral*—whatever their levels of seniority. Those in senior grades are also *politically restricted* (see pp. 132 and 453). Despite being required to avoid political bias, however, officers are expected to provide councillors with policy advice based on their knowledge and experience. Their roles are to:

- *advise*—defined by the Widdecombe Report as giving 'politically impartial' information and support to aid councillors in their decision-making;

- *support* the executive, non-executive, and scrutiny arms of the local authority—that is, to help *all* councillors, not only the most senior ones—as outlined in 2000 by the then Department for Transport, Local Government and the Regions (DTLR).

Each department is headed by its own equivalent of a Whitehall **permanent secretary.** Among the most influential of these are the leading civil servants in the biggest spending areas: the director of social services, and the chief planning, transport, and education officers.

Higher up still are three officials whose role is to oversee the workings of the council as a whole:

- the *chief executive*—also known as the **head of the paid service,** the chief executive is the council's main policy adviser, manager, and co-ordinator, and is expected to have the requisite experience and maturity to be able to carry out this role effectively. Chief executives often perform the role of 'acting returning officer' at elections, on behalf of the official **returning officer**—normally, the council chairperson or mayor (see pp. 135–7 and 455). He or she also has statutory duties to oversee local emergency procedures;

- the *monitoring officer*—the job of the monitoring officer is to report to members, in consultation with the chief executive, any acts of mal-administration or breaches of good conduct by officers or councillors, and to uphold the council's *code of conduct* (see pp. 436–8). He or she is normally also the council's chief legal officer and should be a trained lawyer. It is also the monitoring officer's role to make sure that the council is acting within its statutory remit at all times—that is, to make sure that it does not overreach the powers granted to it;

- the *chief financial officer* (or *treasurer,* or *director of finance*)—responsible for overseeing the administration of the council's finances, the chief financial officer must be a member of a recognized accountancy body. He or she may also be known as the 'director of central services' or 'section 151 officer' (a reference to the statutory provision from which his or her authority derives).

Under the LGA 2000, chief executives are formally barred from being appointed as monitoring officers. In addition, like any other officer, chief executives, monitoring officers, and chief financial officers can all be subject to a statutory disciplinary procedure that could ultimately lead to their dismissal in the case of any misconduct.

To streamline administration of its affairs, improve efficiency, and avoid duplication, each council now has a chief officers' management team. This is a group of senior officers, headed by the chief executive, that meets weekly or fortnightly to discuss policy ideas that might be put forward for councillors' consideration at meetings and/or issues that are relevant to more than one department.

New models for service delivery—how officers' roles are changing

Until the 1980s, the bulk of local authority services—from refuse collection and street cleaning, through to building, equipping, and maintaining schools and care homes—were carried out directly by council employees. But over the past 25 years, there has been a fundamental shift in the role of councils from being *direct providers* to being *enablers*. Whereas everyone from local parking attendants to account clerks would all once have been local authority employees, today, they are likely to be on the payroll of a private company, voluntary organization, or agency. Rather than delivering local services through the aegis of their own officers and departments, councils are charged with financing, coordinating, and 'commissioning' those services—and the private and voluntary sectors have as much chance of winning contracts to provide them as do local authorities themselves.

The system that ushered in this system of contract-based local service delivery was known as 'compulsory competitive tendering' (CCT). Introduced in the Local Government, Planning, and Land Act 1980, this was a means by which local authorities were forced to put services out to tender—that is, to invite bids from public, voluntary, and/or private sector organizations. The idea was that the most 'cost-effective' bid would be successful, cutting waste and bureaucracy, and giving local taxpayers better value for money—while having the added benefit of curbing the influence of unions, following the mass strikes of the 1970s.

Initially, CCT applied largely to 'blue collar' areas of service provision, such as building maintenance and construction work, but it was extended by the Local Government Act 1988 to cover refuse collection, street cleaning, school catering, and other areas. A further extension was introduced by the Local Government Act 1992, which enabled councils to outsource so-called 'professional' and/or 'support services', such as their information technology (IT), marketing, and PR roles. Councils that wished to continue providing services in-house were required to set up their own arms-length 'companies' to compete for the contracts on an equal footing with the private and voluntary sectors. The name given to council-owned companies competing for building and/or maintenance contracts for things such as schools, care homes, and council housing was 'direct labour organizations' (DLOs). Those vying to provide services such as refuse collection and school catering were called 'direct service organizations' (DSOs).

In practice, the CCT system was constrained by the following factors:

- exceptions to the need to tender for service provision were granted to smaller councils—notably, shire districts—under the *de minimis* principle;

- contracting out of corporate and administrative services was eventually given a blanket exemption from CCT;

- following early complaints about service cutbacks after contracting out, ministers were eventually forced to accept advice that the ability to provide a service at a cheap price should *not* be the only criterion for awarding contracts.

Despite these restrictions, councils were soon complaining that they were being 'forced' to contract services out to private providers. Other criticisms of CTT are listed in Table 13.3, which can be found on the Online Resource Centre that accompanies this book.

Although DLOs and DSOs had a hard time fending off competition from the private sector, in practice CCT had some positive knock-on effects for them. Many councils decided to group together a number of DSOs and/or DLOs covering different services under a senior chief officer—known as 'contract services divisions'—giving them a more professional overall management structure and producing some of the economies of scale enjoyed by large private companies. When 'support services' such as personnel (or human resources), legal, and finance departments are run in-house by councils, they are regulated by a formal contractual arrangement called a 'service level agreement' (SLA).

When Labour returned to power in 1997, they scrapped the existing CTT framework. But anyone hoping for a wholesale reversal of the policy of forcing councils to put local services out to tender was to be disappointed, because it was simply replaced with a new system: Best Value (BV). The party's 1998 local government Green Paper—*Modernizing Local Government: Improving Local Services through Best Value*—introduced a new statutory obligation for councils to hire the most suitable provider—whether public, private, or voluntary.

Ministers spelt out four 'defining elements' of BV to which they must adhere:

- attaining 'economic, efficient, and effective' services (the '3 Es');
- regular service reviews within which they must demonstrate that they had provided Best Value—by comparing their services to those of other private and public providers, and consulting local businesses and residents;
- auditing and measuring their performance, with the aim of cutting costs and raising quality. Performance would be monitored through 'Best Value performance reviews' (BVPRs), against 'Best Value performance indicators' (BVPIs), and disseminated through 'Best Value performance plans' (BVPPs);
- being prepared for government intervention if Best Value was not attained.

In theory, introducing Best Value meant that less emphasis would be paid to the wisdom of contracting out services to the private sector for the sake of it—unless it could demonstrably offer local people a better deal. There was a perception that, in the past, some councils had opted to outsource work purely to cut costs and what had often resulted was an inferior alternative delivered by a company, the first priority of which was to pay its shareholders, rather than to provide a high-quality service for local taxpayers. The 1998 Green Paper accused CTT of 'neglecting' service quality, and producing 'uneven and uncertain' efficiency gains, 'antagonism' between rival providers, and 'significant costs for employees', including high staff turnover and demoralization. Despite such statements, councils are still expected (if not legally compelled) to put contracts out to tender—and, even though price is no longer the biggest factor in determining successful bids, many argue that Best Value is CTT in all but name.

The means by which central government monitors whether councils are indeed delivering Best Value and makes this information available to the public are examined in Chapter 14.

The politicization of council officers—the rise of political assistants

While local government officers are expected to be politically neutral, as early as the Widdecombe Report, it was recognized that senior councillors might benefit from access to professional political advice from central government-style special advisers (see pp. 117–19). Widdecombe envisaged 'political assistants' being hired in the following circumstances:

- for councils the chief executives of which are 'by disposition' managers—not political;
- where a council is 'hung', with three parties all holding the balance of power.

The Report emphasized that appointees must be *overt*—that is, that no council should employ officers who acted unofficially as political advisers. Its ideas were further elaborated on by the 1989 Act, which allowed councils to employ political assistants under terms listed in Table 13.4.

In addition, elected mayors under the new local government models introduced by the LGA 2000 would be entitled to appoint their own political assistants. As mayors of London, Ken Livingstone and his successor, Boris Johnson, hired several *spin doctors,* in addition to special policy gurus such as US public transport expert Bob Kiley, the former's adviser on the part-privatization of London Underground, and Lord Rogers, his architecture guru. While both of these were effectively consultants, journalists should be wary when dealing with a local authority or its leadership through political assistants, as opposed to press officers. As political appointees, they are not expected to give as objective a view as their press office colleagues, who are essentially politically neutral officers.

Table 13.4 Conditions of employment for political assistants

Condition	What it means
Terms of employment	Councils must issue formal **standing orders** relating to appointments before they are made
Restrictions on numbers	No more than three such posts were made available
Fair allocation between the parties	Each political grouping to have only one assistant
Objective recruitment process	Appointments to be made on merit
Restricted salaries	The gross annual salary of such appointees did not exceed a set level (in October 1995, £25,044). It would be reviewed periodically by the Secretary of State.
Limits to political activity	The post was treated as *politically restricted*, like those of senior officers. Contracts were fixed-term, ending no later than 12 months after the next local election.
No electioneering	Assistants only allowed to carry out political work for councillors 'in their capacity as councillors' and not for any other purposes (e.g. canvassing at election time)
No executive powers	No functions of the council itself were delegated to assistants

▌ The local government hierarchy under the pre-LGA 2000 system

Prior to the LGA 2000, one fundamental truth applied to all councillors, irrespective of whether the parties to which they were affiliated held overall power on their local authorities: they each had a *direct say* in at least some policy decisions taken by that council. Policies were initially referred for debate to specialist subcommittees, or committees of councillors covering the relevant areas, and had to be approved at that level before ever being presented for final approval to the full council. If they were rejected at this first hurdle, the full council would never get to discuss them. If reworded, diluted, consolidated, or otherwise amended at this early stage, then the version of the policy voted on by the full council had usually been substantially shaped by the committee. Because every councillor—whether from the ruling political group, a minority party, or none at all ('independents')—sat on at least one such committee, they each had a direct input, however minor, into the policymaking process. Committee decisions were normally couched as 'recommendations'—that is, they were subject to final approval by the full council. The council also reserved the right to reject their rulings, or to *refer back* items for reconsideration. Committees did, however, constitute an important part of the day-to-day policymaking function of their local authorities. This 'bottom-up' approach to policymaking is illustrated by the flow chart in Figure 13.1.

Figure 13.1 A flow chart depicting the decision-making process in 'old-style' local authorities and district councils continuing to operate under 'alternative arrangements'

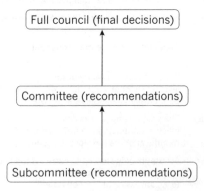

In addition to giving all councillors a direct say in policy decisions—and treating them all as 'equals' when it came to voting in full council—the pre-LGA 2000 local authority set-up preserved a simple hierarchy of councillors not dissimilar to that seen among MPs in the House of Commons. A political party that won sufficient seats in a local election to secure an 'overall majority' on the council would become 'the government' in all but name, and its leader would automatically be appointed *leader of the council*—effectively, local 'prime minister'. But beyond this, there were no visible divisions in 'status' between members of the ruling party—or ruling group—and the other councillors on the authority.

There were three types of local authority committee under this pre-LGA 2000 model:

- *standing (statutory)*—that is, *permanent* committees set up to discharge a specific function (for example, to take decisions on planning, education, environmental services);

- *ad hoc*—often given briefs directly related to the above, but set up to consider specific issues in greater detail than was possible on standing committees;

- *area-based*—formed to look at policy governing specific geographical areas under a council's control. They sometimes contained members of the local community beside councillors and even had budgets delegated to them.

As in Parliament, the political composition of committees and subcommittees tended to reflect the balance of power in the main council chamber at any one time. If the Tories were in overall control of the council, a majority of committee chairpersons would hail from that party and overall membership of committees would be more or less proportionate to the distribution of seats between parties on the full council. Where no political group had overall control of the authority, standing committees sometimes had no permanent chair; instead, a different chairperson was elected to serve on a meeting-by-meeting basis.

Other conventions governing old-style committees included:

- they could 'co-opt' non-councillors to serve on them, either temporarily or on an ongoing basis. These de facto members did not have voting rights—unless they were church representatives sitting on an education-related committee;

- mayors, council chairpersons, and leaders were treated as *ex officio* members of *all* committees in addition to those of which they were normal members. Significantly, this gave them the right both to attend *and* vote on these committees;

- councils had to avoid any perceived or real conflicts of interest by ensuring that committees with related functions had different memberships;

- in addition to committees, councils often set up working parties comprising both councillors and officers to consider policy options in detail. There has been some controversy about these de facto bodies, because they did not necessarily open their doors to the media and it was a moot point whether they were obliged to do so.

Despite the influence of committees, like the governing party at Westminster, ruling groups tended to come up with many of the policy ideas debated at full council meetings, even under the 'old-style' system. Indeed, assuming that they had big enough majorities after a local election, they could normally muster sufficient votes to drive through their proposals. The leader was also usually appointed chairperson of the single most powerful local authority committee on the council: the *policy and resources committee.* Because this committee controlled the council's purse strings, it had to approve any major policy decision likely to involve significant resources and could veto those it considered too costly. Most councils covering fewer than 85,000 inhabitants have now abolished this committee (see p. 401), although some have retained an equivalent 'board' or 'panel'.

But beyond these powers, the ruling group had little real 'executive power' in the sense that the government and prime minister do at national level. The leader could appoint a cabinet of senior colleagues, but it had no authority to make executive policy decisions behind closed doors, as commonly occurs at Westminster. Moreover, in practice, the limited majorities attained by ruling groups in many local elections meant that coalitions were commonplace—forcing the largest party to compromise many of its policy ideas.

At present, the 'old-style' decision-making system is retained by certain councils. Some dragged their feet, preferring the existing model to the new ones introduced by the LGA 2000, but others—primarily, district councils covering fewer than 85,000 people—were permitted to use 'alternative arrangements' indefinitely by the government. They have been allowed to bypass the new-style executive models on condition that they adopt a committee-based system with sufficient scrutiny powers to carry out the same functions competently. Arrangements were agreed by the Secretary of State on a case-by-case basis, but after the initial grace period, firm deadlines have now been put in place by which all authorities must convert to one of the new models. County councils across the UK had to have switched by 31 December 2008 at the latest. The last possible changeover dates for the other types of council are 31 December 2009 for London borough and metropolitan district councils, and 31 December 2010 for district and borough councils.

▶ Local government hierarchies since the LGA 2000

So all local authorities have been given notice to adopt one of the new forms of executive management introduced by the LGA 2000—but what form do these hierarchies take? The main difference between the 'old-style' decision-making system and its principal replacements is that, under the new structures, the balance of power between 'ordinary councillors' and those in the ruling group has shifted radically in favour of the latter. Whereas once all councillors were active participants in the local legislative process, today's council leaders—or, where adopted, *directly elected mayors*—hold a disproportionate level of power. Their cabinets, too, have moved from being largely nominal entities to ones with the power to take executive decisions that the rest of the council has little chance to overturn.

The three types of executive management introduced by the LGA 2000 were:

- the leader of the council and cabinet;
- the directly elected mayor and cabinet;
- the directly elected mayor and council manager.

Although actively encouraged by central government to adopt one of the LGA 2000-style models for local authority decision-making, councils must go through the following two-stage consultation process before introducing their chosen new system on the ground.

1. They must issue an explanation to the public of the three models of executive structure.

2. They must carry out a more detailed formal consultation among local people.

Once a decision has been taken to adopt one of the new models, the council must agree the wording of a formal constitution with the Communities Secretary. Any subsequent attempt to change it would require the constitution to be rewritten in consultation with ministers.

Under all three of the new models, the position of the leader or mayor is of paramount importance. All LGA 2000-style councils are further divided hierarchically into the following functions: *executive, non-executive*, and *scrutiny*. As is the case at national level, the term 'executive' refers to the powers exercised by most senior councillors—that is, members of the cabinet, plus the leader (or mayor). Like the prime minister and his or her **Cabinet,** these individuals may meet and initiate policy in private—even taking final decisions on more minor matters—without the need first to consult committees and subcommittees, as was the case under the 'old-style' system.

The terms 'scrutiny' and 'non-executive' both apply to committees and subcommittees. Each describes one of the two (diluted) roles undertaken by committees under the post-LGA regimes.

'Scrutiny' refers to the committees and subcommittees charged with focusing on specific policy proposals related to the workings of individual spending departments—for example, education, social services, or transport. Their role, then, is like a watered-down version of the standing or statutory committees and subcommittees that existed under the 'old-style' model: like parliamentary standing committees, they have the ability to amend proposals, raise concerns, and call witnesses, but little power to reject or overturn executive decisions. Some local authorities, such as Durham County Council, have adopted a scrutiny system featuring a range of subject-specific subcommittees, beneath a single committee—known as the **overview and scrutiny** committee—with overall responsibility for the scrutiny function.

'Non-executive' decisions, meanwhile, are taken by the other form of new-style local authority committee. Unlike scrutiny committees, non-executive committees actually have **delegated powers** to take decisions—that is, to reject or give final approval to a matter brought before them. The range of matters referred to non-executive committees is extremely limited, however, compared to those deliberated over by committees under the 'old-style' model. A planning subcommittee or committee, for example, might take a decision to reject or approve an application brought before it—without the need for it to be referred on to the full council or cabinet for final approval—but this would only apply to *minor* applications (for example, relating to a small extension to someone's house). The outcome of such applications will already largely have been dictated by the local authority's existing planning rules, as previously agreed by the full council. More major applications—for example, a bid by Tesco to open an out-of-town superstore—will have to go to the full council for final approval.

One of the Blair government's principal arguments for the new-style hierarchies was a desire to 'speed up' the pace of council decision-making. By reducing the ability of committees and subcommittees to hold up final policy decisions, it hoped to streamline council business. But the stark division between the influence on policymaking exerted today by cabinet members as against 'ordinary' members of the council has led to severe criticism of the Blair reforms—not least from veteran councillors who have suddenly found themselves with less of a 'voice' than ever before in the running of their local authorities. The new-style models are widely viewed as having introduced 'two tiers' of councillors, as at Westminster: a powerful 'front bench' and a noisy, but ultimately toothless, 'back bench'.

Under all three 'new-style' executive models, the full council (which used to have to give final approval for virtually all policies before they were implemented) is now only concerned with the most significant decisions. These proposals—defined as those affecting two or more wards or electoral divisions of the authority—are called *key decisions*. An example of a key decision might be one used to determine a proposal for a *Council Tax* rise, or a planning application by developers keen to build a new road (by definition, this is almost certain to affect more than one ward, because it is likely to cut through several). Each month, in the interests of transparency to local electors, every authority is required to publish a *forward plan* of all key decisions that it intends to take in the coming four weeks.

Whatever internal decision-making framework they favour, there are certain other terms that are common to all local authorities in relation to their proceedings:

- the specific roles and powers delegated by a council to its committees, subcommittees, and cabinet/executive are known as *prescribed functions;*
- whenever final decisions are taken on a matter before a committee, the full council, or cabinet, these are known as *resolved items.*

Figure 13.2 illustrates the top-down decision-making process that defines the chain of command in post-LGA councils. Table 13.5 gives an overview of arguments for and against the LGA 2000 hierarchical models.

The 'leader and cabinet' model

Of the three new executive management options introduced by the LGA 2000, that with the most similarities to the existing system is the 'leader and cabinet' model. As was the case under the 'old-style' council hierarchy, the leader is normally the head of his or her party—usually, that which secured the most seats in the preceding local election. Like 'old-style' leaders, he or she will choose a cabinet made up of close confidantes on the council, normally drawn from his or her own party, or (where no single party has overall control) his or her party and any others with which it is in coalition.

But this is where the similarities between 'old-style' and 'new-style' leader-and-cabinet systems end. The new-style cabinets—increasingly referred to as 'executives'—are much more like those formed by prime ministers than the ones that preceded them. Individual cabinet members are given their own policy briefs—for example, education, social services, or housing—and

Figure 13.2 A flow chart depicting the decision-making process in post-LGA 2000 councils

Table 13.5   Arguments for and against the LGA 2000 management models

For	Against
Allowing leaders, elected mayors, and cabinets to take some executive decisions without having to gain permission from committees makes the local legislative process faster—and more effective—than when committees had to approve everything.	The new models have created a 'two-tier' internal council structure, in which frontbench councillors not only have more influence on policymaking than backbench ones—but sometimes are the *only* councillors with any obvious influence on decisions.
Introducing elected mayors is a way of engaging people more closely with local democracy—giving them a direct say in decisions over the leadership of their council. In this sense, it is more democratic and councils are more accountable than under the old system.	By giving small groups of individuals executive powers, we are replicating the 'elective dictatorships' sometimes perceived to exist at national level—with a handful of councillors, at most, driving the agenda. Councils are therefore *less* democratically accountable, if anything, than in the past.
The LGA 2000 laid down a process by which local electorates could demand referenda on the introduction of elected mayors—an example of bottom-up local democracy in action. It also introduced the concept of local constitutions, which allows local authorities to change their leadership structures, subject to the government's agreement.	Introducing three alternative models for council leadership has led to a patchwork landscape of local authority hierarchies across the UK. This confuses voters and can lead to inconsistent local representation.

the delegated powers necessary to enable them to devise policy and, in some cases, make executive decisions. Although they are generally expected to consult with cabinet colleagues, in some cases, they may take executive action with little input from any other councillors—either 'backbench' or 'frontbench'. The same applies to the leader.

The committee system has therefore gone from being a *proactive* agent in policymaking to a largely *reactive* one. Meanwhile, meetings of the full council—which, at least nominally, still has the final say over whether a policy is approved—are portrayed by critics of the new system as mere 'rubber stamps' for decisions already finalized behind closed doors in cabinet. Similar charges are made of the second of the three models.

The 'directly elected mayor and cabinet' model

As explained in Chapter 11, there is a long-standing tradition among district and borough councils and metropolitan district councils of appointing mayors. The office of mayor has customarily, however, been a ceremonial one—with elected councillors taking it in turns to spend a year in the role, before passing on their chain of office to a colleague. While serving as mayor, the individual will officiate over civic duties (opening fetes, visiting schools, etc.), as well as chairing meetings of the full council. In this capacity, like the *Speaker* of the Commons, he or she will temporarily drop his or her party allegiances and his or her right to take part in policy votes.

Directly elected mayors occupy an entirely different position. Firstly, unlike both council leaders and old-style mayors, they are not themselves councillors; elected mayors are instead voted in by their local electorates in a separate ballot run *alongside* the main council elections in their areas. When the Conservative candidate for London mayor, Boris Johnson, thwarted Ken Livingstone's bid to win a third term in May 2008, the separate election for members of the *Greater London Authority (GLA)* saw the Tories lose one seat to Labour (although they remained the biggest party, having eight seats to Labour's six). In this respect, the post of elected mayor bears more similarities to that of the US president than the British prime minister. While no Labour prime minister could remain in post long after a general election in which the Tories won more seats, the same is not true of presidents: the 2006 US congressional elections returned narrow Democrat majorities in both the Senate and the House of Representatives, but Republican president George W. Bush stayed in post for two more years. This mirrored the 2004 London mayoral contest, in which Mr Livingstone won his second term, despite Labour's losing control of the GLA (dropping to five seats, against the Tories' nine).

Before being permitted to introduce elected mayors, local authorities are required to hold a *referendum* of the local electorate; conversely, if 5 per cent of that electorate decides that it favours the mayoral system, it may *demand* a referendum—whatever the council's own view. Where referenda are held, the question used adopts the following standard wording:

> ❝ Are you in favour of the proposal for [name of city/borough] to be run in a new way, which includes a mayor, who will be elected by the voters of [that place], to be in charge of the council's services and to lead [name of authority] and the community it serves? ❞

Labour's hope was that *all* councils would have initiated a consultation within 6–9 months of the passage of the LGA 2000—and that many would favour the mayoral option. In practice, it took until February 2002 for most English councils to publish proposals and, when they did, 80 per cent opted for the leader-and-cabinet model. As of September 2008, only 13 had introduced elected mayors. The Greater London Authority Act 1999 made the GLA the first council to adopt it. The slow pace of reform elsewhere has been put down, in part, to the fact that whenever a referendum is lost, another cannot be held by the same council for at least five years. Of the 35 such referenda held so far, 23 failed to secure a majority in favour of an elected mayor. In addition, campaigns are under way at time of writing in four local authority areas to abolish the post: Stoke-on-Trent, Doncaster, Lewisham, and Hartlepool (where the position has twice been won by the Hartlepool United Football Club mascot, 'H'Angus the Monkey'—alias Stuart Drummond). The 13 councils operating an elected mayoral system as of September 2008 are listed in Table 13.6.

In an effort to increase the number of elected mayors, the government published a raft of new proposals under the title *Communities in Control* in July 2008, which aimed to make it easier for local electors to trigger a referendum on introducing mayoral elections, by enabling those campaigning for 'yes' votes to recruit supporters through online petitions. The plans were announced shortly after the failure of a campaign led by the *Birmingham Mail* to recruit the 36,000 electors required to kickstart a mayoral contest in Birmingham.

Table 13.6   Local authorities with directly elected mayors (September 2008)

District	Type	Mayor	Party
Bedford	District	Frank Branston	Independent
Doncaster	Metropolitan borough	Martin Winter	Labour
Hackney	London borough	Jules Pipe	Labour
Hartlepool	Unitary authority	Stuart Drummond	Independent
Lewisham	London borough	Steve Bullock	Labour
London	Region of England	Ken Livingstone	Labour, first elected as independent
Mansfield	District	Tony Egginton	Independent
Middlesbrough	Unitary authority	Ray Mallon	Independent
Newham	London borough	Robin Wales	Labour
North Tyneside	Metropolitan borough	John Harrison	Labour
Stoke-on-Trent	Unitary authority	Mark Meredith	Labour
Torbay	Unitary authority	Nicholas Bye	Conservative
Watford	District	Dorothy Thornhill	Liberal Democrats

NOTE: A regularly updated version of this table can be found on the Online Resource Centre that accompanies this book.

The same policy document set out a number of other proposals for bringing council decision-making closer to electors. In particular, it emphasized the idea of so-called 'double *devolution*'—that is, devolving lower-level, day-to-day decisions on how to run amenities such as parks and community centres from elected councils to community-based groups led by their users.

The 'mayor and council manager' model—and its demise

One of the most contentious aspects of the new-style council management models introduced by the LGA 2000 is the extent to which power to take executive decisions can now be delegated to individuals or small groups of individuals—with little input from the majority of councillors. And it is not only frontbench councillors who have the authority to make such decisions: senior *officers* are also increasingly being handed delegated powers.

The starkest illustration of this move towards officer-led decision-making—seen by some as seriously undermining councils' democratic accountability—may be found in the third of the executive management models proposed in the LGA 2000: the 'elected mayor and council manager' model. Under this system, executive decision-making powers are vested in only one individual other than the elected mayor: the council manager, who is a senior officer appointed (rather than elected) to the second most influential position in the authority.

That more has not been made of this questionably democratic set-up in the national media must largely be down to the lack of interest expressed in it by local authorities: by 2006, only one council in England—Stoke-on-Trent—had adopted it. Stoke is in the process of negotiating a new constitution that will almost certainly lead to its abandoning the role of council manager (a post filled by its chief executive) by the end of 2009. It is looking to replace its current management model with one of three alternatives—the third of which would require a private Bill to be passed by the Commons, because it would be unique to the city:

- an *elected mayor and cabinet*—in which a mayor would be elected by the voters and would then choose a cabinet from existing councillors;
- a *leader and cabinet*—in which a councillor would be appointed by other councillors as leader for a four-year term, with a cabinet;
- a *directly elected executive*—in which a group of candidates would be directly elected by the voters to form a leader and cabinet.

In the wake of Stoke's abandonment of the leader and council manager model, the government is expected to push all local authorities covering a population of 85,000 people or more to adopt one of the above three models. This proposal, set out in a 2006 White Paper, entitled Strong and Prosperous Communities, stipulates that council leaderships will in future serve a four-year term - whichever model is adopted.

→ Further reading

Boynton, J. (1986) *Job at the Top: Chief Executive in Local Government*, London: Financial Times/Prentice Hall. **Concise, but authoritative, text examining the emergence and growing influence of the role of local authority chief executives and other senior officers.**

Hodge, M., Leach, S., and Stoker, G. (1997) *Local Government Policy: More Than the Flower Show—Elected Mayors and Democracy*, London: Fabian Society. **Pamphlet arguing for the merits of directly elected mayors, prior to their introduction by the Blair government.**

Randle, A. (2004) *Mayors Mid-term: Lessons from the First Eighteen Months of Directly Elected Mayors*, London: New Local Government Network. **Impeccably researched booklet from the NLGN think tank citing quantitative and qualitative data to examine the impact at grass-roots level of the introduction of directly elected mayors.**

Rogers, S. (1998) *Performance Management in Local Government: The Route to Best Value*, 2nd edn, London: Financial Times/Prentice Hall. **Second edition of guide, principally aimed at local government professionals, focusing on the new management standards introduced by Labour and giving tips for achieving Best Value.**

? Review questions

1. Outline the main difference between the responsibilities of 'officers' and 'councillors'. Who has the more power and who is more accountable to local people?

2. Describe the main changes to internal local authority hierarchies introduced under the Local Government Act 2000. Which model is the most democratically accountable?

3. What is the difference between the traditional role of mayor and that of directly elected mayors? How does a town or city go about introducing the latter?

4. Who has the power to take executive action under the three forms of local authority leadership introduced by the LGA 2000? Why have the changes been so contentious?

5. How are councillors currently remunerated? What are the arguments for and against increasing their payment and/or introducing paid professional councillors?

 Online resource centre

www.oxfordtextbooks.co.uk/orc/Morrison

Visit the Online Resource Centre that accompanies this book for web links and regular updates.

14

Local government accountability and elections

British local authorities are responsible for spending more than £65bn a year in taxpayers' money between them. Perhaps understandably, then, the decisions that they make on behalf of those whose interests they represent are subject to increasing scrutiny.

Councils are accountable to their local citizens in the following principal ways:

- by publishing their own *standing orders*, *codes of conduct*, and constitutions;
- through independent auditing of their accounts and publication of performance data;
- by allowing press and public to attend their meetings, and to access *agendas* and reports;
- by giving local people a say through the ballot box at local authority elections.

This chapter focuses on the range of ways in which both councillors and officers are held accountable.

▌ Local government post-Nolan—the new era of transparency

As with central government, there have long been systems, rules, and procedures to which local authorities have been expected to adhere in conducting business. But the extent to which councils were required to *demonstrate* their integrity and openness underwent a profound shift in the aftermath of the succession of high-profile scandals at national level in the early 1990s that led to the findings of the Nolan Inquiry (see pp. 61-2).

The immediate effect of Lord Nolan's recommendations, published in 1996, was to compel all public officials—starting with members of Parliament (MPs), but extending down to local councillors and their officers—to uphold the 'Seven Principles of Public Life': selflessness, integrity, objectivity, accountability, openness, honesty, and leadership (see p. 62). But he and the prime minister who commissioned his inquiry, John Major, had a desire to go further—an aspiration shared by Mr Major's successor, Tony Blair, who consolidated his reforms in the Local Government Act (LGA) 2000. Today, the new processes introduced to police the behaviour of MPs at national level are also being widely implemented by local authorities.

The emergence of council constitutions

As discussed briefly in the previous chapter, under the terms of the LGA 2000, every local authority now has an obligation to draw up—and agree with the Secretary of State—its own *council constitution*. Within reason, this constitution can take any number of forms—whether a broad mission statement, or a more detailed breakdown of the council's responsibilities and services. The very fact that individual councils were free, initially, to come up with their own wording reflects an acknowledgement by government that the particular issues that different councils face in running their affairs vary. As of 19 December 2000, however, *all* constitutions have had to contain all of the components listed in Table 14.1.

Section 37 of the 2000 Act goes on to specify that copies of the constitution must be available for inspection by members of the public 'at their principal office' and 'at all reasonable hours'. Personal copies must also be supplied by the authority to anyone requesting them—subject to the payment of a 'reasonable fee' determined by the authority.

Table 14.1 The compulsory components of a local authority constitution since 19 December 2000

	Component
1	A summary and explanation of the purpose and content of the constitution
2	A description of the composition of the council, the scheme of ordinary elections for members of the council, and their terms of office
3	A description of the principal roles and functions of the members of the council, including the rights and duties of individual members
4	The scheme of allowances for members of the authority
5	A description of the rights and responsibilities of local inhabitants, including their rights to vote in local elections, access information about local services, and access council, committee, subcommittee, and cabinet/executive meetings
6	A description of the roles of the authority itself
7	Any rules governing the conduct and proceedings of meetings of the authority itself
8	A description of the roles and functions of the chairman of the council (including mayors), the leader/**directly elected mayor**/council manager, the cabinet/executive, individual cabinet members, and individual officers with delegated executive powers
9	A description of the arrangements for the operation of **overview and scrutiny committees**, their terms of reference, membership, and any rules governing them
10	Any provisions in the local authority's executive arrangements with respect to the appointment of committees of the executive
11	The membership, terms of reference, and functions of committees and subcommittees, and any rules governing the conduct of their meetings
12	A description of the roles of the local authority's standards committee and any parish council subcommittee of the standards committee (plus details of membership)
13	A description of the roles and membership of any area committees of the authority
14	A description of any joint arrangements made with any other local authorities
15	A description of the roles of officers of the authority, including senior management
16	The role and functions of the **chief executive**, monitoring officer, and chief finance officer
17	The code of conduct for local government employees issued under the Act, plus any details governing their recruitment, disciplinary procedures, etc.
18	Any protocol established by the authority in respect of relationships between members of the authority and officers of the authority
19	A description of the arrangements that the authority has in place for access of the public, members of the authority, and officers of the authority to meetings of full council, the cabinet/executive, committees, subcommittees, and joint committees
20	A description of the arrangements that the authority has in place for access of the public, members of the authority, and officers of the authority to information about decisions made—or to be made—by any of the above meetings
21	A register stating the name and address of every member of the local authority executive, the ward or division (if any) that they represent, and the name of every member of each committee of the executive

(continued)

	Component
22	A description of the rules and procedures for the management of the authority's financial, contractual, and legal affairs, including procedures for auditing its accounts
23	The local authority's financial rules and regulations, and those governing procedures in respect of contracts and procurement (including authentication of documents)
24	The rules and procedures for legal proceedings brought by and against the authority
25	A description of the register of members' interests of all full and co-opted members of the authority, and the procedures for publicizing, maintaining, and updating it
26	A description of the rules and procedures for review and revision of the authority's constitution, and its management structure
27	A copy of the authority's standing orders and code of conduct

The foundation stones of council constitutions

What, then, of the various technical terms highlighted in the government's criteria for the content of constitutions? The concept of 'standing orders' is one that should be familiar to anyone who has worked for any public sector organization (and, indeed, many of those in the private and voluntary sectors). In broad terms, it refers to the overall system of rules and guidelines governing the day-to-day conduct of local authority business. Like the constitution as a whole, individual councils set their own standing orders—meaning that, in theory, they can be as detailed or as vague as they wish. Some authorities may choose to incorporate into their standing orders rules governing the propriety of councillors and officers—for example, the requirement that those with financial interests in a matter due to be discussed by a committee in which they are involved declare this fact and remove themselves from the meeting. Others may confine their standing orders to mundane procedural issues—for example, most contain, as a bare minimum, a breakdown of the customary order of business at council, committee, and *cabinet* meetings (discussed in more detail later in this chapter).

The remaining terms singled out by the LGA 2000 in instructing councils how to frame their constitutions all refer to the post-Nolan preoccupation with enforcing national standards of ethical conduct by public officials. Most councils have long had an agreed code of conduct specifying a list of 'do's and 'don'ts' by which they expect their members to abide. In the wake of the sleaze allegations of the 1990s, however, a new onus was placed on those in public life at all levels to clean up their acts—in particular, keeping their 'outside interests' separate from the duties that they carry out on the public's behalf.

Given the essentially unpaid nature of councillors' work and the fact that many are juggling their duties with earning a living elsewhere (often in the same town or city), the potential for conflicts of interest in local government is arguably even greater than that faced by MPs at Westminster. The councillor who is a member of his or her authority's planning committee, but also sits on the board of a company with development interests in the area, poses an all-too-familiar conundrum—and for this reason. most authorities have long had in place clear rules compelling members to make a ***declaration of interest*** in relation to any outside pecuniary interest. The LGA 2000 attempted to standardize this process, however, requiring *every* council to publish a reworded constitution reflecting Lord Nolan's 'Seven Principles'. Declarations of interest, meanwhile, must now be made at the point at which someone first stands for election as a councillor. As with MPs and peers, they are required to enter all interests on a ***register of members' interests*** (see p. 60), which—given that new interests can emerge at any time—must be regularly updated. Councillors must also declare an interest at the start of any meeting in which they are due to participate should there be an agenda item in which they have a personal involvement. In such circumstances, they should remove themselves from the meeting—but only for the duration of that item.

So much for the rules: who actually polices them? As explained in the last chapter, each local authority has a designated ***monitoring officer***, whose job is to ensure that the council as a whole—and its constituent parts—act within the law and do not overreach their powers. The introduction of codes of conduct and registers of members' interests—coupled with the new onus placed on officers, as well as councillors, to make themselves accountable—has, however, been accompanied by a new emphasis on objective scrutiny. To this end, each council must now appoint a ***standards committee***, like that at Westminster, to monitor the actions of its officials and to raise concerns about any unethical conduct. Its independence is theoretically assured by the fact that, in addition to two or more members of the council itself, it must include at least one individual who is neither a councillor, nor an officer of that or 'any other relevant' authority.

The principal roles of standards committees are to:

- promote and maintain high standards of conduct by members and co-opted members;
- assist members and co-opted members of the authority to observe its code of conduct;

- advise the authority on the adoption or revision of a code of conduct;
- monitor the operation of the code of conduct;
- advise, train, or arrange to train members and co-opted members of the authority on matters relating to the code of conduct.

On a day-to-day basis, standards committees often devolve many of their functions to a subcommittee of the authority, but the composition and precise remit of that subcommittee must be formally agreed with the involvement of local parish councils.

At the other end of the scale, the conduct of English and Welsh local authorities, their councillors, and officers is ultimately overseen by a *quango*, the *National Standards Board for England and Wales*. Although it has no legal powers, in certain circumstances, it may formally investigate complaints brought to its attention by a local authority standards committee. Its main roles are listed in Table 14.2.

Helpfully for the media, the Board normally discloses when formal complaints have been made, issuing full details of its eventual decisions, and any sanctions arising from them.

Best value, comprehensive performance assessment (CPA) and comprehensive area assessment (CAA), and the growth of performance data

The growing emphasis placed on promoting high ethical standards among public officials has emerged hand in hand with what critics have decried as a growing government obsession with performance targets, league tables, and ratings systems focusing on the quality of their actual work. The concept

Table 14.2 The main powers of the National Standards Board for England

	Power
1	Requiring councils and other authorities to inform it how well they are dealing with complaints about their members' conduct
2	Working with standards committees to help them to improve their handling of complaints
3	Giving standards committees and councillors guidance on understanding the code of conduct, and how to deal with complaints about the conduct of council members
4	Removing the power of a standards committee to receive complaints about its members
5	Investigating serious cases when the local standards committee believes it is not best placed to deal with the matter and the Board agrees with that verdict
6	Publishing information about how councils and other authorities are dealing with complaints about their members

of 'Best Value' (BV) was introduced in the previous chapter, but it is worth spending a little time here examining how the various Best Value performance indicators (BVPIs) ushered in under its umbrella have been applied in practice.

Prior to the 1998 *Green Paper*, which detailed how the government proposed to implement BV, an earlier consultation document had outlined 12 provisional 'principles' that would be used to define its meaning. The 1998 Paper then outlined four key 'dimensions of performance'—that is, criteria—against which BVPIs for specific local services should be measured:

- *strategic objectives*—why the service exists and what it seeks to achieve;
- *service delivery outcomes*—how well the service is being run to achieve the above;
- *quality*—the quality of the services delivered, explicitly reflecting users' experience of services (that is, not only 'how many' or 'how quickly', but 'how *good*');
- *fair access*—ease and equality of access to services.

Since the introduction of BV, there has been an explosion of BVPIs—some covering local services as a whole; others specific aspects of individual services, such as education and social services. Early BVPIs covered areas such as 'service delivery' (the actual standard of local services from the public's perspective), and 'corporate health' (a category that itself contained a further 18 indicators, relating to everything from 'customers and the community' to 'partnership working'). Altogether, there are now more than ninety BVPIs.

The advent of BV was only the beginning of a new era of monitoring, auditing, and evaluating local authorities' performance. In December 2002, a new system of service-by-service performance ratings was introduced, known as *comprehensive performance assessment (CPA)*. Overall responsibility for monitoring individual councils' performance in England and Wales—taking action when it is judged necessary—now falls to a central government quango, the *Audit Commission*, which discharges this role through a network of *district auditors* (each overseeing a specific authority area). Scottish local authorities are held to account by Audit Scotland, while Northern Irish ones have their books pored over by designated officers from the Northern Ireland Audit Office (NIA).

Initially covering only 'top-tier' local authorities (county councils and unitaries), CPA was subsequently extended to encompass districts/boroughs, and fire and rescue authorities. Its statistics were grouped into three different frameworks, according to the type of authority:

- single tier and county councils;
- district councils;
- fire and rescue authorities.

One of the main differences between BV and CPA were that the latter statistics were made public, allowing local taxpayers and the media to judge the performance of their council in specific service areas against that of other authorities in much the same way that they might view hospital league tables, or school exams performance data.

CPA used a four-star ratings system and broke each of its frameworks down into a list of service areas. Councils were rated on a department-by-department basis in relation to the quality of the different services that they provide. So, for example, the same county or unitary authority might have scored highly in relation to its social care provision, but poorly in education—or vice versa. Star ratings were also applied to councils overall in the following four assessment categories:

- corporate efficiency;
- use of resources;
- quality of services;
- direction of travel—that is, whether they were improving and how rapidly.

The public could visit the Commission's website at any time to access their local council's CPA 'scorecard', while its annual reports would 'name and shame' the best and worst of the previous year. To cite an example, in its 'Scores and Analysis Report' for 2007, published in February 2008, the Commission praised Somerset County Council for improving its overall 'star category' and 'direction of travel'. It is now a 'four-star improving strongly' council.

Anyone expecting the introduction of CPA to be the last word on government targets for local authorities, however, was to be disappointed. In

Table 14.3 Other recent measures for assessing local authority performance

Measure	What it is
'Beacon Council' scheme	Launched by the Improvement and Development Agency (IDeA) in 1999 through the Department for the Environment, Transport and the Regions (DETR)—with 42 councils singled out as 'beacons' (examples of best practice) in year one.
More 'freedoms' for successful councils	A pilot scheme was launched by ministers in September 2000 to reward high-performing councils with more financial autonomy in exchange for meeting ambitious performance targets, in the form of new public service agreements (PSAs). Of the 20 pilot authorities that signed PSAs in September 2000, few had met many of their targets by January 2002.
Citizens' charters	John Major's government introduced a much-derided 'Citizens' Charter' under which the public could complain about poor-quality public services. Many individual councils have since replicated this initiative: both Cambridgeshire and Lincolnshire county councils still have citizens' charters, while Lewes District Council has a similar 'customer charter'.

addition to these 'quality assurance' standards, several other performance measures have been introduced. These are explained in Table 14.3.

From April 2009, the Department for Communities and Local Government (DCLG) was to replace the CPA system with so-called *comprehensive area assessment (CAA)*. In contrast to CPA, CAA focuses not on the performances of individual local authorities, but on the overall experience of public services for people living and working in a given area. The resulting data—focusing on the quality of life for local residents and businesses—reflects a growing belief that people are more concerned about the standard of *services* than the notional 'performance' of organizations that deliver them, whether public, private, or voluntary.

Like CPA, CAA incorporates four key elements—with strong similarities to the existing ones:

- a joint risk assessment undertaken by all local services inspectorates;
- a scored 'direction of travel' judgement for every local authority;
- a scored 'use of resources' judgement for every local public sector body;
- the publication of performance and assessment statistics against a reduced national indicator set.

The last resort—the role of the Local Government Ombudsmen

Of course, targets, league tables, and performance data can only take things so far. What should an individual do when they feel they have been the victim of an injustice at the hands of his or her local authority—or when he or she believes that he or she has lost out because a council has, say, taken an incorrect decision on his or her eligibility for services to which he or she is entitled?

The answer, since the Local Government Act 1974, has been for the individual to lodge a formal complaint with the **Local Government Ombudsmen**— better known today as the **Commission for Local Administration**. The Commissioner's remit is to investigate allegations of maladministration—that is, the negligent or incompetent running of local services). He or she is not there simply to look into complaints relating to decisions about which people are unhappy—*unless* those decisions show evidence of maladministration. Since 1988, complainants have been able to take their cases direct to the Commissioner, without the need to use their local councillor as an intermediary. This change had an immediate impact on the number of complaints made: in the first year alone, they soared by 44 per cent.

There are three Commissioners operating in England, each responsible for a specific geographical area:

- London, Buckinghamshire, Berkshire, Hertfordshire, Essex, Kent, Surrey, Suffolk, and Sussex;
- Birmingham City, Solihull MBC, Cheshire, Derbyshire, Nottinghamshire, Lincolnshire, Warwickshire and the north of England;
- the rest of the country.

Complaining to a Commissioner is subject to the conditions outlined in Table 14.4.

As more people become aware of the role and remit of the Commissioners, so the number of complaints investigated each year continues to increase. In 2007–08, the last period to date for which precise data is available, the Commissioners received 17,628 new complaints. A breakdown of the areas into which they fell is given in Figure 14.1.

Understandably, journalists are always keen to find out about cases being heard by the Ombudsman, because they tend to concern major complaints and to be highly newsworthy as a result. At times, however, these stories can

Table 14.4 The conditions for filing complaints with the Local Government Commissioner

Condition	Explanation
Timeliness	Complaints must be made 'in time'—i.e. lodged with the Commissioner or a member of his or her staff within 12 months from the date on which the alleged matters took place
Fairness to other party	Before a Commissioner investigates, he or she must be satisfied that the complaint has been brought to the notice of the authority to which the complaint relates and that the authority has been given a reasonable opportunity to investigate and reply to it
Within remit	Commissioners will not usually investigate a complaint if there is a right of appeal to a tribunal or minister, or if there is a remedy through the courts
	They may not investigate a complaint about action that affects all, or most, of the inhabitants of the authority's area (i.e. it must relate to an individual)
Not a court matter	Commissioners may not investigate the conduct of civil or criminal court proceedings, specified commercial transactions, action in respect of appointments, removals, pay, discipline, superannuation, or other personnel matters, or the instruction or conduct, curriculum, internal organization, management, or discipline in any local authority school or other educational establishment
Within time frame of Act	A Commissioner may not investigate anything done before 1 April 1974

be very frustrating: while the Ombudsman's final adjudications are always made public, because the identities of those involved are usually kept anonymous, the resulting reports are rarely as revealing as the press (or public) would like.

The surcharging of councillors and officers

In exceptional circumstances, it is possible for individual councillors and senior officers found culpable of major financial or managerial irregularities to be personally *surcharged* by the Audit Commission on behalf of their local authorities. The most infamous example of wilful misconduct of this kind in modern times was the so-called 'homes for votes' scandal of July 1987, which saw the former leader of Westminster City Council, Dame Shirley Porter, and her colleague, David Weeks, conspire to sell off 500 council houses a year to potential Tory voters living in marginal *wards*, in an effort to engineer

Figure 14.1 A breakdown of complaints to the Commissioner 2007–08

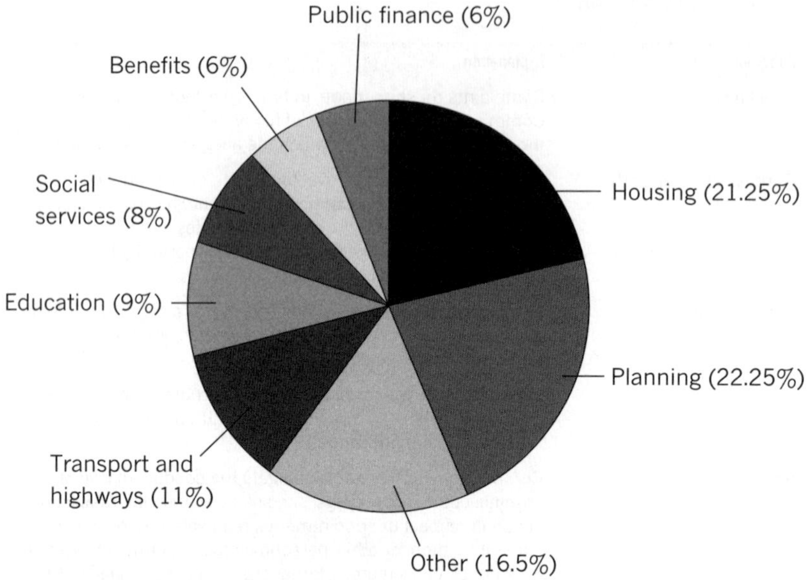

Public finance (6%)

Benefits (6%)

Social services (8%)

Education (9%)

Transport and highways (11%)

Housing (21.25%)

Planning (22.25%)

Other (16.5%)

Source: Local Government Ombudsmen (2009) *Annual Report 2007–08*

Conservative victories in forthcoming elections. The mass sell-off—dubbed 'Building Stable Communities'—was made possible by the Thatcher government's 'Right to Buy' scheme (see pp. 528–31), but Dame Shirley's motives were exposed after an investigation by district auditor John Magill, who condemned her actions as 'disgraceful and improper gerrymandering'. After a legal battle lasting for much of the 1990s, the Tesco heiress was ordered to repay £27m to the council, plus interest and legal costs. Having initially claimed that she had little more than £300,000 to her name, in 2004 she finally relented—reimbursing it to the tune of £12m.

▌ Access to local authority meetings and business—the 'old' system

Until recently, the rights of press and public to attend meetings of local authorities, their committees, and subcommittees were straightforward and widely understood. The Local Government (Access to Information)

Act 1985—which arose out of a *private member's Bill (PMB)* introduced by Conservative *backbencher* Robin Squire—enshrined their right to attend *all* such meetings, unless information due to be discussed was 'confidential' or 'exempt'. The former category refers to specified classes of information supplied by government departments, or matters the disclosure of which is prohibited under statute or by the courts. An example might be details relating to national security or crime prevention prohibited by either the Official Secrets Act or an anti-terror law. 'Exempt' information is any of the following:

- details judged to be 'personal' and/or 'commercially sensitive'—for example, those relating to the terms of a contract the public disclosure of which might have a negative impact on the local authority's future ability to negotiate value for money for local taxpayers;

- matters 'in the process of being negotiated'—for example, details of contractual negotiations with competing companies that the council is considering hiring to provide a service;

- issues 'protected by legal privilege'—for example, when a council's members are discussing confidential legal advice given to it in relation to litigation by or against it, or contractual matters that they are seeking to resolve through the courts.

Under these arrangements, councils tended to use one of two methods for excluding the press and public from meetings—or, more usually, specific *sections* of meetings. Most commonly, local authorities chose to divide their meetings into a 'part one' and 'part two'—with all confidential and/or exempt items (commonly known as 'below the line') held back until the second section. Alternatively, they might hold a vote to exclude the press and public for the duration of a single specified agenda item. The vote had to be formally proposed, seconded, and carried by the members of the relevant committee—and a *reason* given to those excluded (usually citing the Schedule to the 1985 Act under which the exclusion was being sought). Should the motion fail, the matter concerned had to be heard publicly, and copies of supporting reports instantly circulated to members of the press and public present.

In addition to granting the press and public automatic access to its meetings, local authorities were also required to provide information in *advance* of the proceedings; after the event, it was incumbent on them to publicize the outcomes of any votes and debates. At the meetings themselves, meanwhile, clerks had to ensure that they did a lot more, in the interests of accessibility, than simply unlock the doors to the press and public galleries. The bulk of these provisions, which apply to open meetings to this day, are listed in Table 14.5.

In the past, councils were frequently accused of going against the spirit of these access requirements—if not exactly the letter. The not uncommon practice of holding meetings on controversial issues in very small rooms— or barring entry on the grounds of 'overcrowding'—was once famously condemned as 'bad faith' by then Lord Chief Justice Lord Widgery.

Other measures that local authorities were encouraged to take to improve their communication with—and accountability to—the press and public included the appointment of public relations (PR) and/or press officers (a

Table 14.5 Access-to-meetings requirements expected of local authorities

Requirement	What it means
Public registers	Each local authority must keep these, listing names and addresses of all elected councillors, and details of the committees on which they serve. Any powers delegated to officers must also be listed.
Copies of agenda papers	The order of business and all reports prepared by officers for consideration at a meeting—and submitted during the open part of that meeting—must be made available on the day. No matters must be heard at a meeting unless listed on the agenda *at least three days beforehand*. The only exception is when urgent issues arise that could not have been predicted. In such circumstances, they should be mentioned during 'matters arising', towards the end of the agenda.
Access to **background papers**	All reports presented for public inspection should list any background papers used to help draft them. The press and public may also examine these (although they may be charged a reasonable fee for doing so).
Minutes of previous meetings	Copies of the minutes of an open meeting should be made available automatically to the press and to local electors, on request. The minutes are a record of the proceedings that *actually* took place at a meeting—including any items debated that were not on the original agenda. They will normally take the form of a detailed 'summing up' of what each person said, rather than an exact verbatim record. The minutes of a local authority meeting will normally be sent to journalists, along with the agenda for a subsequent meeting.
'Reasonable accommodation' for the press and public	This must be provided for both press and public. This normally means that there should be sufficient numbers of seats and, whenever possible, press benches. At meetings expected to be unusually popular (e.g. a planning committee or full council meeting at which a decision is due to be made about a major housing development), 'overflow rooms' should be provided. If it is oversubscribed, an audio and/or video feed of proceedings should be made available to those forced to sit or stand outside the meeting room, to enable them to see/hear proceedings.

move suggested in the Bains Report). The remit of such paid PR people would be strictly to promote council initiatives and policies in a broad sense, rather than to generate positive publicity for a specific political grouping. Councils were also expected to give journalists some access to individual councillors—particularly committee chairmen or cabinet members—to obtain quotes justifying political decisions, and even senior officers, should they require *technical* explanations for background to their articles.

In practice, by the mid-1990s, a large number of councils still had no press office.

Access to local authority meetings and business—the 'new' system

The LGA 2000 introduced significant new limitations on the extent to which the press and public would be allowed access to local authority meetings in 'new-style' councils—that is, those adopting a leader and cabinet, elected *mayor* and cabinet, or mayor and council manager management structure. While full council, committee, and subcommittee meetings remain as open to the public as ever under these new arrangements, access to others has become more restricted. Because many final decisions are now effectively taken by cabinets and related bodies with *delegated powers* (none of which are required to open their doors), critics argue that—contrary to the rhetoric—this makes councils *less* transparent than in the past. The main requirements for openness in council decision-making under the Act are listed in Table 14.6.

Table 14.6 Changes to access-to-meetings criteria under the Local Government Act 2000

Change
1 Full council, committee, and subcommittee meetings to continue meeting in public, subject to 'access to information' requirements under the 1985 Act.
2 Executive or cabinet bodies *not* required to meet in public (although they may do so if they wish). They must, however, publish decisions after they have been taken.
3 Decisions of mayors or individual executive politicians are subject to the 1985 Act—but a 'record' of their decisions must be published after they are taken.
4 Overview and scrutiny committees—and other scrutiny bodies—to meet in public, subject to existing 'access to information' requirement.

The principal differences between the 'old-style' and 'new-style' systems in relation to their openness to press and public scrutiny are therefore twofold. Because many significant decisions about policy formulation and implementation are now taken in cabinet—or even individually, by elected mayors, leaders, or cabinet members (and, in some cases, officers) with delegated executive powers—by holding such meetings in private, councils can stop the public from finding out anything about their plans until after the event. Meanwhile, meetings that *are* still open to the public—those of subcommittees, committees, and even the full council—are slowly being reduced to talking shops, with little or no executive decision-making powers.

The new system has attracted influential critics. In February 2000, while the LGA was still being debated in Parliament, a critical briefing paper designed to mobilize opposition to the changes was jointly published by the Local Government Information Unit and two constitutional pressure groups, Charter 88 and the Campaign for Freedom of Information.

Criticisms aside, the press and public continue to have a right to the following:

- three days' notice of meetings open to the press;
- agendas and *minutes* of council meetings;
- registers of planning applications;
- records of payments to councillors;
- the council constitution, code of conduct, standing orders, and
- a statutory register of members' interests;
- copies of any reports into allegations of maladministration by the Local Government Commissioner (Local Government Ombudsman);
- the council's annual accounts, annual audit (including the rights to inspect certain items), and performance indicators;
- statutory plans, including the Best Value performance plan;
- general financial information;
- the council's full annual report (including comparative data, indicating how well it has performed as against 'similar authorities').

The order of business in local authority meetings

All meetings of local authority members—whether committee, full council, or executive—follow the same format as they did under the old system, as outlined in Table 14.7.

Table 14.7 The order of business in council, committee, and subcommittee meetings

Order of business	What happens
Publication of agenda	The agenda—a document outlining the matters to be discussed at a meeting and the proposed order of business—is prepared by the council's chief executive, a secretary, or the director of administration—and made available in advance.
Approval of minutes	The meeting opens with formal approval of the minutes of the previous meeting of the same body.
Questions	Usually written down in advance by specific councillors, these are put to committee chairpersons. At full council meetings for local authorities that have adopted a post-LGA 2000 constitution, questions are put to the elected mayor, leader, or most relevant cabinet member.
Public questions	Observers on the public benches are given the chance to question committee chairpersons (optional).
Petitions	Any petitions from electors (e.g. in protest over the proposed site of a new landfill site) are presented to the full council by the local councillors representing the relevant ward or electoral division. Actual debates on these issues, however, will be held at relevant later committee meetings.
Consideration of reports	In full council, reports from committees are considered, while committees will consider those of subcommittees. Debates often arise at this stage if a matter raised is politically controversial. Councillors with strong objections to a given proposal may ask for the matter to be amended or even 'referred back' to the committee (or cabinet, if related to a cabinet decision).
Notices of motion	Individual councillors should table these in advance if they wish them to be debated. These usually cover issues not formally listed on the agenda. In LGA 2000-style councils, any notices that impinge on executive issues must be referred to the executive/cabinet for a final decision.

▌ Local elections

Until 1974, local elections were held throughout the first week in May, but the Local Government Act 1972 changed this, stipulating that they be held on the *first Thursday in May* (unless the Home Secretary fixed another day). The Act also clarified—for the first time—that *all* councillors must be directly elected. Up to this point, archaic offices had remained in certain areas—for example, 'aldermen', who were elected only by other councillors.

All councillors are now elected for four years—except those voted in as a result of a by-election caused by the death of a sitting councillor, or their resignation or disqualification from office in mid-term. Councillors elected in by-elections sit for the remainder of the term of the member that they are replacing, before standing for re-election at the same time as their colleagues. If a councillor dies or otherwise leaves office after the September of a year preceding a local election, his or her seat remains vacant until polling day—that is, it is considered too near the general poll to bother with calling a by-election.

Local authority constituencies

Councillors, like MPs, have their own constituencies (albeit covering far smaller geographical areas than parliamentary ones). Unlike Commons *constituencies*, however, those used in council elections are represented by up to three councillors at a time.

The terms used to refer to council constituencies differ from one type of local authority to another:

- 'county divisions' (or *electoral divisions*) are the constituencies in county council elections in England and Wales. Some unitaries also use electoral divisions. They tend to be geographically bigger, and represent more people, than those for other types of council;

- 'wards' are the constituencies in district or borough, metropolitan borough, London borough, and most unitary authority elections in England and Wales. All Scottish local authority constituencies are called wards.

In general, whether a ward or electoral division is represented by one, two, or three councillors is determined by the size of the local electorate. As a rule, most urban wards contain roughly the same number of electors and, because they are based in towns, tend to have fairly high populations. As a result, they will generally be represented by three councillors. In rural electoral divisions and wards in mixed rural/urban areas, in contrast, population levels can be significantly more varied—meaning that some will have only one councillor, while others will be designated 'multimember divisions or wards' and have up to three.

There were 10,661 wards and electoral divisions in the UK as a whole as of 6 October 2004 (the most recent date for which figures are available from the UK Statistics Authority—formerly the National Office of Statistics). The average population for a ward or electoral division was 5,500. Table 14.8, which can be found on the Online Resource Centre that accompanies this book, gives an overview of the number of wards and electoral divisions in each of the four countries of England, Wales, Scotland, and Northern Ireland.

Local authority election cycles

The precise election cycle followed by a local authority—that is, the years in which it holds its elections—will depend on the type of council. Present cycles are listed in Table 14.9.

As should be clear from the explanations above, local election cycles in the UK can be somewhat confusing for electors. This is especially true for those living in two-tier areas, who will face elections more often than most, given that they are covered by not one, but two councils: a district/borough and a

Table 14.9 The electoral cycles for the different types of English local authority

Type of local authority	Electoral cycle
County council	Held *every four years*, with the whole council retiring at the same time. Elections were last held in 2005, and are due again in 2009, 2013, 2017, etc.
London borough councils	Elections held *every four years*, again with whole councils retiring at the same time. To avoid conflicting with county polls, London boroughs hold their elections in different years. The last were in 2006 and the next will be 2010.
Metropolitan borough councils	Elections held in *three out of every four years*, with a third of councillors retiring each time—this roughly translates as one councillor per ward. Elections never take place in these areas in the same year as county council elections are held elsewhere. Elections were last held in 2006, 2007, and 2008, and will next be held in 2010, 2011, and 2012.
District/borough councils	Can choose to hold elections *either* in three out of every four years, again with a third of the council retiring each time, *or* all in one go, with the whole council standing down en masse. If districts or boroughs opt for the 'three out of four year' cycle, their electoral calendar is the same as that for metropolitan boroughs, but if they decide to stage 'Big Bang' polls every four years, these are held midway between those of counties—i.e. in 2007, 2011, etc.
Unitary authorities	Follow the same pattern as district and borough councils (i.e. they, too, have a choice), but special arrangements are made in areas where there is a *hybrid* council structure (i.e. one or more unitary authorities coexisting with a two-tier system—see pp. 353–5). When a new unitary authority is created out of the amalgamation of a pre-existing district and county, a statutory order may be passed stating that the new unitary authority should initially sit for a period of *less than four years*—to stop elections clashing with future county ones.
Parish, town, and community councils	Elections held *every four years*, with the whole council retiring at same time: in 2007, 2011, etc. Each parish council has to have at least five councillors and actual numbers are fixed by the local district council. Some parishes follow a ward-based system (like their parent authorities).

county. In some areas, where district/borough and county elections are occasionally held in the same year, the process can be particularly confusing.

Among the many other changes that it ushered in, the LGA 2000 envisaged the patchwork election cycles of local authorities gradually being rationalized over time. The Act tried to facilitate this by recommending that all councils adopt one of the following three models:

- the whole council being elected *every four years* at the same time;
- half of the council standing for election *every two years*;
- one third of the council standing in *three out of four years*.

Because it was left up to individual councils to decide whether—and when—to reform, little has come of the Act's recommendations on the ground. In January 2004, following a lengthy consultation, the **Electoral Commission** warned in a report that public confusion about electoral cycles was contributing to the general malaise afflicting local democracy, by further eroding turnouts already dwindling due to widespread political apathy. It cited research conducted on its behalf in April 2003 by MORI, which found that a quarter of British people did not know whether elections were due to be held in their area that May. Only one in six were able to say how often elections were held locally. The findings prompted the Commission to make the following recommendations—yet to be acted on by the government:

- that all local authorities in England should hold whole-council elections every four years;
- that county councils and the **Greater London Authority (GLA)** should hold elections in different years to boroughs/districts, unitaries, metropolitan, and London boroughs.

Quite apart from their baffling nature, the present local electoral cycles have produced curious quirks. Because individual district and **borough councils** are permitted to choose whether to follow a whole-council election model or one in which votes are held in three out of every four years, there are some counties in which, in any one year, an election may be held for a borough, a district, a county, and potentially even a neighbouring unitary authority. By the same token, two district or borough councils sitting side by side in the same county may choose to adopt different electoral cycles, meaning that—despite being the same type of council—they only hold elections on the same day as each other a maximum of once in four years.

Who can stand as a councillor?

As at general elections (see pp. 131–2), any citizen of the UK, Irish Republic, or a Commonwealth country who lives in Britain and is *over 18 on the day that her or she is nominated* may stand as a candidate—provided that he or she can prove one of a range of verifiable connections with the area in which he or she is standing and is not disqualified in law for any of the reasons listed in Table 14.10. There is no requirement for an election deposit.

Unlike at general elections, candidature is also open to EU citizens who meet these criteria. To be nominated, a prospective councillor has to obtain the signatures of both a *proposer* and a *seconder*—both of whom must be registered to vote in the relevant local authority area. Candidates must also be able to prove that at least one of the following is true of them:

- that he or she is a legitimate elector listed on the local *electoral register*—that is, the list of registered voters kept by the local electoral registration officer;

Table 14.10 The disqualifications for candidacy as a councillor

Category of person	Details of disqualification
Some bankrupts	Prospective candidates are barred if they are undischarged bankrupts subject to a bankruptcy restriction order under the Enterprise Act 2002 in England and Wales. These are made by the Insolvency Service (an **executive agency** of the Department of Business, Enterprise and Regulatory Reform) if a bankrupt individual is found to have acted dishonestly, or in an otherwise 'blameworthy' way. In Northern Ireland, anyone adjudged bankrupt is barred from standing, while in Scotland, anyone whose estate has been sequestered is banned.
Certain recent convicts	Those convicted of a criminal offence with a minimum penalty of three months in prison within the five years before the election.
Electoral fraudster	Have been convicted of a corrupt or illegal election practice in the previous five years.
Politically restricted officials	Work for the local authority for which they are intending to stand, or hold a post with any other council that is politically restricted (e.g. a senior officer position in which they are expected to work closely with elected councillors and give dispassionate advice free from any personal political bias—see pp. 114 and 419). Civil servants working for Whitehall departments above 'Grade 7' may only stand in local elections with the permission of their employers. Most senior ones are banned.

- that he or she has been resident in the area for the 12 months before the nomination process;
- that he or she has had a 'principal or only place of work' for the whole preceding year in the area;
- that he or she has owned property in the area for the whole of the preceding year.

The ability of EU citizens to stand as councillors and the rather fluid test of 'residency' within a council's area make the qualifications for local authority candidates seem rather less stringent than those for prospective MPs. Unlike in general elections, this liberal attitude extends to peers entitled to sit in the Lords, who, although barred from standing for the Commons, may become councillors. Labour peer Lord Bassam (currently a minister in the government Whips Office) was, for a time, leader of Brighton and Hove Council in the 1990s.

Who can vote in a local election?

Only those people whose names are on the electoral register for a given local authority area are entitled to vote. To be eligible for inclusion on the register, a person must be:

- at least 18 years old or attain that age during the 12-month period covered by the register (*provided* that this is by the date of voting);
- a UK, Commonwealth, Irish Republic, or other EU citizen;
- qualified on the basis of normal residency, service in the Armed Forces or as a merchant seaman, or a declaration as a voluntary mental patient;
- not barred because he or she:
  - is a foreign nationals from outside the EU and Commonwealth;
  - is detained compulsorily under mental health legislation;
  - is a convict detained in prison or a mental institution;
  - has been convicted within the previous five years of corrupt or illegal practices.

As with general elections, it is the electoral registration officer's responsibility to ensure that every household completes a *compulsory* electoral registration form. Anyone moving from one council area to another may have his or her name added to the electoral register at the start of a given month under a system of 'rolling registration' introduced in 2000.

The local election process

The basic procedure governing local elections is summarized in Table 14.11.

Of the various other rules governing the legitimate conduct of local elections, most notable are those limiting the sums that candidates are allowed to spend on campaigning. The spending cap was most recently raised in March 2005, by **statutory instrument**, at the request of the Electoral Commission. Those standing as councillors are now allowed to spend £600 on campaign expenses, while mayoral candidates may spend up to £2,000 (both sums are broadly equivalent to 5p per elector). The decision to more than double spending limits (council candidates had previously been forced to keep their expenditure below £242) was, in part, a belated response to the impact of the Representation of the People Act 1983, which, for the first time, required candidates to declare the financial value of 'benefits in kind' such as free use of stationery, offices, or other facilities. To ensure that limits are

Table 14.11 The local election procedure in Britain

Stage	Procedure
Notice of election	Must be published *at least 25 days before an election*
Nomination papers submitted	To be handed in *by noon 19 days before the election*
Publication of candidates' list	Must be published *by noon on the 17th day before the election*
Candidate withdrawals	This can happen *no later than 16 days before the election*
Appointment of officials	Each local authority appoints a returning officer to preside over the election night count (normally the mayor or chairperson of the council, but whose role will be taken on the day by an 'acting' or 'deputy returning officer', usually the chief executive—see pp. 136 and 415). It is his or her responsibility to appoint presiding officers and poll clerks to attend polling stations during the day, to supervise the counting of votes, to rule on whether any ballot papers have been 'spoiled', and to publish the finished results
Polling stations open	Usually based at local schools and community centres, these open from 8 a.m. to 9 p.m. for local elections
Votes cast	When electors (or their proxies) arrive at a polling station to vote, their names are checked against the register and issued with a ballot paper. If an elector has applied for a **postal vote**, they must send it to a designated place other than the polling station

not exceeded, agents must send inventories of their candidates' expenses to their *returning officer* after the poll.

Moves towards improving local election turnout

Dwindling engagement in local elections has long been a cause of concern to UK governments. Compared to many EU countries, the turnout in Britain's local polls is extremely poor: in a survey by the then Office of the Deputy Prime Minister (ODPM) carried out in 2000, it came bottom of the European league, with an average turnout of just two out of every five electors (a drop of 37 per cent since 1987). Between two and four million people are estimated to be absent from the electoral register at any one time—whether intentionally (in an attempt to avoid being charged *Council Tax*), or because of apathy towards the democratic process.

The present government, aided by the Commission, continues to review the local election process, with an eye to boosting turnout. Among its proposals are:

- introducing *anonymous registration* for those reluctant to have their names listed;
- opening polling stations at supermarkets, workplaces, colleges, doctors' surgeries, etc;
- allowing voting over a period of a few days, rather than the usual one;
- introducing universal postal voting;
- electronic voting—that is, via email, Internet, text messaging, etc.;
- holding *annual* elections for at least a portion of each council, to make councils more accountable to electors by forcing them to campaign for votes continually.

Since 2001, the task of reviewing the electoral arrangements of English local authorities—and overall structures and boundaries—has been the responsibility of a specially formed statutory committee of the Commission, the *Boundary Committee for England* (a successor to the Local Government Commission for England). The Committee is charged with carrying out periodic electoral reviews (PERs) every few years, to ensure that the number of electors represented by each councillor is broadly the same across the country.

The most 'successful' local elections—such as the 2008 vote for London mayor and the GLA—are often viewed through the prism of what is happening on the national and global political stages, rather than interpreted as true tests of public opinion about the merits of candidates and parties locally. The results of so-called 'mid-term' local elections—that is, those held partway through a Parliament, when voters are often disenchanted with the serving government—frequently send a shot across its bows, and are consequently styled as 'protest votes' by political commentators and opinion pollsters. The 2008 local elections were an object lesson in protest voting. Barely a week after Mr Brown's government had meekly pledged to compensate low-earners hit by the abolition of the 10p starting rate of Income Tax—many of them its own grass-roots voters—Labour fell to its worst election result for more than forty years. It polled barely 24 per cent, coming one point behind the Lib Dems and 20 shy of the Tories—a share that would sent it to a crushing defeat at a general election.

→ Further reading

Johnston, R. and Pattie, C. (2006) *Putting Voters in Their Place: Geography and Elections in Great Britain*, Oxford: Oxford University Press. **Thoughtful examination of geographical differences in voting and turnout patterns in local, national, and European elections around the UK. Examines issues including the emergence of safe seats, and the roles of marginal wards and constituencies in winning polls.**

Knowles, R. (1993) *Law and Practice of Local Authority Meetings*, 2nd edn, London: ICSA Publishing. **Updated second edition of an indispensable guide to the statutory rules and regulations governing access for the press and public to local authority meetings.**

Pratchett, L. (2000) *Renewing Local Democracy? The Modernisation Agenda in British Local Government*, London: Frank Cass. **Thoughtful assessment of the impact of the 'New Labour' reform agenda in local government, focusing on its attempts to increase public participation in local democracy through mayoral elections and new forms of voting.**

Rogers, S. (1998) *Performance Management in Local Government: The Route to Best Value*, 2nd edn, London: Financial Times/Prentice Hall. **Second edition of guide, principally aimed at local government professionals, focusing on the new management standards introduced by Labour and giving tips for achieving Best Value.**

? Review questions

1. Outline the electoral cycles for district/borough councils, county councils, and unitary authorities. Why might a district council have an election in a year when a neighbouring borough council does not, and vice versa?

2. What are the qualifications for candidates and electors in local elections? Who oversees the running of local government elections and to whom besides this individual might one complain about the handling of electoral procedures?

3. In what ways besides elections can local councillors be held accountable for their actions? What mechanisms exist to punish them for misusing their positions?

4. Outline the main ways in which the performance of local authorities in service delivery is assessed, exposed, and regulated.

5. What rights do the press and public have to attend and access information from meetings of local authorities, and their committees and subcommittees? How were the access rights changed by the Local Government Act 2000?

Online resource centre

www.oxfordtextbooks.co.uk/orc/Morrison
Visit the Online Resource Centre that accompanies this book for web links and regular updates.

15

Local authorities and education

At the start of Chapter 6, we described the health service as a subject with an almost unique ability to shape the news agenda. But if there is any other political issue with the capacity to occasionally give it a run for its money, that is education. Whether it is local unrest over changes to school catchment areas, anger over disruption caused by striking teachers, reports about soaring undergraduate student debt, the annual rows over 'grade inflation' when General Certificate of Secondary Education (GCSE) and A level results are published, or the frantic scramble for university places through the Clearing system each summer, the trials and tribulations of parents and pupils are seldom out of the media for long.

The involvement of British local authorities in this huge policy area stretches across all four 'phases' of the education process: primary, secondary, tertiary—or *further education (FE)*—and higher education (HE). These phases are explained in Table 15.1.

In addition, local authorities have a statutory responsibility to ensure that suitable preschool education is available across their areas, through nurseries, registered *childminders*, and other forms of recognized early years childcare. This chapter examines each layer of state education in detail, beginning with perhaps the most important and certainly the most controversial: the school system.

Table 15.1 The structure of the British education system

Phase	Structure
Primary phase	Education in all of the subjects of 'primary' importance (e.g. English language, maths, basis history, and science). This takes place in primary schools (ages 5–11), or in two stages, at infant school (ages 5–7) and junior school (ages 7–11), or, in some areas of the UK, first school (ages 5–8/9), then middle school (ages 8/9–12/13).
Secondary phase	Education for 11–16-year-olds (or 13–16-year-olds in some areas) in both core subjects such as English and maths, and with increasing specialization in other areas after children take their 'options' at the age of 13 or 14. Compulsory secondary education in England, Wales, and Northern Ireland leads to final assessment between the ages of 14 and 16, through GCSEs and/or new vocational diplomas. GCSEs are awarded through a mix of exams and coursework across eight grade bands: A*–G. In Scotland, the GCSE equivalent is the Standard Grade (levels 1–7). Standard Grades take up the first half of a four-year National Qualification (NQ) programme, which encompasses the Scottish equivalent of the gold standard pre-degree qualification in the rest of the UK, A levels. This is called the Scottish Higher. The majority of school-age qualifications and many taught at FE and HE level are recognized by the Qualifications and Curriculum Authority (QCA) and accorded a 'level' on its National Qualifications Framework (NQF).
Further education (FE) phase	'Sixth-form' education in chosen subjects to A level in England, Wales, and Northern Ireland, Advanced Subsidiary (AS) Level (taken during the first year of a standard two-year A level course), vocational diploma, or International Baccalaureate (IB) (a qualification modelled widely taught outside the UK). In Scotland, pupils study for intermediate-level certificates, followed by Scottish Highers. 'Catch-up' tuition for the less academic and/or those seeking to retake GCSEs/Standard Grades is also offered at this stage. BTEC National Diplomas, foundation degrees, and other practical, trade-based post-GCSE certificate are also often taught in school sixth forms, and at further education (FE), technical, or tertiary colleges.
Higher education (HE) phase	University education to degree—Bachelor of Arts (BA) and Bachelor of Science (BSc)—and postgraduate—Master of Arts (MA), Master of Science (MSc), Doctor of Philosophy (PhD)—level for those who gain the requisite A levels or equivalent qualifications.

▶ The origins of state schools and the rise of comprehensive education

Until Victorian times, many children in Britain had little or no formal education. The offspring of the aristocracy and the bourgeois middle classes that emerged during the Industrial Revolution fostered the growth of a burgeoning private education system for those who could afford it. But for the large number of less well-off households, paying the high fees charged by these schools was out of the question. Poor parents were forced either to teach their children themselves, or to rely on piecemeal philanthropy from any local churches, charities, or guilds—that is, groups of wealthy merchants and tradesmen—prepared to fund local schools for the working classes. In the absence of a state system, the opportunity for children from poorer families to gain an education varied hugely from place to place—an early 'postcode lottery'.

By the late nineteenth century, however, there was a growing clamour for the government to provide some form of recognized schooling across the board for the nation's children. Campaigns by civil rights movements such as the Chartists and Radicals had brought social inequality into sharp focus. Morality aside, there was also a belated recognition that allowing 'the masses' to remain uneducated might be limiting Britain's potential to compete on the world stage economically.

The foundation stone of the modern 'state school' system—or 'maintained sector'—was the Elementary Education Act 1870, which introduced the first nationwide 'elementary schools'. The term 'elementary' is key here: even at this stage, poorer children were only to be offered the most basic level of teaching, and only up to the age of 13—that is, at what would later be termed *primary school* level. Neither was this limited schooling guaranteed to be within the financial grasp of all parents: local school boards elected to manage the system on the ground—and set up new schools in areas devoid of ones provided by a church or guild—charged families up to 9 pence a week to send their children. While boards were given discretion to waive this fee for the poorest households, they could only do so for a limited time. It was not until the Education Act 1891 that elementary education became free for most pupils, and 1918 that every last fee was abolished. This reform was initiated by county councils, which, as of 1901, were designated local education authorities (LEAs).

The path towards introducing secondary schools was even more protracted. Not until after the Education Act 1944 did a nationwide system that was open to all children—regardless of their parents' ability to pay—come into being. When the 1870 Act had been passed, the compulsory school leaving age for children was just 10 (despite the fact that elementary schools were prepared to teach them up to the age of 13). This was increased incrementally—first to the age of 11, then 13, then 14—by three subsequent Acts, in 1893, 1899, and 1918, respectively. But it was only the advent of Tory Education Minister Rab Butler's 1944 Act that introduced secondary schooling for all in England and Wales (a provision extended to Northern Ireland in 1947).

Despite the widespread welcome given to the new universal free secondary schools, the Butler Act was far from uncontentious. Its most controversial innovation was the introduction of not one, but three types of secondary school:

- *grammar schools*—for the most academically gifted;
- *secondary modern schools*—a more standard alternative for the less able;
- *technical schools*—offering a practical, vocationally orientated education for the least academic.

The decision whether a child was admitted into one or other was based on their performance in a new exam that they would sit at normal elementary school leaving age—the '11 plus'. Table 15.2 offers a timeline charting the major education reforms up to, and including, the 1944 Act.

The ideological divisions caused by the introduction of this system of academic selection and the repeated efforts of Labour governments to scrap grammar schools (still unfulfilled in some areas) are discussed in detail later this chapter. One such government, however—Harold Wilson's first administration, elected in 1964—went further than most towards abolishing the tripartite secondary school framework ushered in by Butler in favour of a more egalitarian system. Under the Conservative governments of the late 1950s and early 1960s, the number of non-selective secondary schools had been gradually increased to cater for the post-war 'baby boom' generation. These schools—focusing on a broad-based academic education—came to be known as *comprehensive schools*. But it was under Labour Education Secretary Anthony Crosland that comprehensives truly earned their name, becoming the norm for the vast majority of British schoolchildren as the government fought to persuade LEAs to begin dismantling what they saw as the 'two-tier system' preserved by grammars. In time, these schools came to be known variously as 'high schools', *community schools* (see p. 470), and in Scotland, 'academies' (not to be confused with today's self-governing *academies*—see p. 471).

The number of grammar schools has since fallen dramatically across the country. In their mid-1960s heyday, there were several hundred, including 179 direct grant schools—that is, fee-paying grammars that agreed to take between a quarter and a half of their pupils from poorer families in return for state subsidies. Today, there are only 164, spread over ten LEA areas, including Devon, Kent, and Lincolnshire. The Conservatives' traditional support for academic selection gave grammars a temporary stay of execution in the 1980s, but few new ones were established. In recent years, however, the great selection debate has reared its head again—not least because of

Table 15.2 A timeline of the major reforms in school education in the UK

Date	Reform	Effect
1841	The School Sites Act	Formally introduced the concept of 'voluntary schools', principally in villages and rural areas. These were schools offering basic teaching of English, maths, and other core subjects built on land donated by local landowners or vicars. Covenants protected the ownership of the land, which remained with the donor.
1870	Elementary Education Act (also known as the 'Foster Act', after Foster)	Set up elected school boards to run voluntary schools as part of a new universal 'elementary education' system in England and Wales, and to introduce new schools where none existed. Boards charged up to 9d a week for teaching, but could subsidize the poorest.
1891	Education Act	Made elementary schools free for most pupils.
1901	Education Act	Abolished school boards and transferred responsibility to newly established county councils—the first local education authorities (LEAs). Councils to offer financial help to these schools through local taxes.
1918	Education Act	Last remaining elementary school fees abolished. School leaving age raised to 14 years old. The first nursery schooling for preschool children introduced.
1944	Education Act (also known as the 'Butler Act')	Introduced comprehensive education in all but name, by raising school leaving age to 15 years old and giving all children access to free secondary schooling. Three types of secondaries introduced: grammar schools, secondary modern schools, and technical schools. The Act also formalized the then three-tier education system—primary, secondary, a further education (FE)—and introduced new measures to support children with disabilities and learning difficulties.
1960s/ 1970s	Wilson/Crosland reforms	Successive Labour governments attempt to persuade LEAs to scrap grammar schools, while rolling out a mass expansion of comprehensive education.
1988	Education Reform Act	Introduction of the National Curriculum, GCSEs replace GCE O levels, and grant-maintained (GM) schools introduced, allowing primary and secondary schools to opt out of local authority control for the first time.
1998	School Standards and Framework Act	GM schools become foundation schools.
2000	Learning and Skills Act	Self-governing, partially selective, city academies introduced as a replacement for CTCs. Later renamed simply 'academies'.
2007	Education and Inspections Act	Concept of trust schools introduced, allowing foundation schools to set up their own charitable trusts to manage their assets and decide admissions policies.
2008	New qualifications launched	New vocational diplomas launched as alternative or complementary qualifications to GCSEs and A levels.

Labour's failure to scrap the remaining grammar schools since returning to office in 1997. A fuller discussion of the impact that the grammar school model continues to have on schools right across the state education system follows later in this chapter.

◗ The 1988 Act—and the birth of 'independent' state schools

Just as it turned its back on forty years of consensus over health policy by introducing the National Health Service (NHS) 'internal market' (see pp. 180 and 186), in 1988, Margaret Thatcher's Conservative government initiated the most profound change in the state education system since secondary schools were first established in the public sector in 1944. The Education Reform Act 1988 marked the culmination of the so-called 'Great Debate' of the early Thatcher years, revolutionizing the way many state schools were managed—liberating them from LEAs, and giving parents and teachers a greater say in their day-to-day running than ever before. It also polarized political opinion between those who viewed the transfer of power from councils to citizens as a triumph of 'localism' over bureaucratic control and ideological defenders of the faith who saw in it an attempt to undermine the philosophy of comprehensive education.

Up to this point, the designation 'independent schools' had been used as an umbrella term for fee-paying schools in the private sector: 'private schools' and 'public schools' (which tend to be older, more costly, and academically prestigious). What the 1988 Act did was to apply the concept of independent *governance* for the first time to schools in the public sector. Schools would be offered the opportunity to 'opt out' of LEA control—in much the same way as GP surgeries were being invited to break away from district health authorities to become fundholding practices (see p. 182). Schools opting out would be renamed 'grant-maintained (GM) schools', and given autonomy to take their own decisions on admissions, staffing, and spending with the help of direct grants from central government. The Tories were effectively handing them de facto independent status, albeit without the freedom to charge fees, in the name of the latest Whitehall buzzword: *localism*. The idea underpinning this term was that decisions on the running of vital public services such as education and, progressively, health and social care should be put in the hands of the people who 'knew best'—those who *used* them—rather than politicians or civil servants. The main provisions of the 1988 Act are outlined in Table 15.3.

Table 15.3 The main provisions of the Education Reform Act 1988

Reform	Effect
Introduction of grant-maintained (GM) schools	Primary and secondary schools with at least 300 pupils allowed to 'opt out' of LEA control, becoming GM schools. Initially, this entitlement was granted as a 'reward' to high-performing schools (i.e. those with high proportions of pupils attaining five or more A–C GCSE passes), but the eventual aim was to extend the system to most state schools. GM schools could set pay and conditions for staff and—most controversially—decide their own admissions policies (some began to select academically). They received direct revenue grants from the government towards their running costs, and could apply for capital grants to fund new equipment and buildings, and repairs to existing ones.
Local Management of Schools (LMS)	Day-to-day financial decisions were delegated to headteachers of GM schools working with their schools' boards of governors.
Introduction of National Curriculum (NC)	This dictated not only the key subjects that all schoolchildren must be taught—or offered as options—at various stages in their schooling, but also the core areas that must be covered in those subjects (e.g. basic spelling and punctuation in English language). The curriculum was to cover broadly the same basic content throughout England and Wales, up to and including GCSE level, with periodic exams, at 'key stages' one, two, and three (ages 7, 11, and 14), through so-called National Curriculum standard assessment tests (SATs). In Wales, however, the Welsh Assembly has been given the authority to make slight adjustments to it—something it acted on soon after its establishment by making the teaching of the Welsh language compulsory in all state schools, alongside English.
Launch of key stages (KS)	Formal stages introduced by which each pupil would be expected to attain certain educational objectives. This would normally be established through testing and/or continuous assessment.
Emergence of parent choice	The first signs of choice were introduced into the schools admissions process, with parents allowed to specify to which local school they would prefer to send their children.
First school league tables	These began publishing school exam results—seen by ministers as a means of providing objective information on the performance of local schools to parents considering where to send their children. Attention today focuses on comparative data relating to truancy, exclusions, and performance in external exams—in particular, GCSEs, and the all-important benchmark of how many children achieve five 'good' passes (A*–C). Since 2007, the A*–C grades recorded by schools for league table purposes have had to include English language and maths, following criticism that many top grades are obtained by students studying 'easier' subjects (although academies are not yet required to specify to which subjects their A*–C passes relate).
Introduction of city technology colleges (CTCs)	A new generation of specialist schools geared to the needs of industry and the technology sector is established, with private companies invited to sponsor them. In time, most of these would be transformed into academies under Labour.

GM schools—and the Local Management of Schools (LMS) scheme that supported them—proved hugely divisive. The element of selection introduced by some popular schools to simplify their admissions procedures and cherry-pick the most 'academic' applicants was seen to favour children with educated, professional parents, and discriminate against those from disadvantaged backgrounds. Critics argued that it would worsen existing inequalities between schools, and lead to a gradual polarization between high-performing schools dominated by the affluent middle classes and poorer ones in working-class areas. The ability of headteachers and governors to set their own pay scales in an effort to attract the 'best' staff was seen to compound this problem: by headhunting high-performing teachers from LEA-run schools, or ones with poorer results, they would be making their own schools yet more 'successful', while further impoverishing those already struggling. This was exacerbated by the fact that government money tended to follow the more successful schools—rewarding them with funding bonuses and extra freedoms, and fast-tracking grant allocations for GM headteachers by enabling them to bypass the cumbersome application procedures used by 'one size fits all' LEAs.

Although it was to adopt its own version of LMS after regaining power, Labour stood firmly opposed to the reforms in 1988. It was all the more embarrassing, then, when it emerged in 1995 that Tony Blair, the party's leader, was sending his eldest son, Euan, to the London Oratory, a GM school. A year later, Harriet Harman, Labour's then health spokesperson, faced backbench calls for her resignation after it was revealed that she was sending one of her sons, Harry, to the same school. Her decision was aggravated by the fact that her other son, Joe, was attending a grammar school.

To some opponents, the idea of introducing 'parent choice' into the GM schools equation set the final seal on an emerging 'two-tier' state education system. If parents were allowed to choose between rival schools in their area, who in their right mind would opt for the one with worse results and less money to spend on its pupils? As these 'successful' schools became richer and still more successful, the less popular ones were likely to become *less* successful and poorer. Moreover, successful schools would realistically have only limited ability to expand to take in the growing numbers of children applying for places and, given their vested interest in favouring those most likely to succeed (in so doing, improving their league table ratings), they would become increasingly selective. All the while, children forced to attend less popular and/or 'failing' schools were likely to fall further behind. Only a few years later, similar arguments would be

Table 15.4 Arguments for and against state schools being allowed to 'opt out'

For	Against
Parents generally know what is best for their own children. Giving them a more direct input into the running of their schools will enable them to cater provision better to individual children's needs, rather than relying on a 'one size fits all' approach imposed from above.	Allowing schools to become self-governing can only worsen inequality in the state school system. Given charge of their own budgets and control of teacher recruitment, they will poach the 'best' from elsewhere—widening the gap between 'successful' and 'failing' schools.
Putting more power in the hands of headteachers and boards of governors (including parents, teachers, and members of the local community) gives them a sense of *ownership* of the school. Ownership increases determination to drive up standards, and equips them with the money and tools to be able to do so.	Giving schools control of their own disciplinary procedures, staff recruitment, and budget decisions could lead to huge inconsistencies in the nature and quality of provision across the sector. It is also the thin end of the wedge: how long before they demand the right to select the brightest pupils—or start using 'social selection' to do so by the back door?
LEAs are unwieldy and bureaucratic organizations that, historically, have been slow to take decisions. Putting power in the hands of governors and headteachers speeds up decision-making and saves money by 'cutting out the middle man'.	Local authorities are run by elected councillors and therefore accountable to all members of their local community. School governing boards are accountable to no one but the parents of children already attending those schools. Who will stop them taking bad or unfair decisions?

raised against the introduction of 'patient choice' and competition in the NHS (see p. 191). Table 15.4 presents a summary of the main arguments for and against schools being allowed to opt out.

The first school to be given grant-maintained status was Skegness Grammar School, in 1988. By the time that GM schools were finally abolished (in name at least) in 1998, there were nearly 1,100 nationwide—three out of five at secondary level.

City technology colleges and the rise of specialist schools

Although pedants might point towards the technical schools established in the 1950s and 1960s as early examples of schools that specialized in specific disciplines—in their cases, practical subjects such as carpentry—the birth of *specialist schools* per se actually came much later. Reviving the notion that some children are less predisposed towards academic subjects and more towards 'vocational' ones—and that more needed to be done to tailor the skills and qualifications with which 16-year-olds and 18-year-olds left school to the demands of industry and the scientific community—the

1988 Act saw the Conservatives introduce a new generation of 'technical schools'.

From the outset, these secondary schools-cum-sixth form colleges—*city technology colleges (CTCs)*—were distinct from anything before them. Taking their inspiration from the US experience of involving business and industry in a more hands-on way through so-called 'charter schools', CTCs saw private companies become involved not only in funding buildings and equipment, but, more controversially, in day-to-day decisions about how they were run. Rather than focusing entirely on teaching practical subjects, as an alternative to the customary *National Curriculum* taught by mainstream comprehensives, they still offered pre-16 children all of the usual subjects. In *addition* to this, however, they were equipped with particular specialisms in the sciences, maths, the emerging field of information technology (IT), and other related disciplines.

But the defining characteristic of CTCs—a source of concern to traditionalists—was the extent of private sector involvement. In capital terms, private 'sponsors' helped to finance up front the expansion and refurbishment of existing schools—and the construction of brand new ones—in return for a long-term leaseback agreement that would make their investments profitable over time. This was one of the first tangible manifestations of the Tories' new 'big idea' for funding expensive public sector projects, the *private finance initiative (PFI)* (see pp. 238–9 and 471). But the sponsorship arrangements went deeper than this: companies investing in CTCs were given seats on the governing boards of those schools—effectively, a stake in their day-to-day management. To the horror of some, certain schools went so far as to 'rebrand' themselves, incorporating the names of sponsoring companies into their official titles and logos. The first CTCs were set up at the tail end of the 1980s in Kingshurst, Birmingham, and Nottingham. But the most controversial early opening—and the first to incorporate the name of its sponsor so blatantly—was Dixons CTC, funded by the high street electrical retailer. The college, which opened in 1990, has since converted into an academy (Labour's equivalent of CTCs—see the next section). At present, only 13 CTCs remain and the bulk of these are in the process of converting.

The purpose of CTCs was not solely to provide an education more geared to the changing demands of industry and business, and the oncoming technological revolution. By granting them a degree of independence from LEA control commensurate with that offered to GM schools, the government was giving headteachers a more decisive say in the running of their schools—but with the quid pro quo that underperformance might be questioned by their increasingly influential boards of governors. These boards—far from being the talking shops of old, there to be 'consulted' by LEAs, but otherwise powerless—gave parents, teachers, local residents, and members of the business community a direct say in school management for the first time. 'Localism' was again on the march and who was to stop it?

Foundation schools, academies, and school autonomy

When Tony Blair was elected in 1997, he surged to power with the mantra 'education, education, education'—and the pledge to improve school standards and opportunities for children from all backgrounds. Labour had opposed both CTCs and the whole principle of schools 'opting out' of LEA control in opposition, and sure enough set about ending both the LMS and CTC programmes within months of entering office. As with the health service, however, it was not long before Mr Blair and his ministers were converted into champions of specialist schools, PFI—which they renamed *public–private partnerships (PPPs)*—and the idea of 'school autonomy'.

Today, the state school landscape is, if anything, even more patchwork than it was when Labour won power. The School Standards and Framework Act 1998 converted all existing GM schools into *foundation schools*. The immediate effect of this was to bring them back under a measure of LEA control—to the extent that, rather than continuing to be funded by direct government grant, they would again have their funds passed to them by their councils. In practice, however, the amounts allocated to each foundation school are largely determined by Whitehall and, in many other respects, foundation schools retain a degree of independence akin to that wielded by GM schools before them. Their boards of governors own the land and buildings from which they operate (unless ownership has been handed, or historically belonged, to a charitable foundation); they also have primary control over their own admissions policies, and they hire and fire their own staff, rather than relying on the local authority to recruit people on their behalf.

The most controversial of these three aspects of foundation school autonomy is the second. If schools are allowed to decide which pupils to admit and which to exclude, argue Labour's backbench critics, is this not essentially reintroducing 'selection' by the back door? How are LEAs and the government to prevent popular schools discriminating between applicants on the basis of their prior academic records, social background, or even appearance?

A layer of complication was added to the debate when, in Mr Blair's final few weeks in office, the Education and Inspections Act 2007 introduced the term *trust school* into the equation. Trust status—a term borrowed, like 'foundation', from the health service—is now offered to foundation schools that choose to set up a charitable trust to manage their affairs. By the end of the first year, some three hundred foundation schools had already either converted into trust schools or were in the process of doing so. A number have been formed through the merger of two or more schools, or the take-over of a 'failing' school by a more successful one. Trust schools are not generally offered any additional funding as an incentive to convert—nor are they allowed to 'opt out' of local authority control to any greater extent than they already had—but in December 2007, Schools Secretary Ed Balls set out several 'sweeteners' to encourage high-performing schools to team up with less successful ones, including the promise of a £300,000 cash injection to smooth over the process.

Alongside foundation schools, the 1998 Act retained two other principal types of secondary school: community schools and voluntary schools. 'Community school' is the umbrella term for all 'ordinary' state comprehensives—that is, those the land and buildings of which are owned by their local authorities, and the admissions policies and staffing procedures of which remain in council hands. Prior to the 1998 Act, these standard comprehensive—or 'high'—schools had for some time been known as 'county schools'. Some community schools have since been renamed 'community *colleges*', as a reflection of the fact that, in addition to teaching the National Curriculum, they also offer adult education and training (normally through evening classes) like that provided elsewhere by FE and tertiary colleges.

'Voluntary schools' are (as their name suggests) the stalwarts of earlier times, which are normally linked to either the Church of England or the Roman Catholic Church. They are divided into two types: *voluntary aided schools* and *voluntary controlled schools*. The former are schools the land and buildings of which are owned by either a church or charitable foundation, and the capital costs of which will often be funded, in part at least, by those same bodies. As with foundation schools, their governing boards determine their admissions and staffing policies—but they, too, receive their revenue funding through the LEA. The principal difference between voluntary aided and voluntary controlled schools is that, in the latter case, the LEA will take control of admissions and staffing procedures, as it does in relation to community schools.

Although the term 'voluntary school' is not generally used in Scotland, since the Education Act 1918, it has been commonplace for secondary schools to specify a denominational bias, with a number labelling themselves 'RC schools'.

The emergence of academies

The most significant additional change to school designations since the 1998 Act came with Labour's belated conversion to the twin ideas of specialization and independent management *within* the public sector. The Learning and Skills Act 2000 introduced 'city academies'—that is, schools with state-of-the-art buildings and facilities, part-funded by the private sector, which would be allowed both to specialize in key subjects geared to the demands of their local community and to manage their own internal affairs (including admissions). Some Labour traditionalists saw in the policy a direct contradiction of the party's initial opposition to CTCs, and a betrayal of the ideals of comprehensive education being entirely funded and managed both within and *by* the public sector—that is, by councils and central government. Labour modernizers like Mr Blair and then Education Secretary David Blunkett saw it as a way of pumping much-needed teaching resources into deprived areas more quickly than if the government were to finance the investment single-handedly, while equipping young people in those areas with the skills demanded by modern industry.

To all intents and purposes, academies (as they are now known) are much the same as CTCs. Buildings and amenities receive significant boosts from private capital in return for complex PFI/PPP leaseback arrangements and often a stake for the companies in the running of the schools. This can be of the 'arms-length' variety—that is, a presence on the governing board—or, increasingly, more hands on: private investors are now directly involved in the day-to-day staffing of administrative, security, maintenance, and/or catering functions at several academies, including William Hulme's Grammar School in Manchester. Pupils attending CTCs will often work slightly longer days than their peers in community, voluntary, and foundation schools, and their terms may be arranged differently. Unlike CTCs, meanwhile, academies do not necessarily specialize in scientific, business, or technological subjects: if the local communities in which they are based lack adequate sports facilities, or if there are specific demands for people with skills in the arts and media, these factors may instead determine choices of specialism.

Perhaps the most controversial of the various 'privileges' granted to academies is the limited freedom that they have to bypass one of the most sacred cornerstones of traditional Labour education policy: its opposition to academic selection: that is, the choosing of pupils on the basis of their prior performance in exams and other assessments. Academies are permitted to select *up to 10 per cent* of their pupils on the basis of 'aptitude' in their specialist subjects. The choice of this word—pointedly distinguished from 'ability' by ministers—has been the cause of considerable controversy (not to mention many a semantic debate among educationalists). While allowing these limited powers, Labour appeared to be trying to keep its distance from the Conservatives' more wholesale traditional support for selective schools—to appease its own **backbenchers**, many of whom regard any form of academic selection as anathema.

In drawing a distinction between a pupil's 'potential' to do well in a subject—that is, their 'aptitude'—and their 'ability' in it, however, Labour left many headteachers nursing headaches as they struggled to put partial selection into practice. In 2003, the House of Commons Education and Skills Select **Committee recommendation** was that aptitude tests were removed, arguing that the government had failed to provide a convincing definition of what it meant by 'aptitude'. Ministers countered that the aim of introducing limited selection was to identify pupils who 'would benefit from' accessing a specialism, rather than those with an already developed ability in it.

Since their introduction, the number of academies has grown steadily, from 17 in the first year to around a hundred at time of writing. Ministers have set a 'five-year strategy' to open two hundred by 2010 and, to speed the process up, Education Minister Lord Adonis recently invited private schools struggling to meet recruitment targets in the face of growing competition in the 'true' independent sector to consider converting into them. Several, including Belvedere School in Liverpool and Bristol Cathedral School, already have. Meanwhile, 12 CTCs have so far been turned into academies, with only three of the remaining 13—Emmanuel College, Gateshead; Thomas Telford School, Shropshire; the British Record Industry Trust [BRIT] School, Croydon—having expressed a firm desire to remain as they are.

Arguments about autonomy aside, the rise and fall of CTCs, and their subsequent metamorphosis into academies, is in many ways only the latest expression of a decades-old debate about the virtue of dividing pupils into 'academic' and 'practical', and gearing education towards the *needs* of industry as well as the *aspirations* of young people keen to develop their intellects in a wider sense. In earlier times, this debate led to the schism between Left and Right over grammar schools (see pp. 462 and 478–80); more recently, it has been played out in arguments over the introduction of new qualifications covering vocational disciplines. As of September 2008, 14–19-year-olds have had the option of studying for new vocational diplomas in addition to—or instead of—GCSEs and/or A levels. These new qualifications, covering subjects as varied as health and social care, creative media, and engineering, and equivalent to six GCSEs or three A levels, are based on proposals published by former Chief Inspector of Schools Mike Tomlinson in 2004.

In addition to the above categories, there are two other terms commonly used to describe certain types of state school. They are often confused with each other, so we will clarify them here.

'Specialist schools' can be a source of confusion not only because their name sounds similar to *special schools*, but because it implies that they are a discrete category of school permitted to specialize in particular subject areas (like academies and CTCs). They are, indeed, schools with specialisms, but the title 'specialist school' is actually an umbrella term used to refer to *all* state schools with a recognized specialism in one or more subjects. The second point is that it is not necessary for a school to become independently managed—foundation school, academy, or CTC—to be granted 'specialist status'; in fact, the majority of secondary schools in the state sector, whatever their designation, now have one or more specialisms. Any secondary headteacher may apply for specialist status to the Department for Children, Schools and Families (DCSF).

Achieving specialist status usually sees the school offered a significant injection of capital and revenue funding to support the development of its new specialism. The specialist schools programme requires those seeking to obtain specialist status first to raise around £50,000 in sponsorship. If granted their wish, they then qualify each year for an extra £100,000 or more in capital grant from government, plus around £130 per pupil, to help put their specialist ambitions into practice. Applications are normally successful if the chosen specialism either:

(a) relates to a genuine area of outstanding achievement by pupils of the school; or

(b) is seen to fill a gap in provision of facilities for the local community in which the school is based.

In return for its funding boost, the school is normally expected to make its new, improved facilities available to other schools and community groups. Like academies, many specialist schools are permitted to select up to 10 per cent of their pupils, on the basis of their aptitude in a relevant subject specialism. Whether schools are allowed to select depends on the nature of that specialism, however—only those specializing in languages, the performing and visual arts, and sport are permitted to do so. In 2007, Shadow Education Secretary David Willetts committed the Tories to extending the right to select a tenth of pupils to all specialist schools if the party were returned to power. But whatever the future holds for these limited selection powers, the response from schools themselves has so far been muted. A report by the Commons Education Committee in 2003 found that, in the first five years of the programme, only 6 per cent of schools eligible to select actually did so.

In contrast to *specialist* schools, 'special schools' specialize in teaching children with learning difficulties, such as dyslexia or autism, or mental or physical disabilities. These were formerly known as 'special needs schools'. To be judged eligible to attend such a school, a child must be 'statemented'—that is, awarded a 'statement of special education need'—by the LEA, following an official diagnosis by a GP or specialist and, in some cases, a formal test of his or her academic ability. Recent years have seen a growing trend for such pupils to be integrated into mainstream schools, to avoid segregating them from their peers, and to help them to attain skills and qualifications that will give them career prospects comparable to those of other children. The extent to which special schools remain distinct from mainstream ones varies from one area to another.

Table 15.5 outlines the main changes in school designations since 1997.

Table 15.5 Changes in school designations since 1997

School name pre-1997	School name since 1997
County	Community school/community college
Grant-maintained (GM)	Foundation/trust
Controlled	Voluntary controlled
Aided	Voluntary aided
City technology college (CTC)	Academy (formerly city academy)
Maintained special	Community special
GM special	Foundation/trust special

The changing role of LEAs

As alluded to earlier in this chapter, LEAs have had their powers increasingly eroded over the past twenty years—caught between the pincer movement of growing self-determination for schools and direct intervention in cases of underperformance by the Secretary of State (see pp. 485). But the single most significant recent reform of local education occurred in the Children Act 2004, passed in the wake of the Victoria Climbié child abuse case (see pp. 547–60). The media inquest into this gruesome tragedy led to a sweeping reorganization, under the 'Every Child Matters' agenda. This saw old-style education departments hand their oversight of schools over to across-the-board 'children's services' departments and the post of chief education officer effectively replaced by a new all-encompassing 'director of children's services' in each county council or unitary authority area. The aim was to join up a range of services affecting children that were seen to have become fragmented, in an effort to better provide for child welfare and make it less likely that warning signs of abuse would be missed in future. ('Every Child Matters' is discussed fully in Chapter 18.)

Despite their overarching role in implementing the provisions of the 2004 Act, local authorities have seen significant reductions in their powers in relation to schools. Today, they tend to be less the principal state education providers in their areas than they are enablers and coordinators. Table 15.6 outlines the ways in which councils' powers over local schooling have been reduced, alongside those that they retain.

The rise of faith schools and other recent trends in schooling

One debate that has been bubbling over recent years concerns the future of 'faith schools'—an umbrella term that is used to describe schools run by, and on behalf of, particular religious communities. The term 'faith school' has traditionally been used interchangeably with 'voluntary school'—that is, a type of school, discussed earlier this chapter, run by either the Church of England or the Roman Catholic Church, with or without the direct

Table 15.6 The powers retained and lost by local education authorities (LEAs)

Retained	Lost
Role in providing and maintaining premises for primary and secondary schools.	Until the Education Act 1993, each LEA had a statutory duty to appoint an education committee. Those operating in areas with voluntary schools would include members of the relevant churches, alongside elected councillors. The obligation to convene committees has gone, but some councils still do so. Education committees that remained under Mr Major were required to involve teachers and governors in decisions, as co-opted (non-voting) members. Labour extended this invitation to parents.
Duty to ensure that every school-aged child in their area has access to a formal state education—even if they do not attend a council-run school.	The 1993 Act also gave the Education Secretary formal responsibility for 'promoting the education of the people of England and Wales'. It made no mention of the role of LEAs and new quangos—the Funding Agency for Schools and the Schools Funding Council for Wales—were introduced. In areas with large numbers of GM schools, the agencies could share with the LEA—or take over—its schools planning and funding role.
Channelling funds to the governors of community, foundation/trust, voluntary, and special schools, and ensuring that all schools follow the National Curriculum.	The School Standards and Frameworks Act 1998 introduced a new requirement for every LEA to prepare an education development plan (EDP) for the Secretary of State. This was seen as an attack on council autonomy, transferring executive power to Whitehall.
Making recommendations for school reform in response to Ofsted reports (see pp. 480–3).	Local authorities have no role in the funding or day-to-day running of academies, and a limited role as a conduit for funding in foundation/trust schools.
Establishing an independent schools organization committee, made up of councillors and representatives of other interest groups, such as the boards of academies and CTCs. It meets every three years to consider a school organization plan, proposed by the council, addressing issues such as prospective mergers, closures, and changes to catchment areas.	
Coordinating the government's 'Building Schools for the Future' programme in their areas. This initially saw £3bn devolved directly to local authorities to spend on improving and maintaining their school buildings, with targets for the school in greatest need in each locality to be renewed with money from the fund by 2011. Every LEA is expected to have started work on at least one major building project by 2016.	

involvement of LEAs. In this context, however, it also denotes schools run by non-Christian faith groups, such as the Muslim, Sikh, Hindu, and Jewish communities. There are some seven thousand faith schools in England, Wales, and Northern Ireland, and a growing number in Scotland. A breakdown of the split between different religions in England and Wales is given in Table 15.7, which can be found on the Online Resource Centre that accompanies this book.

Faith schools were championed by Mr Blair, whose eldest son, Euan, attended the RC London Oratory School. He and other advocates argue that they have above-average attendance rates compared to standard primaries and comprehensives, and high achievement rates. They have also been praised for instilling a strong sense of discipline and respect among pupils. Mr Blunkett famously said that he wanted to 'bottle' the essence of faith schools and use it as a template for reform elsewhere. Two *White Papers* advocating further integration of faith schools into the state sector followed: one in 2001, focusing on all denominations, and a second, in 2005, specifically aimed at Muslim schools, as part of the government's wider efforts to tackle the perceived cultural isolation of some localized Islamic communities.

Yet there has been plenty of opposition. Although most faith schools are subsidized by the state, non fee-charging, and obliged to follow the National Curriculum, critics such as the National Secular Society regard the idea of any child being educated from a young age at a school with a prescriptive underlying world view as a form of brainwashing incompatible with one of state education's primary roles—that fostering freedom of thought and expression. Others, including some politicians and teaching unions, have argued that maintaining single-faith schools—whether inside or outside the state system—is promoting ghettoization and undermining efforts elsewhere to promote understanding between communities with different beliefs. Some also object to their being allowed to exercise limited selection, albeit faith-based rather than academic, unlike any other state schools save academies and grammar schools. In 2002, Labour backbencher Frank Dobson tabled an unsuccessful amendment to the Education Bill (for England and Wales) that would have limited the ability of faith schools to select pupils according to faith and force them to offer at least a quarter of places to those from other religious—or, indeed, secular—backgrounds. Undeterred, in March 2008, the National Union of Teachers (NUT) proposed a novel approach to paving the way for an end to single-faith schools: by requiring *all* state schools to become 'multi-faith' institutions, offering faith-based instruction, a choice of religious holidays, and varied prayer facilities.

It is not only Muslim schools that have been singled out for criticism: in April 2006, it emerged that the Emmanuel Schools Foundation (sponsored by Christian car dealer Sir Peter Vardy), the schools of which include the King's Academy in Middlesbrough, was teaching 'creationism' alongside Darwin's theories of evolution as an alternative view of the origins of the universe.

Other recent trends include the announcement by Mr Balls of additional help for schools struggling to improve their GCSE pass rates. Those with fewer than 30 per cent of pupils achieving five A*–C grades will be rewarded extra money to channel into top-up tuition via a new 'National Challenge for Schools' programme. In a further sign of a shift towards 'carrots' and away from 'sticks', as of April 2008, new 'school improvement partners' (SIPs) have been introduced in many areas of England—that is, individuals or organizations with relevant expertise who provide an outside consultancy role to schools to help them to improve standards.

New Labour, David Cameron, and the great 'grammar school' debate

The origins of the debate about the rights and wrongs of selection were outlined earlier this chapter. To recap, academic selection—allowing schools to decide whether to accept pupils on the basis of their prior assessment results, normally in a one-off exam called the '11 plus'—was introduced in 1944 and has since been a mainstay of Conservative administrations.

Between the late 1960s and the later 1970s, successive Labour and Tory governments engaged in a game of educational ping-pong over the future of the grammar schools established under the 1944 Act. Mr Wilson's 1960s government instructed LEAs to start dismantling the system, but this process had scarcely begun by the time he was defeated by Conservative leader Ted Heath in the 1970 election. Mr Heath's Education Secretary, one Margaret Thatcher, promptly reversed the Wilson directive, meaning that councils yet to abolish their grammars—many of them Tory and in favour of selection—managed to retain them. When Labour was re-elected in 1974, it swiftly overturned Mrs Thatcher's instructions, but a sluggish response in certain areas meant that, by the time she was elected prime minister in 1979, a number still remained. But Mrs Thatcher (herself an ex-grammar school pupil) was to do more to encourage selection than simply saving the 11 plus. In 1980, she introduced the 'assisted places scheme'—a means by which pupils from lower-income families who passed entrance exams for schools in the independent sector would be entitled to state financial aid with tuition fees, according to a sliding scale.

Labour scrapped assisted places when it returned to power in 1997. Yet the 11 plus remains in many of the areas in which it survived the axe in the 1970s, thanks to the more consensual way in which the party broached the issue of grammar schools under Mr Blunkett. Rather than abolishing grammars (infuriating many of its newfound middle-class supporters into the bargain), the School Standards and Framework Act 1998 instead gave local people in the relevant areas a direct say in whether the 166 remaining should be kept or scrapped. To this end, two types of ballot (effectively local *referenda*) were held:

- *area ballots*—in areas of the country where *the majority of* secondary schools were grammars, *all* parents would be balloted. One county in which this process was due to be used, Kent, was ultimately exempted from the ballot, due to what the government described as logistical problems;
- *feeder ballots*—in areas where *some* secondary schools were grammars, all parents of children attending 'feeder' primary schools—that is, those in the catchment areas of the grammars—were to be balloted. In Ripon, where this was first done, two out of three parents voted to retain grammar schools.

Labour's failure to make good on its long-standing pledge to abolish grammar schools—despite having a huge Commons majority—infuriated many of its own backbenchers. These rumblings of unease grew louder when it emerged that ministers were planning to *introduce* a degree of selection in academies (see pp. 471–2).

But it is not only Labour's leadership that has trouble containing its backbenchers over the selection issue. In 2006, then newly elected Tory leader David Cameron provoked a fight with party traditionalists—portrayed in some parts of the media as his 'Clause 4 moment' (see pp. 162–6)—by announcing that a future Conservative government would not be founding any new grammar schools. Instead, the Tories would focus on building on Labour's academy programme, with its limited powers of selection, and using more streaming and setting *within* schools to group pupils by ability. The following May, after months of infighting over the issue, he accused his critics of '*clinging on to outdated mantras that bear no relation to the reality of life*', adding that most parents did not '*want children divided into successes and failures at 11'*. He was later forced to make a significant concession to rebels, however, after the party's Europe spokesman, Graham Brady, resigned over the issue. In what was widely portrayed as an embarrassing climbdown, Shadow Education Secretary David Willetts reassured diehard '11 plus' supporters that a Tory government *would* consider building more grammar schools in areas in which they already existed—but only if their populations expanded and local people expressed a desire for more.

Monitoring school standards—'parent choice' and Ofsted

As explained earlier this chapter, the other great school debate currently raging in Britain is over the idea of 'parental choice'. At the heart of this issue is the long-standing notion that families should be free to apply to send their children to whichever local school they choose. Dividing lines have been sharpened, however, by the introduction of two key innovations designed to inform parents better about the relative academic merits of the various schools in their areas: school league tables and a national inspectorate, the *Office of Standards in Education (Ofsted)*.

League tables of school exam results were first introduced under the 1988 Act, but took a while to catch on with parents. The more decisive agent of parental choice was arguably the introduction of systematic school inspections. Until 1992, school standards were enforced by inspectors from two bodies: Her Majesty's Inspectorate and LEAs themselves. But the Education (Schools) Act 1992 and the School Inspections Act 1996 established Ofsted (in Wales, *Estyn*), with a view to providing a more consistent nationwide framework. Ofsted was headed by a new Chief Inspector of Schools.

Ofsted's task was to inspect all state schools within its first four years; thereafter, they would be visited on a six-yearly basis. In recent years, however, inspections have become more and more frequent, and shorter and shorter notice has been given to schools of Ofsted's intention to visit—with the aim of giving them less scope to engineer positive reports by 'cleaning up their acts' at the last minute.

As of 1 April 2007, Ofsted was renamed the Office for Standards in Education, Children's Services and Skills. Today, it inspects the following types of school:

- nursery and primary schools;
- secondary schools;

- special schools;
- service children's education—for offspring of those in the Armed Forces;
- pupil referral units—schools set up for children 'who cannot attend' normal schools, such as pregnant teenagers, those with specific medical problems, and children excluded from mainstream schools for bad behaviour;
- some independent schools, excluding members of the Independent Schools Council (ISC) and Focus Learning Trust, which are inspected by the Independent Schools Inspectorate (ISI) and School Inspection Services (SIS).

Ofsted reports rate schools in one of four categories—'outstanding', 'good', 'satisfactory', or 'inadequate'—and are made available to the public on the inspectorate's website. After the inspection itself, a school will be expected to act on any recommendations that the report contains, according to the process outlined in Table 15.8.

So to what extent has the advent of league tables and Ofsted intensified competition for school places? In short, they have promoted 'the best' schools, and named and shamed 'the worst'—in so doing, creating a thriving market

Table 15.8 The process for responding to recommendations in an Ofsted report

Stage	Process
School action plan	The initial summary report is considered formally by the school's governing body, which has to produce an action plan within 40 working days. Both the report and the school's response are open to public inspection.
Local authority report	If the report contains significant recommendations, the local LEA is required to produce its own report (even if the school is not council-run).
Special measures	Where a report finds that a school is 'failing to give its pupils an acceptable standard of education'—i.e. is dubbed a 'failing' school—it can be deemed to be placed in 'special measures'. In such cases, an action plan must be submitted to the Secretary of State, who will monitor closely the school's progress over the following two years.
Fresh Start	If no appreciable signs of improvement follow, the school's management and teaching staff will normally be replaced and it will be reopened under a scheme known as 'Fresh Start'. This normally involves the headteacher and all other existing teachers being sacked, and replaced with new recruits from elsewhere. In such cases, it is common for a 'super-head' to be parachuted in from a more 'successful' school, at the request of the authority or Secretary of State. One example is German-born Torsten Friedag, who was headhunted for a £70,000-a-year salary (£20,000 above the norm) from Croydon's BRIT School to take over Islington's George Orwell School in 1999. The latter was later reopened as Islington Arts and Media School.

for places at successful ones and an exodus of middle-class families from those deemed to be 'failing'. There has been no starker illustration of this pattern than the East Brighton Centre of Media Arts (COMART)—a 'failing' comprehensive that went through not one, but two name changes, and a costly PFI building programme, before finally closing in summer 2005. Based in one of Brighton's most deprived areas, Whitehawk, the school consistently had the worst rates of GCSE passes and truancy in Brighton and Hove. Better-off parents voted with their feet—reducing the school's social mix and overall pupil numbers, and sending its standards plummeting still further.

Critics argue that the advent of 'parent choice' has parallels with the current direction of the NHS, in which 'patient choice' has seen successful hospitals oversubscribed and failing ones avoided. While a growing number of 'failing' schools are closing, 'successful' ones gain greater financial rewards and freedoms—enabling them to headhunt the most experienced staff and improve further. Devoid of these privileges, underperforming schools can become locked in a downward spiral.

From a journalistic viewpoint, particularly for local media outlets, Ofsted reports provide 'easy-hit' bread-and-butter stories that can be hugely valuable in filling space or airtime. As Ofsted inspections have become more frequent and the process more widely understood, however, the inspectorate itself cannot be relied on to send out reports proactively to newspapers or television and radio stations, so it is usually up to journalists to chase them. Reporters should also be wary about relying on a school's own account of its inspection and Ofsted's findings: as with most things in journalism, it is always best to go straight to the horse's mouth for the full story.

Another area of controversy related to the growing national obsession with school league tables is that of testing. Ministers have consistently come into conflict with headteachers and unions in recent years over the sheer volume of assessment with which schoolchildren are now faced—and the pressure that this puts on both pupils and teachers. Opposition to the culture of testing intensified in summer 2008 when ETS Europe, the commercial company contracted to oversee marking of the Key Stage 2 and 3 tests for 11 and 14-year-olds, was responsible for a marking fiasco. Results for some schools suffered severe delays and there were reports of packages of exam papers lying uncollected, and unmarked, in headteachers' offices weeks after the exams had been sat. The government launched an independent inquiry into the scandal, headed by Lord Sutherland, and in August, ETS Europe had its £156m five-year contract terminated by the *Qualifications and Curriculum Authority (QCA)*. It had been paid £39.6m for 2008 alone.

In a surprise olive branch to critics of school testing, in October 2008, Mr Balls announced in the Commons that *National Curriculum standard assessment tests (SATs)* for 14-year-olds were to be scrapped with immediate effect. In the same statement, Mr Balls pledged to introduce a new US-style 'report card' in 2011 for each primary and secondary school child, giving an overall grade from A to F covering not only his or her exam results and performance, but also his or her attendance and/or truancy rate, behaviour, and health.

The future of school catchment areas

The trends in school applications fostered by the extension of 'parental choice' have had an inevitable impact on the question of catchment areas—that is, the geographical patches within which families need to live to be eligible to send their children to a particular school. Pressure on popular schools to admit more pupils—potentially at the expense of maintaining the high standards for which they are renowned—has seen some councils take drastic steps to 'ration' places, in an effort to keep their numbers sustainable, and improve the social mix and performance of other institutions.

Brighton and Hove provides the most dramatic example of this social engineering to date. In 2008, the council controversially began allocating places at its three highest-performing secondary schools—all based in the city's so-called 'Golden Triangle'—by 'lottery'. Many families living in this area had paid high prices for houses in the expectation of being automatically entitled to send their children to one of these popular schools. Under the new system, the schools' catchments were extended to cover areas until now devoid of comprehensives, and children living in outlying districts are theoretically just as likely to be admitted as those who live on their doorstep. Indications are that the Brighton experiment will soon be rolled out across the UK: in January 2007, several months after Brighton and Hove Council narrowly agreed to introduce a lottery, then Education Secretary Alan Johnson announced a new admissions code urging headteachers of oversubscribed schools to determine who should be offered places effectively by drawing names out of a hat. The new guidelines—intended to stamp out 'selection by the back door'—also banned schools from interviewing parents, considering their backgrounds, or otherwise excluding people by, for example, stipulating that they buy uniforms from expensive suppliers.

Concern about the use of lotteries and rationing to ensure that state schools have a better social mix has seen a growing number of middle-class parents 'defect' to the independent sector, angry that their children are no longer guaranteed places in 'good' schools near home. Some are fear that, by admitting more youngsters from deprived backgrounds, the high-performing schools to which they currently send their children will compromise their academic standards. Furthermore, oversubscribed schools have, on occasion, reportedly turned away the siblings of children already attending them because of pressure on spaces—making the 'school run' increasingly complicated and galling for parents. This has further fuelled the flight to the private sector. According to a 'census' published in April 2008 by the Independent Schools Council (ISC), 50,000 more children were being sent to private school than in 1997—with parents paying up to £27,000 for the privilege. This is despite Labour's record investment in state schools and the fact that the overall number of school-aged children in the UK has dropped since 1997. Neither were parents put off by the fact that independent school fees had risen by 6.2 per cent—twice the rate of *inflation*—in the same period.

To bolster the state sector—and, ministers would argue, break down a false divide between state and independent schools—the government recently instructed the Charity Commission to impose new conditions on private and public schools seeking to retain their charitable status (which entitles them, among other things, to significant tax breaks not enjoyed by companies). The biggest condition was a requirement to earn this privilege by opening up their playing fields and other facilities to state schools and community groups in their areas. These moves were denounced at a hearing of the Commons Children, Schools and Families Select Committee by Chris Parry, short-lived head of the ISC, as provoking a new 'Cold War' between the independent and state school sectors. Undeterred, ministers have pointed to other developments, including a recent invitation to independent schools to sponsor academies (accepted by the £18,000-a-year Wellington School, whose headmaster is Mr Blair's biographer, Anthony Seldon), and to share amenities and expertise with the new trusts, as proof of their desire for an equal partnership between the two sectors.

Guaranteeing fairness—the role of schools adjudicators

Ofsted is not the only new body to have been introduced in the 1990s to police the state school system. The 1998 Act saw the establishment of a second: the *Office of the Schools Adjudicator (OSA)*. Despite its title, like Ofsted (which employs a number of inspectors) the office does not have only one adjudicator, but ten. One of these is known as the 'chief adjudicator'.

There are many misconceptions about the OSA—the most common of which is that it is there to rule on complaints by parents about their children's failure to get into their chosen school. In fact, that role is taken by independent appeals panels. The OSA, in contrast, has statutory duties to:

- determine objections to admission arrangements and appeals from schools against directions from the local authority to admit a particular pupil;
- resolve local disputes on statutory proposals for school reorganization, or on the transfer and disposal of non-playing field land and assets;
- decide on competitions to set up new schools where the local authority has entered the contest with its own proposals;
- decide on requests to vary already agreed admission arrangements.

Intervention of last resort—the role of the Secretary of State

As the powers of local authorities to control state education in their areas has diminished with the emergence of new types of self-governing school, conversely, the powers of the Secretary of State have been resurgent. Direct intervention by the Schools Secretary can now take any of the forms outlined in Table 15.9.

Other issues affecting schools

As explained at the start of this chapter, the state of Britain's schooling is rarely out of the news for long. But besides the customary slew of stories about damning Ofsted reports, catchment areas, and league tables, there has been a significant amount of coverage in recent times about more positive developments. These have included the joint pledge by the DCSF and the Department of Culture, Media and Sport to provide at least five hours of sport and five hours of 'quality culture' per week for every state school child aged between 5 and 16 by 2010. In February 2008, Schools Secretary Mr Balls and Culture Secretary Andy Burnham announced that local authorities would be invited to compete in a three-year £25m pilot project across ten council areas, dubbed 'Find Your Talent'. The aim of the programme is

Table 15.9 The modern-day powers of the Schools Secretary

Power	Effect
Intervention 'in default'	Intervening to prevent unreasonable uses of power by local authorities and 'acting in default' when particular bodies fail in their statutory duties to children.
Managing the availability of school places	Directing LEAs to reduce surplus places in schools by merging and/or closing unpopular ones, or to increase provision where there is a high demand through expansion or by building new schools.
Intervening in 'failing schools'	Placing individual schools under special measures if they are judged to be 'failing', and instigating the Fresh Start initiative should they fail to improve. In March 2000, Mr Blunkett announced at the National Union of Teachers (NUT) conference that he wanted LEAs to consider 'fresh starts' for any schools where fewer than 15 per cent of pupils achieved five or more GCSE passes at grade C or above. First in the firing line was Gillingham Community College in Medway, Kent, where not one of the pupils had achieved a C.
Tackling inequalities of educational opportunity	In Labour's first term, Education Action Zones (EAZs) were introduced in areas of long-standing academic underachievement (normally deprived areas). Such areas were given around £1m a year in combined government and private sector money to help to fund innovative pilot projects designed to improve engagement and achievement by local schoolchildren. Some 47 EAZs were set up in the end—each with a five-year lifespan. Because they were accountable direct to Whitehall, rather than councils, there were questions over their transparency to the press and public. The Secretary of State continues to intervene directly in the interests of educational opportunities—Mr Johnson's recent direction to local authorities to ensure a good social mix at schools in their areas being an example.

to identify and nurture pupils with an aptitude in areas such as acting, film-making, singing, or playing a musical instrument by providing them with high-quality tuition, and free trips to theatre shows, cinemas, galleries, and museums. Mr Burnham later extended the scope of the arts scheme to offer free theatre tickets to all young people under the age of 26.

But not all stories are so uplifting. In October 2008, it emerged that Mr Balls was planning to issue a new code to require teachers who suspected their pupils of having extremist views—or being in danger of becoming 'radicalized' as potential terrorists—to report them. The move, introduced alongside efforts to demystify fundamentalist beliefs by discussing them more openly in the classroom, angered some headteachers, who said that it was tantamount to asking them to 'spy' on children. But it was broadly welcomed by union leaders, including Christine Blower, acting general secretary of the National Union of Teachers (NUT), who declared:

ff Terrorist threats have to be tackled. It's worth remembering that groups such as those from the far right can pose intimidatory threats to their communities, as serious as those from al-Qaeda. *jj*

▌ The role of local authorities in further education

Councils have had an on–off relationship with the FE sector over the past twenty years. Like schools, FE colleges—at the time, generally known as 'technical colleges'—were both managed and financed by county councils up to 1988. But the sweeping education reforms introduced by the 1988 Act included the removal of FE and sixth-form colleges from LEA control, giving them a 'semi-independent' status *within* the state sector analogous to that granted first to GM schools and CTCs, and later to foundation and trust schools, and academies.

Labour initially did little to challenge FE colleges' newfound autonomy. In 2001, it established the *Learning and Skills Council (LSC)*—Britain's largest single education funding body, with an annual budget of some £11bn—to finance provision in the sector across England and Wales. This replaced the existing Further Education Funding Council (FEFC), set up by the Tories. In Scotland, the Scottish Further Education Funding Council was transformed into a joint body in 2005, charged with overseeing the funding of the country's 43 FE colleges and 19 HE institutions: the Scottish Further and Higher Education Funding Council (SFC).

The LSC is administered at local level by 47 satellite councils. The government also introduced the concept of the 'Centre of Vocational Excellence' (COVE)—an accolade linked to the reward of additional funding for individual colleges, departments, or courses, in recognition of high achievement.

By way of answering some of the criticisms levelled at FE colleges under the self-governing regime introduced by the Tories, in the Learning and Skills Act 2000, Labour extended Ofsted's scope to cover FE. Since September 2001, all FE and sixth form colleges have been inspected on a four-year cycle. This decision was, in part, an attempt to address growing concerns about the lack of transparency in management of some colleges, shorn of direct LEA scrutiny. To cite two examples, in 1998, Stoke-on-Trent College received a bottom grade for management from government inspectors, following a succession of scandals that led to an £8m deficit, and the dismissal of a principal accused of bullying staff and running a pub in Wales while on extended sick leave. At Gwent Tertiary College, meanwhile, the principal was suspended, then resigned, after it emerged that he had made a £7m loss.

Under Mr Brown's government, the tone of FE policy in some ways began shifting away from college autonomy. While ministers have so far stopped short of taking the UK's 385 English and Welsh FE colleges back into LEA control wholesale, they are now thought to advocate greater council involvement. To this end, they have relieved the LSC of its responsibility for funding 16–19-year-olds—the core FE target market—and given this back to councils. But nearly two-thirds of all LSC funding will shortly be transferred to LEAs and the Council is ultimately expected to be wound up entirely. Nonetheless, at least nominally, FE colleges remain self-governing, in the same way as an ever-growing number of state schools. The governing bodies—that is, the 'boards' or 'corporations'—of colleges have primary autonomy over their day-to-day management, with local authorities providing a *strategic* role, in much the same way as **strategic health authorities (SHAs)** direct the work of other local NHS bodies (see p. 187).

The role of LEAs in higher education

LEAs play a much more limited role in HE. For decades, they were responsible for providing mandatory awards—or education maintenance grants—to students undertaking full-time degree courses at university or other HE institutions. In 1997, however, after being 'frozen' for seven years, state grants were scrapped by Labour, in favour of a further roll-out of the Student Loans system introduced by the Tories in 1990. Following fierce opposition from many families, then Education Secretary Charles Clarke announced the return of grants in 2004—albeit only up to £1,000 a year initially and only then for students whose parents earned less than £10,000. The value of grants (and the number of people entitled to them) has twice increased since then. As of September 2008, students whose parents have a joint income of less than £25,000 are entitled to a 'full' grant of £2,835 a year and to have their university tuition fees paid for them. Those with parents earning up to £60,000 (up from £39,300 previously) still receive a partial grant. The government claims that 50,000 more students a year will receive the full grant under the new scheme, while 100,000 will qualify for something.

Over and above the mandatory undergraduate grants for students from poorer backgrounds, LEAs also retain the power to make discretionary awards to those who follow courses that do not benefit from this system—for example, postgraduate degrees.

Funding and monitoring fairness in higher education

As in Scotland, higher education funding in England and Wales is the responsibility of a *quango*: the *Higher Education Funding Council for England (HEFCE)*. The principal roles and purpose of the Council are to:

- distribute public money for teaching and research to universities;
- promote high quality education and research in a 'financially healthy' sector;
- play 'a key role' in ensuring accountability and promoting good practice.

To this end, HEFCE has its own board and committees with the following, more specific, remits:

- quality assessment, learning, and teaching;
- widening participation;
- research;
- business and the community;
- leadership, governance, and management.

The task of ensuring that HE institutions operate 'fairly'—particularly in relation to the thorny issue of admissions policy—falls to the Office for Fair Access (OFFA), led by a 'Director for Fair Access'.

The primary job of OFFA is to ensure that institutions that opt to charge tuition fees above the 'standard level' produce an 'access agreement' detailing how they intend to make sure that their courses do not exclude people from disadvantaged backgrounds. In practice, many universities have sought to do this voluntarily, even before OFFA started work in 2006–07, by offering a range of new bursaries and scholarships targeted at high achievers from low-income households, those with disabilities, and people from under-represented minority groups.

OFFA arose, in part, out of the perceived continuing bias of some 'top' universities towards children from independent school backgrounds. Concern about this issue has been rumbling since Mr Brown publicly condemned

Magdalen College, Oxford, in 2000, for failing to offer Laura Spence, a pupil at Monkseaton Community High School in Whitley Bay, North Tyneside, a place to read medicine—despite the fact that she had achieved ten A* passes at GCSE and was predicted to gain five A grades at A level. In the event, Ms Spence (who secured straight As) won a £65,000 scholarship to Harvard. As recently as September 2007, however, *The Times* was reporting that a third of all Oxbridge places were still being taken by pupils from 3 per cent of elite independent schools. One of England's foremost public schools, Westminster College, successfully groomed half of its sixth-formers to win places at either Oxford or Cambridge. The figures were criticized by the Sutton Trust, an educational charity formed to promote greater equality of opportunity in the British school system. Sir Peter Lampl, the Trust's chairman, urged universities to recognize the 'unevenness of the system' from which applicants are drawn and to ensure they were *'nurturing and developing talent, not honing a finished product'*.

OFFA's job has become harder, argue critics, since the government's introduction of 'top-up fees' in England and Wales in 2006–07. In an effort to enable the HE sector to raise more income for investment to enable it to meet a target of luring 50 per cent of British 18-year-olds into HE by 2015, ministers have permitted individual institutions to charge additional fees over and above their basic tuition costs for students from families with combined incomes above a certain level. Opponents of this system—rejected in Scotland—say that it favours youngsters from well-heeled backgrounds and will only worsen the social mix of universities, because those from low-income households just over this threshold will be deterred from applying.

▶ The growth of free preschool education

LEAs today have limited direct involvement in providing preschool or nursery education in their areas. Prior to 1997, the Conservatives left it up to individual councils whether to fund free nursery education for children from lower-income backgrounds. Given the choice between squeezing more money out of already tight budgets and leaving it to 'the market' to provide where there was sufficient demand, many authorities voted with their feet. A 1986 audit found that free provision ranged from zero to a maximum of 27.5 places per 100 children—hardly a ringing endorsement of council investment. Many LEAs today run at least some nurseries themselves, but the majority are provided by the private and voluntary sectors. In addition, money directed to enable children from poorer backgrounds to access preschool education tends to come direct from central government, rather than via local authorities (as with many schools).

In the early 1990s, the Conservatives made a limited inroad into providing free nursery care for preschool children. So-called 'nursery vouchers'—'virtual' money used to 'buy' access for children aged 4 and over to nursery education and/or childcare worth up to £1,100—were introduced in 1996, but abandoned by Labour. The voucher system had baffled many parents: although billed as an extension of the 'parent choice' being encouraged in the school sector, it could not compensate for the fact that—however willing families were to shop around for a desirable nursery—in many areas, there simply were not enough places to go round.

Labour's solution was to scrap the voucher system (which had also proved hugely expensive to administer) and launch its first National Childcare Strategy, which concentrated in the short term on two priorities:

- increasing the number of childcare places available;
- guaranteeing all 4-year-olds a nursery place from April 1998 onwards.

Provision has been gradually extended. Since April 2004, LEAs have been obliged to guarantee free nursery places to all 3 and 4-year-olds for up to 12.5 hours a week (to be taken in up to five 2.5-hour sessions), for 33 weeks a year. In late 2008, Mr Brown used his Labour conference address to signal plans to further extend this to two-year-olds.

Improving access and accountability in preschool education

While responsibility for 'early years education' rests with the devolved administrations in Scotland, Wales, and Northern Ireland, in England, a new programme was established in 1999 to drive through the government's aims of guaranteeing high-quality provision for children from low-income households: *Sure Start*. Although its primary focus is on welfare and educational development, Sure Start has extended its support to the whole of a child's family, in an effort to improve their financial and social prospects.

The 'Sure Start' concept arose out of New Labour's conviction that early years education is crucial to a child's social and emotional well-being, and that families prevented from accessing it miss out on a vital development tool. Ministers' conviction that preschool teaching should be seen as a core entitlement, rather than an optional 'add-on' accessible only to the middle classes, was based on a body of research into its impact in later life and the outcomes of experiments in similar schemes pioneered in Scandinavian countries.

Sure Start aims to:

- increase the availability of childcare for all children;
- improve health and emotional development for young children;
- support parents as parents and in their aspirations towards employment.

Sure Start operates through a network of children's centres, often based at the heart of deprived estates, in community centres and church halls. Staffed by multidisciplinary teams of professionals, including health visitors, teachers, and social workers, they have become focal points for liaison between families and a whole range of support services over and above those concerned with childcare—from *Jobcentre Plus*, to expert antenatal and postnatal advice for new parents. In a modest extension of their duties in relation to preschool children, local authorities were recently given overall 'strategic responsibility' for developing Sure Start centres in their area.

Where Sure Start ensures everyone has *access* to preschool education, Ofsted monitors the *standard* of that provision. Its remit was recently increased to cover nurseries, nursery schools, and also playgroups and childminders (see pp. 559–60).

→ Further reading

Crook, D., Power, S., and Whitty, G. (2000) *The Grammar School Question: A Review of Research on Comprehensive and Selective Education*, London: Institute of Education. **An examination of comparative qualitative and quantitative data relating to selective and non-selective state schools.**

Jones, K. (2002) *Education in Britain: 1944 to the Present*, Cambridge: Polity Press. **Historical and sociological examination of the evolution of schooling in the maintained sector since the Second World War.**

Mansell, W. (2007) *Education by Numbers: The Tyranny of Testing*, London: Politico's Publishing. **Informed overview and critique of recent British governments' increasing reliance on targets, league tables, and academic testing.**

Phillips, R. and Furlong, J. (2001) *Education, Reform and the State: Twenty-Five Years of Politics, Policy and Practice*, London: Routledge Falmer. **Critical overview of the major trends and debates in educational reform in the UK over the past quarter-century, starting with the 'great debate' and moving towards school autonomy.**

? Review questions

1. Outline the structure of state education in Britain, identifying the main differences between England, Wales, Scotland, and Northern Ireland.

2. What are the main types of school operating in the UK state sector? How have their names changed since the advent of New Labour?

3. Describe what is meant by 'localism'. What are the main types of self-governing state school and how do their levels of autonomy differ? What are the main issues surrounding higher education in relation to student access? How has Labour sought to address them?

4. Outline the role of Ofsted and local league tables. What impact have they had on the relative popularity of different schools and the growth of the independent sector?

Online resource centre

www.oxfordtextbooks.co.uk/orc/Morrison
Visit the Online Resource Centre that accompanies this book for web links and regular updates.

16

Planning policy
and environmental protection

Education may be the local policy area that is closest to the hearts of the British public, but if there is one subject—other than rising *Council Tax* bills—that is guaranteed to get them even more agitated, it is planning. Local newspapers are crammed with stories about planning controversies on a daily basis: from rows about out-of-town superstores 'sucking the life-blood' from town centres, to protests by 'not in my backyard' (NIMBY) residents about proposed sites for New Age traveller camps or drug treatment centres.

But away from all the placard-waving and sensationalist headlines, planning is a deeply serious issue for everyone. Without planning policy, there would be no schools, hospitals, offices, care homes, supermarkets, or village shops. Before a developer can start work on a site, and a company or public sector organization can get anywhere near opening new premises, or altering existing ones, they will need to obtain planning consent. And decisions by local authorities about whether to grant that consent will be dictated by overarching guidelines—some set out by central government, others by councils—designed to make overall patterns of development as harmonious as possible, to provide the most effective infrastructure, and to limit its impact on the natural environment.

Compared to other areas of local authority responsibility—particularly highways, transport, and public health—planning policy (traditionally known as 'town and country planning') has emerged relatively recently. Its three basic underlying principles are to:

- ensure that all development is supported by appropriate infra-structure—for example, roads, traffic crossings, bus routes, leisure facilities;
- make sure that any impact that it has on the environment is sustainable;
- ensure that it is located on land that is unlikely to be affected by factors, such as flooding.

To this end, there is a single Town and Country Planning Code that is designed to control all development in England and Wales, which arose through nine principal Acts:

- the Town and Country Planning Act 1947;
- the Town and Country Planning Act 1968;
- four separate Acts passed in 1990;
- the Planning and Compensation Act 1991;
- the Planning and Compulsory Purchase Act 2004;
- the Planning Act 2008.

The planning process itself is divided into two broad categories:

- *forward planning*—the drawing up of strategic development plans, by individual local authorities at area level and regionally by regional assemblies (as of 2010, *regional development agencies*). These map out long-term planning strategies for each area, acting as a guide to councils in their planning decisions;
- *development control*—where authorities respond to individual planning applications and decide whether to approve or reject proposed material changes to existing land or buildings, or to carry out physical development, such as construction or demolition.

The role of the Communities Secretary in relation to planning is outlined in Table 16.1.

Table 16.1 The role of the Communities Secretary in relation to planning procedures

Role	Responsibilities
Provides guidance	Lays down guidelines on how local planning authorities should carry out their responsibilities by issuing periodic **statutory instruments**, known until recently as 'planning policy guidance notes' (PPGs), but now renamed 'planning policy statements' (PPSs). These are supplemented by more specific regional spatial strategies (RSSs)—formerly regional planning guidance (RPGs)—produced by government Offices for the Regions.
Sets general ground rules	Draws up fixed rules about the types of land suitable for development.
Arbitrates in disputes	Acts as final arbiter in disputes between individuals and authorities, and can appoint independent inspectors to convene public planning inquiries to determine a disputed application.
Final rulings in last resort	Can 'call in' controversial planning applications to give a final ruling where even a planning inquiry has failed to resolve the issue.

▶ Forward planning

Since the 1991 Act, there have been three varieties of local authority development plan, the names of which vary according to the type of council responsible for drawing them up. All three—structure plans for counties, local plans for districts and boroughs, and unitary plans for metropolitan and unitary areas—are in the process of being abolished, to be replaced by a more *regional* approach to development planning. In practice, however, they remain in place in many areas, as transitional arrangements in lieu of the introduction of the new system. The three types are explained in Table 16.2, which can be found on the Online Resource Centre that accompanies this book. The procedures by which structure and local plans are adopted are outlined in Table 16.3, also found on the Online Resource Centre.

As with most issues concerning local government, here and there, the system produces exceptional quirks. In most hybrid counties—those with a **two-tier structure** sitting alongside one or more unitary authorities—countywide development plans, encompassing the elements of structure, local, and unitary plans, have tended to be produced by a joint strategic planning authority. In London, in addition to the unitary plans produced by individual boroughs, the **Greater London Authority (GLA)** oversees a joint strategic planning authority for the whole city.

The 2004 Act began the process of replacing all of the above with a simplified system, which the government claimed would both speed up and harmonize the process of development planning across the UK, by giving a handful of regional bodies the power to take strategic decisions for huge swathes of the country. Under this system, development planning has steadily been reduced to a simple two-tier process, as follows.

- *Regional spatial strategies (RSS)* are overarching 20-year planning frameworks for each of England's eight regions and are produced by designated *regional planning bodies.* Up until recently, these were the eight regional assemblies, but in 2010, they will be wound up and regional development agencies will take over this duty. The capital is covered by an overarching London Spatial Development Strategy, while each of the three devolved countries has its own single spatial plan.

- *Local development documents* are local planning strategies produced by individual local planning authorities—that is, borough/district councils, and unitary authorities. These are effectively 'watered-down' local and unitary plans, because the authority will be unable to deviate from the strict guidelines set out by the RSS. Local development documents are further constrained by the terms of *local development schemes*—broad statements of intent by authorities about their long-term planning strategies, open to public inspection, which dictate the terms within which specific plans are proposed.

To critics (including many local councillors and officers), RSSs are a centralizing mechanism designed to undermine the ability of local authorities to determine the direction of planning policy in their areas. Indeed, the 2008 Bill arguably takes this trend further, by introducing the concept of centrally determined 'national policy statements' (NPSs). Opponents argue that ministers can impose unsympathetic and/or unsustainable development on local authorities in the interests of national targets. An example is the ongoing dispute between Whitehall and town halls over the top-down 'housing quotas' designed to address the shortage of homes for key workers and low earners (see p. 535), particularly in less-developed rural areas.

Criticism has also been directed at the bodies responsible for determining strategic planning policy under the new arrangements, which lack councils' transparency and democratic accountability. In England, responsibility for producing RSSs was initially handed to the eight regional assemblies set up by former Deputy Prime Minister John Prescott as a first step towards introducing directly elected regional chambers. But since the abandonment of plans for English regional *devolution,* following overwhelming rejection of the idea in a *referendum* in the north-east in November 2004 (see p. 41), all assemblies except London's have trundled on under their previous member-ship. Although 60 per cent of these are elected councillors seconded from relevant local authorities, they have no direct mandate in their regional role and the remainder of their colleagues are appointed. Critics argue that taking power away from elected councils and handing it to distant regional bodies with no clear accountability to local people conflicts with the spirit of 'localism' that is increasingly championed by all of the major parties in relation to most other walks of life. Although regional assemblies are in the process of being phased out and their powers handed to existing regional development agencies, these, too, are appointed rather than elected.

Such concerns may soon be academic, in relation to many of the more significant infrastructural developments that currently preoccupy assem-blies/agencies in drawing up their RSSs, such as major road-building pro-grammes, energy projects such as nuclear power stations and wind farms, and construction on the *greenbelt* (see pp. 507–12). The 2008 Bill stipulated that decisions on these issues would, from April 2009, be handed to a new national Infrastructure Planning Commission. Its members—although bound by NPSs devised by the Department for Communities and Local Gov-ernment (DCLG)—would be independent of government. Perhaps most im-portantly for the public, the Commission would hold its hearings in public and take the final say on infrastructural planning away from the Secretary of State—theoretically replacing political decisions with pragmatic ones based on impartial expertise.

▮ Development control

Although long-term development plans have a significant impact on the lives of British families and businesses, it is specific planning applications that tend to arouse the strongest emotions. This is invariably reflected in the nature of press coverage about planning issues: while most people would struggle to remember the last time that there was a notable debate about their council's structure plan—and many are unlikely even to have heard of 'regional spatial strategies' yet—most will be familiar with local disputes about the proposed locations of new sewage works and landfill sites. And how many can claim never to have been riled by a neighbour's plans to extend the size of his or her property, or the increase in traffic and parking problems caused by a local developer turning a handful of houses into multiple flats?

As stated earlier in this chapter, the procedure used by local planning authorities to determine the success or otherwise of individual planning applications is known as 'development control'. The right to build on a site from scratch, or to make major structural alterations to an existing development, is known as *planning permission.* Some minor material alterations to an existing building may require no permission, or only a 'one-stop' decision from the planning authority to give consent. But most 'new-build' applications, however big or small, require planning permission in two stages:

1. *outline planning permission*—that is, consent 'in principle' for a site to be developed. Obtaining outline permission is often used by building developers as a way of 'testing the water' with a proposal that they may not pursue once they have investigated further to decide its commercial viability—for example, a proposed shopping centre. Plots of land are often sold to prospective developers with outline permission already in place. Outline permission lasts for five years from the date on which it is granted, but if the developer has not proceeded to the next planning stage within three years, it will also lapse;

2. *detailed (full) planning permission*—once outline permission has been obtained and a developer decides to proceed with the prospective development, he or she will apply for detailed permission. With any major scheme, the outline planning process will usually have highlighted particular 'gaps' in detail that the developer will now have to fill—for example, a detailed proposal for an out-of-town retail park will need to address concerns about transport and access, environmental impact, etc. It will also need to specify the exact location, dimensions, and makeup of the proposed development—for example, how many shops the retail park will include, how many car parking spaces, etc. Like outline permission, detailed permission lapses if not acted on within five years.

When deciding whether to grant planning permission, authorities have three options:

- *unconditional consent*—that is, approval of the application with no alterations;

- *conditional consent*—that is, approval subject to provisos (for example, better access to the site, improved or new traffic crossings, additional parking, environmental adaptations). A developer will often be given outline permission with attached conditions and he or she will be expected to satisfy these before being granted detailed consent;
- *refusal*—that is, the outright rejection of an application.

Before any planning authority can decide whether to grant permission for a proposed development, it must follow a detailed process designed to give every 'interested party'—that is, those who are likely to be most directly affected by its approval—the chance to air their views. This procedure is described in detail in Table 16.4.

Table 16.4 The stages of the development control planning process

Stage	Process
Completing an application	Official forms must be obtained from the local authority responsible for development control (i.e. district or **borough council** in two-tier areas, unitary authorities, or metropolitan/London borough councils).
Entering on the register	The application appears in the formal register of applicants and immediate neighbours are immediately notified by the council. Parish and/or community councils will also be fully consulted at this stage.
Advertising application	Certain kinds of application must be advertised in the local press to enable others who 'may be affected by it' to make representations.
Public consultation and exhibition stage (major applications only)	Proposals for a major development will see the authority organize a public exhibition, often involving detailed plans and models, either at its own offices or at a local library or other council-run venue.
Subcommittee, committee, and full council decisions	Routine and small-scale planning applications (e.g. extensions to a domestic garage) will normally be determined at subcommittee or committee level, purely on the basis of existing regulations. Major applications will be treated as **key decisions**, and will have to go before both the **cabinet** and full council for a final verdict.
Appeal	If an application is turned down, the applicant has six months to lodge an appeal with the Secretary of State. Each stage of an application must be determined within two months (unless granted an extension due to its complexity). If it is not, the application may apply for a ruling from the government on grounds of 'non-determination'.
'Calling in'	The Secretary of State may 'call in' particularly controversial planning applications for a decision—normally, when a bid raises issues of national or regional importance, arouses 'more than local opposition', raises 'unusual issues', or becomes 'unreasonable' to expect the local planning authority to adjudicate on it alone.

Small-scale planning applications—and changes of use

While a tight rein is kept on more ambitious development plans, because of their potential to affect large numbers of people other than the applicants, it is not always necessary to obtain formal permission for minor material alterations to land or buildings. Under the Town and Country Planning (Use Classes) Order 1987 and the Town and Country Planning (Use Classes) Order 1995, various kinds of land and property are split into 'classes' and a material change of use 'within the same class' will normally not need planning consent; neither will certain changes of use between **related** classes—provided that no major building work is required.

For example, a greengrocer may be changed to a newsagent with no need for planning permission, because both are class A1 business premises, and therefore considered sufficiently similar not to require it. Restaurants, meanwhile, can be changed into shops without permission, because both are within the same overall 'class order' (the former A1 and the latter A3). The same is not always true in reverse, however—changing a shop into a restaurant, for example, may also involve making further applications, including obtaining a liquor licence. Neither is it possible to change from an A to a B-class establishment without permission. Table 16.5 outlines the changes that are currently allowed without planning permission.

In addition to the above permitted changes of commercial use, the 1995 Order allows home extensions to go ahead without the need for planning consent—provided that they comply with specified conditions. Local authorities

Table 16.5 Changes of use allowed without acquiring planning permission

From	To
A1 (shop)	A1 (shop, plus single flat above)
A2 (professional and financial services)	A2 (plus single flat above)
A2 (when premises have a display window at ground level)	A1
A3 (restaurants and cafes)	A1 or A2
A4 (drinking establishments)	A1 or A2 or A3
A5 (hot food takeaways)	A1 or A2 or A3
B1 (business) (permission limited to 235m^2 of floor space in the building)	B8 (storage and distribution)
B2 (general industrial)	B1 (business)
B2 (general industrial) (permission limited to 235m^2 of floor space in the building)	B8 (storage and distribution)
B8 (storage and distribution) (permission limited to 235m^2 of floor space in the building)	B1 (business)

have discretion, however, to pass an 'Article 4 Direction' removing some of these permitted development rights—particularly if the extension is likely to have a negative impact on the view and/or quality of light enjoyed by a neighbouring property. Planning consent is not usually required to lop or cut down a tree—provided that it is not under a tree preservation order (TPO), or in a *conservation area.* If the former is violated, the local authority has the power to prosecute.

In contrast to all of these exceptions, applications for planning permission are *always* required for material changes of use involving amusement centres, theatres, scrapyards, petrol filling stations, car showrooms, taxi firms, car hire businesses, and youth hostels—all of which are categorized as *sui generis.*

Planning appeals and inquiries

As outlined earlier, it is possible for either an applicant or opponent to appeal against a council's approval or rejection of a planning application—provided that he or she does so within six months of the date of the decision letter. If permission is refused, or only conditional consent granted, applicants may lodge appeals free of charge with a Planning Inspectorate in England and Wales (there is one for each of the two countries).

There are three ways in which an appeal can be decided:

- a planning inspector's consideration of written representations by both parties, alongside a brief site visit;
- a formal hearing with both parties present;
- a full *planning inquiry*—which is by far the lengthiest and most costly option.

At present, four-fifths of appeals are decided by the 'written method', 16 per cent by hearings, and 4 per cent after an inquiry.

In Scotland, the Planning (Scotland) Act 2006 altered the previous appeal system—which saw them referred directly to the *Scottish Government's* Directorate for Environmental and Planning Appeals—to bring decision-making closer to the ground. Until recently, appeals had been due to be heard by local member review bodies of councillors from 2009, but this now seems unlikely, because of controversy about the rigour of the process. Similar plans for appeals about minor developments to be heard by panels of councillors, rather than inspectors, in England and Wales have also been shelved, due to objections from members of Parliament (MPs) and peers. In

Northern Ireland, the planning appeal process remains the responsibility of the Planning Appeals Commission.

The most high-profile planning inquiries tend to be those called in response to objections to an approved development—rather than appeals by unsuccessful applicants. Stansted Airport has been the subject of two such inquiries in recent years, both related to the expansion plans of its owner, BAA. The first—the findings of which were still awaiting formal government approval at time of writing—related to its attempts to increase its current annual passenger limit of 25 million a year. The second, ongoing, inquiry was into BAA's application for permission to build a second terminal and runway (as recommended in a 2003 Air Transport *White Paper*). The company's plans for a fifth terminal—finally realized in 2008—were subjected to an earlier inquiry, which lasted nearly four years, starting in May 1995.

Even after an inquiry, the Secretary of State may occasionally intervene to make a final judgement, based on the recommendations included in an inspector's report. This was the case in the recent debacle over Brighton and Hove Albion Football Club's ultimately successful application to build a new 22,000-seater stadium near the village of Falmer in East Sussex, which prompted two separate planning inquiries.

The only way that the Secretary of State's 'final decision' in these exceptional cases may be challenged is in the High Court, by a judicial review based on a point of law. Both the appellant and the council may apply to the inspector for the other side to pay its costs should the judgment go their way. In the Brighton stadium case, then Secretary of State Mr Prescott's decision to back the proposal in October 2005 led to an immediate pledge by its main opponents—Lewes District Council, Falmer Parish Council, and the South Downs Joint Committee—to mount a challenge. But after his successor, Hazel Blears, reaffirmed his verdict, in July 2007, they reluctantly dropped their plans.

The procedure surrounding planning inquiries is outlined in Table 16.6.

Other issues affecting major developments

Although notionally highly rigorous, the convoluted consultation procedure surrounding planning applications has often been dismissed as no more than a paper exercise in local democracy. Despite its supposed transparency,

Table 16.6 The procedure for planning inquiries

Stage	Procedure
Advertisement	Planning inquiries to be publicized in advance—with invitations sent to any formal objectors to the plan, anyone with a legal interest in the site, and the local parish/community council to address the hearings. An independent inspector (in exceptional cases, two) is appointed by the Secretary of State to chair proceedings and make a recommended judgement at the end.
Convening hearings	Formal hearings are held, often over a period of weeks, with all of the above allowed to speak. At their discretion, the inspector *may* allow individuals other than those 'with a right to be heard' to speak at the hearing.
Presentations of evidence	Inspectors will listen to evidence for and against, and make site visits to the proposed development area in question. One or more site visits are likely to occur.
Verdict	Often made by the inspector, a few weeks or more after the completion of the inquiry hearings. With some major inquiries, the inspector may refer his or her recommendations to the Secretary of State for a final decision.
Appeal	An application for leave for a judicial review may be filed with the High Court—but only on a 'point of law' or human rights issue.

councils have been criticized for doing too little to make the public aware that a 'consultation' is actually taking place—sticking poorly photocopied notices to trees and lampposts, rather than proactively leafleting homes or knocking on doors. The planning process was memorably lampooned in Douglas Adams's novel, *The Hitchhiker's Guide to the Galaxy*, in which the hero, Arthur Dent, awakes to find a bulldozer about to demolish his house to make way for a bypass about which he knows nothing. On questioning the developers, while lying in front of the bulldozer, he reflects on the tortuous lengths to which he had to go to view the plans while they were 'on display'—by taking a torch into a disused toilet bearing a sign with the legend: 'Beware of the Leopard!'

In real life, too, if a proposed development is not in breach of the law, the odds have historically been stacked in favour of major developments—especially where they are likely to bring new jobs and other economic benefits—and councillors have frequently been criticized for their propensity to be won over by grand gestures and promises of prestige. One recent example of this was Brighton and Hove Council's ultimately ill-fated decision to grant detailed planning permission to a consortium of developers and architects, including Frank Gehry, who designed Bilbao's world-famous Guggenheim museum, for an ambitious £290m residential block comprising two 'crumpled tin can' towers, a sports centre, a GP surgery, cafes, and restaurants directly overlooking the sea. Although toned-down from earlier designs—including one that would have seen four towers, each up to 25 storeys high—the plan infuriated residents of the signature Regency townhouses and apartments that line Hove's seafront, many of whom argued that it would blot out their views.

Planning contribution (or planning gain)

One way in which developers have increasingly sought to persuade local authorities to look kindly on their applications is by offering them 'sweeteners', in the form of additional infrastructural improvements that they would otherwise struggle to afford. For example, a company seeking permission to build a new luxury apartment complex might offer to build some social housing elsewhere in the same area at a reduced price, in the hope of inducing councillors to back its principal project. This offer of a 'benefit in kind' is known as *planning contribution (or planning gain)*. Gain is also intended to avoid major new developments putting an unnecessary strain on existing infrastructure, by ensuring that necessary changes are made to accommodate them.

Although it had operated informally for a number of years beforehand, the concept of planning gain was formally recognized in the Planning and Compensation Act 1991. Up to that point, it had been the convention for developers only to provide the infrastructure—that is, the roads, crossings, and community amenities—*within* the bounds of the housing estate or business development that they were building. All external roads, access points, traffic crossings, etc. tended to be financed by the council. But in 1991, all of this changed and it became commonplace for developers to provide both *on-site* and any *off-site* gain required to enable the proposed development to function properly—for example, both to give people access to and from the site, and even to transport them there. Although, in theory, this saved councils a lot of money and 'penalized' developers, the quid pro quo was that applicants were able to use the incentive of off-site planning gain as a 'carrot' to wave before councils more liberally than in the past. In this sense, planning contribution is arguably as much a 'gain' for the developer as it is for the authority.

Nonetheless, planning gain has undeniably helped to finance much that is worthwhile. Recent examples of large-scale gain have included the £2.5m invested by London's Canary Wharf (a privately owned estate) in the Tower

Hamlets Further and Higher Education Trust—a grant-giving body designed to provide educational opportunities for people from deprived backgrounds. And it is not only commercial businesses that get involved in negotiations over planning gain: the government has occasionally been a direct party to it, too. In June 2008, Environment Secretary Hilary Benn announced that he was writing to every local authority to ask it to consider 'volunteering' to become the location of a deep geological disposal facility for waste from Britain's nuclear power stations. The prize should they agree? More local jobs and 'other benefits', including improved infrastructure and services.

Indeed, ministers have been looking for even more imaginative ways of helping local authorities to profit from commercial development. In its 2006 White Paper (the first of two that formed the basis of the 2008 Bill), Labour pledged to introduce a new 'planning gain supplement'—a tax of up to 20 per cent on the profits made by landowners selling off land for development. The idea was that up to 70 per cent of the proceeds would be pumped back into the local area to help finance the building of the schools, roads, and community amenities needed to support the government's huge house-building programme. But, following extensive lobbying by the building industry, which argued that less land would be available for housing as a result, the plan was shelved by Chancellor Alistair Darling in his 2007 Pre-Budget Report. The 2008 Bill promises a new levy of some kind on development land—called the 'community infrastructure levy'—but it is unclear exactly what form this will take.

Planning gain is not the only means by which local authorities enter into bilateral agreements with developers to secure additional benefits for communities. The 1990 Act (as amended by the 1991 Act) introduced 'section 106 agreements'—a means by which, having already granted outline permission for a site, councils may subsequently require developers to sign legally binding contracts requiring them to provide specified community infrastructure, avoid damaging existing infrastructure, and even transfer ownership of development land to the authority or another body for 'safekeeping'. Examples include:

- the developer giving an area of woodland to the council, together with a suitable fee to cover its future maintenance;
- the developer being required to plant a specified number of trees and maintain them for a number of years—or only to use some of the land for a specified amenity purpose;

- a requirement for the developer to build a specified amount of social housing at a specified location, to provide funds for a school or other community facilities local to a housing estate that it has constructed, or to create a park, playground, or nature reserve.

Developers cannot be *forced* into signing section 106 agreements. In practice, however, they have often been happy to do so—not least in relation to controversial developments that are likely to be the subject of appeals by local residents or businesses—because they offer as much legal protection to them as councils. The aforementioned proposal for a tower block in Hove was made subject to a section 106 agreement shortly before its backers pulled out in July 2008.

A related idea worth mentioning here is the concept of 'per cent for art'—a now widely used device whereby local authorities can compel developers to set aside a small percentage of their total project cost to provide public art. This can take the form of anything from a modernist or classical sculpture erected outside the development site itself, to a payment in kind to the council to go towards the cost of, for example, a local arts festival or street art displays elsewhere in the locality. Such schemes currently operate in areas as diverse as Brighton and Hove and Teignbridge in Devon.

Greenfield versus brownfield sites—and the decline of the greenbelt

An enduring conflict facing planning authorities is their struggle to balance the perceived need for certain kinds of development—housing estates, schools, hospitals, and shopping centres—with their legal and ethical obligations to conserve and protect the natural environment. At a basic level, councils have to take decisions almost daily about whether to approve applications to build on *greenfield sites*—that is, plots of land that have either never been built on before, or have remained 'natural' for prolonged periods. Obvious examples of greenfield land include agricultural fields, parks, and public gardens. The alternative to greenfield sites—and that favoured publicly by the present government—is the *brownfield site*. This is a plot of land, normally in a town centre or suburb, that was the site of a previous development. It may be the location of an abandoned office block or car park, or a largely derelict scrap of land devoid of extant buildings.

National planning policy has fluctuated dramatically in recent decades between the conflicting priorities of building new homes, offices, and retail outlets on the one hand, and preserving green spaces for 'quality of life' reasons on the other. Between the 1960s and 1980s, successive governments liberalized the planning laws to make it easier for developers to build on so-called 'out of town' or 'edge of town' greenfield sites, in recognition of the pressure on space in tightly developed town centres (many of which had originally developed in an unplanned, organic way). By the late 1990s, however, a significant backlash had begun against such developments, with town centre businesses complaining of losing custom to the then new breed of out-of-town superstores, and growing social and infrastructural problems afflicting housing estates in outlying areas—many the preserve of low-income families, benefit claimants, and especially the unemployed.

In its first few years in office, Labour sought to redress the balance, introducing new guidelines to encourage councils to lure developers into town centres. The aim was twofold: to regenerate eyesore urban sites, and to provide housing and amenities in the heart of the community, in so doing integrating previously marginalized groups, and making it easier for them to obtain work and to contribute meaningfully to society.

But times change—and so too do government priorities. The soaring house prices of the past decade have seen many British people—particularly low-paid 'key workers', such as nurses and teachers—unable to climb onto even the lowest rung of the property ladder. The limited space offered by brownfield sites for development on the scale that the government believes is necessary to tackle the 'national housing shortage' has led to sweeping quotas being imposed on many regions and local authorities. This trend has necessarily led to development being targeted more at rural areas, including the greenbelt—that is, areas formally designated by local authorities around towns and cities to be preserved from development, to prevent urban sprawl and to protect wildlife (see pp. 507–12).

Introduced in 1935, by the then Greater London Regional Planning Committee, the notion of a ring of land protected from urbanization for the foreseeable future quickly became fashionable in smaller centres. It was eventually formalized by central government, firstly, in the Town and Country Planning Act 1947 and, more recently, in Planning Policy Guidance Note 2 (PPG2, introduced in 1995). As of the 1993 structure and local plans—the last drawn up to date—around 13 per cent of the English countryside is designated greenbelt, covering 14 discrete areas in all.

PPG2 outlines that the five purposes of greenbelts are to:

- check the unrestricted sprawl of large built-up areas;
- prevent neighbouring towns from merging into one another;
- assist in safeguarding the countryside from encroachment;
- preserve the setting and special character of historic towns;
- assist in urban regeneration, by 'recycling' derelict and other urban land.

Once an area has been defined as greenbelt, it is expected to provide the following:

- opportunities for access to the open countryside for the urban population;
- opportunities for outdoor sport and outdoor recreation near urban areas;
- the retention of attractive landscapes and enhanced landscape near where people live;
- the improvement of damaged and derelict land around towns;
- the securing of nature conservation interests;
- the retention of land in agricultural, forestry, and related uses.

For many years, greenbelts were treated as sacrosanct by local authorities, but, with a rapidly rising population and diminishing land space in already developed areas, they are increasingly compromising their long-held resistance to expansion into these zones. And government policy, again, is making it hard for them to resist.

Since 1996, developers proposing to build new supermarkets on the outskirts of towns, or within relatively easy reach of a town, have been forced to satisfy both a 'needs test' and an 'impact test' to be eligible for planning permission. The former requires them to prove that a new superstore is 'needed' in that location, given lack of choice for consumers elsewhere, while the latter is meant to ensure that there will be no negative impact on trade in the nearby town centre. A government consultation document currently under consideration proposes to relax this provision, by combining the twin tests—a move that, according to the Association of Convenience Stores, led to a notable rise in the number of out-of-town stores when adopted in Scotland.

Greenbelts are not the only designation used to protect land from development. Some areas of countryside and coastline are regarded as so exceptional in terms of their beauty, and the richness or rarity of their flora and fauna, that they qualify for designation as one of the following, under the terms of the National Parks and Access to the Countryside Act 1949:

- an *area of outstanding natural beauty (AONB)*—that is, an area recognized as being deserving of special protection to conserve and enhance the natural beauty of its landscape, to meet the need for quiet enjoyment of the countryside by the public, and to have regard for the interests of those who live and work there;

- a *national park*—that is, an area of countryside with additional statutory protection against development, commercial exploitation, and habitation.

Until recently, both AONBs and national parks were designated by the Countryside Agency, but this job now falls to its replacement: *Natural England.*

According to its mission statement, Natural England is committed to '*conserve, protect, and manage the natural environment for the benefit of current and future generations*'. It seeks to promote:

- a healthy natural environment;
- enjoyment of the natural environment;
- sustainable use of the natural environment;
- a secure environmental future.

Natural England, like most government *quangos,* is run by an executive board, in the manner of a company or charity, with a chief executive and a chairman. Despite the fact that its remit is to protect AONBs, national parks, and green spaces more generally, the organization has not been afraid to challenge some long-standing 'sacred cows' since its inception in October 2006. In 2007, chairman Sir Martin Doughty used its first anniversary speech to argue that 'the sanctity of greenbelt land should be questioned', in light of the government's drive to find space for three million more homes by 2020 (see p. 535).

There are currently 35 AONBs in England and Wales (covering 18 per cent of their combined countryside); there are four in Wales—one straddling the border with England—and nine in Northern Ireland. The smallest AONB is the Isles of Scilly (designated in 1976), which is just 16 km², and the largest is the Cotswolds (covering 2,038 km²). Although they notionally qualify for

greater protection than mere greenbelts, in practice, councils are not required by law to preserve AONBs and have little power to do so, other than by
applying standard planning controls more vigorously.

Perhaps because of this, significant development has continued on or
alongside AONBs, leading to vociferous protests from countryside pressure groups, most notably the Campaign to Protect Rural England (CPRE),
fronted by bestselling author Bill Bryson. In 2006, it highlighted the plight
of three in particular. Dorset AONB was threatened by major road plans,
while the Kent Downs were the target of a proposal by Imperial College,
London, to build thousands of new homes and offices. The Brighton stadium
debacle (see p. 503) was particularly sensitive because of the scheme's prox-
imity to the Sussex Downs AONB.

National parks are a higher form of designation that, unlike AONBs, is afforded greater statutory protection from development. To this end, they are
protected by their own *national park authorities*. There are 14 in total—nine
in England, three in Wales, and two in Scotland, where AONBs do not exist;
the nearest equivalent being national scenic areas (NSAs). A fifteenth is expected to be confirmed shortly, in the South Downs. In England and Scotland,
7 per cent of countryside is designated national park land, while in Wales, it
is 20 per cent. The existing national parks are listed in Table 16.7.

Table 16.7 National parks in the UK

Key	National park	Established	Area (km^2)
1	Peak District	1951	1,438
2	Lake District	1951	2,292
3	Snowdonia (Welsh: *Eryri*)	1951	2,142
4	Dartmoor	1951	956
5	Pembrokeshire Coast (Welsh: *Arfordir Penfro*)	1952	620
6	North York Moors	1952	1,436
7	Yorkshire Dales	1954	1,769
8	Exmoor	1954	693
9	Northumberland	1956	1,049
10	Brecon Beacons (Welsh: *Bannau Brycheiniog*)	1957	1,351
11	The Broads	1988	303
12	New Forest	2005	580
13	South Downs	2008	1,641
14	Cairngorms	2003	3,800
15	Loch Lomond and the Trossachs	2002	1,865

In addition to AONBs, national parks, and greenbelts, successive govern-ments have tried to conserve at least some of Britain's wooded areas in the teeth of ever-increasing demand for development land. The quango respon-sible for preserving woodland for public benefit is the Forestry Commission, headed by a chairman and up to ten regional commissioners.

Land banks and the great supermarket stranglehold

A planning issue that has come to prominence only recently is the growing practice by some big developers and their clients of building up 'land banks'. This term refers to the idea of purchasing pockets of land—and often obtain-ing outline planning permission to develop them—without actually doing so for prolonged or indefinite periods. The use of land banks is viewed as highly unscrupulous by its critics: although developers argue that they are merely trying to guarantee themselves 'first refusal' to build on a site, the fact that they are 'sitting on it' without doing so is seen as an anti-competitive move pri-marily designed to stop anyone else getting in first. In some cases, land banks have proved even more controversial, with developers or their clients buying up land only to sell it on to third parties—in so doing, writing clauses into sales agreements preventing the sites being developed by rival companies.

Of all alleged 'land-bankers', the one most often cited is supermarket chain Tesco. In St Albans, the company is believed to have purchased more than four acres of land, which has lain undeveloped for more than five years. Perceived threats to the town's historic marketplace have prompted the for-mation of a media-savvy 'St Albans Stop Tesco Group' and captured national newspaper headlines, as well as being covered by several BBC reports.

Compulsory purchase orders and planning blight

Sometimes, plans are approved for developments on such a mammoth scale—or with such a significant likely impact on surrounding environments—that it is necessary for land and buildings that might otherwise stand in its way to be 'cleared' before work can proceed. Examples of such projects include the building of new airport runways, such as those mentioned above, or new roads, waterways, harbours, or new towns (see pp. 522–3). In such cases, it is sometimes necessary for planning authorities to force homeowners and businesses to move, so that their premises can be bulldozed to make way for the development. In this case, councils serve a *compulsory purchase order* (CPO), in a process outlined in Table 16.8, which can be found on the Online Resource Centre.

CPOs are not the only means by which local authorities sometimes find themselves having to pay compensation to the owners of property as a result of their planning decisions. Should the value of a property drop because of a decision by a council to approve a controversial application—for example, for a sewage works—the property might be regarded as 'blighted'. In such cases, the owners can effectively force the authority to buy their blighted homes from them—a type of 'CPO in reverse'. People owning property the value of which has been cut by a minimum threshold amount due to fumes from public works that began after 1971 may also claim compensation.

 The process for lodging a planning blight claim is outlined in Table 16.9, which can be found on the Online Resource Centre.

Other quirks of the planning system

Authorities now have the power to decline to consider planning applications on the grounds that the Secretary of State has refused a 'similar' one, on appeal, within the preceding two years. In addition, there are various ways of *enforcing* planning controls, as well as monitoring to ensure developments granted are lawful, as listed in Table 16.10.

Table 16.10 Other forms of planning notice

Action	Effect
Certificate of lawfulness of existing use or development (CLEUD)/Certificate of lawfulness of proposed use of development (CLEPUD)	Can be issued on a planning authority by anyone wishing to find out if an existing or proposed use of land is lawful
Enforcement notice	Served on a developer by the council if no planning application has been made for a development—or if the terms of a consent or refusal have been breached. This will describe the nature of the breach and spell out the steps to be taken within a specified period of time
Stop notice	Served on a developer by the council if a breach is 'in the process of being committed'
Developer appeal to Secretary of State	The individual or company concerned may appeal to the Secretary-of-State against any such notice—normally prompting an inquiry. If the notice served is ultimately quashed, the authority may be liable for compensating the appellant. But if the appeal fails, the authority may take further action—including prosecuting the individual or company for a criminal offence (the maximum fine in a magistrates' court is £20,000)

▌ Other planning-related issues—building regulations

Even when formal planning permission per se is not required for a new build or to adapt an existing building, *building permission* (under *building regulations*) invariably will be. The reason for such regulations is primarily to ensure that buildings are structurally sound from a point of view of safety, health, and design—and an inspector (normally from the local authority) will visit the property during work to ensure that it meets the specified regulations.

Other than in inner London, which has its own system, the standard of regulations is the same across the country. It derives from the Public Health Act 1961—which stopped councils making their own building *by-laws* and returned that power to ministers—and the Health and Safety at Work Act 1974. The process for applying for regulations is as follows:

- plans for the building work must be submitted to the planning authority;
- if they comply with the basic regulations and are not in any other way defective, prima facie, they must be approved; if not, they must be rejected.

Building regulation cases are usually overseen by trained inspectors, rather than councillors, because of their technical complexity. Local authorities can order buildings without regulation consent to be demolished, or remedial work to be undertaken by the owner. Alternatively, they can carry out the work themselves—but at the owners' cost.

Listed buildings and conservation areas

Although buildings of historic or architectural interest are not immune to being demolished if they are in a severe state of disrepair, their owners can obtain substantial help with their upkeep by getting them 'listed'. Local authorities may choose to pursue this route to protect premises that they fear might otherwise be unsympathetically altered or knocked down by developers.

Buildings are listed—on the advice of the quango *English Heritage*—because they are:

- deemed to be of 'architectural interest'—for example, the recently renovated grade II* Morecambe Bay Hotel in Lancashire, regarded as a classic example of Art Deco;
- of 'historical interest'—that is, reflective of a particular period or movement (a criterion that might also apply to the above example);
- linked to nationally important people or events—for example, Charleston, the grade II listed country home of the Bloomsbury Set, near Lewes in East Sussex;
- have 'group value' as an architectural or historical unit, or a fine example of planning—for example, the grade I Brunswick Square of Regency townhouses in Hove.

There are three 'grades' of listing:

- *Grade I*—buildings judged 'exceptional' (for example, the Royal Pavilion in Brighton);
- *Grade II**—fractionally lower down the pecking order than grade I, these include the Shakespeare Memorial Theatre in Stratford-upon-Avon;
- *Grade II*—buildings judged to be 'particularly important'.

A decision to list a building ultimately has to be approved by the Secretary of State for Culture, Media and Sport, under the Listed Buildings Act 1990. Although there has traditionally been a reluctance to list post-war buildings, in 1988 a rolling '30-year rule' was introduced, stipulating that any structure deemed of sufficient interest for one of the above reasons and at least 30 years old could be listed.

When buildings are listed, the lists themselves must be published and notified to local planning authorities, and their owners and occupiers. Once listing has taken place, any alteration or addition to a building entails the owner obtaining **listed building** consent in addition to other forms of permission. Among the new constraints will be limitations on the types of materials that they are permitted to use—and an obligation to keep the property in a good, and characteristic, state of repair. Unauthorized work on a listed building will see the planning authority issue a listed building enforcement notice requiring it to be reversed.

If local authorities wish to protect 'non-listed' buildings threatened with demolition or serious alteration, they may place building protection notices on them—a process commonly referred to as 'spot-listing'. This covers the building for six months, during which time the Culture Secretary must decide whether to list it formally.

One further way of protecting groups of buildings—or whole areas of a village, town, or city deemed to have 'special architectural or historic interest'—is for them to be designated as 'conservation areas'. Introduced by the Civic Amenities Act 1967, conservation areas offer particular protection for buildings from unsympathetic and/or inappropriate cosmetic alterations. Special attention is paid to conservation areas whenever a planning application arises within them. Some 'permitted development rights', which allow changes of use of buildings without the need for planning permission, do not apply to those in conservation areas, and councils can make 'Article 4 directives' to increase their control over issues such as the insertion of replacement doors and windows.

Councils must advertise in a local paper notice of any planning application in a conservation area that might affect its 'character or appearance'—and the public has 21 days in which to object. It is a criminal offence to lop or cut down a tree in a conservation area.

→ Further reading

Bryan, H. (1996) *Planning Applications and Appeals*, Oxford: Architectural Press. **Helpful guide, for public and professionals alike, to handling the complexities of the planning process.**

Cullingworth, J. B. and Nadin, V. (2006) *Town and Country Planning in the UK*, 14th edn, London: Routledge. **The 14th edition of this standard text offers a typically comprehensive overview of the planning process at local level and updates its core sections to take into account the impact of recent government reforms, including moves to speed up of applications.**

Hall, P. (2002) *Urban and Regional Planning*, 4th edn, London: Routledge. **Fourth edition of classic text charting the history of town and country planning in Britain from its inception up to the early years of Tony Blair's government and the introduction of spatial strategies.**

Smart, G. and Holdaway, E. (2000) *Landscapes at Risk? The Future for Areas of Outstanding Natural Beauty in England and Wales*, London: Spon Press. **Insightful look at the challenges facing AONBs in an era when land is in increasingly short supply. It examines the new economic pressures being tackled by AONB managers in an effort to preserve them.**

? Review questions

1. Outline the application and decision-making process for standard planning proposals. What is the difference between 'outline' and 'detailed' consent?

2. What is 'planning contribution' (or 'planning gain')? Who benefits from the 'gain'
   concerned—local authority or developer? Give some examples.

3. What devices are available to local authorities and other public bodies to force
   property owners to comply with planning regulations?

4. What is the difference between building regulations and listed building consent?

5. Outline the planning appeals process, and explain to whom appeals should be
   made in England, Wales, Scotland, and Northern Ireland.

Online resource centre

www.oxfordtextbooks.co.uk/orc/Morrison

Visit the Online Resource Centre that accompanies this book for web links and
regular updates.

17

Local authorities and housing policy

One of the most contentious issues in Britain in recent times has been housing—and, more specifically, the lack of 'affordable' homes for those on low incomes and others without the means to climb onto the property ladder. Local authorities have traditionally been responsible for the following aspects of housing policy:

- building and maintaining their own council housing stock;
- liaising with *housing associations*, other voluntary bodies, and private companies to promote developments that bring low-cost or social housing to their local rented sector, and affordable homes to the ownership market;
- granting *planning permission* for appropriate public, private, and voluntary sector housing schemes in locations best suited to meet demand;
- providing night shelters, temporary accommodation, and, where necessary, longer-term advice and support for the homeless;
- assessing claims for *Housing Benefit* and administering it locally.

Until the mid-1980s, local authorities generally played a direct role in providing social housing for the poor and unemployed, by building council flats and houses, and making them available for rent at subsidized rates. But during Margaret Thatcher's premiership, the stock of council housing began steadily to diminish, as long-term tenants were given the right to buy their homes at discounted prices and councils' ability to build more to replace them was curbed, in favour of an expansion of the role of the voluntary and private sectors in social housing provision.

Today, while two million homes remain in local authority ownership nationwide and about the same number are managed by voluntary housing associations (see pp. 531–3), in some areas, the number of 'council homes' surviving is piecemeal; in others, it is non-existent. Much of the rented accommodation currently available is now in the hands of private agencies, professional and semi-professional landlords, and a new generation of amateur 'buy-to-let' developers. Meanwhile, as successive governments have asserted the public's 'right' to aspire to own their homes, much of their focus has switched towards expanding the private sector, and making houses and flats more affordable for ordinary working people.

▌ From prefab to new town—a potted history of social housing

Providing fit and proper public housing has been one of the prime purposes of local government since embryonic council services first emerged in the nineteenth century, predominantly in response to public health problems of the time. Eliminating overcrowding and poorly constructed housing—in so doing, integrating proper sanitation and sewerage systems, and improving hygiene—was a vital part of the fight against diseases such as cholera, dysentery, and typhoid fever.

But it was partway through the twentieth century, between the First and Second World Wars, before any real revolution occurred in the provision of *social housing*: houses and flats built on a mass scale for families who had previously been unable to afford roofs over their heads, or had lost their homes during the 1914–18 conflict.

Public housing and the prefab

Between the world wars, there was a period of major public housing activity. A campaign dubbed 'Homes Fit for Heroes' arose out of concern about the poor physical health of many young servicemen from poorer backgrounds recruited to bolster the ranks of the forces in the trenches and, under the

Housing Act 1919, a start was made on clearing the worst slums. New planned estates were constructed in their place, largely in existing urban areas. But it was not until after the Second World War that a housebuilding boom began, as the struggle to provide shelter for people rendered homeless by Hitler's bombing campaigns became a national emergency.

Ironically, the Blitz (although it could hardly be described as a blessing) helped to clear the way for development. The large areas of wasteland created by the bombings of Britain's major cities offered ample scope for big housing projects and it was not long before the new spirit of collectivism that had been channelled into the 'war effort' was being harnessed to build cheap, functional homes for those returning from the fighting, and the many families left dispossessed by its impact on their homeland.

Displaced families needed housing at a time when materials were in short supply, so the 'prefab' was developed—literally, a prefabricated, single-storey compact house, made not from conventional bricks and mortar, but from anything from shipping containers to surplus aluminium aircraft parts. Prefabs could be manufactured off-site and erected quickly. Their lifespan was intended to be limited, but they fared so well that they survived into the 1970s and can be viewed in building museums to this day.

Prefabs were not the only weapon in the post-war Labour government's bid to provide new housing. In October 1945, Lord Reith was appointed chairman of a 'new town housing committee' charged with devising a workable solution to the growing problem of city overspill. His suggested solution was to draw inspiration from the British New Town movement of Victorian philanthropist Ebenezer Howard, who created the garden cities of Letchworth and Welwyn, both in Hertfordshire: government-backed development corporations would be formed and tasked with acquiring land for construction within 'designated areas'. The resulting New Town Act 1946 designated Stevenage (again in Hertfordshire) as Britain's first official 'new town' and, within a decade, a further ten were designated.

The rise of high-rise living

Population growth during the 1950s 'baby boom' inevitably led to increasing demand for housing and, by the end of the decade, ministers had decided to empower councils to clear away many of the jerry-built prefabs, to demolish the last inner-city slums, and to set about a mammoth new housebuilding programme.

Under the terms of a series of Acts beginning with the Housing Act 1957, local authorities (LHAs) embarked on extensive slum clearance schemes,

using *compulsory purchase orders* (see p. 512) to obtain sufficient land at
sufficient speed to facilitate the construction of suitable alternative housing.
But no sooner had they done so than they faced an immediate dilemma that
continues to echo to this day in the decision-making of urban planners: how
were they to accommodate a rapidly rising population without resorting to a
similar tactic to their forebears—that is, cramming homes together in high-
density Victorian-style terraces, or on overcrowded estates? Their solution
was to build upwards, rather than laterally, as in the past—in so doing, creating the first generation of high-rise tower blocks.

Although a number of multi-storey blocks still exist in and around major
towns and cities, there has been a growing backlash against them since the
1970s by town planners, politicians, and public. Tight terraces and sink
estates might have been shoddily built and poorly served by infrastructure,
but at least many of those homes had their own backyards or small gardens, facilitating interaction and cooperation between neighbours. Neither
were residents forced to share the entrances into their blocks, or to take a
temperamental lift up ten or twenty floors before reaching their own flat.
Many tower blocks were initially of sturdier construction than the social
housing that preceded them, but, over time, their sheer height and overall
scale begat major long-term structural weaknesses. The lack of accessible
shared social spaces and amenities—especially for those living on higher
levels—contributed to serious social problems, such as drug-taking, vandalism, violent crime, and general isolation. Today, like the sprawling slums
before them, tower blocks are viewed by many as ghettoes for a forgotten
'underclass', cut off from mainstream society.

In recent decades, tower blocks have been the location of ugly scenes.
Broadwater Farm in Tottenham, north London, was depicted as one of the
worst places to live in Britain in Alice Coleman's influential 1985 book about
the perils of 'one size fits all' urban planning, *Utopia on Trial*. Later the
same year, it witnessed one of the most notorious riots of the 1980s. The
Aylesbury estate in Walworth, south-east London—these days a favourite
backdrop to everything from party political broadcasts to rap videos and
episodes of ITV1's *The Bill*—has one of the UK's lowest ACORN (A Clas-
sification of Residential Neighbourhoods) demographic classifications,
principally due to its infamous crime rate. According to a *Guardian* article
on 18 May 2005, a crime was reported there every four hours. Less than
a year later, Southwark Council issued a demolition notice on residents
of the estate's main tower block, arguing that knocking it down was necessary if the area was to be regenerated. A proposed £350m redevelop-
ment plan, involving the transfer of council homes to a housing association

(see pp. 531–3), remains the source of an as yet unresolved dispute between tenants and the local authority.

The great 'new town' boom

Given the limited capacity of tower blocks to cater for rapidly rising population levels across the board and the social deprivation increasingly associated with them, by the 1960s it was perhaps unsurprising that both central and local government had begun looking for yet another 'new way' of providing low-cost housing on a mass scale for those unable to buy homes on the open market.

A consensus quickly emerged that there should be a further rollout of new towns and, in the decade from 1960, a further ten were founded in as many years. By far the most famous centre to emerge from the ensuing English new town programme was Milton Keynes in the Midlands—a new-build city founded from scratch in 1967. In other cases, the term 'new town' was something of a misnomer: the ancient cathedral city of Peterborough in Cambridgeshire was designated a new town in 1967, with Northampton following suit a year later. In effect, these designations gave the towns—along with nearby Warrington—a licence to expand, with the help of government capital investment, on a scale that was out of step with other parts the country.

The advantages of new towns over other housing solutions were manifold. By effectively starting out with a blank slate, urban planners were given free rein to design roads, estates, and other infrastructure in an ergonomic and 'human-centred' way, making the maximum use of space and integrating vital community facilities to enhance the quality of life of those who would end up living in them. The housing itself tended to be built on a more domestic scale, with two to three-storey homes arranged along a clear street pattern, with individual gardens and focal spaces.

But new towns had their downsides: established urban areas rarely provided enough building space for them, so they tended to be developed in largely rural locations, becoming satellite or dormitory towns from which residents would have to commute, often over considerable distances, to the established towns and cities in which they worked. Efforts were, however, made to ensure that the new towns were as self-sufficient as possible, with their own shops, sports and leisure centres, cinemas, and, in time, employment opportunities. In some cases, new towns became so populated that new local authorities had to be set up to cater for their services.

Despite the demonstrable benefits of new towns for families on modest incomes who had previously found it difficult to afford their own homes or to find any accommodation in overcrowded town centres, in practice, they brought limited benefits for those at the bottom of the heap. During the 1970s and 1980s, a growing divide opened up between poorer households who were fortunate enough to live in a new town in which there had been sufficient investment in new council houses and the large number of council tenants in older towns still confined to tower blocks.

Over time, the English new town experiment has been extended to the rest of the UK, with Scotland acquiring six, and Wales and Northern Ireland two each. Table 17.1 lists all 31 existing British new towns, together with their populations.

Table 17.1 A list of new towns currently designated in Britain

New town	Population
Basildon	102,400
Bracknell	52,243
Central Lancashire (Preston, Chorley, and Leyland)	365,000
Corby	53,000
Craigavon	57,685
Crawley	99,727
Cumbernauld	51,300
Cwmbran	47,254
East Kilbride	73,820
Glenrothes	38,927
Harlow	80,600
Hemel Hempstead	83,000
Irvine	33,090
Livingston	50,826
Londonderry	83,652
Milton Keynes	230,000
Newtown	12,783
Northampton	194,400
Peterborough	161,800
Redditch	79,216
Runcorn	61,252
Skelmersdale	38,813
Stevenage	79,790
Warrington	158,195
Washington	60,000
Welwyn and Hatfield	97,546

▌The Housing Revenue Account (HRA)

As explained in Chapter 11, every local authority that maintains its own stock of social housing is required by law to record all income and expenditure relating to it on a separate account to that used for its general revenue funds. This discrete balance sheet is called the **Housing Revenue Account (HRA)**. The HRA is split into two halves: one covering revenue income and spending; the other, capital payments. The majority of revenue income generated by the HRA comes in the form of rent, but councils can also charge one-off fees for arrears or damage to property, and the account may accrue interest. The primary purpose of the capital component of the HRA is to record all income generated from house and flat sales under 'Right to Buy' (see pp. 528–31).

Council tenants' rights and how they qualify

Council tenancies have a number of advantages over the standard shorthold tenancies available when renting in the private sector, including:

- security of tenure;
- no deposit;
- rent set at a level that is substantially below the market average;
- the right to buy their home at a discount (see pp. 528–31).

Unsurprisingly, social housing is much prized among those on low incomes. To ensure that they are allocating their limited stock of social housing as fairly and equitably as possible, local authorities have traditionally kept a *housing register* (more colloquially known as a 'housing waiting list'). Anyone aged over 16 who met certain basic eligibility criteria was able to apply to enter the register and certain types of applicant were prioritized—for example, due to their perceived vulnerability, or long-standing connection to the local area. This system was changed by the Homelessness Act 2002, which introduced a 'points system' to prioritize applicants. It stipulated that 'reasonable preference' should be given to anyone falling into a set of specified categories, although other long-standing factors favouring certain households over others must also be taken into account. These are outlined in Table 17.2. For those granted council homes, tenancy has traditionally been given for life, but in November 2008 it emerged that Housing Minister Margaret Beckett was considering new Whitehall proposals to relieve waiting lists by terminating tenancies for people whose financial positions significantly improved during their occupancy.

Table 17.2 The criteria for prioritizing social housing applicants

'Reasonable preference' under the Homelessness Act 2002	General criteria
The 'unintentionally' homeless (see pp. 537–8)	Residency—does the applicant live in the area in which they wish to be housed?
People living in uinsanitary, overcrowded, or unsatisfactory housing	Financial circumstances—is the applicant on benefits, or in paid employment? Benefit claimants and low earners are normally treated as priority cases.
Those who need to move on medical or welfare grounds	Tenancy record—does the applicant have a good record, or has he or she accrued rent arrears? Although social housing is aimed at people on low incomes (many of whom may have had past debt problems), councils are wary of 'defaulters'.
People who need to move to a particular locality in the district of the authority, where failure to meet that need would cause hardship to themselves or to others (e.g. a parent with a child in a local school)	Time on register—applicants may gain extra points if they have been on the housing register for some time (a throwback to the 'waiting list' days).

In addition, some councils will use their discretion to *disqualify* certain people from applying for social housing (thus making the job of finding homes for 'qualifying' applicants that much easier). Alnwick District Council in Hampshire bars anyone from applying who has previously left a social housing tenancy owing £250 or more, or who lived in a council flat or house locally at a time when 'nuisance to neighbours' or damage to the property occurred. Burnley Borough Council in Lancashire writes into its tenancy agreements a clause allowing the social housing provider to evict any tenant for antisocial behaviour (a sanction authorized by the Housing Act 1996). The government has recently clambered onto this conditional tenancy bandwagon, too: in spring 2008, then Housing Minister Caroline Flint mooted the idea of requiring new council tenants to sign 'commitment contracts' promising to look for work (see p. 250). Her proposal was prompted, in part, by several studies, including a report by Professor John Hills of the London School of Economics, published in February 2007, which found that people living in council housing were twice as likely to be unemployed as the average person—largely because of the 'neighbourhood effects' of living in deprived areas.

Once their home is secured, the occupants of social housing have recourse to a number of measures should they be in any way unhappy about the way in which it is managed, or the quality of the property itself. These are outlined in Table 17.3.

Table 17.3 The safeguards for social housing tenants

Device	Effect
The Council Tenant's Charter	Tenants must be consulted before major decisions on housing management are taken by the council or other provider.
'Tenants' Choice'	The Housing Act 1988 gave tenants the right to choose an alternative 'approved landlord', with voluntary sector housing associations normally fulfilling this role.
Recompense for own investment	The Leasehold Reform, Housing and Urban Development Act 1993 strengthened tenants' rights to have repairs carried out at their local authority's expense—and the right (when they were required to move home) to be compensated for any improvements that they had made themselves.
Independent regulation	A social housing regulator—the Tenant Services Authority (TSA)—was launched in 2008 to handle complaints about poor rent and maintenance issues.

Other local authority housing responsibilities

Local authorities not only have to provide *new* houses and flats for rent, but are required to maintain and improve existing social housing—as well as to monitor the state of private sector accommodation in their areas. Many councils have now combined their housing and environmental health departments, following a series of court actions brought against landlords under various Public Health Acts. The 1990 Act outlined councils' duty to inspect existing buildings in their area to detect 'statutory nuisances'—defined as including premises prejudicial to health, as well as menaces such as smoke, dust, fumes, rubbish, and noise pollution. The Act gives local authorities the power to secure the 'elimination' of the statutory nuisance.

Local authorities may also take action over houses deemed 'unfit for human habitation'. Most of this work relates to the private sector. When assessing if a house is 'unfit', housing authorities will look at its state of repair, freedom from damp, natural lighting, ventilation, water supply, drainage, and sanitation. The Housing Act 1985 gave councils the power to serve 'repair notices' on the owners of individual unfit homes. Alternatively, they were permitted to carry out specified repairs to bring dwellings up to a habitable standard themselves, charging the owner afterwards for the privilege. In exceptional circumstances, they were allowed to serve 'closure notices' (ordering owners to cease using a dwelling for that purpose) or 'demolition notices' (ordering owners to demolish the dwelling). Or they can go further—buying unfit houses outright and taking them into their own housing stock. Before any demolition or closure order is agreed, the council must give the owner the opportunity to carry out any remedial work. They must also rehouse occupiers and potentially pay compensation.

Councils may occasionally take action against an entire 'area', requiring or undertaking improvements or demolition. Demolished areas are known as 'clearance areas'. Before a clearance order can be made, the authority must make provision to rehouse all tenants and finance the work. The Housing, Grants, Construction and Regeneration Act 1996 enables councils to pay discretionary relocation grants to displaced people to help them buy at least a part-share in a new home in the same area.

In addition to the above, the Local Government and Housing Act 1989 empowered local authorities to declare whole districts 'renewal areas' for a period of up to ten years. These normally encompass a minimum of 300 dwellings, at least 75 per cent privately owned, and a third of the inhabitants of which are receiving benefits. Once a renewal area is designated, the authority may acquire the land by agreement or through a compulsory purchase order, and provide new housing, improve existing stock, and dispose of property to a suitable third party for future management.

Privately owned accommodation can also benefit from council help. Under the Housing, Grants, Construction and Regeneration Act 1996, a range of means-tested, mostly discretionary, grants were introduced to help private homeowners unable to afford essential adaptations themselves. More recently, various new 'green' grants—funded by central government—have also been introduced to help tenants and homeowners improve their energy efficiency, in an effort to reduce both their fuel bills and carbon footprints. The main types of grant are listed in Table 17.4.

▌ Thatcherite housing policy and the decline of the council home

As with many areas of policy, such as health, education, and the utilities, the Thatcher government had a profound effect on the availability of social housing in Britain. Less than a year after gaining office in 1979, the Conservative

Table 17.4 Local authority grants available to private homeowners

Name of grant	How it works
Renovation grants	Designed to improve or repair a dwelling. This is discretionary and only available to owners or tenants who have occupied a dwelling for three or more years. It is usually made available for a specific purpose—e.g. repairs to satisfy a statutory notice, provision of basic facilities, adequate space, heating and insulation, and means of escape in a fire.
Disabled facilities grant	These mandatory grants provide facilities for a disabled person in that person's home or in the common parts of a building containing that home. They are available to all owners/tenants under the expectation that the occupier will be resident for at least five years 'or such shorter period as his health or other circumstances permit'. Grants are payable for providing access to and within a dwelling, facilities for sleeping, cooking, and washing, and measures for the safety of a disabled person.
House in multiple occupation (HMO) grant	To improve or convert a house in multiple occupation. These are discretionary.
Warm Front (England)/Warm Deal (Scotland)/Home Energy Efficiency Scheme (Wales)/Warm Homes Scheme (Northern Ireland)	Means-tested energy-efficiency grants targeted at benefit claimants, pensioners, and low-income families with young children.

prime minister embarked on the first step in a radical overhaul of the extant council house framework—giving long-standing tenants the chance to buy their homes at a knock-down price and compelling local authorities to sell to them. Within the decade, responsibility for building and maintaining social housing had moved decisively away from local authorities, towards new not-for-profit organizations independent of direct democratic control—'housing associations'—overseen by a similarly unaccountable national *quango*: the Housing Corporation.

Things would never be the same again.

'Right to Buy' and the privatization of council housing

One of the defining election-winning policies of the Thatcher era—and, in many ways, the death knell for traditional council housing—was the so-called 'Right to Buy' programme ushered in by the Housing Act 1980 in England and Wales, and the Tenants' Rights (Scotland) Act 1980 north of the border. Under this scheme, some five million 'long-term' council tenants were given the opportunity to purchase their homes at a discount on the price that they were estimated to be worth on the open market.

Tenants eligible for 'Right to Buy' could initially claim the following discounts:

- those who had lived in their homes for at least three years were allowed to buy at a 33 per cent discount for a house, or a 44 per cent discount for a flat;
- people who had rented from a council for more than 20 years were entitled to a 50 per cent discount on either a house or a flat;
- the Housing Act 1985 increased the value of discounts significantly, as follows:
  - tenants living in houses for more than two years could claim a 32 per cent discount, plus 1 per cent for each complete year by which the qualifying period exceeded two years—up to a maximum of 60 per cent;
  - flat tenants resident for two years or more could claim 44 per cent, plus 2 per cent for each complete year by which the qualifying period exceeded two years—up to a maximum of 70 per cent.

Between 1980 and 1995, a total of 2.1 million homes previously in the local authority, housing association, or new town social sectors were transferred to private ownership. Since then, social housing has continued to be sold off at a rate of around 60,000 a year—with the result that some areas, such as Leicester and parts of Argyll and Bute in Scotland, now have little, or no, council-owned stock remaining.

'Right to Buy'—lauded by Mrs Thatcher in the Tories' 1983 election manifesto as the 'the biggest single step towards a homeowning democracy ever taken' and 'the transfer of property from the State to the individual'—was understandably popular with aspirational working-class voters. By the time of the party's 1987 general election victory, even Labour had dropped its formal opposition. On the face of it, the policy also provided a welcome boon to hard-pressed councils, liberating them from responsibility for financing the upkeep of often aged and creaky accommodation, and raising millions of pounds in capital receipts that (at least in theory) could be spent in other areas of need. According to social policy think tank the Joseph Rowntree Foundation, proceeds from council home sales between 1987–88 and 1989–90 generated £33bn—more than the windfalls from privatizing BP, British Telecom, British Gas, British Airways, and Rolls Royce put together.

But critics maintain that 'Right to Buy' has had a devastating impact on the ability of local authorities and housing associations to provide homes for future generations devoid of the financial means to rent or buy in the private sector. Perhaps its most controversial feature was the strict controls imposed by the government on councils' ability to spend the capital receipts generated by 'Right to Buy' sales on improving or increasing their remaining social housing stock. Initially, they were limited to spending only 20 per cent of this income on housing, rising to 25 per cent following the Housing Act 1989. But what the 1989 Act gave with one hand, it took away with the other: it stated that the 75 per cent of receipts remaining must be spent not on building new schools, care homes, or roads, but on paying off their debts. Arguments for and against 'Right to Buy' are explored in Table 17.5.

Despite its manifest attractions for aspiring homeowners of limited means, the 'Right to Buy' scheme contained certain caveats designed to deter people from cashing in on the policy. If a house was sold within three years of being bought by a tenant, part of the discount had to be repaid—pro rata the time

Table 17.5 Arguments for and against the 'Right to Buy' policy

For	Against
'Right to Buy' offers low-income families and individuals who would never otherwise be able to afford their own home a chance to buy one. It is a progressive policy that fosters opportunity, aspiration, and ownership among the poor.	Under 'Right to Buy', local authorities have only been allowed to spend a fraction of the capital receipts from council house sales on maintaining the rest of their accommodation and building more. This means that there is less available for poor people who might need it in future.
Council tenants have traditionally been at the mercy of their local authorities while waiting for repairs and essential maintenance to be carried out—often having to wait months, or even years, for work to be done. Enabling them to buy their homes has liberated them from the shackles of the bureaucratic local government machine—giving them the flexibility to pay for repairs as and when they need them, and motivating to keep their property to a high standard.	The distribution of local authority housing around the UK has historically been quite unequal and some councils are more pro-active about promoting 'Right to Buy' than others. A council tenant's ability to buy his or her home is therefore subject to the whims of a 'postcode lottery'—and those on low incomes forced to rent from private landlords have no such opportunity.
'Right to Buy' raises significant amounts of revenue for local government, which can be used to pay off debt that it has run up elsewhere. Less debt means healthier finances, because more money will be left to pay for essential services—and savings may feed through into lower Council Tax.	Selling off council housing has enabled local authorities to offload the punitive cost of repairs and maintenance onto former tenants. While initial sale prices may be attractive, the poor state of repair of some former council homes has left those who purchase them with high ongoing depreciation costs.

that had elapsed since its purchase. The general thrust of the government's approach, however, was to do everything in its power to persuade tenants to purchase their council housing and local authorities to part with it. If a council was felt to be doing too little to promote the scheme, the Secretary of State could appoint a commissioner to investigate and, if necessary, enforce the policy. Some Labour councils—such as Norwich City Council—actively tried to sabotage it and ended up footing the legal bill for their unsuccessful fight to preserve their housing stock.

Ministers also introduced the concept of 'Right to Buy mortgages', to be administered by local authorities—although, in time, this was replaced by a 'rent-to-mortgage' scheme introduced under the Leasehold Reform, Housing and Urban Development Act 1993. Under these initiatives, the price fixed for a house or flat was comprised of two elements:

- an *initial capital payment*—that is, a form of partial mortgage paid in regular instalments set at the same or a similar level to the rent for which they would previously have been liable;
- a *deferred financial commitment*—that is, a lump sum that accrued no interest, but was repayable on the sale of the property, the death of the purchaser, or by means of a voluntary payment that could be made at any time.

These models were the forerunners of the shared ownership schemes that are commonplace today, under which 'tenants' buy a share of a property from a housing association, with the help of a normal home loan, paying rent on the remainder. A cash incentive scheme was also launched in time, to enable tenants to borrow cash at a low *interest rate* to help them to buy property in the private sector.

From housing associations to social landlords

The 1957 Act had formalized local authorities' responsibilities as the primary providers of social housing in their communities. But when the 1985 Act supplanted it as the 'principal' housing law on the British statute book, this mantle was passed squarely to the new breed of not-for-profit housing associations. Coming at the same time as Mrs Thatcher's government was waging war on the Greater London Council, metropolitan *borough councils*, and so-called 'loony lefty' authorities elsewhere, the decision to dilute the powers of local housing departments was viewed by some as another direct assault on the autonomy of elected councillors. Local authorities, it seemed, were caught in a carefully orchestrated pincer movement—between individuals and families keen to buy up their council homes, on the one hand, and the newly emancipated housing associations (backed by Whitehall), on the other.

Sometimes called the 'third arm of housing', Britain's 2,200 housing associations are generally—although not universally—registered by the Housing Corporation, a quango set up in 1964. (Scottish Homes and Housing for Wales are the equivalents in those countries, but Northern Ireland has no comparable body.) Most housing associations are registered as industrial and provident societies. All have committees of management elected by their membership—which is voluntary work for which members can claim only expenses. Some have no professional staff, while others are large—formed from amalgamation or takeover—and have substantial workforces.

Local authorities may loan money or provide guarantees to registered housing associations, in return for interest income. They normally have the right to nominate 50 per cent of council home tenants in their areas to housing association schemes.

The primacy of housing associations was cemented by the introduction of 'Tenants' Choice' in the Housing Act 1988, under which local authorities came under pressure to promote them as alternative social housing providers. But rather than simply giving tenants the right to move into a housing association property, the Act sought to facilitate the transfer of the houses and flats themselves into association hands. In truth, even some Labour-run authorities (whatever their ideological objections) were attracted by the prospect of offloading their stock, given the high running costs and other complexities associated with repairs and maintenance. By July 1996, 51 local authorities had transferred their entire council home stock to housing associations—totalling some 220,000 properties.

Further undermining of local authorities' status as the pre-eminent provider of social housing was to follow. The 1993 Act and the detailed regulations that followed introduced the concept of 'tenant management organizations' (TMOs). Under the Act and the regulations, groups of council tenants living in a designated area could set up a TMO to take over the day-to-day management of their housing and its associated finances—effectively, *replacing* the local authority and forming their own de facto housing association. The formation of a TMO was subject to approval of its competence by a recognized development agency and a ballot of local tenants. Well over a hundred TMOs are now up and running.

A further development came with the passage of the Housing Act 1996, which introduced the concept of the 'social landlord'—an umbrella term used to define a variety of different models of shared social housing management.

Whatever precise form they take, social landlords are overseen, like housing associations, by the Housing Corporation. They include a new type of local not-for-profit 'housing company'—often partnered with, but not directly controlled by, local authorities and tenants themselves—and 'housing co-ops' (a variation on the idea of TMOs).

The outcome of this flurry of reforms was precisely what the Conservatives had set out to foster—that is, in their own words, 'a more pluralist and more market-oriented system'. A symbolic final seal was set on the logical direction of the party's policies, when the Local Government and Housing Act 1989 explicitly freed local authorities from any obligation to retain their own social housing stock.

The rise of owner-occupancy and the 'affordable housing' debate

Recent surveys suggest that, despite years of spiralling house prices and the well-reported financial obstacles faced by first-time buyers, Britain has indeed gone some way towards becoming that great 'homeowning democracy' heralded by Mrs Thatcher back in 1983. Figures 17.1 and 17.2 provide a comparison between the breakdown of dwelling types in 1961 (the year in which records began) and 2006 (the latest year for which statistics are available). Information from the census of 31 March 1961 revealed that, of the 13.83 million dwellings in which UK inhabitants were then living, 6,068 (44 per cent) were owner-occupied houses and flats, while 4,377 (32 per cent) were rented from private landlords, or as part of a job or business for which the residents worked, and 3,382 (24 per cent) were rented from local authorities (that is, council housing). Forty-five years later, in a 31 March 2006 survey conducted by the National Statistics Authority on behalf of the Department for Communities and Local Government (DCLG), out of a total of 21,989 dwellings the number of owner-occupied properties had soared to 70 per cent (15,442), with the number rented from private landlords having fallen by nearly two-thirds, to just 12 per cent (2,611). While the number of people living in social housing had held up better—falling by only a quarter, to 18 per cent (3,936)—significantly, only 9.5 per cent of these were traditional council houses and flats. The rest were properties rented from various types of social landlord, such as housing associations, housing co-ops, and TMOs. The statistics therefore demonstrate two key trends: a decisive shift in the number of people living in owner-occupied accommodation, as opposed to renting, and the steady decline of local authorities as the principal providers of social housing.

Figure 17.1 Where UK residents were living as of 31 March 1961

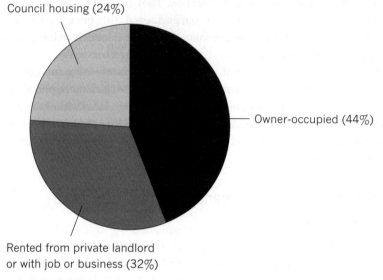

Source: Department for Communities and Local Government (DCLG)

Figure 17.2 Where UK residents were living as of 31 March 2006

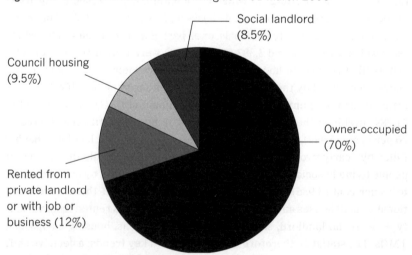

Source: Department for Communities and Local Government (DCLG)

Despite the growth in home ownership, however, many people—particularly those on low incomes and single public sector professionals living in south-east England—have found it next to impossible to enter the property market during the housing boom of the past decade. As a consequence, recent years have seen much government rhetoric—and significant chunks of policy—geared towards helping out those who would not qualify for conventional social housing, yet are unable to afford their own homes. Particular emphasis has been placed on the plight of so-called 'key workers'—that is, public servants such as teachers and nurses (especially those living in areas, such as inner London, where house prices are disproportionately high).

To guarantee that the market provides more houses that are 'affordable'—the latest government buzzword—ministers aim to build three million new homes by 2020, at a projected cost of £8bn. In theory, by targeting the homes at areas with a shortage of affordable private sector housing, the move will both provide bricks and mortar up front, and, by increasing housing supply, force prices down across the board. A 2007 *Green Paper* outlined new priorities, as listed in Table 17.6.

The sheer scale of development proposed for some areas has generated fierce opposition. In many areas across the south-east, where some 200,000 new houses are due to be built, councils and local residents alike have

Table 17.6 The highlights of the 2007 Housing Green Paper

Measure	Effect
More affordable homes	An increased number of homes, with a wider range of options available to people on limited incomes seeking to buy their own homes—including more long-term mortgages (i.e. longer than the standard 25-year repayment term).
More social housing	Of the 70,000 new affordable homes to be built each year from 2010–11, 45,000 should be social homes—more than double the total for 2004.
'Greener' homes	As many homes as possible to meet high environmental standards, through improved energy capture and efficiency, and low carbon footprints. Solar panels, wind turbines, improved insulation, and more efficient boilers are a priority.
Fast-track planning process	Speeding up planning approval for new housing developments that meet the government's priorities, with more land released for construction—and local authorities barred from dragging their heels.
New *executive agency* to drive change	Homes and Communities Agency launched by the DCLG in 2008 to drive forward the homebuilding programme sustainably.

objected to the 'quotas' that they have been handed by ministers. The Sussex Downs *area of outstanding natural beauty (AONB)* is likely to be the location of thousands of new homes, many necessarily in the flood plain—to the fury of local parish councils and environmental campaigners. There is also considerable controversy over the government's pledge to give preferential planning permission to sustainable housing developments—so-called 'eco-towns'. Criticisms have included the fact that, in order to establish these supposed paragons of environmental friendliness, large tracts of as-yet-undeveloped countryside will need to be given up for housebuilding. Green campaigners also argue that some of the sites earmarked for such developments are in rural areas where there is little or no existing public transport infrastructure—a factor that is likely to lead to even higher than average levels of car ownership among those who end up moving there, in so doing making a mockery of their 'eco' credentials. Protests about the mass housebuilding programme have been held from Wales and the south-west, to the north-east.

Despite all of this, some experts claim that the government's housebuilding plans are, if anything, too modest. In October 2007, the National Housing and Planning Advice Unit (a quango set up to advise ministers) predicted that typical house prices in the UK will have reached nine-and-a-half times the average salary by 2026 unless the government raises its target significantly. By 2016, it argued, 270,000 new homes will need to be built each year to avert a crisis in home ownership among people on low and middle incomes—as opposed to the 240,000 a year currently planned.

Whatever the truth of the matter, by autumn 2008, the arguments for and against the onset of a new 'new town' era were beginning to look increasingly academic: the severe economic downturn, coupled with a collapse in the housing market, saw many developers involved in the government's plans bring their housebuilding programmes to a standstill. At the same time, the escalating crisis of confidence in the banking sector saw a dramatic slump in the number of new mortgages agreed by banks and building societies. In the year to June 2008, the number of approvals slumped by 70 per cent, according to the British Bankers' Association.

To jump-start the housing market, the government unveiled a range of measures designed to help first-time buyers in September of that year. These included a one-year 'stamp duty holiday' for homes sold for less than £175,000, a shared equity plan offering low and middle-income families free loans worth up to a third of a property's value, and a 'mortgage rescue scheme' designed to stave off the threat of repossession for those experiencing difficulties with their repayments. Chancellor Alistair Darling also made it a condition of the £50bn rescue package offered to Britain's major high street banks and building societies after the October 2008 stock market crash that they use some of the money pumped into the system by the government to start approving more mortgage loans (see p. 221).

Housing policy and the homeless

Local authorities have a statutory duty to house the 'unintentionally homeless' and those threatened with homelessness *within 28 days of being made aware of their predicament* under the Housing (Homeless Persons) Act 1977 (as amended by the Homelessness Act 2002). Under the Housing Act 1996, however, the ambit of 'homelessness' was narrowed to allow councils to take into account available accommodation across the UK and even 'elsewhere'. The aim of this reform was to help out local authorities presented with disproportionately high numbers of homeless people, particularly asylum seekers, because it would be unreasonable for them to be expected to house all applicants in their own areas. Ensuing regulations also tightened up the law with regard to the eligibility of asylum seekers for help with housing full stop: anyone who did not claim asylum-seeker status at the port of their arrival was rendered ineligible (barring refugees and those granted 'exceptional or unconditional leave to remain in the UK'). The Act also introduced a limit of two years on the provision of accommodation in certain cases and a review of all cases after that.

The following categories of homeless people are treated as priority cases:

- people with dependent children;
- people made homeless by an emergency and disaster (flood, fire, etc.);
- people vulnerable because of old age, or mental or physical disability;
- pregnant women and their households.

When assessing applications from homeless people for permanent housing and while waiting for flats to become available, local authorities are often forced to use short-stay, hostel, and/or so-called 'bed and breakfast' accommodation (in reality, often little more than bedsits or studio flats within multi-occupancy dwellings).

The overriding controversy over local authorities' responsibilities towards the homeless, however, relates to its rather wide-ranging definition of 'unintentional homelessness'. Under the law, the 'intentionally homeless' include people evicted from private sector accommodation for falling behind with rent and even those fleeing their home 'voluntarily' to escape domestic abuse. Nonetheless, if an intentionally homeless person fits into a priority category, the authority must provide them with advice, assistance, and temporary accommodation.

Anyone whose application for housing is turned down on the grounds that they are 'intentionally homeless' may challenge the local authority by judicial review proceedings on the grounds that they have been unfairly defined as such.

Tony Blair's government made a high-profile effort to tackle the problem of street homelessness—or 'rough sleeping'—during his first term in office. Under a new Rough Sleepers Unit, headed by 'Homelessness Tsar' Louise Casey, he launched the Rough Sleepers Initiative, initially in central London, but then across several other cities with high levels of homelessness, including Bristol and Brighton. Its stated aim was initially to provide places in short-term hostels and leased places in 'move-on' accommodation, before rerouting street sleepers to permanent homes, high-dependency specialist care homes, and special accommodation for people with drink and/or drug problems. The initiative officially ended in March 2002, having (according to the government) more or less achieved these aims in most areas.

But not everyone was convinced by the figures that officials produced to demonstrate the reduction in street homelessness. Over the period of the initiative, 'spot counts' of rough sleepers were periodically carried out on the streets of the target cities—but controversy erupted when several charities and support groups accused those involved in the counts of massaging the figures by using questionable criteria to determine whether someone was or was not a rough sleeper. In December 2002, volunteers working with the homeless in Waterloo and Westminster alleged that rough sleepers had been moved out of the London boroughs two nights before a count to gerrymander their figures downwards, while a Bristol-based volunteer wrote to a national newspaper alleging that, a year earlier, street sleepers were moved prematurely into a temporary night shelter just ahead of a count there. This had the effect of taking 19 sleepers off the streets on that night—artificially slashing the headcount as a result.

Local authorities and Housing Benefit

In addition to providing social housing and looking after the unintentionally homeless, local authorities administer Housing Benefit on behalf of the Benefits Agency. Housing Benefit is a payment that is equivalent to part, or all, of the rent charged to a tenant in private, public, or voluntary sector accommodation who is on a low income.

There are two types of Housing Benefit, depending on individuals' circumstances:

- *Standard Housing Benefit*—paid to those in work, but on low earnings;
- *Certificated Housing Benefit*—for those on **Jobseeker's Allowance**, **Income Support**, Incapacity Benefit, and other benefits related to an inability to work.

Local authorities are paid a subsidy by central government to cover the cost of assessing claimants' eligibility and administering the benefit on the ground (although, as this is equivalent to just 95 per cent of the actual cost, councils have often complained that this role places an unfair burden on them). In addition to processing claims and ensuring that regular payments reach successful applicants (either through their bank accounts, or as direct payments to their landlords), councils are responsible for inspecting accommodation at the point at which applicants make their initial claim, to assess how much rent the council believes the property is 'worth'. This can bring them into conflict with claimants who are being charged a higher rent by their landlords than the housing department feels is warranted—effectively putting the onus on the claimant to top up his or her Housing Benefit with money from their other benefits.

Alongside Housing Benefit, local authorities also operate *Council Tax* Benefit schemes.

→ Further reading

Bramley, G., Munro, M., and Pawson, H. (2004) *Key Issues in Housing: Policies and Markets in 21st-Century Britain*, London: Palgrave Macmillan. **Examination of the most burning contemporary housing issues in Britain, including the supply of social and affordable homes, new demographic pressures, and the threats to greenbelt sites.**

Jones, C. and Murie, A. (2006) *The Right to Buy: Analysis and Evaluation of a Housing Policy*, London: WileyBlackwell. **Thorough and balanced evaluation of the legacy of the Thatcher government's 'Right to Buy' policy for selling off council homes. Policies are set in the context of the Blair housing reforms.**

Lund, B. (2006) *Understanding Housing Policy*, Cambridge: Policy Press. **Up-to-date appraisal of issues in social and low-cost housing, focusing on the decline of local authority housing, and growth in the involvement of housing associations, co-ops, and other providers.**

Malpass, P. (2005) *Housing and the Welfare State: The Development of Housing Policy in Britain*, London: Palgrave Macmillan. **In-depth historical critique of the evolution of housing policy in Britain since the Second World War.**

? Review questions

1. What is the difference between 'social housing' and 'affordable housing'?

2. Who are the main providers of social housing in Britain today and how did this multi-agency system come about?

3. Explain what is meant by the term 'Right to Buy'. How and when was it introduced, and what are its benefits for council tenants?

4. What is the Housing Revenue Account (HRA)? Outline how it works.

5. What meant by 'unintentional homelessness' and what responsibilities do local authorities have to house the unintentionally homeless?

 Online resource centre

www.oxfordtextbooks.co.uk/orc/Morrison
Visit the Online Resource Centre that accompanies this book for web links and regular updates.

18

Children's services and adult social care

One of the most intricate (and occasionally explosive) aspects of local authority policy delivery is 'social services'—an umbrella term that refers to the provision of everything from foster care and adoptive parents for vulnerable children, to residential and nursing homes for the elderly and disabled. Today, 1.5 million people in England rely on support from social services—400,000 of whom are children.

Although the title 'social services' may not be used as often in the media as the 'NHS' or 'health service', stories relating to its work—and, more often than not, to negligence arising from that work not being conducted properly—are seldom far from the news agenda. Controversies have ranged from complaints about errant social workers failing to identify cases of domestic child abuse until it is too late (Victoria Climbié's death at the hands of her *foster parents* and the 2008 'Baby P' case), to screaming headlines about discharged mental patients running amok during the era of the now notorious 'Care in the Community' drive (the 1992 murder of musician Jonathan Zito by schizophrenic Christopher Clunis).

Most of these stories, however, have arisen out of atypical circumstances and, with the exception of specialist sections such as *Society Guardian*, the British media is often accused of neglecting the complexities of this 'difficult' policy area in favour of sensationalism. But given some of the current demographic and social trends in the UK—the liberalization of the *adoption* laws, rising diagnoses of mental illness, and a rapidly ageing population— only a foolish editor would be unwilling to engage with the underlying issues that determine the direction of policy (and, occasionally, give rise to some of the more dramatic situations about which we so often read and hear).

Until the early twentieth century, such social welfare services as existed were provided on an ad hoc basis by charities and voluntary foundations, or in workhouses or infirmaries provided by the parish under the Poor Law. But growing social reform under the modernizing governments of David Lloyd George and Clement Attlee saw the introduction of more widespread and coordinated social care provision, paralleling the nationwide establish- ment of the National Health Service (NHS) and the welfare state. The main landmarks included a seminal report by the Inter-Departmental Committee on Local Authority and Allied Personal Services (otherwise known as the 'Seebohm Report'), which in turn led to the decision, two years later, to form discrete social services departments from the merger of the pre-existing health and welfare, and children's, departments by the Local Authorities Social Services Act 1970. The new departments worked closely with existing housing departments (part of a district or *borough council* in two-tier areas) and the NHS.

Until 2004, when children were given their own dedicated department following the Climbié case, social services departments were responsible for three broad policy areas:

- child protection (often known as 'children and families');
- domiciliary and residential care for the elderly and disabled;
- care for those with mental health problems.

▶ Child protection

Until recently, child protection was overseen collaboratively by social ser- vices departments, in partnership with a number of other bodies:

- local education departments (normally within the same local authority);
- police child protection units;

- *NHS trusts* and *primary care trusts (PCTs)*;

- the National Society for the Prevention of Cruelty to Children (NSPCC);

- registered adoption agencies.

These various agencies liaised through an area review committee (ARC), which determined the child protection procedures that each of them should follow and carried out reviews of cases when those processes had failed to prevent 'non-accidental injury' from taking place. Information on vulnerable children was shared between them through a local child protection register maintained by the ARC.

The Children Act 2004—passed in the wake of the Climbié case—took steps to scrap ARCs in favour of a new breed of *children's trusts*: all-in-one bodies bringing together all of the statutory agencies involved in promoting child welfare and comprising multidisciplinary teams of experts, including social workers, health visitors, paediatricians, and child psychologists. These were due to be in place in every local authority area by the end of 2008. Local child protection registers are being replaced by *child protection plans*, to be drawn up by professionals following an initial child protection conference to assess the child's degree of risk.

The sweeping changes, ushered in under the 'Every Child Matters' banner (see pp. 475 and 547–52), saw all services relating to children—from education to social care—combined under a discrete heading 'children's services', overseen by a director of children's services. Adult social care remains within the remit of social services, albeit under new directors of *adult* services.

Children's social services are required to:

- promote the general welfare of children;

- encourage the upbringing of children by their families (wherever possible);

- pay regard to the wishes and feelings of the child;

- work in partnership with parents in the best interests of the child;

- provide accommodation for children if there is no person with 'parental responsibility' for them (see next section), if the child is lost or abandoned, or if the person responsible is unable to provide care;

- advise, assist, and befriend any child who leaves local authority care—and provide financial assistance and support to find accommodation.

The following two sections primarily focus on the web of regulations and guidelines that currently govern child protection policy in England and Wales, as derived from two key Acts:

- the Children Act 1989 (the 1989 Act);
- the Children Act 2004 (the 2004 Act).

The 1989 Act and the definition of 'parental responsibility'

The Children Act 1989 sought to harmonize the existing body of public and private law on the care, protection, and safe upbringing of children, giving it a more cohesive focus than it had in the past. It came into force in England and Wales in 1991, and in Northern Ireland in 1996, after minor alterations.

As had long been the case, the Act's presumption was that the best place for children to be brought up was at home with their parents or guardians—unless there was serious concern for their welfare should they remain there. To this end, councils were given a 'general duty' to 'keep a child safe and well', and to provide suitable support services to help them to remain with their families. The Act's definition of the term 'family' is quite fluid, however—referring to any adult(s) who have 'parental responsibility' for a child in law. It defines 'parental responsibility' as meaning '*all the rights, duties, powers, responsibilities and authority which by law a parent of a child has in relation to the child and his property*'.

The main categories of 'children in need' set out in the Act were defined as those who are:

- disabled—that is, blind, deaf, dumb, or with a mental disorder or physical handicap;
- unlikely to have—or to have the opportunity to have—'a reasonable standard of health or development' without the help of services from a local authority;
- unlikely to progress in terms of health or development;
- unlikely to progress in health or development without the help of local authority services.

The Act entitles any parent, guardian, or carer who feels that his or her child might be eligible for services to contact the relevant department for a 'needs assessment'. This assessment, carried out by a qualified social worker, should take into account not only the child's needs, but also those of his or her parent(s) or guardian(s). For example, the child might need remedial educational support or therapy, but the adult with parental responsibility might qualify for financial assistance, counselling, or—depending on the circumstances—respite care (a short break from caring, perhaps involving a stay away from home, while the child is looked after by professionals). Since 2000, assessments have been conducted in a 'multi-agency' way, under the terms of the Department of Health's Framework for the Assessment for Children in Need and their Families. This means that, in addition to providing for a child's immediate physical, mental, and emotional needs, a more holistic plan must be put in place—catering for any ongoing specialist social, financial, or educational requirements.

The range of services available under the 1989 Act includes:

- short break services;
- holiday play schemes;
- care at home—including help with washing, dressing, and mobility;
- some aids and adaptations—for example, stair lifts, hoists, wheelchairs;
- financial help—for example, to pay for fares to hospital visits.

Services can be arranged by the council on the child and family's behalf, with social services providing some of them, and outside agencies and charities usually contracted to deliver others. Alternatively, the parent or guardian may request the use of a new direct payment scheme. This involves cash payments being made directly to the family, giving them the freedom to 'shop around' for the services of their choice, rather than being left to make do with the 'one size fits all' approach of the council. Direct payments—based on a similar principle to that fuelling current proposals to extend 'patient choice' reforms in the NHS (see p. 191)—was piloted in the context of care packages for the elderly as early as 1996, but recently extended, controversially, to severely mentally impaired adults (see pp. 560–3).

In addition to setting out the range of day-to-day services available for children in need, the 1989 Act addressed the thorny issue of local authorities' role in the wider question of child welfare. In particular, it defined the circumstances in which social services should be prepared to intervene to ask the family courts to decide where, and with whom, a child felt to be 'at risk' of neglect or abuse at the hands of his or her parents, guardians, or other relations should live. The Act set out four types of court order—collectively known as 'section 8 orders' (see Table 18.1).

Table 18.1 Types of 'section 8 order' under the Children Act 1989

Order	Effect
Contact order	An order requiring the person with whom a child is to live to allow the child to visit or stay with another named person (e.g. another parent), or for that person and the child to have other specified contact with each other.
Prohibited steps order	An order that certain 'steps' related to the role of a person with parental responsibility for a child must not be taken without the express prior agreement of the court (e.g. to prevent a parent with whom the child is not living from taking him or her away on holiday, in circumstances where there is thought to be a danger that the parent will abscond with the child). During some family proceedings—particularly those relating to a serious custody dispute between a separated couple—the court may go further and make the child a ward of court. This is where the court itself, as opposed to social services, takes the child into its care temporarily. Again, this is normally used to prevent one parent leaving the country with the child unlawfully.
Residence order	An order specifying that a child must live with a named person, often outlining other specific arrangements.
Specific issue order	An order made to determine a 'specific question' that has arisen, or may arise, in relation to the care of a child (e.g. where a child should go to school, if parents or guardians disputing custody of the child each want him or her to attend one near to their homes).

From time to time, the level of intervention by social services departments permissible under the above orders is insufficient to deal with the care needs of a child; at other times, the terms of an order may be breached, again putting the child at unacceptable risk. In these circumstances, it may be necessary for the local authority to consider taking children 'into care'—that is, away from the adult(s) with parental responsibility for them. The procedure for doing this and the range of care options available to children once removed from their own homes is discussed in the section on *care orders*, fostering, and adoption later in this chapter.

The 1989 Act only applies to England and Wales, although most of its provisions are reflected in the Children (Scotland) Act 1995. The one significant difference is that, under Scottish law, legal proceedings surrounding child welfare follow a distinct process, known as the 'children's hearings system', first established in the early 1970s, which determines any compulsory measures of supervision that a minor may need. The 1995 Act's one notable strengthening of existing procedures was in its emphasis on the role of 'safeguarders'—that is, individuals with relevant professional backgrounds (normally lawyers, social workers, or teachers) appointed to act as the 'voice of the child'.

The 2004 Act and the 'Every Child Matters' agenda

The 2004 Act focused less on introducing additional duties of care or legal powers for local authorities and the courts, than on radically shaking up the *culture* of child protection. Its main emphasis was on improving communication between professionals and early intervention, following the horrific case of Victoria Climbié.

In 2000, 8-year-old Victoria died of hypothermia, with 128 separate injuries on her body, after two years of systematic torture and abuse at the hands of her great aunt, Marie Thérèse Kouao, and the latter's boyfriend, Carl Manning, at their London bedsit. She had been sent to Britain in the hope of a better life by her parents, who both live on the Ivory Coast. During the months before her death, Victoria was systematically beaten, burnt with cigarettes and scalding water, tied up, and forced to sleep in a bath with only a bin liner over her naked body. Police, social workers, and even the NSPCC failed to treat the warning signs sufficiently seriously—closing a child protection investigation that was opened at one stage on the basis of a paediatrician's mistaken diagnosis that scars on her skin were caused by scabies.

After Victoria's treatment was finally exposed, both Kouao and Manning were jailed for murder at the Old Bailey; a number of social workers at Haringey Council were sacked and three major investigations were prompted, one by the local authority, another by the **Independent Police Complaints Commission (IPCC)**, and the third a public inquiry chaired by senior social worker and former Chief Inspector of Social Services Lord Laming. The latter, which reported in January 2003, made a series of 17 recommendations for the reform of child protection procedures, the most significant of which are explained in Table 18.2.

The government's response was to publish a **Green Paper** entitled *Every Child Matters*. It dwelt on four key 'themes' in relation to the issue of child protection:

- increasing the focus on supporting families and carers—described as 'the most critical influence on children's lives';
- ensuring that necessary intervention takes place before children reach crisis point and protecting children from falling through the net;
- addressing the underlying problems identified in the report into the death of Victoria Climbié—weak accountability and poor integration;
- ensuring that the people working with children are valued, rewarded, and trained.

Table 18.2 The main recommendations of the Laming Inquiry

Recommendation	Details
Government to take lead with new ministerial board	A Children and Families Board to be established at the heart of government, chaired by a minister of **Cabinet** rank. Like a **Cabinet committee**, it should be made up of ministers or other senior representatives from all departments concerned with the welfare of children and families.
New regulator	A new Children's Commissioner for England (Children's Commissioner) should be established, who would also be chief executive of a National Agency for Children and Families. He or she would report directly to the Board. The new agency would be responsible for: (a) assessing and advising the board about the impact of proposed policies; (b) scrutinizing any relevant new legislation and guidance; (c) advising on the implementation of the **United Nations (UN)** Convention on the Rights of the Child; (d) advising on setting 'nationally agreed outcomes' for children, and how best to monitor and achieve these; (e) ensuring that policies are implemented at local level and monitoring this process through its own regional offices; (f) reporting annually to Parliament on the quality and effectiveness of children and family services.
Major case reviews by government	The agency to conduct 'serious case reviews' in the event of the death or serious deliberate injury of a child.
New local authority committees	Each local authority responsible for social services to establish its own committee of members for children and families, to include lay members of the management committees of key services.
Proper coordination of local services	Local authority **chief executives** to chair management boards for services to children and families, which must report to the above committees.
Full inspection of delivery and support services	Government inspectorates responsible for monitoring children and family services must in future inspect not only service delivery on the ground, but also the effectiveness of inter-agency arrangements surrounding those services.
Tighter fostering procedures	Ministers should review the law regarding registration of private foster carers.
Full recording and information-sharing between partner agencies	Every individual agency involved in the care of a child should record basic information about him or her—including name, address, age, the name of primary carer, GP, and the name of school (if of school age).
Stripping away jargon	The Department of Health to establish a new 'common language' for the effective identification of, and intervention in, child protection issues, to be disseminated to all agencies involved in the area. The existing local child protection register system to be replaced by 'a more effective system'.

Recommendation	Details
National database	The government should carry out a feasibility study with a view to setting up a national children's database containing the details of all children under the age of 16.
Improved training for professionals	Local management boards to ensure proper training in child protection—on an 'inter-agency' basis—and this to be monitored by government inspectorates.

Following a widespread public consultation and a further paper, *Every Child Matters: The Next Steps*, many of Lord Laming's recommendations were put into effect by the 2004 Act. The Act revolved around five so-called 'Every Child Matters outcomes', which set out to enable all children to:

- be healthy;
- stay safe;
- enjoy and achieve;
- make a positive contribution;
- achieve economic well-being.

To drive forward the pursuit of these outcomes, the government created 'children's trusts'—new multidisciplinary teams composed of professionals of all types involved in promoting the 'well-being' of children. To improve the coordination of children's services on the ground, the idea was that these trusts should bring together these various professionals at a single location in the local community, such as a children's centre or school. Between them, they would be expected to carry out the following:

- joint needs assessments for a child in need;
- shared decisions on priorities relating to a child's well-being;
- identification of all available resources suited to improving a child's well-being;
- joint plans to deploy those resources, to avoid duplication or overlap.

Even before trusts were in place in every area, plans were unveiled in June 2008 for their remit to be widened to encompass aspects of youth justice previously overseen by the Police Service and the Prisons Service Agency. Children's Secretary Ed Balls announced a feasibility study into the idea of transferring responsibility for the 2,900 under-18s in young offender institutions, privately run secure training centres, and local authority secure units to the new trusts. The stated aim, should the policy be implemented, is to replace the existing, more punitive approach to youth justice with an early-intervention, welfare-orientated strategy designed to 'catch' potential career criminals early and prevent repeat offending. The policy—the cause of a rift between Mr Balls and Justice Secretary Jack Straw, who, as Home Secretary, had earlier shaken up the system by introducing the Youth Justice Board—arguably marked a return to the 'tough on crime, tough on the causes of crime' view once espoused by Tony Blair in his days as Shadow Home Secretary.

To steer the changes, an independent *Children's Commissioner* was appointed in March 2005, in the shape of Professor Al Aynsley-Green, a former national clinical director for children in the Department of Health. The Commissioner's remit is to:

- promote awareness of the views and interests of children among all sectors;
- work closely with organizations the decisions of which affect all aspects of children's lives, including the police, schools, hospitals, and voluntary groups;
- have regard to the framework of the five 'Every Child Matters' outcomes and the rights of children under the 1989 UN Convention on the Rights of the Child.

In the run-up to the Commissioner's appointment, consultation among children found that their main concerns included bullying, personal safety, and pressure in education (especially from exams). Many also stressed the problems that they faced coming from deprived and minority social backgrounds.

A further significant reform instigated in the wake of 'Every Child Matters' was the introduction of a new requirement for local social services authorities to establish discrete children's services departments, and to develop an integrated children's system to coordinate needs assessments, planning, early intervention, and periodic reviews of children's services. As of April 2006, social care services for under-16s were taken out of the general social services arena and combined with education provision under this new all-embracing umbrella. The Act also stipulated that every county council or unitary authority—except those with an 'excellent' rating under *comprehensive performance assessment (CPA)/comprehensive area assessment (CAA)* (see pp. 438–41)—must publish a periodic children and young people's plan (CYPP), to which every agency should contribute, detailing all services for children and young people in their area, and the shared objectives of partner organizations for improving these services.

The local authority-run boards demanded by Lord Laming were introduced under the 2004 Act in the guise of *local safeguarding children's boards (LSCBs)*. Each children's services authority is obliged to create such a board to work out exactly how the various agencies involved in delivering those services will collaborate and to monitor the effectiveness of their work once it is under way. The Act defined three levels of action to be taken by boards, as outlined in Table 18.3.

To facilitate a more joined-up approach to providing care and support to children in need on the ground, meanwhile, a new database, ContactPoint, was due to be launched in early 2009, to make it easier for different agencies involved in the care of an individual child to communicate, share expertise, and coordinate their efforts. It was due to record the following basic details for each child in England up until his or her 18th birthday:

- name, address, gender, date of birth, and a unique identifying number;
- name and contact details of the child's parent or carer;
- contact details for services working with the child, including (as a minimum) educational setting (e.g. school) and GP practice, but also other services, where appropriate;
- a means of indicating whether a practitioner is a lead professional and if he or she has undertaken an assessment under a new common assessment framework (CAF).

Table 18.3 The three levels of responsibility of local safeguarding children's boards

Type of responsibility	Meaning
Activities	To prevent maltreatment—or 'impairment of health or development—by introducing better mechanisms to identify cases of abuse or neglect, and providing clear, accessible contact points for children seeking to report them.
Proactive work	Outreach activities targeted at specific groups—e.g. children identified as 'in need', but not suffering abuse or neglect.
Reactive work	Responding more quickly and effectively in instances where children are suffering neglect or abuse at the hands of family members, other adults known to them, other young people, professional carers, and strangers.

Months before ContactPoint had even launched, it was already generating controversy. Despite reassurances from the government that only professionals involved in the care of children would be able to access it—and then only subject to passing advanced Criminal Records Bureau (CRB) checks, to ensure that they had no previous offences involving children—the Conservatives and several charities expressed concern at potential security breaches. They cited the experience of the succession of then recent data breaches by government departments relating to everything from the personal details of Child Benefit claimants, to the domestic arrangements of military personnel (see p. 629). Eyebrows were also raised about the fact that the details of young people would remain on the database until they reached the age of 25—well into their adulthood. Some, including the Tories, accused the government of hiding a sinister agenda—that is, a 'Big Brother' obsession with keeping tabs on the every move of British citizens—behind the more respectable cloak of 'child protection'.

Care orders

The reforms described so far this chapter illustrate the extent to which social services and the various other agencies working to promote child protection have become increasingly interventionist, due at least in part to pressure from the media, the general public, and families themselves. But sometimes they are required to be more proactive still, in the interests of a child whom they believe to be at serious risk of abuse or neglect if he or she remains in the care of a parent or guardian. The Climbié case highlighted what can happen if early warning signs are not noted or acted upon by professionals. Similarly, there have been numerous high-profile cases of abuse going unreported—or unimpeded—in local authority care, not least the recent scandal over Jersey's Haut de la Garenne children's home. Yet, paradoxically, the media—and the wider public—are often quick to criticize conscientious social workers who, fearing a child is living in an abusive environment, intervene overzealously to remove them.

Perhaps the most infamous example of heavy-handed intervention by the authorities occurred in Cleveland in 1987, when 121 cases of suspected child abuse were diagnosed by two Middlesbrough-based paediatricians, Dr Marietta Higgs and Dr Geoffrey Wyatt. A number of children were removed from their families by social services in the ensuing investigation using a type of court order introduced under the Children and Young Persons' Act

1969, known as a 'place of safety order'. In the end, 26 children from 12 families were found by judges to have been wrongly diagnosed and cases involving a further 96 alleged victims were dismissed by the courts.

More recently, several newspapers—notably, the *Daily Mail*—castigated Portsmouth City Council for being too ready to take children into care following the death of a 17-month-old girl, Anna Hider, who drowned in her foster parents' swimming pool, allegedly while they were entertaining guests. At the time of writing, though, the pendulum was swinging back the other way, with widespread calls for the sacking of professionals involved in the welfare of 'Baby P'—a 17-month-old boy killed by the stepfather and a family lodger in Haringey just streets away from where Victoria Climbié died.

Recent Acts have seen successive governments attempt to walk the tightrope between guaranteeing high standards of child protection, on the one hand, and preventing cavalier intervention by social services and other agencies, on the other. Since the 1989 Act, the principal means by which local authorities have been able to take children into care for an indefinite period—often against the will of their parent or guardian—is by applying to a family court for a care order. Under these circumstances, the parent or guardian must still be allowed 'reasonable access' to the child—unless the court explicitly prohibits it—but the local authority assumes parental responsibility in law and has the power to determine the *degree* of any contact. Occasionally, the need to safeguard a child's welfare is perceived to be so urgent that a local authority can apply to a court for a 'fast-tracked' care order to remove him or her from a threat at home. This is known as an **interim care order**, or **emergency protection order**. Initially granted for up to eight days, but renewable for a further week, emergency protection orders may only be granted if a court is satisfied that there is 'reasonable cause to believe that the child is likely to suffer considerable harm' if left in situ. Since the Family Law Act 1996, the emphasis has been on removing 'the source of danger'—rather than the child (e.g., applying for a non-molestation order against a named individual will lead to his or her removal—not the child's).

Local authorities also have the power to apply for a lesser action known as a 'supervision order'—a device enabling them to 'supervise' parents or guardians in a closer way than normal, to ensure that a child they fear may be at risk is being properly cared for. Under the 1989 Act, a court may only make a supervision order if it is satisfied that:

- a child is suffering, or likely to suffer, significant harm if one is not granted;

- the harm, or likelihood of harm, is attributable to the care given to the child (or likely to be given if the order were not made) not being what it is 'reasonable to expect a parent to give', or the child's being 'beyond parental control'—that is, likely to be persistently truant from school, and/or to commit crime;

Under supervision orders, it is the duty of the council to take steps to 'advise, assist, and befriend' the child and to approach the court for a variation of the order—that is, to convert it into a care order—if it is felt to be insufficient in practice. Likewise, the authority may apply to the court for the order to be lifted should it feel it to no longer be necessary. Where the request for an order is specifically in relation to a child's non-attendance at school or his or her parents' refusal to send him or her, a local education authority may apply for a specific 'education supervision order'.

Fostering and other forms of local authority care

We have established that there are various ways in which children can be removed from their home environments, should professionals and the courts be sufficiently concerned for their welfare. But where do these children—known as 'looked-after children'—actually *live* while under council protection?

Whether a child is under an emergency protection order or a full care order, he or she will normally be accommodated by social services in one of two ways:

- in a registered community children's home;
- with foster parents (sometimes known as a 'foster home').

Children's homes

As with other forms of residential accommodation for vulnerable groups (see the sections on nursing and care homes for the elderly and mentally infirm later this chapter), these days, children's homes may either be run directly by local authorities or by any number of other registered providers, from private companies, to specialist charities such as Barnardo's. Although far removed from the grim Victorian orphanages and children's homes of yesteryear, many of those operating today still contain shared dormitories, as well as individual rooms. They tend to take both boys and girls, rather than being single sex, and house up to a hundred or more children at any one time (although most tend to limit their intake to double figures).

The roles of children's homes are to:

- keep young people safe;
- give them consistent boundaries and routines;
- give them assistance in accessing education;
- promote their health and well-being;
- provide quality of life—for example, games, leisure activities, external trips.

Children's homes—like adult care homes—used to be inspected by their local authorities, but in 2000, this role was taken over by a nationwide *quango*: the National Care Standards Commission. This was abolished in April 2004 and replaced by the *Commission for Social Care Inspection (CSCI)*, which rates the local authorities in which area a children's home is based on a three-star system, based on their 'overall performance' and 'capacity to improve' (see pp. 569–70).

As of 2006–07, adult and children's services have been assessed separately.

Foster parents

Fostering can be arranged on a long-term or a short-term basis by children's social services, often with the help of an independent foster agency. It is usually seen by councils as preferable to keeping a child in a community children's home, because the involvement of designated foster parents places them in a familiar, domestic-style setting, rather than in an impersonal institution. Children placed in long-term foster care will normally be located with 'parents' with at least one other child of their own. They may continue to live in this environment for a number of years, although (unless formally adopted) if they leave home at the age of 16, their foster carers will no longer have any legal rights over them. If their stay proves to be very long-term, however, their foster parents may apply at some stage to adopt them. Assuming that their application is successful, the foster parents will then become the legal parents.

There are various forms of foster arrangement, the main ones of which are explained in Table 18.4. The strict vetting procedure for prospective foster parents is outlined in Table 18.5.

Table 18.4 The different types of fostering arrangement

Arrangement	How it works
Emergency	Where children need somewhere safe to stay for a few nights—normally after an emergency protection order is granted.
Short-term	Carers look after children for a few weeks or months, while plans are made for the child's future (while an interim care order is in place).
Short breaks	Disabled children or children with special needs or behavioural difficulties enjoy a short stay on a pre-planned and/or regular basis with another family, and their parents or usual foster carers have a short respite break.
Remand fostering	Where young people in England or Wales are 'remanded' by the court to the care of a specially trained foster carer in relation to a criminal conviction. Scotland does not use remand fostering, because young people usually attend children's hearings, rather than court. The hearing might, however, send a young person to a secure unit and some Scottish schemes hope to develop fostering as an alternative to secure accommodation.
Long-term	For children who choose to live with long-term foster carers until they reach adulthood and are ready to live independently.
'Family and friends' or 'kinship' fostering	Children looked after by a local authority are put into the care of relatives, friends, or other people whom they already know.
Private fostering	Where the parents make an arrangement for the child to stay with some-one else who is not a close relative and has no parental responsibilities, and the child may stay with that person (the 'private foster carer') for more than 27 days. Although this is a private arrangement, special rules are put in place to determine how the child is cared for. The council must be told about the arrangements and visit to check on the child.

Table 18.5 The vetting procedure for foster parents

Procedure	What happens
Background investigation	Children's social services staff must provisionally approve prospective foster parents, following an investigation into their family lives, and medical and criminal backgrounds. Anyone convicted of causing or permitting bodily harm to a child is barred from fostering. Anybody living in the same house as someone with such a background is usually prohibited, as it is with those who have had orders made against them to remove a child from their care.
Regular spot checks	Social workers retain the right to see foster children on request at regular intervals and can remove them from care without notice if they believe that this is in the child's interests. Such actions can, however, prompt foster parents to apply to a court for a residence order, asserting their right to keep the child with them.
Training for foster parents	Prospective foster parents are required to attend groups where they are taught about the statutory responsibilities of foster carers. Although this is not yet compulsory, many also study for formal qualifications: in England and Wales, a National Vocational Qualification (NVQ) Level 3 in Caring for Children and Young People; in Scotland, a Scottish Vocational Qualification (SVQ) can be pursued.

The number of children in foster care in the UK has risen by almost a third in recent years—from 32,300 in 1995, to 41,700 a decade later. Yet, in light of the growing preference for foster care over traditional children's homes, there is a national shortage of eligible carers, with some estimates suggesting that at least 10,000 more are needed to provide for all of the youngsters waiting to be placed. Some campaigners have blamed the shortfall on the financial burdens of fostering. In 2007, the charity Fostering Network called for foster carers to be paid a professional salary. A survey published at the start of its campaign found that 75 per cent of foster carers received less than the minimum wage and that 40 per cent received nothing at all.

Despite this, all foster carers qualify for an allowance to cover the basic cost of clothing, feeding, and otherwise providing for them. If a fostering arrangement has been negotiated through an agency, the level of this allowance will be set by that agency and is usually dependent on the child's age, with carers of older children qualifying for more. As of April 2007, in recognition of the wide disparities in foster allowances from agency to agency, the government introduced guaranteed minimum levels for the first time in relation to different age groups—as outlined in Table 18.6, which can be found on the Online Resource Centre that accompanies this book.

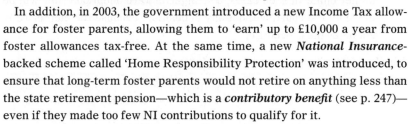

In addition, in 2003, the government introduced a new Income Tax allowance for foster parents, allowing them to 'earn' up to £10,000 a year from foster allowances tax-free. At the same time, a new *National Insurance*-backed scheme called 'Home Responsibility Protection' was introduced, to ensure that long-term foster parents would not retire on anything less than the state retirement pension—which is a *contributory benefit* (see p. 247)—even if they made too few NI contributions to qualify for it.

The adoption process

The principal distinction between fostering and adoption is that, while the former is theoretically a finite arrangement, the latter is permanent. At any point, there are up to four thousand children across the UK looking for adoptive parents. By law, children can only be adopted through an adoption agency—that is, either a social services authority, or a government-approved registered adoption society (a voluntary adoption agency). Most agencies cover a radius of around 50 miles from their offices. Not all agencies actually arrange placements themselves, but all of them may carry out adoption assessments, to ensure that prospective adoptive parents are suitable.

So, who is entitled to adopt? Until very recently, the right was mainly restricted to married heterosexual couples, with those under the age of

40 more likely to be successful than older applicants, who would be of mature age by the time their adopted children had grown up. But much of this changed with the passage of the Adoption and Children Act 2002, which opened adoption up to single people, as well as to one partner in an unmarried couple (whether straight or gay). The law was further tweaked in 2005 to enable unmarried couples to apply to adopt jointly—effectively giving them the same rights as married ones. For gay couples, the procedure is usually quicker if they are in a civil partnership, but provided that they are living together, they will normally stand as much chance of success as straight couples. Qualifying conditions for adopters are listed in Table 18.7.

There are two different types of adoption process, depending on whether the natural parent(s) of the child have given their consent for the child to be adopted:

- *single-stage adoption*—that is, a placement made with the full cooperation of the child's natural parents. This is the procedure followed when, for example, the child was conceived during rape, or when a young woman or a girl below the age of consent (16 years) becomes pregnant and feels unable to take on the responsibility of bringing up her child. In such cases, a straightforward adoption order will be made by the court, without any opposition, because the mother fully endorses the procedure;

Table 18.7 The criteria for prospective adopters

Criterion	Meaning
Age	They must be over the age of 21, and be able to prove that they are happy to make space in their life and home for a child, and that they are patient, flexible, energetic, and determined to make a real difference to a child's life. There is no official upper age limit, although agencies may sometimes favour younger couples.
Criminal checks	They must not have been convicted of any serious offence against a child. More minor offences will have to be looked into, but may not exclude them.
Relationship status	A single person, or one partner in an unmarried couple—heterosexual, lesbian, or gay—may adopt. Unmarried couples may also apply to adopt jointly.
Good health	Prospective adopters must have a medical examination and health issues (including any hereditary conditions) will need to be explored.
Ethnic/cultural background	People from all ethnic origins and religions may adopt. Preferential treatment is often given to prospective parents of the same ethnic and racial identity as a child. This follows research into the well-being of minority-adopted adults who grew up with families who did not match their ethnic and racial identity.
Disability access	People with disabilities may adopt, subject to conditions set down on a case-by-case basis.

- *two-stage adoption*—When a child's natural parent(s) object to his or her (or their) child being adopted, an adoption agency will have to apply to a court for a freeing order—that is, an order to remove the child from his or her parents' custody against their will. At this stage, the parents of the child are often not usually identified in court.

The usual adoption procedure for applicants follows a similar, if slightly more rigorous, route to that for fostering, as explained in Table 18.8.

Childminding

'Childminding' is the term used to describe a type of day care provided for children, usually under school age, outside of nursery or preschool. A registered *childminder* will look after the child in his or her own home, normally while the parents or guardians are at work. Since the passage of the Care Standards Act 2000, regulation of childminding has been in the hands of the *Office for Standards in Education (Ofsted)*, rather than local social services departments, as in the past.

Ofsted's role is to:

- provide a register of people who receive payment for looking after children under the age of five, on an area-by-area basis;

Table 18.8 The adoption process

Procedure	What happens
Initial meeting(s)	Following an application through an adoption agency, a social worker will meet prospective adopter(s), together and individually if in a couple, on several separate occasions.
Background investigation	The prospective adoptive parents' personal backgrounds will be investigated and they will be asked about their reasons for wanting to adopt. Confidential enquiries will be made through their local social services department and the police.
Personal references	These will need to be supplied by at least two friends of the adopters and they will be put through a medical examination by their GP.
Independent adoption panel	A hearing by a panel linked to the agency through which the prospective adopter(s) have applied will consider their case and decide if they should progress to the final stage: an opportunity to meet the panel in person.
Provisional care agreed	Once adopters are approved in principle, the child will be put into their provisional care (children's social services authorities or adoption panels must be notified of this if done through an approved adoption society, rather than the local authority).
Adoption order confirmed	This decision is made by a family proceedings court, sitting in private, three months after notification to the authority.

- inspect the homes of anyone applying to be registered as a childminder, to ensure that there are adequate facilities, including toilets and play equipment.

Registration, when granted, is subject to various conditions covering the facilities to be provided; the number of staff, and their qualifications/experience of working with children, and the maximum number of children who may be minded at one time (particularly babies and those aged under a year).

Following initial inspections, further ones can take place at any time. If registration conditions are breached at any point, registration can be revoked or modified to reduce the maximum number of children to be minded.

The Protection of Children Act 1999

Introduced following a series of high-profile scandals about the abuse of children in residential care homes, the Protection of Children Act 1999 saw the launch of a statutory list of all people considered unsuitable to work with children. The consultancy service index, a list along these lines, had been kept by the Secretary of State since 1993, but the 1999 Act—in Scotland, the Protection of Children (Scotland) Act 2003—formalized the process by enforcing it as a statutory list, to which all existing names were added.

It requires childcare organizations to inform the government if:

- they transfer or dismiss someone who has harmed a child, or put a child at risk;
- an individual evades disciplinary action along these lines by resigning or retiring.

▶ Adult social services and the rise of community care

Although children's services account for the bulk of local authorities' social care budgets—and attract by far the most media coverage into the bargain—councils retain significant responsibilities in relation to both the elderly, and adults of working age who suffer from enduring physical and mental illnesses or disabilities.

Until relatively recently, much of the care provided for people falling into these categories was delivered in an institutional environment—that is, long-stay residential care homes (like adult versions of the children's homes mentioned earlier), or nursing homes for those who had reached a stage at which they could no longer wash or dress themselves, or perform other basic functions without assistance.

People with mental disorders severe enough to prevent them continuing to live at home were often transferred for prolonged periods into NHS-run mental hospitals, or into specialist secure asylums managed by their local authorities. The oldest of these asylum facilities had been established in the early 1800s and many of them continued in more or less uninterrupted use for the best part of two hundred years. But under the last Conservative government, during the transition between Margaret Thatcher and John Major, a revolution occurred that was to transform the culture of social care for not only the mentally ill, but for all other categories of adult 'service user'.

This transformation came in the form of the National Health Service and Community Care Act 1990, which restyled patients as 'clients' and ushered in the now-notorious policy of 'Care in the Community'. In simple terms, its aims were to:

- place greater emphasis on *community care*—that is, providing support services for elderly people, and those with mental and physical illnesses and disabilities, in their homes, wherever possible, with a view to enabling them to remain in a community setting for longer periods, while reducing the pressure in acute wards and residential facilities;
- make the delivery of social care more cost-effective and to increase choice for service users, through the greater involvement of providers from the private and voluntary sectors, including charities.

Although few opposed the idea of empowering the vulnerable to continue living in their own homes in *theory*, many were alarmed by the way in which the NHS and local authorities set about implementing the Act in practice. Long starved of funding for the so-called 'Cinderella service' of mental health, and with many of their homes and asylums severely underoccupied and therefore uneconomical to maintain, a number of councils and trusts used the freedom granted by the Act to shut down half-empty units, discharging inpatients to return to 'the community' irrespective of the strength of their personal support networks or their ability to fend for themselves.

Soon newspapers were reporting a slew of scare stories about assaults, and even killings, by prematurely discharged mental patients. Perhaps the most infamous case was the 1992 murder of musician Jonathan Zito by a paranoid schizophrenic who had been released from mental hospital just weeks earlier under the 'Care in the Community' scheme. Mr Zito's death prompted the establishment of the Zito Trust by his wife, Jayne, which continues to campaign for changes to mental health policy in the best interests of both patients and public. Other high-profile cases included the 1996 murders of Lin Russell and her 6-year-old daughter, Megan, by Michael Stone on a country lane in Kent. Stone, who had a severe personality disorder, had been out of prison and receiving a package of community care since 1992.

At the time of the murders, it was not only the 1990 Act that came in for criticism in the media, but also the Mental Health Act 1983, which, it was claimed, contains a loophole preventing mental health professionals providing care for people suffering from untreatable conditions, such as Stone's, even when they ask for help (Stone had repeatedly pleaded to be admitted to Broadmoor). The *British Medical Journal* has subsequently cast doubt on this suggestion, yet criticisms of Stone's case remain.

But not everything about the renewed emphasis on community care has proved negative. For many people—particularly the elderly and physically disabled—the channelling of social services funding into care packages tailored to their individual needs, and home adaptations designed to make their domestic environments more comfortable and user-friendly, has proved liberating—enabling them to spend crucial extra years living near to friends and family that might otherwise have been lost had they been prematurely admitted to a residential home.

The responsibilities with which social services authorities are charged under the 1990 Act in relation to community care are as listed in Table 18.9.

The scale of the controversy surrounding 'Care in the Community' proved so damaging and long-lasting that, when Labour finally returned to power two elections later, in 1997, it wasted little time in officially scrapping the initiative (although, in practice, the 1990 Act remains the main legal basis for the provision of social care). Community care is still the government's preferred option for caring for the elderly and disabled, at least until such time as they require full-time nursing; the balance has been redressed somewhat between domiciliary and residential care arrangements.

Table 18.9 The main provisions of the Community Care Act 1990

Measure	Meaning
Emphasis on 'Care in the Community', rather than residential care	Local authorities to promote domiciliary (home care), day care (attendance at day centres and activity groups), and respite services (short breaks for both carers and cared for), to allow people to live in their own homes.
Emphasis on practical support to promote self-reliance	Ensuring that all agencies and authorities involved in providing services make practical support a high priority.
Detailed needs assessment	Carrying out 'proper assessment' of a person's needs, followed by good case management by an appointed key worker (normally a social worker).
Promoting partnerships	Developing a flourishing independent/private sector alongside good public services.
Long-term care planning	Preparing strategic plans for community care arrangements, working with NHS authorities, publishing them, and keeping them under review, in consultation with bodies in the public and voluntary sectors. Collaboration between the NHS and local government to improve non-hospital services had first been introduced under the National Health Service Act 1977, when joint consultative committees (JCCs) were set up, consisting of representatives from all relevant statutory agencies.

Labour's biggest reforms include the following:

- the Health Act 1999—which introduced new forms of NHS structure and, with them, new partnerships with the healthcare sector, formally abolishing the joint consultative committees established in 1977;

- the National Carers' Strategy—built on the Carers (Recognition and Services) Act 1996, which gave statutory recognition to the work of unpaid relatives or friends looking after people in receipt of community care in their own homes. It enabled these informal carers to access their own support (see pp. 565–6).

Community care—what the state provides

Social services authorities have a duty to assess the needs of people who require care due to their age, infirmity, or disability. If an assessment shows that someone requires services, the authority must determine the services required and inform them of the details of their assessment, and of their right to appeal. Some authorities have been accused of raising the bar in relation to when people become eligible for services (so-called 'eligibility criteria') because of budgetary concerns, and the courts have ruled that it is appropriate for councils to take their financial resources into account when setting those criteria.

The principal community care services provided by social services department, whether delivered directly by them, by a voluntary organization, or through a private agency, include:

- home help (help with washing, dressing, and sometimes cleaning the home);
- hot meals ('meals on wheels');
- help with shopping and financial management;
- advocacy (advice and support with accessing other services, paying bills, etc.);
- telephone access;
- cheap travel (disabled and OAP bus passes, free transport to appointments);
- free and accessible parking, through the 'disabled badge holder' scheme;
- day care (access to day centres for structured activities, day trips etc.);
- respite care;
- home modifications and aids to daily living (stair lifts and hoists usually provided by housing departments on the advice of social services; wheelchairs and other mobility aids are often accessed through the NHS or charities).

In addition, training and employment can be provided for disabled people in sheltered workshops, while day nurseries and centres are available for the children of the disabled.

These days, 'packages' of community care are put together by a client's key worker (or case worker). Because most social care professionals now work in multidisciplinary teams designed to improve coordination between social services, the health service, and the other agencies by bringing them together under one roof, this may be a social worker, a community psychiatric nurse (CPN), or an occupational therapist. The latter's expertise lies in assessing individuals' capacity to perform basic tasks for themselves and in providing support in carrying them out where it is needed.

Key workers have a statutory duty to produce—and regularly update—a care plan that is individually tailored to their client's needs. This should be made available in writing to the client and/or their carer, on request, and cover the following ground:

- the services to be provided, by whom they will be provided, when and where this will happen, and what is intended to be achieved by providing them;
- a contact point at which to deal with problems about service delivery;
- information on how to ask for a review of the services being provided if the client's and/or carer's circumstances change.

Specific concern about the plight of people with serious mental health issues led to the introduction, in 1991, of a more rigorous care plan procedure, known as the 'care programme approach' (or 'care plan approach'). This is broken down into four stages:

1. an initial assessment of the client's needs;
2. consultation with all professionals involved, any informal carer, and (depending on their degree of mental capacity) the client themselves;
3. the appointment of a key worker;
4. the coordination of services agreed on the basis of the initial assessment by that key worker.

The role of home carers

Britain's rapidly ageing population, coupled with the growing emphasis on community-based care over residential arrangements, has led to a huge rise in the number of carers—defined as people who spend at least part of their lives looking after elderly and/or disabled relatives or friends in their or the other person's home. Some six million Britons identified themselves as carers in the 2001 census.

Long-running campaigns by support groups set up to help home carers have led to belated recognition of their work, initially through the 1996 Act (which entitled them to limited respite care), but, more recently, through the National Carers' Strategy established by former Prime Minister Tony Blair in 1999. This ten-year strategy, renewed by Gordon Brown in 2008, made the commitments listed in Table 18.10, which can be found on the Online Resource Centre.

In practice, although it has undeniably improved the situation for some, the strategy was just that. Recent studies suggest that many carers continue to feel isolated, undervalued, and bewildered by the often labyrinthine network of services and providers that are theoretically available, and the bureaucratic, jargon-laden processes involved in accessing them. Of the four hundred carers interviewed in a survey of carers' views in summer 2006 for the Princess Royal Trust for Carers' 'Duty to Care' campaign, more than half confessed to having felt like walking out on the person for whom they cared. Fifty-six per cent said that they felt 'depressed', 71 per cent 'stressed', and 86 per cent 'frustrated'.

Choice in community care—the rise of direct payments

As if negotiating the maze of options available to those in community care—and the mountains of paperwork that often come with them—was not already mind-boggling enough, recent governments have sought to put clients and carers more directly in the driving seat, as part of their 'choice' agenda (see p. 191). The Tories introduced this concept, through the aegis of the Community Care (Direct Payments) Act 1996. This enabled cash payments to be made by local authorities to dependent individuals to enable them to 'buy' their own care services from the providers of their choice. This approach was not mandatory and authorities were required to ensure that any individual to whom they paid money had the capacity to take informed decisions about their own needs, and to locate and access suitable services. In some cases—when there was evidence that the money had been spent on things other than services related to the client's needs (for example, on alcohol or gambling)—councils had the power to cease direct payments and even to require that the money paid thus far be refunded.

In 'policy and practice guidance' issued in 2000, the Labour government made it clear that it intended to retain the direct payment system, stating that it wanted to see 'more extensive use made' of the system. In January 2006, a **White Paper** entitled *Our Health, Our Care, Our Say* outlined plans to roll it out further, taking in groups of clients who, until now, had been seen as having insufficient capacity to make decisions for themselves, due to the nature of their conditions. These included:

- young disabled people whose parents have managed a direct payment on their behalf and whose payments may have to stop when they reach the age of 18;

- people with dementia, where the use of direct payments is not set out in a power of attorney (PoA) agreement—that is, a legally binding document detailing the individual(s) authorized to handle the affairs of their estate;
- people with more profound learning disabilities.

The new 'individual budget' system has, perhaps predictably, been heavily criticized by campaigners for the elderly and mentally ill—many of whom argue that people in dire need of treatment may end up losing out on help to which they are entitled because of the complexity of negotiating the system and managing their own accounts.

Care homes, nursing homes, and the rise of the private sector

When it is agreed that a person is no longer well and/or capable enough to continue living in his or her own home, or that of a carer, arrangements will normally be made for him or her to move into either a long-term residential care home, or one with nursing provision—commonly known as a 'nursing home'. The former is usually a relatively 'low dependency' environment, in which residents can enjoy a relatively independent lifestyle in the company of a number of other people of a similar age, or with comparable physical and/or mental health needs. A nursing home, in contrast and as its name suggests, is targeted at individuals with more severe physical and/or mental impairments—often the very old, or those at an advanced stage in the progression of their conditions—who require care that is provided or supervised by a registered nurse.

Broadly speaking, the process followed when an elderly person reaches the point of requiring residential accommodation is as follows:

- they are assessed by a key worker in a multidisciplinary team and placed in a home that best suits their needs (whether local authority or private);
- where a private home is chosen, the ability of the person to pay 'the full economic cost' of their care is assessed—taking into account the value of property in their name, which might be sold to contribute to care home fees.

Since the late 1980s, there has been a marked increase in the amount of residential care provided by private companies, rather than social services themselves. In many local authority areas, there are no longer any homes maintained by the council directly: all are owned and managed by the private or voluntary sectors. Under the terms of the Tories' 'mixed economy of care', residents in private homes could claim a 'social security residential care allowance', which they had to pay over to the owner, and a small 'personal allowance', which they were permitted to keep for themselves.

But those in local authority homes were not entitled to claim the residential care allowance—a fact that meant that the final 'bill' presented for the care of individuals admitted to them often appeared superficially higher. This was used by the government as leverage to argue that councils were being 'excessive' with their charges. Opposition leaders at the time accused ministers of using this as a pretext to expand the private sector and undermine councils, particularly when a special transitional grant (STG) was made available to them, on condition that they spent 85 per cent of the money provided on arranging private sector residential placements.

In tandem with the expansion of private sector provision and the rising fees that followed, Mr Major's government risked infuriating the 'grey vote' with new moves to divide the cost of residential care between the state and the individual. Under the 1990 Act, anyone with assets of £16,000 or more— including the value of the homes in which they lived until being admitted into residential care—was expected to pay for themselves up to the point at which that money was exhausted, at which stage, the state would take over. In practice, this meant that many people—particularly widows and widowers whose homes were entirely in their possession—ended up being 'forced' to sell the houses and flats for which they had spent much of their working lives paying. The 'capital/assets limit' remains in place, but was raised to £18,500 in 2001 and rose further to £22,250 in 2008.

Another source of tension that emerged around the same time was that between social services departments and the NHS over how best to provide for people not yet considered to be in need of residential care, but who experienced frequent, sometimes prolonged, periods of ill health necessitating hospital treatment. Hard-pressed acute hospitals—already struggling with long waiting lists—increasingly became the subject of newspaper and television news reports as they combated 'bed blockage' ('bed-blocking'): the need to cater for vulnerable patients too sick to be sent home, but for whom a residential care space was either not yet felt to be necessary, or not yet *available*.

Given that more than half of people aged over 65 now have a disabling condition requiring long-term care and the British population is steadily ageing, it is no wonder that bed-blocking remains a serious issue to this day, as local authorities struggle to find enough care home places to meet demand—particularly for those with unusual and/or debilitating ailments. Yet, critics argue that the government's answer has merely been to intensify the pressure, by getting tough with local authorities found 'guilty' of contributing to bed-blocking, rather than concentrating its efforts on boosting the number of residential care places. Under the Community Care (Delayed Discharges etc.) Act 2003, NHS hospitals may fine their local councils up to £120 a day for every 'blocked' bed—a rule condemned by the Local Government Association (LGA). The Act was motivated, in part, by a 2001 *Audit Commission* report that found that two out of three patients in English hospitals at a time are over the age of 65—and around five thousand people on any given day are unnecessarily stuck on acute wards.

The regulation of the social care sector

To ensure reasonable standards of care are being adhered to by private, public, and voluntary sector providers, in 2004, the government set up a new regulator, the Commission for Social Care Inspection (CSCI)—effectively, the Ofsted of the social services sector. It inspects and imposes national standards on the following care sector organizations: day centres, care homes for the elderly and mentally ill, domiciliary care agencies, nurses' agencies, children's homes, and residential *special schools*. As of April 2009, the Commission was due to be combined with the *Healthcare Commission* to become a new Care Quality Commission (CQC) (see p. 198).

All residential care and nursing homes must be formally registered under the Registered Homes (Amendment) Act 1991 (previously the Registered Homes Act 1984), but, since 2004, the 18,500 listed homes have also had to register separately with the Commission. On inspection, all care organizations, including agencies, are rated under a star system. The meanings of these classifications are as follows:

- no stars—poor;
- one star—adequate;
- two stars—good;
- three stars—excellent.

Following an inspection, or subsequent investigation, the commission may decide to use its statutory powers either to demand that an organization meets specified 'conditions to improve', to bring them up to the agreed national minimum standards, or, in extreme cases, to force their immediate closure. In addition, instances of abuse or neglect may be referred to the police and/or Crown Prosecution Service (CPS). The Commission is especially vigilant in relation to adults with serious mental or physical disabilities or impairments that are seen to put them at greater risk of abuse—in line with the 'Protection of Vulnerable Adults' (POVA) scheme introduced in July 2004. As with children in social care, anyone directly involved in the care of vulnerable adults is required to undergo periodic Criminal Records Bureau (CRB) checks and there are bans on those who have harmed such people in the past from continuing to work with them.

Although the advent of the Commission has theoretically tightened up regulation of the increasingly disparate social care 'market', serious concerns have been raised on more than one occasion about the rigour with which its inspections are carried out. In June 2008, an investigation by Radio 4's *Today* programme found that many of the Commission's own inspectors were unhappy with the frequency and quality of its care home inspections. More than two hundred CSCI staff participated in an anonymous questionnaire, with one commenting: '*I wouldn't leave my dog in 90 per cent of our care homes.*'

The programme's reporter was also told by an insider that, whereas the Commission had tried in the past to inspect most care homes at least twice a year and very poor ones every few weeks or months, some were likely to be inspected only once every three years in future, given the financial pressures facing the regulator.

The 'sectioning' of the mentally ill

Since the Mental Health Act 1983, councils have had limited powers in relation to mentally infirm adults not in residential care, as outlined in Table 18.11.

The Mental Health Act 2007

Before it finally received *Royal Assent* in July 2007, Labour's Mental Health Bill (originally published more than four years earlier) had endured one of

Table 18.11 The powers of social services in relation to the mentally infirm

Power	Effect
Application for compulsory observation	Approved mental health practitioners (AMHPs)—formerly approved social workers (ASWs)—have the right to apply for a person to be admitted to hospital for up 72 hours for compulsory observation, under s. 136 of the Mental Health Act 1983. AMHPs may either be social workers, nurses, occupational therapists (OTs), or psychologists. Their application must be supported by two responsible clinicians—formerly responsible medical officers (RMOs). These may be social workers, nurses, OTs, or psychologists—not only GPs and/or psychiatrists, as was the case previously. In 'emergencies', applications may go ahead with only one RMO's endorsement.
Appointment of 'nearest relatives'	Applications for people to be admitted to hospital for treatment are normally subject to consent by the nearest relative. If the AMHP believes that consent is being withheld 'unreasonably', however, he or she can apply to the courts for an order appointing someone else to be given 'nearest relative' rights.
Application to extend observation	An observation order may be granted for up to 28 days if a hospital psychiatrist sees fit, under s. 2 of the Act. Following this (or sometimes from the outset), a six-month renewable treatment period may be agreed, under s. 3 of the Act. This may be renewed after the initial six months, subject to approval by a mental health review tribunal (MHRT) and with the patient and/or their nearest relative given a right to appeal against the decision. A further renewal may be made after 12 months and thereafter at yearly intervals.
Application for warrants	If an AMHP believes that a mentally disordered person is being ill-treated or neglected on private property, he or she may make an application to a magistrate for a warrant to search the premises.
Assumption of the role of 'guardian'	Social services authorities can be appointed as 'guardians' to mentally ill people unlikely to respond to hospital treatment, but in need of protection. Private individuals can be appointed, too—but only with the council's consent.

the rockiest rides of any approved piece of new legislation in living memory. At the heart of the Bill were two key proposals that provoked fury among mental health and human rights campaigners, and a high-profile campaign by *The Independent on Sunday*:

- new powers to enable doctors to detain people with serious mental health conditions who might pose a potential risk to themselves or others primarily for the protection of the public—rather than to receive treatment;

- that clinicians (doctors and psychiatrists) were to be given authority to 'impose' treatment on the severely mentally ill, regardless of their wishes and even if judged to have the mental capacity to make their own decisions.

At various stages, the Bill was opposed by campaign groups across the gamut—most notably, the Mental Health Alliance, a coalition of 78 organizations, including Mind, the King's Fund, and various bodies representing practitioners in the field. In the end, it was watered down, although the ability of doctors to prescribe enforced medication remained in the final version.

The Act's other main features are listed in Table 18.12.

Table 18.12 The main provisions of the Mental Health Act 2007

Provision	Effect
New definition of 'mental disorder'	Rationalized the system by abolishing references to different types of condition.
Detention only if relevant treatment available	Introduction of a new 'appropriate medical treatment' test to prevent patients being compulsorily detained unless medical treatment appropriate to their disorder and all other circumstances of the case is available to them. A pre-existing 'treatability test' has been abolished.
Extension of 'sectioning' powers to wider range of professionals	A broadening of the group of professional practitioners allowed to take on the functions previously performed by ASWs and RMOs (now AMHPs and responsible clinicians).
New rights for patients to challenge 'nearest relatives'	Patients given the right to apply to displace their nearest relative, with county courts also allowed to do so, on 'reasonable grounds'. Civil partners to be treated as nearest relatives, in the same way as husbands and wives.
More community supervision of discharged patients	Supervised community treatment (SCT) to be introduced for patients following a period of detention in hospital. The aim is to allow 'a small number' of patients with mental disorders to live in the community while subject to certain conditions under the 1983 Act (as amended by the 2007 Act), to ensure that they continue with the medical treatment they require. The intention is to address the so-called 'revolving door', whereby some patients are discontinue their medication in the community and end up being detained again.
Fast-track mental health review process to safeguard patient and 'nearest relative' rights	A reduction in the amount of time before a case must be referred to the MHRT, and the introduction of a single Mental Health Review Tribunal for England, modelled on the existing single one for Wales.
Services customized more to different age groups	Improvement of 'age-appropriate services'—ensuring that people under the age of 18 are accommodated suitably, rather than on adult wards.
Professional advocacy for all patients	Every detained patient to be entitled to an independent mental health advocate.
More emphasis on therapy and non-invasive treatments	New safeguards to limit the use of electro-convulsive therapy (ECT).

Prior to the final passage of the 2007 Act, Labour introduced a marginally less controversial reform in the guise of the Mental Capacity Act 2005, which sought to enshrine the rights of people with severe mental health issues to take decisions relating to their own care that had previously only existed in common law in statute. The Act covered only England and Wales, but similar provisions had earlier been made north of the border, under the Adults with Incapacity (Scotland) Act 2000.

The Act also introduced the following new measures:

- a new Independent Mental Capacity Advocate Service (IMCAS) for England and another for Wales to come into force in 2007;
- new criminal offences introduced of 'wilful neglect', and 'ill treatment';
- service users to be allowed to nominate 'substitute decision-makers' under a new lasting power of attorney (LPA);
- the introduction of a new Court of Protection, with extended powers.

→ Further reading

Blackman, T., Brody, S., and Convery, J. (eds) (2001) *Social Care and Social Exclusion: A Comparative Study of Older People's Care in Europe*, London: Palgrave Macmillan. **Thoughtful and informative comparisons between the different approaches taken by six states—including Britain—to providing social care for the elderly.**

Leff, J. (1997) *Care in the Community: Illusion or Practice?*, London: WileyBlackwell. **Critical evaluation of the impact of the Conservative Party's 'Care in the Community' policies on the mentally ill and those who treat them.**

Philpot, T. (2007) *Adoption: Changing Families, Changing Times*, London: Routledge. **Examination of the British adoption laws, focusing on real-life stories, and recent changes to open up the process to same-sex and unmarried couples.**

Stanley, J. and Goddard, C. (2002) *In the Firing Line: Violence and Power in Child Protection Work*, London: WileyBlackwell. **Thoughtful insight into the pressures faced by child social workers and other social services professionals in identifying and protecting children in need. Examines recent case studies evidencing failures in the system.**

? Review questions

1. What is the definition of 'children in need'? Outline the main responsibilities of local authority social services departments in relation to such children.

2. What were the main reforms arising from the Victoria Climbié Inquiry and the 'Every Child Matters' agenda? What are 'children's trusts'?

3. What is the difference between adoption and fostering? Outline the processes for adopting or fostering, and the range and types of people entitled to adopt or foster under British law.

4. What is meant by the term 'community care'? What are the main types of support available to the elderly and mentally ill under this policy?

5. Outline the purpose and powers of the Commission for Social Care Inspection.

Online resource centre

www.oxfordtextbooks.co.uk/orc/Morrison

Visit the Online Resource Centre that accompanies this book for web links and regular updates.

19

Transport, environment, and 'quality of life' issues

As we have seen from the previous chapters, the bulk of local authorities' time and money is spent raising and allocating funds, administering the planning process, and managing—if not always directly delivering—core services such as schools, housing, and social care. But beyond these complex and costly policy areas, councils are also responsible for a range of other things, from maintaining roads and arranging them into bus routes, to licensing pubs and nightclubs, inspecting hotels and restaurants, and running museums, theatres, and libraries. This broad sweep of service areas—covering everything from public transport to environmental health and trading standards—is where the basic utilitarian needs represented by the core spending areas listed above make way for those that might broadly be described as being about 'quality of life'. It is these areas that are the focus of this penultimate chapter.

▶ Highways and public transport

As described in Chapter 11, one of the prime motivators behind the emergence of local government in the UK was the promotion of production and trade, and the need to service the rapidly evolving agricultural and manufacturing economy ushered in by the Industrial Revolution. To this end, the embryonic councils of the nineteenth century became preoccupied with two broad areas of policy designed to facilitate the expansion of this new economy:

- *highways and transport*—specifically, the movement of workers and goods from country to town, and between markets, and the maintenance of proper roads;
- *public health*—the provision of housing and sanitation of sufficiently high quality to cater for the workers on whose labour the new economy was founded. Today, this is split between local authorities' housing functions (see Chapter 17), and environmental health and waste management services, as explored later this chapter.

For hundreds of years, the only public highways of a decent navigable standard across the UK were the remains of Roman roads and others built from the Tudor period onwards by local parish councils. But the growth of commerce and long-distance trade in the eighteenth century meant that industrialists and merchants began to wake up to the need for their goods to be transported as speedily and safely as possible, and this led to an increase in the level of private investment in highways.

The main developments early on in the history of highways and public transport are outlined in Table 19.1.

Types of road and the highways authorities responsible for them

The construction and maintenance of Britain's labyrinthine road network is divided between multiple authorities. Minor roads, and some of the more major ones linking two or more towns together, are usually maintained by the relevant local authorities (county councils, unitary authorities, or metropolitan **borough councils**), but the longest—and widest—are normally the direct responsibility of the Secretary of State for Transport. Upkeep

Table 19.1 A timeline of the emergence of road-building in Britain

Date	Development
Eighteenth century	The emergence of 'Turnpike trusts' (effectively an early form of public–private partnership), with locally based companies given parliamentary powers, under a series of 2,000 Acts, to build and maintain specific sections of road. This was financed by levying tolls on road users—a system currently being revisited in some areas of the UK.
1816	In Bristol, John Macadam pioneers a convex road-building technique designed to improve the camber for transporting heavy loads and to facilitate better drainage. The system is subsequently adopted across the country.
1888	Responsibility for maintaining public roads in their area is handed to the newly emerging county councils (in two-tier areas, this remains their responsibility to this day).
1959	The first section of the M1, Britain's first major national trunk road—or motorway (M road)—is opened, between Berrygrove, Hertfordshire, and Crick, Northamptonshire.
1968	Final stretch of the M1 is completed, after being extended several times into Yorkshire.
1973	The first section of a London orbital motorway, the M16 (later to be renamed the M25), is built between South Mimms and Potters Bar, both in Hertfordshire.
1986	The M25 is officially opened by Margaret Thatcher, with the completion of the section between junctions 22 and 23 (London Colney and South Mimms).

of these primary roads falls to the **Highways Agency**, an **executive agency** of the Department of Transport (DoT). The main road designations and the authorities responsible for them are outlined in Table 19.2.

New highways are usually either the result of new local and/or central government road-building schemes—in which case, they will automatically be 'adopted' as the responsibility of the relevant authority once built—or an incidental effect of the laying out of a new housebuilding programme. In the latter case, the developer behind the scheme will normally enter a formal agreement with the planning authority to ensure that it can hand over responsibility for the roads concerned as soon as the development is complete. Such agreements are backed with 'bonds' issued by banks or building societies to ensure that, if the developer goes into receivership or defaults, the roads will be finished without expense to local taxpayers.

In some circumstances, however, highways—normally footpaths or bridleways—may be closed or diverted to enable development. There are two main ways in which this is done:

Table 19.2 The types of road and the authorities responsible for them

Road type	Definition	Authority
Trunk roads (M and major A roads)	Major roads linking one town or city with another, and often connecting them to ports and airports. Normally divided into at least a dual carriageway layout, the biggest of these are multi-lane motorways. The M25 is in the process of becoming an eight-lane motorway, with one stretch (between junctions 12 and 14) boasting ten	Secretary of State for Transport and the Highways Agency
County roads (A roads)	Major arterial roads (almost all A roads) linking smaller towns together and normally falling within the boundaries of a single county	County councils, unitary authorities, metropolitan borough councils, and individual London boroughs
Secondary roads (B roads), and public bridleways and footpaths	B roads and smaller roads in both rural and urban areas, particularly those linking villages, hamlets, and smaller settlements. Bridleways and footpaths are often little more than dirt tracks, following the lines of medieval or more ancient routes, and paths through fields and woodland	Local authorities (as above)
Private roads	Highways contained within the boundaries of a private estate, such as Canary Wharf in east London, or the City of London	Private estates and related businesses (e.g. Canary Wharf)—unless the road has been formally adopted by the relevant local authority under the Private Street Works Act 1892

- if a highway is being closed because it is no longer being used, the authority must apply to magistrates for an 'extinguishment order' under the Highways Acts (this will not be granted if there is a proven objection on the basis that the highway *is* still used);

- a highway can sometimes be *realigned* to run around a development, rather than through it, by the granting of a 'public path diversion order' under the terms of various Town and Country Planning Acts.

Developers must carry out detailed research before embarking on their plans to ensure that they have applied for any necessary extinguishment or diversion orders. This is done by consulting a 'definitive rights of way map' maintained by the highways authority.

The role of the Secretary of State and the Highways Agency

Because of their major infrastructural significance, motorways are designated as 'special roads' by the government. In relation to both motorways and *trunk roads (other major roads)*, the Secretary of State is ultimately responsible for the following:

- *overall policy*—that is, whether and where to build new motorways and A roads, the use of tolls and other forms of road pricing, and the balance between road-building and investment in public passenger transport via the rail network and airports;
- *planning, improvement, and maintenance*—the logistics of building, repairing, and maintaining major roads, and the implementation of policies on the ground;
- *financing and controlling* the trunk road and motorway programme through taxation.

In practice, many important decisions are taken in regional government offices, and much of the maintenance and improvement is overseen by the Highways Agency, which, in turn, subcontracts the hands-on engineering work to other companies—for example, UK Highways. In addition, although county councils have long undertaken road maintenance in their areas on behalf of the Secretary of State, this, too, is franchised out to private contractors.

There is also an increasingly complex system by which primary, secondary, and unclassified roads can be 'designated' to lower-tier authorities to take control of their day-to-day maintenance, to ensure the smooth flow of traffic, and to tackle issues such as congestion and pollution from noise and petrol fumes. In this way, the Secretary of State can 'designate' responsibility for maintaining motorways and major A roads to London boroughs, while county councils can 'designate' to their local borough and/or district councils.

The Highways Agency, established in 1994, is overseen by its own board, under a chief executive earning £180,000 a year. It boasts seven regional control centres and a further 28 outstations from which its traffic officers operate. According to its website, its official statutory responsibility is to oversee the '*operation and stewardship of the strategic road network in England on behalf of the Secretary of State*'. The more specific roles of the Highways Agency include:

- managing traffic;
- tackling congestion;
- providing information to road users;
- improving journey times, road safety, and reliability;
- minimizing the impact of the road network on the environment.

The Highways Agency, in consultation with the Secretary of State and individual local authorities, is responsible for consulting on holding wide-ranging consultations when major road projects are planned. The main stages in this process are outlined in Table 19.3.

In practice, even at this late stage in the process, road projects often go far from smoothly. A number of high-profile protests have occurred in recent years against major road-building projects, the most famous being that over the so-called 'Newbury Bypass'—a 9-mile stretch of dual carriageway built around the market town of Newbury in Berkshire. From January to April 1996, some seven thousand protestors—ranging from hardcore environmentalists, based at a series of 20 roadside camps along the route, to middle-aged professionals and pensioners—picketed a 360-acre site in an effort to thwart the building programme, which involved the felling of 120 acres of ancient woodland. In the end, the work went ahead, but not before the cost of policing the protest (dubbed 'Operation Prospect') had broken through the £5m mark, and that of hiring private security firms to put up fences and patrol the perimeter had topped £24m.

Other notable protests include those over the construction of the A30 between Exeter and Honiton in Devon, which saw a network of tunnels and tree houses built at a road camp near Fairmile. These protests made a media celebrity out of 'Swampy' (aka self-proclaimed eco-warrior Daniel Hooper), whose later antics included a one-off stint as a panellist of BBC1's current affairs comedy quiz show, *Have I Got News for You*.

Table 19.3 The main stages in the consultation process for major road projects

Stage	Procedure
Consultation document published	Document must cover the following criteria: (a) a description of potential alternative routes; (b) the project's projected cost, including an explanation of the differences between the various alternative options; (c) an environmental impact assessment (EIA) disclosing details of any potential environmental issues arising from the project, as stipulated by various EU Directives; (d) other relevant factors (e.g. any potential impact on historical sites).
Comments invited on proposal	A copy of the consultation document is sent to all local authorities affected by the proposals. A public exhibition is arranged at which the proposal is explained and alternative solutions discussed.
Invitation for alternative schemes	Opponents are offered a chance to submit their objections formally to the Secretary of State.
Assessment of objections	Views of objectors are examined in detail following the end of the consultation period.
Approval or rejection of proposal	The Secretary of State publishes a final decision on the plan, in the form of a statement giving his or her reasons for advocating the project and the benefits that it will bring.
Detailed plans for implementation of proposal drafted	Draft orders covering proposed route drawn up—including any *compulsory purchase orders (CPOs)* necessary for it to go ahead.
Public inquiry	This will discuss in detail any objections to the draft order, with directly affected parties invited to speak. It will focus solely on questions about the viability of the route, its design, and the case for it.
Final decision	The final say is had by the Secretary of State once the inquiry inspector has heard the case for and against the plans, and produced his or her report.

Recent national reforms of traffic policy

Road-building continues to be an issue of huge controversy across Britain, not least because there is little evidence that the continuing expansion of the network has done much to ease congestion. In some cases, studies suggest that the funnelling of government spending away from public transport and into major building programmes is, if anything, *increasing* the likelihood of traffic jams—by encouraging more people to drive. An independent study by transport consultant Halliburton published in 2002 predicted an increase in congestion in the M25 corridor of a third by 2016 unless radical steps were taken to lure people out of their cars and onto public transport. It recommended the charging of tolls and the introduction of a luxury bus service around the motorway to persuade people to get out of their cars.

Concern about road policy is arguably one of the rare issues to unite both supporters and opponents, albeit from different perspectives: to environmental campaigners, road expansion and congestion represent a cause of serious pollution and long-term ecological damage, while to motorists and long-distance hauliers, traffic jams are a huge source of discomfort and frustration. Perhaps unsurprisingly, the government has launched a number of initiatives in recent years to address congestion and pollution, as listed in Table 19.4.

Despite these initiatives, many road and rail users are united in the view that Britain has some way to go before it can boast of anything like the 'integrated transport policy' first promised by then Deputy Prime Minister John Prescott in 1999. His successor as Transport Secretary, Alistair Darling, enraged environmental groups in 2003 by bowing to pressure from motoring organizations such as the AA by announcing a £5.5bn road-building programme, to involve widening parts of the M1, and expanding major roads around London and Birmingham.

Local traffic management, road pricing, and congestion charging

The term 'traffic management' was, for long years, synonymous with little more than road crossings, signs, signals, and diversions—in short, the bread-and-butter mechanisms used to direct traffic from A to B, to help pedestrians cross it, and to 'warn' motorists about everything from changes in speed limits to school crossings, steep slopes, sharp bends, and bumpy road surfaces. To a large extent, the day-to-day work of highways authorities remains preoccupied with these and other humdrum concerns—many of which continue to excite the attention of local newspapers and television news outlets. The more workaday responsibilities of highways departments include planning, installing, and monitoring the effectiveness of the following:

- traffic lights;
- major and mini roundabouts;
- sleeping policemen (speed bumps) and other forms of 'traffic calming' measures;

Table 19.4 The major government traffic and transport initiatives since 1997

Initiative	Proposals
Traffic Reduction Act 1997	Requires new highway design to take account of the need to cut traffic, by increasing the number of bus lanes and park-and-ride schemes, to encourage more people to travel by passenger transport.
A New Deal for Transport: Better for Everyone (1999)	**White Paper** outlining the need for an 'integrated transport policy' to increase use of trains and buses.
Transport Act 2000	Created a new Commission for Integrated Transport responsible for:
	(a) advising ministers on how to implement an integrated transport policy;
	(b) monitoring developments across transport, environment, health, and other areas;
	(c) reviewing progress towards government objectives.
Transport 2010: The Ten-Year Plan	Published in July 2000, this gave effect to many of the ideas in the 1999 White Paper. It enshrined the following broad key proposals:
	(a) a target to cut traffic congestion by 5 per cent by 2010;
	(b) local highways authorities allowed to levy charges to ease congestion (see pp. 584–7);
	(c) Highways Agency to change from being a 'road builder' to being a 'road network operator' (effectively, a highway equivalent to **Network Rail**), charged with improving and operating the trunk road network, using outside contractors;
	(d) 60 per cent of trunk roads to be retained as 'core' network of nationally important routes, with others 'detrunked' and transferred to councils;
	(e) future trunk road planning to be overseen by regional planning guidance (RPG);
	(f) Highways Agency to work closely with rail companies to improve 'interchanges' between public and private transport—and other types of public transport;
	(g) local authorities required to formulate five-year local transport plans to coordinate and improve public transport, promote walking and cycling, foster green transport plans for journeys to work, school, and elsewhere, and reduce social exclusion, especially in rural areas, by improving bus routes;
	(h) by end of 1999, in run-up to the plan's official launch, councils expected to have produced draft transport plans covering the period 2000–05 (these replaced the existing transport policies and programmes (TPP) system).

- zebra crossings, pelican crossings, and crossings manned by 'lollypop ladies';
- road signage;
- one-way systems;
- 'park and ride' schemes—that is, free bus services to and from out-of-town car parks;
- dedicated bus and taxi lanes, and cycle lanes/paths.

In recent years, traffic management has entered a new phase, as the frustration with mounting congestion of pedestrians and motorists alike has met with growing calls from both the environmental lobby and the business community for radical action to address what is widely perceived as an unsustainable growth in private car ownership. The prime concern of environmentalists remains the pollution caused by carbon monoxide exhaust fumes and the noise generated by heavy traffic. Business leaders, meanwhile, are increasingly alarmed by the impact of lengthy traffic delays on the smooth running of the economy. A 2005 survey by the Institution of Civil Engineers (ICE) estimated that road traffic was costing UK businesses up to £20bn a year, because so many employees were arriving late for work. This figure is also consistently quoted by the Confederation of British Industry (CBI).

Faced with the prospect of roads becoming even more clogged up, if left unchecked, with all of the associated impacts on people's quality of life, the government and the Highways Agency have been looking to other countries for inspiration in an effort to find a way of luring people out of their cars and onto passenger transport. Given the high cost of travelling by rail and the severe congestion experienced by train commuters on many routes—particularly in south-east England—the 'carrot' of public transport has historically failed to persuade sufficient numbers to leave their cars at home. As a result, policymaking has gradually shifted towards adopting more of a 'stick' approach, focusing on the following:

- congestion charging;
- road pricing (tolls).

Congestion charging

Originating in Singapore, where it was introduced as far back as 1975, congestion charging is the system by which flat-rate fees are charged to the drivers of vehicles entering a specified 'congestion charge zone' (usually in or around a town or city) between specific hours on a given day. In Britain, the most famous example of congestion charging to date was introduced by former London Mayor Ken Livingstone in February 2003, initially within a limited central zone broadly defined by the capital's inner ring road. It was extended to cover much of west London in February 2007, although at the time of writing it is unclear whether this will remain the case, in the wake of the election of Conservative Mayor Boris Johnson. The charge operates between 7 a.m. and 6 p.m., Monday to Friday, and was initially set at £5 a day. It is currently £8 a day for all qualifying vehicles (or £7 for fleet lorries). Drivers may now pay by credit or debit card over the phone, by mobile phone text messaging (SMS), via a dedicated website, or over the counter in shops equipped with a PayPoint facility. Those who fail to pay are fined £120 (or £60 if they make payment within 14 days of receiving the fine).

The congestion charge has won praise from both business leaders and green lobbyists, with various reports suggesting that it has successfully cut traffic jams in central London by anything from 8 to 20 per cent. It has won fans in the medical community, too: according to a 2008 study in *Occupational and Environmental Medicine* magazine, its impact on pollution may have already 'saved' up to 1,888 extra 'years of life' among London's seven million residents. Perhaps unsurprisingly, however, the charge has infuriated many motorists—particularly shift workers forced to arrive at, or leave, work in central London at unsocial hours, when little or no public transport is available (thus forcing them to pay the charge in relation to the half of their journey that falls within the time frame of the charge).

On its launch, the charge became the subject of a high-profile campaign by stage actors, including Tom Conti and Samantha Bond ('Miss Moneypenny' in the Pierce Brosnan James Bond films), who cited the plight of low-paid shift workers, but also argued that the timings of the daily charge period would adversely affect the size of audiences for West End performances, by penalizing theatregoers for entering the zone in early evening.

Nonetheless, the perceived overall success of the charge has seen major international cities from New York to Stockholm racing to imitate it, and the British government (initially sceptical of Mr Livingstone's plans) has committed itself to rolling it out to other towns and cities. To this end, in June 2008, then Transport Secretary Ruth Kelly approved the biggest congestion charge scheme so far introduced anywhere in the world, in the form of a dual–ring zone around Greater Manchester covering an area 12 times bigger than the original London zone. The zone, intended to be introduced in 2013, would have operated at peak times only (from 7–9.30 a.m. and 4–6 p.m.), and Ms Kelly vowed it would not come into force until the city had a 'world-class public transport system' in place—funded by £2.8m in public investment, £1.5m of which would come from central government and the remainder from the Association of Greater Manchester Authorities (AGMA). However, in December 2008 the plan was thrown into disarray when local residents rejected it outright in a referendum, with 79 per cent voting against and just 21 per cent for it. Despite this, other schemes are still proposed for Bristol and Bath, although Norwich and Edinburgh (whose voters previously rejected the charge) have shelved theirs indefinitely.

In addition to congestion charging itself, in February 2008, Mr Livingstone introduced a new 'low-emission zone' encompassing the whole of Greater London—an area covering some 610 square miles (1,580 km^2). The worst polluting lorries, buses, and coaches were to be fined £200 per day for entering the capital. On its launch, Mr Johnson condemned the charge as 'the most punitive, draconian fining regime in the whole of Europe'—leading to speculation that he would scrap it once established in office. The introduction of the low-emission zone did little to endear Mr Livingstone to the owners of so-called 'Chelsea tractors'—gas-guzzling, four-wheel-drive vehicles, popularly used by parents for the so-called 'school run' (that is, to ferry their children to and from school at the start and end of each weekday)—many of whom had already been hit by the congestion charge.

Road pricing

Congestion charging may be the flavour of the month among highways authorities seeking to battle traffic problems (while raising a million or two to invest in other local services), but the idea of forcing motorists to pay up front to use roads is hardly a new one. In Britain, 'road pricing' was first mooted by John Major's Conservative government, which outlined proposals to introduce a network of privately financed toll roads on major routes, modelled on the system used on motorways in France and other mainland European countries. To date, the UK has only one private toll motorway—a 27–mile stretch of the M6 between Coleshill, Warwickshire, and Cannock, Staffordshire, which opened in December 2003. But in July 2004, then Transport Secretary Mr Darling announced plans for two 50-mile 'pay as you go' expressways to run alongside the M6 between Wolverhampton and Manchester.

The Labour government remains ambivalent about the long-term future for private toll roads overall, in light of recent research into the impact of road pricing. In January 2005, an answer to a parliamentary question to the DoT revealed that congestion on and around the M6 near Birmingham had actually *increased* since the opening of the existing toll road. Junctions to the south had seen traffic levels rise daily by up to 10,000 vehicles, with those to the north seeing 5,000 extra a day. Altogether, 38,000 additional cars and lorries a day were using both the toll route and the free M6. Ministers' focus has been sharpened by the scale of apparent public opposition to increased road pricing. In February 2007, 1.7 million people signed an online petition objecting to more tolls—prompting outgoing Prime Minister Tony Blair to write to them collectively, stressing that the government's mind had not yet been decided and the debate was only 'beginning'.

Other aspects of highways and transport policy

Street lighting

Street lighting tends primarily to be the preserve of the local highways authority—that is, the county council in two-tier areas. As with parking policy (see later in this chapter), however, district/borough councils often have responsibility for maintaining and repairing roads and pathways delegated to them, along with the budget required to contract out the necessary work. The advent of *quality parish councils* (see pp. 361–2) has also increasingly seen maintenance of individual roads in smaller towns, villages, and other rural settlements delegated to an even lower level.

Public transport

Since the privatization of the National Bus Company—Britain's nationwide bus service provider—in the 1980s, the subsequent deregulation of local routes, and the introduction of dedicated passenger transport authorities in metropolitan areas, local authorities have played a diminishing role in providing public transport. As in many policy areas, they have largely been reduced to the status of 'enablers'—monitoring the provision of bus, tram, underground, and river boat services by the free market, and stepping in to act as 'providers of last resort' where unacceptable gaps and/or inconsistencies in services emerge.

Under the Local Government Act 1972, the then newly established metropolitan county councils were charged with providing bus services through 'passenger transport executives' designed to promote 'integrated' local transport. But in 1985, this changed when Margaret Thatcher's government replaced the metropolitan counties with metropolitan borough councils and scrapped the GLC, and introduced independent passenger transport authorities in these areas, the most famous being London Transport—now *Transport for London (TfL)* (see later in the chapter). At the same time, local authorities' responsibility for providing transport links to and from airports and docks was transferred to new joint boards. The one abiding legacy of the 1972 Act was the transfer of highways and transport responsibilities from borough and district councils to county councils. This remains the case to this day, with the qualification that, outside two-tier areas, this role has been assumed by unitary authorities.

The effective privatization of local transport was formalized in the Transport Act 1985, with councils expected to provide only 'socially necessary' services—for example, those linking villages and smaller towns—directly and only then when the market had failed to do so. A year later, the system was formally deregulated, to allow any number of bus companies to compete on a specific route—known as a 'registered bus route'—provided that they first obtained a 'public service operator's licence' from the *Traffic Commissioners*. Trams, such as those operating in Manchester, had to be similarly licensed.

Under the present licensing regime, there are seven regional Commissioners. Their main responsibilities are to:

- license operators of delivery lorries, or heavy goods vehicles (HGVs), and the operators of buses and coaches—known as 'public service vehicles' (PSVs);
- register local bus services;
- grant vocational licences, and take action against drivers of HGVs and PSVs.

The Traffic Commissioner for Scotland has additional powers that, in England and Wales, are exercised individually by officers in local authority highways departments. These include determining appeals against taxi fares, as well as those against charging, and removing improperly parked vehicles in Edinburgh and Glasgow.

One effect of deregulating local bus services was to undermine councils' ability to subsidize public transport. While, in some areas, the introduction of competition did improve services by pushing down fares, in others, the loss of council-run buses deprived residents of heavily subsidized tickets that found no replacement in the privatized marketplace. Among the most celebrated local services were the cut-price buses ushered in by Mr Livingstone in the days of the Greater London Council and the record-breaking 2p fares introduced by future Home Secretary David Blunkett while leader of Sheffield City Council in the 1970s.

Contracting out bus services has also been blamed for the increasing isolation of some local communities, particularly those based in remote villages and hamlets, because—shorn of state subsidies—private companies have been reluctant to maintain, let alone initiate, unprofitable routes. On occasion, poorer suburbs of towns and cities have also been left isolated by private operators' refusal to continue running services there—normally in response to outbreaks of vandalism, or verbal and/or physical violence towards drivers. In June 2006, one of Britain's biggest private bus operators, Stagecoach, briefly suspended services to Hull's Orchard Park estate after receiving 16 separate reports of missiles being thrown at buses in just four days.

While bus service licensing has long since passed to the Traffic Commissioners, county councils, unitary authorities, and metropolitan boroughs retain responsibility for issuing licences to the operators of taxi services and minicab firms, including Hackney carriages outside London (where they are licensed by the Commissioner of the Metropolitan Police).

Although deregulation of the buses may have produced a patchy service in many areas, with some now being very poorly served, recent years have seen the introduction of generous *concessionary fare schemes* for those who meet certain criteria, such as students, the disabled, and old age pensioners (OAPs). Local authorities fund the schemes by subsidizing local bus operators with the equivalent of the full fares that they are 'losing' by implementing them. As of April 2006, the government ordered all local authorities to provide a bare minimum of free off-peak bus fares for pass-holders. In an even more far-reaching initiative—launched in April 2008—the government gave registered OAPs and the disabled entitlement to free off-peak travel anywhere in England and Wales, rather than simply in their local authority area, as had been the case before. 'Off-peak' is defined as between 9.30 a.m. and 11 p.m.—that is, not the morning rush hour.

Transport for London (TfL)

Formerly London Transport, Transport for London (TfL) is a *quango* charged with managing—if not directly running—the following passenger transport services:

- London buses, Croydon Tramlink, and the Docklands Light Railway;
- the London Underground (the 'Tube') network;
- the Transport for London Road Network (TLRN);

- London River Services—that is, licensed passenger ferries along and across the Thames.

It is also responsible for:

- delivering the Integrated Transport Strategy published by the mayor in July 2001, and revised in 2004 and 2006, in consultation with the Greater London Assembly (GLA);
- regulating taxis and minicabs;
- helping to coordinate the Dial-a-Ride and Taxicard schemes for door-to-door services for transport users with mobility problems;
- installing and maintaining traffic lights across London;
- promoting the safe use of the Thames for passenger and freight movement.

To help the mayor to deliver the strategy for London, in 1998, a Transport Committee for London was set up by the GLA to replace the four pre-existing bodies in charge of overseeing the Underground, buses, taxis, most main roads running into and through the capital, and the Docklands Light Railway (a privately owned company).

While all of this may sound very cooperative and harmonious, at times in the past few years, the process of taking decisions about the future of London's transport network has been far from that. Between 1997 and 2001, Mr Blair's government was locked in a tortuous stalemate with Mr Livingstone and London Transport Commissioner Bob Kiley over ministers' insistence on the 'part-privatization' of the underground. Despite widespread criticism about the shambolic privatization of the national rail network, the government went to huge lengths to persuade the mayor to accept a *public–private partnership (PPP)* arrangement (see pp. 238–9), which saw a near-identical model adopted for the Underground, with franchises to run services on individual lines contracted out to competing private companies, while the tracks, signals, stations, and even rolling stock itself remained in the hands of a separate authority (in this case, TfL). With the Underground, the proposed management/ownership split was actually three-way, rather than two-way, as with the railways—with companies contracted to carry out a £13bn, 15-year programme of improvements on the Underground infrastructure given a stake in it, too. But under an 11th-hour compromise agreed between Mr Blair and Mr Kiley, the Commissioner was ultimately offered a 'golden share' in the infrastructure companies—giving him the power to sack their chief executives, appoint his own representatives to their boards, intervene in their maintenance programmes, and even challenge their internal budgets and share policies.

More recently, TfL was involved in the protracted negotiations over the proposed new £16bn overland train link bringing 24 overland rail services an hour through the heart of London from Maidenhead, Berkshire, in the west, eastwards to Essex. The project—dubbed 'Crossrail'—was finally approved in September 2007, after a decade of deliberation. A third of its cost will be financed up front by the government, with the remaining two-thirds split between borrowing against future fares and a levy on London business rates.

Car parking

Responsibility for administering and policing car parking is broadly divided between local authorities in the ways outlined in Table 19.5.

Until relatively recently, car-parking responsibilities were split fairly straight in two-tier areas between borough and district councils, on the one hand, and counties, on the other, with the former managing off-road car parks and the latter on-street parking. Today, in many areas, these distinctions are blurred, with some district councils entering into agency agreements with neighbouring counties, and vice versa, effectively to contract out these functions to the other. To confuse the public further, while the fixed-penalty fines system tends to be administered by county councils or unitary authorities, the actual issuing of penalty notices—that is, the action of placing them on parked vehicles—has traditionally been performed by traffic wardens employed by local police forces. This recently changed, with council-employed parking attendants taking over the role in most areas and, at time of writing, this system, too, was due for a makeover—with wardens about to be renamed 'civil enforcement officers'.

Table 19.5 The types of local authority responsible car parking services

Type of parking	Local authority
On-street car parking and residents' parking schemes	Traditionally, county councils and unitary authorities, but now administered by all types of local authority, subject to local arrangements
Open-air car parks on public or council-owned land	Traditionally, district/borough councils and unitary authorities, but now depends on local arrangements
Multi-storey car parks	Private firms, such as National Car Parks Ltd (NCP)
Car parks at hospitals, colleges, universities, and business premises	Run by organizations themselves, increasingly via the aegis of private contractors

As with traffic management, parking issues have a habit of raising the ire (and blood pressure) of motorists—and, as a result, they provide the raw material for just as many news stories. A common misconception—fuelled by countless local newspaper reports to this effect—is that wardens and attendants are paid commissions or 'bonuses' related to the number or value of the fixed-penalty notices that they issue. In actual fact, the government legislated to prevent this happening in the Traffic Wardens and Parking Attendants Act 2005.

So combustible has the car-parking issue become in recent years, however, that ticket recipients may now appeal to a National Parking Adjudication Service (NPAS).

Waste management and environmental health

Public health has been on the local authority agenda for longer than almost anything else. A chronology of major Public Health Acts and other relevant legislation is given in Table 19.6.

The task of making sure that housing, businesses, and local amenities in a given area conform to basic hygiene and safety standards today falls to the environmental health departments of district/borough councils and

Table 19.6 A chronology of public health legislation in the UK

Law	Reform
Public Health Acts 1872 and 1875	Local boards of health and sanitary authorities first set up
Public Health Act 1936	Public health responsibilities transferred to newly created local authorities
Public Health Acts 1948–74	Public health responsibilities—other than those covering environmental health—gradually transferred from local authorities to the NHS
Environmental Protection Act 1990	Earlier Acts consolidated to summarize councils' responsibilities, creating new environmental services departments
Food Safety Act 1990 (adapted for Scotland and Northern Ireland)	New powers of inspection and criminal prosecution given to environmental health officers
Food Safety Act 1999	Food Standards Agency established, roles of local inspectors clarified, and more all-encompassing environmental services departments introduced

unitary authorities. Of their myriad responsibilities, by far the most costly and complex are those related to the effective monitoring of waste management services—an area so broad that it requires the active involvement of every type of council.

Waste collection, recycling, and waste disposal

There are two overriding aspects to waste management, each handled by a different type of local authority in two-tier areas:

- *waste collection*—the responsibility of district or borough councils, unitaries, and metropolitan boroughs;
- *waste disposal*—the responsibility of county councils, unitaries, and metropolitan boroughs.

Waste collection

Throughout the UK, household and business waste collection has traditionally been carried out in the form of a weekly door-to-door service. In recent years, however, the nature of rubbish collecting (as it is more commonly known) has changed somewhat, with a growing emphasis on recycling, rather than the simple disposal of refuse at 'rubbish tips', or landfill sites. At the same time, while councils have been looking at more imaginative and environmentally sustainable ways of disposing of waste, pressure on resources has led to some reducing the frequency of their basic door-to-door collections.

As with most areas of local service delivery, waste collection is periodically put out to tender under the Best Value system (see p. 417–18), with the result that many 'bin men and women' are now employed not by councils directly, but by the private contractors hired to carry out collections on their behalf. Having started out with kerbside recycling points at supermarkets, parks, and other public amenities, many collection authorities in England and Wales now tend to operate at least a fortnightly door-to-door recycling service. The operator contracted to collect the normal, non-recyclable household and/or business waste (food waste, plastics, etc.) will not always be the same one that collects the recycling.

Despite having dramatically increased its levels of recycling in recent years, Britain has been slow to embrace it in comparison to most other developed countries. As a result, the government has been looking at increasingly fiendish ways of cajoling or forcing householders and businesses to recycle more waste—the most controversial of which is the introduction of 'pay as you throw' fines for people who chuck away too much 'black bin waste', with commensurate 'rebates' for those who disproportionately use their green bins. Then Environment Secretary David Miliband announced plans to give councils the power to charge for excessive black bin waste in May 2007, as part of the government's drive to force councils to recycle at least 40 per cent of waste by 2010 and 50 per cent by 2020. Under the terms of the Climate Change Act 2008, trials of bin taxes were due to begin in 2009 in five pilot areas, to be announced nearer the time by the Department for the Environment, Food and Rural Areas (Defra). In March 2008, Mr Miliband's successor, Mr Benn, announced that the role of traditional council waste management officers in policing the new system would be handed over to a new breed of unelected quangos, known as 'joint waste authorities', and that they would be given the power to set the new taxes.

The willingness of ministers to take such unpopular action is a response to an even bigger threat than the prospect of being punished at the polls. A 1999 European Union (EU) Directive specifies that the amount of biodegradable waste dumped at landfill sites in Britain—equivalent to 18.1m tonnes in 2003–04—rather than composted or recycled must have been cut to 13.7m tonnes by 2010, 9.2m tonnes in 2013, and 6.3m in 2020. If it fails to meet these targets, the British government will be fined £180m a year by the *European Commission*.

Not content to wait for the outcome of the government's pilots, some local authorities have already taken the 'pay as you throw' concept into their own hands. After a series of alarmist reports of supposed 'Big Brother' tactics being used by Woking Borough Council to monitor the amount of recyclable waste that local householders were throwing away in black bags, rather than recycling as they should, in September 2006 the authority (one of the 'greenest' in Britain) confirmed that it had installed electronic chips capable of weighing this 'residual' waste in its wheelie bins. It insisted, however, that these had yet to be activated.

Waste disposal

The Environmental Protection Act 1990 required all waste disposal authorities to form arm's-length local authority waste disposal companies (LAWDCs) to dispose of waste on their behalf—a form of direct service organization (DSO) (see p. 417). In turn, these were required to 'hire' waste disposal contractors—in practice, either the company itself or another franchisee—to:

- provide the waste transfer and landfill sites to which householders can take large items of waste (for example, electrical goods) for landfill or destruction;
- dispose of items collected from local people's homes by collection operators;
- recycle waste or sell it for scrap.

Contractors running waste disposal sites on behalf of a local authority must obtain a waste management licence (WML) from the *Environment Agency* in England and Wales. In Scotland, applications must be made to the Scottish Environmental Protection Agency (SEPA), and in Northern Ireland, to the Department of the Environment (Environment and Heritage Service).

Because the EU has stepped up its use of targets to promote recycling and reduce the reliance of member state governments on landfill, the issue of straightforward rubbish dumping has become one of acute political sensitivity in Britain. Over the past 15 years, faced with rapidly dwindling capacity at the country's existing landfill sites, successive governments have sought to deter local authorities from continuing to dump waste in the age-old tradition. Perhaps the most contentious mechanism they have used in doing so is the Landfill Tax. Introduced under the Conservatives in the Finance Act 1996, this was initially levied on councils, waste disposal companies, and other organizations involved in dumping rubbish at a standard rate of £7 a tonne and a reduced rate of £2 a tonne. In its 1999 Budget, Labour raised the standard rate to £10 a tonne and introduced a 'Landfill Tax accelerator' designed to increase it by a further £1 a tonne each year until 2004. In his 2002 Pre-Budget Report, then Chancellor Mr Brown announced further stepped rises, with the medium to long-term aim of charging £35 a tonne. As at September 2008, the two rates are as follows:

- *standard rate*—£32 a tonne (rising by a further £8 a tonne each year until 2010–11) for household waste that may decay and/or contaminate land;
- *reduced rate*—£2.50 a tonne for rocks and soils, ceramics and concrete, unused minerals, furnace slag, ash, low-activity inorganic compounds, and water.

To ameliorate the impact of the Landfill Tax on site operators, the Tories introduced a Landfill Tax credit scheme designed to reward them with a 90 per cent tax credits against any donations that they made to an environmental body registered with the scheme's regulator, Entrust. This was, however, capped at 20 per cent of their Landfill Tax liability.

Rows over the Landfill Tax and recycling targets are not the only reasons why the issue of waste disposal has been in the news recently. In 2005, an investigation for BBC1's *Real Story* programme found that 500 tonnes of supposedly recycled waste from UK households had actually been dumped by contractors in Indonesia—raising concerns that British citizens might be salving their consciences over recycling at the expense of developing countries. Around the same time, EA figures revealed that around half of the 8m tonnes of green waste generated each year in Britain ends up overseas.

Air quality, noise pollution, fly-tipping, and dog fouling

The local authority officials charged with inspecting domestic and business premises to ensure that they meet statutory environmental health standards are called *environmental health officers*. One of their main duties is to investigate complaints relating to waste collection and disposal—or, more accurately, the *lack* of collection and disposal, in cases when, for example, a property owner or occupier has failed to leave out his or her rubbish at the right time and day, or to place it in the correct place for removal by the collection authority. They will also be called on to investigate incidents of so-called 'fly-tipping'—the unscrupulous practice of dumping rubbish on someone else's doorstep or backyard, often used by residents or businesses to offload refuse on a neighbouring street after missing their own collection day. Complaints will often arise through a neighbour who reports an unpleasant smell, or the unsightly presence of overloaded bin bags days before—or after—they are—or were—due to be collected. In extreme cases, rotting waste that has been inadequately stored in bags or dustbins, or left out for days on end before the next collection is due, may attract mice, rats, or other forms of vermin, necessitating direct intervention by the local environmental health department to remove them. The cost of doing so and of ridding the area of vermin will normally be passed straight on to the offending party—and the council may also choose to prosecute that party under environmental health legislation. A conviction will usually lead to a fine.

Another menace accorded greater priority in recent years has been dog fouling. After years of campaigning by environmental groups and others concerned about the potential danger that contact with dog mess poses to young children, so-called 'poop scoops' and dog litter bins became a common feature of most parks and public rights of way in the mid-1990s. Yet many areas remain blighted by it today—at least according to the revelation, in June 2008, that local authorities are increasingly using closed-circuit television (CCTV) cameras to spy on errant dog owners who fail to clean up after their pets. On learning of this fact, the Local Government Association (LGA) wrote to all councils in England and Wales urging them to use security cameras to police only more 'serious' misdemeanours, such as fly-tipping. But several authorities, including Hartlepool Borough Council, broke ranks to argue that local residents regarded dog fouling as far from trivial.

In response to growing pressure on the UK to conform to EU Directives, the Environmental Protection Act 1990 placed a new onus on local authorities to control any industrial emissions in their areas with the potential to produce significant pollution affecting air, land, or water. This was superseded by the Pollution Prevention and Control Act 1999, which made councils responsible for exercising 'local authority pollution prevention and control' (LAPPC) in relation to so-called 'Part B' installations. These include smaller power plants, glassworks, waste disposal sites, sewerage works, and municipal and hospital incinerators. More major polluting installations—such as oil refineries, nuclear power stations, steelworks, and large chemical plants—were designated as 'Part A1' and placed under an 'integrated pollution prevention and control' (IPPC) designation overseen by the Environment Agency, SEPA, or the Northern Irish Department of the Environment. There is also a third category of process, known as 'Part A2', which relates to medium-range installations. This, like Part B, is policed by local authorities in the following way:

- applications for a process to be carried out must be made to the relevant authority (if refused, appeals can be lodged to the Secretary of State);
- if an enforcing authority believes that an operator has breached an authorization, it can serve an enforcement notice specifying the nature of the breach, the steps that need to be taken to rectify it, and a deadline for that work to be completed;
- if the authority feels that external factors are creating an imminent risk of serious pollution, even if unconnected with the process itself, it can serve a prohibition notice.

An especially newsworthy issue in recent years has been the growing intolerance of noise pollution. In certain circumstances, authorities may now seize offending equipment, such as stereos or drills. The Noise Act 1996 gave them the power to send in officers to investigate the sources of excessive noise at night and to *measure* levels of noise pollution. Where it exceeds a statutory limit, a warning notice may immediately be served on whomever is responsible. Failure to comply is a criminal offence and officers may subsequently enter a property without a warrant to seize offending equipment. Prosecution often also follows—a fact that, when the first round of cases started to emerge in the late 1990s, provided an endless source of amusement for local newspaper editors and, presumably, readers alike.

Noise pollution has also been a notable target of government crackdowns on 'antisocial behaviour'—and the introduction of *antisocial behaviour orders (ASBOs)* (see p. 371). The use of ASBOs to tackle it has produced some highly newsworthy, and occasionally outlandish, outcomes. In March 2005, Andrew Gordon and his 18-year-old son, Phillip, were banned from their own home in Dunfermline for three months under the Anti-Social Behaviour (Scotland) Act 2004 because of severe noise and disruption caused due to drinking, cursing, fighting, and drug-taking at the house at times when Mr Gordon was away.

Action taken against 'unpleasant' smells has also made plenty of headlines. One contentious case involved an award-winning vegetarian cafe in Greenwich, which was ordered to stop serving cooked food in June 2008 after neighbours complained about the smells that it produced.

Environmental health officers also oversee various other areas, as listed in Table 19.7.

Environmental health and food safety

One of the most widely understood duties of environmental health officers (or 'inspectors', as they were previously known) is the role that they play in promoting food safety, by ensuring that restaurants, cafes, pubs, and shops serving food to the public are preparing, cooking, and storing meat and other items of suitable quality under appropriate conditions. This role—memorably satirized in the classic 'Basil the Rat' episode of BBC1 sitcom *Fawlty Towers*—covers all aspects of food hygiene, including its sale, importation, preparation, transportation, storing, packing, wrapping, displaying, serving, and delivery.

The Food Standards Act 1999 set up a new Food Standards Agency to oversee food hygiene and animal husbandry issues at a national level, while building on existing legislation to introduce two criminal offences for businesses failing to meet minimum standards: those of rendering food 'injurious to health' and of selling food 'unfit for human consumption'. The Act also

Table 19.7 The additional responsibilities of environmental health officers

Responsibility	Definition
Litter	Local authorities, 'statutory undertakers' (companies contracted by councils to run services on their behalf), and other public landowners are legally bound to keep their land free of litter. If the local authority designates a specific 'litter control area', it becomes an offence for anyone to throw down, drop, or dispose of litter on land owned by a public body in that area.
General health risks	If measures for preserving public health fail and diseases such as dysentery, smallpox, typhoid—or, more recently, foot and mouth—break out, the authority must inform the NHS and the local community physician or Director of Public Health.
Maintaining public areas	These range from public parks and playgrounds, to cemeteries.
Vermin control	Taking action to tackle infestations of rodents, insects, etc.—if necessary, charging private individuals after the event, should the infestation relate to privately owned land or property.
Contaminated land	Management of land contaminated by, e.g., industrial processes or military tests involving radiation is still covered by the 1990 Act. Borough/district councils or unitary authorities are responsible for identifying and registering contaminated land in their areas. If a serious problem is noted, the authority must designate a 'special site' and notify the EA/SEPA, which will then take responsibility for enforcing any action to be taken. The enforcing authority serves a remediation notice on the person or business responsible, specifying the action needed to remedy the problem. In Northern Ireland, contaminated land issues are overseen by the country's Department of Health under the terms of the Radioactive Contaminated Land Regulations (Northern Ireland) 2006.
Air quality	The following types of emission are prohibited under the Clean Air Act 1993 (which built on the provisions of the Clean Air Act 1956, introduced to eliminate winter smog): (a) 'dark smoke' issuing from chimneys; (b) excessive smoke, grit, dust, and fumes from chimneys; (c) excessively high chimneys; (d) excessive exhaust emissions; (e) smoke emissions in designated 'smoke control areas'. In addition, the Environment Act 1995 required councils to review present and likely future air quality in their areas. Where air was not meeting the desired standard, councils were given powers to designate 'air quality management areas' covered by air quality action plans.
Statutory nuisances	The 1990 Act empowers local authorities to serve 'abatement notices' on those responsible for statutory nuisances deemed prejudicial to health. In addition to vermin and noise pollution generated by premises, vehicles, machinery, or equipment in the street (e.g. by road workers), these include smoke, gas, or fumes; dust, steam, or effluvia; and accumulations of rubbish.
Public lavatories	Providing sufficient public conveniences to a hygienic standard, including accessible toilets, baby-changing facilities, etc.

introduced new, all-encompassing local authority environmental services departments, specifying that environmental health officers had the responsibility for:

- inspecting and seizing suspicious food;
- issuing improvement notices to owners of food businesses;
- serving emergency prohibition notices to close down businesses in the case of perceived serious health risks;
- liaising with the National Health Service (NHS) whenever they feel it necessary to take action in relation to potentially communicable disease risks;
- issuing additional enforcement notices dictated by central government in instances of sudden crisis—for example, the ban on the sale of beef on the bone as a consequence of the bovine spongiform encephalopathy (BSE), or 'mad cow disease', crisis in the late 1980s and early 1990s.

The aforementioned 'outbreak' of BSE presented one of the biggest instances in recent memory of environmental health issues breaking into the wider public health arena. The alarm generated by the first diagnoses of BSE in cattle, in November 1986, and subsequent identification of symptoms of Creutzfeldt-Jakob Disease (CJD) in several British people became of international concern—leading to a ten–year ban on the export of UK beef to EU countries, from 1996 to 2006.

Other examples of recent environmental health scares have included a succession of outbreaks of foot-and-mouth disease in British livestock. The major one occurred in 2001, and led to a mass cull of sheep and cattle— including tens of thousands of healthy animals—in what was widely portrayed in the media as a panicky, botched, and unnecessarily costly reaction. Two more localized outbreaks occurred in 2007, attracting more measured responses. Under the law, where a landowner suspects an outbreak of a communicable (infectious or contagious) disease among his or her animals, he or she must inform the police, the local authority, and Defra. Once an outbreak has been confirmed, the movement of animals 'from the land' or 'within and beyond the local area' is prohibited, other than through a licence granted by an inspector.

More usually, environmental health officers will be called in to individual business premises to take away samples of food for laboratory analysis, after receiving complaints about food poisoning, unpleasant tastes or odours, or outdated food labels from the public. Among the more common-place—if potentially dangerous—food safety issues arising is the identification of bacteria such as E. coli or salmonella. In one of the most notorious examples of overreaction by government to the latter, in 1988, gaffe-prone Junior Health Minister Edwina Currie provoked widespread alarm by erroneously telling reporters:

❝ Most of the egg production in this country, sadly, is now affected with salmonella. ❞

Food safety authorities also oversee the regulation of slaughterhouses in accordance with EU rules and inspect the quality of any meat bought from them. They also have the power to provide their own public slaughterhouses, cold stores, and refrigerators.

▌ Trading standards and the new licensing laws

While environmental health officers are responsible for verifying the *safety* of food sold to the public, wider consumer protection issues relating to its sale and presentation fall to **trading standards officers** to police. Under the terms of the Food Safety Act 1990, there are two main criminal offences relating to trading standards:

- selling food '*not of the nature or substance or quality demanded by the purchaser*';
- '*falsely describing or presenting food*'—usually without advertisement or labelling.

In addition to these food-related responsibilities, trading standards officers are responsible for ensuring that businesses comply with government policy in a number of other areas.

General consumer protection

General consumer protection involves monitoring the accurate description of goods, the use of credit, and the safety of goods sold—for example, household tools and appliances, and children's toys. Trading standards departments are also responsible for ensuring that trade is being carried out 'fairly' in their areas, under the terms set out by the *Office of Fair Trading (OFT)* (see pp. 216–18). So time-consuming and costly can general consumer protection work be that some authorities have even established dedicated consumer advice departments to pool resources with their local Citizens Advice Bureaux (CABs) and the Consumers Association.

The Fair Trading Act 1973 introduced a Director General of Fair Trading, who has the authority to ask anyone in the course of business '*acting in a way detrimental to the interests of consumers*' to give assurances as to his or her future conduct. If he or she fails to do so, the Director General can take the individual to a county court or the Restrictive Practices Court, which has the power to accept an assurance that he or she will not repeat the offence—or to make an order. Civil claims under the Sale of Goods Act 1979 must be brought by individuals through county courts.

Weights and measures

Each authority must appoint a 'chief inspector of weights and measures' to ensure that all traders in its area are complying with authorized weights and measures (the 'metric system' of metres and litres used throughout the EU, rather than the previously familiar 'imperial system' of yards and ounces, which dates back to the Middle Ages).

The history of Britain's reluctant conversion to metric standards is almost as long and tangled as that of its relationship with the EU itself. It began in earnest with the passage of the Weights and Measures Act 1963, which formally redefined yards and pounds in terms of metres and kilograms, and abolished a number of archaic imperial measurements, such as 'scruples', 'rods', and 'minims'. In 1965, under pressure from industry, the then President of the Board of Trade committed the state to adopting the metric system fully within a decade and, by 1968, a Metrication Board had been established to promote its benefits. The pledge was reaffirmed on Britain's entry into the European Economic Community (EEC) in 1973.

Despite several concrete moves, such as the decimalization of the UK's currency in 1971, subsequent governments further delayed full implementation of metrication and it was only with the advent of two EU Directives—in 1995 and 2000, respectively—that Britain was finally ordered to introduce the metric system across the board—first for packaged goods and then for bulk-sold goods (for example, fresh fruit and vegetables sold on market stalls).

This diktat did not stop some traditionalists continuing to resist. The first few years after the introduction of metrication in fruit and vegetable markets was marked by a succession of high-profile court cases that captured the imagination of the popular press—with so-called 'metric martyrs' continuing to label their goods in pounds and ounces in defiance of EU law. In September 2007, in the face of continuing widespread defiance, the resistance finally scored a pyrrhic victory when the EU Commissioner responsible for the single market, Gunther Verheugen, announced that they would be permitted to continue labelling their items in imperial measures after all—provided that they also did so in metric measurements. The EU subsequently relaxed its stance even more, to allow most traders to continue using only imperial measures, but some local authorities still insisted on prosecuting those who did so. Victory for the cause of the metric martyrs finally came when, in October 2008, the Department for Innovation, Universities and Skills (DIUS) issued new guidelines to councils to urge them to take 'proportionate' action against refuseniks in future. This was widely interpreted in the media as the final nail in the coffin for the metric movement in Britain.

In addition to checking that goods are itemized in metric measures, inspectors regularly check market stalls and shops to ensure that food is not sold in 'short weight'—that is, that scales are being used correctly and that consumers are being sold the correct quantities of goods. Short weight is treated as a criminal offence. Weights of manufactured goods are checked at factories, while those of loose food, fuel, and beer are checked at the point of sale.

Sunday trading

The Deregulation and Contracting Out Act 1994 marked the first major liberalization of Britain's retail laws, which, up to that point, had been among the strictest in Europe—with most shops commonly opening only between 9.30 a.m. and 5.30 p.m., and few being allowed to trade on Sundays out of respect for Christian worshippers. The 1994 Act gave, for the first time, individual traders the freedom to decide their own shop-opening hours, and other employment practices on weekdays and Saturdays. A Bill introduced by the Tories to remove all remaining restrictions—particularly those relating to Sunday opening—initially collapsed on its *second reading* in the early 1990s, but change was finally introduced in the Sunday Trading Act 1994, which stipulated that:

- 'large shops'—that is, those with internal sales areas of 280 m² or more—could open for up to six hours between 10 a.m. and 6 p.m., but must remain closed on Easter Sunday and Christmas Day (if the latter falls on a Sunday);

- smaller shops could open as and when they chose to;

- certain measures were to be introduced to protect the rights of shop workers who did not wish to have to work on a Sunday—especially those who wished to attend church.

Trade descriptions

It is a criminal offence under the Trade Descriptions Acts of 1968 and 1972 for 'false descriptions' to be given to goods, or 'false indications' given as to their sale price—for example, for labelling not to include VAT as part of the cover price.

The licensing of pubs and clubs, and drinking by-laws

The Licensing Act 2003, which finally came into force in February 2005, ushered in so-called '24-hour drinking' by allowing pubs and bars to apply to vary their existing liquor licences so that they could open until later than the customary 11 p.m. closing time on weekdays and Saturdays, and 10.30 p.m. on Sundays. At the same time, nightclubs and restaurants were given the option of applying for 'late licences' allowing them to stay open beyond their usual 2 a.m. shutdown. In liberalizing the drinking laws, the Labour government's stated aim was to tackle Britain's rising epidemic of 'binge drinking' by ending the frantic 'last orders' culture, which often saw drinkers racing to buy two or more drinks just before closing time in an effort to get the most out of the limited time available to them. The hope was that, in time, this more relaxed approach to buying and drinking alcohol would foster more of a Continental-style 'cafe' culture, with a steadier stream of drinkers drifting in and out of bars at different times, and fewer of the sudden explosions of violence and rowdy behaviour traditionally witnessed at 'chucking out' times.

The 2003 Act also introduced significant changes in terms of the way in which licences were issued and policed. Until 2005, local magistrates' courts were responsible for awarding and varying liquor licences, but the Act transferred this duty to local authorities. Councils would henceforth work together with the police to ensure that the terms of licences were adhered to, obtaining formal orders from magistrates to revoke them in the event of a breach.

The new licensing laws have had a mixed reception from licensees, public, and police alike. One of the main complaints made by pub landlords and nightclub owners in the early days related to the complexity of the revised system. Rather than having to apply simply for a personal licence to serve alcohol between stated hours on stated days and a single public entertainment licence giving them the freedom to stage occasional events, such as concerts or other types of performance, they were now required to apply for both the former and a separate premises licence or temporary event notice for each and every occasion on which they planned to stage any entertainment—from a live acoustic band, to a karaoke competition.

Following a high-profile run-in between the Musicians' Union, various other groups representing performers, and the Department of Culture, Media and Sport (DCMS), the government ministry charged with implementing the reforms, the wording of the Act was tweaked to avoid any unintended consequences, such as deterring pubs from putting on shows or plays. In rationalizing this aspect of the law, however, ministers unwittingly made it easier for licensed premises to put on all manner of other performances: lap dancing, for example, was recategorized alongside other forms of more innocuous public entertainment, meaning that premises no longer needed to apply for separate 'sexual encounter' licences, as before, to stage it. Perhaps unsurprisingly, there has since been a huge increase in the number of clubs and bars offering shows involving at least partial nudity—with the pressure group Object identifying some three hundred in Britain today, compared to a handful in the late 1990s, and a report by the Lilith Project, run by the charity Eaves Housing, numbering between 58 and 70 in London alone. Research by the Lilith Project has also pointed towards an apparent link between the proliferation of lap dancing and striptease clubs, and increased rates of rape or other sexual crimes in neighbouring areas. It found that, in the three years following the opening of four large clubs in Camden Town, north London, rapes in the area increased by a half and sexual assaults by 54 per cent.

The Licensing Act has also been criticized by some police forces and residents in some of Britain's towns and cities for allegedly turning their town centres into 'no-go areas' for older residents, particularly on Friday and Saturday nights. In 2008, in its submission to a government review of the impact of the 2003 Act, the LGA described it as 'a mistake'; at the same time, its chairman, Sir Simon Milton, declared in an interview with the *Daily Telegraph* that it had 'failed miserably'. The policy has also been openly condemned by everyone from the Archbishop of Canterbury, Rowan Williams, to former Labour Health Secretary Frank Dobson. A Freedom of Information Act request by the *Telegraph* to all 43 police forces in England and Wales, made just ahead of the publication of the Home Office's official review in February 2008, appeared to support their reservations, by uncovering official statistics confirming that 12 forces had seen a 46 per cent rise in the number of antisocial incidents with which they dealt since the Act was enforced—with 16 reporting an increase of 5 per cent in alcohol-related assaults, harassment, and criminal damage. Nationwide, serious violent offences in the early hours of the morning had risen by a quarter.

In the end, buoyed by reports from a number of individual police forces that pointed towards no significant increase in criminal offences—and, in some cases, suggested that crime rates had fallen—the government's review recommended retaining the 'new' licensing regime when it was finally published in March 2008. Ministers did, however, move to introduced one or two notable amendments—including a new 'two-strikes rule' designed to deter off-licences from selling alcohol to underage drinkers.

In practice, despite the initial expectation that 24-hour drinking would become a feature of most town centres, statistics obtained from 86 per cent of licensing authorities in November 2007 found that fewer than five hundred pubs and clubs in England and Wales had actually ever been granted 24-hour licences. Most 'late licences' have tended to cover only an additional hour or two of business, and only then at weekends in many cases. Of the 5,100 venues in all that were operating 24-hour licences between April 2006 and March 2007, 3,300 were hotels, 910 supermarkets, and 460 pubs and clubs.

On a related note, local authorities have long had powers under statute to curb public drinking. In the early 1990s, Plymouth City Council and Bristol City Council were among the first to invoke **by-laws** forbidding public consumption of alcohol in specified locations within their areas of jurisdiction and similar measures have since been more widely implemented. Additional powers were introduced under the Criminal Justice and Police Act 2001, which enabled councils to pass alcohol-free zone orders—or, to use their official title, 'alcohol consumption in designated public places orders'—again related to specified locations. Once such a zone is in place, police officers may require individuals spotted drinking there to stop immediately and, where necessary, confiscate their alcohol from them. In the last resort, those who fail to comply may be prosecuted and, if convicted, fined a maximum of £500. Some individual authorities have gone still further: within days of his election as London Mayor in May 2008, Boris Johnson announced that all drinking would be banned from the London Underground and other public transport throughout the capital as of 1 June that year.

Not to be outdone, less than a week after Mr Johnson's election, Communities Secretary Hazel Blears launched a new crackdown on problem drinking and related antisocial behaviour, in the guise of new *alcohol disorder zones (ADZs)*. Ministers gave individual local authorities the power to designate specific areas as needing extra policing to curb drink-related crime and disorder. The cost of the additional patrols would be met by pubs, bars, and other licensees themselves, in the form of a £100-a-head fee. Perhaps unsurprisingly, councils have been less than enthusiastic about embracing the new policy: only one in three had agreed to set up such a zone by the time at which it was officially introduced.

Such measures notwithstanding, unlike smoking (which was banned in all workplaces and enclosed public spaces, including bars and pubs, as of 1 July 2007), Labour's attitude towards licensing has been seen as highly liberal on the whole. This liberalism also extended for a time towards another popular British pastime—gambling—which former premier Mr Blair and Culture Secretary Tessa Jowell planned to popularize still further by giving the go-ahead to at least one 'super-casino' in a major city and a network of smaller casinos in other towns. The government's stated aim was to use the casinos as an engine to attract more industry, jobs, and private sector investment into deprived areas of the competing cities.

In January 2007, Manchester became the surprise choice of location for the super-casino project—beating off competition from, among others, Blackpool and London's former Millennium Dome. The plan had been for a venue containing up to 1,250 unlimited-jackpot gaming machines, with a further eight large casinos in cities including Hull, Milton Keynes, and Great Yarmouth, and eight smaller ones in areas as diverse as Bath and northeast Somerset, and Dumfries and Galloway. Within a short time of entering Downing Street, however, Mr Brown lived up to his puritanical image by scrapping the super-casino plans.

▌ Leisure and cultural services

Providing for citizens' quality of life does not only mean managing public transport, clearing up refuse, and maintaining a social environment that is relatively free of crime and disorder. Among the 'softer services' traditionally offered by local authorities—directly or indirectly—are those that fall beneath the broad umbrellas of 'leisure services' and/or 'cultural services'. These terms—increasingly fused together by some councils—cover everything from the maintenance of local swimming pools and sports centres, to the provision of theatres, museums, and galleries, and the financing of local festivals, such as the Edinburgh International Festival or England's largest equivalent, the Brighton Festival.

Swimming pools, leisure centres, parks, and playgrounds

Under the Local Government (Miscellaneous Provisions) Act 1972, local authorities were given the discretion—and ability to raise finance through local taxation—to provide 'such recreational facilities as they think fit'. These amenities included:

- sports centres;
- pitches for team games and athletic events;
- swimming pools;
- tennis courts;
- stadiums, and premises for athletic and other sporting clubs;
- golf courses and bowling greens;
- riding schools;
- campsites;
- facilities for gliding, boating, and water-skiing;
- staff—including instructors—for any of the above.

As in most other areas of local service provision, compulsory competitive tendering was introduced under Mrs Thatcher to force local authorities to compete with private contractors for franchises to run leisure centres (a practice continued under Best Value). Wearing another 'hat', however, councils still have responsibility for ensuring that *standards* of service meet statutory requirements, not least in terms of health and safety, and disabled access.

Libraries, museums, galleries, and the performing arts

Under the Public Libraries Act 1850, emerging local authorities were empowered to *provide* libraries, but not actually to stock them with books. This changed under the Public Libraries 1919 Act, which allowed them to '*spend more than a rating limit of one penny in the pound on books'*. Today, there is no statutory limit and authorities are charged with *'providing a comprehensive and efficient library service'* covering not only books, newspapers, and periodicals, but also records, CDs, DVDs, and video and audio tapes. Public libraries have also been required to provide free Internet access to the public since 2002, funded by the New Opportunities Fund 'Community Access to Lifelong Learning' (CALL) programme.

Although the statutory requirements are less stringent, local authorities are also 'allowed' to provide museums and galleries, and to require other, neighbouring, councils to contribute towards the expense of doing so. Museum 'activities' over and above collecting, maintaining, and displaying objects—that is, public events such as readings, lectures, performances, or classes—were, until recently, coordinated through area museum councils. This role has since been taken on by new 'hubs' set up by the Museums, Libraries and Archives Council (MLA)—normally museums in larger towns. The Local Government Act 1972 also gave councils the power to establish theatres, concert halls, and other places of entertainment, to maintain their own bands or orchestras, and to foster the arts and crafts.

The use of the broad-brush term 'cultural services' to encapsulate these many and varied types of 'quality of life' provision has been increasingly criticized in recent years—not least by those directly employed by the organizations concerned. Whenever central government offers local authorities a less-than-generous financial settlement—forcing them to tighten their belts, as has frequently happened in recent years—'added value' services such as libraries, museums, and theatres are usually the first to suffer, as councils move to protect 'core' areas such as education and social services from serious cutbacks. The museums sector, for one, has suffered, as long-serving curators have retired without being replaced, while councils have sought to make economies by introducing job shares and substituting specialist curatorial jobs with generalist managerial positions.

Hard-pressed local authorities have often also been 'forced' to withdraw funding from theatres and other performance venues. In 1990, Derby Playhouse faced closure after its annual £130,000 revenue grant from Derbyshire County Council was withdrawn overnight, following the authority's decision to scrap its entire arts budget to save money. although thrown a lifeline at the time by the Arts Council, the playhouse again narrowly avoided permanent closure in 2007, after Derby City Council withdrew a £40,000 grant, criticizing the theatre's poor management and what it described as 'unsustainable' losses.

In addition to their overarching role in promoting cultural venues and events for the benefit of local people, councils play a part in encouraging tourism and monitoring its effects on their local economies. The DCMS is formulating a new nationwide 'Tourism Prospectus' that is intended to define the future role of local authorities in promoting tourism alongside regional tourist boards, *regional development agencies (RDAs)*, and the national quango Visit Britain (formed from the merger of the British Tourist Authority and English Tourism Council in April 2003).

→ Further reading

Docherty, I. and Shaw, J. (2003) *A New Deal for Transport: The UK's Struggle with the Sustainable Transport Agenda*, London: WileyBlackwell. **Critical overview of the Blair government's sustainable transport policy, evaluating its impacts against its professed aspirations by experts on transport and highways.**

Gumpert, B. and Kirk, J. (2001) *Trading Standards: Law and Practice*, Bristol: Jordans. **Comprehensive overview of statutory trading standards regulations, and how they work in theory and practice. Aimed at professionals, companies, and members of the public.**

Lane, K. (2006) *National Bus Company: The Road to Privatisation*, Shepperton: Ian Allen. **Affectionate, but balanced, account of the last years of the National Bus Company monopoly, and the revolution in public passenger transport ushered in by the Thatcherite privatization and deregulation reforms of the mid-1980s.**

Lang, C., Reeve, J., and Woolard, V. (eds) (2006) *The Responsive Museum: Working with Audiences in the Twenty-First Century*, Aldershot: Ashgate. **Thoughtful examination of the present-day challenges facing public museums in light of diminishing financial support from the state and local government, and increasing competition from other attractions and leisure pursuits.**

Morgan, S. (2005) *Waste, Recycling and Reuse*, London: Evans Brothers. **Practical evaluation of the Western world's mounting waste management problem, with suggested solutions, focusing on the new 'three R's'—reducing, reusing, and recycling.**

Waters, I. and Duffield, B. (1994) *Entertainment, Arts and Cultural Services*, London: Financial Times/Prentice Hall. **Informative look at changes in the provision and funding of arts, entertainment, and other aspects of cultural services during the 1990s, emphasizing the tensions between different parts of the sector.**

? Review questions

1. Who are the main highways authorities and how are their responsibilities divided up?

2. What are the main weapons available to local authorities and central government to tackle traffic congestion? Give some recent examples of ideas being put into practice.

3. Explain the distinction between 'waste collection' and 'waste disposal'. What policies are being used to promote greener waste management in Britain?

4. What are the main duties of environmental health officers? How are their responsibilities in relation to food distinct from those of trading standards officers?

5. Outline the range of leisure and cultural services provided by local authorities.

 Online resource Centre

www.oxfordtextbooks.co.uk/orc/Morrison
Visit the Online Resource Centre that accompanies this book for web links and regular updates.

20

The Freedom of Information Act 2000

The bulk of this book has been concerned with explaining *how* Britain is governed—both politically, and in terms of the nuts and bolts of public administration. We began with an examination of the UK constitution and the place within it of core institutions such as Parliament, the government, and the monarchy. We went on to explore the concept of *devolution*, the place of individual spending departments, *executive agencies*, and unelected *quangos*, and the role that local authorities play in delivering day-to-day services to citizens.

This final chapter focuses not on who wields power, what that power amounts to, and how it is exercised, but on the means by which journalists (and the public) can *find out* about the inner workings of these institutions and hold them to account. Where can citizens go to obtain information about the composition and remit of the various bodies—many of them unelected— that hold sway over their lives? What rights, if any, do they have to question or challenge those bodies, and how can they exercise those rights? In a way, this is a chapter to which the whole of the rest of this volume has been leading. We now know how government in Britain works (at least in theory)—but how can it be made to work *better*?

▌ The origins of the Freedom of Information Act 2000—what is 'freedom of information'?

In essence, the concept of 'freedom of information' rests on the notion that, in a democracy, taxpayers and voters should be entitled to know as much as possible about the actions and decisions of the politicians that are elected to represent them. More important still, to many, is the principle that participating citizens should be able to find out how public money—largely derived from the taxes that they pay on their earnings from work—is spent on their behalf.

Freedom of information was a long time coming in the UK. At least seventy other states had legislation in place enshrining the rights of their citizens to access information about how their money was being spent by the 'powers that be' long before the Freedom of Information Act 2000—in Scotland, the Freedom of Information (Scotland) Act 2002—received *Royal Assent* at Westminster. It was not until Tony Blair's election in 1997 that Britain gained a government committed to implementing such reforms. Even then, it was several years into New Labour's first term before the party's manifesto pledge was put into action—and in somewhat watered-down form at that. It was not until 1 January 2005, towards the end of its second term, that the full force of the new law came into effect, under the then Department of Constitutional Affairs (now the Ministry of Justice).

The concept of freedom of information has long been celebrated in the USA, which has passed a nationwide Freedom of Information Act based on the principle of democratic accountability, as well as numerous state-specific laws governing access to public documentation and the records of tax-levying entities. These Acts are collectively known as 'sunshine laws'. Elsewhere in Europe, where freedom of information legislation is also commonplace, freedom of information Acts are generally known as 'open records'. The European Union (EU) as a whole, meanwhile, is governed by Regulation 1049/2001, passed by the *European Parliament (EP)* and the Council of Ministers on 30 May 2001, which sets out a detailed system of rules regarding public access to the main EU institutions, including the *European Commission*, and the Council and Parliament themselves.

Lest blinkered constitutional historians try to convince us that Britain is the seat of democracy it so often purports to be, it is worth noting that the earliest known 'open record' was passed in Sweden as far back as the late eighteenth century, in the form of the Freedom of the Press Act 1766. And while some might scoff at the idea of openness and accountability operating under dictatorships, it is also intriguing to note that, since 1 January 2008, even China has had a freedom of information in law in place—at least notionally—in the form of the Regulations of the People's Republic of China on Open Government Information.

Given the huge number of freedom of information laws of one kind or another in force around the world, perhaps unsurprisingly, there is little conformity in their exact wording or provisions. With some exceptions, however, these laws do share one or two general traits—in particular, the principle that the 'burden of proof' tends to fall on the institution from which information is being sought, rather than the individual seeking it. In other words, the person making a request is not normally required to explain why he or she is asking for the information, whereas the organization being questioned must give a valid reason should it fail to supply the details requested. What constitutes a 'valid reason' is, of course, open to debate. The next section seeks to answer this question in relation to the UK.

Who and what the Act covers—and who and what are exempt

The freedom of information (FoI) legislation operating in the UK applies to more than 100,000 'public authorities', ranging from individual schools and hospitals, to local councils, quangos, and entire government spending departments. If a legitimate FoI request is made under one of the two Acts, the authority asked must first tell the questioner whether it holds the relevant information and, assuming that it does, then supply it *within 20 working days* of the request.

The authority may, however, *refuse* to confirm or deny the existence of the information—and/or to provide it—if any of the following conditions apply:

- if an exemption applies;
- if the request is vexatious or similar to a previous request;
- if the cost of compliance exceeds an 'appropriate limit'.

The term 'exemption' might invite the idea that an authority in possession of information has free rein to refuse to disclose it, but, according to the Acts, even exempt material should sometimes be made available.

There are two broad classes of exemption: 'absolute' and 'qualified'. While the former may not be disclosed under any circumstances, the latter may be, if the 'public interest' in disclosing it outweighs that in keeping it secret. For example, a public authority involved in security policy might legitimately refuse to disclose exempt information that could compromise public safety by jeopardizing counter-terrorism operations, but it would be hard pressed to do so if the information that it was withholding was likely to *improve* safety—by, for example, revealing the expected time and location of an impending attack.

In addition to absolute and qualified exemptions, there are several entire categories of information that are exempt. Authorities may also refuse requests that they consider 'likely to prejudice' the interests of the UK abroad or law enforcement. The three categories of exemption are listed in Table 20.1.

These, then, are the categories of information that carry exemptions, but what of the Acts' definitions of 'public authority'? Are any organizations or individuals that might be considered to fall under this umbrella term exempted from FoI requests per se?

In short, 'yes'.

The Queen and the Royal Household

The Royal Family's website defines the status of the Queen and Royal Household thus:

❝ The Royal Household is not a public authority within the meaning of the FOI Acts, and is therefore exempt from their provisions. ❞

It goes on to cite the 'fundamental constitutional principle' that communications between the sovereign of the day and his or her ministers and other public bodies remains confidential—not least to ensure that the royals do not compromise their 'political neutrality'. As the site goes on to stress, however, the fact that the Royal Household is not bound by the FoI Acts does *not* mean that it is unwilling to make certain information available voluntarily.

To this end, it is happy to '*account openly for all its use of public money*'. It does this by posting online every June a consolidated report, including a full annual account and breakdown of the *Civil List* and Grants-in-Aid (see

Table 20.1 Exemptions under the Freedom of Information Act 2000

Absolute	Qualified	Categories
Information supplied by, or relating to, bodies dealing with security matters	Intended for future publication	Information relating to investigations and proceedings conducted by public authorities
Court records and information related to an impending prosecution	Related to national security (other than information supplied by, or relating to, named security organizations, in which case a duty to consider disclosure in the public interest does not arise)	Court records
Information that would infringe **parliamentary privilege**	Which might limit the defence of the British Isles, or the 'capability, effectiveness, or security' of any of the Armed Forces	Formulation of government policy
Personal information of *either* of the following kinds: (a) that relating to the person making the request, which could be obtained under the Data Protection Act 1998; (b) about another individual, if it would breach data protection principles	Potentially prejudicial to international relations between the UK and any other state, international organization or court, or the UK's interests abroad	
Information held by the House of Commons or the House of Lords that may be prejudicial to the effective conduct of public affairs	Information that might prejudice relations between administrations within the UK	
Information provided in confidence	Information likely to prejudice the financial and/or economic interests of the UK	
Prohibitions on disclosure where a disclosure is prohibited by an enactment or would constitute contempt of court	Information relating to investigations and proceedings conducted by public authorities	
	Information likely to prejudice law enforcement—defined as the prevention or detection of crime, prosecution of offenders, assessment of taxes, etc.	
	Information relating to a public authority with audit functions in relation to another public body (e.g. the **Audit Commission**)	

Absolute	Qualified	Categories
	Information relating to the formulation of government policy, communications between ministers, or the operations of a ministerial office	
	Information held by public authorities other than the House of Commons or the House of Lords that may be prejudicial to the effective conduct of public affairs	
	Information relating to communications between the Queen, her ministers, and/or other public bodies, including those in relation to the honours system	
	Information likely to endanger the health and/or safety of any individual	
	Environmental information, which the authority concerned is obliged to make public under s. 74 of the Act	
	Personal information believed by the institution not to breach data protection principles, but in relation to which the individual who is the subject of the request serves notice that disclosure would cause 'unwarranted substantial damage or distress'	
	Subject to legal professional privilege	
	Information regarded as 'trade secrets', or otherwise liable to prejudice the commercial interests of any person (including the public authority holding it)	

p. 27). In addition, the Prince of Wales voluntarily publishes details of his income from the Duchy of Cornwall estate—both before and after tax—on his own website.

What the sites fail to emphasize is the fact that no information about the Royal Household's funding was made public by it until 2001, when it was persuaded to agree to greater openness as part of its negotiation with HM

Treasury over a new ten-year financial settlement from the government. Perhaps even more remarkable is the amount of detail about its dealings that the Royal Family still will *not* disclose. For example, nowhere will British taxpayers find details of the size of the Privy Purse (see p. 28)—that mysterious treasure trove derived from the estate of the Duchy of Lancaster, which is reserved for the personal expenditure of the reigning monarch; nor will they be able to access details about other aspects of the royals' personal finances, such as the incomes derived by several members of the family from service in the Armed Forces, the annual income derived by the Duke of Wessex from his television and film company, Ardent Productions, the Duchess of York's royalties for her series of *Budgie the Helicopter* children's books, or the dividends and profits derived from family members' numerous shareholdings and other investments.

The list of specific FoI exemptions for the Queen and the Royal Household are detailed in Table 20.2.

Despite this array of exemptions, which place the Royal Family in a significantly more privileged position than any other, recent annual disclosures of their public accounts have shed light on the huge lengths to which members still appear to be going to defend FoI applications. According to the Royal Household's 2006–07 accounts, it spent £180,000 of taxpayers' money in that one year shielding itself from FoI requests. Buckingham Palace explained at the time that the sum was spent reminding government departments of the exemption to prevent them releasing details of communications with the household.

Table 20.2 Specific FoI exemptions relating to the Royal Household

Exemption	Details
Financial and other personal matters	Information relating to the personal affairs of the sovereign and of members of the Royal Family—including their private finances and activities in their personal and private capacity—are exempt under s. 40 of the FoI Act and s. 38 of the Scottish FoI Act (Data Protection Act provisions)
Correspondences with deceased family members	Personal information on recently deceased members of the Royal Family that relates to communications with the Queen, other members of the family, or the Royal Household, and if contained in records less than 30 years old, may be exempt under s. 37 of the UK FoI Act (s. 41 of the Scottish FoI Act)
Other information relating to deceased royals	Information relating to recently deceased members of the Royal Family the disclosure of which would damage 'the right to family life' of the deceased's relatives may be exempt under s. 44 of the UK FoI Act and s. 26 of the Scottish FoI Act, and under art. 8—'Private Life and Family'—of the Human Rights Act 1998

In addition, it is normally possible for more resourceful journalists to find ways of circumventing the royals' exemption. In June 2008, an FoI request to the Ministry of Defence unearthed the cost of Prince William's controversial flight in an RAF Chinook helicopter to an exclusive stag party on the Isle of Wight. The trip—one of five 'familiarization exercises' undertaken by the prince, which saw him stop off en route to pick up his brother, Prince Harry, in London—set taxpayers back £8,716.

The utilities, train companies, and other passenger transport operators

To widespread dismay among journalists and supporters of open government, including the Campaign for Freedom of Information, the privatized utilities—that is, water, electricity, gas and telecommunications providers, and rail-operating companies—were excluded from automatic coverage by the FoI Acts when they entered their final draft stages. After they were included in the remit of the government's 1997 *White Paper, Your Right to Know*, hopes were high that they would be subject to scrutiny under the Act when it was finally passed. But intensive lobbying by the companies concerned—many of which argued that being subject to the Acts could jeopardize commercially sensitive operations—they were eventually omitted.

The decision to exclude companies involved in supplying British taxpayers with such vital 'natural monopolies' as energy and water was enough to infuriate many, but more baffling still for some was the fact that even *Network Rail*—the not-for-dividend, massively subsidized company set up by the government to take over the maintenance of the railway infrastructure after the collapse of private firm Railtrack in 2001—was also exempted. In a test case ruling in January 2007, the *Information Commissioner*—the individual appointed to hear FoI appeals (see pp. 626–9)—clarified that Network Rail was a 'private company' and therefore not a 'public authority' under the terms of the Act. His ruling came in response to an appeal against the company's refusal to answer a request made in May 2005, under the Data Protection Act 1998, regarding information about a flood beside a railway line.

Although utility companies themselves are not subject to the FoI Acts, the regulators set up by the government to monitor them—such as the *Office of Gas and Electricity Markets (Ofgem)* and the *Office of Communications (Ofcom)* (see pp. 232–3)—*are*. This fact has been used as an argument by organizations such as the Confederation of British Industry (CBI) for retaining the 'light touch' approach to the utilities, in response to recent murmurings that the Justice Secretary might be considering amending the Schedule to the Act to incorporate them.

Academies

One of the most contentious examples of an organization exempt from current FoI legislation is that of *academies*—the new generation of 'independent' secondary schools operating within the state sector (see pp. 469–74). Their exemption—granted because of the involvement of private companies in financing them and, in some cases, running their ancillary services, such as catering and cleaning—is widely viewed as a double standard, given that all other state schools are required to comply with the Acts. Some have even suggested that it is a convenient way of masking the relatively sluggish academic performance of these schools, which, when first introduced in 2002, were trumpeted as a way of turning round 'failing' comprehensives by pumping in large amounts of private capital. Academies' quasi-independent status in law enables them to present information on their exam results in a different way to other schools—for example, omitting details of the subjects in which GCSE A–C grades have been obtained—making it difficult for parents to make informed decisions about whether their performance is relatively better or worse than that of their rivals.

Some critics of the academies exemption have also pointed to a clear contradiction between the government's public insistence that, despite being largely privately financed, they are in the public sector—and not the start of a creeping privatization of the state schooling system. If this is so, argue some, why are they not subject to the same conditions of openness of all other state schools?

The Security Service, MI6, and other intelligence agencies

Just as most security-related material is exempt from the provisions of the FoI Acts, there is a blanket exemption for any information relating to the work of the Security Service (MI5), MI6, and all other British intelligence agencies. Similar exemptions apply within the Armed Forces to special forces, such as the Special Air Squadron (SAS).

The Trades Union Congress, individual unions, the Confederation of British Industry, and public limited companies

Neither trade unions nor employers' organizations, such as the CBI or the Institute of Directors (IoD), are required to divulge information under the FoI Acts. Similarly, an exemption applies to all businesses, including public limited companies (plcs). The latter fact—and the qualified exemption for sensitive information defined as being of 'commercial interest'—pose a frequent source of frustration for journalists seeking to hold public authorities, such as councils and government departments, accountable for their use of tax-payers' money. With more and more public sector work being carried out by private sector companies contracted to do so on an authority's behalf—rather than the authority itself—some reporters see the 'commercial interest' exemption as being open to abuse by organizations using it as a smokescreen to cover up for waste and inefficiency—particularly in cases of contractual negotiations that have given the public purse poor value for money.

How to make an FoI request—and how not to

Around 120,000 FoI requests are made each year in the UK—six out of ten by members of the public, one-fifth by businesses, and just 10 per cent at time of writing by journalists. That said, the exhaustive nature of some journalistic enquiries has taken its toll on public authorities' time and resources. Media-related requests reportedly take up significantly more time than those from private individuals and companies between them. The overall cost of complying with FoI requests was estimated at £35.5m in 2005 alone.

However fruitful the results that they are producing, the Acts are certainly capturing people's imaginations. So how does one go about making a request? Although the exact procedure varies from one public authority to another, it entails writing to the organization either by email or by post, detailing the specific question(s) to which an answer(s) is requested. If there is any ambiguity in the wording of a request, the authority is encouraged to enter into a proactive dialogue with the maker of the request to clarify what is being asked and to supply the information as quickly as possible, provided that it is not exempt. Authorities are also expected, where relevant or necessary, to supply additional explanatory material if it is likely to elucidate otherwise complex or confusing information, and avoid the necessity for a prolonged correspondence with the questioner. As in other states, the questioner must give his or her name and contact details when filing the request, but he or she is not expected to divulge his or her 'reason' for requesting the information. In principle, FoI requests are free and it is highly unusual for organizations to charge for answering them.

In addition to the exemptions listed earlier this chapter, authorities may refuse to respond to requests in certain other circumstances. If a single request to a central government department or other body is likely to cost more than £600 in terms of the time and staffing needed to locate the desired information (£450, in the case of other public authorities), it may be refused outright. Alternatively, the authority concerned may levy a charge to the requester. There is also provision in law for authorities to decline to respond to other so-called 'vexatious' requests. The definition of this term was clarified by the Information Commissioner's Office (ICO) in a guidance note issued in July 2007. It ruled a request to be 'vexatious' if it would impose a 'significant burden' on the public authority, in terms of expense or distraction, *and* meet at least one of the following criteria:

- that it clearly does not have any serious purpose or value;
- that it is designed to cause disruption or annoyance;
- that it has the effect of harassing the public authority;
- that it can otherwise fairly be characterized as obsessive or manifestly unreasonable.

Examples of 'vexatious' enquiries cited by the ICO included the case of an individual refused information by Birmingham City Council after making more than seventy previous requests. Their final one consisted of multiple questions and would have cost £3,500 to answer—making it a 'significant burden'. In another case, West Midlands Transport Executive estimated that it had spent 175 hours responding to one person's requests. *Transport for London (TfL)*, meanwhile, reported that it had received so many letters from a single enquirer that it had had to devise a new internal management strategy to cope with them. But perhaps the most burdensome FoI addict to date was the individual who sent no fewer than 347 requests to police forces, 412 to the Ministry of Defence, and 22 to the *Cabinet* Office. In a joint decision notice, the individual was judged by the Commissioner to be 'vexatious' on the following basis:

❝ It is entirely appropriate to consider the aggregated effect of dealing with all the requests known to have been made across the public sector. ❞

Just as authorities may reject vexatious requests, they may also refuse to answer 'repeated' ones—that is, those that are identical to others to which they have previously responded in full, or refused to respond, particularly if they originate from the same individual or organization.

The Environmental Information Regulations 2004

The FoI Act was not the only new legislation designed to promote greater government openness to come into effect in 2005. Under the requirements of EU law, the Environmental Information Regulations (EIR) 2004—in Scotland, the Environmental Information (Scotland) Regulations 2004—came in at the same time, giving the British public access to information about the state of their natural environment, particularly in relation to potential hazards such as pollution.

Unlike the FoI Acts, EIR requests—also generally made by post or email, and subject to a 20-day maximum delay in response times—do not have to be made in writing and may be lodged verbally. They also cover a number of private sector organizations currently outside the remit of general FoI legislation. For example, EIR requests may be made to privatized utilities, such as water and electricity companies—many of the activities of which have a direct impact on the environment.

Environmental information covered by the Regulations falls into six categories:

- the state of the 'elements of the environment', such as air, water, soil, land, fauna (including human beings);
- emissions and discharges, noise, energy, radiation, waste, and other such substances;
- measures and activities such as policies, plans, and agreements affecting, or likely to affect, the state of the elements of the environment;
- reports, cost–benefit, and economic analyses;
- the state of human health and safety, and contamination of the food chain;
- cultural sites and built structures—to the extent that they may be affected by the state of the elements of the environment.

As with the FoI Acts, there are certain 'absolute' and 'qualified' exemptions to the provisions of the EIR. These are explained in Table 20.3.

Unlike FoI requests, enquiries made under the EIR tend to incur a charge to the questioner, provided that it is set at a 'reasonable' level and that the authority publishes a schedule of all its charges. It may not, however, refuse a request on grounds of cost alone.

The FoI Act and the Data Protection Acts

The Data Protection Act 1984 (as amended by the Data Protection Act 1998) relates to the notion of protecting individuals' privacy, as its name suggests. On the face of it, this may appear to conflict with the more 'free for all' aspects of information disclosure ushered in by the FoI Acts. In practice,

Table 20.3 Exemptions under the Environmental Information Regulations 2004

Absolute	Qualified
Information is not held by the authority (if so, it has a 'duty' to refer the request on to the relevant body)	Information's release would breach the confidentiality of legal proceedings
The request is 'manifestly unreasonable'	Information might prejudice international relations between Britain and other states or international bodies, public security, or national defence
The request is 'too general' (although the authority should still fulfil its duty to advise and assist)	Information might jeopardize the course of justice and the right of citizens to a fair trial
The request is for unfinished documents or data (in which case, an estimated time for completion must be given)	Commercially confidential information
The request is for internal communications	Certain information related to intellectual property rights
	Information related to personal and/or voluntary data
	Information related to the work of environmental protection

however, the two Acts largely complement and build on each other—a fact assured by the government's decision to give the task of policing both of them to the Information Commissioner as of 2005 (see pp. 626–9).

The 1998 Act applies to 'personal data'. This is defined as *'any data which can be used to identify a living person'*—such as names, addresses, telephone, fax, and mobile phone numbers, email addresses, and birthdays. It applies, however, only to data that is—or is intended to be—held on computer or in another 'relevant filing system'. The scope of the Act is fairly broad in this latter context: an individual's paper diary may be considered a 'relevant filing system', if it is used for commercial purposes. The Act is underpinned by seven 'key principles' relating to the handling of personal data by public authorities, private sector companies, and other organizations, as outlined in Table 20.4.

The Act gives anyone whose personal data is processed the right to:

- view any data held by an organization for a small fee (known as 'subject access');

- request that incorrect information be corrected. If the organization ignores his or her plea, a court may order the data to be corrected or destroyed, and compensation may be paid;

Table 20.4 Conditions relating to the use of personal data under the Data Protection Act 1998

Condition	Details
Focus	Data may only be used for the specific purposes for which it was collected.
Privacy	It must not be disclosed to other parties without the consent of the individual to whom it relates, unless there is legislation or other overriding legitimate reason to share the information (e.g. the prevention or detection of crime). It is an offence for other parties to obtain this personal data without authorization.
Accessibility	Individuals have a right of access to information held about them, subject to certain exceptions (e.g. information held for the prevention or detection of crime).
Time-sensitivity	Personal information may be kept for no longer than is necessary.
Protection	Personal information may not be transmitted outside the European Economic Area (EEA) unless the individual to whom it relates consents, or adequate protection is in place (e.g. by the use of a prescribed form of contract). Entities holding personal information are required to have adequate security measures in place. Those include technical measures (such as computer firewalls) and organizational measures (e.g. staff training).
Regulation	All entities that process personal information, subject to one or two specified exceptions, must register with the Information Commissioner.

- require that data is not used in a way that causes 'damage or distress';
- require that his or her data is not used for direct marketing.

So how do the two Acts—governing 'data protection', on the one hand, and 'freedom of information', on the other—work together in practice?

The first point that must be made is that many enquiries that individuals might think of making under the FoI Act, in relation to information specifically relating to them, will be exempt under that Act. This is, however, only because the correct procedure for accessing that information actually falls under the 1998 Act. If, however, an individual seeks to make a request relating to themselves that will also disclose information about a third party, the correct Act to use is likely to be the FoI Act. Confusingly, however, the authority asked to supply this information must consider the 'data protection principles' applicable under FoI before deciding whether to release the details. Because many FoI requests tend to concern what might broadly be termed 'corporate' information—that is, procedural, statistical, and/or constitutional matters—rather than personal data, in practice, the number of serious conflicts between the application of the FoI and 1998 Act is relatively limited. There have, however, been some notable altercations between the media and local authorities—particularly in relation to the salaries and perks of *chief executives* and other senior officers. Councils have often tried to hide behind 'data protection' legislation when asked for such details under FoI, arguing that—because they are not elected representatives, unlike councillors—such information constitutes information of a personal nature, which should therefore be treated as confidential. The Commissioner has sought to clarify the legal position surrounding this, by making a distinction between information relating to the private lives of public officials (which should be exempt) and that relating to the discharge of their public duties.

In March 2008, members of Parliament (MPs) played the data protection card, too, in an effort to limit disclosures about the generous expenses packages for which they are eligible in relation to their London homes (see p. 63). Details of the so-called 'John Lewis list' had been obtained under an FoI request by the Press Association, but the House of Commons challenged the publication of a full run-down first in an Information Tribunal hearing and then in the High Court—arguing that it would compromise data protection principles by potentially revealing personal details such as their *constituency* addresses. Their efforts failed and the somewhat anticlimactic full breakdown was duly published in May.

FoI appeals and the role of the Information Commissioner

Anyone refused information under the FoI Acts has a right to appeal, initially through the authority's own internal review procedures, but ultimately by complaining to the Information Commissioner's Office (ICO)—the regulator that replaced the pre-existing Data Protection Commissioner's Office in 2005, following the passage of the FoI Act. In addition to its central London office, the ICO has three offices based in the capitals of the devolved regions—Edinburgh, Cardiff, and Belfast.

It is the job of the ICO, among other things, to make sure that the 23 exemptions contained in the Act are not abused by authorities seeking to keep secret information that they regard as embarrassing, but which is not actually exempt in law. In Scotland, complaints are made through the Scottish Information Commissioner. By way of underlining the importance of disclosure wherever possible, the public also has a further right to appeal over and above the Commissioners themselves, via the Information Tribunal.

To aid designated public authorities in complying with the FoI Acts, the ICO has published on its website 'Ten Top Tips' for them to follow. These are listed in Table 20.5.

Table 20.5 The Information Commissioner's Office's 'Ten Top Tips' for handling requests

Tip	Explanation
'Be positive'	Remember that transparency is 'good for the public and democracy'
'Be active'	Publish as much material as possible proactively under the terms of publication of the Act, because this will save time, effort, resources, and money
'Anticipate requests'	Do not wait to be asked
'If in doubt, disclose'	Remember that there is a presumption for disclosure—public authorities should meet people's requests unless there is a good reason not to do so and organizations do not have to withhold unless an absolute exemption applies
'Get talking'	A dialogue between the requester and the public authority can help to resolve requests more quickly
'Don't fear precedent'	All decisions should be made on their own merits and on a case-by-case basis at the time of the request
'Give clear reasons for turning down a request'	Write a clear 'refusal notice', because properly drafted and explained refusals can avoid reviews and complaints
'Give more if it helps'	Supply additional information where it is useful, such as an explanation of the data being supplied
'Meet it or beat it'	The 20-day deadline must be met—and improved upon, if possible
'Help yourself'	Look at the ICO's guidance online at www.ico.gov.uk for more information

Complaints may be made to the ICO if a public authority fails to:

- provide the information requested;

- respond to a request within 20 working days (or to explain why longer than 20 working days is needed);

- give proper advice and help;

- give information in the form requested;

- properly explain any reasons for refusing the request;

- correctly apply an exemption under the Act.

Complainants must provide the following material:

- a covering letter, giving the ICO details of the complaint;

- details of their initial request;

- a copy of the public authority's initial response (known as the 'refusal notice');

- a copy of the complaint that they made to the public authority's internal review or complaints procedure;
- a copy of the public authority's response;
- any other information that they think is relevant;
- their contact details.

The stories in which the Information Commissioner has played a prominent role in recent times have, ironically, had more to do with data protection than FoI issues. In June 2008, he confirmed that he would be serving formal enforcement notices—the toughest sanction available to him—against both HM Revenue and Customs (HMRC) and the Ministry of Defence over what he described as 'deplorable failures' leading to 'serious data breaches'.

The Commissioner was referring to two major data protection fiascos that caused huge embarrassment to the government during Mr Brown's early months in Downing Street. On the first occasion, in November 2007, HMRC confessed to losing two unencrypted data discs containing personal details of 25 million Child Benefit recipients—effectively, every family in Britain with a child under the age of 16. The information—including names, addresses, dates of birth, *National Insurance (NI)* numbers, and bank details—had been en route from the HMRC offices at Waterview Park, Sunderland, to the National Audit Office in London. At time of writing, the discs had still not been found.

Table 20.6 Priority types of information covered by the FoI 'public interest test'

Category	Definition
Matters of public debate	Covers issues in relation to which a public debate has been generated, debate cannot properly take place without the disclosure of the information, the issue affects a wide range of individuals and/or companies, the government has put its views on the issue on the record, and the issue may in some way affect the legislative process
Public participation in political debate	Covers situations in which local interest groups need sufficient information to be able to represent those interests, and requests relate to the facts behind a major policy decision—particularly one of 'unprecedented importance'
Accountability for public funds	Matters relating to government accountability for the sale of public assets, or legal aid spending, the need for openness relating to tender processes and prices relating to public spending and services, the misappropriation of public funds, when accountability of elected officials whose propriety has been called into question, and the need for public bodies to obtain value for money in spending receipts from taxpayers
Public safety	Information relating to air safety, nuclear plant security, and public health, contingency plans in an emergency, and potential damage to the environment

The second breach, revealed in January 2008, concerned the theft of an MoD laptop containing confidential details of 600,000 service personnel. In reporting the crime to the Commons in a statement, Defence Secretary Des Browne revealed that two further thefts of departmental laptops had also occurred since 2005.

There is a welter of guidance on the ICO's website about the rights of public and media to access information under the various Acts that it administers. One of the most useful for journalists is the guidance notice—based on specified precedents set by both British and international FoI authorities—explaining how public authorities should weigh the 'public interest' of a request against any potential qualified exemptions (see Table 20.6).

▶ Freedom of information and the headlines—some case studies

Perhaps unsurprisingly, news reporters working on everything from local weekly free sheets to national dailies have been quick to embrace the FoI Acts as a source of potential stories—not least because they enable a modicum of what might loosely be termed 'investigative journalism' to be carried out within the increasingly restrictive parameters of the modern newsroom environment. Widespread cutbacks—from the offices of regional publishers to those of major national newspapers—have seen the size of many papers' reporting staff dwindle steadily in recent years. Papers are facing growing competition from the Internet and other forms of new media, and, as a result, new recruits are expected to be able to 'multitask' as everything from video journalists and photographers, to designers, sub-editors, and online writers. At the same time, the ever-tighter economies being imposed on newsrooms means that what conventional reporting is still being done is increasingly having to be carried out over the telephone and/or email, rather than in the more face-to-face, hands-on fashion of days gone by.

The FoI Acts, therefore, offer a means by which journalists with the ability to think up suitably forensic questions and target them at the right public authorities can effectively hold the 'powers that be' to account 'on the cheap'. Whereas once they might have had to resort to cloak-and-dagger tactics and invest significant amounts of time (and money) in rooting out information that organizations were doing everything in their power to keep out of the public domain, much of this information can now be obtained—at least in theory—by sending a simple email.

The FoI bonanza did not take long to kick off. In January 2005, within days of the 2000 Act coming fully into force, *The Observer* ran a story listing a 'who's who' of celebrities and businesspeople who had been wined and dined by then Prime Minister Tony Blair at his country retreat, Chequers, since 2001. The luminaries—whose names it had obtained under the new FoI rules—included entertainer Des O'Connor, former Spice Girl Geri Halliwell, television presenter Esther Rantzen, Lord Lloyd Webber, Olympic champion rower Sir Steve Redgrave, and Tesco chief executive Sir Terry Leahy.

In August of the same year, BBC2's *Newsnight* used an FoI request to expose a secret that saw Harold Macmillan's British government sell Israel sufficient quantities of uranium 235 and heavy water to enable it to develop its nuclear weapons programme. In a statement to the International Atomic Energy Agency (IAEA), then Foreign Office Minister Kim Howells denied that Britain had been a party to any such sale, but in March 2006, *Newsnight* used a further FoI request to expose sales of plutonium to Israel during Harold Wilson's first term in office.

Perhaps even more shocking was the disclosure, in December 2005, of a hushed-up report by a Scotland Yard detective, Inspector Tom Hayward, into a brutal torture camp operated by British forces in post-war Germany. *The Guardian* used an FoI request to obtain a copy of the document, which detailed the outcome of interrogations of 372 men and 44 women at the Bad Nenndorf camp, near Hanover. Among the grisly details included was an account of how two men suspected of being Communists were starved to death, another was beaten to a pulp, and numerous others suffered serious injuries or lost toes to frostbite. Four months later, the paper published images of emaciated prisoners after winning an appeal against the MoD's refusal to release photographs of the victims contained in the report.

In July 2006, under its FoI Act obligations to publish proactively information in the public interest, the Foreign Office released an alarming gazetteer of allegations against foreign diplomats showing that, between 1999 and 2004, they had been accused of 122 separate criminal offences—including murder, child abuse, rape, and sexual assault. No charges had been brought against any of them because, under international law, officials on diplomatic business have immunity from prosecution. Criminality seemed to be catching around that time: in the same month, statistics published by 13 UK police forces revealed that at least 174 serving officers had convictions, ranging from drink driving, to criminal damage and public order offences. Some had committed crimes while employed by the police.

But FoI requests do not always throw up such sensational outcomes. In most cases, they 'unearth' more humdrum information—much of it unexciting and lacking in any obvious news value. Indeed, there is a feeling in some quarters—not least in the offices of the less well-staffed public authorities—that some journalists have come to rely on the Acts a little too heavily. Before the concept of 'freedom of information' had passed into British law, reporters were forced to rely on those timeworn qualities—guile, ingenuity, and perseverance—to tease out material that organizations would rather have kept under their belts. If they received tip-offs that councillors were fiddling their expenses, or that public officials were taking overseas flights using taxpayers' money, they would often have to confront the relevant authority's press office head on, citing phrases such as 'the public interest' and 'public domain' to remind them of their obligation to confirm or deny such activities, and, where necessary, supply details. Reluctant though authorities invariably were to expose themselves to criticism by admitting such abuses, more often than not they grudgingly put their hands up. Today, able to hide behind the cloak of having to 'dig out the information' or 'go through all of the files', the same authorities can cheerfully take far longer to make their disclosures—using the benefit of the statutory 20-day time limit to craft polished excuses and put off answering questions until any newsworthiness derived from them has dwindled, if not entirely passed.

Seasoned FoI users—particularly those experienced enough to know the difference between a story that requires the Act and one that can be stood up using more conventional tactics—cite the counter-argument that, given the relative ease and effectiveness of the legislation, far too few journalists are taking advantage of it. Used in a targeted way, it is certainly true that FoI provides an excellent source of off-diary stories—gold dust for news editors—that, until recently, simply was not available.

▶ The future of freedom of information— and moves to restrict it

The Labour government made a big noise about its commitment to freedom of information during its first term in office, but, more recently, it has appeared to regret laying itself open to quite so much scrutiny. Ministers' discomfort with some of the outcomes of FoI began to emerge in May 2007, when Conservative **backbencher** David Maclean introduced a **private member's Bill**

(PMB) into the House of Commons—the Freedom of Information (Amendment) Bill, the principal proposals of which included effectively exempting MPs from the 2000 Act, ostensibly to protect details contained in their private correspondences. It also proposed incorporating the cost of the time that officials spend 'thinking' about whether (and how) to make an FoI disclosure within the £600 limit above which requests become chargeable. Around the same time, it was reported that then *Lord Chancellor*, Lord Falconer, was privately drawing up his own proposals to curb FoI requests relating to MPs' affairs—so it came as little surprise when Mr Blair declined to condemn Mr Maclean's Bill when challenged to do so publicly.

The issue came to a head (for the time being at least) in June that year after the Bill was provisionally passed by the Commons and moved up to the House of Lords, where it appeared that ministers were seeking a sympathetic peer to 'sponsor' it. When no such peer came forward, and the Bill was roundly condemned by both the Commons Constitutional Affairs Select Committee and the Lords Constitution Committee, it finally fell—but not before then *Leader of the House* Jack Straw had announced that he would be issuing new guidelines to public authorities to ensure that MPs' personal details were not compromised by the release of any correspondences between them and their constituents.

It is not only public authorities themselves that have begun to gripe about the FoI Acts. In May 2007, the Information Commissioner himself used his address to the annual Freedom of Information Conference to urge people to act with more 'restraint' when making requests. He cited an enquiry about how much the Foreign Office spent on Ferrero Rocher chocolates and another asking about the number of eligible bachelors in the Hampshire Police Force as examples of frivolous, time-wasting queries. Mr Thomas went on to announce plans to produce a new 'charter' for 'responsible' FoI requests.

Beyond measures to *restrict*—or otherwise qualify—the application of the Act, there are signs that its scope might well be extended in coming months, in response to pressure from the Campaign for Freedom of Information (CFOI) and others. In February 2008, the Ministry of Justice published a consultation paper mooting the idea of rolling out the Act to cover not only bona fide public authorities, but also private companies providing services on behalf of the public sector and those carrying out 'public' functions, such as utility companies. The extension could potentially cover independently run care homes with residents funded by social services departments, private sector providers involved in diagnosing and/or treating NHS patients, private prison operators and security firms, and, of course, privately funded academy schools.

→ Further reading

Brooke, H. (2006) *Your Right to Know: New Edition—A Citizen's Guide to the Freedom of Information Act*, London: Pluto Press. **Comprehensive step-by-step guide to making effective Freedom of Information Act requests—and getting the results you want. Includes an introduction by Ian Hislop, editor of *Private Eye,* on his magazine's prolific use of the Act.**

Carey, P. (2004) *Data Protection: A Practical Guide to UK and EU Law*, Oxford: Oxford University Press. **This handy jargon-busting guide, now in its second edition, offers succinct explanations of the UK's data protection laws and the EU rules from which much of their content is derived—including the Directive on Privacy and Electronic Communication, which came into force in December 2003 and governs the potential for electronic privacy infringement arising from abuse of the Internet, telecommunications, and CCTV.**

Macdonald, J., Crail, R., and Jones, C. (eds) (forthcoming) *The Law of Freedom of Information*, 2nd edn, Oxford: Oxford University Press. **Second edition of this acclaimed legal handbook, which offers a forensic breakdown of the law and how it applies in practice to public authorities in the UK.**

Wadham, J., Griffiths, J., and Harris, K. (2007) *Blackstone's Guide to the Freedom of Information Act 2000*, 3rd edn, Oxford: Oxford University Press. **Revised third edition of this popular, user-friendly FoI guide, which contains clear pointers to making worthwhile FoI requests, what not to bother requesting under the Acts, and a full explanation of the various exemptions.**

? Review questions

1. What are the main stated aims of the Freedom of Information Act 2000 and Freedom of Information (Scotland) Act 2002?

2. Outline the main types of exemption from the FoI Acts and give some examples of how these exemptions apply in practice.

3. How and to whom does an individual make a formal complaint about a refusal by a public authority to disclose information under the FoI Acts?

4. How do the FoI Acts relate to the Data Protection Act 1998? Do they complement or contradict each other?

5. Give some examples of news stories to have been unearthed by FoI requests.

Online resource centre

www.oxfordtextbooks.co.uk/orc/Morrison
Visit the Online Resource Centre that accompanies this book for web links and regular updates.

Glossary

academy Labour's successor to the Conservatives' **city technology college (CTC)**, this is a semi-independent state secondary school, funded by injections of private capital and allowed to specialize (although it must teach the **National Curriculum**). Up to 10 per cent of pupils may be selected on the basis of aptitude in the specialism.

acceptable behaviour contracts (ABCs) written agreements that young people identified as having caused a public nuisance in their area are required to sign, with the consent of their parents or guardians, as part of the government's 'Respect' agenda. They are a form of pledge that the signatories will refrain from future antisocial behaviour.

adoption the process by which registered 'children in need' are taken into the permanent care of a family other than their biological one. Their adopters become their legal parents; recent reforms have extended this right to gay and unmarried heterosexual couples, as well as those that are married (cf **foster parent**).

Advisory, Conciliation and Arbitration Service (ACAS) a **quango** charged with mediating between employers and employees in industrial disputes. It is often asked to intervene by one of the two parties to prevent industrial action, such as strikes, being taken in the first place, but can be called in later on to bring the opposing sides back to the negotiating table in pursuit of a peaceful settlement.

agenda an outline of the timetable for a meeting of a subcommittee, committee, full council, **cabinet**/executive, or other body.

alcohol disorder zone (ADZ) a locality that has traditionally been the scene of alcohol-related public disorder, often adjacent to at least one licensed premises, this can be formally designated by a local authority as requiring more intensive policing. Local licensees will be charged a £100 fee to help to finance the additional patrols.

antisocial behaviour order (ASBO) a form of punishment issued by the police and local authorities for 'antisocial behaviour' that falls short of a criminal offence (e.g. shouting and swearing in the street). An ASBO can be used to impose restrictions on an individual's movements or actions, and its breach can result in prosecution.

Appeals Service a **quango** that handles appeals from the public on a range of issues, from the refusal of entitlement to social security benefits and tax credits, to complaints about vaccine damage.

area of outstanding natural beauty (AONB) a geographical area designated for special legal protection from development and commercial exploitation because of its natural beauty, and/or rare or unique flora and fauna.

Audit Commission the national **quango** employing the **district auditors** who award local authorities their star ratings under **comprehensive area assessment (CAA)** (**comprehensive performance assessment (CPA)** prior to April 2009). Individual councils' CAA 'scorecards' can be accessed via the Commission's website.

b

backbencher a term referring to the majority of members of Parliament in the House of Commons, who represent a **constituency**, but have no additional job title or responsibilities within the government or opposition, and therefore tend to sit on the 'back benches' (the seats behind the front row on either side of the house).

background paper a document or file produced by a local government officer for consideration as support for a policy proposal to be considered at a subcommittee, committee, **cabinet**/executive, or full council meeting.

balance of payments the difference in value between imports to and exports from the UK in a given financial year, *including* all types of payment. It encompasses both 'visible' items (such as cars and refrigerators) and 'invisible' ones (such as legal and financial services), as well as the value of financial transfers and debt payments to foreigners. If the value of imports exceeds that of exports, Britain is in a 'balance of payments deficit'; if the reverse is true, it is in a 'balance of payment surplus' (cf **balance of trade**).

balance of trade the difference in value between imports to and exports from the UK in a given financial year, *excluding* financial transfers and debt payments to foreigners. If Britain is importing consumer goods and services worth more than those it is exporting, it is in a 'balance of trade deficit'; if the reverse is true, it is in a 'balance of trade surplus' (cf **balance of payments**).

Bank of England Britain's central bank, based at Threadneedle Street in the City of London. It has its own governor and was given independence from government by then Chancellor Gordon Brown within days of Tony Blair's 1997 election victory.

basic allowance a standard fee (usually modest) paid to all councillors out of the revenue budgets of their local authorities. It can vary from one area to another.

billing authority the local authority that sends out **Council Tax** bills to local households, collects the money, and keeps a register of who has and who has not paid. This is the responsibility of district councils or **borough councils** and unitary authorities (cf **precepting authority**).

borough council a type of local authority with exactly the same powers as a district council, but which has the right to call itself a 'borough' because of an historical connection to the Crown.

Boundary Commission for England a national **quango** responsible for periodically reviewing the sizes and boundaries of English parliamentary **constituencies** to ensure that they cover approximately the same number of voters.

Boundary Committee for England a national **quango** tasked with periodically reviewing boundaries between wards and electoral divisions to ensure that each is represented by the correct number of councillors relative to its population size. It replaced the Local Government Commission for England.

brownfield site an area of land (usually in a built-up area) that has previously been used for development and may still have extant buildings on it (cf **greenfield site**).

building permission/building regulations additional consent required by private individuals or developers on top of **planning permission** in relation to work on extant buildings, normally relating to internal structural alterations. To attain *building permission*, developers must meet a series of *building regulations*, relating to health and safety, energy efficiency, etc.

by-law a form of **delegated legislation** that may be invoked by a local authority to combat a specific problem. For example, many councils have invoked by-laws allowing them to ban the drinking of alcohol in the street in order to improve public order (cf **statutory instrument**).

C

Cabinet the committee of senior government ministers, which meets at least once a week in Downing Street (cf **cabinet**).

cabinet a form of executive arrangement introduced under the Local Government Act 2000, which mimics the Westminster **Cabinet** system. Most members of the local government cabinet will be drawn from the party with the greatest number of seats on the council and each will be handed a specific portfolio, or brief (e.g. housing).

Cabinet committees subsets of the **Cabinet**, usually made up of groups of three or more senior ministers whose departmental responsibilities are related in some way. There are three types: standing (permanent); ad hoc (temporary); ministerial (permanent, but made up not of ministers, but of senior civil servants from related spending departments).

capital expenditure the share of a local authority's annual budget spent on building and repairing infrastructure, such as roads, schools, care homes, and libraries (cf **revenue expenditure**).

capping the process by which central government (particularly under the Conservative Party) has sometimes stopped local authorities raising **Council Tax** above a certain level. It has also occasionally been used to cap spending in particular areas.

care order an umbrella term for a type of court order, for which a local authority must apply in order to take a child away from his or her parents and into protective care. This can be a temporary arrangement (e.g. with a **foster parent**), or a permanent one (**adoption**).

Chairman of the Conservative Party the title held by an official (often a member of Parliament) whose responsibility is to mastermind the public image of the party as a whole, and to coordinate its national fundraising operation and membership recruitment.

chief constable the most senior officer in a local police force, responsible for hiring and firing junior officers and ensuring that resources are spread effectively across the area that the force covers. He or she is held accountable by his or her local **police authority**.

chief executive (also known as the head of the paid service) the most senior officer working for a local authority. The chief executive will frequently take the role of 'acting **returning officer**' for his or her area at local, general, and European elections.

child protection plan formerly known as the 'child protection register', this is a list of all recognized 'children in need' in each local authority area, which is shared between the various public, private, and voluntary organizations involved in protecting them.

childminder an individual registered to look after children, normally in his or her own home, during the daytime while their parents or guardians are at work.

Children's Commissioner a government regulator appointed under the 'Every Child Matters' agenda to ensure that all professionals and organizations involved in protecting recognized children in need are discharging their duties effectively.

children's trust an all-in-one body, formed in 2008, comprising multidisciplinary teams of professionals involved in the care of recognized children in need, including social workers, paediatricians, and child psychologists.

city council a purely honorary title bestowed on certain district councils, **borough councils**, and metropolitan borough councils that have been granted Royal Charter status.

city technology college (CTC) a type of semi-independent state secondary school, introduced by the last Conservative government to specialize in maths, sciences, and information technology (IT), often with hands-on involvement from the private sector (cf **academy**).

Civil List one of two sources of taxpayers' money that is used to finance the monarchy. Until recently, all members of the Royal Household (that is, the immediate Royal Family), other than the Prince of Wales, received annuities from the Civil List, but this now only applies to the

Queen and the Duke of Edinburgh. Seventy per cent of Civil List money is used to pay the salaries of royal servants and 30 per cent is used to fund annual royal garden parties.

code of conduct a system of rules governing the behaviour of councillors and officers that, since the Local Government Act 2000, has had to be formally adopted by each local authority. It must set out details of unacceptable conduct and any penalties incurred.

collective responsibility the principle that all members of a parliamentary party's front bench (and especially of the government) should either 'sing from the same hymn sheet' publicly, whatever their personal views on some of their party's policies, or be prepared to resign. The late Labour **Leader of the House** Robin Cook resigned in 2003 in protest at the UK's impending invasion of Iraq (cf **individual ministerial responsibility**).

Commission for Equality and Human Rights (CEHR) a **quango** formed as a result of the amalgamation of the Commission for Racial Equality (CRE) and the Equal Opportunities Commission (ECO), to ensure the equal treatment of employees in the workplace, regardless of their gender, race, or age.

Commission for Local Administration (also known as the **Local Government Ombudsmen**) independent body established to investigate complaints from the public, businesses, and other organizations about alleged incompetence by local government officials.

Commission for Social Care Inspection (CSCI) a government inspectorate responsible for evaluating the quality of service providers across the social care spectrum, from community nursing agencies, to care homes for the elderly, children in need, and the mentally ill. It awards homes a star rating between '0' and '3'.

Commission of the European Union (also known as the **European Commission**) the European Union's Civil Service, spread over 27 departments known as 'Directorates-General'. Unlike the British Civil Service, however, it *initiates* policy as well as implements it on behalf of elected politicians. Each Directorate-General is headed by a commissioner.

committee recommendations the form that the outcomes of subcommittee and committee meetings usually take, rather than definite decisions. The recommendations are referred on to the **Cabinet** (if at national level) and/or full council (if at local level) for their final say.

committee stage the third stage of a Bill's passage through Parliament, this gives a committee of **backbenchers** the chance to scrutinize it line by line and to suggest amendments. The type of committee that examines Bills is known as a 'standing committee' (or 'public Bill committee') and normally sits in a room outside the main Commons chamber. Emergency legislation, however, and committee stages of international treaties due to be incorporated into British law tend to be heard on the floor of the Commons itself—a so-called 'Committee of the Whole House' (cf **report stage**).

Common Agricultural Policy (CAP) one of the most expensive areas of annual European Union expenditure, amounting to some 44 per cent of its revenue budget, this offers a system of financial subsidies for EU farmers, to compensate them in years of poor yields and to enable them to compete on world markets by reducing their overheads.

community care an umbrella term for social care provided to the elderly and adults with mental health issues in their own homes, or in the home of a friend or relative. Examples of help available under community care include 'meals on wheels'.

community school the umbrella term used for state secondary schools under 'New Labour'. Some community schools are known as 'community colleges', because they provide adult education and evening classes on top of their primary role as day schools.

Competition Commission formerly the 'Monopolies and Mergers Commission' (MMC), this regulatory **quango** vets prospective company mergers and takeovers to ensure that they are not likely to have the effect of compromising free market competition.

comprehensive area assessment (CAA) a system for monitoring the quality of key services provided in each local authority area, replacing **comprehensive performance assessment (CPA)** from April 2009.

comprehensive performance assessment (CPA) a system in place to April 2009 that measures the performance of individual councils, awarding each service area between no and four stars (cf **comprehensive area assessment (CAA)**).

comprehensive school the umbrella term used to refer to all types of maintained secondary school other than **grammar schools**.

Comprehensive Spending Review (CSR) a method used by the Treasury to encourage individual spending departments to plan strategically for the future by announcing how much money it intends to allocate to them on a three-yearly basis, rather than annually through the Budget. Two spending reviews—in 1998 and 2007—have been dubbed 'comprehensive' because of their more detailed nature.

compulsory purchase order (CPO) an enforceable statutory order used by local authorities to force home owners and businesses to sell up and move out of their properties, so that they can be demolished to make way for a new development.

concessionary fare schemes types of discount bus fare scheme, often operated by individual councils and passenger transport authorities, to allow qualifying individuals—such as children, pensioners, or students—to travel at a reduced rate. The government launched a nationwide concessionary fare scheme in April 2008, allowing all pensioners to travel free of charge on local buses anywhere in the UK.

conservation area a district of a city, town, or village that is characterized by buildings of a particular historical and/or architectural vintage, and offered statutory protection from unsympathetic alteration (particularly to exterior appearance).

Conservative Campaign Headquarters the new title for the national headquarters of the Conservative Party and for the building that it occupies at Victoria Street, Westminster.

constituency the geographical area represented by a member of Parliament. There are 646 constituencies in the present House of Commons and all members (including ministers) must stand for re-election when a general election is called.

Consumer Council for Water the consumer watchdog focusing on the water industry.

consumer prices index (CPI) the government's preferred measure of **inflation**, this charts the movement in a notional 'basket' of goods regularly bought by a typical British household. Unlike the **retail prices index (RPI)**, it does not include mortgage payments and its readings therefore tend to be lower.

contributory benefits an umbrella term for more generous social security benefits to which British people are entitled (subject to meeting other criteria) if they have made sufficient **National Insurance** contributions during previous periods in employment. For example, Incapacity Benefit is a contributory benefit that is related to illness and disability (cf **non-contributory benefits**).

council constitution each local authority has been obliged to adopt its own constitution since the Local Government Act 2000, outlining its chosen form of executive decision-making arrangements and other procedural matters.

Council of Europe an alliance of 47 European member states formed in 1949, prior to the European Union. It aims to promote common legal and ethical standards in all member states, and its most celebrated achievement is the European Convention on Human Rights (ECHR).

Council of Ministers of the European Union (also known as the **Council of the European Union**) the European Union's supreme decision-making body. It is composed of senior ministers from each member state and its precise composition varies according to the issue being debated. For example, if health policy is on the **agenda**, each state will send its most senior health minister. The Council is chaired by a leading politician from the country holding the EU presidency, which rotates on a six-monthly basis.

Council Tax a form of local taxation currently paid by UK residents. It is charged to households and is predominantly property-based (under a banding system from A–H, related to the capital values of the home), but with elements of a 'head tax'. It was introduced in 2003 to replace the unpopular Community Charge (or 'Poll Tax').

county road a major arterial road—normally an 'A' road linking one town or city to another—the whole length of which falls within the boundaries of a single county (cf **trunk road**).

d

debt charge the money that local authorities must set aside each year in their revenue budgets to pay back the interest on outstanding loans taken out for capital projects.

declaration of interest an admission made by a councillor at the beginning of business in full council, committee, subcommittee, or **cabinet** that he or she has an outside vested interest in an issue due to be discussed and/or voted on. He or she will be expected to leave the meeting for the duration of that item.

Dedicated Schools Grant (DSG) a **ring-fenced grant** from central government paid to local authorities on the proviso that it is only spent on school staffing and maintenance.

delegated legislation (also known as secondary legislation) a 'lower-tier law', derived from a parent Act of Parliament, which may be implemented by ministers without the need to pass further Bills. There are three main types: **statutory instruments**; **by-laws**; Orders in Council.

delegated powers policy responsibilities handed to a particular individual, or group of individuals, by the full council or **cabinet**. For example, some decisions on rules and regulations governing local schools may be delegated to the **cabinet** member responsible for education.

designated public places order (DPPO) applied by local authorities to specified 'public places' (e.g. streets and parks) that have become trouble spots for drink-related antisocial behaviour, this gives local police the authority to remove alcohol forcibly from people in those areas and, if necessary, charge them with an offence.

devolution the constitutional concept of delegating a degree of power from a central parliament to regional and/or local assemblies. In the UK, Scotland, Wales, and Northern Ireland were all granted devolution in 1998—with the first of these gaining the most power, including the right to vary Income Tax by up to three pence in the pound. Devolution is distinct from independence, which is the handover of full sovereignty.

direct taxes an umbrella term for taxes, such as Income Tax and Corporation Tax, that are taken directly from the individual or company on whom they are levied, normally at a progressive rate determined by their income levels in a given financial year (cf **indirect taxes**).

directly elected mayor the most senior and powerful local politician in towns and cities that have voted in a local **referendum** to adopt one of the three new forms of executive arrangement outlined in the Local Government Act 2000. They can run their administrations either with the aid of a **cabinet**, or a council manager (senior officer). Ken Livingstone, the inaugural **mayor** of London, was Britain's first elected mayor.

dispersal order applied by local authorities to antisocial behaviour 'black spots' in which groups of two or more people alleged to be causing 'harassment, alarm, or distress' may be forcibly broken up by neighbourhood wardens or police officers.

dissolution the procedure by which Parliament is formally 'dissolved' following the resignation of a government and before a general election.

district auditor the official employed by the Audit Commission to monitor the performance of local authorities in a given geographical area using the **comprehensive area assessment (CAA)** system.

district valuer See **valuation officer**

e

elected hereditary peerage peerages that are passed from one generation to the next. Until 1999, all hereditary peers were entitled by birthright to sit in the House of Lords, but all except 92 (who have since been elected to remain by their colleagues) had this privilege removed in the House of Lords Act 1999 (cf **life peerage**).

election deposit a £500 deposit paid by each candidate who stands in a general election. The payment is lost if they fail to poll votes from more than 5 per cent of the registered electorate in the **constituency**. It was introduced in 1929 as a deterrent to 'frivolous candidates', but has been criticized recently for being too affordable.

Electoral Commission the **quango** responsible for ensuring that the correct procedures are followed in parliamentary, local, and European elections, and for enforcing rules on party finance. Its responsibilities include keeping campaign spending by election candidates within agreed statutory limits, and it may refer cases to the Crown Prosecution Service if it feels that electoral law has been broken.

electoral division the term used for the **constituencies** represented by county councillors and some unitary authority councillors. Each has between one and three councillors, depending on the size of its population.

electoral register the official list of all electors registered to vote in local, general, and European elections in a given local authority area. It is compiled by an electoral registration officer employed by a district council or **borough council**, or unitary authority.

emergency planning officer an officer employed by a county council or unitary authority to oversee strategic planning for civil emergencies, such as floods.

emergency protection order *(also known as an interim care order)* a type of **care order** allowing a local authority to take a child into care immediately, because of a perceived threat to his or her well-being. It initially applies for eight days, but may be renewed for up to a further week.

Energywatch a consumer watchdog set up to monitor prices and service standards in the gas and electricity markets. It has no statutory powers, unlike **Ofgem**.

English Heritage a national **quango** responsible for managing heritage monuments and properties, such as Stonehenge, on behalf of the government. English Heritage administers the listed buildings programme.

enlargement a term referring to the expansion of the European Union. It has been enlarged twice in the past decade, with a number of former Soviet countries joining for the first time: ten new states joined in 2004, and a further two—Bulgaria and Romania—in 2007.

Environment Agency the executive agency of the Department of the Environment, Food and Rural Affairs (Defra), responsible for regulating the quality and safety of water in rivers and streams, and for strategic planning for flood protection.

environmental health officer an officer employed by a district council or **borough council**, or unitary authority, to investigate complaints about environmental health hazards, such as vermin infestation, rotting waste, and noise pollution, and to inspect business premises serving food for their hygiene.

euro (€) the single European currency, introduced in all European Union member states bar the UK, Denmark, and Sweden as of 1 January 2002. The Labour government has pledged to hold a **referendum** before joining the euro, but Gordon Brown, when Chancellor, said that it would not do so until 'five economic tests' were met.

European Central Bank (ECB) based in Frankfurt, the central bank of the European Union, which issues the euro.

European Commission See **Commission of the European Union**

European Court of Human Rights (ECtHR) based in Strasbourg, the ultimate court of appeal for citizens of states that have signed up to the European Convention on Human Rights (ECHR) and passed it into their own domestic law. Britain belatedly ratified the convention by passing the Human Rights Act 1998. The Court was established by the **Council of Europe** and has no link to the European Union.

European Court of Justice (ECJ) the European Union's main legal body, this ensures that EU law is correctly implemented in member states. Each state contributes one judge—making 27 in all—although only 13 ever sit in session together. Only major cases go to the full ECJ, with others being heard by the General Court (formerly the Court of First Instance). Warring parties have their cases presented to the judges by one of 11 advocates-general.

European Parliament (EP) based primarily in Brussels, but moving to Strasbourg for one week in every month, this Parliament is elected every five years. Members of the European Parliament (MEPs) sit in political groupings, rather than along national lines. For example, the British Labour Party sits with the Socialist Group.

European Regional Development Fund (ERDF) the European Union fund to which local authorities and other public bodies may apply for financial aid to help with major capital projects designed to improve infrastructure and industry in deprived areas.

European Social Fund (ESF) the European Union fund to which local authorities and other public bodies may apply for financial aid to invest in training and employment opportunities in deprived areas.

executive agency a subset of a large government spending department, staffed by civil servants, charged with delivering a particular area or areas of its policy. Examples include the Health and Safety Executive, within the Department of Health, and the Highways Agency, in the Department for Transport.

f

federalism the flipside of subsidiarity, this is the idea promoted by Eurosceptics that further extension of the powers of the European union will lead to individual members states surrendering autonomy for their internal affairs to centralized institutions, turning the Union into a 'United States of Europe', or 'European super-state'.

first reading the formal introduction of a proposed Bill to the House of Commons. The reading usually consists solely of the full title of the Bill being read out by a minister (cf **second reading**; **third reading**).

forward plan a list of all key decisions due to be taken in a given calendar month that must be made public before the start of that month.

foster parent an adult who is registered to look after children in need in his or her own home, often for a short period of time, while a more permanent situation is sought (cf **adoption**).

foundation school like the Conservative Party's grant-maintained (GM) school, this is a self-governing state secondary school, permitted to spend its budgets as it pleases, within certain conditions set by central government. Money is allocated to it via its local education authority (LEA), but it may hire and fire its own staff, and set its own admissions and disciplinary policies distinct from those of LEA-run schools.

foundation trust the most successful hospital trusts (those with the highest star ratings) may apply for 'foundation' status, allowing them greater autonomy over running their own internal finances, setting their own pay scales, etc.

FT100 Share Index (FOOTSIE) the *Financial Times* Stock Exchange 100 Share Index (to use its full title) is the most famous of a number of 'indices', or lists, of major companies listed on the London Stock Exchange. It lists the hundred highest valued companies at any one time, in order of their share value.

further education (FE) an umbrella term for education and training provided by tertiary colleges and school sixth forms. It can encompass resits of A levels and other qualifications aimed at those of school age, but primarily focuses on vocational courses and diplomas.

g

general block grant a generic term for revenue grants paid by central government to local authorities that may be used for any service area, according to local needs and priorities. It is often used as a synonym for the **Revenue Support Grant (RSG)**.

globalization a term describing the gradual convergence of national economies into a bigger international whole. It is used increasingly in relation to the idea of free trade and the free movement of labour between countries, and the expansion of the Internet.

grammar (selective) school a type of maintained secondary school, phased out in much of the UK, which admits only pupils who have passed an academic test known as the '11 plus'. Those who fail it are admitted to standard **comprehensive schools**.

Greater London Authority (GLA) London's overarching 'council', which came into being in 2000 at the same time as the city gained its first **directly elected mayor**. Individual London boroughs retain their own councils to run local services at ground level, but the GLA is responsible for taking strategic decisions for the whole capital.

Green Paper a consultation document on a tentative government policy proposal that may, in time, evolve into a **White Paper**, and from there into a proposed Bill. All government Bills (other than emergency legislation) will go through at least one Green Paper stage, although if the public and/or interest groups react strongly against a proposal, it is unlikely to go much further.

greenbelt a term used for designated zones around towns and cities that have deliberately been kept free of development to prevent urban sprawl and to protect wildlife.

greenfield site an area of land on which there has been little, or no, prior development (cf **brownfield site**).

gross domestic product (GDP) the total profit from all goods and services generated in Britain in a given financial year, irrespective of which state benefits from them (cf **gross national product (GNP)**).

gross national product (GNP) the total profit from all goods and services generated by British-based companies in a given financial year, irrespective of where they are physically produced. For example, Far Eastern call centres owned by UK companies such as BT or Virgin would still count towards the state's GNP (cf **gross domestic product (GDP)**).

G8 (Group of 8) a loose organization, or forum, devoted to promoting economic free trade and globalization, made up of the world's eight leading industrial nations—currently the USA, the UK, Japan, France, Germany, Italy, Canada, and Russia.

h

Hansard the official record of all parliamentary business in both Houses. Protected by legal privilege and now available to read online, it is nonetheless not an entirely verbatim record of proceedings (except for the words used by the serving prime minister).

head of the paid service See **chief executive**

Health and Safety Executive (HSE) an executive agency of the Department of Health, which is charged with setting and enforcing health and safety legislation in the workplace across the UK. It recently merged with the Health and Safety Commission (HSC), which had previously drawn up health and safety rules.

health service scrutiny committee a statutory body set up by a county council or unitary authority to monitor the quality of health service provision in its area. Each committee is composed of 15 members, including a chairperson, local councillors, and representatives from relevant voluntary sector organizations.

Healthcare Commission a government inspectorate that monitors the standard of medical care provided by National Health Service hospitals and primary care services. Patient complaints are directed to the Commission, but only after they have first gone through the appropriate formal complaints process with the relevant NHS body.

Higher Education Funding Council for England (HEFCE) a **quango** that channels public money for teaching and research into universities.

Highways Agency the executive agency of the Department for Transport responsible for building and maintaining Britain's major roads.

honours list a generic term used for two annual lists of individuals chosen to be honoured with ceremonial titles by the Queen in recognition of their worldly achievements. The lists are compiled by ministers and shadow ministers, and honours are awarded in the Queen's Birthday Honours List and the New Year's Honours List.

House of Lords Appointments Commission a **quango** that vets potential candidates for **life peerages** after they have been nominated by a political party leader. It may have an enhanced role as and when the last hereditary peers are finally removed from the House after the next general election.

housing association a not-for-profit organization overseen by the Housing Corporation **quango**. Housing associations are the principal providers of social housing in Britain today, often working with, or on behalf of, local authorities.

Housing Benefit a means-tested benefit for the unemployed and low earners, ultimately paid by **Jobcentre Plus**, but administered by district councils or **borough councils** and unitary authority housing offices.

Housing Revenue Account (HRA) a discrete local authority account for the housing budget, which draws its main income from council home rents, and receives **ring-fenced grants** from central government to fund repairs and upkeep.

hybrid structure a type of local government structure that exists in some counties in England and Wales, in which a **two-tier structure** remains in certain areas while others have adopted the newer **unitary structure**. East Sussex is an example of a hybrid county: Lewes is covered by both a district and a county council, while neighbouring Brighton and Hove has a **city council**, which is a unitary authority.

i

Income Support a basic level of benefit paid to a range of people who satisfy certain needs-based criteria, but have paid insufficient prior **National Insurance** contributions to qualify for **contributory benefits**. It is available to certain people between the ages of 16 and 60 who are not in full-time work, such as carers or single parents.

Independent Police Complaints Commission (IPCC) a national **quango** responsible for investigating complaints against **chief constables** and/or their forces. The Commission will automatically launch an investigation whenever a civilian is killed by a police officer.

independent remuneration panel a body comprising at least three non-councillors, which was set up in each local authority area under the Local Government Act 2000 to adjudicate independently on any application by the council to increase its member allowances.

indirect taxes often referred to as 'hidden' or 'stealth' taxes, these are embedded in the cost of items bought by individuals or companies. Value-Added Tax (VAT) and excise duties on tobacco and alcohol are examples of indirect taxes. Because they are charged at a flat rate on relevant items, they are seen as regressive—i.e. they do not take account of an individual or company's ability to pay (cf **direct taxes**).

individual ministerial responsibility the principle that a **secretary of state** should be prepared to 'fall on his or her sword' and resign if a major failing is exposed in his or her department. In practice, ministers often have to be pushed by their prime minister (as happened in the case of then Chancellor of the Exchequer Norman Lamont after 'Black Wednesday' in 1992) (cf **collective responsibility**).

inflation changes in the prices of goods and services from one month to the next. This is calculated using either the **consumer prices index (CPI)** or **retail prices index (RPI)**, which monitor fluctuations in the values of a notional 'basket' of goods containing items regularly bought by a typical British household.

Information Commissioner a statutory official appointed to police the implementation of the Freedom of Information (FoI) Act 2000, adjudicating on complaints from individuals and organizations of lack of transparency by public authorities in response to legitimate FoI requests.

interest rates an instrument of monetary policy used to promote saving and investment, and reduce consumer spending. Since the 1980s, raising interest rates has been the preferred method of controlling **inflation**. The **Bank of England**'s **Monetary Policy Committee (MPC)** meets monthly to decide whether or not to raise or lower interest rates.

interim care order See **emergency protection order**

j

Jobcentre Plus this replaced the Benefits Agency in 2002 as the main body responsible for administering benefits of all kind, from **Jobseeker's Allowance (JSA)** and **Income Support**, to sickness and disability-related benefits, and maternity benefits.

Jobseeker's Allowance (JSA) a benefit paid to people over the age of 16 who are registered as unemployed and actively seeking work. There are two types of allowance: contributions-based (which is related to prior **National Insurance** payments) and income-based.

k

key decision a policy decision affecting two or more wards or electoral divisions in a local authority area. They are judged to be so significant that they must be presented for a final say to the full council and cannot be taken solely in **cabinet**.

l

leader of the council the most senior and powerful local politician in authorities that have either adopted the third new executive arrangement outlined in the Local Government Act 2000, or retained their pre-existing one. Like the prime minister at Westminster, they are normally the leader of the party with the greatest number of seats on the council.

Leader of the House the government minister responsible for organizing the weekly House of Commons timetable, and for proposing changes to its working hours and orders of business.

Learning and Skills Council (LSC) a national body formed in 2001 to fund certificated further education courses recognized by the **Qualifications and Curriculum Authority (QCA)**.

life peerage honorary peerages conferred on individuals for life in one of the two annual honours lists. As their name suggests, these titles die with their recipient and therefore cannot be passed on to his or her children (cf **elected hereditary peerage**).

listed building　an individual building, or small group of buildings (e.g. a Georgian crescent), offered statutory protection against alteration or demolition because of its link to specific historical personalities, events, or architectural movements. There are three levels of listing: grades I, II*, and II.

listing officer　an official employed by one of the 85 regional offices of the Valuation Office Agency (VAO) to place individual homes in property bands for **Council Tax** purposes.

local development framework **(LDF)**　an umbrella term for strategic plans produced by individual local authorities, along the lines of the now defunct local plan, structure plan, and unitary plan. Made up of schemes composed of individual documents, the LDF is useful for guidance, but is subject to more binding **regional spatial strategies (RSSs)**.

local government association　the regional coalitions of local authorities that lobby Parliament and central government on their behalf. There is also a national Local Government Association (LGA).

Local Government Ombudsmen　See **Commission for Local Administration**

local involvement networks **(LINks)**　the replacement for patients' forums in the National Health Service, these are groups of local service users, working together with voluntary sector professionals, who channel complaints and feedback on local health service bodies and social services care providers to those organizations.

local safeguarding children's board **(LSCB)**　the committees set up by every county council and unitary authority under the Children Act 2004 to coordinate the efforts of all organizations involved in looking after recognized children in need.

Lord Chancellor　a centuries-old office held traditionally by Britain's most senior judge and a member of the House of Lords. The title is in the process of being phased out, along with some of its customary responsibilities (the role chairing debate in the Lords was recently passed to a new **Lords' Speaker**). Jack Straw, the Lord Chancellor at the time of writing, generally goes under the title 'Justice Secretary', and is the first non-peer to hold the post.

Lords' Speaker　a recently introduced post designed to mimic that of the Commons **Speaker**, this title is given to a peer elected by his or her colleagues in the House of Lords to chair debate in the chamber.

Lords Spiritual　a collective term for the 26 senior Church of England bishops, led by the Archbishop of Canterbury, who remain entitled to sit in the House of Lords.

m

mayor　a ceremonial title that has traditionally been rotated between councillors on local authorities on a year-by-year basis. Its recipient spends 12 months chairing full council meetings on a non-partisan basis and attending civic events.

member of the European Parliament (MEP) an elected representative who sits in the **European Parliament**, of which there are 732, elected every five years. Each state contributes a number of members that reflects its population size.

minister of state an umbrella term for all ministers in government departments, including junior ministers.

minutes the written record of the proceedings of a meeting of a subcommittee, committee, full council, **cabinet**/executive, or other body.

Monetary Policy Committee (MPC) a committee of the **Bank of England** that meets once a month to decide whether or not to raise or lower **interest rates**, on the basis of the previous month's **inflation** figures.

monitoring officer a senior local authority officer responsible for monitoring councillors' and officers' compliance with their council's **code of conduct**, and recording and reporting to members any cases of suspected maladministration.

n

National Assembly for Wales the full title of Wales's **devolved** assembly, which is based in a purpose-built chamber in Cardiff Bay.

National Curriculum the compulsory content that must be taught in maintained (state) schools in Britain in certain core subjects, such as English language and maths.

National Curriculum standard assessment tests (SATs) academic tests taken by state school pupils at three key stages in their **National Curriculum** learning. Key stages 1, 2, and 3 take place at the ages of 7, 11, and 14, respectively.

National Executive Committee of the Labour Party (NEC) often referred to as 'Labour's ruling **1922 committee**', a senior policy committee composed of representatives of all of the main branches of the Labour Party, including members of Parliament, **constituency** Party members, and trade unionists. Major changes to the Party's constitution must be approved by this committee.

National Institute for Health and Clinical Excellence (NICE) a **quango** set up to vet medication before it is made available on the National Health Service, and to carry out its own research into potential cures and treatments. It is headed by a chief medical officer.

National Insurance (NI) a system of contributory payments deducted from employees' wages and topped up by employers, to finance entitlement to future benefits should they be needed. The system was originally set up in 1911 to protect workers from poverty should they become unable to work through sickness or injury.

national non-domestic rates (NNDR) (also known as the **uniform business rates**

(UBR)) the local taxation paid by companies, the bills of which are calculated according to the rateable values of business premises and a national multiplier set each year by the government (e.g. 50 pence in the pound). The money is collected locally, but then funnelled through the Treasury and redistributed around the country according to need.

National Offender Management Service (NOMS) an executive agency of the Ministry of Justice responsible for recruiting and employing the UK's 48,000 prison staff, and overall policy regarding the day-to-day running of its 135 jails. The Prisons Service is now a part of NOMS and is responsible only for publicly funded jails

national park one of the 14 geographical areas of Britain designated for the highest degree of protection from development or commercial exploitation possible under UK law.

national park authority the managing authority of each UK **national park**, which is charged with maintaining it up to a statutory standard on behalf of the public.

National Standards Board for England and Wales a national **quango** that has the final say on complaints about breaches of codes of conduct or other failures in ethical high standards referred to it by a local authority **standards committee**.

Natural England a **quango** responsible for conserving, protecting, and managing the natural environment in England for current and future generations.

neighbourhood policing teams community-based teams made up of serving police officers, **police community support officers (PCSOs)**, and volunteers, which are intended to increase the visibility of patrols on the streets. Since April 2005, 3,600 neighbourhood policing teams have been set up across the UK.

neighbourhood warden a salaried, community-based official, based in a local authority area, whose job is to patrol areas with reputations for antisocial behaviour, graffiti, and criminal activity. The warden is employed by the Department for Communities and Local Government's Neighbourhood Renewal Unit.

Network Rail the not-for-dividend company set up by the government in 2001 to take over repairs and maintenance of the UK overland rail network (tracks, signals, and stations) from Railtrack, the private monopoly initially given those responsibilities following the privatization of British Rail in the early 1990s.

NHS trust an umbrella term referring to hospitals, ambulance services, and mental health services provided on the National Health Service. The term 'trust' was coined in the early 1990s and relates to the new levels of autonomy given to these bodies to run their own affairs. Each has its own board, like a company, and is designated a service 'provider'—rather than a 'commissioner', like **primary care trusts (PCTs)**.

1922 Committee often referred to as 'the influential 1922 Committee', this is made up of all of the backbench Conservative members of Parliament at any one time. The 'mood' of the Committee is a crucial test of the likely lifespan of its leadership and it was widely credited with delivering the knockout blow to Margaret Thatcher's premiership after she was challenged by Michael Heseltine in 1990.

non-contributory benefits an umbrella term for lower-level social security benefits to which British people are entitled (subject to meeting other criteria) irrespective of their previous **National Insurance** contributions. **Income Support** is an example of a purely 'needs-based', non-contributory benefit that is paid to people in lieu of a higher level entitlement (cf **contributory benefits**).

North Atlantic Treaty Organization (NATO) a military alliance made up of 26 predominantly Western powers, NATO was formed with the signing of the North Atlantic Treaty in Washington DC in 1949. It was initially designed to act as a bulwark during the Cold War against the expansion of the Soviet Union and the Warsaw Pact.

o

Office of Communications (Ofcom) a **quango** dubbed a 'super-regulator' because of its all-embracing responsibilities for overseeing the telecommunications and broadcast media industries (radio, television, and the Internet). Ofcom may fine broadcasters, including the British Broadcasting Corporation (BBC),

for breaking the rules governing taste and decency, and it monitors their public service content (such as current affairs and news output).

Office of Fair Trading (OFT) a national regulatory **quango** established to ensure that free and fair competition operates in a given market for the benefit of the consumer on a day-to-day basis. The OFT investigates complaints about restrictive practices, cartels, and other anti-competitive behaviour.

Office of Gas and Electricity Markets (Ofgem) a regulatory **quango** that oversees Britain's privatized energy market to ensure that there is free and fair competition between suppliers, and that bills are kept within acceptable bounds. It is headed by a Director General of Gas and Electricity Markets.

Office of Standards in Education (Ofsted) a central government inspectorate, headed by a Chief Inspector of Schools, which visits maintained schools, pre-schools education providers, and **further education** colleges on a rolling basis to monitor standards of teaching and administration, and awards grades from '1' to '4'.

Office of the Qualifications and Examinations Regulator (Ofqual) a new national regulator established in 2008 to monitor the standard of qualifications, exams, and tests in England. Ofqual is headed by a ruling committee. It is part of the **Qualifications and Curriculum Authority (QCA)**.

Office of the Schools Adjudicator (OSA) a national regulator that rules on complaints from parents over major administrative decisions affecting schools, such as proposals to close or merge schools, or to change admission criteria.

Office of Water Regulation (OFWAT) (also known as the **Water Services Regulatory Authority**) one of three statutory regulators of the privatized water industry, OFWAT monitors the transparency of individual water companies' accounts and share policies.

outline planning permission the first stage of obtaining consent to develop a site, during which permission is granted 'in principle', subject to the submission of a more detailed plan (cf **planning permission**).

overview and scrutiny committee an overarching 'super-committee' adopted by some local authorities under the Local Government Act 2000, which scrutinizes the workings of council departments, and decisions taken by **cabinet** and senior officers. There will normally be several scrutiny subcommittees that focus on more specific policy areas.

p

pairing a convention allowing a member of Parliament (MP) or peer who is unable to attend an important vote in the Commons or Lords to 'pair up' with an MP or peer on the opposing bench, both agreeing to stay away, and thereby 'cancelling each other out' to no net advantage on either side.

parish meeting the lowest form of local authority, this is a de facto parish council that convenes once a year in small villages to discuss the provision of local services and to make representations to the statutory authorities on behalf of local people.

Parliamentary Commissioner for Administration (also known as the **Parliamentary Ombudsman**) also responsible for overseeing administration in the National Health Service, the Commissioner hears complaints from members of the public and organizations about alleged maladministration by Parliament, rather than corruption.

Parliamentary Commissioner for Standards a post created on the recommendation of the Nolan Inquiry, which was prompted by a series of 'sleaze' scandals involving Conservative members of Parliament in the early 1990s, including the 'cash for questions' affair, when Neil Hamilton was accused of taking payments from Harrods owner Mohamed Al Fayed to ask parliamentary questions on his behalf. The Commissioner polices the rigorous system of disclosure of outside interests that was introduced after these scandals.

Parliamentary Labour Party (PLP) Labour's equivalent of the **1922 Committee** in the Conservative Party, this is the collective term for all Labour **backbenchers**.

Parliamentary Ombudsman See **Parliamentary Commissioner for Administration**

parliamentary private secretary (PPS) a
very junior government post often
offered to an upcoming member of
Parliament judged to have ministerial potential. PPSs are the 'link'
between senior ministers and the
ordinary **backbenchers** in their
party, and are often used to float
potential policy ideas to 'test the
water' among their parliamentary
colleagues.

parliamentary privilege the constitutional
convention allowing members of
Parliament and peers to speak
freely within their respective
chambers, even criticizing named
individuals without fear of being
prosecuted for defamation. Even
under parliamentary privilege, certain terms are banned in reference
to their fellow MPs or peers, including the word 'liar'.

parliamentary sovereignty the constitutional principle derived from the
1689 Bill of Rights that elevated Parliament to a position of supremacy
over the sovereign in governing
England and Wales (and, in due
course, the whole of the UK).

parliamentary under-secretary the lowest
form of government minister, this
is a junior minister below the level
of minister of state and **secretary of
state**.

parole the procedure by which prisoners are released early from their
sentences for 'good behaviour'.
Those convicted of more minor
offences are usually granted automatic early release after serving

half the length of their sentences,
but serious offenders, such as rapists and serial murderers, will usually serve at least twenty years.

Passenger Focus (also known as the
Rail Passengers' Council) a consumer
watchdog representing the interests
of overland rail commuters and
passengers.

permanent secretary the most senior
civil servant in a government department. He or she will offer day-
to-day advice to **secretary of state**
and other ministers, and therefore
occupies a politically restricted post.

planning contribution (or planning gain) an
offer by a developer of added value
for a local authority in exchange for
being granted **planning permission**
for a major project. For example,
the developer may offer to finance
a new playground for children in a
deprived ward as a form of 'sweet-
ener' to help its bid to build a new
supermarket.

planning inquiry a public inquiry held
into a contentious development
proposal to which there is strong
opposition. It will be chaired by an
independent inspector appointed
by the Secretary of State for Communities and Local Government,
and those immediately affected by
the proposal will be allowed to speak
at it.

planning permission consent given to an
individual, company, or other organization to build new premises, or to
extend or adapt an existing one (cf
outline planning permission).

police authority the local authorities of the UK Police Service, these are composed of a mix of local councillors and laypeople, and are charged with hiring and firing **chief constables** and their deputies, and holding them to account for their policies.

police community support officers (PCSOs) formerly known as 'special constables' (or 'specials'), these officers are employed as auxiliary police officers, with the power to arrest and issue some minor punishments, such as fixed penalty fines.

policy and resources committee traditionally the most powerful local authority committee, because it is in charge of the council's overall budget, this committee must be consulted on major decisions (e.g. to build a new road), because it will have to approve the funding.

political sovereignty the constitutional concept of an institution or individual holding political supremacy (or 'sovereignty') over the citizens of a nation. In Britain, political sovereignty originally rested with the reigning monarch (or 'sovereign'), but passed to Parliament after the 1689 Bill of Rights.

politically restricted post the contractual position held by senior public officials (civil servants and local government officers) who are barred from canvassing openly for a political party at elections, or standing for office, due to their close day-to-day working relationship with politicians.

Postal Services Commission (Postcomm) the regulatory **quango** monitoring the quality and reliability of postal delivery services in the UK.

postal vote a means of casting a vote in an election by post, rather than in person. The British government is committed to extending rights to vote by post across the country, following several recent pilots, but this has provoked criticism from some quarters because of the perceived risk of fraud in multi-occupancy households.

Postwatch a consumer watchdog with no statutory recognition, which channels complaints from the public and businesses to the government.

precepting authority all local authorities that receive some of their revenue funding through the **Council Tax** are precepting authorities. The term 'precept' refers to the 'invoice' that such authorities present to the **billing authority**, outlining the sum that they wish to raise through the Council Tax in the coming financial year.

prescribed function a role and responsibility formally delegated by a council to its committees, subcommittees, **cabinet**/executive, and individual cabinet members.

Press Complaints Commission (PCC) the independent, self-regulatory industry body responsible for handling complaints from the public about newspapers and magazines. It has 17 members, including editors, and representatives of the public relations (PR) and marketing industries, and enforces a code of practice to which all print journalists must adhere. This prohibits practices such as major intrusions into personal privacy.

primary care trust (PCT) a body headed by general practitioners (GPs), community nurses, and other primary care professionals based in a given area, and responsible for 'commissioning' the vast majority of National Health Service care on behalf of local people. PCTs are responsible for 80 per cent of the NHS revenue budget and cover up to 600,000 people each.

primary schools maintained schools that deliver primary teaching to pupils in core subjects such as English, maths, and science between the ages of four (reception class) and 11.

private finance initiative (PFI) the main way in which major capital projects are now funded, this is an arrangement between a public authority (e.g. a council or government department) and a private company, under which the latter foots most of the initial bill and the former pays it back (with interest) over a period of years (cf **public–private partnership (PPP)**).

private member's Bill (PMB) a Bill proposed by an individual **backbencher**, normally on an issue dear to his or her heart, and/or one that concerns his or her constituents. While they may cast the media's spotlight onto an issue, most PMBs are never allotted sufficient parliamentary time to pass into law, but there have been exceptions, including the 1967 Abortion Bill, introduced by future Liberal leader David Steel.

Privy Council an ancient committee of state, originally formed as a group of close confidantes for the reigning monarch to counteract the power of the Great Council or *Magnum Concilium*, composed of peers of the realm. Today, all serving and past **Cabinet** ministers and leaders of the Opposition are appointed members for life, and advise the monarch on matters such as the use of the Privy Purse (their personal pot of money, derived from the Duchy of Lancaster estate) and the making of Orders in Council.

proportional representation (PR) an umbrella term for alternative electoral systems to the 'first past the post' (FPTP) process used in British general elections. Most Western countries use PR, including Ireland, which uses the single transferable vote (STV). The Liberal Democrats have been campaigning for STV to be adopted in Britain, arguing that is fairer than the UK system, because the number of seats won by a party tends to bear more of a relationship to the votes cast for them than does FPTP.

prorogation a term that denotes the procedure by which Parliament is temporarily suspended (or 'prorogued') at the end of a parliamentary session.

public Bill committee a temporary parliamentary committee convened to scrutinize and debate a Bill or another prospective Act of Parliament. They were formerly known as 'standing committees' because, being only temporary, their members are notionally not in their positions for long enough to warrant permanent seats at the committee table.

public limited company (plc) a type of larger registered company in the UK that makes its shares available to the general public to buy by 'floating' itself on the London Stock Exchange. It has a legal obligation to maximize profits for its shareholders. Most household name companies in Britain are plcs (e.g. BP).

public–private partnership (PPP) a financial arrangement used to fund major capital projects, such as roads and prisons, whereby a government department or other public authority will share the cost of the initial outlay with a private company or companies. The bulk of the up-front investment is usually made by the private sector and the public sector will pay it off (with interest) over a period of years. PPP is 'New Labour's' successor to the Conservatives' private finance initiative (PFI).

public sector net cash requirement (PSNCR) formerly the 'public sector borrowing requirement' (PSBR), this is the sum of money that the British government will need to borrow through commercial loans or from the public in a given financial year to meet its public spending commitments—that is, it is the difference between the total taxation that the Exchequer expects to raise in a year and its actual outgoings.

Public Works Loan Board (PWLB) a body that can lend money to local authorities for major capital projects at a lower rate of interest than those offered by the banking sector. The PWLB is part of the UK Debt Management Office, a Treasury executive agency.

q

Qualifications and Curriculum Authority (QCA) the national quango from which recognition is required for certificated school and further education qualifications in England and Wales. Recognized qualifications appear on the Authority's National Qualifications Framework (NQF).

qualified majority voting (QMV) a system of voting in the Council of Ministers of the European Union that enables certain issues to be decided by a majority vote in favour or against, rather than unanimity. Under QMV, each member state is allocated a certain number of votes in proportion to its population, meaning that some have substantially more say in matters than others and that decisions are taken on a 'qualified' majority basis. The UK, for example, has 29 votes, while Malta has just three.

quality parish council a form of parish council made up of elected councillors from a village or small town that has performed its limited duties (e.g. maintaining local play facilities) so efficiently that it has been rewarded with additional responsibilities—and resources to act on them—by the statutory local authorities.

quango (quasi-autonomous non-government organization) a non-departmental body set up by a government department, and partly funded by the taxpayer, to regulate, monitor, or otherwise oversee a particular area of policy delivery. UK quangos have their own executive boards, like companies, and include the Arts Council England and the **Commission for Equality and Human Rights (CEHR)**.

Queen's Speech an annual address given by the Queen at the State Opening of Parliament in October or November. The speech is actually a list of legislation to be proposed by the government during the coming parliamentary session (year) and is written not by the monarch herself, but by the prime minister and the **Cabinet**.

Question Time sessions of parliamentary business during which **backbenchers** and/or peers on all sides have the opportunity of questioning individual departmental ministers on the conduct of their ministerial business. Major spending departments each have a question time session at least once a fortnight, while the most famous is 'Prime Minister's Questions', held every Wednesday lunchtime.

r

Rail Passengers' Council See **Passenger Focus**

rateable value the sum of money that a business premises would be able bring in on the rental market. Both **national non-domestic rates (NNDR)** and the rates—that is, the property-based domestic tax that preceded the Community Charge—are (or were) based on rateable values.

recession an economic term used to describe a rapid slowdown or negative growth. Technically, it refers to a period of two successive economic quarters during which the economy has 'shrunk'—i.e. consumers have stopped spending, sales of goods and services have dwindled, and manufacturers have reduced production.

refer back a term used to describe when a local authority **cabinet**/executive and/or full council meeting asks a committee or subcommittee to rethink a recommendation.

referendum a public vote on a single issue. In Britain, referenda are rare, but a national referendum was held in 1975 on the question of whether the country should remain in the European Community, and the people of Scotland, Wales, and Northern Ireland were consulted in referenda about whether they wanted **devolved** government.

regional development agency (RDA) one of eight **quangos** covering each of England's eight regions, charged with promoting sustainable development and economic prosperity.

regional planning body a generic term used for overarching administrative organizations responsible for drawing up **regional spatial strategies (RSSs)** outlining proposed developments in each of England's eight regions over the ensuing twenty years. Until 2010, regional assemblies will have this role, but they will then be replaced by the existing **regional development agencies (RDAs)**.

regional spatial strategy (RSS) a long-term development plan drawn up every twenty years for each of England's eight regions. RSSs have been introduced as replacements for local plans, structure plans, and unitary plans.

register of members' interests under the Local Government Act 2000, each local authority must keep a register listing the outside business and other interests of all of its councillors. The register was adapted from the parliamentary register used for members of Parliament, following the Nolan Inquiry.

report stage the stage immediately after the **committee stage**, when the committee's chairperson will 're-port back' to the Commons with its recommendations.

resolved items the matters concluded at the end of a committee, full council, or **cabinet**/executive meeting. A vote will normally be taken to make the final decision.

retail prices index (RPI) the measure of **inflation** (changes in prices of goods and services) preferred by most economists to the **consumer prices index (CPI)**, this charts the movement in the value of a notional 'basket' of goods regularly bought by typical British households. Because it includes mortgage payments, it is usually higher than the CPI.

returning officer the official responsible for overseeing local and general election procedures on the day of a poll, ordering recounts where necessary, and announcing the result. Officially, this post is held by the chairperson or **mayor** of a neighbouring or coterminous local authority, but a senior council officer will usually perform the duties in practice—often a **chief executive** or electoral registration officer.

revenue expenditure the share of a local authority's annual budget spent on the day-to-day running costs of schools, libraries, offices, and other local services (cf **capital expenditure**).

revenue support grant (RSG) one of three types of formula grant allocated to local authorities by central government for their revenue spending, this is traditionally the biggest single chunk of money that they receive. It is calculated on the basis of a formula relating to the demographic make-up of the local area and, unless stipulated by ministers, it may be used by the council in any area of revenue spending.

ring-fenced grant one of two types of **specific grant** for local authority revenue spending (cf **unfenced grants**), which must be used for a purpose stipulated by central government.

The **Dedicated Schools Grant (DSG)** is the most famous.

Royal Assent the 'rubber stamp' given to a Bill by the reigning sovereign to make it an Act of Parliament. In practice, the Royal Assent is a formality today and no monarch has refused to give it since Queen Anne attempted to do so in 1707.

Royal Prerogative a constitutional term used to refer to the (now largely notional) idea that power in the UK derives from the authority of the reigning sovereign. In practice, today the majority of prerogative powers (e.g. the ability to declare war, and to appoint ministers) rests with the elected prime minister of the day.

rule of law a constitutional principle, derived from 1215's Magna Carta, stipulating that no one is 'above the law of the land', including (in theory) the sovereign.

s

Schengen Agreement the collective term for two European Union treaties—signed in 1985 and 1990, respectively—which formally abolished systematic border controls between member states.

Scottish Government (Scottish Executive) the title used by the **devolved** administration in Scotland.

Scottish Parliament Scotland's **devolved** assembly, which is based in a purpose-built parliamentary building at Holyrood, at the foot of the Royal Mile in Edinburgh.

second reading the first stage at which the main principles of a Bill are formally read out to the House and debated. This normally takes place within a few weeks of the **first reading** and may lead to an early vote on some aspects of the Bill (cf **third reading**).

secondary legislation See **delegated legislation**

secretary of state an umbrella term for the most senior government minister in a spending department (e.g. the Secretary of State for Health).

select committee a permanent parliamentary committee charged with scrutinizing the day-to-day workings of a government department, and other public authorities related to the responsibilities of that department. For example, the Culture, Media and Sport Select Committee examines the work of the Department for Culture, Media and Sport, as well as that of the British Broadcasting Corporation (BBC).

separation of powers a principle stipulating that the three main seats of constitutional authority in the UK—the executive, legislature, and judiciary—should be kept separate to avoid concentrating power in too few hands. In practice, there are overlaps, with the prime minister and **Cabinet** (executive) also sitting in Parliament (legislature).

Speaker a member of Parliament elected by his or her peers, on a motion moved by the Father of the House (the member with the longest unbroken service to the chamber) following a general election, to serve as chairperson of debates and maintain discipline in the Commons for the coming Parliament.

special responsibility allowance a top-up fee added to the **basic allowance** for a councillor in recognition of additional responsibilities, such as sitting on, or chairing, a local authority committee. The allowance can vary according to the level of responsibility.

special school a state school dedicated to teaching children with learning difficulties and/or mental or physical disabilities.

specialist school a generic term for all state schools that are permitted to specialize in one or more subjects over and above teaching the **National Curriculum**. **Academies** are, by nature, specialist schools—but, in practice, most **community schools** also have subject specialisms, enabling them to draw down extra funds to improve facilities.

specific grant one of two different categories of non-formula grant given to local authorities each year to help with revenue spending (cf area-based grants). Specific grants can either be **ring-fenced grants** or **unfenced grants**.

spin doctor a layperson's term for a type of special adviser usually employed by a senior figure in a political party to put a positive 'spin' on their policies to the public and the media. Alastair Campbell, the former Downing Street director of communications, became one of Britain's most infamous spin doctors during Tony Blair's ten years in power.

standards committee a committee set up by each local authority under the Local Government Act 2000 to monitor councillors' and officers' compliance with the council's registers of members' interests and **code of conduct**. The committee must have at least one lay member.

standing order the system of rules adopted by individual local authorities to govern the day-to-day conduct of business in the full council, and its committees, subcommittees, and/or **cabinet**.

statutory instrument (SI) a type of **delegated legislation** that takes the form of a rule or regulation that is needed to implement a policy approved by Parliament 'on the ground'. Statutory instruments can be issued by a government minister under the authority of a parent Act of Parliament, without the need to pass a further Bill. For example, the detailed guidelines issued to local authorities and the police to put into practice the Licensing Act 2003 were issued by the Culture Secretary Tessa Jowell, who devised them on the basis of the general provisions in the Act itself (cf **by-law**).

strategic health authority (STA) a body that is responsible for the administration of the Department of Health 'on the ground'. There are 28 STAs, which replaced 96 pre-existing health authorities (HAs). Although they take an arms-length approach to commissioning National Health Service services from hospitals and other trusts, they are charged with producing three-yearly health improvement plans (HIPs) to promote healthier lifestyles and to guard against illness.

subsidiarity a loose constitutional principle underpinning the European Union, which holds that member states retain primary sovereignty over their internal affairs, with the EU acting as last port of call if individual self-determination falters.

supplementary estimate when a local authority is calculating the level of revenue funding that it will need in the next financial year, it will ask each department to make an estimate of its projected spending. Occasionally, departments underestimate their needs and, at a later date, ask for an additional sum—the supplementary estimate.

Sure Start a government programme launched in 1999 to improve access for low-income families to early years teaching and other support services.

t

tactical voting a type of strategic voting by electors voting in 'first past the post' (FPTP) elections, which sees them vote for a candidate other than their 'sincere preference' in the knowledge that to do so would be 'wasted vote'. Tactical voters instead opt for their 'least worst option'—choosing a 'bearable' third party, in order to stop the candidate they most oppose winning.

Ten-Minute Rule one of three ways in which **private members' Bills**

(PMBs) may be introduced into Parliament and the one that most often grabs headlines. A member of Parliament must have their idea for a Bill proposed and seconded by colleagues, and obtain a further eight members' signatures, and they will then be given ten minutes in which to introduce their proposals to the Commons. A MP who opposes the Bill will then have the same amount of time to make a speech outlining his or her objections.

third reading the final stage of a Bill's passage through the House of Commons. It is at the third reading that members of Parliament are confronted with the final version of the Bill's wording, so it is an occasion for any major disagreements to be fought out in a formal vote (cf **first reading; second reading**).

trading standards officer an officer employed by a county council or unitary authority to ensure that local businesses are adhering to regulations regarding issues such as product labelling, and weights and measures.

Traffic Commissioner one of seven regional commissioners, who are employed to license public transport routes and operators, and long-distance haulage companies.

Transport for London (TfL) the **quango** responsible for strategic planning and day-to-day running of London's transport network, including the London Underground, Docklands Light Railway, city bus services, and river ferries.

trunk road a major arterial road—an 'A' road or a motorway—linking towns and cities, and sometimes crossing the boundaries between counties (cf **county road**).

trust schools a new form of **foundation school** introduced under the Education and Inspections Act 2006. These are primary and secondary schools supported by charitable trusts that employ their staff, manage assets, and set admissions policies.

two-tier structure a type of local government structure established under the 1974 reorganization of local authorities, in which there are two levels of council operating in the same area: district councils and/or **borough councils** responsible for services such as waste collection, housing, and environmental health; and an overarching county council providing countywide services, such as education and highways (roads).

u

unfenced grant one of two types of **specific grant** for local authority revenue spending (cf **ring-fenced grant**), it may be spent in whatever way a council sees fit, subject to certain conditions. For example, the Housing and Planning Delivery Grant (HPDG) must be used for planning, but councils may choose precisely how to spend it.

uniform business rates (UBR) See **national non-domestic rates (NNDR)**

UNISON the main local government trade union, it counts among its members many departmental officers, social workers, and health professionals.

unitary structure a type of local government structure that has replaced the **two-tier structure** in many areas, in which a single—unitary—local authority is responsible for all local services, from waste collection, to education and social care.

United Nations (UN) a global peacemaking body formed in 1945, as a successor to the defunct League of Nations established after the First World War. The UN is headquartered in New York. Its main constitutional bodies include the UN General Assembly and the UN Security Council (which debates international conflict).

v

valuation officer an official who manages one of the 85 regional offices of the Valuation Office Agency (VOA), the government body responsible for valuing homes into bands for the purpose of charging the **Council Tax**.

virement a process allowing local authorities limited discretion to transfer money from one spending area to another during a given financial year, if the former is showing a surplus and the latter a deficit. Councils' ability to use virement has been severely curtailed in recent years, as the government has issued more **ring-fenced grants**.

voluntary aided school a type of school in the state sector, the land and buildings of which are owned by a charity or local church. Although such schools receive some funding through the local authority, they are more autonomous than **voluntary controlled schools**, employing their own staff and setting their own admission policies.

voluntary controlled school a type of school in the state sector, the land and buildings of which are owned by a charity or local church. They have less autonomy than **voluntary aided schools**, and their admissions policies will be controlled and staff employed by the local authority (like those in other council-run schools).

w

ward a term used to describe a **constituency** represented by district council, **borough council**, and some unitary authority councillors. Each has between one and three councillors, depending on its population size.

Water Services Regulatory Authority See **Office of Water Regulation (OFWAT)**

Welsh Assembly Government (Welsh Executive) the title adopted by the elected **devolved** administration in Wales.

whip members of Parliament and peers with the job of 'whipping into line' their parliamentary colleagues, by making sure that they attend important debates and votes, and that they 'toe the line' by supporting their party.

White Paper a crystallized version of a **Green Paper**, containing more concrete proposals. If a proposed government Bill has got this far, it will normally proceed further into a formal draft Bill, and may well subsequently become an Act of Parliament.

Bibliography

a

Atkinson, H. and Wilks-Heeg, S. (2000) *Local Government from Thatcher to Blair*, Cambridge: Polity Press.

b

Bartholomew, J. (2006) *The Welfare State We're In*, London: Politico's Publishing.

Blackman, T., Brody, S., and Convery, J. (eds) (2001) *Social Care and Social Exclusion: A Comparative Study of Older People's Care in Europe*, London: Palgrave Macmillan.

Bomberg, E. and Stubb, A. (eds) (2008) *The European Union: How Does it Work?*, Oxford: Oxford University Press.

Boynton, J. (1986) *Job at the Top: Chief Executive in Local Government*, London: Financial Times/Prentice Hall.

Bramley, G., Munro, M., and Pawson, H. (2004) *Key Issues in Housing: Policies and Markets in 21st-Century Britain*, London: Palgrave Macmillan.

Brooke, H. (2006) *Your Right to Know: New Edition—A Citizen's Guide to the Freedom of Information Act*, London: Pluto Press.

Brown, C. and Ainley, K. (2005) *Understanding International Relations*, London: Palgrave Macmillan.

Bryan, H. (1996) *Planning Applications and Appeals*, Oxford: Architectural Press.

Budge, I., Crewe, I., McKay, D., and Newton, K. (2007) *The New British Politics*, 4th edn, London: Longman.

Burnham, J. and Pyper, R. (2008) *Britain's Modernised Civil Service*, London: Palgrave Macmillan.

c

Campbell, A. (2007) *The Blair Years: Extracts from the Alastair Campbell Diaries*, London: Hutchinson.

Cannon, J. and Griffiths, R. (1998) *The Oxford Illustrated History of the British Monarchy*, Oxford: Oxford Paperbacks.

Carey, P. (2004) *Data Protection: A Practical Guide to UK and EU Law*, Oxford: Oxford University Press.

Challis, P. (2003) *Local Government Finance*, London: Local Government Information Unit.

Crewe, I. (ed) (1998) *Why Labour Won the General Election of 1997*, London: Frank Cass.

Crook, D., Power, S., and Whitty, G. (2000) *The Grammar School Question: A Review of Research on Comprehensive and Selective Education*, London: Institute of Education.

Crossman, R. (1979) *The Crossman Diaries: Selections from the Diaries of a Cabinet Minister, 1964–1970*, London: Book Club Associates.

Cullingworth, J. B. and Nadin, V. (2006) *Town and Country Planning in the UK*, 14th edn, London: Routledge.

d

Daniels, P. and Ritchie, E. (1996) *EU: Britain and the European Union*, London: Palgrave Macmillan.

Denver, D. (2006) *Elections and Voters in Britain*, 2nd edn, London: Palgrave Macmillan.

Docherty, I. and Shaw, J. (2003) *A New Deal for Transport: The UK's Struggle with the Sustainable Transport Agenda*, London: WileyBlackwell.

e

Edwards, P. (2003) *Industrial Relations: Theory and Practice in Britain*, 2nd edn, London: WileyBlackwell.

Evans. G. and Newnham, R. (1998) *The Penguin Dictionary of International Relations*, London: Penguin.

f

Fischel, W. A. (2005) *The Homevoter Hypothesis: How Home Values Influence Local Government Taxation, School Finance and Land-Use Policies*, Cambridge, MA: Harvard University Press.

g

Gallagher, M. and Mitchell, P. (2008) *The Politics of Electoral Systems*, Oxford: Oxford University Press.

Glendinning, C. and Kemp, P. (2006) *Cash and Care: Policy Challenges in the Welfare State*, Bristol: Policy Press.

Grimsey, D. and Lewis, M. (2007) *Public Private Partnerships: The Worldwide Revolution in Infrastructure Provision and Project Finance*, London: Edward Elgar.

Gumpert, B. and Kirk, J. (2001) *Trading Standards: Law and Practice*, Bristol: Jordans.

h

Hall, P. (2002) *Urban and Regional Planning*, 4th edn, London: Routledge.

Ham, C. (2004) *Health Policy in Britain: The Politics and Organisation of The National Health Service*, 5th edn, London: Palgrave Macmillan.

Hansen, R. S. (2001) *Citizenship and Immigration in Post-war Britain: The Institutional Origins of a Multicultural Nation*, Oxford: Oxford University Press.

Hardman, R. (2007) *Monarchy: The Royal Family at Work*, London: Ebury Press.

Harrison, K. and Boyd, T. (2006) *The Changing Constitution*, Edinburgh: Edinburgh University Press.

Hazell, R. and Rawlings, R. (2007) *Devolution, Law Making and the Constitution*, Exeter: Imprint Academic.

Hennessey, P. (2001) *The Prime Minister: The Job and Its Holders Since 1945*, London: Penguin.

Hodge, M., Leach, S., and Stoker, G. (1997) *Local Government Policy: More Than the Flower Show—Elected Mayors and Democracy*, London: Fabian Society.

Hollis, G., Davies, H., Plokker, K., and Sutherland, M. (1994) *Local Government Finance: An International Comparative Study*, London: LGcommunication.

j

Jackson, R. and Sorensen, G. (2003) *An Introduction to International Relations: Theories and Approaches*, Oxford: Oxford University Press.

Johnston, R. and Pattie, C. (2006) *Putting Voters in Their Place: Geography and Elections in Great Britain*, Oxford: Oxford University Press.

Jones, A. (2007) *Britain and the European Union*, Edinburgh: Edinburgh University Press.

Jones, B. (2004) *Dictionary of British Politics*, Manchester: Manchester University Press.

Jones, B., Kavanagh, D., Moran, M., and Norton, P. (2006) *Politics UK*, 6th edn, London: Longman.

Jones, C. and Murie, A. (2006) *The Right to Buy: Analysis and Evaluation of a Housing Policy*, London: WileyBlackwell.

Jones, K. (2002) *Education in Britain: 1944 to the Present*, Cambridge: Polity Press.

Jones, N. (2002) *The Control Freaks: How New Labour Gets Its Way*, London: Politico's Publishing.

k

Klein, R. (2006) *The New Politics of the NHS: From Creation to Reinvention*, Abingdon: Radcliffe Publishing.

Knowles, R. (1993) *Law and Practice of Local Authority Meetings*, 2nd edn, London: ICSA Publishing.

l

Lane, K. (2006) *National Bus Company: The Road to Privatisation*, Shepperton: Ian Allen.

Lang, C., Reeve, J., and Woolard, V. (eds) (2006) *The Responsive Museum: Working with Audiences in the Twenty-First Century*, Aldershot: Ashgate.

Leach, R., Coxall, B., and Robins, L. (2006) *British Politics*, London: Palgrave Macmillan.

Leff, J. (1997) *Care in the Community: Illusion or Practice?*, London: WileyBlackwell.

Lowe, R. (2004) *Welfare State in Britain Since 1945*, 3rd edn, London: Palgrave Macmillan.

Lund, B. (2006) *Understanding Housing Policy*, Cambridge: Policy Press.

m

Macdonald, J., Crail, R., and Jones, C. (eds) (forthcoming) *The Law of Freedom of Information*, 2nd edn, Oxford: Oxford University Press.

Malpass, P. (2005) *Housing and the Welfare State: The Development of Housing Policy in Britain*, London: Palgrave Macmillan.

Mansell, W. (2007) *Education by Numbers: The Tyranny of Testing*, London: Politico's Publishing.

Marr, A. (2008) *A History of Modern Britain*, London: Pan Books.

McCormick, J. (2008) *Understanding the European Union: A Concise Introduction*, London: Palgrave Macmillan.

Michie, R. C. (2001) *The London Stock Exchange: A History*, Oxford: Oxford University Press.

Midwinter, A. F. and Monaghan, C. (1993) *From Rates to the Poll Tax: Local Government Finance in the Thatcher Era*, Edinburgh: Edinburgh University Press.

Monbiot, G. (2001) *Captive State: The Corporate Takeover of Britain*, London: Pan Books.

Moran, M. (2006) *Politics and Governance in the UK*, London: Palgrave Macmillan.

Morgan, S. (2005) *Waste, Recycling and Reuse*, London: Evans Brothers.

n

Norton, P. (2005) *Parliament in British Politics*, London: Palgrave Macmillan.

p

Phillips, R. and Furlong, J. (2001) *Education, Reform and the State: Twenty-Five Years of Politics, Policy and Practice*, London: Routledge Falmer.

Philpot, T. (2007) *Adoption: Changing Families, Changing Times*, London: Routledge.

Pollock, A. M. (2006) *NHS plc: The Privatisation of Our Health Care*, London: Verso Books.

Pollock, A. M. and Talbot-Smith, A. (2006) *The New NHS: A Guide to Its Funding, Organisation and Accountability*, London: Routledge.

Pratchett, L. (2000) *Renewing Local Democracy? The Modernisation Agenda in British Local Government*, London: Frank Cass.

r

Randle, A. (2004) *Mayors Mid-term: Lessons from the First Eighteen Months of Directly Elected Mayors*, London: New Local Government Network.

Reiner, R. (2000) *The Politics of the Police*, 3rd edn, Oxford: Oxford University Press.

Rogers, R. and Walters, R. (2006) *How Parliament Works*, 6th edn, London: Longman.

Rogers, S. (1998) *Performance Management in Local Government: The Route to Best Value*, 2nd edn, London: Financial Times/Prentice Hall.

Roy, D. (2005) *Liberals: A History of the Liberal and Liberal Democratic Parties*, London: Hambledon Continuum.

s

Sanders, A. (2006) *Criminal Justice*, London: LexisNexis UK.

Seldon, A. and Snowdon, P. (2004) *The Conservative Party*, Stroud: The History Press.

Smart, G. and Holdaway, E. (2000) *Landscapes at Risk? The Future for Areas of Outstanding Natural Beauty in England and Wales*, London: Spon Press.

Stallion, M. and Wall, D. S. (2000) *The British Police: Police Forces and Chief Officers 1829–2000*, London: M. R. Stallion.

Stanley, J. and Goddard, C. (2002) *In the Firing Line: Violence and Power in Child Protection Work*, London: WileyBlackwell.

Stevens, A. (2006) *Politico's Guide to Local Government*, 2nd edn, London: Politico's Publishing.

Stewart, J. (2003) *Modernising British Local Government: An Assessment of Labour's Reform Programme*, London: Palgrave Macmillan.

Swann, D. (1988) *Retreat of the State: Deregulation and Privatisation in the United Kingdom and the United States of America*, London: Prentice-Hall.

t

Thorpe, A. (2001) *A History of the British Labour Party*, 2nd edn, London: Palgrave Macmillan.

w

Wadham, J., Griffiths, J., and Harris, K. (2007) *Blackstone's Guide to the Freedom of Information Act 2000*, 3rd edn, Oxford: Oxford University Press.

Waters, I. and Duffield, B. (1994) *Entertainment, Arts and Cultural Services*, London: Financial Times/Prentice Hall.

Wilson, D. and Game, C. (2006) *Local Government in the United Kingdom*, London: Palgrave Macmillan.

Wilson, D., Ashton, J., and Sharpe, D. (2001) *What Everyone in Britain Should Know about the Police*, London: Blackstone Press.

Wrigley, C. (2002) *British Trade Unions Since 1933*, Cambridge: Cambridge University Press.

y

Young, J. and Kent, J. (2003) *International Relations Since 1945: A Global History*, Oxford: Oxford University Press.

Index